AIA Guide to the Twin Cities

Publication of the

AIA Guide to the Twin Cities

has been made possible

through a grant from

AIA Minnesota
A Society of The American Institute of Architects

and through generous gifts from

John R. Camp

George A. MacPherson Fund

Elmer L. and Eleanor J. Andersen Fund

Bean Family Fund for Business History

North Star Fund of the Minnesota Historical Society

Larry Millett

AIA Guide to the Twin Cities

The Essential Source
on the Architecture
of Minneapolis and St. Paul

Minnesota Historical Society Press

www.mnhs.org/mhspress

The Minnesota Historical Society Press is a member of the
Association of American University Presses.

Manufactured in Canada

·10 9 8 7 6 5 4 3 2 1

♾ The paper used in this publication meets the minimum requirements of the American National Standard for Information Sciences—
Permanence for Printed Library Materials, ANSI Z39.48-1984.

International Standard Book Number 13: 978-0-87351-540-5 (paper)
International Standard Book Number 10: 0-87351-540-4 (paper)

Library of Congress Cataloging-in-Publication Data
Millett, Larry, 1947–
    AIA guide to the Twin Cities : the essential source on the
    architecture of Minneapolis and St. Paul / Larry Millett.
    p. cm.
Includes bibliographical references and index.
    ISBN-13: 978-0-87351-540-5 (pbk. : alk. paper)
    ISBN-10: 0-87351-540-4 (pbk. : alk. paper)
 1. Architecture—Minnesota—Minneapolis—Guidebooks.
 2. Minneapolis (Minn.)—Buildings, structures, etc.—Guidebooks.
 3. Architecture—Minnesota—Saint Paul—Guidebooks.
 4. Saint Paul (Minn.)—Buildings, structures, etc.—Guidebooks.
 I. Title.

NA735.M5M53 2007
720.9776′579—dc22

                                                    2007000520

To John Camp, friend and patron

Contents

Part II St. Paul

Maps of Minneapolis

Maps of St. Paul

Foreword

Picture a genial, bespectacled, middle-aged man on a bright summer day unloading a bicycle from his van in a St. Paul or Minneapolis neighborhood and setting out on the leafy streets, scanning the buildings for noteworthy architecture. Passing the river, parks, and lakes, he stops occasionally to chat with a resident, ponder an interesting discovery, or perhaps jot down an observation. He does this for three summers, researching at home through the winter, even though he already knows more about Twin Cities architecture than anyone. The man is Larry Millett: architectural critic for the *St. Paul Pioneer Press* for more than two decades, author of two popular books tracing the Twin Cities' past and present architecture, and author of this book, *AIA Guide to the Twin Cities.*

I like this image of the patient man on a bicycle both because it speaks of the passionate commitment and depth of knowledge that informs this book and also because I think Larry's dedicated explorations say something of the character of the culture, people, and architects that have shaped this community. Though we have our landmarks and curiosities that would appear in any architectural guide, the soul of Twin Cities architecture is the quiet and genial fabric of high-quality "ordinary" buildings that make up much of our downtowns and neighborhoods and much of this guide. In nearly all areas of the Twin Cities one can find likeable and well-built structures like the warehouse buildings of each downtown, the variety of architect-designed and vernacular houses in the neighborhoods, the lake and park districts' larger homes and other buildings, the riverfront's former mills, and the village-like commercial clusters of Linden Hills or Grand Avenue. The buildings are cared for as uses change from generation to generation; some are removed, some are added, but for the most part the neighborhoods continue to function well as attractive and practical infrastructure for quality urban living.

Larry's career as a critic is evident as he leavens concise descriptions with opinion—both positive and negative. The book is not a civic booster's promotion for Twin Cities living, nor is it merely descriptive. You will read that many of our landmark buildings, from the capitol to the Guthrie Theater, are the result of civic leaders and citizens banding together around a high-minded community vision. You will also read of ambitious plans with unintended consequences: the demolition of vast areas of serviceable and sometimes historic buildings for urban renewal; freeways linking city to suburb but slicing up neighborhoods; the ill effects on street life of our vaunted skyway system; missed opportunities for inspired architecture in recent redevelopment areas. This willingness to critique coupled with an uncynical belief in the possibility of positive change, even visionary change, is indicative of the Twin Cities' character. Our quality of life and our buildings and urban fabric in particular have benefited from a strong progressive and optimistic civic-mindedness. The working river genesis of this place, the northern European progressive political heritage, the long winters, the distance from the coasts, the wide-open abundance of land, and the agricultural origins of the economy may account for this. Whatever the reasons, as you read about and visit the buildings and places in this book—both landmark and ordinary—consider how the individual entries add up to the whole, for perhaps our best architecture is manifested less in individual buildings than it is in the collective striving to build the urban fabric of everyday life and make a better community.

THOMAS MEYER, FAIA, president, AIA Minnesota

Symbols Used in this Guidebook

! A building or place of exceptional architectural and/or historical significance

N Individually listed on the National Register of Historic Places or included within a National Register Historic District

★ A building or place that has been designated as a National Historic Landmark

Ȳ A structure that has been designated as a Historic Civil Engineering Landmark

L Locally designated as a historic property or within a local historic district

i A property in which all or part of the interior is included within local historic designation

Abbreviations Used for Select Architectural Firms

ESG Architects	Elness, Swenson Graham Architects
HGA	Hammel, Green and Abrahamson
KKE Architects	Korsunsky Krank Erickson Architects
MS&R Architects	Meyer, Scherer and Rockcastle Architects
SOM	Skidmore, Owings and Merrill
TKDA	Toltz, King, Duvall, Anderson and Associates

This book is the first large-scale, neighborhood-by-neighborhood architectural guide to Minneapolis and St. Paul. As such, it represents my own work as a writer and architectural historian, but it's built upon a broad foundation of research by many others—academics, neighborhood historians, planners, and preservationists—who have labored to document the Twin Cities' rich architectural environment. It's also the product of personal experience, of a lifetime of living in the Twin Cities.

I grew up in North Minneapolis, and among my earliest memories is riding one of the old yellow trolleys downtown and marveling at the big buildings that loomed up all around. I also remember winter days sledding down the high hill in Farview Park, which offered a grand vista of the downtown skyline, including what was probably the first building I ever knew by name, the Foshay Tower. Although I was born and raised in Minneapolis, I later took the highly adventurous step of moving to St. Paul, where I worked as a newspaper reporter for 30 years. Because of these experiences, I know both cities well and have come to appreciate their similarities and their differences.

In addition to the usual kinds of reading and research that went into this guide, I also took to the streets in pursuit of knowledge. Over the course of several summers, I bicycled through every part of Minneapolis and St. Paul on what might be called a personal expedition of discovery. Everywhere I went I found interesting buildings—some well-documented, others seemingly below all the usual radar screens—and a number of my "finds," such as the delightfully peculiar George Pilmer House in St. Paul, are now entries in this book.

As with many guidebooks, I suspect, this one began with great dreams and ended in a certain amount of regret, simply because I could not, due to limitations of space and time, include all of the buildings and places I had hoped to. Quite a few personal favorites had to be jettisoned as I pared down the manuscript, and I have no doubt that some local readers will be disappointed as well to find that a building or place they particularly admire did not make the final cut. However, I can offer some solace in this regard. All of the basic information I've gathered about thousands of Twin Cities buildings now resides in a database maintained by the Minnesota Historical Society. Soon, the MHS will launch an interactive website to make this information available to any and all who have an interest in the architecture of the Twin Cities.

Guidebooks by their very nature are built upon a series of choices about what to include and what to omit, and this one is no exception. I would like to tell you that my criteria for selecting entries were precise and unfailingly consistent, but that wouldn't be entirely truthful. This is, for better or worse, one man's guide to the architecture of Minneapolis and St. Paul, and I make no claim that the selection process was free of subjectivity. I did, however, use a system in deciding which buildings to include in the guide, dividing candidates into three categories, conveniently labeled A, B, and C.

The A buildings are generally those I consider to be of national significance, including grand monuments like the State Capitol in St. Paul or smaller works, such as the Purcell-Cutts House in Minneapolis, that are widely regarded as masterful architectural achievements. I also took historic significance into account in deciding whether to assign a building to the A list. In most cases, A buildings receive the longest and most detailed entries in the guidebook.

The B category encompasses buildings that, while not of national importance, are among the best works of architecture in the Twin Cities and may also have considerable historical significance. Examples of this type include Westminster Presbyterian Church in Minneapolis and the Church of St. Louis King of France in St. Paul. Both are well-known, well-designed local buildings, but they don't necessarily possess national stature. For B buildings, I generally provide a paragraph-length entry.

The large and rather amorphous C category is the most subjective of all. Here, I included buildings that nicely represent a particular style or era, that stand out in their surroundings, or that offer an architectural or historic quirk that makes them of more than passing interest. Entries for C buildings are usually no longer than a sentence or two.

Readers will also find two special types of entries in the guidebook. POI (Point of Interest) entries provide information about buildings and places that are primarily of historic value. For example, parks with no large or distinguished works of architecture typically are entered under this heading. I have also provided a sampling of "Lost" buildings in the guide as a way of acquainting readers with some of the prominent architectural ghosts that haunt many sites in the Twin Cities. Those who want to learn more about vanished buildings will find a much fuller treatment of the subject in my earlier book, *Lost Twin Cities*.

In planning this guidebook, I decided early on to limit its scope to Minneapolis and St. Paul proper with the exception of two unique suburban areas: Falcon Heights and Fort Snelling–Mendota. I made this decision largely as a practical matter. There is so much new and historic architecture of note in the suburbs (the Lake Minnetonka area alone could generate a guidebook) that I felt it was far beyond my means to try to take in the entire Twin Cities metropolitan area. However, I included Falcon Heights, which is nestled into St. Paul's northern border, because it's home to three large and important architectural sites: the University of Minnesota's St. Paul campus, the Minnesota State Fairgrounds, and the University Grove neighborhood. Fort Snelling and Mendota were incorporated because of their important roles in the founding of the Twin Cities. I also added entries for a few close-in suburban buildings, such as the Terrace Theater in Robbinsdale, that I especially like.

Most guidebook entries include at least three pieces of basic information: a building's name, the name of its architect, and the year it was completed. Additions, if any, are also listed by year. Significant artwork that adorns a building may be mentioned as well. Of course, there are buildings that have no known or verified architect. Rock-solid completion dates can also be elusive, particularly for nineteenth-century houses, and even building permits can be misleading. In any case, I've tried to provide the most accurate completion dates I can, though I readily acknowledge that errors are inevitable.

To identify buildings, I use the current name (as of late 2006) whenever possible, followed by the original or historic name, if known, in parentheses. I am well aware that this approach is not ideal, since building names change frequently. But I felt that this guidebook would be of greatest immediate use to readers if it listed buildings with their most up-to-date names. In the case of private homes, however, I've followed convention by listing them under the names of their first owners, if known. Here, I insert a standard guidebook caveat: respect people's property and privacy. Feel free to look at buildings, but don't venture onto private property unless you have the owner's permission.

Guidebook entries may also include special logos that indicate a building is listed on the National Register of Historic Places (**N**) or is locally designated as historic (**L**). Many buildings carry both designations. Other buildings may not be individually designated but are within the boundaries of national and/or local historic preservation districts.

The entries themselves are organized into neighborhood-based chapters, which in turn may be subdivided into several sections. The downtown chapters for each city are arranged in a series of looped walking tours. In the neighborhoods, where the architectural attractions tend to be more widely scattered, I've numbered entries so that they follow a more or less continuous path suitable for walking, biking, or driving. Probably the most efficient way to tour the neighborhoods is by bicycle, but I leave it to each reader to decide how best to take in the architectural sights.

Finally, I would add that although this guidebook is full of commentary, it is not intended to offer anything like the last word on the fifteen hundred or so buildings and places it covers. I expect that readers will agree with some of my observations and judgments and take great issue with others. That is as it should be. My hope is that this book will serve more than anything else as a thought-provoking companion, one that will help urban tourists of all kinds look at the Twin Cities with fresh and curious eyes.

Many organizations and individuals helped make this book possible. The American Institute of Architects (AIA) Minnesota provided financial support and sponsorship; in particular, I thank AIA Minnesota executive vice president Beverly Hauschild-Baron for her help. I must add, however, that the opinions expressed herein are mine alone.

John Camp, an old friend and longtime fellow reporter at the *St. Paul Pioneer Press*, also provided financial assistance. Known to the world as best-selling mystery novelist John Sandford, John is perhaps more of an art than an architecture buff, but he's also one of the most generous people I know, and his help was crucial in moving this project forward.

During the three years I worked on the book, I had the help of many dedicated volunteers recruited by the Minnesota Historical Society or AIA Minnesota. Darleen Hauck and Robin MacGregor were my two stalwarts, taking time out from their own busy lives to track down innumerable details. I owe them both a huge debt of gratitude. Other historical society volunteers—Robert Bauman, Douglas Chapel, Neal Dodge, Tony Krosschell, Harriette Lemke, and Helen Newlin—also pitched in at critical moments to provide research and fact-checking assistance. Diane Brown took reference photographs of every site in my long list of potential entries for the book. Diane Sherman typed details into the vast database of buildings. Volunteers from AIA Minnesota provided final-round fact-checking assistance: Mina Adsit, Christine Albertsson, Dave Alstead, Stephanie Alstead, Shannon Bambery, Rick Bronson, Jon Buggy, Bryan Desma, Janet Deutch, Vince DiGiorno, Dawn Eikamp, Sean Gilbertson, Dan Grothe, Tom Hysell, Catherine Mullinax Jones, Lee Jorgensen, Jennifer Kingsbury, Maria Lavenas, Erin McKiel, Timothy Mennel, Tonya Nicholie, Paula Pentel, Darryl Pratte, Michael Schrock, Brian Tempas, Lee Tollefson, Brian Tucker, Kathy Wallace, Jeff Walz, and Christopher Yungers. My thanks go to all of them.

On my biking trips through the Twin Cities, Gar Hargens—an architect of distinction and a good friend—often came along for the ride. His sharp eye for detail and knack for finding good restaurants were both much appreciated. Together, we pedaled our way to many discoveries, the most breathtaking of which is that St. Paul really does have a lot of high hills.

Paul Larson, who can fairly be called the dean of Twin Cities architectural historians, read the entire manuscript, providing valuable suggestions as well as numerous corrections that saved me from errors large and small. I also thank St. Paul historian Jim Sazevich, who provided a wealth of detailed information that greatly enhanced the chapter on the historic West Seventh and Irvine Park neighborhoods.

Another local historian, Thomas Balcom of Minneapolis, led me on a wonderful tour of that city's Tangletown neighborhood.

I also benefited from the help of State Historic Preservation Officer Susan Roth, who provided access to National Register nomination forms and other documents relating to historic buildings in the Twin Cities. At the Ramsey County Historical Society in St. Paul, director Priscilla Farnham and her staff, including Maureen McGinn, were unfailingly helpful in providing access to Historic Site Survey forms, building permits, and other sources of information. The Minneapolis Collection at the Minneapolis Public Library was another excellent resource. At the University of Minnesota's Northwest Architectural Archives, director Alan Lathrop and his assistant, Barb Bezat, provided their usual expert assistance when I came to them with questions. My thanks go as well to Amy Spong, planner for the St. Paul Heritage Preservation Commission, and to Amy Lucas, who until recently held a similar position with the Minneapolis Heritage Preservation Commission. Both opened up their files and provided much important information, especially during the early stages of my research.

My editor at the Minnesota Historical Society Press, Shannon Pennefeather, performed especially heroic service. An architectural guidebook such as this one—with well over a thousand individual entries plus scores of maps, photographs, special headings, and innumerable other complications—can easily devolve into an editor's worst nightmare. Shannon managed to orchestrate all the details of the project with great skill and, equally important, with consistent good humor. Sally Rubinstein also helped with the editing, while design and production manager Will Powers worked with book designer Cathy Spengler and typesetter Allan Johnson to deliver what I believe is an attractive and highly usable guidebook. Press director Greg Britton was an enthusiastic supporter of the book from the very beginning. To all of them go my thanks.

Most importantly, I wish to thank my youngest children, Lexy and Corey, for their understanding during what proved to be a difficult period for all of us. My thanks also go to Jodie Ahern, who became a wonderful friend and companion at a time when I needed both.

AIA Guide to the Twin Cities

An architect from London once spent a day touring Minneapolis and St. Paul. It was his first visit to the American Midwest, and after he had seen all the usual sights, he had a simple question: Where, he asked, is the city? The question is not as strange as it sounds. With long blocks of single-family houses standing on 40- or 50-foot-wide lots along well-wooded streets amid thousands of acres of lakes and parks and winding waterways, the Twin Cities would strike almost any European as essentially suburban, in places almost rural, in character. Fly across the Twin Cities on a summer day, and what you see is mostly forest and water, with the skyscrapers of the two downtowns providing the best evidence of urbanity somewhere down among the trees.

Built upon a highly diversified economy that grew out of the region's agricultural riches, Minneapolis and St. Paul also lack many of the grittier features of other American cities. There are no vast, sooty industrial zones or great expanses of urban wasteland or slums that seem beyond all hope of redemption. To be sure, the Twin Cities are not immune to the usual urban ailments—crime, poverty, decay, racial tension. Yet they remain very livable and inviting places, in part because of what might be called their anti-urban qualities.

With a combined population of 670,000 people (385,000 in Minneapolis and 285,000 in St. Paul) spread across 114 square miles, the twins are among the least dense American cities, not only because of the predominance of detached single-family homes but also because so much of the natural world is integrated into their urban texture. A midwestern sense of space, of urban living as a kind of compacted continuation of rural life, may well be the Twin Cities' defining quality. It is perhaps only fitting that the Minnesota State Fairgrounds, home to a giant annual extravaganza founded on the rituals of the harvest, lies midway between the two cities, on a typically expansive site.

The architectural world of Minneapolis and St. Paul is not, overall, uniquely different from that of most other American cities, especially those in the Midwest. Despite much fine work by local architects over the years, the Twin Cities never became known for a distinctive kind of design such as the commercial style that emerged in Chicago in the 1880s. Instead, architects in Minneapolis and St. Paul have generally been content to follow the prevailing styles of the day, with the usual individual variations.

Even so, a number of Twin Cities-based architects—ranging from Harry Jones, Long and Kees, Purcell and Elmslie, and, more recently, Ralph Rapson in Minneapolis to Cass Gilbert, Clarence H. Johnston, and Allen H. Stem in St. Paul—have produced works of national stature. Both cities (though Minneapolis much more so than St. Paul) can also boast of buildings designed by acclaimed outside architects, including major works by McKim, Mead and White, Holabird and Root, Erich Mendelsohn, Frank Lloyd Wright, Philip Johnson, Edward Larrabee Barnes, Cesar Pelli, Michael Graves, Frank Gehry, Jean Nouvel, and Herzog and de Meuron, among others.

Although it's fair to say that no more than 50 or so buildings and structures in the Twin Cities can be classified as nationally significant, it's equally true that Minneapolis and St. Paul possess a rich body of architecture that often matches the best contemporaneous work elsewhere in the United States. There are in addition some one-of-a-kind architectural oddities scattered around the Twin Cities; though their number is not large, they tend to be genuine delights.

Both Minneapolis and St. Paul also have what might be called signature neighborhoods. Minneapolis's defining place is the Lake District, a meeting of land and water like none other in urban America. Lakes Harriet, Calhoun, Isles, Cedar, and Brownie string out here in a lost valley of the Mississippi River. Ringed by parks and parkways and connected by canals, the lakes form the centerpiece of a gorgeous residential zone that remains the most coveted ground in the city as well as a kind of giant summer playground for the entire metropolitan area.

St. Paul's great treasure is the Historic Hill District and the long street that bisects it, Summit Avenue. The Hill District contains one of the nation's outstanding collections of upper middle-class Victorian housing, while Summit is perhaps the finest and most intact grand residential boulevard of its era left in the United States. The Hill District also resonates through the timeless realm of literature: F. Scott Fitzgerald grew up in the neighborhood, a not-so-rich boy who transmuted his experiences at the fringes of great wealth into such melancholy masterpieces as *The Great Gatsby*.

How Minneapolis and St. Paul came to grow up side by side is a story with geological roots that go back 12,000 years to a time when great rivers, among them the Mississippi, coursed through a landscape newly shaped by glaciers. Because of these ancient forces, the Twin Cities occupy a unique region where the Mississippi and its valley undergo a dramatic transformation.

In St. Paul, settled in the 1830s by a group of outcasts from nearby Fort Snelling, the Mississippi flows through a broad, deep valley that forms an S-shaped gash through the heart of the city. The Mississippi is St. Paul's great physical fact, its presence seen or felt in almost every corner of the city, which is built on a series of terraces, bluffs, and high hills that extend out from the river valley. The river scenery is much different in Minneapolis, which was established in the 1850s along the west bank of St. Anthony Falls. In Minneapolis, the Mississippi is largely out of view, running between low banks north of downtown and within a narrow, 70- to 100-foot-deep gorge south of the falls. Much of Minneapolis is built on prairie, and it has the feel of a Great Plains city in a way that St. Paul does not.

It was precisely because of this abrupt change in the river that St. Paul and Minneapolis developed into large, wholly separate cities just a few miles apart. Through most of St. Paul, the Mississippi follows a valley carved out by the mighty Glacial River Warren, an ancestor of the present Minnesota River. Just east of downtown St. Paul, this glacial torrent plunged into an old valley scoured out by the Mississippi before one of its many changes of course. Here, too, the River Warren encountered a layer of hard limestone over a bed of softer sandstone. As the thundering river dug down into the sandstone, it formed a waterfall (located near today's Robert Street Bridge in downtown St. Paul) that at its maximum extent was wider and higher than Niagara.

Over thousands of years, this waterfall receded upstream before dividing at the confluence of the Mississippi and Minnesota rivers, a strategic location where Fort Snelling—the first permanent white settlement in the Twin Cities area—was established in 1820. Moving north up the Mississippi, the cataract carved out a rocky gorge and had migrated to about a mile south of its present site in downtown Minneapolis by the time Father Louis Hennepin named it St. Anthony Falls in 1680.

This waterfall, by far the river's largest, made the Twin Cities. St. Paul became the head of navigation on the Mississippi because the river upstream through the gorge was generally too fast and rocky for steamboats to negotiate. By 1860, St. Paul was home to over 10,000 people and was both Minnesota's largest city and its capital. A flourishing steamboat trade, which soon gave way to railroading, turned the city into a major regional distribution center. Among those drawn early on to St. Paul was James J. Hill, who arrived in 1856 and eventually become the city's richest and most influential citizen.

In Minneapolis, the falls became the basis of a vast industrial complex centered around flour and saw milling. The first settlement at the falls was located on the east side of the river and was known as St. Anthony. Minneapolis (a coined name combining the Dakota word for water and the Greek word for city) was established in 1855 on the falls' west bank after a treaty with the indigenous Dakota opened the way for settlement. The west bank, as it turned out, was the place to be, and in 1872 Minneapolis absorbed St. Anthony.

Minneapolis's rapid growth was propelled by development of the falls—a 16-foot-high cataract with another 50 or so feet of drop in the rapids below, a superb source of power. With vast pineries to the north and endless prairies ideal for growing wheat to the south and west, Minneapolis was perfectly positioned to become a center of milling. By 1881, the two largest flour mills in the world (one operated by the Pillsbury family, the other by the Washburns) stood on either side of the falls, while just upriver scores of sawmills chewed away at the ever dwindling bounty of the northern forest.

Although the Mississippi separates much of Minneapolis and St. Paul, there's a stretch of a mile or so in the aptly named Midway area where the two cities abut, so that you can simply walk across the street from one to the other. In some places, such as along Franklin Avenue, this transition is very noticeable because of zoning differences between the adjacent neighborhoods; on other streets, like University Avenue, there are few visual clues that you've made the crossing, except for a sign welcoming you to either Minneapolis or St. Paul.

The two cities' proximity and the ease of movement between them naturally leads to a question: are they different from each other in any important ways, or can they be better understood as a single place with the inconvenience of separate names? The answer is that while Minneapolis and St. Paul have much in common—both are midwestern grid cities that grew up in traditional fashion around rivers, railroading, agriculture, and industry—they are different. Or, to put it another way, their urban DNA may be similar, but it's by no means identical.

A variety of clichés have been trotted out over the years to explain how the cities differ. Minneapolis, it's said, is a "small big city" that's western, progressive, Protestant, and Scandinavian. St. Paul, by contrast, is usually characterized as a "big small town" that's eastern, conservative, Catholic, and Irish. There's some truth to this, especially when it comes to the city-town comparison. Minneapolis, though it has only about 100,000 more people than St. Paul, does indeed feel much more like a big city than its twin, and it has a kind of urban hustle, not to mention a desire to be hip and stylish, that its more meat-and-potatoes neighbor doesn't share. Then again, Minneapolis usually tallies at least twice as many murders annually as St. Paul. Once famous as a gangster hideout, St. Paul is now a pretty quiet place, charmingly tribal in its politics (feuds and disputes can go on for years) and so strongly identified with its neighborhoods that it often seems more like a boisterous confederation of villages than a city.

Yet the truth is that the geographical, social, cultural, political, historical, and, yes, architectural differences between Minneapolis and St. Paul are far more subtle and complex than a few broad brushstrokes, however well chosen, can convey. If you spend enough time in both cities you will begin to understand that they are twins with quite dissimilar personalities.

The architectural differences between Minneapolis and St. Paul are due in large measure to the fact that, until well after World War II,

architects from one city seldom worked in the other. This design seg-
regation was especially rigid in the period from about 1880 to 1930,
when the intercity rivalry was at its most intense. About the only
St. Paul architect who worked regularly in Minneapolis during these
years was Clarence H. Johnston, and his was a special case: he became
state architect in 1901 and thus designed many buildings for the University of Minnesota. Minneapolis firms such as Kees and Colburn
occasionally won commissions in St. Paul, as did mansion designer
William Channing Whitney and theater architects Liebenberg and
Kaplan, but for the most part the wall of architectural separation
remained inviolate.

Because there was so little architectural crossover between the
cities, a building from, say, 1900 in Minneapolis will almost always display certain traits that set it apart from a St. Paul building of the same
period. These discrepancies, however, tend to be at the level of detail,
reflecting variations between designers rather than major differences
in form and style. A good place to observe such differences is in the
two cities' downtown warehouse districts, which were built up at the
same time. Minneapolis warehouses, often decorated with terra-cotta
or carved stone, tend to be a little more ornate than those in St. Paul,
where rigorous plainness was usually the order of the day.

While their architectural differences can be subtle, Minneapolis
and St. Paul are markedly disparate when it comes to geography and
streets. One obvious difference is their orientation: Minneapolis's main
axis is north-south, whereas St. Paul runs east-west, so that together
the cities form a sort of giant L. These orientations reflect the course
of the Mississippi, which actually runs in a northeasterly direction
through much of St. Paul.

Minneapolis has a few steep glacial ridges such as Lowry Hill, but
it's mostly a wide-open prairie city with a street grid that in many
places is regular to the point of monotony. Its streets, especially downtown, are also quite wide, up to 100 feet in some cases. St. Paul has
some level sections along the West Seventh Street plateau and farther back from the river bluffs, but because of the enormous Mississippi valley at its center, much of the city is rough and hilly, with over
350 feet of elevation between the lowest and highest points. Like
Minneapolis, St. Paul is largely a grid city, but the grid is often very
irregular, and streets can be narrow, especially in older residential
neighborhoods.

Minneapolis's street naming and numbering system is very orderly, perhaps reflecting the mindset of the highly efficient New Eng-
landers who played a large role in founding the city. The system is
largely numeric, with numbered streets and avenues (followed by one
of six different directional indicators) extending outward from downtown to every section of the city. Many of Minneapolis's named streets
also follow some sort of order, either alphabetical or, in the case of
the Northeast neighborhood, chronological according to the names
of U.S. presidents (an arrangement intended as a history lesson for
immigrants). Yet for all its devotion to logic and order, the Minneapolis street system can be confusing if, say, you can't remember whether
you're looking for the intersection of 26th Avenue and 25th Street or
26th Street and 25th Avenue.

St. Paul's street system, by contrast, is an ad hoc affair, famously
described by former Minnesota governor Jesse Ventura as being laid
out by "drunken Irishmen." This slur upon the Celtic peoples did not
go unnoticed in St. Paul, but even longtime city residents will admit
that the street system can be trying at times. St. Paul has just a handful
of numbered streets (beginning at Second—First vanished long ago—
and ending at 14th, with two Sevenths thrown in just to make matters
interesting). All the other streets in St. Paul are named, in no particular
order. It is, in other words, a street system that has to be memorized.

Interestingly, even though St. Paul has fewer people and is a bit smaller in physical size than Minneapolis, it has about 300 more streets than its twin. This apparent anomaly may stem in part from the physical differences between the cities. Streets in St. Paul often end abruptly at bluffs, hills, ravines, or other natural barriers, whereas they can run for great distances across the plains of Minneapolis. St. Paul also has a much different address numbering system than does Minneapolis. Numbers in St. Paul don't change by the hundreds from block to block as they do in Minneapolis. As a result, the highest street address in St. Paul is around 2500, compared to about 6300 in Minneapolis. Finally, it is worth noting that while Minneapolis has a St. Paul Avenue (an obscure block-long street south of Cedar Lake), St. Paul has no Minneapolis Avenue and, it's a good bet, never will.

Although St. Paul and Minneapolis are both over 150 years old, their existing building stock doesn't, for the most part, reflect their age. The Twin Cities' oldest documented building is the heavily restored Ard Godfrey House, built in 1849 by a pioneer miller and later moved to its current site in southeast Minneapolis. St. Paul's oldest property, in the Irvine Park neighborhood near downtown, is a house that dates to 1850. All told, Irvine Park and the adjoining West Seventh neighborhood have about two dozen pre–Civil War houses, by far the biggest such group in the Twin Cities. Most of the pioneer-era buildings in the Twin Cities are long gone, however, overtaken by commercial expansion as Minneapolis and St. Paul outgrew their original downtowns.

Buildings from the 1860s and early 1870s, when both cities were still quite small, aren't especially common either. Even so, a substantial number remain, particularly in St. Paul. Two stone mansions—the Burbank-Livingston-Griggs House (1863) and the Alexander Ramsey House (1872)—are among the most notable survivors, as is another St. Paul landmark, Assumption Catholic Church, built in 1874 and a significant example of the Romanesque Revival style. Most extant buildings of this era in the Twin Cities are either vernacular in character or follow popular romantic styles such as Italianate and French Second Empire. They also tend to be fairly provincial, reflecting the small size and relative remoteness of Minneapolis and St. Paul at the time.

By the mid-1870s, both cities began to shed their small-town ways and acquire the rudiments of urbanity. Horsecar lines started operating, sewer systems were dug, streetlamps powered by coal gas began illuminating the downtowns, and the first paved streets (wood or granite blocks being the favored materials) appeared. Meanwhile, the combined population of the two cities had grown to 50,000 or so and would reach almost 90,000 by 1880. There was plenty of work for the newly arrived masses. In Minneapolis, advances in technology and the influx of capital transformed the milling district around St. Anthony Falls into an industrial powerhouse, while across the river in St. Paul James J. Hill and his associates were laying the foundations of a railway empire that in the 1890s would stretch to the West Coast and become known as the Great Northern.

Everything came together in the Twin Cities, with astonishing human force, in the 1880s, fed by waves of European immigrants as well as arrivals from the eastern states and Canada. Minneapolis's population soared from 46,000 to 164,000 between 1880 and 1890; St. Paul's rise, from 41,000 to 133,000, was almost as spectacular. Both cities greatly enlarged their boundaries in response to this unprecedented growth. St. Paul reached its present size of about 56 square miles in 1887. Minneapolis was also close to its final dimensions of 58 square miles by that year but didn't fill in all the way to its southern boundary at 62nd Street until 1927.

As the cities grew into full-fledged urban adults, they came ever more strongly to view themselves as competitors, with notably impolite results. Newspapers flung insults back and forth, politicians cast aspersions on their cross-river rivals, and in 1890 the two cities even engaged in an all-out court battle over census figures, each accusing the other of chicanery in padding the numbers (it was discovered, for example, that a St. Paul census taker somehow managed to find a resident population of a dozen or so worthy fellows in a downtown barber shop). This acrimonious dispute set the tone for other intercity dust-ups to follow, as Minneapolis became the dominant twin, much to St. Paul's dissatisfaction.

The establishment of the Minneapolis Park Board in 1883 was another of the decade's signal events, opening the way for the city to develop a superb park system. It was also the park board that around 1900 in effect created the lake district by "improving" (that is, dredging) the city's lakes, which in their natural and often unpleasantly swampy state had been better known for attracting mosquitoes than high-class homes.

Perhaps the most far-reaching event of this era in the Twin Cities, however, was the arrival of electric streetcars. Successfully tested in 1889 and widely in use within just a few years, streetcars helped establish an early pattern of sprawl that continues to this day. But it's not fair to pin anything like sole responsibility for sprawl on the trolleys, which ran until 1954. Instead, sprawl was all but inevitable given the devotion of Twin Citians to the ideal of the single-family home (row houses have always been rare, while apartment buildings weren't constructed in large numbers until the 1920s) and the ready availability of developable land in every direction. The Twin Cities have no major natural barriers to expansion such as Lake Michigan at Chicago or the Hudson and East rivers in Manhattan; as a result the metropolitan area (as of 2007 home to 3 million people) has over more than a century spread out into an unfathomable conglomeration, its fuzzy, ever shifting edges now a good 50 miles or more from the old downtown cores.

Today, the architectural legacy of the 1880s and early 1890s (the boom ended with the depression of 1893) is still visible throughout Minneapolis and St. Paul. It includes thousands of houses ranging from mansions to cottages, commercial buildings small and large (the oldest Twin Cities' skyscraper, the Lumber Exchange in Minneapolis, dates to 1887), factories and mills, school and institutional buildings, and churches. It's an incomplete legacy, however. Many of the Twin Cities' best downtown buildings from this period are gone, as are numerous mansions and, in some cases, entire neighborhoods, especially in Minneapolis.

The architects who created this new urban world in the 1880s were almost all locally based, although many had been born and trained elsewhere. What drew them to the Twin Cities, of course, was the opportunity to build. St. Paul in the 1880s was home to a pair of especially outstanding architects—Clarence H. Johnston, whose work was mostly limited to Minnesota, and Cass Gilbert, whose elegant and assured design for the Minnesota State Capitol (first submitted in 1893, when he was just 34 years old) ultimately catapulted him to a national career in New York.

No figure of Gilbert's stature came out of Minneapolis in the 1880s, but designers like the team of Frederick Long and Frederick Kees, as well as the versatile Harry Jones, produced scores of wonderful buildings. And for many years beginning in the 1880s another Minneapolis architect, LeRoy Buffington, claimed that he had invented that most American of buildings, the steel-framed skyscraper. The patent courts didn't agree. However, Minneapolis engineers such as Charles Haglin and C. A. P. Turner were in fact at the forefront of American building technology at the turn of the twentieth century. Haglin designed and built the first cylindrical concrete grain elevator in 1900 (it still stands just outside Minneapolis), while Turner was a pioneer in concrete frame construction.

Although the late Victorian era produced many first-class buildings in Minneapolis and St. Paul, the golden age of architecture in the Twin Cities came between about 1895 and 1920. Still growing, but not as rapidly as they once had, the two cities began a process of what might be called architectural consolidation. Public and private institutions erected new buildings to reflect their growing wealth and prestige, as did many businesses and industrial enterprises. The moneyed class, meanwhile, raked in the proceeds and used them to erect numerous splendid mansions, along Summit Avenue, on Lowry Hill, and at other favored locales. Not as prosperous but equally devoted to good design, the middle class contented itself with bungalows that to this day remain among the best small houses ever built in the Twin Cites.

Classical styles, however, dominated the public and institutional architecture of the time. Cass Gilbert's State Capitol (1905) in St. Paul provided Minnesota government with all the white-marbled splendor it's ever likely to need. A decade later, the French-born architect Emmanuel Masqueray turned out a pair of vast if somewhat peculiar baroque-inspired churches—the Basilica of St. Mary in Minneapolis (1914) and the St. Paul Cathedral (1915)—that rank among the nation's largest houses of worship. Meanwhile, the renowned New York firm of McKim, Mead and White designed the Minneapolis Institute of Arts, a marble palace completed in 1915. But it was a lesser-known New York architect, Electus Litchfield, who designed what is perhaps the apogee of Beaux-Arts classicism in the Twin Cities: the St. Paul Central Library and James J. Hill Reference Library (1917).

Along with this revival of classical ideals came the so-called City Beautiful movement, whose advocates dreamed of creating something like baroque grandeur out of the old Victorian clutter of American cities. Civic leaders in both Minneapolis and St. Paul hired Chicago architect Edward Bennett (an associate of the famed Daniel Burnham) to draw up grand plans. Neither plan (Minneapolis's was published in 1917, St. Paul's in 1922) led to much in the way of concrete development, although Minneapolis in 1915 built the Gateway Pavilion (gone), a classical monument designed to dress up what had become a down-and-out portion of downtown. St. Paul managed to build Kellogg Boulevard beginning in the late 1920s, but other grand ideas fizzled. Cass Gilbert was among the big dreamers, preparing three plans (the last in the 1930s) for a vast mall extending south from the State Capitol. It wasn't until the 1950s, however, that a mall, not of Gilbert's design, finally appeared.

Yet even as architectural monuments rose all around the Twin Cities in the early 1900s, a very different current of design flowed through both communities. Progressive or organic architecture, as its practitioners called it, came out of the broad Art and Crafts impulse but was transformed into a very particular kind of high art by Frank Lloyd Wright in Chicago. His so-called Prairie houses, which began appearing in the late 1890s, were brilliantly modern works decades ahead of their time, and they soon arrived in the Twin Cities via the firm of William Purcell and George Elmslie, formed in 1910. Both men were well versed in the Wrightian manner: Purcell hailed from the Chicago suburb of Oak Park, where Wright lived and worked, while the Scottish-born Elmslie had long been the chief draftsman for Louis Sullivan, Wright's mentor.

Purcell settled in Minneapolis first, in 1908, and designed a church and several small houses (with Elmslie providing a helping hand from Chicago) before Elmslie joined him in 1910. The firm soon established its own distinct identity within the so-called Prairie School (a term used to describe early followers of Wright). Purcell and Elmslie designed more than a dozen homes in the Twin Cities, mostly in south Minneapolis, as well as several small commercial buildings. Their masterpiece, the Purcell-Cutts House (1913) on Lake Place in Minneapolis, is among the greatest of all Prairie houses.

Other local designers also produced distinctive residential work during this time, and certain types of houses became unique to each city. In St. Paul, both Cass Gilbert and Clarence H. Johnston, beginning in the mid-1890s, designed a series of foursquare stone houses with a vaguely Medieval tinge that have no real counterparts in Minneapolis. Similarly, there is nothing in St. Paul quite like the broad mansions, influenced by the Chicago work of Louis Sullivan and others, that began appearing atop Minneapolis's Lowry Hill around 1905.

Both progressive and Classical Revival architecture had peaked in the Twin Cities by the 1920s, when developing neighborhoods in both cities filled with houses in various Period Revival styles such as Tudor, Norman, Spanish Colonial, French Provincial, English Cottage, and Storybook. Little-known St. Paul architect Kenneth Worthen was the local master of this pictorial brand of architecture, and a number of his 1920s houses (including his own, built in 1926 on Mississippi River Boulevard in St. Paul) are so far over the top that they have the quality of grand hallucinations.

It was also in the 1920s that the streetcar era reached its high point in Minneapolis and St. Paul. As more and more Twin Citians bought automobiles, streetcar ridership began a long, steady decline. Still, both downtowns remained vibrant through the 1920s, when a new generation of tall office buildings, mostly in the art deco style, rose to new heights. The 32-story Foshay Tower (1929), an obelisk modeled on the Washington Monument, was the most dramatic of these new skyscrapers in more ways than one: its builder and namesake—Wilbur Foshay—went to federal prison on stock swindling charges not long after the building opened.

However, the Twin Cities' greatest art deco monument was built during the Great Depression. Designed by Holabird and Root of Chicago and completed in 1932, the St. Paul City Hall–Ramsey County Courthouse is most notable for its dazzling interiors, including a main concourse that qualifies as a masterpiece of American art deco. Later in the 1930s, a handful of Twin Cities architects kept current by designing houses and other buildings in the late phase of art deco known as the Moderne. The Abe and Mary Engelson House (1939) in St. Paul is the most significant of these Moderne works.

What most people think of as architectural modernism made its Twin Cities debut in the late 1930s in several houses designed by Winston and Elizabeth Close. Frank Lloyd Wright's Willey House of 1934 also made a modernistic statement. However, it wasn't until after World War II that buildings of the modernist persuasion became common. Flat-roofed, one-story, overtly utilitarian houses began appearing in scattered outer neighborhoods, especially near Minnehaha Creek in far south Minneapolis and in the Highland area of St. Paul. Immediately north of St. Paul, in suburban Falcon Heights, the unique community of University Grove has a particularly fine collection of architect-designed modernist houses from the 1950s and 1960s.

Some of the best buildings of the post–World War II period in the Twin Cities were the work of prominent outside architects. In Minneapolis, Finnish-born Eliel Saarinen designed, just before his death, the exquisite and highly influential Christ Lutheran Church (1949). Another career finale came in St. Paul, where Erich Mendelsohn's Mount Zion Temple (1955) on Summit Avenue was completed two years after he died. Nearby, Chicago architect Barry Byrne produced one of his characteristically odd churches, St. Columba (1951), while back in Minneapolis the Neils House (1951) by Frank Lloyd Wright demonstrated that the octogenarian architect had lost none of his creative juice.

By the 1960s, modernism was the everyday currency of architecture in the Twin Cities. Much of the new building in this period took place in the suburbs, which were already starting to grow outward in one ring after another. In response to this inexorable suburban expansion, civic leaders in Minneapolis and St. Paul pushed ever harder for downtown renewal. The surviving downtown buildings from this time tend to be predictable and bland, but there are some shining exceptions.

Ralph Rapson, who trained under Eliel Saarinen at Cranbrook Academy near Detroit, assumed leadership of the University of Minnesota's architecture school in 1954 and quickly established himself as the leading modern architect in the Twin Cities. Unfortunately, his most famous and in many ways most lovable building, the Guthrie Theater (1963), was razed in late 2006. Minoru Yamasaki's templelike Northwestern National Life Insurance Co. building (now ING 20 Washington) of 1965 in downtown Minneapolis is another of the decade's gems, as is Val Michelson's extraordinary and powerful St. Paul's Priory (now the Benedictine Center of St. Paul's Monastery), also from 1965.

For many Twin Citians, however, the architectural legacy of the 1950s and 1960s is measured more by what was destroyed than by what was built. Urban renewal, freeway construction, and other interventions brought about enormous changes, not always benign, to both cities. The Gateway urban renewal program in downtown Minneapolis excised the city's historic heart, claiming in the process such singular monuments as the Northwestern Guaranty Loan (Metropolitan) Building. St. Paul waited until the 1960s to begin surgical removal of much of its downtown core, with generally unhappy results.

The construction of interstate highways 35 and 94 through both cities began in the 1960s and was largely complete by 1980. These freeways came at the usual cost: long swaths through both cities were cleared of houses and other historic buildings. The area around downtown St. Paul was especially hard hit by clearance, and many fine old buildings were lost. The interstate was routed a bit farther from Minneapolis's downtown core, while the provision of a tunnel beneath Lowry Hill helped preserve some of the major monuments there.

One by-product of all this destruction was the development of a strong historic preservation movement in the Twin Cities. The first city and national historic districts were established in the 1970s. Minneapolis now has 17 historic districts; St. Paul has eight. The restoration and renovation of the old federal courthouse (now Landmark Center) in downtown St. Paul from 1972 to 1978 was perhaps the defining moment for historical preservation in the Twin Cities. Even so, preservation remains a challenge, and it is now proving especially hard to save early modernist buildings, which lack the "curb appeal" of their Victorian and early twentieth-century ancestors.

The massive rebuilding of the 1960s also laid the groundwork for the skyway systems in both downtowns. These systems of second-story bridges and corridors, now extending across many blocks, have proved to be a kind of urban drug: they make life much more pleasant during the long winter months, but they've had some unpleasant side effects when it comes to downtown street life. Minneapolis in the 1960s also built the Nicollet Mall, one of the few American downtown malls than can be regarded as a continuing success.

The seminal building of the 1970s in the Twin Cities was the IDS Center (1973) in downtown Minneapolis, designed by Philip Johnson and John Burgee. The IDS not only brought unprecedented height (57 stories) to the Minneapolis skyline, it also inaugurated an era of "starchitecture," which became particularly pronounced in the 1980s as well-known architects like Cesar Pelli, Helmut Jahn, and William Pedersen were hired to design major downtown buildings. Today, an international field of designers has found work in the Twin Cities (or, at least, in Minneapolis), and the trend seems likely to continue.

The most recent building boom in the Twin Cities has centered on housing. Since 2000, new condominium towers have been built or planned in both downtowns. In addition, there have been innumerable historic conversions of old warehouse and industrial buildings into loft-style apartments. Elsewhere, low-rise condominium buildings seem to be cropping up everywhere. A number have already been built near the Hiawatha Light Rail Line, which opened in Minneapolis in 2004, and if a similar line is built along University Avenue in St. Paul, as seems likely to happen, an apartment-building frenzy will probably occur there as well.

Unfortunately, all too much of this recent architecture has demonstrated little in the way of imagination or rigor, in part because Minneapolis and St. Paul have come under the thrall of neo-traditional town planning. The neo-traditionalists, who seek to create attractive new buildings and communities by reviving historic principles of city making, have the best of intentions. However, their approach has so far yielded consistently uninspiring results. Quasi-historic brick boxes designed with the idea of giving no offense have become an architectural plague in both cities, and truly creative work now seems largely reserved for occasional showpiece projects like art museums, theaters, and churches.

Yet the biggest issue for Minneapolis and St. Paul in the coming years will likely be population density and whether it should be greatly increased, especially if growth can be tied to good mass transit. Cultural, geographical, and historical forces have all combined to keep population densities quite low in the Twin Cities. At some point, however, the sprawling pursuit of elbow room will hit a wall (for social, economic, political, and ecological reasons). It will then make sense to accommodate growth through density rather than dispersal. Both Minneapolis and St. Paul clearly have the capacity to become denser cities; the trick will be to ensure that, in doing so, they do not fatally compromise the green and open qualities so vital to their nature.

AIA Guide to the Twin Cities

1 Downtown Minneapolis

Overview

Downtown Minneapolis has the broad, spacious feel common to midwestern prairie cities. Its wide streets—measuring 80 to 100 feet across—are arranged in a standard gridiron of square blocks, and there are no bluffs or deep valleys, as in St. Paul, to provide a sense of containment. Walk out onto a street in the middle of downtown, and you are in a world that looks as though it could go on forever. Downtown Minneapolis is well defined vertically, however, by the giant crop of skyscrapers that cluster near its center and serve as potent symbols of the city's wealth and prestige.

As it's evolved over the years, downtown consists of five distinct districts. The central core—running along the Nicollet Mall, Marquette Avenue, and streets to the east—includes virtually all of downtown's skyscrapers as well as its major shopping venue. Along and to the north and west of Hennepin Avenue is the city's historic warehouse district, which offers a mix of theaters, bars, restaurants, and loft-style apartments and offices. The central riverfront, which has seen explosive development over the past decade, extends down to the old milling complex around St. Anthony Falls and features much new upscale housing as well as cultural institutions like the Mill City Museum and the Guthrie Theater. The Elliot Park neighborhood on the southeastern side of downtown is a classic mixed-use area. So, too, is the Loring Park neighborhood, which has perhaps the most diverse array of buildings anywhere in the Twin Cities.

Much of downtown Minneapolis is the product of modern-era (post–World War II) development; only in the warehouse district will you find entire blocks still populated by historic buildings. The oldest portion of downtown, the so-called Gateway area along Hennepin and Nicollet avenues near the Mississippi River, was swept away by the hard, unsparing brush of urban renewal in the 1950s and 1960s. This early commercial center formed in the 1850s, as did the huge complex of mills a few blocks to the south at St. Anthony Falls. The completion in 1855 of the first Hennepin Avenue Suspension Bridge, which linked Minneapolis to the slightly older village of St. Anthony on the east side of the river, helped spur growth. The area near the new span became known as Bridge Square, and by the 1870s it was already lined with small brick and stone buildings, including the first Minneapolis City Hall (1873, now gone).

From this starting point, downtown gradually spread back from the river like an irresistible tide, reaching something close to its present dimensions by about 1920. Along the way, most of its first generation of buildings disappeared, a trend that was to continue through the twentieth century. Today, little remains from the early age of downtown development. The destruction of the Gateway area, including such monuments as the Northwestern Guaranty Loan (Metropolitan) Building (1890), is the best-known episode of urban renewal gone amok in downtown Minneapolis. Over the years, however, scores of other historic buildings fell one by one—to fire, to old age, or simply to make way for something bigger and newer. As a result, downtown's stock of nineteenth-century buildings is quite small.

Much of what survives, however, is choice, beginning with the magnificent Minneapolis City Hall (started in 1889 but not completed until 1906). Other Victorian-era monuments include such early high-rise buildings as the Lumber Exchange (1886 and later) and the Masonic Temple (1888–90), warehouses like the Langford-Newell Block (1887), churches such as First Baptist (1886) and Wesley Methodist (1891), and even a few mansions in the Loring Park neighborhood.

During the early decades of the twentieth century, downtown continued to grow both outward and upward, often in spurts reflecting the general state of the American economy. One wave of development began early in the century and culminated in the 16-story First National Bank–Soo Line Building (1914), the city's tallest skyscraper to that point. The so-called City Beautiful movement also flourished at this time, and all manner of schemes were proposed for remaking downtown (and other parts of Minneapolis) on a grand scale. Most of these plans turned out to be no more than grandiose reveries, but one did bear fruit: Gateway Park and Pavilion (1915, gone), which was in many ways the first urban renewal project in the city's history.

Another big burst of development came in the 1920s, when art deco–style skyscrapers reached new heights. The Foshay Tower (1929) remains the best known and most beloved of these Jazz Age monuments. The art deco skyscraper era in Minneapolis was very brief, however, and ended in 1932 with the completion of the Qwest (Northwestern Bell Telephone) Building.

By the end of World War II, downtown looked much as it had in the 1920s. Streetcars rumbled along thoroughfares, shoppers crowded into Nicollet Avenue's four big department stores, and numerous theater marquees illuminated the night on Hennepin. By the early 1950s, however, downtown showed signs of serious decline as half the city, or so it seemed, began moving away to the suburbs. Civic leaders believed that downtown needed to be modernized or risk losing its place at the center of urban life. What followed was a period of astonishing change.

The Gateway project, which got under way in the 1950s, was only the beginning. Over the next two decades, several other seminal developments helped reshape downtown. One was the establishment of the skyway system, which debuted in 1962 with a single glass-and-steel bridge across Marquette Avenue. Five years later, the Nicollet Mall opened, providing downtown with a parklike spine that was also carefully designed to serve the needs of transportation and commerce. A third key development was the IDS Tower. Completed in 1973, the tower not only provided a dominating new presence on the skyline but also set a high standard for design. Since then, 20 or so other skyscrapers—many designed by "starchitects" with international reputations—have grown up around it. The 1970s also saw large-scale redevelopment of the Loring Park neighborhood, including creation of the Loring Greenway (1976).

In the 1980s, city leaders began to look to downtown's past for inspiration. Two historic areas—the warehouse district and the riverfront—became the focus of redevelopment. The transformation of the riverfront, once a derelict industrial landscape, has been especially spectacular. Here, the defining moment may well have been the 1994 reopening (for pedestrians and bicyclists) of the Stone Arch Bridge, a monument from 1883 that now serves as the riverfront's visual and symbolic centerpiece. Parks, museums, restaurants, the new Guthrie Theater (2006), and a seemingly unlimited number of upscale apartments and condominiums have cropped up in recent years along the riverfront, now one of the city's trendiest precincts.

Residential development, in fact, has fueled downtown's most recent building boom, although a "market correction," as the experts like to call it, was already evident by 2006. Overall, however, Minneapolis has done remarkably well in creating the kind of vibrant downtown that many other American cities of its size can only dream of.

Minneapolis Central Core Map 1

1   Nicollet Mall
2   ING 20 Washington
3   Marquette Plaza
4   Minneapolis Public Library
5   Renaissance Square
6   Gaviidae Common
7   City Center:
    City Center Shopping Mall
    33 South Sixth Street
    Marriott Hotel City Center
8   Restaurant
9   Macy's Department Store
10 IDS Center
11 US Bancorp Piper Jaffrey Center
12 Medical Arts Building
13 Young Quinlan Building
14 900 Nicollet
15 VNU Business Media
16 LaSalle Plaza
17 Oakwood Minneapolis
18 First Baptist Church
19 University of St. Thomas
20 Continental Apartments
21 Westminster Presbyterian Church
22 Peavey Plaza
23 Orchestra Hall
24 Lafayette Building
25 WCCO-TV Building
26 Target Plaza North and South
27 Perkins and Will Building
28 Handicraft Guild Building
29 W Foshay Hotel
30 Baker Center
31 Minneapolis skyway system
    (oldest bridge)
32 Wells Fargo Center
33 Westin Hotel
34 Rand Tower
35 Parking ramp
36 501 Marquette
37 510 Marquette

L1 Minneapolis Public Library,
    Globe Building
L2 Donaldson's Department Store
L3 Conservatory
L4 Northwestern National Bank
    Building

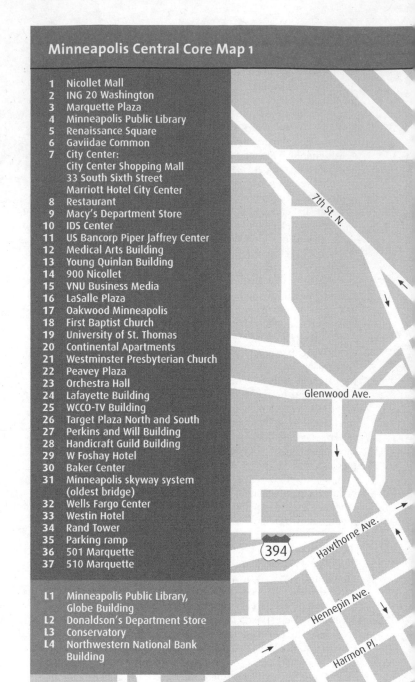

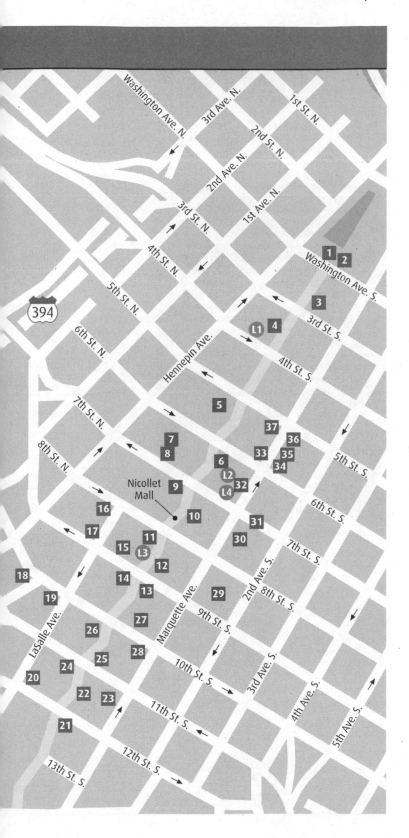

Minneapolis Central Core Map 2

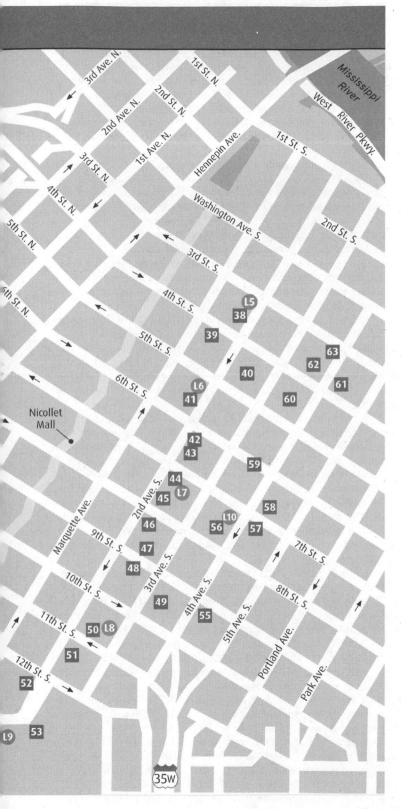

The Central Core

The gridiron of streets forming the heart of downtown Minneapolis was laid out in 1854 by surveyor Charles Christmas on behalf of John Stevens, one of the city's first permanent residents. There's nothing unusual about the plat, which like those of many other American downtowns is aligned in relation to a major geographical feature—in this case, the Mississippi River. Years later, Stevens wrote that the streets should have followed the cardinal points of the compass, but the angled downtown grid is actually a good thing, creating a dynamic twist in what is otherwise a very foursquare city.

Stevens made another crucial decision when he established a standard street width of 80 feet, 20 feet wider than in neighboring St. Paul. Although he subsequently regretted this choice as well (narrower streets, he said, would have saved on "the great cost of paving"), it's hard to argue with the result. One reason Minneapolis's downtown grid has remained largely intact over the years is that streets did not have to be widened or moved to accommodate increasing traffic, as was frequently the case in St. Paul. Unfortunately, Stevens failed to set aside any land for public use along his broad streets, and so Minneapolis has nothing comparable to St. Paul's downtown squares.

Although Stevens's plat survives, many of his original street names have not. Marquette Avenue, for example, was called Minnetonka, while Third Avenue South was Oregon. Portland Avenue, which ends at St. Anthony Falls, was—appropriately enough—known as Cataract. Most of Stevens's named streets were assigned numbers in the standard Minneapolis manner after the city merged with St. Anthony in 1872.

In the early years, the central business core was between Washington Avenue and the river in what is now called the Gateway District. Houses (including many early Victorian mansions), churches, and institutional buildings gradually filled in the area to the south from Fourth Street all the way to Ninth and Tenth streets. By the late 1870s, however, as the city began its most spectacular period of growth, the business core was already creeping south, swallowing up homes and churches along the way. In 1902, when George Draper Dayton built his department store at Seventh Street and Nicollet Avenue, the intersection became downtown's "100 percent corner"—a status it still enjoys.

Despite a lack of anything like professional city planning, the central core by the 1920s had organized itself into three distinct corridors. Theaters and other entertainment venues clustered along Hennepin Avenue. Retailing, including four major department stores, was the focus of Nicollet Avenue. Marquette Avenue was home to many banks and other financial institutions. This three-pronged arrangement is still in evidence today, though not quite as strongly as it once was.

The Nicollet Mall, created in 1967, is the most significant modern-era intervention in the downtown core (though it could be agued that the skyway system, which dates to 1962, has had an even greater impact). The mall functions as a linear park as well as a pedestrian path and busway, and it is downtown's signature public amenity.

Because of its dynamic history of development, the central core has only a dozen or so buildings constructed before 1900. There are, however, many fine art deco and modern-era buildings scattered throughout the core. These include the wonderfully peculiar ING Building (1965), Marquette Plaza (formerly the Federal Reserve Bank, built in 1972), the new Minneapolis Public Library (2006), the supremely elegant IDS Tower (1973), and two first-class art deco skyscrapers from 1929, the obelisk-shaped Foshay Tower and the Rand Tower.

The Nicollet Mall and Back

Nicollet Mall

1 Nicollet Mall !

Washington Ave. South
to Grant St.

Lawrence Halprin and Associates (San Francisco) with Barton-Aschman Associates (transportation consultants), 1967 / expanded, 1982 / rebuilt, BRW Architects, 1990 / Art: sculptures, fountains, bus shelters, benches, planters, and other works by many different artists

Downtown pedestrian malls were once the height of urban fashion, widely viewed as a way to counteract urban decay and bring back shoppers fleeing to the green pastures—and convenient parking lots—of suburbia. Kalamazoo, MI, inaugurated the mall era in 1959, and over the next 25 or so years at least 200 American cities built downtown malls. Most turned out to be failures. The Nicollet Mall, by contrast, has endured, so much so that downtown Minneapolis would be almost unthinkable without it. The mall's success is due in part to the fact that it was the first to include a transitway for buses and taxis. Even now, not everyone likes this dual arrangement, but it's doubtful a pedestrian-only mall would have worked over a length of 12 blocks (the mall was originally eight blocks long but was expanded four blocks to the south in 1982).

Nicollet Avenue was a natural choice for a mall because it had been downtown's prime shopping street since at least the 1880s. By the 1950s, however, Nicollet was losing shoppers to the suburbs, and it was during this anxious period that planning for the mall began. In 1958, the city brought in Barton-Aschman Associates to study transportation needs on Nicollet. Four years later, landscape architect Lawrence Halprin came on board to design the mall. The design's visual signature was a sinuous transitway, which Halprin likened to a medieval street. Halprin rounded out his design with fountains, benches, lights, and bus shelters. Works by such leading sculptors as Alexander Calder added to the mall's pleasing ambience when it opened in 1967. After two decades of hard use, however, the older portions of the mall began to look a bit tacky, even though Mary Tyler Moore's famous hat toss had made it something of an international architectural celebrity. In 1990 the mall was rebuilt with a new palette of materials, new street furniture, new artwork, and new plantings (including Austrian pines that proved no match for Minnesota winters). The curvature of the transitway was also reduced. Halprin groused that the city had "trashed" his design, and while some might argue with that wording, there's no doubt that the original mall—a free-spirited child of the 1960s—is gone. By contrast, the new mall brings to mind an elderly hippie who's finally been forced to don a suit and get a real job. Be that as it may, the mall remains the long stick of glue that holds downtown together.

ING 20 Washington, 1965

2 ING 20 Washington (Northwestern National Life Insurance Co.) !

20 Washington Ave. South

Minoru Yamasaki and Associates, 1965 / Art: Sunlit Straw *(metal sculpture),* Henry Bertoia

A temple to the gods of underwriting, built by an insurance company and mixing luxury and high camp in a way that, say, Liberace would have fully appreciated. Along with Ralph Rapson's now demolished Guthrie Theater (1963), it ranks as a high point of 1960s modernism in Minneapolis. Dubbed by an anonymous wag as the "Japanese Parthenon," the building's highlight is an attenuated, 85-foot-high portico that visually terminates the Nicollet Mall. Japanese-born architect Minoru Yamasaki is most remembered today as the designer of the destroyed World Trade Center towers in New York City. However, ING 20 Washington is more typical of his work from the 1960s, when he was among a number of American architects who produced buildings in a

formal, classically inspired modernist style.

Marquette Plaza

3 Marquette Plaza (Federal Reserve Bank) !

250 Marquette Ave.

Gunnar Birkerts and Associates (Bloomfield Hills, MI), 1972 / renovations and addition, Walsh Bishop Associates, 2002

A hunk of heroic modernism that is now both more and less than it used to be. Built for the Minneapolis Federal Reserve Bank, it employed a novel structural system, with long floors supported by steel arches suspended from towers at either end. This setup allowed the building to span a plaza below much like a suspension bridge. The design made structural sense because it minimized the number of columns that would penetrate into what was actually the largest portion of the building—a system of underground vaults and secure work spaces.

Birkerts's inventive design didn't wear well over time. The building's curtain walls leaked, and the narrow office floors proved inefficient. In 1997, the Federal Reserve moved out, and it looked as if the building might be demolished. Instead, a developer decided to renovate and expand it for office use. The project included replacing the curtain walls and attaching an 11-story addition. This work was nicely done. Even so, the building in its new configuration has lost a fair share of its original swagger, but it's a better outcome than not having the building at all.

Minneapolis Public Library

4 Minneapolis Public Library !

300 Nicollet Mall

Cesar Pelli and Associates (New Haven, CT) with Architectural Alliance, 2006

When Cesar Pelli was selected to design this new central library, not everyone was pleased. Pelli is not an especially edgy designer, and at a time when new libraries have often taken on highly unconventional forms (Rem Koolhaas's Seattle library being the prime example), Pelli's proposal seemed conservative. As it turned out, there was no need to worry. While the library might not satisfy the *avant garde* crowd, it's a luminous building that seems to have instantly endeared itself to Minneapolitans. It's easy to understand why. Suave and gracious, the library delivers that most precious of architectural gifts—natural daylight. Warm, buttery light pours into every corner through bands of fritted glass windows. The result is a building that conveys a sense of clarity and openness perfectly in keeping with the idea of what a library should be.

On the outside, the building is quite straightforward. Its floors— five on one side and four on the other—are stacked like glass trays, separated by narrow bands of Mankato-Kasota stone. The fritted glass windows depict four common Minnesota scenes: water, evergreens, birch trees, and prairie grass. The building goes for one spectacular gesture in the form of a giant wing that takes flight atop the roof and thrusts out over Nicollet Mall. This aggressive protuberance seems too flamboyant for such an otherwise decorous building, but it does indeed catch the eye.

Inside, the library is organized around a wedge-shaped atrium that functions as a kind of hinge as the building bends to follow the converging lines of Hennepin Ave. and the mall. The bright, welcoming atrium sets the tone for the entire building. It's also impeccably detailed: you see quality in everything from structural connectors to railings to stairway treads. The library's loft-style floors, which have no bearing walls, were designed for maximum flexibility, since no one knows for sure what the next big thing in information technology may be. Despite its overall openness, the library has several well-defined interior spaces, including a marvelous children's library with abstract tree forms. Plans also call for the addition of a planetarium, thereby restoring a beloved feature of the 1960s-vintage library that once occupied this site.

LOST 1 *Lost buildings of note on this site include the previous **Public Library** (1961–ca. 2002, razed), and the **Globe Building** (1889–1959, razed), an early skyscraper.*

5 Renaissance Square (Andrus Building)

512 Nicollet Mall

Long and Long, 1898 / remodeled, Miller, Hanson, Westerbeck and Bell, 1983

The mall's old-timer, given a showy—if not historically correct—remodeling of the kind common in the 1980s. The second-floor arches aren't original.

Gaviidae Common interior

6 Gaviidae Common

651 Nicollet Mall

portion between Sixth and Seventh Sts., Cesar Pelli and Associates (New Haven, CT), 1989 / portion between Fifth and Sixth Sts., Lohan Associates (Chicago), 1991

Taking its name from the Latin term for Minnesota's state bird, the loon, this upscale mall was built in two sections by different architects, and it's a decidedly schizoid affair, at least inside. The two sides are connected across Sixth St. by downtown's only double skyway, one at the second story and the other at the fourth. The older portion, designed by Cesar Pelli, features a skylit mall modeled on the airy glass-and-iron arcades of the late nineteenth and early twentieth centuries. It's serenely elegant, almost too much so for the frenetic business of getting and spending. The mall's newer portion, across Sixth St., was designed by Lohan Associates, and its gaudy interior can only be described as the id to Pelli's superego. The, um, high point of the design is a fourth-floor food court that looks to be on loan from a traveling carnival.

LOST 2 *The portion of Gaviidae Common between Sixth and Seventh Sts. was long home to* **Donaldson's Department Store** *(1883 and later). The vacant store was destroyed by fire on Thanksgiving Day, 1982.*

7 City Center

Block bounded by Nicollet Mall, Hennepin Ave., and Sixth and Seventh Sts.

Skidmore, Owings and Merrill (Chicago), 1983

City Center Shopping Mall, Nicollet Mall and Seventh St.

33 South Sixth Street (office tower), 33 Sixth St. South

Marriott Hotel City Center, 30 Seventh St. South

This big architectural oaf includes a fortresslike mall and a 52-story office tower, both clad in precast concrete panels designed, quite successfully, to achieve maximum unattractiveness. The glitzy Marriott Hotel is a bit better, with mirrored glass walls that at least offer some semblance of urbanity, a quality woefully lacking in the complex as a whole.

8 Restaurant (Forum Cafeteria interior) i

Off Seventh St. in City Center

George Franklin, Magney and Tusler, 1929 / 1978 (interior dismantled) / 1983 (interior moved)

Buried within City Center is a reconstituted version of one of the city's finest art deco interiors, salvaged from the Forum Cafeteria once located on this block. The Forum, a fantasy in black and gray glass, was a remodeling job, installed in 1929 inside an old movie theater on Seventh St. The interior was dismantled after the Forum closed in 1978 and reinstalled, with many changes, in a restaurant space that as of late 2006 was vacant.

9 Macy's (Dayton's) Department Store

700 Nicollet Mall

Charles S. Sedgwick, 1902 / additions, Larson and McLaren, 1937, 1947, and later

Known for nearly a century as Dayton's, this retail emporium—now Macy's—is a Minneapolis icon. Still well patronized, the store sprawls across a city block and offers 12 floors of merchandise, along with restaurants, an auditorium, and other amenities.

Macy's Department Store, 1902 section

Long the flagship of the Dayton's chain, the store consists of buildings from several eras. The oldest section at Seventh and Nicollet is the most ornate, while the newer portions toward Eighth St. are in the Moderne style of the 1930s and 1940s.

IDS Center, 1975

10 IDS Center !

717 Nicollet Mall

Philip Johnson and John Burgee (New York) with Edward Baker, 1973 / renovated (Crystal Court), HGA, 1998

An extraordinary retailing, office, and hotel complex. Far taller and larger than any previous downtown building, IDS Center

brought a new level of modern elegance and a new scale to the

IDS Center Crystal Court, 1975

city, and it has lost none of its luster over the years. Although later office towers have risen to within a few feet of the IDS, none so far has come close to matching the overall quality of its design or its gracious urban presence.

When it opened in 1973, the 57-story skyscraper (built for Investors Diversified Services, now part of American Express) soared 300 feet above the Foshay tower, long the city's tallest building. Given its bulk, the IDS Tower could easily have been a rude giant. Instead, Johnson and partner John Burgee, assisted by Minneapolis architect Edward Baker, turned out a very large building that carries itself with a ballerina's grace. Much of the building's seeming delicacy stems from the way in which its thin metal window frames project slightly from the walls of blue green glass, producing an airy, cagelike effect. The architects also produced a commercially savvy design that yields up to 32 corner offices per floor. They accomplished this feat of prestige enhancement by means of stepbacks (or "zogs," as Johnson called them) at the tower's corners.

At the heart of the center, which includes the Marquette Hotel, is the Crystal Court, so called because of a glass roof that rises in a series of faceted setbacks from a height of three to eight stories. Johnson once called the court "a frolic space," and while it may be a bit too formal for uncontrolled cavorting, it certainly is fun. It's also the crossroads of downtown; 50,000 people pass through it on a typical weekday. The court was remolded in 1998 with the addition of a fountain, new benches, and black olive trees that added much-needed greenery to the space.

11 US Bancorp Piper Jaffray Center

800 Nicollet Mall

Ellerbe Becket, 2000

A competent if hardly eye-catching 30-story skyscraper. It's part of a three-block project along this side of the mall that began in the late 1990s, replacing a mix of mostly small, older buildings with skyscrapers, a Target store, shops, and restaurants.

LOST 3 *In 1987, a costly shopping mall and office complex opened on this site. Known as the **Conservatory**, it was a bust from the start. It stood only 11 years before being razed, making it one of the shortest-lived downtown buildings in Minneapolis history.*

12 Medical Arts (Yeates) Building

825 Nicollet Mall

Long and Thorshov, 1923 / addition, Long and Thorshov, 1929 / renovated, Shea Architects, 1993

This Gothicized office building, notable for its creamy terra-cotta, was designed to cater to doctors and dentists. Although the building has been modernized in places, its vaulted lobby—resplendent with marble, bronze, and terrazzo—remains largely intact.

13 Young Quinlan Building i

901 Nicollet Mall

Frederick Ackerman (New York) with Magney and Tusler, 1926 / renovated and restored, Ellerbe Becket, 1989

In 1924, Elizabeth Quinlan, who had opened her first women's clothing shop in Minneapolis 30 years earlier, made plans for a new store that would offer "the austerity and simplicity of the finest Italian art." The result was this exquisite Renaissance Revival building designed by New York architect Frederick Ackerman. Rusticated Mankato-Kasota

Young Quinlan Building, 1929

stone sheathes the ground floor, while stone pilasters and columns frame windows set in the brick walls above. Within, the store features a marble staircase, crystal chandeliers, and superb iron, brass, bronze, and pewter metalwork. Quinlan died in 1947, but her store operated until 1985. In 1989 the building was handsomely renovated by new owners and now combines retail and office space. One of the building's lovely brass and pewter elevators is the last in the city still operated by an attendant.

14 900 Nicollet (including Target Store and Retek Tower)

900 Nicollet Mall

Ellerbe Becket, 2001

Taking its cue from theme parks and the spectacular deceits of Las Vegas, 900 Nicollet consists of a group of facades intended to mimic a traditional downtown streetscape with a variety of buildings. The complex, which includes a Target store as well as an office building known as Retek Tower, uses numerous shades of brick and stone, along with terra-cotta accents, to achieve its effects. The message here seems to be that modern architecture has run out of ideas and that the best that can be done along downtown's most famous street is to play a game of pretend.

15 VNU Business Media (Minnesota Theater storefronts)

50 Ninth St. South (at LaSalle Ave.)

Graven and Mayger, 1928 / theater razed, 1959 / remainder of building remodeled, ca. 1960s

This two-story building occupies part of the site of the Minnesota (later Radio City) Theater, a lavish movie palace that opened in 1928. With just over 4,000 seats and a vast lobby, it was the largest movie theater ever built in the Twin Cities. Never a financial success, it fell to the wrecker after standing for only 31 years. Although this building dates to the 1960s, it was probably built using the steel frame of a shop and office structure that fronted the theater along Ninth St.

16 LaSalle Plaza

800 LaSalle Ave.

Ellerbe Becket, 1991

Most of the architectural theatrics here are within, where you'll find an arcade with one of the most elaborate interiors of the postmodern era in the Twin Cities. The highlight is a copper fountain that burbles beneath an oculus sporting fiber-optic stars and neon lights.

17 Oakwood Minneapolis (Central YMCA)

36 Ninth St. South

Long, Lamoreaux and Long, 1919 / renovated, J. Buxell Architecture, 1994

A handsome exercise in Gothic Revival, built as a YMCA and designed by the architects who produced the similarly styled Medical Arts Building nearby. The YMCA moved to a new facility next door in the early 1990s, after which this building was converted into an apartment hotel.

18 First Baptist Church

Tenth St. and Harmon Pl. (1021 Hennepin Ave.)

*Kees and Fisk (later Long and Kees), 1886 / addition (**Jackson Hall**), Long and Thorshov, 1923 / addition, Station 19 Architects, 1983*

First Baptist, founded in 1853, is among the city's oldest congregations. Its first two churches were wood-frame structures located in or near the Gateway District. In 1886 the congregation completed this double-towered church, which is built of Mankato-Kasota stone and blends the Romanesque and Gothic Revival styles. The church lost its original steeples in a 1967 windstorm. Within, there's an auditorium with radial seating and a sloping floor. This arrangement, used for many Protestant churches, is called the Akron plan, after the Ohio city where it was developed.

19 University of St. Thomas

1000 LaSalle Ave.

*includes **Terrence Murphy Hall**, Opus Architects, 1992 / **Opus Hall**, Opus Architects, 1999 / **Law School**, Bulfinch Richardson and Abbott (Boston), 2003 / **Schulze Hall**, Opus Architects, 2005 / Art: The Seven Virtues (fresco, Terrence Murphy Hall), Mark Balma, 1994*

Four modern buildings wearing Gothic Revival drapery. The highlight here is Mark Balma's 1,900-square-foot ceiling fresco in the Terrence Murphy Hall lobby. The fresco, one of the largest in the United States, presents a vision of the seven virtues, at least some of which most college students are probably acquainted with.

20 Continental (Ogden) Apartments N *L*

66–68 12th St. South (at LaSalle)

Adam Lansing Dorr, 1910

A six-story building originally constructed as an apartment hotel. Clad in three colors of brick, the Continental is in a classical style sometimes called Second Renaissance Revival.

21 Westminster Presbyterian Church N

83 12th St. South

Charles S. Sedgwick and Warren H. Hayes, 1897 / renovation, Purcell and Elmslie, 1910–12 / additions 1937 (Magney and Tusler), 1952, and later / sanctuary renovated, 1998

A twin-towered Gothic Revival church that forms a big stone anchor near the south end of the mall. It's home to one of the city's oldest Protestant congregations, founded in 1857. This church replaced an earlier one (on the

Westminster Presbyterian Church, 1898

site of the Macy's store at Seventh and Nicollet) that burned down. Despite the church's massive appearance, the sanctuary is bright and airy, with 1,300 seats circling beneath a glass dome. Although it retains much of its historic integrity, the church—built largely of local limestone—has seen many additions and remodelings, including a kindergarten room renovated by Prairie Style masters William Purcell and George Elmslie. As early as 1904, part of the front gable had to be rebuilt because of damage from a windstorm. Additions to the church include a parish house and chapel (1937) as well as an education wing from the 1950s.

22 Peavey Plaza

Nicollet Mall and 11th St.

M. Paul Friedberg and Associates, 1975

A very "architectural" plaza, rather hard-edged but on the whole beautifully designed. Though only an acre in size, the plaza has something for everyone—pools, fountains, walkways, grassy nooks shaded by honey locust trees, and all manner of places to sit. The park is also used by the Minnesota Orchestra for a popular series of summer concerts.

Orchestra Hall, 1982

23 Orchestra Hall

1111 Nicollet Mall

Hardy Holzman Pfeiffer Associates (New York) with HGA, 1974 / renovated, Hardy Holzman Pfeiffer Associates, 1997

This building's aggressive modernism brought industrial chic to Minneapolis. The "power plant" style of the lobby, complete with exposed vents, drew grumbles from those expecting the usual symphony hall. It was in fact a very deliberate architectural gesture, designed to remove the taint of class and privilege from the symphony-going experience. Whether this populist strategy succeeded remains open to debate, but the building has won acceptance over the years (though its lobby, revamped in 1997, has never seemed as spacious or inviting as it ought to be). The hall itself, home to the Minnesota Orchestra, is impeccable. An oblong brick box, it seats over 2,500 people and is justly renowned for its rich, lively acoustics (by Cyril Harris), achieved in part with the help of 100 or so sound-deflectors sprinkled across the ceiling like giant cubes of sugar.

24 Lafayette Building

1108 Nicollet Mall

Croft and Boerner, 1922

One of the small glories of the mall, this building wears its polychromed terra-cotta ornament like fine jewelry. The style is Renaissance Revival with a Spanish-Moorish twist.

The Central Core

25 WCCO-TV Building

Nicollet Mall and 11th St.
(90 11th St. South)

Hardy Holzman Pfeiffer Associates (New York), 1983 / renovated, Beecher Walker and Associates (Salt Lake City), 2005

This building, supposedly designed to resemble a television tower, is clad in copper and exceptionally large and beautiful blocks of Mankato-Kasota stone. It's well done, but you'd think a television station would have sought a more lively, modern, and technologically sophisticated image than the one conveyed by this rather ponderous structure.

26 Target Plaza North and South

1000 Nicollet Mall

Ellerbe Becket, 2002

A pair of office buildings, one 15 stories and the other 33, that serve as headquarters for the Target Corp. and also provide retail space along Nicollet Mall. The tall south tower features a sophisticated architectural light show provided by tall glass pipes within the uppermost floors.

27 Perkins and Will (Essex) Building

Nicollet Mall and Tenth St.
(84 Tenth St. South)

Ernest Kennedy, 1913 / renovated, Perkins and Will, 2001

A gracious example of the Classical Revival style. The two lower stories are sheathed in terracotta with brick above. An architectural firm now occupies much of the building.

28 Handicraft Guild Building *L*

89 Tenth St. South

William Channing Whitney, 1907 / addition, 1914

This Georgian Revival building was once home to the Minneapolis Handicraft Guild. Founded by 12 women in 1904, the guild served as the local outpost of the Arts and Crafts movement then sweeping the United States. The building provided studios and workshops for artisans as well as galleries, classrooms, an auditorium, and a store. In 1918 the guild was dissolved when many of its educational programs were merged into a new art department at the University of Minnesota.

Foshay Tower, 1929

29 W Foshay Hotel (Foshay Tower) **! N L**

821 Marquette Ave.

Magney and Tusler (Leon Arnal, chief designer), 1929 / renovated, Setter Leach and Lindstrom and Shea Architects, 1992 / renovated, 2007–8

A giddy bottle of art deco champagne uncorked just in time for what turned out to be the last big party of the 1920s. Modeled on the Washington Monument, it's the nation's only obelisk-cum-skyscraper. At 447 feet, the Foshay was for over 40 years the Twin Cities' tallest building, and its open-air observatory provided a thrilling view to generations of schoolchildren. The tower was the brainchild of Wilbur Foshay, a stock plunger whose mastery of creative accounting was such that he eventually earned a three-year berth in federal prison for mail fraud. Before this unhappy turn of events, Foshay had been the toast of the town during festivities to mark the tower's opening in August 1929. John Philip Sousa's band played a march composed for the occasion, and girls dressed as water nymphs cavorted for the crowd. Then the stock market crashed. Foshay's fortune went down with it, so quickly that even his check to Sousa bounced.

The tower, clad in Indiana limestone, is more than just an unusual shape: it's also a superior example of art deco architecture. Rising from a broad two-story base lined with storefronts, the Foshay features four identical windows per floor on each side of the tower. Because of the inward slant, however, corner windows are slightly different on every floor, an inconvenience when it comes to ordering drapes. Foshay's name is carved in ten-foot-high letters beneath the observatory, which wraps around a stepped pyramidal roof. The public corridors in the ground floor of the tower's two-story base feature terrazzo floors with inlays, along with such ornamental details as images of the tower worked into elevator doors. These hallways originally converged near an open courtyard later filled in with a parking ramp.

Wilbur Foshay, whose luxurious office suite still remains on the upper floors, was pardoned by President Harry Truman in 1947 but never returned to the world of high finance. He died in Minneapolis on August 30, 1957, exactly 28 years after the dedication of his one-of-a-kind tower. As of 2007, work was under way to convert the Foshay into a luxury hotel.

30 Baker Center

Block bounded by Marquette and Second Aves. South and Seventh and Eighth Sts.

various architects, 1926, 1928, 1968 and later

includes **Baker Block,** 706 Second Ave. South

Larson and McLaren, 1926

A complex of four interconnected office buildings, including three from the 1920s. The gem of the group is the Baker Block, a 12-story building sheathed in Kettle River sandstone but sporting terra-cotta ornament in a style so elusive it's been labeled everything from Byzantine to Gothic Revival.

31 Minneapolis skyway system !

various architects, 1962 and later

Minneapolis's downtown skyway system, the largest in the world, consists of over 70 bridges and eight miles of corridors linking about 80 blocks. Its impact has been profound: skyways now shape every aspect of downtown life. The first skyway appeared in 1962 when Leslie Park and his partner, architect Edward Baker, built a bridge (gone) from their new Northstar Center to a building across Marquette Ave. A year

Skyway near Seventh and Marquette

later, they built a second bridge (which still stands) across Seventh St. to the Baker Block.

Park and Baker did not originate the idea of elevated pedestrian walkways. Various urban dreamers had long envisioned such walkways as a means of separating pedestrian and vehicular traffic. In Minneapolis, however, traffic separation wasn't the impetus for skyways; instead, the aim was to boost downtown businesses by sheltering workers and shoppers from Minnesota's extreme weather. As with Park and Baker's early bridges, most Minneapolis skyways are built and maintained by individual property owners. As a result, bridges vary widely in style. A few, such as those designed in 1973 for the IDS Center, are exceptionally elegant, but most are fairly simple. The second-story corridors that radiate from these bridges also vary in quality and style.

The system's pluses and minuses have long been debated. Skyways have undoubtedly helped the central core remain vibrant, providing an all-weather connection from one end of downtown to the other. Yet they have also sucked life up and away from the streets. As a result, ground-floor retailing has become a dicey proposition in much of downtown. The lack of obvious connections between street level and the skyways is also a problem. What is certain is that the skyways are here to stay, and however fashionable it may be to decry their mournful effect on street life, the fact is, come January, just about everyone who can use them, will.

32 Wells Fargo (Norwest) Center !

90 Seventh St. South

Cesar Pelli and Associates (New Haven, CT), 1989

Along with the IDS Center and 225 South Sixth, this is one of three 50-plus-story skyscrapers that rule the Minneapolis skyline (the IDS Tower is the tallest of the trio by a matter of feet).

Wells Fargo Center pays homage to the General Electric (RCA) Building at Rockefeller Center in

Wells Fargo Center

New York City. The slablike form and sculpted setbacks of that art deco masterpiece are echoed here in Mankato-Kasota stone with white marble accents. The result is a very large building that nonetheless manages to maintain a slender, pleasing profile from most vantage points. It's also quite urbane at street level. Within there's a rotunda (at Sixth St.) that's supposed to be an update of the grand bank lobbies of old, but somehow it doesn't impress quite as much as it should.

LOST 4 *Wells Fargo Center occupies the site of the* **Northwestern National Bank Building,** *constructed in 1929. The building was best known for its rooftop Weatherball. The 14-story building was destroyed, along with the neighboring Donaldson's Department Store, in a fire on Thanksgiving Day 1982.*

33 Westin Hotel (Farmers and Mechanics Bank)

520 Marquette Ave.
(also 88 Sixth St. South)

McEnary and Krafft, 1941 / additions, McEnary and Krafft, 1955, 1961 / renovated, 2007 / Art: relief sculptures, Warren T. Mosman, 1941

Converted to a luxury hotel in 2007, this longtime home to the Farmers and Mechanics Savings

Bank is a major monument in the Moderne phase of art deco. Faced in Mankato-Kasota stone, the building is most notable for

Westin Hotel

bold relief sculptures (of a farmer and a mechanic, naturally) that frame the main entrance. Their designer, Warren T. Mosman, headed the sculpture department at the Minneapolis Institute of Arts. Within, a walnut-paneled banking hall (now the hotel's lobby) was designed to impress—but not overawe—the bank's unpretentious clientele. The tall wings that wrap around the old banking hall were built as offices but today house 214 hotel rooms.

Rand Tower, 1928

34 Rand Tower ! N i

527 Marquette Ave.

Holabird and Root (Chicago), 1929 / renovated and restored, Shea Architects, ca. 2001 / Art: Wings (sculpture in lobby), Oskar J. W. Hansen, 1929

A skyscraper that's strong in profile but dainty in its details. Chicago architects John Holabird and John Wellborn Root, Jr., were art deco masters, as they were to demonstrate conclusively with

their St. Paul City Hall–Ramsey County Courthouse (1932). This 26-story tower displays classic art deco features: emphatic corners, dramatic verticality, setbacks, and exquisite ornament. The tower is especially fine at street level, where a delicate scrim of metalwork frames the windows.

The must-see lobby includes a terrazzo floor inlaid with stars and crescents, marble walls, frosted glass, a spiral staircase, and red elevator doors with nickel-plated ornament. Here, too, you'll find *Wings*, a bronze sculpture by Oskar J. W. Hansen. The statue, as well as references to aviation in the building's ornamental program, reflects the man behind the tower, Rufus R. Rand. A member of a prominent Minneapolis business family, Rand served in the Lafayette Flying Corps during World War I and was involved with the aviation industry for much of his life.

35 Parking ramp (Scandinavian Bank Building)

517 Marquette Ave.

Bertrand and Keith, 1895 / rebuilt, Gage and Vanderbilt, 1925

A bit of Egyptian Revival–style exotica now impaled by a skyway and serving no purpose other than to screen a parking ramp. Long live the pharaoh!

36 501 Marquette (Soo Line–First National Bank Building) L

501 Marquette Ave. (also 105 Fifth St. South)

Robert W. Gibson (New York), 1914

Before the Foshay and Rand Towers came along in 1929, this 16-story building was the tallest downtown. Like most skyscrapers of its era, it follows a tripartite design scheme with a clearly defined base, a long mid-section treated repetitively, and ornate upper stories beneath a full cornice. It was built as joint headquarters of the First National Bank and the Soo Line Railroad.

37 510 Marquette (First Federal Reserve Bank)

510 Marquette Ave.
(also 75 Fifth St. South)

Cass Gilbert, 1922 / addition, Larson and McLaren, 1955 / renovated, Cerny and Associates, 1974–77

You can't tell it now, but this was Cass Gilbert's greatest work in Minneapolis, built for the newly minted Ninth District Federal Reserve Bank. Gilbert designed a stone vault of a building, bristling with colossal columns and pilasters and offering nary a window in its lower walls. In the 1950s, a ten-story addition was built above the original structure. After the bank moved in 1972, Gilbert's columns and other classical details were removed during another remodeling.

Skyscraper City

38 330 Second Avenue South

330 Second Ave. South

KKE Architects, 1980

A cookie-cutter modern office structure, notable only because of what used to be on its site.

Northwestern Guaranty Loan Building, 1892

LOST 5 *The **Northwestern Guaranty Loan (Metropolitan) Building,** at the corner of Second Ave. South and Third St., was Minneapolis's one indisputable masterpiece of Victorian commercial architecture. Built in 1890 and designed by E. Townsend Mix, the 12-story building, clad in sandstone and granite, was especially renowned for its magnificent iron and glass atrium. The building was torn down in 1962.*

39 Schiek's Palace Royale (Farmers and Mechanics Bank Building) *L*

115 Fourth St. South

Long and Kees, 1891–93 / enlarged and remodeled, William Kenyon, 1908

The last small Classical Revival–style bank building that remains downtown. Today, it's home to a topless bar and restaurant. If you step inside for a view of the, ahem, scenery, you'll discover a glass dome that once illuminated a "ladies banking lobby" but is now the scene of activities not everyone would consider ladylike. Incidentally, the only known natural cave beneath downtown Minneapolis was discovered in this vicinity in 1904 and is sometimes called "Schiek's Cave."

40 Qwest (Northwestern Bell Telephone) Building

224 Fifth St. South
(425 Second Ave. South)

Hewitt and Brown, 1932

In the 1930s, long before Ma Bell gave birth to a fractious set of babies, the phone monopoly constructed large office and equipment buildings—mostly in the art deco style—in cities across the United States. These buildings were often of very high quality, as is the case with this 26-story skyscraper, clad in Minnesota limestone and granite. Designed in a version of art deco sometimes called Zigzag Moderne, the building features symmetrical setbacks culminating in a

Qwest Building, 1944

square tower, now topped, not very attractively, with a crown of modern electronic equipment.

One Financial Plaza

41 One Financial Plaza (First National Bank)

120 Sixth St. South

Holabird Root and Burgee (Chicago) with Thorshov and Cerny, 1960 / renovated, Skidmore, Owings and Merrill (Chicago), 1981

The first big post–World War II skyscraper in Minneapolis, built for the old First National Bank. With its metal-and-glass skin, this 28-story building brought a sense of modernity to a skyline that in 1960 was still dominated by art deco towers. Its basic form—a

vertical slab mounted atop a long, low base—was widely used for skyscrapers of the time, while its minimalist detailing shows the influence of Chicago architect Ludwig Mies van der Rohe.

LOST 6 *One of the city's finest nineteenth-century office structures, the New York Life Building, once occupied this site. It opened in 1890 and included a magnificent lobby with two spiral staircases. The building was razed in 1958.*

225 South Sixth Street

42 225 South Sixth Street (First Bank Place)

225 Sixth St. South

Pei Cobb Freed and Partners (New York), 1992

The newest of the three 50-plus-story skyscrapers that hold sway over the city's skyline. Designed by James Ingo Freed, it rises from an L-shaped site in a series of cylindrical and rectilinear forms, culminating in an illuminated crown that shines over the city like a halo. A mix of gridded and horizontal cladding adds to the complexity of the building, which includes an 18-story section in addition to the main 56-story tower. Lacking vertical momentum, the building isn't as graceful as its two skyline competitors—the IDS Tower and Wells Fargo Center. Within, a winter garden provides some green solace during Minnesota's longest season.

43 Grand Hotel Minneapolis (Minneapolis Athletic Club)

615 Second Ave. South

Bertrand and Chamberlin, 1915 / renovated, HGA, 1992

An old downtown athletic club that has taken on a second life as a ritzy hotel. It's one of several early twentieth-century buildings of identical height (12 stories) that stand along or near Second Ave. South. This uniformity is the result of height limits imposed by the city until about 1920.

44 707 Second Avenue South (Ameriprise Financial Center)

707 Second Ave. South

HKS Architects (Dallas), 2000

A 31-story skyscraper with cellular, stone-clad facades that project from a curving background of glass.

Lutheran Brotherhood Building, 1955

LOST 7 *An early modernist gem, the* **Lutheran Brotherhood Building,** *opened on this site in 1955. Designed by Perkins and Will of Chicago, it was the first glass-walled office building downtown and was notable for its dainty elegance. It was razed in 1997.*

45 Minneapolis Club

729 Second Ave. South

Gordon, Tracy and Swartwout (New York) with William Channing Whitney, 1908 / addition, Hewitt and Brown, 1911 / addition, Setter Leach and Lindstrom, 2002

The Minneapolis Club was founded in 1883 by members of the city's business, professional, and social elite. The club was at several other locations before constructing this building in 1908. With its clubby English feel, it's the kind of building that new money orders up when it wishes to appear old. The brick building has aged gracefully, abetted by a luxuriant growth of ivy.

46 St. Olaf Catholic Church

215 Eighth St. South

Thorshov and Cerny, 1955 / addition (including **Chapel of Saints John and Paul),** *Bentz, Thompson and Associates, 1980 / addition (parish center), Opus Corp., 1990 / renovated, HGA, 2000*

Founded in 1940, St. Olaf initially occupied an 1880s stone church here built for a Protestant congregation. After that building was destroyed by fire in February 1953, the parish built this modernistic church. Faced in Mankato-Kasota stone, the church is in the form of an elongated hexagon, with high windows illuminating the nave. There's also a tower that has nine bells salvaged from the old church. An addition from 1980 includes an exquisite barrel-vaulted chapel designed by Milo Thompson. A parish center was added in 1990.

47 Campbell-Mithun (Piper Jaffray) Tower

222 Ninth St. South

HGA, 1985

A big glass box with a funny top, which sums up a lot of skyscrapers from the 1980s.

48 Oakland Flats

213–15 Ninth St. South

Harry Jones, 1889

Two round windows set within an ornate panel above the entrance add a lively, if somewhat peculiar, note to this brick and brownstone apartment building, which has looked a bit forlorn in recent years. With development surging around it, you have to wonder how long it will survive.

Ameriprise Financial Client Service Center Winter Garden

49 Ameriprise Financial Client Service Center and Winter Garden

901 Third Ave. South

HKS Architects (Dallas) and Maya Lin (Winter Garden), 2002

A surprisingly elegant corporate back office building that includes a Winter Garden designed by Maya Lin. Occupying a glassy enclosure set in front of the main mass of the building, the garden is Lin's only work in the Twin Cities, and it has some of the quietly affecting qualities of her most famous design—the Vietnam Veterans Memorial in Washington, DC. The garden makes especially imaginative use of water, which flows down a portion of the windows like a moving scrim and even freezes over in winter.

50 Leamington Municipal Ramp and Transit Hub

220 11th St. South
(1001 Second Ave. South)

Ellerbe Becket, 1992

Deconstructivism—a style that aimed to subvert normal architectural expectations by creating what look to be elaborately disordered buildings—never enjoyed much popularity in the Twin Cities. But here's a stab at it in a parking ramp that features lots of weird angles.

LOST 8 *The ramp is named after the* **Leamington Hotel,** *once one of the largest in the city. The hotel stood on this block from 1905 until its demolition in 1990.*

Ivy Tower, 1974

51 Ivy Hotel and Residence (Ivy Tower) *L*

1115 Second Ave. South

Kimball, Steele and Sandham (Omaha, NE), 1930 / additions, Walsh Bishop Associates, 2007

A skyscraper in miniature that, like a child in a roomful of grown-ups, can be hard to spot. Never intended to stand alone, it was supposed to be one of four towers at the corners of a giant new Second Church of Christ Scientist (now located elsewhere on this block). Alas, 1929 was an inauspicious year for grand plans, and this tower was the only part of the church ever completed. The tower—which once included offices, classrooms, and a reading room—is a suave design that mixes the ziggurat form of art deco with mideastern overtones. Its pebbly concrete walls are also distinctive. Renamed Ivy Tower in the 1980s, the building stood vacant and in jeopardy of demolition for over a decade. A plan was finally approved in 2005 to incorporate the building into a condominium and hotel complex that will include new 17- and 25-story towers.

52 Architects and Engineers Building *N L*

1200 Second Ave. South

Hewitt and Brown, 1920 / restored, MacDonald and Mack Architects, 1985

An elegant building in the Renaissance Revival style. It was designed as a cooperative that included both private offices and shared spaces for the design professionals who were its chief occupants. The names of great architects such as Christopher Wren and Filippo Brunelleschi are displayed in gold lettering above the third-floor windows. Within, there's a vaulted lobby.

53 Minneapolis Convention Center

1301 Second Ave. South

Convention Center Design Group (Leonard Parker Associates, Setter Leach and Lindstrom, LMN Architects, and others), 1991 / addition, Convention Center Design Group, 2002 / Art: Seasons of the City (mural), Anthony R. Whelihan, 2003

A convention center that's not the overpowering architectural gorilla such buildings tend to be. Opened in 1991 and enlarged 11 years later, the center's well-defined entry towers, glassy lobbies, and carefully detailed precast concrete cladding give it a welcoming presence. Four of the exhibition halls within are topped by low domes. Conservatively styled, the center isn't especially exciting, but its does what it's supposed to do in a pleasant Minnesota sort of way.

LOST 9 *The six square blocks consumed by the convention center were home to many buildings, including the **Minneapolis Auditorium,** built in 1927 and razed in 1988.*

Wesley United Methodist Church

54 Wesley United Methodist Church i

101 Grant St. East

Warren H. Hayes, 1891 / restored, MacDonald and Mack Architects, 1988–98

One of the city's finest nineteenth-century churches. It was built for the oldest Methodist congregation in Minneapolis, founded in 1852. The church, which has undergone extensive renovation since the 1980s, offers a colorful take on the Richardsonian Romanesque style. Its walls are built of quartzite from southwestern Minnesota, with softer brownstone used for trim. There's also a good deal of Byzantine-style ornament. The 120-foot corner tower originally had a tall wooden cap, but it was removed after a 1949 windstorm. The massive exterior yields within to a radiant auditorium that seats over 1,000 people beneath a delicate stained-glass dome.

Gethsemane Episcopal Church, 1890

55 Gethsemane Episcopal Church N *L*

905 Fourth Ave. South

Edward S. Stebbins, 1884

A church that serves the city's first Episcopal parish, founded in 1856. It's constructed of local limestone in a rural English Gothic style that conveys an aura of quaint charm. A corner tower topped by embattlements, rather than the usual spire, is perhaps the church's most distinctive feature. The interior includes open beams, a richly carved screen between the sanctuary and altar, and a stained-glass window designed by Louis Tiffany that depicts the Garden of Gethsemane.

56 Accenture Tower in Metropolitan Centre (Lincoln Centre)

333 Seventh St. South

Kohn Pedersen Fox (New York), 1986

With its oddly placed midblock lobby and unusual shape, this office tower has always seemed awkward. In fact, the building was designed to have two mirroring towers, with a shared lobby between them. The second tower never got off the ground, however, and its site is now a grassy plaza. Still, what's here qualifies as a good example of 1980s postmodernism, its design hinting at everything from Beaux-Arts Classicism to art deco. The lobby is especially sumptuous.

LOST 10 *The **John Bradstreet Shop and Crafthouse** occupied part of this site from 1904 to 1919. Regarded as the city's leading decorator, Bradstreet incorporated many Japanese elements in the crafthouse, which was a remodeled and enlarged 1870s mansion. The crafthouse closed five years after Bradstreet's death in an auto accident.*

701 Building

57 701 Building

701 Fourth Ave. South

Murphy-Jahn Associates (Chicago), 1984

German-born Chicago architect Helmut Jahn was one of the *wunderkinds* of the 1980s skyscraper boom, designing bright, hyperactive buildings that usually lie somewhere beyond the confining bounds of good taste. Here, Jahn produced a blue glass octagon with salmon-colored accents, and the result is a building as cheerfully inviting as a big lollipop.

58 Thrivent Financial (Lutheran Brotherhood) Building

625 Fourth Ave. South

Skidmore, Owings and Merrill (Chicago), 1981

Pretty wild stuff for Lutherans. Constructed for Lutheran Brotherhood (which became Thrivent in a 2001 merger), this 17-story building's cascading glass curtain wall ends in a barrel-vaulted dining room poised like a giant glass Tootsie Roll above Fourth Ave. The effect is undeniably dramatic. The other side of the building—a large blank wall—is undeniably uninteresting.

Hennepin County Government Center

59 Hennepin County Government Center

300 Sixth St. South

John Carl Warnecke Associates with Peterson Clark and Associates, 1977

A vision of government as numbing bureaucracy, this 24-story, granite-clad building consists of two towers—one for county offices and the other for courts—separated by an atrium. The building spans Sixth St., creating a darkly uninviting tunnel for pedestrians but leaving room for plazas to either side, including one with a large reflecting pool that faces Minneapolis City Hall. Within, the public spaces feel cold and oppressive, and the center as a whole seems designed to convey the might and majesty of county government more than anything else. It doesn't make for a pleasant experience. The original atrium design, with open balconies, also proved to be a suicide magnet, and all the balconies later had to be enclosed with glass.

Minneapolis City Hall, 1958

Minneapolis City Hall, Father of Waters *statue, 1926*

60 Minneapolis City Hall (Municipal Building) ! N i

350 Fifth St. South

Long and Kees, 1889–1906 / restoration, MacDonald and Mack Architects, 2001, 2004 / Art: Father of Waters (statue in rotunda), Larkin Mead, 1906 / Hubert Humphrey *(statue at Fifth St. entrance), Roger M. Brodin, 1989*

A thundering granite pile that when it rose block upon mighty block in the 1890s must have seemed like the city's dream of itself—powerful, resourceful, built for the ages. No other civic building in the Twin Cities conveys a comparable sense of mass, and the fact that it was constructed in a treacherous swamp of politics, controversy, and debt only makes it more remarkable. Placed on a site well away from the heart of downtown, the building in its early years stood like a stony giant amid rows of small frame houses that served as reminders of the tiny riverside village Minneapolis had been less than half a century earlier.

Known as the Municipal Building, it was designed for both city and county government. This division, saturated in politics, proved awkward. There was also debate over the site, a compromise between downtown and "south side" interests. Financing problems plagued the project as well, the cost ballooning from an early estimate of $1.5 million to a final total of $3.6 million. Even the selection of an architect proved controversial despite a design competition. The local duo of Frederick Long

and Frederick Kees won the job only after much politicking. Given these issues, it's no surprise that the building took nearly two decades to complete.

It was worth the wait. An outstanding example of the Richardsonian Romanesque style, the building is modeled on Boston architect H. H. Richardson's Allegheny County Courthouse in Pittsburgh (1884–88). The sparsely adorned exterior is built of granite from Ortonville, MN, with some blocks weighing over 20 tons. The design displays many Richardsonian Romanesque features, including deep-set arched entries, bands of windows grouped under elongated arches, turrets and dormers, and two towers, the largest of which (on the Fourth St. side) rose to 345 feet, making it the tallest structure in the city until the Foshay Tower opened in 1929. As built, the tower had a crow's-nest lookout from which visitors could obtain a view of the city. The lookout is gone, but the tower's 15-bell carillon and its clock (once said to be the world's largest) remain.

The interior, which originally included an open central courtyard, wasn't substantially completed until 1906. It offered an array of splendid spaces, including courtrooms, the mayor's reception room, and the city council chambers. The building's chief interior spectacle, however, is provided by a rotunda off Fourth St. Here, Larkin Mead's gloriously over-the-top statue of a reclining Father of Waters presides over an ornate space featuring a marble staircase, stained glass, carved stonework (including sculptor Andrew Gewond's delightful grotesques), and superb ironwork by Winslow Brothers of Chicago.

Over the years, the building has undergone many remodelings and modernizations, mostly of less than stellar quality. In the 1980s the city and county finally developed a restoration plan. So far, the Fourth and Fifth St. entrances, the city council chambers, and, most recently, the rotunda have been restored. Looking better than it has in quite awhile, the building seems ready to go for another 100 or even 1,000 years, should Minneapolis last that long.

Grain Exchange Building

61 Grain Exchange (Chamber of Commerce) Buildings ! N i

400 Fourth St. South

*Kees and Colburn, 1902 / **Annex,** Long, Lamoreaux and Long, 1909 / addition (trading room enlarged), Bertrand and Chamberlin, 1919 / **North Building,** Edmund J. Prondzinski, 1928 / addition (three floors added), 1955 / renovated and restored, ca. 1985*

These three buildings were constructed for the Minneapolis Chamber of Commerce, established in 1881. Later renamed the Minneapolis Grain Exchange, the complex was home to as many as 500 commodities traders. The oldest of the trio—a ten-story, brick-clad building at the corner of Fourth St. and Fourth Ave. South—is one of the city's finest early skyscrapers as well as the first constructed with an all-steel frame. Its heavy corner piers, tawny terra-cotta ornament, and exquisite hardware derive from the work of Louis Sullivan, especially his Guaranty Building

(1896) in Buffalo, NY. The heart of the building is a fourth-floor trading room that includes a trading pit, 32-foot-high ceilings, and a balcony with murals furnished by decorator John Bradstreet. The building also has a beautiful main lobby finished in marble, brass, iron, terra-cotta, and ornamental plaster.

A narrow, 12-story Classical Revival–style annex was added to the east side of the building in 1909, and it's nicely done, with boldly scaled terra-cotta ornament. A third building, completed to the north in 1928, offers little of architectural interest.

62 U.S. Courthouse and Federal Building

300 Fourth St. South

Kohn Pedersen Fox (New York), 1997 / Art: plaza, Martha Schwartz, 1997

This courthouse could have served as an elegant, modernist foil to City Hall. Instead, it comes across as blandly corporate. To be sure, it has some nice features— the courtrooms are well handled, and the lobby is by no means unpleasant—yet the building overall isn't very compelling. Neither is its plaza, by artist Martha Schwartz, which consists of a field of grassy lumps representing drumlins, a kind of glacial hill found in Minnesota. As high-concept art, the plaza must have looked peachy on paper, but it's proved to be of little earthly use to the public.

63 Flour Exchange N L

310 Fourth Ave. South

Long and Kees, 1893 / addition, Kees and Colburn, 1909

Holding down one corner of the block otherwise occupied by the U.S. Courthouse, this brick office building is the earliest surviving example in Minneapolis of the straightforward skyscraper style pioneered by Chicago architects in the 1880s. The first four stories date to 1893. The top seven floors, all but identical to those below, were added in 1909.

Hennepin Avenue and the Warehouse District

Named after Father Louis Hennepin, who "discovered" St. Anthony Falls, Hennepin Avenue is among the city's oldest streets, following a trail that led from the riverbank near Nicollet Island, where the Mississippi could be forded, to Lake Calhoun and points west. The first bridge anywhere across the Mississippi, built in 1855, was at Hennepin, linking Minneapolis to the village of St. Anthony on the east bank of the river.

In its gaudiest days, Hennepin was called the "Broadway of the Northwest." The first large opera house in Minneapolis, the Pence, opened on Hennepin in 1867, and theaters eventually spread down the avenue all the way to Tenth Street. At one time or another, at least 25 theaters operated on Hennepin, which also became home to hotels, the first Minneapolis Public Library (1889, gone), restaurants, bars, arcades, dime museums, and strip joints. Streetcar service made the avenue's attractions readily accessible.

Hennepin's luster faded in the 1960s and 1970s as theaters shut down one by one while porn houses and rough-and-tumble bars flourished. Block E between Sixth and Seventh streets became especially notorious. Its attractions included the legendary Moby Dick's Bar, which generated up to 600 police calls a year—still believed to be a municipal record. The city cleared the block in 1987, and it is now occupied by a truly dreadful hotel-entertainment complex completed in 2003. The reopening of the historic State and Orpheum theaters in the early 1990s was a more positive development, and today much of Hennepin has gone upscale, its old lewd charms largely a memory.

To the north of Hennepin lies the Historic Minneapolis Warehouse District, a gathering of mighty brick buildings that has evolved into one of the city's most desirable places to live, work, and play. Most of the 30-square-block neighborhood now lies within national and local preservation districts, and its trendy transformation would surely astonish the sober businessmen who began building their warehouses and factories here in the 1880s.

Along First and Second Avenues North, development has focused on the renovation of old warehouse buildings for use as offices and housing. Elsewhere in the district, hundreds of new apartments and condominiums have sprung up, many proclaiming themselves—on thin evidence—to be "lofts." Most of this new architecture is of the inoffensive brick box variety, although of late edgier buildings like the Bookmen Stacks (2005) have embraced a more modern look.

Rail lines—the first arrived in 1867—drove development of the warehouse district, which by the 1890s was a bustling mix of sawmills (along the river), saloons (mainly along Washington Avenue), and wholesale and manufacturing firms, including numerous farm implement dealers. The district's sturdy brick buildings—mostly constructed between 1885 and 1920—were designed by some of the city's leading architects. At least one, Harry Jones's Butler Brothers Warehouse (now Butler Square) of 1906, is among the city's architectural masterpieces.

The trade didn't last forever, and as early as the 1930s the fortunes of the warehouse district began to decline. But because its buildings weren't generally in the path of development, they largely escaped the convulsions of urban renewal in the 1950s and 1960s. Instead, they waited like dormant plants for new life. It came in the form of tax credits for historic renovations in the 1970s, along with a deepening public interest in preservation. Artists and entrepreneurs formed the vanguard of this urban renaissance, which has become one of the great stories in the city's history.

Hennepin Avenue and the Warehouse District

1 Hennepin Avenue Suspension Bridge
2 Federal Reserve Bank
3 Lumber Exchange
4 Hiawatha Line Warehouse District/
   Hennepin Avenue Station
5 Minnesota Shubert Performing Arts
   and Education Center
6 Hennepin Center for the Arts
7 Murray's Restaurant
8 Block E
9 Pantages Theater and Simpson
   Building
10 Girard Building
11 State Theater
12 Chambers Hotel
13 Orpheum Theater
14 First Avenue and 7th Street Entry
15 Target Center
16 Gluek Building
17 Butler Square
18 Wyman Building
19 300 First Avenue North
20 Fourth Street Ramp, Fifth Street Ramp,
   Seventh Street Ramp

21 Ford Centre
22 Wells Fargo Branch Bank
23 Bookmen Stacks
24 Traffic Zone Center for Visual A
25 Pacific Block
26 Andrews Building
27 Tower Lofts
28 HGA Offices
29 Ames and Fischer Building
30 Itasca Lofts
31 Minnesota Opera Center
32 Gaar Scott Historic Lofts
33 River Station
34 Creamette Historic Lofts
35 Heritage Landing
36 Riverwalk Condominiums
37 Riverwalk Condominiums
38 Ribnick Furs Building
39 Prisma International
40 Chicago House
41 Foster House
42 Theatre de la Jeune Lune

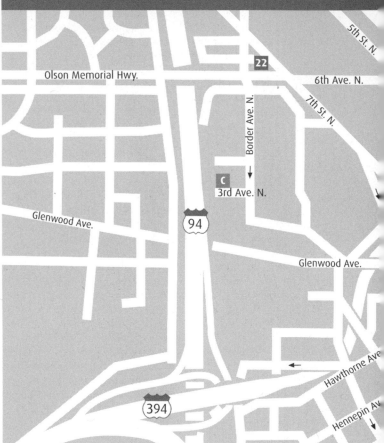

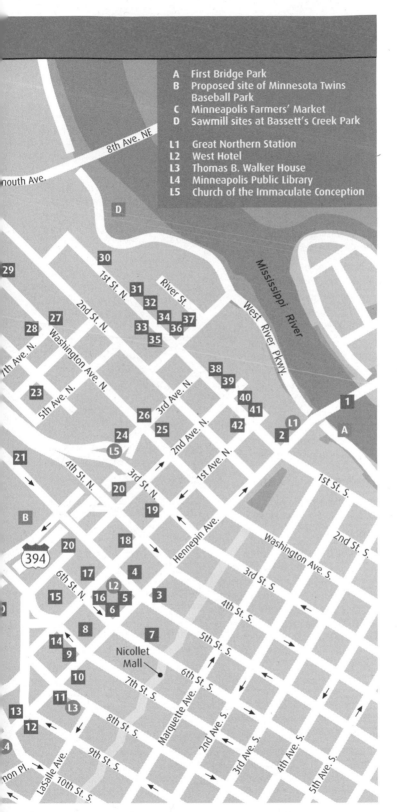

A   First Bridge Park
B   Proposed site of Minnesota Twins
    Baseball Park
C   Minneapolis Farmers' Market
D   Sawmill sites at Bassett's Creek Park

L1   Great Northern Station
L2   West Hotel
L3   Thomas B. Walker House
L4   Minneapolis Public Library
L5   Church of the Immaculate Conception

Hennepin Avenue and the Lower Warehouse District

Hennepin Avenue Suspension Bridge

1 Hennepin Avenue Suspension Bridge N *L*

Across Mississippi River to Nicollet Island

Howard Needles Tammen and Bergendorf (engineers), 1990

This stubby suspension bridge was built in part to "recall" two earlier suspension spans here. But there was no structural rationale for it, since suspension bridges these days are normally used for spans of several thousand feet. This bridge crosses only 625 feet, which explains why the towers are so low compared to those of other, far more graceful suspension bridges elsewhere.

POI A First Bridge Park N *L*

Beneath Hennepin Avenue Bridge at West River Pkwy.

2001

Here you'll find excavated footings of the first three Hennepin Ave. bridges—suspension spans built in 1855 and 1876 and a steel arch bridge completed in 1891 and replaced by the present bridge. Part of the iron anchoring for the 1876 bridge is also on display.

2 Federal Reserve Bank N *L*

90 Hennepin Ave.

Hellmuth Obata and Kassabaum (Kansas City), 1997

The first two Federal Reserve banks in Minneapolis were muscular buildings that conveyed a sense of the institution's power and prestige. This building, by contrast, tries hard not to be monumental. Instead, it offers a wall of curving glass, a dainty clock tower that looks as though

it might have come from a 1950s Scandinavian town hall, and a riverfront plaza designed to show that the bank can be a good urban neighbor. Call it the kinder, gentler Federal Reserve, but don't call it a bold, imaginative, or exciting work of architecture.

LOST 1 *For many years this was the site of the* **Great Northern Station,** *which opened in 1914 and replaced an earlier* **Union Depot** *just across Hennepin Ave. The station had a stately, colonnaded facade and was one of the city's prominent monuments. Like many another old train depot, it ended its days as a vacant hulk; it was torn down in 1978.*

Lumber Exchange, 1957

3 Lumber Exchange N *L*

425 Hennepin Ave.

Long and Kees, 1886, 1891 / addition (top two stories), Harry Jones, ca. 1909 / remodeled, Wheeler Hildebrant, 1980

Downtown's oldest "skyscraper," and the city's tallest when it was built in 1886. Like Long and Kees's contemporaneous Minneapolis City Hall, the building—with its arched entrances and walls of rough-cut granite and sandstone—is in the Richardsonian Romanesque style. Its undulating bay windows and lack of ornamentation except around the entrances also show the influence of period Chicago skyscrapers. The building was enlarged in 1891 along its Hennepin Ave.

side. Later, two stories (faced in brick) were added to the top. It was originally home to many lumber dealers, but that trade largely vanished with Minnesota's pineries by 1910.

4 Hiawatha Line Warehouse District/Hennepin Avenue Station

Fifth St. between Hennepin Ave. and First Ave. North

ESG Architects, 2004

This station is at the northern end of the Hiawatha Line, which opened in 2004 and restored light rail service to Minneapolis 50 years after streetcars rattled off to oblivion. The line connects downtown to the Minneapolis–St. Paul International Airport and the Mall of America. So far it's exceeded ridership goals, though critics lambasted the $715 million cost while others contended the line was built in the wrong place. It was. Much of the line follows an industrial corridor along Hiawatha Ave. that provides limited opportunities for dense, transit-oriented development. A link between downtown St. Paul and Minneapolis along University Ave. would have made more sense. (It's likely that if a second line is built it will be along or near University.)

The line's 17 stations, all designed by local architects, vary in style. Some go for a glassy, high-tech modern look, while others drift in the direction of nostalgia. This station seems to fall between those two poles.

5 Minnesota Shubert Performing Arts and Education Center (Sam S. Shubert Theater) N *L*

516 Hennepin Ave.

William Albert Swasey (New York), 1910 / renovated, Miller Dunwiddie Architecture, 2008

A monument to either the wisdom or the folly of historic preservation, depending on your point of view. This playhouse turned movie theater, which had been vacant for nearly 20 years, was

moved here in February 1999 at a cost of $4.7 million even as critics questioned whether it was a wise expenditure of public dollars.

The 1,100-seat theater, downtown's oldest, features a creamy terra-cotta facade with classically derived ornament. Although hardly a great building, it has historic value as the last theater of its kind in Minneapolis. The theater—all 5.8 million pounds of it—was moved because it stood in the path of development plans for the so-called Block E. Artspace, a nonprofit developer, bought the building (minus its floor and stage house, which couldn't be moved). The city then paid to move the structure so that it could be renovated into an arts center. However, it took Artspace seven years to raise enough money (including $11 million allocated by the state legislature) to begin renovations. The Shubert is now scheduled to debut in its new guise in 2008.

LOST 2 *The* **West Hotel,** *the finest in the city when it opened in 1884, once occupied this site. The hotel had over 400 rooms and a huge skylit lobby. It was demolished in 1940.*

Hennepin Center for the Arts, 1900

6 Hennepin Center for the Arts (Masonic Temple) N *L*

528 Hennepin Ave.

Long and Kees, 1888–90 / renovated, Svedberg-Vermeland Architects, 1979

A fine old Victorian, its craggy walls of Ohio sandstone animated by intricate carvings, quasi-Egyptian columns, projecting bays and balconies, and whatever else the architects could think of to stir up some Masonic excitement. Two Moorish onion domes once capped the composition, but they succumbed to age and rot and were removed. As designed, the temple included retail and office space plus four large Masonic halls stacked one atop the other at the building's northeast corner. The largest of the halls occupied most of the top floor. The building has been an arts center since 1979, and plans call for linking it via an atrium to the Shubert Theater next door.

7 Murray's Restaurant

26 Sixth St. South

ca. 1880s (original building) / remodeled, 1946, 1954, 1984 (Paul Pink and Associates)

This restaurant opened in 1946 and since then has offered the luscious promise of a "silver butter knife steak" behind a late Moderne facade that, like the restaurant's signature dish, is well aged.

8 Block E

Hennepin Ave. between Sixth and Seventh Sts.

Antunovich Associates (Chicago), 2002–3 / includes stores, restaurants, bar, and parking; **Graves/601 Hotel;** *and* **Crown Theatres 15**

A cartoon of a development that presents architecture as a kind of entertainment for the same masses who crowd into Disney World or roam the Las Vegas strip. It's easy to dislike everything about this complex, from its cheap-looking stucco and precast concrete details to its almost complete divorce of structure from facade, but it's much harder to dismiss the reality of what it represents. Commercial architecture of all kinds is growing ever lighter, showier, and more disposable, and Block E in its own crummy but calculated way perfectly expresses these trends.

9 Pantages (Mann, RKO Pan) Theater and Stimson Building i

700–10 Hennepin Ave.

Kees and Colburn and B. Marcus Priteca (Seattle; auditorium), 1916 / renovated, 1926, 1946, 1961 / restored, HGA, 2002

This old vaudeville theater stood vacant for 18 years before the City of Minneapolis stepped in to buy and restore it. Reopened in 2002, it now serves as a venue for touring shows, concerts, and other live performances. When it opened in 1916, it was part of a circuit operated by Alexander Pantages. The theater went through three names and an equal number of remodelings before beginning its long hibernation in 1984. The 1,000-seat auditorium has lavish plasterwork, a skylight, and a two-level balcony. Today, the Pantages is one of three restored theaters that create a distinctive entertainment zone along Hennepin between Seventh and Ninth Sts.

Girard Building

10 Girard (Teener) Building

727–29 Hennepin Ave.

Magney and Tusler, 1922

A sliver of a building, faced in terra-cotta and one of the last of its kind downtown. Many original downtown lots were only 20 feet wide, leading to clumps of narrow buildings that once formed highly varied streetscapes. It's anyone's guess how long this little gem will survive.

State Theater

11 State Theater i

805 Hennepin Ave.

J. E. O. Pridmore (Chicago), 1921 / restored, Ellerbe Becket with Ray Shepardson, 1991

When it opened on February 5, 1921, this was the largest and most opulent theater yet built in Minneapolis, its terra-cotta facades adorned with floral ornament, droopy Ionic column capitals, eagles, and even four grinning faces mounted along the cornice. Architect J. E. O. Pridmore described the style as "Free Italian Renaissance." Make that very free, and you've probably got it right. Within, the theater is equally ornate. The auditorium, which seats just under 2,200, features colorful plasterwork, crystal chandeliers, and murals depicting "bountiful" (i.e., bosomy) nudes. Though built to accommodate stage and film presentations, the State functioned mainly as a movie theater until it closed in 1975. A church later occupied the building, which was purchased by the city and restored in 1991 as part of the LaSalle Plaza project in the same block.

LOST 3 *The Thomas B. Walker House occupied this site from 1876 to about 1920. Walker was a lumber and real estate baron and a great collector of art. A public gallery he established at his house in 1887 evolved into what is now the Walker Art Center.*

12 Chambers Hotel (Fairmont Apartment Hotel)

901 Hennepin Ave. (also 9 Ninth St. South)

Adam Lansing Dorr, 1908 / renovated and enlarged, Rockwell Group (New York) with Shea Architects, 2006

An old apartment hotel that doesn't look anything like it used to after receiving an upscale makeover. It's one of many projects that have changed the texture and feel of this part of Hennepin in recent years.

Orpheum Theater, interior

13 Orpheum (Hennepin) Theater i

910 Hennepin Ave.

Kirchhoff and Rose (Milwaukee), 1921 / renovated, Miller Dunwiddie Architects, 1989 / renovated and restored, HGA, 1993

With 2,650 seats, this old vaudeville house is the largest of the three restored theaters along Hennepin. In fact, it was once billed as the "biggest vaudeville theater west of New York." The theater is actually two separate but connected structures: a long, fingerlike lobby that extends back from a narrow facade along Hennepin, and the auditorium itself, which is well to the back paralleling Hawthorne Ave. Much remodeled over the years, the restored lobby includes six terra-cotta bas-relief sculptures inspired by the Roman art of Pompey. The auditorium is a testament to the colorful art of the plasterer, offering a ripe abundance of garlands, swags, medallions, and the like. There's also a ceiling dome that glitters with 30,000 squares of aluminum leaf. Originally, the theater had a shallow stage, but it was extended by 20 feet as part of the restoration project so that the theater could accommodate large Broadway shows.

LOST 4 *The first* **Minneapolis Public Library,** *a fine Richardsonian Romanesque building, was built in 1889 at Tenth St. and Hennepin Ave. at what is now the site of a parking lot for First Baptist Church. The library was demolished in 1959.*

First Avenue, 1990

14 First Avenue and 7th Street Entry (Greyhound Bus Depot)

701 First Ave. North
(29 Seventh St. North)

Lang and Raugland, 1936 / remodeled, ca. 1970

Known for its association with performers like Prince, this nightclub began as a Greyhound bus depot designed in the Streamlined Moderne variant of art deco, with sweeping curves and bands of windows. After Greyhound left, the building reopened in 1970 as a club. Now painted black with a field of white stars, the old depot retains many original interior features. If the music ever dies, the building—an important Moderne monument—might be a candidate for restoration.

15 Target Center

600 First Ave. North

KMR Architects, Pfister Architects, 1990

It's too big for its site, its facades have the look of bad wallpaper, it rebukes its historic surroundings,

its steeply pitched nosebleed seats will give you instant vertigo, and it's home to a consistently mediocre basketball team—the Minnesota Timberwolves. The only good news is that, given the typical life span of arenas these days, it probably won't be around for very long.

16 Gluek Building *L*

16 Sixth St. North

Boehme and Cordella, 1903 / interior rebuilt after fire, 1989 / Art: mural, Herman Krumpholz

A terra-cotta facade with baroque aspirations makes this one of downtown's liveliest little buildings. There's also a *trompe l'oeil* mural on one side. The building was constructed for the Gluek Brewing Co., which operated a brewery in northeast Minneapolis until 1965.

Butler Square, 1913

17 Butler Square (Butler Brothers Warehouse) ! N *L*

100 Sixth St. North

Harry Jones, 1906 / renovated, Miller Hanson and Westerbeck with Arvid Elness, 1976–81 / Art: Circus Flyers (figures suspended in atrium), George Sefal, 1981

One of the city's architectural masterpieces, a sternly poetic mass of wine-colored brick that conveys the commercial might of Minneapolis at the dawn of the twentieth century. It's also significant as the first, and still the finest, warehouse renovation in the historic district here. The job wasn't done perfectly—the windows, for example, should have been set farther back in their reveals—but it paved the way for many other renovations to come.

The building was constructed for Butler Brothers, a Boston-based wholesaler that later established (in 1927) the Ben Franklin chain of variety stores. The design was entrusted to Harry Jones, and it proved to be the outstanding work of his long and varied career. He produced a building of great power that also offers many subtle details: a corbeled (stepped out) cornice, narrow windows grouped vertically so as to resemble oversized Gothic lancets, twin belt courses that define the building's base, and deeply inset ground floor openings that reveal the heft of its masonry walls. Within, the building was a timber-framed loft structure designed to meet the heavy demands of warehousing. The architects of the renovation that began in 1976 carved an atrium out of the interior and surrounded it with glass-walled offices inserted into the building's timber framework, all with beautiful results.

18 Wyman (Wyman Partridge and Co.) Building N L

400 First Ave. North

Long and Kees, 1896 / addition, Kees and Colburn, 1910

Renaissance Revival elements applied to a standard brick warehouse. Bands of terra-cotta ornament and a Doric frieze enliven the ground floor, while five large arches and a heavy cornice balance off the composition at the top. This building served as headquarters of Wyman Partridge and Co., a dry goods wholesaler. The company once owned several other buildings nearby, including a 12-story factory building—the warehouse district's tallest—at 110 Fifth St. North.

19 300 First Avenue North (Langford-Newell Block) N L

300 First Ave. North

William H. Dennis, 1887 / renovated, KKE Architects, 1985

An impressive building notable for stone and brick arches that seem to lift it above the street as

300 First Avenue North, 1974

though it were mounted on stilts. The building's terra-cotta ornament includes lion heads and a bulging corner cartouche that displays a train and a clipper ship. Built for businessman Robert Langdon (memorialized by a decorative "L" in the terra-cotta), the building was once occupied by the wholesale grocery firm of George L. Newell and Co., which later became SuperValu.

20 Fourth Street Ramp, Fifth Street Ramp, Seventh Street Ramp

Second Ave. North between Third and Tenth Sts.

Stageberg Beyer Sachs, 1989 (Fifth St.), 1991 (Seventh St.), 1992 (Fourth St.)

Three city-built parking ramps that—unlike many other post-modern structures with pretensions of being "contextual"—actually do fit into their historic environment.

POI B Proposed site of Minnesota Twins Baseball Park

Block bounded by Third Ave. North, Fifth and Seventh Sts. North, and railroad tracks

HOK Sport (Kansas City) and HGA, 2010

A $522 million, 42,000-seat open-air baseball park for the Minnesota Twins is scheduled to open here in 2010. Early renderings suggest the park will try to blend in with the warehouse district's brick and masonry industrial buildings.

21 Ford Centre (Ford Assembly Plant) N

420 Fifth St. North

Kees and Colburn with John Graham (Seattle), 1914

The Ford Motor Co. produced 400 Model T automobiles a day here before moving its operations to the assembly plant that still operates in St. Paul (but will close in 2008). Now offices, Ford Centre is a well-designed specimen of the lightly classicized, concrete-frame industrial architecture of its time.

POI C Minneapolis Farmers' Market

312 East Lyndale Ave. North

1933 and later

This popular market, located beside an elevated stretch of Interstate 94, lies at the southern edge of what was once a genteel neighborhood of Victorian homes known as Oak Lake.

22 Wells Fargo (Northwestern National) Branch Bank

615 Seventh St. North

Ackerberg and Associates, 1969

Grand kitsch from the 1960s. With its sloping walls, restless massing, and aura of otherworldly oddness, this two-toned brick wonder would make a fine temple for a religious cult. Alas, the only almighty it serves at present is the dollar.

23 Bookmen Stacks

345 Sixth Ave. North

James Dayton Design, LSA Design, 2005

A glass- and zinc-clad building that brings a welcome dose of aggressive, forthright modernism to the nostalgia-prone warehouse district. While the building wouldn't turn many heads in

California (where its architect, James Dayton, once worked for

Bookmen Stacks

the modern master Frank Gehry), it certainly stands out here and plays off nicely against the masonry structures around it.

24 Traffic Zone Center for Visual Art (Moline, Milburn and Stoddard Co.) N

250 Third Ave. North

Joseph Haley, 1886 / addition, 1925 / renovated, 1995

A rugged stone industrial building converted in 1995 to artist studios and offices. It's a strict and economical design for its time, with nary a hint of Victorian ornament. The building, which received a seamless three-story addition in 1925, achieves its effects through the massing of its limestone walls, the rhythmic pattern of its windows, and the use of belt courses between the floors. It was built for the Moline, Milburn and Stoddard Co., a farm implement manufacturer.

LOST 5 *The **Church of the Immaculate Conception,** predecessor of the Basilica of St. Mary, was built at the corner of Third St. and Third Ave. North in 1872. As warehouses swallowed up much of this neighborhood, church leaders decided to erect a new basilica, which opened in 1914 on a site near Loring Park. The old church was then demolished.*

From Lumber to Lofts

Washington Avenue

This long avenue, which connects North Minneapolis to downtown and the University of Minnesota, has a right-of-way of 100 feet, among the widest of any street in the Twin Cities. It was designed as the main avenue in the first plat of Minneapolis made for John Stevens in 1854. Though still an important street, it's not as heavily traveled as it once was because traffic has shifted to Interstate 94.

25 Pacific Block N L

218–28 Washington Ave. North

ca. 1865 (possibly later) / renovated, Adsit Architecture and Planning, 2004

This one-time hotel is believed to be the oldest building in the warehouse district. Note the second- and third-floor windows, which have arches of varying curvature, an arrangement that does much to enliven the building's long facade.

26 Andrews (Jackson) Building N L

300–12 Washington Ave. North

Ernest Kennedy, 1897 / addition (fifth floor), Ernest Kennedy, 1899

Like Butler Square, this building uses Gothic detailing—such as pointed-arch windows on the fourth floor—to dress up what is otherwise a utilitarian structure. The glassy ground floor was built to serve as a storefront, while the upper floors were warehouse space. The fifth floor is an addition, tacked on just two years after the building opened.

27 Tower Lofts (Northern Bag Co.) N

700 Washington Ave. North

Hewitt and Brown, 1920 / renovated, ESG Architects, 2005

The tower that gives this building its name is a landmark along this part of Washington Ave. Like so many other large industrial structures from the early 1920s,

the building has a Gothic air to it, but there are also hints in the tower's subtle setbacks of the art deco style to come. The building became an artists' cooperative in the 1980s but was later converted to condominiums.

28 HGA Offices (Loose-Wiles Biscuit Co.) N

701 Washington Ave. North

Hewitt and Brown, 1910 / renovated, HGA and Miller Dunwiddie Architects, 2002

Now home to one of the state's largest architectural firms, this old biscuit factory is an impressive specimen of industrial design. The building's style is elusive: the ground floor hints at Renaissance Revival, but the terra-cotta panels pinned to the upper corners like big brooches seem to be in the spirit—if not the exact style—of Chicago architect Louis Sullivan.

Ames and Fischer Building

29 Ames and Fischer Building (Deere and Webber Co.) N

800 Washington Ave. North

Kees and Colburn, 1902, 1910 / renovated, 2000, 2005

One of the finest buildings in the warehouse district. The six-story portion went up first, in 1902. The taller section to the north was added in 1910. The building's sloping lower walls, arched entrance, deeply inset windows, curving parapet (on the six-story section), and clean lines are all reminiscent of Chicago warehouses designed by Louis Sullivan. There's even some Sullivanesque ornament around the restored entry. Used today for offices, the building originally served the Deere and Webber Co., a branch of the Illinois-based John Deere Co.

POI D Sawmill sites at Bassett's Creek Park

West River Pkwy. near Eighth Ave. North

The land that forms the park at the mouth of Bassett's Creek is all fill. Much of it was dumped by sawmills—there were at least seven at one time or another—that began clustering along the river here in the early 1850s. All were gone, as were most of Minnesota's pineries, by 1910. Bassett's Creek, which is diverted into a tunnel through the downtown area, is named after Joel Bassett, a settler from Maine who homesteaded a farm near here in 1852 and later operated the first steam-powered sawmill on the west bank of the river at the foot of Seventh Ave. North.

Itasca Lofts

30 Itasca Lofts (Itasca A and B warehouses) N *L*

702–8 First St. North

Long and Kees, 1886 / renovated, Cuningham Architects, 1984

Although this yellow brick building looks like one structure, it's a pair of identical warehouses separated by an internal wall.

With their broad brick arches, including a pair that recedes into the parapet, the warehouses have a light and fanciful quality that sets them apart from the weightier buildings all around. They were among the first warehouses here to be converted into housing. The plain red brick buildings to the north, which date to 1906, are also part of the complex and were originally known as the C and D warehouses.

31 Minnesota Opera Center (S. J. Cooke Co. warehouses) N *L*

620 First St. North

Frederick A. Clarke, 1892 / renovated, Phillips Klein Companies, 1990

32 Gaar Scott Historic Lofts (S. J. Cooke Co. warehouses) N *L*

614 First St. North

Frederick A. Clarke, 1892 / renovated, Paul Madson and Associates, 2001

These buildings offer two dramatic examples of historic preservation. The Gaar Scott Lofts—named after a farm implement manufacturer that once occupied the building—was for decades covered by a green metal screen. When the screen was finally removed, the effect was both startling and beautiful. The adjacent building that's now part of the Minnesota Opera Center suffered a fire that destroyed its interior, but architects were able to insert three floors of new space inside the shell while preserving the entire five-story facade.

33 River Station N *L*

First St. and Sixth Ave. North (560 Second St. North)

J. Buxell Architecture, 1998–2002

One of the largest housing developments in Minneapolis history, consisting of 348 units in 12 buildings. Too bad, then, it has so little architectural character. Instead, the buildings retreat behind timid brick shells, as though terrified of anything that smacks of modernity.

34 Creamette Historic Lofts (Champion Reaper Co. Warehouse) N *L*

428–32 First St. North

Long and Kees, 1897 / addition and renovation, Paul Madson and Associates, 1998

A fine Richardsonian Romanesque building. Dominating the composition is a sandstone arch, a staircase set within it, that makes for a most emphatic front entrance. Originally an implement warehouse, the building was purchased in 1916 by what later became the Creamette Co., a pioneer in developing fast-cooking elbow macaroni. An addition was constructed in 1998 when the building was converted to housing.

35 Heritage Landing N *L*

415 First St. North

BKV Group, 2000 and later

With its neo-Victorian corner turret, mansard roof, and brash colors, this brazen confection—which includes housing as well as some retail space—is so close to pure pop architecture that you almost expect to see costumed Disney characters rappelling down the walls. Still, give this garish devil its due: it's got some life and energy to it, which is more than can be said of the neutered brick boxes that often pass for modern architecture elsewhere in the warehouse district.

Riverwalk Condominiums

36 Riverwalk Condominiums (Lindsay Brothers Building) N *L*

400 First St. North

Harry Jones, 1895, 1909 / renovated, Oertel Architects, 1987 / 2004

37 Riverwalk Condominiums (Chicago, St. Paul, Minneapolis and Omaha Railroad freight house) N *L*

50–56 Fourth Ave. North

1880–1928

The old Lindsay Brothers Building is another impressive design from Harry Jones. Although it has Gothic-style windows, the building's overall design is reminiscent of H. H. Richardson's seminal Marshall Field Warehouse of 1887 in Chicago. It was constructed for Lindsay Brothers Co., a farm implement wholesaler. Converted to housing in 1987, the warehouse was renovated a second time in 2004 to create loft-style condominiums. A new building called **Lindsay Lofts** was constructed just to the north in 2001. The Riverwalk complex also includes a brick freight house built for the Omaha Road. It's one of the largest railroad remnants in the warehouse district, where the Omaha and two other railways—the Northern Pacific and the Soo Line—once maintained tracks and large yards along First and Second Sts. North. These old rail corridors have now been almost completely filled in with new development.

38 Ribnick Furs (Berman Brothers) Building N *L*

224 First St. North

William D. Kimball, 1884 / addition, Jack Boarman, 1988

A delightful little building with oversized keystones that punctuate the second story like exclamation points.

39 Prisma International (Hennepin Hotel) N *L*

204 First St. North

1888

40 Chicago House N *L*

124 First St. North

Carl F. Struck, 1884

41 Foster House N *L*

100 First St. North

1882 / 1884 / 1886

A number of small hotels for workingmen were built along this part of First St. in the 1880s. These three charmers, all restored, are among the surviving examples.

Theatre de la Jeune Lune

42 Theatre de la Jeune Lune (Realty Co. Warehouse) ! N *L*

106 First Ave. North (also 105 First St. North)

Edward S. Stebbins, 1889 / remodeled, Cass Gilbert, 1902–6 / remodeled, Paul Madson and Associates, 1992

One of the warehouse district's outstanding buildings, the fortunate recipient of two brilliant remodelings that came 90 years apart. The first transformation was the work of Cass Gilbert. Between 1902 and 1906, Gilbert—then still busy with his Minnesota State Capitol—gave the warehouse a Gothic makeover, unifying the main facade with a series of inset arches. In 1992, Paul Madson and Associates of Minneapolis undertook an equally superb intervention, converting the cavernous warehouse, used for cold storage for many years, into a lively and highly flexible new home for Theatre de la Jeune Lune.

The Central Riverfront

For many decades, most of the central riverfront was the flour-dusted industrial heart of Minneapolis, a densely built environment of mills and factories powered by a subterranean maze of racing waterways. What made it all possible was St. Anthony Falls, where the Mississippi River in its natural state fell 75 feet through a mile-long tumult of cascades and rapids. The falls also happened to be in just the right place, poised between pineries to the north and prairies—ideal for growing grain—to the south and west. Although sawmilling initially flourished at the falls, flour millers soon became dominant as wheat poured in from farms along an ever expanding system of rail lines.

The first mills appeared along the western side of the falls in the 1820s, built by soldiers from Fort Snelling to grind flour and saw logs. But it wasn't until the 1850s, when the west bank opened to settlement and a power canal was excavated, that the flour milling industry began a period of astonishing growth. By the 1880s, 25 mills clustered along the west bank, forming one of the largest water-powered industrial complexes in human history. Railroad tracks threaded around and through the mills, some crossing the Mississippi on James J. Hill's Stone Arch Bridge, built in 1883. Meanwhile, subsidiary industries—including bag and barrel makers and manufacturers of milling machinery—sprang up nearby to feed the roaring colossus of flour.

The mills were of masonry construction, with heavy timber interior frames, and the largest of them, such as the Washburn A (1880, now Mill City Museum), could turn out over a million pounds of flour a day. Yet for all its might, the milling industry couldn't withstand the power of changing market forces that gradually ate away at Minneapolis's flour production in the early twentieth century. The west bank's first flour mill, the Cataract, closed in 1928, and more were shuttered in the 1930s when Buffalo, NY, became the nation's largest flour miller.

By the 1960s, when the last of the mills shut down, the falls area had become a landscape of loss and decay. But cities can be surprisingly resilient, and the seeds of an urban revolution were already in the air by 1971, when most of the old milling quarter was placed within the St. Anthony Falls Historic District. A wave of trendy redevelopment occurred in the 1980s, when several old mills—including the Standard (1879, now Whitney Landmark Residences) and the Crown Roller (1880, now offices)—were renovated with the aid of historic tax credits and large infusions of public money. The reopening of the Stone Arch Bridge in 1994 for pedestrian use was another milestone.

Around 2000 a second and much larger wave of development, fueled by a booming housing market, began to sweep through the district, utterly transforming it. Piece by piece, the old industrial order gave way to a new and decidedly upscale precinct of parks, museums, theaters, office buildings, restaurants, hotels, and apartments. This triumph of the latte and loft culture has not been without its critics, but there's no question that what happened here was a remarkable feat of urban revitalization.

The new and remodeled buildings that have now all but filled the district include the usual examples of tepid historicism, but some outstanding works of modern architecture can also be found here. Among the best are Meyer Scherer and Rockcastle's Mill City Museum (2003), carved from the burned-out hulk of the Washburn A Mill; the broodingly blue Guthrie Theater (2006), designed by the French architect Jean Nouvel; and Humboldt Lofts (1878), a mill converted to apartments in 2003 by Julie Snow Architects.

Central Riverfront

1	U.S. Post Office	14	Guthrie Theater
2	Carlyle Condominiums	15	The Depot
3	Third Avenue Bridge	16	Federal Office Building
4	Crown Roller Building	17	Dunn Bros. Coffee
5	Ceresota Building		
6	MacPhail Center for Music		
7	Whitney Landmark Residences and Whitney Garden Plaza	A	Gateway Park and the Historic Gateway Area
8	Upper Lock and Dam and Visitors Center	B	Mill Ruins Park
		C	St. Anthony Falls
9	Stone Arch Bridge	D	Stone plaque
10	North Star Lofts		
11	Washburn Lofts		
12	Mill City Museum and offices	L1	Minneapolis Union Depot
13	Humboldt Lofts		

Gateway Park, 1916

U.S. Post Office

POI A Gateway Park and the Historic Gateway Area N L

South and east of First St. and Hennepin Ave.

Minneapolis Park Board, 1963

Today's Gateway Park, a bland plaza from the 1960s, is nothing like the first park built here in 1915. That park, which occupied a triangle between Hennepin and Nicollet Aves., was known for its pavilion, a classical structure with curving, colonnaded wings. The park and pavilion were fruits of the so-called City Beautiful movement of the early 1900s. The idea was to create monumental streets, buildings, and parks that would express the grandeur of American civilization while clearing away Victorian-era detritus. It was, in other words, a high-minded species of urban renewal. In fact, two blocks of old buildings, among them the first Minneapolis City Hall (1873), were demolished for the original Gateway Park.

But the park failed to transform the larger Gateway area, which by the 1950s had become the city's undisputed skid row. The pavilion came down in 1953 while the park itself was rebuilt after urban renewal had cleared away much of the historic Gateway. About 180 buildings, most from the nineteenth century, were razed for the Gateway urban renewal project and replaced by modern structures or parking lots. Today, about the only reminder of the historic park is the **George Washington Memorial Flagstaff.** Now located near First and Hennepin, it features an ornate base designed by Daniel Chester French and was installed in the old park in 1917.

1 U.S. Post Office N L

100 First St. South

Magney and Tusler (Leon Arnal), 1934 / addition and remodeling, HGA, 1991

A very good art deco building in a bad place, cutting off access to the riverfront for three blocks along First St. In the 1930s, however, the building's location made perfect sense, providing easy access to the rail lines that delivered much of the mail. As built, the post office was fronted along First by Pioneer Square Park. The park was lost to urban renewal in the 1960s, and an apartment building now occupies its site, obscuring distant views of the post office's monumental facade.

The post office, designed by the same architects responsible for the Foshay Tower (1929), displays an art deco–classical blend characteristic of the 1930s. Sheathed in Mankato-Kasota stone, the building stages a long, rhythmic march down First, the broad piers and inset windows of its lower three floors producing the effect of a classic colonnade. The stepped-back fourth story and blocky corner entrances, however, are art deco hallmarks. Inside, there's a block-long, virtually pristine art deco lobby outfitted with marble walls and much brasswork. The brass light fixture that runs the length of the lobby is said to be the longest in the country.

LOST 1 *Before the post office was constructed, much of its site was occupied by the **Minneapolis Union Depot,** which opened in 1885. The depot stood until 1914, when the much larger **Great Northern Depot** (also gone) was built just across Hennepin.*

2 Carlyle Condominiums N *L*

100 Third Ave. South

*Humphreys and Partners
Architects (Dallas), 2007*

At 39 stories, this is—as of 2007—
the tallest residential tower in
Minneapolis. The style appears to
mix faux classicism with hints of
art deco.

3 Third Avenue Bridge N *L*

Across Mississippi River

*Concrete Steel Engineering Co.
(New York), Frederick Cappelen,
and Kristoffer Oustad, 1914–18 /
renovated, Loren Pierce and
Conrad Wurm (engineers), 1980*

Spanning St. Anthony Falls, this
bridge's graceful double curve
stems from a happy convergence
of form and function. The curve
was dictated by the need to place
four river piers just so in order to
avoid holes in the limestone ledge
at the falls. Renovated in 1980,
the bridge is the oldest of five
concrete-arch spans that cross the
Mississippi between St. Anthony
Falls and the Ford Dam.

Crown Roller Building

4 Crown Roller Building
(Crown Roller Mill) N *L*

105 Fifth Ave. South

*W. F. Gunn (engineer), 1880 /
addition (boiler house), 1908 /
renovated, Architectural Alliance,
1986*

With its mansard roof, this may
be the handsomest of the old
mill buildings around the falls,
although much of what you see
today is a reconstruction. Operating until the early 1950s, it was
one of the last mills to close on
the west bank. A fire in 1983
destroyed the interior and roof
of the vacant structure, and for a
time it looked as though it would

be torn down. Preservationists
convinced the city to save what
remained, however, and in 1986
the old mill—with a new interior
and new roof—reopened as an
office building.

5 Ceresota Building
(Northwestern Consolidated
Elevator A) N *L*

155 Fifth Ave. South

*G. T. Honstain (engineer), 1908 /
renovated, Ellerbe Becket, 1988*

An old grain elevator converted
into offices arranged around a
new atrium. The large Ceresota
sign—identifying a former owner
of the elevator—was preserved
as part of the renovation.

6 MacPhail Center for Music

ca. 501 Second St. South
(at Fifth Ave. South)

James Dayton Design, 2007

The MacPhail Center for Music
was founded as a violin school in
1907 and now offers a variety of
education and performance programs. This project will provide
studio, classroom, and performance spaces in an angular, Frank
Gehryesque building clad in
Cor-Ten steel and glass.

7 Whitney Landmark Resi-
dences (Standard Mill) and
Whitney Garden Plaza N *L*

150 Portland Ave.

*W. D. Gray, 1879 / renovated, Miller,
Hanson, Westerbeck and Bell, 1988 /
renovated, Tanek Architects, 2006*

Built by Dorilus Morrison, Minneapolis's first mayor, this brick
mill ground its last flour in the
1940s. It was converted into
a luxury hotel in the 1980s. An
adjoining plaza includes a giant
chessboard. In 2006 the former
mill was renovated a second time
into condominiums.

8 Upper Lock and Dam
and Visitors Center N *L*

1 Portland Ave.

U.S. Army Corps of Engineers, 1963

Although the suspicion persists
that the Upper Lock and Dam

Mill Ruins Park

project was federal pork at its most succulent, it did produce this solid piece of 1960s industrial architecture. The lookout area atop the visitor center offers a fine view of the falls as well as information about its history.

POI B Mill Ruins Park ! N *L*

First St. South and Portland Ave.

URS Corp., 2001 and later

This park is like a three-dimensional map of a lost world, offering a cutaway view of the complex engineering that underlay the west side milling district. The ruins—a maze of building foundations, walls, tunnels, and pits—were uncovered in 2001 after being hidden for years beneath fill excavated during construction of the St. Anthony Falls Lock and Dam in the 1960s.

The key to the milling district was a canal built in 1857 and later enlarged twice. Fourteen feet deep, the canal (long since filled in) extended 900 feet beneath First St. Taking in water at a gatehouse above the falls, the canal ran to the eastern end of the Washburn milling complex. By the 1860s, mills lined the canal, gulping water to power turbines lodged at the bottom of wheel pits. Dropping by up to 40 feet, the water created such force that a single turbine could drive all of a mill's machinery. After serving its purpose, the water was sent back to the river via tailrace tun-

nels and a main tailrace channel that is now a centerpiece of the park. The park includes ruins of several mills, among them the Minneapolis Mill (built in 1865), the Pillsbury B Mill (1866), the Excelsior Mill (1870), and the Northwestern Mill (1879). Most of these mills were demolished in the early 1930s, though the Excelsior survived until 1961.

St. Anthony Falls, 1934

POI C St. Anthony Falls

*includes **Falls of St. Anthony (Upper) Dam**, Charles H. Bigelow (engineer), 1858 / many later modifications and improvements*

Although no match for Niagara, St. Anthony Falls in its natural state—set amid rolling prairies and patches of woodland—must have been one of the great spectacles of the continent. Today, after nearly two centuries of industrial use, almost every natural feature of the falls has been obliterated or altered. Before dams, tunnels, channels, canals, spillways, walls, and other structures harnessed the power of the falls, the Mississippi poured over

Stone Arch Bridge, 1942

a 16-foot-high limestone ledge, then roared through a series of rapids into the only gorge on its 2,500-mile-long course. Because the river level has been raised by dams below the falls, the rapids are no longer visible. The last major construction project at the falls occurred in the 1960s, when the U.S. Army Corps of Engineers built the Upper Lock and Dam. This allowed barges and other river traffic to navigate past the falls—long a dream of Minneapolis boosters.

9 Stone Arch Bridge ! N ⅄ L

Across Mississippi River below St. Anthony Falls

Charles C. Smith (engineer), 1883 / two spans replaced, U.S. Army Corps of Engineers, 1963 / renovated, Minnesota Department of Transportation and A. J. Lichtenstein and Associates (New York), 1994

The most poetic of all Twin Cities bridges and a spectacular feat of Victorian engineering. Sweeping across the river at a diagonal and then curving to follow the western shore, the 2,100-foot-long structure is the Mississippi's only stone arch bridge. It's also the second-oldest railroad bridge (next to the 1874 Eads Bridge in St. Louis) on the river. Since reopening as a pedestrian bridge in 1994, it's become a symbol of the reinvigorated riverfront.

The bridge, designated a National Engineering Landmark

in 2000, was built by James J. Hill, who called it "the hardest thing I ever had to do in my life." He needed the bridge to bring his St. Paul, Minneapolis and Manitoba Railroad (predecessor of the Great Northern) into downtown Minneapolis. Scoffers called the project "Jim Hill's folly," pointing to the difficulty of constructing a bridge of any kind—let alone a curving stone bridge with 23 arches—across the treacherous waters below St. Anthony Falls. Despite its difficult site, Hill's "folly" was finished in less than two years, consuming 100,000 tons of stone, including limestone quarried on site.

When the bridge opened in November 1883, even the skeptics had to admit it was a work of rare magnificence. The bridge, with some modifications—including the replacement of two arches with a steel truss in the 1960s to provide clearance for the new lock at St. Anthony Falls—carried Great Northern trains across the river until 1978. In 1992 the State of Minnesota acquired the bridge and over the next two years renovated it for use as a pedestrian span. Today, a walk across the bridge, which received dramatic new lighting in 2005, is one of the great experiences of the city, offering an unmatched vista of St. Anthony Falls and the milling district as well as the tactile pleasure of feeling beneath your feet a structure truly built for the ages.

10 North Star Lofts (North Star Woolen Mill) N *L*

117 Portland Ave.

1864 / addition, ca. 1885–90 / addition, Pike and Cook, 1922 / old portion rebuilt, C. F. Haglin and Sons, 1925 / renovated, Paul Madson and Associates, 1999 / addition (Stone Arch Lofts), Paul Madson Associates with LHB Architects, 2001

Although it was almost entirely rebuilt in 1925, portions of this building date to the North Star mill's founding in 1864. The mill specialized in wool blankets and for many years supplied them to the Pullman Co. for use in its railroad cars. Closed in the late 1940s, the mill was later used as a warehouse. The conversion to condominiums was skillfully accomplished in 1999. A new section to the rear of the building, known as the **Stone Arch Lofts,** was added in 2001.

11 Washburn Lofts (Washburn Utility Building)

700 Second St. South

Hewitt and Brown, 1914 / renovated, Paul Madson and Associates and LHB Architects, 2001 / Art: terra-cotta figures (atop Second St. side of building), John Karl Daniels, 1914

Now apartments, this industrial building originally included various shops and offices serving the A mill complex. The terra-cotta figures high on the Second St. facade show milling techniques through the ages. The figures on the left and right depict men grinding grain by hand, while the larger central figure tends to a mechanized roller of the kind used in modern mills.

Washburn A Mill Complex ! N ★ *L*

Second St. South between Park and Chicago Aves.

various architects and engineers, 1880–1928

This is hallowed industrial ground and one of the most significant historic sites in the Twin Cities. It includes portions of what was, when built, the largest flour mill in the world. Using novel techniques to grind high-grade flour from hard spring wheat, the A mill helped put Minneapolis on the world map. At least nine structures once comprised the complex, which included elevators, engine houses, a wheelhouse, a wheat house, and a small office building.

The mill's concrete grain elevators, built between 1906 and 1928, were especially fascinating to European *avant garde* architects like Le Corbusier. Architectural historian Reyner Banham, in his 1986 book *A Concrete Atlantis*, wrote that "it could be argued, and with very little exaggeration, that Elevators A, B, and C of the Washburn-Crosby complex constitute the most internationally influential structures ever put up in North America."

The man behind the mill was Cadwallader Washburn, a Maine-born entrepreneur who with his brother William got in on the ground floor of the flour milling business around St. Anthony Falls. He built his first mill here in the 1860s. In 1874, fresh from a stint as governor of Wisconsin, Washburn constructed a second and larger mill, known as the A (his earlier mill next door, now the smaller of the two, was renamed the B). Despite its massive stone walls, the first A mill had a short life. On May 2, 1878, the structure was literally blown to pieces in an explosion that claimed the lives of 18 workers and damaged or destroyed five adjoining mills.

Washburn and his partner, John Crosby, made immediate plans to rebuild. The new A mill, completed in 1880, was also built of stone, but it incorporated many advances in milling technology that made it far superior to its doomed predecessor. Rollers were used instead of stones to grind the flour, and the mill also came equipped with middlings purifiers, devices that removed all traces of bran from hard spring wheat, thereby producing a perfectly white, if notably fiber

Mill City Museum

deficient, flour. Powered by twin turbines, the mill could turn out over a million pounds of flour a day. The A mill complex ground flour until 1965, when it was shut down by General Mills, the successor firm of the Washburn Crosby Co. A sign advertising the firm's "Gold Medal" flour still stands atop a grain elevator that forms part of the complex.

The mill, with much of its historic machinery intact, stood vacant for the next quarter century. Then, in 1991, a fire—probably set by homeless people—all but destroyed the structure. Fortunately, portions of the walls survived, and they were eventually stabilized as part of a plan to create a museum in what remained of the mill. Today, Washburn's mill and its auxiliary buildings serve new purposes but remain a centerpiece of the milling district.

12 Mill City Museum and offices (Washburn A Mill and Wheat House) !

A Mill, 704 Second St. South

Adolph Fischer and William de la Barre (engineers), 1880 / rebuilt after fire, 1928 / interior destroyed by fire, 1991

Wheat House, 710 Second St. South

Adolph Fischer and William de la Barre (engineers), 1881 / rebuilt after fire, 1928 / interior destroyed by fire, 1991

Mill City Museum

renovation and new construction, MS&R Architects, 2003

This dazzling example of historic renovation refutes the misguided notion that the best way to honor the past is to imitate it. Instead, modern and historic architecture are intertwined here in a way that honors both. At the heart of the project is the Mill City Museum, operated by the Minnesota Historical Society and devoted to telling the story of the flour industry.

In designing the museum to fit within the derelict and fire-devastated A mill complex, architect Thomas Meyer of Meyer Scherer and Rockcastle in Minneapolis wisely avoided trying to create any kind of nostalgic pastiche. Instead, he left the exteriors of the old mill and wheat house largely intact while creating new spaces within, including the museum and four floors of office space above. But Meyer and his team also made a bold modern statement, inserting a glass walled structure into the oldest and most heavily damaged portion of the mill. The remainder of the ruins was then left open to form a walled courtyard.

The design works brilliantly, glass playing off against stone something in the manner of I. M. Pei's pyramid at the Louvre in Paris, so that the museum manages to be at once rigorously modern and highly romantic—a rare combination. Inside, the museum features a spacious lobby with an intriguing wooden ceiling scrim, a variety of exhibit spaces, and a ride known as the "flour tower" that provides an interpretive history of the milling industry. Meyer's design also ensures that museumgoers have an excellent view of the biggest exhibit of all—the old mill itself.

POI D Stone plaque

Above the entrance to the Mill City Museum's plaza, First St. South

This plaque, dating to 1880, commemorates the 14 "faithful and well tried employees" killed in the May 2, 1878, explosion of the first A mill. Four men working in neighboring mills also died in the blast, which was so powerful that it lifted the mill's roof by 200 feet and hurled chunks of stone up to eight blocks away. It remains the worst industrial accident in the city's history.

13 Humboldt Lofts (Humboldt Mill)

750 Second St. South

J. T. Noyes and Sons, 1878 / addition, 1913 / renovated and enlarged, Julie Snow Architects, 2003

The historic portion of these apartments was built in 1878 as the Humboldt Mill, which later became the Washburn E Mill. Architect Julie Snow designed a crisp addition to the long-vacant mill as part of its conversion to condominiums. The two-level units are interlocked, an ingenious trick first used by the architect Le Corbusier in the 1940s for an apartment block in France.

Guthrie Theater

14 Guthrie Theater !

818 Second St. South

Jean Nouvel (Paris) with Architectural Alliance, 2006

Large, dark, and rather mysterious, this new riverfront landmark is like a play full of wonderful moments that doesn't quite achieve its full dramatic potential. It's drawn plenty of comparisons to Ralph Rapson's groundbreaking 1963 theater for the Guthrie. That theater was small, funky, and rather cheaply built—not quite a flower child, perhaps, but possessing some of that old hippie spirit. The new Guthrie, by contrast, conveys a sense of mass and power, so much so that you could image real electricity, as opposed to the theatrical kind, being generated here.

The Guthrie is French architect Jean Nouvel's first completed work in the United States, and what may be most impressive about it is how he and his team (including the Architectural Alliance of Minneapolis) responded to the site. The theater's proximity to the Washburn A Mill was not lost on Nouvel, and it explains the Guthrie's robustly industrial look. A gentle, delicate building simply would not have worked on this site. The building's midnight blue skin, which displays screen-printed images from old Guthrie plays, has provoked much discussion. It is indeed a startling color choice. But if you keep in mind that the Guthrie is in many ways a building designed to celebrate the night, then the color makes sense.

Inside, Nouvel's design is less compelling. To be sure, the three performance spaces—a thrust-stage theater virtually identical to Rapson's original, a proscenium theater, and a small "studio" for experimental works—are well done. The studio also has the building's coolest space: a projecting "amber box" lobby that provides stunning views of the riverfront. On the other hand, what passes for the Guthrie's main entrance lobby is a hallway-like room of no architectural distinction. To reach the theaters, you have to ride long, walled-in escalators to the second floor, where you'll discover more corridors doing double duty as lobbies. The overall tone of these quasi lobbies is so noirish that in places you'll almost feel as though you've wandered into some wise guys' hangout in New Jersey.

The building's peculiar circulation patterns were dictated in part by its most dramatic feature—a long cantilevered walkway (called the "endless bridge") that projects out toward the river. Because of the bridge, there's a central crossroads on the second floor that can easily become congested during intermissions. Nor does it help that the ramps leading out to the bridge are unusually steep. If the bridge delivered some fabulous benefit, it might have been worth the trouble, but in truth the view from its small open-air balcony isn't significantly better than if Nouvel had simply created a large window on the river side of the theater.

All that said, the Guthrie is a strong design that never fails to be interesting, even when it's most irritating (as in, for example, its lack of a publicly accessible skyway link to a parking ramp across the street). It's the kind of building that inspires curiosity: if you walk by you'll want to step inside to see what all the fuss is about. That's not a bad thing. The Guthrie's directors wanted a new building that would provide the

theater with an unmistakable architectural identity, and Nouvel's design—whether you like it or not—does just that.

The Depot (former train shed), 1974

15 The Depot ! N i

225 Third Ave. South

Milwaukee Road Depot, *Charles S. Frost (Chicago), 1899 / renovated, ESG Architects, Shea Architects, 2001*

Courtyard by Marriott and Residence Inn, *ESG Architects, 2001*

Once the Milwaukee Road Depot, this stately old brick and granite building has found new life as a hotel and event center, while its historically significant iron train shed now shelters an ice skating rink. Redevelopment did not come easily. After the depot closed in 1971, reuse schemes came and went in a cloud of bankruptcies and foreclosures, and it wasn't until 2001 that the depot—joined by a pair of hotels—finally reopened in its new guise.

As built, the Renaissance Revival–style depot's outstanding feature was a pinnacled clock tower modeled on that of the Giralda in Seville, Spain. Unfortunately, high winds ruined the ornate pinnacle in 1941, leaving the tower with the unsatisfactory flat top it retains to this day. Within, the waiting room—now known as the Great Hall—included marble floors, arched doorways, and a decorative plaster ceiling. The depot's glory, however, was its 625-foot-long iron train shed. Now used for parking as well as skating (behind a new glass curtain wall), the iron shed is one of only about a dozen such structures believed to remain in the United States.

16 Federal Office Building (U.S. Post Office)

220 Washington Ave. South
(212 Third Ave. South)

*Supervising Architect of the
U.S. Treasury (James Knox Taylor),
1915 / renovated, 1927*

A solid specimen of Beaux-Arts classicism with an impressive two-story-high colonnade done in the rather exotic Roman composite order. Designed as a U.S. post office, the building never worked very well for that purpose. It was converted to a federal office building in 1937, not long after a new post office opened two blocks away. The Selective Service System had its offices here, and the building was the scene of protests during the Vietnam War era as well as a 1970 bombing that damaged the Second St. entrance.

17 Dunn Bros. Coffee (Milwaukee Road Freight House) N *L*

201 Third Ave. South

*Charles Haglin, 1879 / rear
portion demolished, 1989 /
front portion renovated, Design
Partnership, 1998*

This two-story brick building was originally the front of a freight house serving the Milwaukee Road Depot. The rear was demolished in 1989, and two modern hotels now occupy the site.

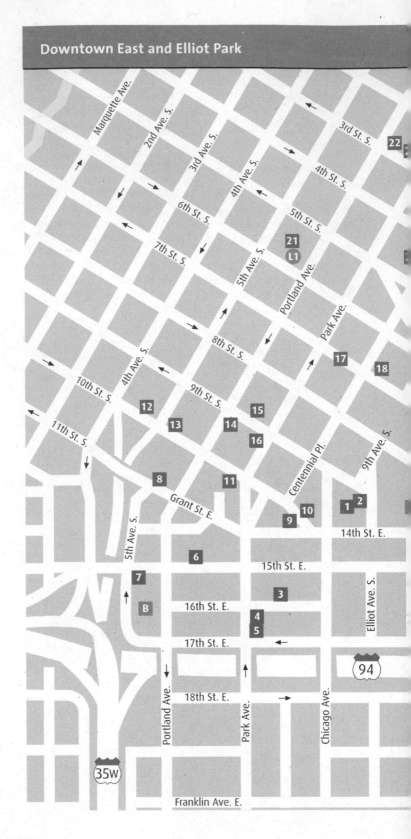

Downtown East and Elliot Park

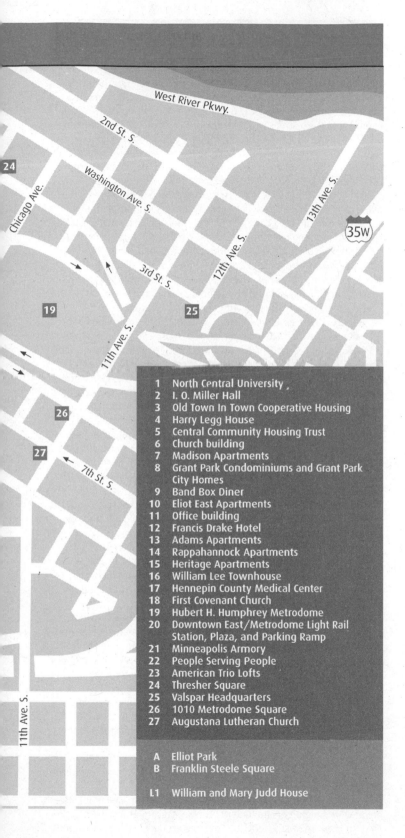

1 North Central University
2 I. O. Miller Hall
3 Old Town In Town Cooperative Housing
4 Harry Legg House
5 Central Community Housing Trust
6 Church building
7 Madison Apartments
8 Grant Park Condominiums and Grant Park City Homes
9 Band Box Diner
10 Eliot East Apartments
11 Office building
12 Francis Drake Hotel
13 Adams Apartments
14 Rappahannock Apartments
15 Heritage Apartments
16 William Lee Townhouse
17 Hennepin County Medical Center
18 First Covenant Church
19 Hubert H. Humphrey Metrodome
20 Downtown East/Metrodome Light Rail Station, Plaza, and Parking Ramp
21 Minneapolis Armory
22 People Serving People
23 American Trio Lofts
24 Thresher Square
25 Valspar Headquarters
26 1010 Metrodome Square
27 Augustana Lutheran Church

A Elliot Park
B Franklin Steele Square

L1 William and Mary Judd House

Downtown East and Elliot Park

These adjoining neighborhoods have quite different architectural characters. Downtown East, perhaps best known today as home to the Hubert H. Humphrey Metrodome (1982), developed largely as an industrial and warehousing district, especially along Washington Avenue and Third Street South. Many of Downtown East's old buildings, including the superb Thresher Square (1900, 1904) and the equally fine American Trio Lofts (1910) have been renovated for housing or offices. The opening of the Hiawatha Light Rail Line will likely spur even more development here in years to come.

By contrast, Elliot Park is a classic mixed-use neighborhood, occupying an intermediate zone between downtown and residential districts to the south. It has one of the city's most diverse array of buildings, from residential and medical high-rises to walk-up apartments to a scattering of single-family homes. Situated at a point where the city's downtown and main north side grids collide, Elliot Park also offers a pleasing jumble of streets. Skewed intersections and oddly shaped building lots abound here, and it's one of the few places in the city where you can easily lose your sense of direction.

Elliot Park derives its name from a small, irregularly shaped park on a site donated to the city in 1883 by Dr. Jacob Elliot, a local physician. Like other neighborhoods around the edges of downtown, Elliot Park—which began to be settled in the 1850s—was at first largely residential, with Swedish immigrants predominating. By the 1870s, however, commercial and institutional uses began to change the neighborhood's character. St. Barnabas Hospital opened on Seventh Street South in 1871. Later, Asbury, Abbott, and Swedish hospitals located nearby. These early hospitals either are gone or have relocated, but the Hennepin County Medical Center—an outgrowth of the old General Hospital, founded in 1887—remains an important institutional presence in Elliot Park. So, too, does North Central University, which occupies the former site of Asbury Hospital.

As commercial and institutional uses pushed farther south into the neighborhood in the 1880s and 1890s, apartment buildings and row houses began to replace much of the original housing stock. A surprising number of Elliot Park's Victorian-era apartment structures have survived, and many are now preserved within the city-designated South Ninth Street Historic District. Today, apartments still dominate the neighborhood, although a few single-family homes can still be found south of 14th Street.

The construction of Interstates 94 and 35W in the 1960s swept away the southern fringes of Elliot Park, destroying many homes and apartments, and the neighborhood lost over half its population from 1950 to 1970. Residents who remained were mostly very poor and lived in crowded apartment buildings. One old row house, for example, had 53 apartments carved out of only seven original units.

Elliot Park began to rebound in the 1970s, fueled by community groups that renovated old housing and built new homes as well. The population decline was stemmed, and the neighborhood is now growing again, in part because of an infusion of Somali immigrants. Recent housing projects—such as the East Village (2001) and Grant Park Condominiums and City Homes (2004)—have further revitalized the neighborhood.

In addition to the South Ninth Street Historic District, Elliot Park's architectural highlights include the Hinkle-Murphy House (1887), the First Church of Christ Scientist (1897), the art deco–style Minneapolis Armory (1936), and the delightful Band Box Diner, a neighborhood institution since 1939.

POI A Elliot Park

1000 14th St. East

*ca. 1880s and later / **recreation center,** 1960s / remodeled and enlarged, Bentz/Thompson/ Rietow Architects, 1982*

An oasis set amid institutional and residential buildings. The recreation center, which sports a conical roof, is a strong postmodern design from a firm—Bentz/ Thompson/Rietow—that does this sort of thing better than anyone else in the Twin Cities.

1 North Central University

910 Elliot Ave.

Originally the North Central Bible Institute, this university was founded in 1930 and relocated here six years later, moving into what had been Asbury Hospital's main building. The university has since spread into a dozen or so other buildings, old and new, clustered around Elliot Park.

I. O. Miller Hall

2 I. O. Miller Hall (Asbury Hospital)

910 Elliot Ave. South

Edwin P. Overmire, 1906 / 1916

A stately brick institutional building that extends for a full block along the west side of Elliot Park. As designed, it included a dome above its central pavilion, which now terminates abruptly in a flat roof. Although it's modestly detailed, the building, with its symmetrical wings and arched entry, conveys a sense of quiet dignity. The building opened in 1906 as the new home of Asbury Hospital but wasn't completed for another ten years due to financial problems. Asbury (now known as Methodist Hospital) later relocated to the suburbs.

3 Old Town In Town Cooperative Housing (Linne Flats) *L*

728, 732, 735, 736, 740 16th St. East

Frederick A. Clarke, 1892 / renovated

Five red brick apartment buildings converted into cooperative housing. Today they're part of the South Ninth Street Historic District.

4 Harry Legg House N *L*

1601 Park Ave. South

George H. Hoit and Co. (builder), 1887

Although Harry Legg is a name rich in comic possibilities, the first owner of this dandy Queen Anne obviously didn't let it slow him down on the road to success: he later built a larger home on Lake of the Isles. This house is one of only a few Victorian-era single-family homes that survive in Elliot Park.

5 Central Community Housing Trust

1625 Park Ave. South

1962

The 1960s abounded in small buildings with big ideas. This is one of them. The roof flutters like a butterfly, the brick walls seem to fly out from the foundation, and the windows come in just about every size and shape except regular.

6 Church building (First Church of Christ Scientist) N *L*

614–20 15th St. East

Septimus J. Bowler, 1897 / addition, Septimus J. Bowler, 1899

Now in a state of ivied decrepitude, this brick building was the first Christian Science church building in the Upper Midwest.

London-born architect Septimus J. Bowler freely adapted forms from Roman and Renaissance models in designing the church, which has a Doric portico, brickwork coursed to imitate the rusticated look of stone, and terracotta trim. Within, the church featured an octagonal auditorium lit by large stained-glass windows, corner galleries, and a central plaster dome. The Christian Scientists moved into a new, larger church at 24th St. and Nicollet Ave. in 1914. This building has been vacant since the 1980s, and its future is uncertain.

POI B Franklin Steele Square

Near 15th St. East and Portland Ave.

ca. 1882

Land for this park was donated to the city by daughters of Minneapolis pioneer Franklin Steele.

7 Madison Apartments (Madison School) *L*

501 15th St. East

Walter S. Pardee, 1887 / 1889 / renovated, 1980s

One of the city's oldest public school buildings, converted to apartments in the 1980s. Built of local brick, the building mixes Romanesque-style arched entries with Queen Anne detailing.

8 Grant Park Condominiums and Grant Park City Homes

500 East Grant St.

Humphreys and Partners Architects (Dallas) and Opus Architects and Engineers, 2004

A 27-story condominium tower with 39 townhomes spread around it in accord with the "new urbanist" bible. The townhomes strive to imitate the Romanesque Revival architecture of the nearby South Ninth Street Historic District but come across as a cartoon version of the real thing.

Band Box Diner

9 Band Box Diner *L*

729 Tenth St. South

Bert Wyman (Butler Manufacturing Co., builder), 1939 / renovated and enlarged, Robert Roscoe (Design for Preservation) and Karen Gjerstad, 2003

The oldest operating diner in Minneapolis. Although modeled on the White Castle chain of burger joints, the Band Box is a homegrown product. Harry Wyman and his wife, Bert, opened the diner—their first—in 1939. By 1950 they operated 15 Band Boxes. The diners, among the first in the city to be open 24 hours a day, featured a signature special—three hamburgers for a dime. Bert Wyman is credited with designing the diner, which has elements of the Moderne look. The Wymans sold the Band Box chain in 1953, and by 1972 all the diners were gone except for this one. New owners bought the diner in 1998 and later renovated and expanded it.

10 Eliot East Apartments (Potter Thompson Rowhouses) *L*

812–26 Tenth St. South

Frederick A. Clarke, 1888

Now used as student housing by North Central University, this row house occupies a distinctive trapezoidal lot. Everything about the building, from its lot to the way its windows are arranged, is a bit odd. The building is part of the South Ninth Street Historic District.

11 Office building (Hinkle-Murphy House) *N L*

619 Tenth St. South

William Channing Whitney, 1887 / renovated, HKA Architects and Design for Preservation, 1997

One of downtown's last surviving mansions, and the first example of the Georgian Revival style (a variation of Colonial Revival) in Minneapolis. Built of structural tile and brick with stone trim, the Hinkle-Murphy House features a double-bowed front of the kind architect William C. Whitney would have seen in Boston, where he trained before arriving in Minneapolis. Compared to the rambunctious Queen Anne houses still popular in the 1880s, this house must have seemed very quiet. Built for businessman William Hinkle, the house was later purchased by William Murphy, publisher of the Minneapolis *Tribune*. He lived in it until his death in 1918. The house is now used for offices.

12 Francis Drake Hotel

416 Tenth St. South

1926

Hotels with names familiar to older Minneapolitans—the Leamington, the Curtis, the Sheridan—once clustered along Tenth St. The Renaissance Revival–style Drake, a center court design from the 1920s, is the only hotel of its era that remains in the vicinity. It's now used as a shelter.

South Ninth Street Historic District *L*

Ninth and Tenth Sts. South between Fifth Ave. South and Chicago Ave.

1989

This district, which is focused along Ninth St. but includes individual buildings as far south as 16th St., showcases some of the oldest row houses and apartments in Minneapolis. Built in response to the city's phenomenal growth in the 1880s and 1890s, the apartments here initially served a fairly wealthy clientele. Later, however, most were subdivided to accommodate a poorer class of tenants. In the 1980s, gentrification produced yet another change in the neighborhood's social dynamics;

today, many of the apartments are upscale condominiums.

13 Adams (Williston) Apartments *L*

500 Tenth St. South

Frederick A. Clarke, 1888

The first apartment building (as opposed to row house) in the district, built of red brick with sandstone trim. The building's arched entries are Renaissance Revival in character, but the turrets and arched windows above suggest the Romanesque.

14 Rappahannock (Rappannock) Apartments *L*

601–9 Ninth St. South

Lemuel Jepson, 1895

A good-sized apartment building notable for its fine wrought-iron balconies.

Heritage Apartments

15 Heritage (Mayhew) Apartments *L*

614–26 Ninth St. South

Frederick A. Clarke, 1886 / renovated, 1990

The oldest and most ornate building in the South Ninth Street Historic District, originally consisting of seven row houses. Early residents included the Reverend Marion Shutter, who wrote a three-volume history of Minneapolis published in 1923. Architect Frederick A. Clarke specialized in apartment buildings, including six others in this district. Later subdivided into 53 tiny apartments, this building was renovated around 1990. It now has 15 apartments.

16 William Lee Townhouse *L*

623–25 (possibly 619) Ninth St. South

William Channing Whitney, 1887 / 1894

The only Victorian-era townhouse left in either downtown Minneapolis or St. Paul. It features fanciful ogee-arched windows on the top floor that lend an Oriental air to the composition.

17 Hennepin County Medical Center

701 Park Ave. South

Medical Facilities Associates General (Liebenberg Kaplan Glotter and Associates, S. G. Smiley and Associates, Thorsen and Thorshov Associates), 1975

General (or City) Hospital, as it was known, opened a block from here in 1887. By the early 1970s, the hospital was an almost incomprehensible jumble of buildings. Hennepin County, which had taken over the hospital in the 1960s, finally cleared away the old campus and in 1975 built this street-straddling behemoth. It's not a pretty sight. Brutalist in style and spirit, the medical center walks on massive piers that look as though they could crush the ground beneath them, and it leaves an unpleasant shadowland beneath its crossing on Seventh St. The design is said to be highly efficient, but you have to wonder whether a hospital that seems to have been designed with the idea of scaring the hell out of patients is really a good thing.

First Covenant Church, 1954

18 First Covenant Church (Swedish Tabernacle)

810 Seventh St. South

Warren H. Hayes, 1887 / addition (classrooms), 1937 / addition, ca. 1960s / restored, MacDonald and Mack Architects, 2004

This Romanesque Revival brick building looks more like a clubhouse or meeting hall than a traditional church. Originally known as the Swedish Tabernacle, it was built for a Scandinavian congregation founded in 1874. With an auditorium seating 2,500 people, it was among the largest churches of its time in Minneapolis.

19 Hubert H. Humphrey Metrodome

900 Fifth St. South

Skidmore, Owings and Merrill (Chicago) and others, 1982

A big beige bulge of a stadium everybody seems to hate even

Hubert H. Humphrey Metrodome

though it's worked quite nicely and at a cost that seems unbelievably low by the standards of today's absurdly expensive sports palaces. The Metrodome's billowing, air-supported fabric roof has been the subject of endless jokes, but it was in fact a good engineering solution to the problem of enclosing a large space at a reasonable cost. Two new stadiums (for the Twins and Gophers) are already in the works, and the Vikings are seeking one as well. Combined, these facilities will cost well over $1 billion, whereas the Metrodome was constructed for a mere $55 million.

The biggest criticism of the Metrodome has always been that it's a poor place to watch baseball, which is true. Yet it's also true that the dome's eccentricities—from its ultra-bouncy infield to its right field "baggy" to its occasionally deflated Teflon-coated roof into which baseballs can disappear like ships venturing into the Bermuda Triangle—have been responsible for many strange and memorable moments. Still, it seems only a matter of time before the Metrodome comes down. Although few will mourn its passing, it could be argued that no other building in Twin Cities history has delivered entertainment to so many at such a modest cost.

20 Downtown East/ Metrodome Light Rail Station, Plaza, and Parking Ramp

Kirby Puckett Pl. and
Fifth St. South

HGA with Andrew Leicester (artist) and Philip Koski (artist), 2003

The light rail station here is tied in with a plaza that serves as a gathering spot in front of the Metrodome. The station and plaza include a series of colorful brick arches that pay homage to the Stone Arch Bridge a few blocks away. Patterns in the brickwork are intended to recall those found in textiles worn by nineteenth-century

immigrants in the Elliot Park neighborhood.

21 Minneapolis Armory ! N

500–530 Sixth St. South

P. C. Bettenburg, Walter H. Wheeler (engineer), 1936 / Art: History of the National Guard (mural), Lucia Wiley, 1936 / Early Minnesota (mural), Elsa Jemne, 1936

A nationally significant example of the Moderne phase of art deco. With its graceful curves and gently rounded edges, the building doesn't quite convey the sense of jut-jawed militarism you'd expect from an armory, although it has an undeniably monumental presence. It's also something of an architectural Houdini, having escaped what looked to be certain destruction thanks to a court ruling in 1993. Unfortunately, surviving into architectural old age is no guarantee of a happy life, and today the armory is a parking garage.

The armory was designed by St. Paul architect P. C. Bettenburg, who was also a major in the Minnesota National Guard. Bettenburg worked with Minneapolis engineer Walter Wheeler, who used a patented flat-slab concrete system for the large floor areas. The building has two sections: a drill hall on the Fifth St. side and four stories of offices overlooking Sixth St. Eight steel arches support the roof of the drill hall, which was also used for sporting events—the Minneapolis Lakers basketball team played here for a time—as well as concerts and other shows.

Virtually all of the building's exterior ornament—which includes a pair of stone eagles with 14-foot wing spans, bronze doors and screens, and Moderne-style lettering that spells out *Armory*—is concentrated around a pair of entrances on Sixth. Within, the finishing is generally plain. However, an old trophy room still contains two Depression-era murals—*History of the National Guard* by Lucia Wiley and *Early Minnesota* by Elsa Jemne.

Minneapolis Armory, 1935

The armory's distinctive style is sometimes called PWA Moderne to denote its association with buildings constructed under the auspices of the Public Works Administration, a New Deal agency established in 1933. A PWA grant paid for about 20 percent of the armory's cost, but most of the money came from the City of Minneapolis. In fact, the state didn't assume ownership of the armory until 1965.

The National Guard vacated the armory in 1983. Six years later Hennepin County purchased the building with the idea of razing it to make way for a new jail. However, the Minnesota Historical Society intervened and in 1993 won its case before the state's supreme court, which ruled that the armory was protected under a state environmental rights act. In 1998 Hennepin County finally sold the building to a developer who turned it into a parking garage. As part of the deal, the developer agreed to maintain the armory's historic appearance and to allow the county to use part of the site for a Veterans Memorial Garden, which opened in 2001.

LOST 1 *Before the armory was built, this block was the site of the* **William and Mary Judd House,** *constructed in about 1873 for a Minneapolis businessman and his wife. The Italian Villa–style house had a tall central tower and beautifully landscaped grounds. Later, the property functioned as a rooming house. It was torn down in 1926.*

22 People Serving People

614 Third St. South

Bertrand and Chamberlin, 1916 / renovated, Neil Weber Architects, 2002

A solemn old warehouse that now serves as an emergency shelter and temporary housing for homeless families. The Portland Ave. facade, which has brickwork arranged into large geometric patterns around small windows, is among the most distinctive of any warehouse in the city.

23 American Trio Lofts (Northern Implement Co.) N *L*

616 Third St. South
(also 250 Park Ave.)

Kees and Colburn, 1911 / renovated, ESG Architects, 2005

A fine brick warehouse building, now apartments, that shows the influence of at least three American architectural masters: Henry Hobson Richardson, Louis Sullivan, and John Wellborn Root, Jr. The broad top-floor arches and wide corner piers are modeled on Sullivan's Chicago warehouses, which in turn were inspired by Richardson's work in the Romanesque Revival style. Another distinctive feature—the subtle chamfer of the corners as they rise toward a flaring cornice—is derived from Root's 1891 Monadnock Building, which still stands in Chicago.

Thresher Square

24 Thresher Square (Advance Thresher Co. Building, Emerson-Newton Plow Co.) N *L*

700–708 Third St. South

Kees and Colburn, 1900, 1904 / renovated, Arvid Elness Architects, 1984–86

A pair of beautifully misleading orange brick warehouses, built four years apart and seemingly identical until you look closely at their facades along Third St. The older of the two, originally constructed for the Advance Thresher Co., has six floors, while the adjoining Emerson-Newton Co. building has seven. However, these differing floor heights are so well disguised that the buildings, united under a common cornice, read as two halves of a single structure. The buildings, which feature swirling terra-cotta ornament, are clearly inspired by the work of Louis Sullivan in Chicago, although the terra-cotta is actually Classical Revival in character. Both buildings, which have massive timber frames, were renovated into offices in the 1980s.

25 Valspar Headquarters (Minnesota Linseed Oil Paint Co.)

1101 Third St. South

Long and Long, ca. 1904 and later / Art: Demolition *and* Sport *(murals), Peter Busa, 1974, 1982*

Colorful, abstract murals by artist Peter Busa add some diagonal gusto to an otherwise plain group of brick buildings that form the corporate headquarters of Valspar, a paint and coatings company. These were among the first large outdoor murals in the Twin Cities.

26 1010 Metrodome Square (Strutwear Knitting Co.)

1010 Seventh St. South

1922 / addition, Long and Thorshov, 1930 / renovated and enlarged, Setter Leach and Lindstrom, 1987

Now an office building, this handsome art deco structure with textile-like patterns in its tower was built for the Strutwear Knitting Co., which took its name from its owners, the Struthers family, and once employed as many as 1,100 workers. A bitter strike in 1935–36 closed the plant for months and at one point led Governor Floyd B. Olson to call out the National Guard.

27 Augustana Lutheran Church

704 11th Ave. South

William H. Dennis, 1883 / later additions

Founded by Swedish and Norwegian immigrants in 1866, this is one of several congregations with Scandinavian roots in Elliot Park. The church itself is a straightforward example of 1880s Gothic Revival, built of yellow brick. A number of additions have been made to the structure.

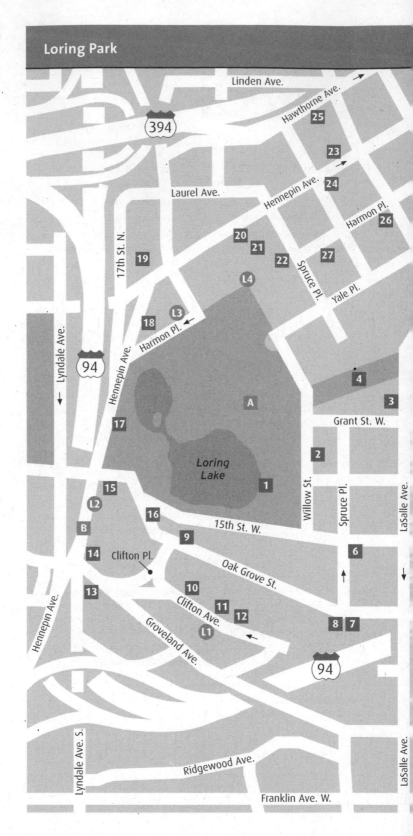

Loring Park

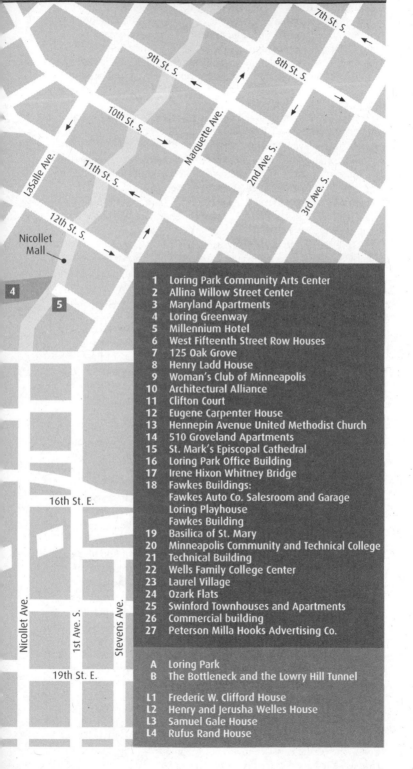

1 Loring Park Community Arts Center
2 Allina Willow Street Center
3 Maryland Apartments
4 Loring Greenway
5 Millennium Hotel
6 West Fifteenth Street Row Houses
7 125 Oak Grove
8 Henry Ladd House
9 Woman's Club of Minneapolis
10 Architectural Alliance
11 Clifton Court
12 Eugene Carpenter House
13 Hennepin Avenue United Methodist Church
14 510 Groveland Apartments
15 St. Mark's Episcopal Cathedral
16 Loring Park Office Building
17 Irene Hixon Whitney Bridge
18 Fawkes Buildings:
     Fawkes Auto Co. Salesroom and Garage
     Loring Playhouse
     Fawkes Building
19 Basilica of St. Mary
20 Minneapolis Community and Technical College
21 Technical Building
22 Wells Family College Center
23 Laurel Village
24 Ozark Flats
25 Swinford Townhouses and Apartments
26 Commercial building
27 Peterson Milla Hooks Advertising Co.

A Loring Park
B The Bottleneck and the Lowry Hill Tunnel

L1 Frederic W. Clifford House
L2 Henry and Jerusha Welles House
L3 Samuel Gale House
L4 Rufus Rand House

Loring Park

Situated at the edges of downtown, this urbane neighborhood offers an intriguing mix of old and new, the result of a complicated history of development, destruction, and renewal. Although the neighborhood's concentration of high- and low-rise apartment buildings makes it the densest residential precinct in the city, it still manages to be quite charming by virtue of the hilly topography at its southern end, its lovely old park, and its angled streets that happily ignore the domineering Minneapolis grid.

Loring Park's architectural diversity is extraordinary. Within its compact boundaries you'll find a 125-year-old park with its own lake, a modern greenway lined with apartments and townhomes, a scattering of Victorian and early twentieth-century mansions, a college campus, three of the city's most spectacular churches, and a historic commercial district that was once home to numerous auto-related businesses. It all calls to mind the kind of mixed-use neighborhoods found in Chicago or large East Coast cities, and there's nowhere else like it in Minneapolis or St. Paul.

First settled in the 1850s, the Loring Park area was initially the site of fairly modest homes but gradually evolved into one of the city's swankiest residential enclaves. Mansion building began in earnest in the 1880s after the opening of what was originally known as Central Park, renamed in 1890 to honor Charles Loring, first president of the Minneapolis Park Board. The park and its pond, the pleasing topography along the flanks of Loring Hill (part of the glacial ridge known farther to the west as Lowry Hill), and the neighborhood's proximity to downtown all appealed to wealthy homebuilders. Many of the largest mansions, such as the rock-ribbed Samuel Gale House (gone) of 1889, were built along Harmon Place on the park's north side. Apartment houses, including several that still stand north of Hennepin Avenue, also began appearing in the 1880s, a sign of things to come.

Loring Park's next great era of change occurred in the early twentieth century as commercial development fueled by the growing automotive business crept south from downtown. Today, the city's Harmon Place Historic District encompasses over 20 buildings that were once used to sell or service automobiles. This period also saw construction of the neighborhood's three landmark churches: St. Mark's Episcopal Cathedral (1910), the Basilica of St. Mary (1914), and Hennepin Avenue United Methodist Church (1916). Meanwhile, apartment buildings filled in the blocks around the park. By the 1920s, as autos and apartments continued to encroach, the neighborhood's historic mansions began to disappear, a trend that would continue for years to come. Today, virtually all of the neighborhood's surviving mansions are along the slopes of Loring Hill south of the park.

By the 1960s, the neighborhood, though not without a certain funky appeal, was at least partway down the road to seed and was losing population at a rapid clip. It was also being pinched in by construction of Interstate 94, which along with the later Interstate 394 cinches around the neighborhood like a thick concrete belt. The decline that became evident in the 1960s paved the way for redevelopment in the next decade. After much debate, the city in 1972 created the Loring Park Development District and powered it with tax increments. Eventually, nearly 40 old buildings, mostly north and east of the park, were torn down to make way for new housing and institutional developments. The Loring Park Greenway (1976), linking Nicollet Mall to the park, was the new district's most notable public amenity.

Although the redevelopment project produced little in the way of memorable architecture, it did succeed in stemming the population

Loring Park

decline and certainly brought a new sense of vitality to the neighborhood, which these days is looking more and more upscale by the minute. Not everyone thinks that's a uniformly good thing, but the trend seems likely to continue.

POI A Loring Park !

1382 Willow St.

Horace Cleveland (landscape architect), 1883 / many later changes / renovated, Diana Balmori (New Haven, CT), 1996 / Art: Berger Fountain, Robert Woodward, 1975 / Ole Bull (bronze statue), Jacob Fjelde, 1897

The closest thing in downtown Minneapolis to a central park (in fact, that was once its name), even if it is well away from the main commercial core. Formally opened in 1883, the park is best known for its pond, which has two distinct bays linked by a narrow channel crossed by a pretty little bridge. Although the park has tennis courts, a playground, and other activity areas, it's primarily a passive green space and a pleasant one at that, despite the presence of Interstate 94 along its western edge. Keep an eye out for the park's squirrels, which may be the plumpest and most brazen in the Twin Cities. Artworks include the lovely, flowerlike Berger Fountain and Jacob Fjelde's statue of the Norwegian violinist Ole Bull.

1 Loring Park Community Arts Center (shelter)

1906 / renovated, Miller Dunwiddie Architects, 2003

Saved from demolition by neighborhood activists in the 1970s, this Mission Revival–style shelter now serves as a recreation and arts center for the Loring Park community.

2 Allina Willow Street Center (Eitel Hospital)

1375 Willow St.

Long, Lamoreaux and Long, 1912

A plain brick building made even more so by the loss of its original cornice. It's primarily of interest as the longtime home of Eitel Hospital, which was merged out of existence in the 1980s. The hospital was founded by Dr. George Eitel, a surgeon, in 1912 and initially served a largely well-to-do clientele. Eitel also operated a large clinic once located just across 14th St.

3 Maryland Apartments (Hotel)

1346 LaSalle Ave.

Long and Long, 1907

A pleasant apartment hotel organized around a center court. At one time, four-story porches extended out from the two wings that face LaSalle.

4 Loring Greenway

Between Nicollet Mall and Loring Park

M. Paul Friedberg and Associates, 1976

Although beginning to show its age, this three-block-long pedestrian corridor, lined with townhomes and apartment towers, is one of the success stories of modern urban planning in Minneapolis. Designed as a centerpiece of the high-density residential community created here in the 1970s, the greenway functions both as a park for nearby apartment dwellers and as a pedestrian link between the Nicollet Mall and Loring Park. One reason the greenway works is that it's not a linear corridor but rather a picturesque sequence of spaces—some soft and green, others more hard edged—that create a sense of movement and variety.

Millennium Hotel

5 Millennium Hotel (Capp Towers)

1313 Nicollet Mall

Ackerberg and Cooperman, 1962 / renovated, 2000

A wonderful 1960s period piece, now remodeled in such regrettably good taste that it's lost its old, kitschy zing. Designed in a jazzy accordion-pleat shape, the hotel originally included a penthouse swimming pool and a domed rooftop cocktail lounge (now used for banquets and meetings). The building belongs to a family of flamboyant modernist hotels built in the 1950s and 1960s by such masters as Morris Lapidus in Miami and Wayne McAlister in Las Vegas.

6 West Fifteenth Street Row Houses *L*

115–29 15th St. West

Adam Lansing Dorr, 1886

The oldest row houses in the Loring Park neighborhood. Their general style is Romanesque Revival. The triple windows spanned by basket-handle arches include stained-glass transoms.

125 Oak Grove

7 125 Oak Grove (Bronzin Apartments)

125 Oak Grove St.

Alexander Rose, 1921

An impressive center-court apartment building, exceptionally well detailed in brick, glazed terra-cotta, and cast-stone (a form of concrete). It was originally known as the Bronzin, a name created by combining those of its owners, Harry Zinman and Solomon Brochin. Note the blue and gold terra-cotta panels above the front windows, some of which sport fire-breathing dragons.

8 Henry Ladd House

131 Oak Grove St.

Harry Jones, 1889

Dark granite or brownstone was generally used for Richardsonian Romanesque mansions in the 1880s and 1890s, but here Harry Jones used golden Mankato-Kasota stone, with pleasing results. The wraparound porch, which features a gridiron-like stone railing, is particularly nice. The house's first owner, Henry Ladd, was in the real estate business.

9 Woman's Club of Minneapolis

410 Oak Grove St.

Magney and Tusler (Leon Arnal), 1927

Founded in 1907 by some of the city's wealthiest women, this club has a diverse membership and remains known for its weekly programs that over the years have attracted everyone from Helen Keller to Frank Lloyd Wright. The Renaissance Revival–style club building is attributed to French-born and -trained Leon Arnal, who worked in the 1920s and 1930s for the local firm of Magney and Tusler.

10 Architectural Alliance (Charles and Kate Bovey House) *L*

400 Clifton Ave.

Howard Van Doren Shaw (Chicago), 1916 / renovated, Architectural Alliance, 1984

A sedate brick house in the Federal variation of Colonial Revival and designed by a prominent Chicago architect. It was built for Charles Bovey, a vice president of the Washburn Crosby Co.

LOST 1 *Among the biggest of the mansions south of Loring Park was the* **Frederic W. Clifford House,** *at 325 Clifton Ave., where a modern apartment tower now stands. The huge Tudor Revival house, designed by Harry Jones, was built in 1905. Clifford was a founder of the Cream of Wheat Co. The house was torn down in 1968.*

Eugene Carpenter House, 1915

11 Clifton Court (Elbert L. Carpenter House) **N** *L*

314 Clifton Ave.

William Channing Whitney, 1906 / renovated, ca. 1974

12 Eugene Carpenter House **N** *L*

300 Clifton Ave.

1890 / rebuilt, Edwin Hewitt, 1906

A pair of mansions originally owned by brothers. Perhaps the most "correct" example of the Federal Revival style in the Twin Cities, the Elbert Carpenter house was built for an Illinois-born businessman who played a key role in establishing the Minneapolis Symphony (now Minnesota) Orchestra in 1903. The house was converted to offices in the 1970s. Eugene Carpenter's house began as a towered Queen Anne but was rebuilt in 1906, emerging from the process as a Georgian variation of Colonial Revival (and a good match for Elbert's mansion). Also an arts maven, Eugene was especially active on behalf of the Minneapolis Institute of Arts.

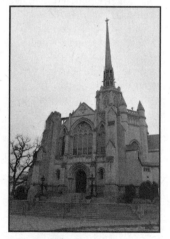

Hennepin Avenue United Methodist Church

13 Hennepin Avenue United Methodist Church !

511 Groveland Ave.

Hewitt and Brown, 1916 / addition (education wing), McEnary and Krafft, 1950 / Art: stained-glass windows, Charles Connick (Boston), 1916 and later

At first glance this church, which overlooks Loring Park, appears to be very traditional, but it's actually a dynamic mix of elements old and new. Although its general style is English Gothic, the church is like nothing from the Middle Ages. Its stonework hides steel, its centralized plan was first used in nineteenth-century Ohio, and its vaulted ceilings are made with a type of interlocking tile patented in 1885 by an architect from Spain. It is, in other words, a characteristically American hybrid, and it's also one of the city's great churches, rising in craggy steps like a small mountain and culminating in a needle-thin, 238-foot-high spire.

Hennepin Avenue Methodist was formed in 1875 and occupied a church at Tenth St. and Hennepin until 1911, when the congregation merged with the Fowler Methodist Episcopal Church. In need of a new church, the congregation settled on this site, which was donated by Thomas Walker, the lumberman and art collector after whom the Walker Art Center is named. Edwin Hewitt, who'd just completed St. Mark's Episcopal Cathedral a block away, was hired to design the church. Born in Red Wing, Hewitt was perhaps the best educated Minneapolis architect of his time, with a résumé that included a degree from the École des Beaux-Arts in Paris. The congregation's building committee instructed Hewitt and his partner (and brother-in-law), engineer Edwin Brown, to create a church that would look "ecclesiastical" (which meant Gothic) but would have an interior "in which the utilitarian should predominate."

Hewitt proved up to the challenge. The church, built largely of stone from Vermont, does indeed look Gothic. Its plan, though inspired by an octagonal lantern built in 1322 at Ely Cathedral in England, isn't Gothic at all, however. Instead of a traditional nave, Hennepin Avenue Methodist has an Akron-plan auditorium of the type favored by many Protestant congregations at the time. Hewitt

employed another modern touch: the starburst vaulted ceiling is built of self-supporting Guastavino tiles, which bear the name of their inventor, Rafael Guastavino. The richly decorated interior also includes stained-glass windows designed by Charles Connick.

14 510 Groveland Apartments

510 Groveland Ave.

Larson and McLaren, 1927 / renovated, Bentz/Thompson/ Rietow Architects

A swank apartment building (now condominiums) that, with a few more stories and a more compact profile, could fit right in on Manhattan's Upper East Side. The T-shaped building, beautifully sited between Hennepin Avenue Methodist Church and St. Mark's Cathedral, is a generally restrained example of the Renaissance Revival style popular in the 1920s. Its boldest gesture is an outsized split pediment that presides over the front entrance.

POI B The Bottleneck and the Lowry Hill Tunnel

Hennepin Ave., Lyndale Ave., and I-94 tunnel, 1971

Before Interstate 94 was built, Hennepin crossed Lyndale Ave. here at an impossibly acute angle, producing the infamous "Bottleneck," a traffic free-for-all in which cars, trucks, and trolleys fought it out. Ideally, a freeway would never have been forced through this historic precinct, but there was no stopping highway builders in the 1960s and 1970s. The 1,500-foot-long Lowry Hill Tunnel, completed in 1971, does lessen the interstate's impact. Yet with so much surface traffic roaring along Hennepin and Lyndale, it's hard now to gain a sense of how Loring Park once related, visually and by means of connecting streets, to the Parade Grounds and Lowry Hill.

St. Mark's Episcopal Cathedral, 1912

15 St. Mark's Episcopal Cathedral !

519 Oak Grove St.

Edwin Hewitt, 1908 (parish house), 1911 (cathedral) / addition (educational wing), Madsen and Wegleitner, 1958 / Art: stained glass, Charles Connick (Boston), 1918 / exterior sculptures, John Rood, 1952

The most traditional of the three large churches that overlook Loring Park. Architect Edwin Hewitt, an active member of the congregation, provided a faithful version of the English Gothic style. Its highlights include a tower modeled on that of Magdalen College at Oxford and a serene nave with plain brick walls, stone-clad columns, and a vaulted ceiling of Guastavino tiles. It's said that Hewitt, a stickler for detail, dressed in monk's robes while designing the church. Originally a parish church, St. Mark's was officially designated in 1941 as the cathedral of the Episcopal Diocese of Minnesota.

The church was built for what was at the time a fairly small Episcopal parish. Founded in 1868, St. Mark's completed its first permanent church three years later on Sixth St. near Nicollet Ave. Plagued by debt, the parish had no real prospects for building a grand new church until a miracle of sorts occurred in 1905: an eastern real estate speculator offered the astounding sum of $275,000—over ten times the appraised value—for the old church and its land. The parish unaccountably stared this gift horse in the mouth for over a year before finally accepting the offer, by then reduced to $250,000.

After securing this prime site from the widow of a longtime parishioner, the parish—under the leadership of Bishop Samuel Cook Edsall—broke ground for its church complex here in 1907. The first services were held in the church three years later.

Among St. Mark's greatest charms is its extensive sculptural program. Exterior sculpture by John Rood is concentrated above and around the main north doors. Rood's work includes a sculpture of Christ as well as figures of St. Mark and St. Peter. Within the archway around the doors Rood also carved 26 delightful bosses (knoblike projections) that depict Minnesota scenes. There is more sculpture within, including an altar screen by Irving and Casson of Boston. The church's stained-glass windows are the work of, among others, Charles Connick, who also designed glass for Hennepin Avenue Methodist Church and the St. Paul Cathedral.

LOST 2 *The **Henry and Jerusha Welles House** once occupied the site of St. Mark's Cathedral and the 510 Groveland Apartments. Welles was a real estate dealer in the early days of Minneapolis. After his death in 1898, his widow sold the 30-room mansion to St. Mark's, after which it was torn down to make way for the new church.*

16 Loring Park Office Building (Northwestern National Life Insurance Co.)

430 Oak Grove St.

Hewitt and Brown, 1924 / Art: murals (in lobby), Harry W. Rubins, ca. 1927

A refined office building originally constructed for a life insurance company. The wedge-shaped building features a monumental entrance in the form of a broad arch with low columned openings to either side—a motif much favored by Renaissance architects. Within, there are murals depicting early Minnesota and Minneapolis scenes.

17 Irene Hixon Whitney Bridge

Over I-94 at Loring Park

Siah Armajani, 1988

A multicolored pedestrian and bicycle bridge that crosses the 16 lanes of traffic separating Loring Park from the Walker Art Center and its sculpture garden. Armajani's design mimics both suspension and arch bridges, though in fact it's neither. If you undertake the crossing, make sure to read the poem by John Ashbery inscribed on the span's upper beams.

18 Fawkes Buildings *L*

Fawkes Auto Co. Salesroom and Garage, 1625 Hennepin Ave.

Bell, Tyrie and Chapman, 1911

Loring Playhouse (Fawkes Auto Co.), 1629, 1633–37 Hennepin Ave.

Bell, Tyrie and Chapman, 1912

Fawkes Building, 1639–49 Hennepin Ave. (also 1620–24 Harmon Pl.)

Bell, Tyrie, Chapman and Gage (1645 Hennepin only), 1916–17

Restaurants, a theater, and other businesses now occupy these buildings, which are part of the Harmon Place Historic District. They were built for Leslie Fawkes, a pioneer auto dealer, and once included showrooms, offices, a warehouse, and a garage. The showpiece here is the Loring Playhouse, a former warehouse featuring a broad central window framed by bands of terra-cotta.

Samuel Gale House, 1900

LOST 3 *A fabulous mansion—the* **Samuel Gale House***—once stood at* Harmon Pl. and Maple St., just east of the Fawkes Buildings. Built in 1889 for a prominent real estate developer, the castlelike house was supposedly designed to last for centuries. In fact, it was razed in 1933, a victim of the Depression and commercial encroachment.

Basilica of St. Mary, 1916

19 Basilica (Pro-Cathedral) of St. Mary ! N i

1600 Hennepin Ave.

Emmanuel Masqueray, 1914 / interior, Slifer and Abrahamson, 1926 / restored and renovated, Miller Dunwiddie Architects, 1990s and later / Art: altar and baldachin, Maginnis and Walsh (Boston), ca. 1926 / stained glass, Gaytee Studios, ca. 1926

Overlooking Loring Park and Lowry Hill, the Basilica of St. Mary has perhaps the most majestic presence of any building in Minneapolis. It's also a grand Beaux-Arts companion piece to the even larger St. Paul Cathedral, designed by the same architect and built at the same time. Compared to the cathedral, the basilica is a more novel—if not necessarily superior—design, combining Renaissance, baroque, and neoclassical elements in a very peculiar way.

The basilica's historic roots go back to the 1860s, when Immaculate Conception parish was established near Third St. and Third Ave. North. By 1900 the parish's old stone church was, in the words of one historian, "an oasis in a Sahara of warehouses." It was also too small, and in 1903 Archbishop John Ireland announced plans for a new church, which would also serve as a secondary cathedral (or pro-cathedral) for

Basilica interior, 1936

the archdiocese. In essence, Ireland had decided to build cathedrals simultaneously in Minneapolis and St. Paul, a daunting proposition.

Ireland, however, was a brilliant fundraiser and a most persuasive man. By 1905 he'd secured a site for the basilica on seven donated lots. He'd also found his architect: Emmanuel Masqueray. Ireland had met the French-born and -trained Masqueray in 1904 at the St. Louis World's Fair, where Masqueray was chief designer. Masqueray soon relocated his offices to St. Paul and began work on the cathedral there and the basilica here.

Masqueray adopted the broad, rectangular form of ancient basilicas here in part because money was an issue and he needed to keep the building relatively simple. As a result, the basilica resembles a huge decorated box, with two towers at one end and a 200-foot-high, squared-off dome at the other. Clad in white Vermont marble, the basilica is not a "correct" design in any historical sense. Instead, Masqueray stirred all manner of things into his architectural pot, from the Renaissance-inspired towers to a neoclassical Doric entry porch to three gigantic "telephone dial" windows (his trademark) that are actually nineteenth century in origin. Uniting it all is Masqueray's taste for bigness—he was obviously an American at heart.

Within, the 82-foot-wide nave (two feet broader than the nave of St. Peter's in Rome) is spanned by a steel truss and girder system hidden above the barrel-vaulted plaster ceiling. The interior's lavish finishing dates to the 1920s. By that time Masqueray was dead, and the work was supervised by two former assistants, Frederick Slifer and Frank Abrahamson. As befitting its prominence, the basilica is loaded with artwork and fine furnishings. Of particular note are the marble altar and baldachin (canopy), wrought-iron grilles made by the Flour City Ornamental Iron Co., and stained-glass windows by Thomas Gaytee of Gaytee Studios in Minneapolis.

The area around the basilica was drastically altered by the construction of Interstate 94. The heavy traffic created damaging vibrations, and by the 1980s age had also taken its toll on the church. The dome was in especially dire shape, leaking profusely. A renovation project began in 1991: workers disassembled and repaired the dome, then sheathed it in new copper. Other improvements included the installation of new bells and renovation of the undercroft (basement).

20 Minneapolis Community and Technical College (includes Minneapolis campus of Metropolitan State University)

1415 Hennepin Ave.

various architects, 1977 and later

Not the most charming college campus you'll ever see. It originally consisted of two separate but adjoining institutions. The community college and the technical college were combined in 1996. Metropolitan State University relocated its Minneapolis campus here as well in 2004. Many of the campus's nine buildings are grouped around a fan-shaped plaza that overlooks Loring Park.

21 Technical Building

1415 Hennepin Ave.

Green Nelson Weaver and Winsor, 1977 / renovated, Bentz/ Thompson/Rietow Architects and Peterson Architects, 1993

The largest campus building and not a pretty one. The structure, clad mainly in striped bands of brick, was designed for energy efficiency—thus the glass panels facing the south—but the architects somehow neglected to make the building even the least bit inviting.

22 Wells Family College Center (Alden Smith House) N L

1403 Harmon Pl.

William Channing Whitney, 1888 / renovated, 1996

The only surviving nineteenth-century mansion on Harmon Pl. Built of brownstone in the Richardsonian Romanesque style, it has a commanding corner tower ringed by small arched windows. Its first owner, Alden Smith, made his money in the sash and door business.

LOST 4 *Among other mansions that once stood near here was the **Rufus Rand House** at 1526 Harmon. Like the Smith House, it was designed by William C. Whitney but was Classical Revival in style. Built around 1890, it came down in the 1970s.*

23 Laurel Village

Hennepin Ave. between 11th and 14th Sts.

Winsor/Faricy Architects, Collaborative Design Group, and others, 1989–91

One of the first modern "urban villages" in the Twin Cities. It includes two apartment towers, townhomes, the historic Swinford complex, and a commercial-restaurant strip along Hennepin. The vaguely postmodern architecture isn't especially interesting.

24 Ozark Flats (Bellevue Hotel)

1225–29 Hennepin Ave.

William H. Grimshaw, 1893 / renovated, 1978

Now condominiums, this apartment hotel is linked to a famous murder. In December 1894, a 29-year-old seamstress named Kitty Ging who lived at the hotel was shot dead near Lake Calhoun. The murder was arranged by her lover, Harry Hayward, son of the hotel's owner. Hayward hired a hotel janitor to perform the actual killing. The motive was money—Hayward had taken out life insurance policies on Ging—though he also seems to have done it for a thrill. Convicted of first-degree murder, Hayward—dressed in a swallowtail coat and pin-striped trousers—was hanged on December 11, 1895, in the Hennepin County Jail. His last words to the hangman supposedly were, "Pull her tight. I'll stand pat."

Swinford Townhouses and Apartments, 1984

25 Swinford Townhouses and Apartments (now part of Laurel Village) N L

1213–21, 1225 Hawthorne Ave.

Hodgson and Sons, 1886 (townhouses) / Harry Jones, 1897 (apartments) / both renovated, Bryan Bowers and Feidt, 1991

These buildings, located in what was once an upper-crust neighborhood near Hawthorne Park (1882, gone), are among the few deluxe urban apartments of their era that survive in Minneapolis. The five three-story row houses offer an amalgam of classically derived styles—from French

Second Empire to Renaissance Revival—done in red brick, brownstone, and terra-cotta. The Classical Revival–style apartment building completed a decade later is just as good. It's alive with distinctive details such as the scrolled arch over the entrance and the bulbous corner bay. As built, the apartments had eight to 12 rooms; they have since been subdivided.

Harmon Place Historic District *L*

Established in 2001, this district encompasses around 25 buildings, most of which were constructed in the early twentieth century for the rapidly expanding automobile trade. Nothing in the district could be construed as a great work of architecture, but as a group the buildings show how designers of the era found ways to accommodate the novel requirements of the automobile in structures that were, by today's rude standards, remarkably urbane.

26 Commercial building (Electric Carriage and Battery Co.) *L*

1207 Harmon Pl.

Purcell and Feick, 1911 / enlarged, HGA, ca. 1990

The oldest automotive building on Harmon Pl. Originally one story (the second floor is a modern addition), it was built for a company that sold electric cars. The building, which once had decorative terra-cotta, is also significant as an early design by William Purcell, who soon teamed with George Elmslie to form a partnership now renowned for its Prairie Style houses and banks.

27 Peterson Milla Hooks Advertising Co. (Oscar M. Nelson Co.) *L*

1315 Harmon Pl.

Carl B. Stravs, 1923

The district's most unusual building, its facade a carnival of patterned brick- and tilework. It was built as an automobile showroom and service garage.

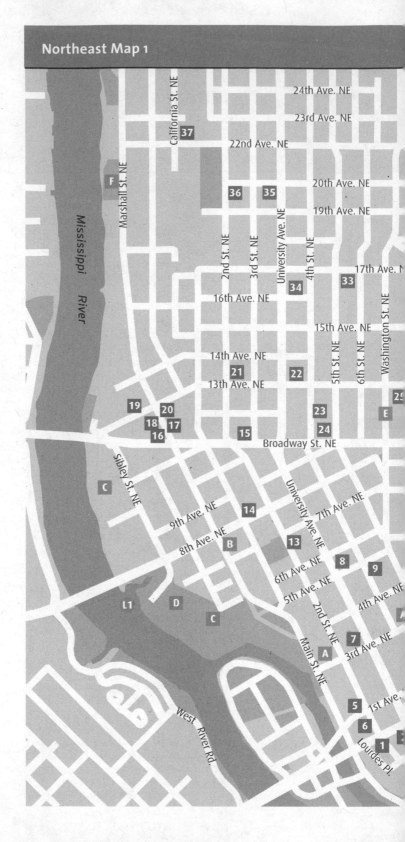

Northeast Map 1

Northeast

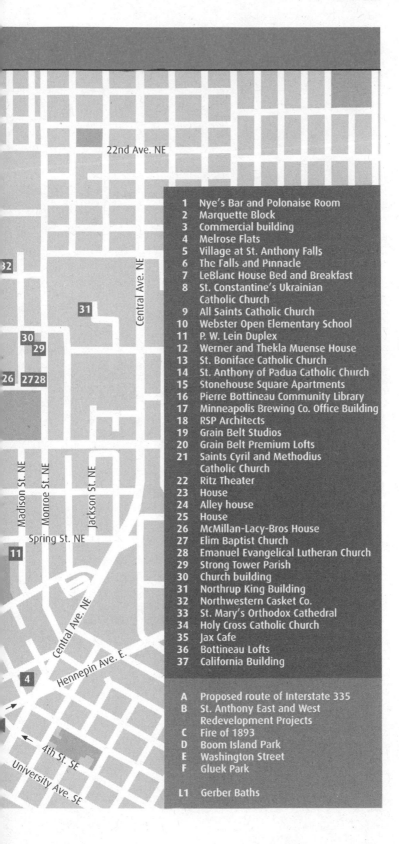

22nd Ave. NE

Central Ave. NE

32

31

30
29

26 2728

Madison St. NE

Monroe St. NE

Jackson St. NE

Spring St. NE

11

Central Ave. NE

Hennepin Ave. E.

4

4th St. SE

University Ave. SE

1   Nye's Bar and Polonaise Room
2   Marquette Block
3   Commercial building
4   Melrose Flats
5   Village at St. Anthony Falls
6   The Falls and Pinnacle
7   LeBlanc House Bed and Breakfast
8   St. Constantine's Ukrainian
    Catholic Church
9   All Saints Catholic Church
10 Webster Open Elementary School
11 P. W. Lein Duplex
12 Werner and Thekla Muense House
13 St. Boniface Catholic Church
14 St. Anthony of Padua Catholic Church
15 Stonehouse Square Apartments
16 Pierre Bottineau Community Library
17 Minneapolis Brewing Co. Office Building
18 RSP Architects
19 Grain Belt Studios
20 Grain Belt Premium Lofts
21 Saints Cyril and Methodius
    Catholic Church
22 Ritz Theater
23 House
24 Alley house
25 House
26 McMillan-Lacy-Bros House
27 Elim Baptist Church
28 Emanuel Evangelical Lutheran Church
29 Strong Tower Parish
30 Church building
31 Northrup King Building
32 Northwestern Casket Co.
33 St. Mary's Orthodox Cathedral
34 Holy Cross Catholic Church
35 Jax Cafe
36 Bottineau Lofts
37 California Building

A   Proposed route of Interstate 335
B   St. Anthony East and West
    Redevelopment Projects
C   Fire of 1893
D   Boom Island Park
E   Washington Street
F   Gluek Park

L1 Gerber Baths

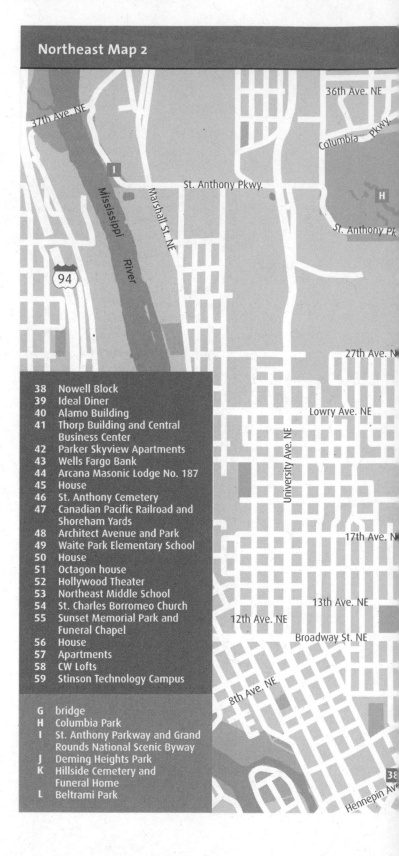

Northeast Map 2

38   Nowell Block
39   Ideal Diner
40   Alamo Building
41   Thorp Building and Central
     Business Center
42   Parker Skyview Apartments
43   Wells Fargo Bank
44   Arcana Masonic Lodge No. 187
45   House
46   St. Anthony Cemetery
47   Canadian Pacific Railroad and
     Shoreham Yards
48   Architect Avenue and Park
49   Waite Park Elementary School
50   House
51   Octagon house
52   Hollywood Theater
53   Northeast Middle School
54   St. Charles Borromeo Church
55   Sunset Memorial Park and
     Funeral Chapel
56   House
57   Apartments
58   CW Lofts
59   Stinson Technology Campus

G   bridge
H   Columbia Park
I   St. Anthony Parkway and Grand
     Rounds National Scenic Byway
J   Deming Heights Park
K   Hillside Cemetery and
     Funeral Home
L   Beltrami Park

Overview

Separated from most of Minneapolis by the Mississippi River, Northeast has long been perceived as having a unique character because of its largely blue-collar population and its ethnic mix, which once included thousands of immigrants from Eastern Europe. Today, however, the neighborhood is rapidly changing. Immigrants now come mostly from Africa, Asia, the Mideast, or Latin America. Artists have also poured in, drawn to the neighborhood's old industrial buildings; there's even a city-designated Northeast Arts District. More recently, upscale condominiums have infiltrated some of the neighborhood's traditional working-class haunts.

Architecturally, what makes Northeast unique in Minneapolis is its intimate tangle of housing and industry. This is especially true in the neighborhood's older sections, where you may find houses on one side of the street and a grain elevator or factory on the other. Such casual commingling of disparate uses is frowned upon by modern zoning codes—the first of which was enacted in Minneapolis in 1924, well after most of Northeast developed—but it's always been a vital feature of the neighborhood's identity. Northeast also has many bars and restaurants, a circumstance stemming in part from an 1884 ordinance that limited where saloons could operate in Minneapolis. As it turned out, a good chunk of Northeast was left open to the temptation of alcohol, and the neighborhood thus became a prime destination for the city's thirsty multitudes.

A portion of Northeast across from downtown lies within the St. Anthony Falls Historic District and was originally part of the town of St. Anthony. Founded before Minneapolis, the town sprang up in the 1840s on the east side of St. Anthony Falls. Industry—especially sawmilling—fueled St. Anthony's growth until it merged into Minneapolis in 1872. Railroads, which arrived in the 1860s, also shaped Northeast's destiny. By 1900, the tracks of four rail lines angled through the neighborhood. The Soo Line was especially important, once employing 1,000 workers at its Shoreham Yards near 28th and Central Avenues. The trains also brought industry. Factories along the tracks turned out everything from coffins to bottles to locomotives, and they made Northeast the most heavily industrialized section of the city.

Industry required workers, who arrived in great numbers between 1880 and 1910. Most of the homes, factories, stores, and churches in what might be called "old" Northeast date to this time. The first settlers had been Yankees and French Canadians, along with Germans, Irish, and Swedes. The second wave of immigration brought in Eastern Europeans, including Poles, Ukrainians, and Russians. As Northeast grew, new residential districts spread out from the old core along the river, a process greatly abetted by the inauguration of streetcar service in 1890.

Northeast's architectural environment is varied not only because of its industrial history but also because it developed over a long period. In the northern reaches of the neighborhood, areas like Waite Park didn't fill with housing until the 1950s. Elsewhere, in the historic St. Anthony East and West communities, there are redeveloped tracts of modern housing built in the 1960s and later. The area around Lowry and Central Avenues, originally called New Boston, is especially diverse. Here you'll find Victorians interspersed among early twentieth-century houses, churches, clusters of brick industrial buildings, and a shopping strip along Central. Farther to the north and east, ranged along hills that rise near Johnson Street, are newer residential neighborhoods from the 1920s and 1930s. To this day, most of Northeast's housing stock is modest and often displays the rough-and-tumble handiwork of do-it-yourself remodelers.

Despite its generally unpretentious character, Northeast does have a number of local monuments. These include the Minneapolis Brewing Co. (Grain Belt) complex (1892 and later), St. Mary's Orthodox Cathedral (1906), Holy Cross Catholic Church (1928), the Cream of Wheat Plant (1928, now loft apartments), and the art deco Hollywood Theater (1935).

Hennepin Avenue East

A continuation of the historic downtown–to–lake district artery, this street has gone by a variety of names over the years, including Bay, Central, and Division. Today, it remains an important dividing line. Above it, streets and avenues have a northeast directional suffix; below, they're all southeast. The most historic portion of East Hennepin is along a four-block stretch between the Mississippi River and Central Ave. Here you'll find many small commercial buildings, the oldest dating to the 1870s. Those east of University Ave. are also within the St. Anthony Falls Historic District.

1 Nye's Bar and Polonaise Room (Minneapolis Brewing Co. Tavern, harness shop) N *L*

112 Hennepin Ave. East

includes **tavern building**, *Boehme and Cordella, 1907 /* **harness shop**, *Ernest Haley, 1905 /* **Polonaise Room**, *1964*

A Minneapolis institution since 1949, known for its Polish cuisine, piano bar, polka band, and ineffably kitschy decor. It consists of two old buildings—a tavern and a harness shop—linked by a 1960s addition dominated by a sign depicting a pianist beneath a candelabra.

2 Marquette Block N *L*

208–24 Hennepin Ave. East

various architects, ca. 1875 and later / renovated, Paul Madson and Associates, 1996

A group of five historic buildings renovated in the 1990s, with shops on the ground floor and apartments above. Twenty new townhomes were also built as part of the project. The oldest building, at 208 Hennepin, is

the Andrews Block, which dates to about 1875 and is a good example of the Italianate commercial style.

3 Commercial building (St. Anthony Falls Bank)

326–30 Hennepin Ave. East

ca. 1893 / remodeled, William Kenyon, 1905

A Victorian-era building hidden behind a Classical Revival facelift. It's one of the nicer temple-style bank buildings remaining in the Twin Cities, with a colossal order of Renaissance-inspired Ionic columns marching along the Hennepin facade.

Melrose Flats

4 Melrose Flats *L*

13–21 Fifth St. Northeast

Charles S. Sedgwick, 1892

A full-bodied Victorian extravaganza. Brickwork in a dazzling variety of patterns, white marble and brownstone trim, fish scale shingles on the bay windows, and multicolored glass transoms all combine to create the kind of rich and busy facade Victorians loved.

5 Village at St. Anthony Falls N *L*

Along First Ave. between Main St. and University Ave. Northeast

ESG Architects, 2001–5

A multi-block project that includes a new retail-apartment building, shops and offices in a renovated 1902 fire barn, a townhouse complex with 48 units, two mid-rise condominium buildings, and a row of luxury "brownstones" along Main St. Overall, the development follows the nostalgic lines dictated by "new urbanist" principles, and it's almost too tidy for its own good: you wonder if you're in a real city or in someone's dream of what a real city should be.

6 The Falls and Pinnacle N *L*

20 Second St. Northeast

Miller, Hanson, Westerbeck and Bell, 1984

Though their busy postmodern styling already seems a bit dated, these high-rise buildings have more panache than many of the newer condominiums along the riverfront.

POI A Proposed route of Interstate 335

Along Third Ave. Northeast east of Main St.

ca. 1960s (right-of-way cleared)

Townhomes and other infill projects occupy a swath of land here that was cleared to make way for proposed Interstate 335, which was intended to complete a high-speed loop around downtown. Fierce opposition from local residents finally killed the highway, and in the 1980s the right-of-way was turned over to the city for redevelopment.

7 LeBlanc House Bed and Breakfast (William LeBlanc House) N

302 University Ave. Northeast

William LeBlanc (builder), 1896

A late Victorian house, more or less Colonial Revival in style. It was built by William LeBlanc, an engineer who worked for the nearby sawmills. The house's most endearing feature is a flaring dormer—topped by a jolly elf's-hat roof—that crowds up against the front gable.

8 St. Constantine's Ukrainian Catholic Church

515 University Ave. Northeast

Hills Gilbertson and Fisher, 1972

A modern version of a Byzantine church, with a colorful central dome covered by mosaic tiles.

All Saints Catholic Church

9 All Saints Catholic Church

435 Fourth St. Northeast

Bard and Vanderbilt, 1939 / Art: stone gargoyles, Barney Cullen, 1939

The second church built by a Polish parish founded in 1916, designed in a somewhat abstracted version of Romanesque Revival. At the rear, circling around the apse, you'll find a group of gargoyles carved by Barney Cullen. Among the faces are Charlie McCarthy (ventriloquist Edgar Bergen's dummy), Joseph Stalin, and Frankenstein's monster. Cullen recalled that the only instruction he received was to "carve any face you want and have fun," which he obviously did.

Webster Open Elementary School

10 Webster Open Elementary School

425 Fifth St. Northeast

Frederick Benz–Milo Thompson and Associates, 1974

Once much praised for its multiple-level, open plan, this school—which closed in 2006 due to budget cutbacks—never worked very well, forcing teachers to create partitions out of filing cabinets, bookcases, and anything else at hand so as to have clearly defined classrooms.

11 P. W. Lein Duplex L

444–46 Madison St. Northeast

1888

A lively trio of bracketed gables turns this otherwise unremarkable double house into something of a showstopper. The bracketing is an Italianate feature you normally wouldn't expect to find on a house built in the late 1880s, but here it brings the whole design to life.

Werner and Thekla Muense House

12 Werner and Thekla Muense House

656 Jefferson St. Northeast

ca. 1885 / Art: Werner Muense, 1967 and later

A monument to the joy of yard art. In the 1960s Werner Muense, a carver trained in his native Germany, began to fill the house and its small yard with a fabulous array of figurines—some new, others reconditioned. The yard's diverse community includes trolls, elves, straw-blond *frauleins,* and a menagerie of animals. Muense died in 1999, but the collection lives on.

13 St. Boniface Catholic Church N

633 Second St. Northeast

1899 (foundation) / Charles A. Hausler, 1929

Established for German immigrants, this is the second-oldest Catholic parish in Minneapolis, dating to 1858. The church is a blend of styles, but the overall

character is Byzantine Revival. It features a triple-arched entry, an ornate rose window, and a sculptural program that includes St. Boniface as well as the 12 apostles.

POI B St. Anthony East and West Redevelopment Projects

Area approximately bounded by Second and Central Aves. Northeast, Broadway St. Northeast, and the Mississippi River

various architects, 1964 and later

This area's housing stock had become aged by the early 1960s, when the city stepped in with a renewal plan. Residents successfully fought to ensure that the plan wasn't of the knock-it-all-down variety. Although 600 properties were demolished, another 1,500 were renovated. Leaving older homes to stand amid the new development proved a wise decision: this seems to be one of those places where urban renewal really did work. Much of the new single-family housing is on and around the former site of the B. F. Nelson Roofing Co. at Eighth Ave. and Main St. Northeast.

1893 fire near Minneapolis Brewing Co.

POI C Fire of 1893

Area approximately bounded by Mississippi River, Marshall St. Northeast, and Sixth and 15th Aves. Northeast, plus portions of Nicollet Island

What one newspaper described as "the worst fire that Minneapolis ever saw" swept through parts of Northeast on August 13, 1893. It started on Nicollet Island, then skipped across a channel to Boom Island, where lumber piles provided fuel. Fanned by southerly winds, the fire crossed to the eastern side of the Mississippi and moved along the riverfront past Broadway. It ultimately incinerated 20 square blocks and destroyed at least 150 buildings, mostly houses. Several hundred families were left homeless by the fire, but no lives were lost.

POI D Boom Island Park N L

700 Sibley St. Northeast

Minneapolis Park Board, 1987

Like Harriet Island in St. Paul, Boom Island is now a misnomer. There was an island here, but the channel separating it from the Mississippi's eastern shore was filled in during a century of industrial use. The island took its name in the 1850s when it became the site of booms used to sort logs being floated downstream to the mills at St. Anthony Falls. After the 1893 fire, the Wisconsin Central Railroad built large yards and a roundhouse here. The iron truss bridge connecting the park to Nicollet Island is a remnant of that rail use.

LOST 1 *Beneath the Plymouth Avenue Bridge a small island formed by sand and sawmill debris was once home to the* **Gerber Baths,** *named after a local alderman who paid for a bathhouse and playground in 1906. Although the Mississippi's water quality in those days cannot have been stellar, the baths survived until 1929, when fire destroyed the bathhouse. The island itself is now gone as well.*

14 St. Anthony of Padua Catholic Church

813 Main St. Northeast

Robert Alden, 1868 / remodeled, 1898 / remodeled, 1948

The oldest Catholic parish in Minneapolis, and one of the oldest churches as well. The parish was established in 1849 on land donated by Pierre Bottineau, one of 50 or so métis (people of mixed French Canadian and Native American heritage) who settled near St. Anthony Falls. Portions of this Gothic Revival–style church's limestone walls date to 1868, but the tower and front are the product of a 1948 remodel-

St. Anthony of Padua Catholic Church

ing. The shaded grounds, among the loveliest in the city, are home to the Shrine of Our Lady of Perpetual Help, dedicated in 1947.

Stonehouse Square Apartments, 1963

15 Stonehouse Square Apartments (Little Sisters of the Poor St. Joseph's Home for the Aged) N L

215 Broadway St. Northeast

Frederick Corser, 1895 / addition (east wing), Frederick Corser, 1905 / addition (west wing), Kees and Colburn, 1914 / renovated, 1979 / remodeled, BKV Group, 2003

Now housing 52 apartments, this neighborhood landmark was built beginning in 1895 by the Little Sisters of the Poor as a home for the aged. The oldest section, which includes a chapel (now a party room) at the rear, faces Broadway. Two side wings were added later. Writer Brenda Ueland in 1944 described the building as "melancholy and picturesque," and with its surrounding wall it does have a stern aura. Yet what seems most remarkable about the building today is its vigorous plainness. Only the arched windows and some of the detail along the roofline place the building in the broad category of Romanesque Revival. The Little Sisters of the Poor cared for the elderly here until 1977, when they moved with their patients to a new home in St. Paul.

Minneapolis Brewing Co. Historic District N L

Two-block area around Marshall St. and 13th Ave. Northeast

16 Pierre Bottineau Community Library (Minneapolis Brewing Co. wagon shed and shops) N L

55 Broadway St. Northeast

1893 (wagon shed) / 1913 (shops) / renovated, RSP Architects, 2003

17 Minneapolis Brewing Co. Office Building N L

1215 Marshall St. Northeast

Carl F. Struck, 1893 / addition, 1910 / renovated, RSP Architects, 2002

RSP Architects

RSP Architects interior

18 RSP Architects (Minneapolis Brewing Co., later Grain Belt Brewery brew house) ! N L

1220 Marshall St. Northeast

Wolff and Lehle (Chicago), 1892 / addition (malt elevator), H. Peter Henshein (Chicago), 1904 / renovated, RSP Architects, 2002

19 Grain Belt Studios (bottling house and warehouse) N L

77 and 79 13th Ave. Northeast

Boehme and Cordella, 1906 (bottling house), 1910 (warehouse) / additions, 1949 and 1957 (warehouse), 1969 (bottling house)

20 Grain Belt Premium Lofts (proposed) N L

13th Ave. and Marshall St. Northeast (next to office building)

ESG Architects, 2007

The block-long brew house that dominates this small historic district is Northeast's greatest architectural monument—a Victorian storybook of a building that erupts at the roofline into a dance of towers, domes, and cupolas. Long vacant after the brewery closed in 1975, its loss would have been unthinkable, and its rebirth serves as a testament to the value of preservation.

The first brewery here (and just the second to be established in Minnesota) was built by John Orth in 1850. Forty years later, as competition led to consolidations in the brewing industry, Orth and three other brewers combined to form the Minneapolis Brewing and Malting Co. Two Chicago specialists in brewery work, Frederick W. Wolff and William L. Lehle, then designed this brew house for the new company. Largely Romanesque Revival in style, it features four distinct sections along Marshall, a visual representation of the merger that created the brewery. Although the sections vary in height and wear different architectural hats, they are tied together by the use of the same wall materials— limestone and cream-colored Milwaukee brick. A malt elevator was tacked on to one end of the brew house in 1904, disrupting its four-part harmony.

A year after the brew house opened in 1892, the company introduced Golden Grain Belt Old Lager, later shortened to Grain

Belt. By 1910 the brewery was the state's second largest, behind only Hamm's in St. Paul. After the repeal of Prohibition in 1933, the brewery began a long period of growth. By the 1960s, production exceeded a million barrels a year, but competition from national brewers proved too much. In 1975 a financier bought the ailing brewery and sold off the Grain Belt label. On Christmas Day of that year, the brewery closed for good. In 1989 the City of Minneapolis bought the building and began looking for someone to renovate it. Schemes of all kinds drifted in, but nothing happened until 1999, when the Ryan Companies put together a plan to redevelop the structure and lease it to RSP Architects.

RSP did a superb job of turning a complicated, irregular old building into modern offices. The architects opened up an atrium, rebuilt wrought-iron staircases that were among the old brew house's only ornamental features, created a conference room beneath the cupola, and brought light into the building. RSP also renovated the former brewery office building across Marshall St. In addition, the brewery's former brick wagon shed and adjoining shops were renovated as a new home for the Pierre Bottineau Community Library. Another pair of brewery buildings—the bottling house and a warehouse—is now known as Grain Belt Studios and has attracted artists. By 2006, new condominiums were also beginning to spring up around the brewery, which has once again become the pride of Northeast.

21 Saints Cyril and Methodius Catholic Church

1305–15 Second St. Northeast

Victor Cordella, 1917

The parish of Saint Cyril (St. Methodius received co-billing in the 1980s) was established in 1891 to serve Northeast's Slovak immigrants. This Renaissance Revival–style brick church, the

parish's second, features a central tower flanked by two balustraded, boxlike wings that screen a long

Saints Cyril and Methodius Catholic Church, 1957

gabled roof to the rear. The tower, which has a kind of baroque swagger, culminates in a copper-clad belvedere that rises above four large scrolls resting on angled, paired columns.

22 Ritz Theater

345 13th Ave. Northeast

Liebenberg and Kaplan, 1928 / renovated, Baker Associates (John Baker), 2006

One of Northeast's two historic movie theaters. It was designed by architects Jack Liebenberg and Seeman Kaplan just before they adopted the new art deco style. Much remodeled over the years, the theater was renovated in 2006 after being acquired by a foundation. Now home to the Ballet of the Dolls dance company, it's also used for a variety of other performances.

23 House

1211 Fourth St. Northeast

ca. 1890s

A cute brick house with two tiny pediments popping up from its front porch like the attentive ears of a cat.

24 Alley house

1115½ Fourth St. Northeast

ca. 1900

So-called alley houses of any kind are rare survivals in the Twin Cities, but this large example is especially unusual in that it appears to be a double house.

Northeast

POI E Washington Street

Home to many immigrants, Northeast was thought by civic leaders to be in need of lessons in American history. Street names were one way to inculcate such worthwhile knowledge, and so it is that over 25 neighborhood streets commemorate U.S. presidents, beginning naturally with George Washington and then moving in chronological order. Thus, if you're one of those rare souls with unerring command of presidential history, you'll know that Taylor St. must lie between Polk and Fillmore. In a few cases, middle names were used to avoid duplication.

25 House

1228 Adams St. Northeast

ca. 1885–90

One of the larger and more peculiar Victorians in this part of Northeast. Partially stuccoed walls, enclosed porches, and other modifications have affected its appearance. Even so, the house retains such picturesque details as a pair of eyebrow windows, the ghost of a bell-shaped tower emerging out of the roof, and an odd half dormer that nestles up against the front gable.

McMillan-Lacy-Bros House

26 McMillan-Lacy-Bros House and carriage house

677 13th Ave. Northeast

C. W. Lunquist (builder), 1886 / addition, 1916

This Queen Anne house was built by an investor named Putnam McMillan in hopes that it would attract wealthy residents to the neighborhood. The first owner was a lumberman named Phineas Lacy, who sold it to William Bros. Later, the mansion was subdivided into 13 apartments. In 1994, new owners renovated the house and returned it to single-family use.

Elim Baptist and Emanuel Evangelical Lutheran churches

Four churches

Block bounded by 13th and 15th Aves. Northeast and Madison and Monroe Sts. Northeast

27 Elim Baptist Church

685 13th Ave. Northeast

A. G. Wass, 1904 / renovated, Armstrong and Schlicting, 1960 / addition (Centennial Hall), Bruce Knutson Architects, 1986

28 Emanuel Evangelical Lutheran Church

697 13th Ave. Northeast

Omeyer and Thori, 1899

29 Strong Tower Parish (Immanuel Lutheran Church)

1424 Monroe St. Northeast

1911

30 Church building (St. Peter's Lutheran Church)

1429 Madison St. Northeast

1905

This block, avers the *Guinness Book of World Records,* is the only one in the world that's home to four churches. The largest of the sacred foursome is Emanuel Lutheran, a two-towered Gothic Revival church overlooking Logan Park. It was built in 1899 for a congregation of mostly Swedish immigrants. Elim Baptist next door was constructed at about the same time but has the broad proportions of the Romanesque Revival style. The other two churches, at the north end of the block, were originally built for what appear to have been dueling Norwegian Lutheran congregations. Strong Tower Parish is the only one of the four that doesn't occupy a corner lot.

31 Northrup King Building

1500 Jackson St. Northeast

ca. 1917 / renovated, ca. 1990s

A complex of ten buildings constructed for Northrup King and Co., a large seed distributor. Northrup King moved out in the 1980s, and the red brick buildings are now occupied by over 130 artists and art organizations as well as several small businesses.

32 Northwestern Casket Co.

1707 Jefferson St. Northeast

1885 and later

One of Northeast's oldest manufacturing firms, founded in 1882 and still doing business in its original brick buildings, which are straightforward examples of Victorian industrial architecture.

33 St. Mary's Orthodox Cathedral

1629 Fifth St. Northeast

Boehme and Cordella, 1906 / addition (chapel), 1966

Another of Northeast's impressive ethnic churches. St. Mary's is modeled on Russian cathedrals and was built for a parish founded in 1887 by immigrants from that nation and other parts of Eastern Europe. The cathedral's traditional features include a front tower and a six-sided dome.

34 Holy Cross Catholic Church

1621 University Ave. Northeast

Cordella and Olson, 1928

A basilican-style church built for the first Polish parish in Min-

neapolis, established in 1886. The church's brick exterior is fairly plain, but inside you'll find marble columns, altars imported

Holy Cross Catholic Church, 1945

from Italy, stained glass, statuary, paintings, and other evidence of decorative abundance.

35 Jax Cafe

1928 University Ave. Northeast

1910 / renovated, 1933 and later

A Northeast institution, opened in 1933 by members of the Kozlak family in a former furniture and hardware store. To the rear is an Old World Garden where you can catch your own trout.

36 Bottineau Lofts (North East Neighborhood House) N

1929 Second St. Northeast

Kenyon and Maine, 1919 / addition, 1927 / renovated, Sjoquist Architects, 2003

This Georgian Revival–style building was originally home to the North East Neighborhood House, a settlement house established in 1915 to serve immigrants. The building was converted to housing in 2003 as part of a project that included construction of new apartments.

37 California Building

2205 California St. Northeast

1915 and later / renovated, 1991 and later

This brick building served as a bottle factory, grain mill, and manufacturing plant before a new group of users—including artists, small businesses, and even the Fraternal Order of Eagles—began to colonize it in the 1970s. Renovated in the 1990s, it's now an arts center.

Louis Gluek House, 1915

POI F Gluek Park

1926 Marshall St. Northeast

1995

This park occupies the site of the Gluek Brewery, founded in 1857 by Gottlieb Gluek and operated for over a century by his descendants. The brewery closed in 1964 and was demolished two years later. Also torn down was a mansion next door to the brewery built in about 1890 for Louis Gluek, one of the founder's sons. The park was closed in 2003 after it was learned that its soil was contaminated with asbestos. Following a cleanup, the park reopened in 2007.

Central Avenue

north of East Hennepin

Central Ave., an old horsecar and later streetcar route, has been Northeast's commercial spine for well over a century. Its lower portions pass through a largely industrial landscape, but farther north shops, restaurants, and other small businesses, interspersed with housing, become more common. The busiest commercial area is around Lowry Ave., in the historic New Boston neighborhood.

38 Nowell Block

509–13 Central Ave.

Adam Lansing Dorr, 1895

Located at the intersection of Central and East Hennepin, this three-story brick building has bay windows, pilasters, and a rhythmic Greek key motif beneath its cornice. Unfortunately, architectural muggers have had their way with the ground-floor storefronts.

POI G Bridge

Central Ave. and Broadway St. Northeast

1987

One of the few intersections in Minneapolis where streets meet in the middle of a bridge. The cross-shaped bridge carries traffic over the tracks of the Burlington Northern Santa Fe Railroad.

39 Ideal Diner

1314 Central Ave. Northeast

1949

It's not much to look at, but this diner is the real deal, an old-fashioned joint with 14 stools and no froufrou stuff on the menu. The sign that beckons customers could be as old as the diner, which opened in 1949.

40 Alamo Building (Imperial Tractor Co.)

1517–19 Central Ave. Northeast

1902

A late example of the use of local limestone for an industrial structure. The building got its name because its stepped central parapet calls to mind the Texas fort where Davy Crockett and other worthies made their last stand. The building now houses an antiques dealer and other businesses.

41 Thorp Building and Central Business Center (Thorp Fire Proof Door Co.)

1618–20 Central Ave. Northeast

1901 / 1937 and later

Many artists have studio space in this old industrial complex. The chief architectural attraction is the Central Business Center, which sports a Moderne facade featuring banded brickwork, polished Rainbow granite, and a nifty metal canopy over the door.

42 Parker Skyview Apartments

1815 Central Ave. Northeast

Bentz/Thompson/Rietow Architects, 1971

Northeast's tallest apartment tower, much better than the average slab of its time. Note how it's scaled down to a single story along Central—a nice gesture toward its low-rise surroundings.

43 Wells Fargo (Central Northwestern National) Bank

2329 Central Ave. Northeast

ca. 1926 / remodeled and enlarged, Gene E. Hickey and Associates, 1972

A truly weird design. With its deep-set arches and sturdy brick walls, this building, which took on its current appearance in 1972, seems to be an amalgam of H. H. Richardson, Louis Sullivan, and something vaguely Islamic.

44 Arcana Masonic Lodge No. 187

2430 Central (also 920 Lowry) Ave. Northeast

1906 / rebuilt after fire, 1957

The 1950s facade of this building isn't impressive, but the lodge room within includes a marble floor, installed in 1967, said to be a "representation" of the floor of King Solomon's temple.

45 House

2619 Central Ave. Northeast

ca. 1900 and later

An eccentric house that seems to have been assembled by anarchists. The roofline is especially peculiar, slanting every which way to accommodate a profusion of gables and dormers. Pray that remodelers with logical thoughts are never allowed to set foot on the property.

46 St. Anthony Cemetery

2730 Central Ave. Northeast

1857 and later

A small Catholic cemetery, originally at 14th Ave. and Marshall St.

Northeast and later relocated to this 13-acre site. Among those commemorated by monuments here is Patrick Judge, one of 18 workers killed in the 1878 explosion of the Washburn A Mill.

Shoreham Yards Roundhouse

47 Canadian Pacific (Soo Line) Railroad Shoreham Yards

2800 Central Ave. Northeast

1887 (yards established)

Roundhouse, west of 28th and Central Aves. Northeast *L*

1887–1919 (portions demolished in 1970)

In 1887, the Minneapolis, Sault Ste. Marie and Atlantic Railway, soon to evolve into the Soo Line, began building shops and yards on this 230-acre site. The railroad had been founded four years earlier by Minneapolis milling interests, who wanted to move flour to eastern markets without having to pay the high prevailing rates through Chicago. The shops were the railroad's main locomotive maintenance and repair facility. Many shop buildings are gone, but a portion of the original roundhouse still stands. Now vacant and dilapidated, the roundhouse faces an uncertain future. Meanwhile, the Soo Line has become a subsidiary of the Canadian Pacific Railroad, which operates a train, truck, and bulk distribution facility at Shoreham.

48 Architect Avenue and Park

West of Central Ave. between Columbia Blvd. and 37th Ave. Northeast

ca. 1905 and later

An urban hideaway that few except the locals know anything

about. Two-block-long Architect Ave. winds around a tiny park and is bordered by a collection of mostly Period Revival houses. Two of the most interesting, both built around 1910, are at 3504 and 3602 Architect.

49 Waite Park Elementary School

1800 34th Ave. Northeast

Magney Tusler and Setter, 1950

Located in one of the last portions of Northeast to be developed, this was the first new elementary school to open in Minneapolis after World War II. With three wings that pinwheel around a small central core, it's typical of the long, low school buildings that were fashionable in the 1950s. Just north of the school is the highest point in Minneapolis, 986 feet above sea level.

POI H Columbia Park

Central Ave. and St. Anthony Pkwy.

Minneapolis Park Board, 1893 and later

Northeast's largest park, encompassing over 180 acres, including an 18-hole golf course. The park's most notable building is Columbia Manor, a Colonial Revival–style reception hall built in 1925.

POI I St. Anthony Parkway and the Grand Rounds National Scenic Byway !

St. Anthony Parkway, 37th Ave. Northeast to I-35E

Minneapolis Park Board, 1912–36

Grand Rounds

Horace Cleveland and Minneapolis Park Board, 1883 and later / rebuilt, Roger Martin, 1970s

St. Anthony Parkway, which winds through the north and eastern portions of the neighborhood, is part of a 50-mile chain of parkways that encircle the city to form what is now known as the Grand Rounds National Scenic Byway. First envisioned

by landscape architect Horace Cleveland in 1883, the Grand Rounds—built over a period of many years—has become a defining feature of Minneapolis and an urban amenity few other American cities can match.

POI J Deming Heights (Grandview) Park

St. Anthony Pkwy. and Fillmore St. Northeast

Minneapolis Park Board, ca. 1924–30

Despite this area's steep hills, the street grid here—like San Francisco's—doesn't accommodate itself to the terrain. As a result, few of the houses near the park have the kind of views that would have been provided by a street layout sensitive to the contours of the land.

50 House

3010 Lincoln St. Northeast

1941

A brick house in the Moderne variant of art deco that almost looks more like a small dentist's office than a home. The corner glass-block windows are especially neat.

51 Octagon house

1120 29th Ave. Northeast

1909 / remodeled, ca. 1930

An eccentric character named Orson Fowler popularized octagon houses in the nineteenth century, but this isn't from one of his pattern books. Instead, it appears to be a fairly standard house that was remodeled to achieve the shape of an octagon.

52 Hollywood Theater *L*

2815 Johnson St. Northeast

Liebenberg and Kaplan, 1935 / renovated, 1949 and later

When this theater opened in 1935, it was proclaimed, perhaps a trifle immodestly, as "the incomparable showplace of the Northwest." If not quite that, it's certainly one of the Twin Cities' best art deco theaters. Its facade features walls of Mankato-Kasota stone incised with lines that turn from vertical to horizontal. A marquee juts past one corner, sheltering the main doors and a

Hollywood Theater

Tower of Memories at Sunset Memorial Park

box office. Within, the lobby includes a fountain, decorative mirrors, and a staircase winding down to a basement lounge. The 750-seat auditorium is an early example of stadium-style seating. Despite at least two remodelings, the theater retains most of its original features. Because of this, both the exterior and the interior have been designated historic by the city, which purchased the Hollywood in 1993, six years after it closed. Although a variety of proposals have been advanced for reusing the theater, as of 2007 it remained vacant.

53 Northeast Middle School

2955 Hayes St. Northeast

Thorshov and Cerny, 1956 / renovated, 2000

An early modernist school originally enlivened by multicolored panels that later were replaced with black glass.

54 St. Charles Borromeo Church

2420 St. Anthony Blvd.

Maguolo and Quinn, 1959

One of the last big Catholic churches of its kind in Minneapolis. Clad in yellow limestone, the church is Italian Romanesque Revival in style and features a broad octagonal dome surmounted by a lantern. The richly decorated front includes a triple-arched entrance.

55 Sunset Memorial Park and Funeral Chapel

2250 St. Anthony Blvd.

*Arthur Nichols (landscape architect), 1927 / **Tower of Memories,** Lovell and Lovell, 1927 / **chapel** and **mausoleum,** Lovell and Lovell, 1927*

Death made elegant, and very sentimental. Located in the city of St. Anthony, this cemetery is divided into 15 themed sections, bearing such names as Haven of Peace and Slumberland. Each section is also marked by a monument, among which are the Temple of Love and the Sylvan Retreat. The cemetery's major architectural work is the 75-foot-high Tower of Memories, which has the look of a small art deco skyscraper.

POI K Hillside Cemetery and Funeral Home

2600–2610 19th Ave. Northeast

1890 and later

This 120-acre cemetery dates to 1890 and is said to occupy some of the highest ground in the city. Among those buried here is former Minnesota governor Elmer L. Andersen.

56 House

1501 18th Ave. Northeast

John Cook (builder), 1889 / restored, 1986

Northeast doesn't have many brick Queen Anne houses, so this one is worth a good look. It includes a shingled tower, a rebuilt front porch, and a festive paint job that avoids the slightest hint of understatement.

POI L Beltrami Park

1111 Summer St. Northeast

1857 / 1908 (acquired as park) / 1948 (park established)

This park is built on the site of Maple Hill Cemetery, established in 1857. The city's health department closed the cemetery in 1890, after which over 1,300 bodies were removed, with many being reinterred at nearby Hillside Cemetery. At least three individual gravestones remain in the park. There's also a monument marking the mass grave of 46 Civil War veterans. The park is named after Giacomo Beltrami, an Italian adventurer who explored northern Minnesota in 1823 in hopes of finding the source of the Mississippi River.

57 Apartments (Margaret Berry Settlement House)

759 Pierce St. Northeast (at Broadway)

1915 / 1922

A remnant of Northeast's immigrant history, now an apartment building. The League of Catholic Women founded the settlement house in 1912, and it operated here from 1915 until the 1960s, when it was merged into what today is known as East Side Neighborhood Services.

58 CW Lofts (Cream of Wheat Co.) *L*

730 Stinson Blvd. Northeast

Walter H. Wheeler, 1928 / later additions / renovated, Walsh Bishop Associates, 2006

A superb work of industrial architecture built on a parklike site in 1928 for a company that had extracted corporate gold from an unlikely source—the milling by-product known as wheat middlings. In 1893, a North Dakota miller hit upon the idea of selling middlings as a hot breakfast cereal, and Cream of Wheat was born. The company

CW Lofts, 1930

soon moved to Minneapolis. Mixing Classical Revival and art deco elements, this brick and concrete building is five stories high and has a corner tower with a pyramidal roof. Within, most of the building is loft space, though there's an elegant lobby that once connected to a well-appointed executive office suite.

The National Biscuit Co. (later Nabisco) bought Cream of Wheat in 1961 but continued to manufacture the cereal here. Nabisco was in turn swallowed by Kraft Foods, which decided it could make Cream of Wheat elsewhere, and the plant closed for good in 2002. Renamed CW Lofts, the building is now home to about 120 condominiums, with additional units in the works.

59 Stinson Technology Campus (Northwestern Terminal)

Stinson Blvd. between Broadway St. Northeast and Hennepin Ave. East

Croft and Boerner, 1919 and later / renovated and expanded, 1999–2003

In 1919, an industrial and warehousing center known as the Northwestern Terminal opened here along Stinson Blvd. Owned by a consortium of Minneapolis business leaders, the terminal was similar in some ways to a modern industrial park. It had its own railroad freight station linked to the industrial buildings by a tunnel system. Many of the terminal's brick buildings were leased to companies. In other cases, large firms such as Cream of Wheat built their own factories. Today, several of the original terminal buildings, including those at 400 and 500 Stinson Blvd., have been redeveloped as part of what is now called the Stinson Technology Campus.

Overview

The University of Minnesota dominates these neighborhoods even though they are on opposite sides of the Mississippi River. The historic East Bank campus, one of the nation's largest, takes in 340 acres and at least 135 buildings in the heart of the University neighborhood. Its ever-expanding orbit also includes the busy commercial district known as Dinkytown; a fraternity row, parts of which are now a historic district; and a nimbus of well-aged rental housing. In the 1960s, the university jumped the river to create a new West Bank campus in Cedar-Riverside. It has since grown to encompass over 25 buildings.

The university's two big campuses, however, are by no means the only areas of architectural interest here. Within the greater University neighborhood, for example, you'll find historic Nicollet Island, an almost bucolic little community. Across from the island is the city's oldest settled ground—the so-called east bank area that developed in the 1840s around St. Anthony Falls. Nearby is the Fifth Street Southeast Historic District, which has many Victorian houses. The University neighborhood is also home to Prospect Park, a genteel "suburb" established in the 1880s. There's industry as well, most notably in the form of skyscraper-like grain elevators that tower over rail yards east of the university.

What is now the University neighborhood dates its urban beginnings to the 1830s, when Franklin Steele, a transplanted Pennsylvanian working as a storekeeper at Fort Snelling, staked a claim to 338 acres along the east side of St. Anthony Falls. A savvy political operator, Steele claimed the valuable waterpower site the minute word reached Minnesota that a treaty had been signed with the Dakota and Ojibwe, clearing the way for settlement. It took Steele a decade to gain official title to the land, after which he and several partners built the first privately owned sawmill at the falls. Steele also began selling lots in the incipient village of St. Anthony. The University of Minnesota entered the picture in 1851, when it was created by the territorial legislature. Lawmakers specified a location for the institution near St. Anthony Falls. By 1858 the university occupied its first permanent building, Old Main (1856, gone), on Pillsbury Drive Southeast, where Shevlin Hall now stands.

Like University, Cedar-Riverside is one of the city's oldest neighborhoods. Known historically as Seven Corners, it was for much of its history a working-class neighborhood quite similar to Northeast. A goodly share of its early residents were Scandinavian and German immigrants, many of whom worked in the mills at St. Anthony Falls, at breweries once located along the river, or for the railroads. First settled in the 1850s, the neighborhood developed well before zoning laws took effect, which meant that housing, commerce, and industry were jumbled together. Even in its early days, the neighborhood had a high percentage of renters living in rooming houses and tenements. Saloons were also a prominent part of the mix, since Cedar-Riverside, like Northeast, was within the city's liquor limits.

Today, Cedar-Riverside has been radically altered by modern interventions. Besides the university's West Bank campus, Cedar-Riverside is also home to other large institutions such as Augsburg College and the Fairview-University Medical Center. The neighborhood, however, may be best known as the location of Riverside Plaza (formerly Cedar Square West), the nation's first "New Town—In Town" and one of the most ambitious, idealistic, and complicated community-building projects ever attempted in the Twin Cities. Because large residential and institutional buildings occupy so much of Cedar-Riverside, it has very few single-family homes: fully 90 percent of its 7,500 residents live in rental apartments.

University

This neighborhood offers a remarkably varied architectural environment. Houses of many styles and vintages, modern apartments, enormous industrial structures, and an eclectic array of institutional buildings on the University of Minnesota campus are all part of the mix here. The most historic buildings, not surprisingly, tend to cluster around St. Anthony Falls. Along the east bank you'll find the city's oldest house (built by miller Ard Godfrey in 1849), the oldest commercial building (the Upton Block of 1855), and the oldest church (Our Lady of Lourdes, parts of which date to 1857). The east bank's most important monument, however, is the Pillsbury A Mill (1881), once the largest flour mill in the world and the foundation of a family dynasty.

Although a good many of University's historic homes have been swept away by the push of progress, both Nicollet Island and the Fifth Street Historic District remain well stocked with Italianate- and Queen Anne–style houses from the 1870s and 1880s. The Prospect Park neighborhood also has fine homes, most notably the exquisite Malcolm and Nancy Willey House (1934), a pivotal work in the career of Frank Lloyd Wright. Another of Prospect Park's landmarks is its water tower (1914), which occupies one of the city's highest points.

The university's sprawling East Bank campus won't win any awards for its architectural ensemble work, but it does include several buildings of exceptional quality. Among them are Pillsbury Hall (1889), a powerful Richardsonian Romanesque design; Folwell Hall (1907), an elaborately ornamented Tudor Revival building; and the shimmering Weisman Art Museum (1993), designed by Frank Gehry.

Nicollet Island

At first glance, this 48-acre island seems like a place out of time, much of it dotted with Victorian houses that evoke images of a nineteenth-century village. The island, however, is in part a re-creation. Some houses were moved in, most were renovated with city financial aid, and all stand on land leased from the Minneapolis Park Board. This unusual arrangement is the result of a deal brokered in 1983 after years of controversy over what to do with the island.

Located just upstream from St. Anthony Falls, the island—linked via bridges to both banks of the river by 1855—once had a more mixed character. The southern end was developed by William Eastman and John Merriam. After their effort to build a tailrace tunnel ended in a disastrous collapse in 1869, the two entrepreneurs brought power to the island via a rope cable ten years later. Industries then established themselves on the island south of Hennepin Avenue.

The upper part of the island, by contrast, became mostly residential and at one time had 40 or so houses. Eastman himself built a mansion as well as three row houses, one of which—Grove Street Flats—remains. In places the island's atmosphere was so pastoral that as late as the 1960s one resident kept a donkey on her property. The city, however, considered much of the island a slum, and by 1970 redevelopment plans were afoot. Discussions dragged on for years, finally resulting in the 1983 agreement, which in effect created a park with houses on it. Today the island is within the St. Anthony Falls Historic District. Its old industrial section is now mostly parkland, while the northern side remains a quiet—and unique—residential enclave.

Nicollet Island and the East Bank

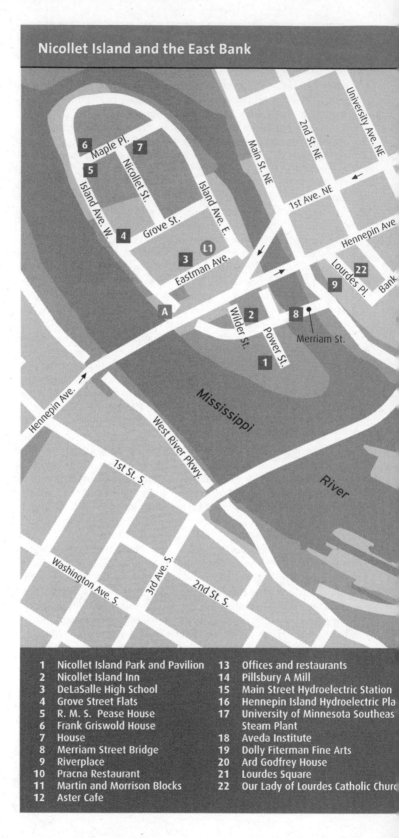

A   Grain Belt Beer Sign
B   Chute's Tunnel and Cave
C   Father Hennepin Bluff Park
    and Pillsbury Park
D   Sixth Avenue Stroll

L1   William King House, Eastman Flats
L2   Winslow House Hotel, Industrial
     Exposition Building, Coca-Cola
     Bottling Plant

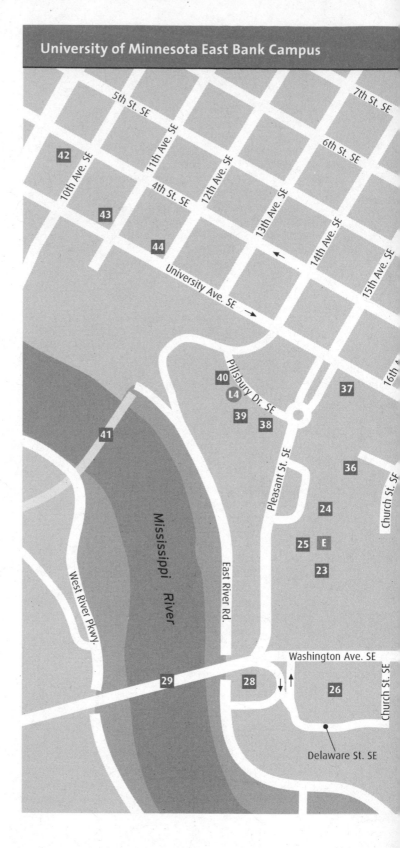

University of Minnesota East Bank Campus

Northrop Mall
Northrop Auditorium
Walter Library
Coffman Memorial Union
Malcolm Moos Health Sciences
Tower and Phillips-Wangensteen
Building
Frederick R. Weisman Art Museum
Washington Avenue Bridge
McNamara Alumni Center and
Gateway Plaza
Williams Arena
Bell Museum of Natural History
Rapson Hall

34 Civil Engineering Building
35 Armory
36 Pillsbury Hall
37 Folwell Hall
38 Eddy Hall
39 Burton Hall
40 Shevlin Hall
41 Pedestrian Bridge
42 Kappa Kappa Gamma Sorority
43 Delta Upsilon Fraternity
44 Phi Gamma Delta Fraternity
45 Phi Kappa Psi Fraternity
46 Phi Sigma Kappa Fraternity

E   Former Northern Pacific Railroad
    main line

L3 Memorial Stadium
L4 Old Main

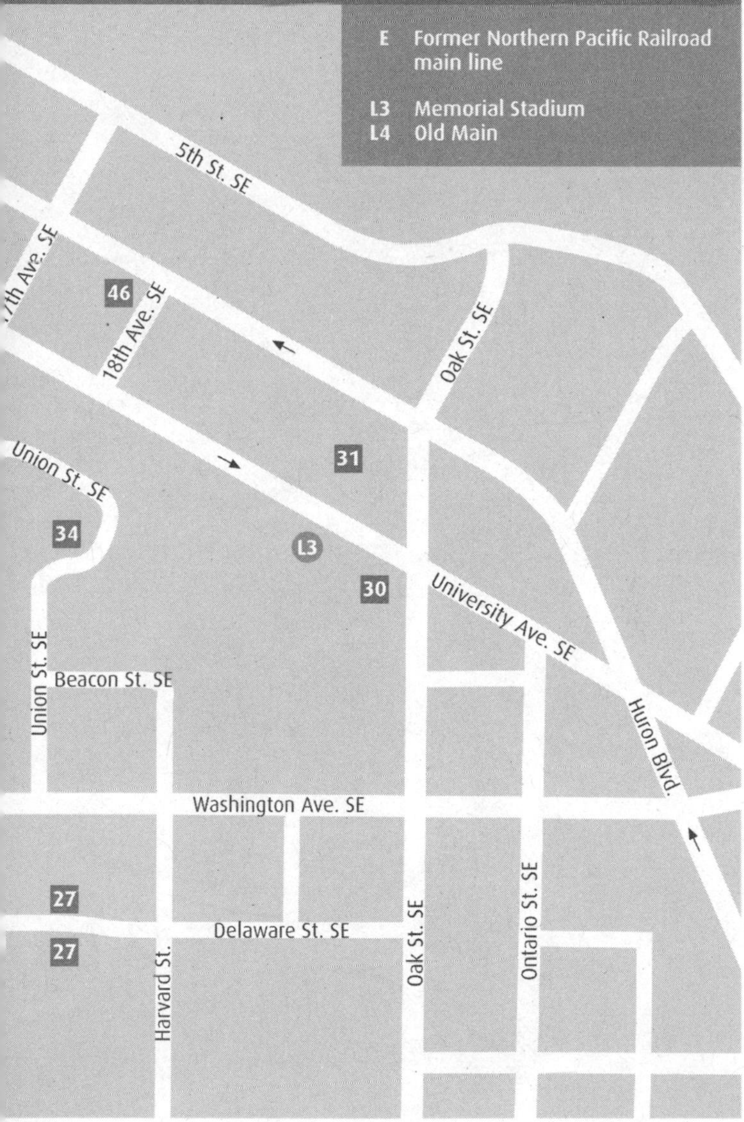

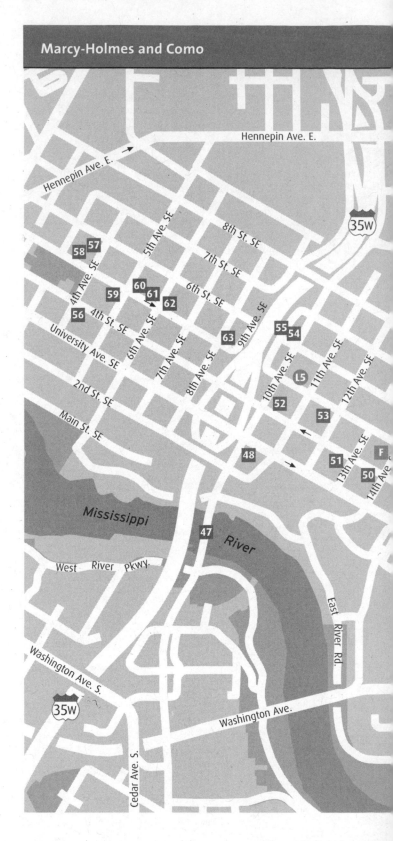

Marcy-Holmes and Como

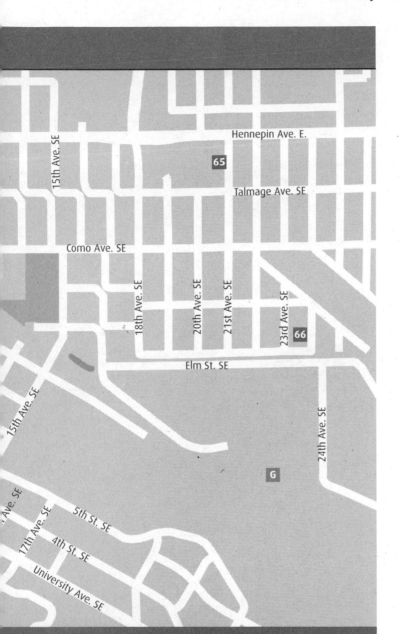

Hennepin Ave. E.

15th Ave. SE

65

Talmage Ave. SE

Como Ave. SE

18th Ave. SE

20th Ave. SE

21st Ave. SE

23rd Ave. SE

66

Elm St. SE

24th Ave. SE

15th Ave. SE

G

Ave. SE

17th Ave. SE

5th St. SE

4th St. SE

University Ave. SE

University

7   Tenth Avenue Bridge
3   Florence Court
9   Dinky Dome
0   Varsity Theater and Cafe
     des Artistes
1   Southeast Community Library
2   Sigma Phi Epsilon Fraternity
3   Gamma Eta Gamma Fraternity
4   Earle Brown House
5   Fred and Susan Pillsbury Snyder House
6   Church
7   Octavius Broughton House
3   Frank Stetson House
9   Woodbury Fisk House

60   John E. Lockwood House
61   Andrews Condominiums
62   William Kimball House
63   First Congregational Church
64   Donald Cattanach House
65   Quinn Violins
66   Double bungalows

F   Al's Breakfast
G   Grain elevators

L5   John S. Pillsbury House

Prospect Park and the East River Road

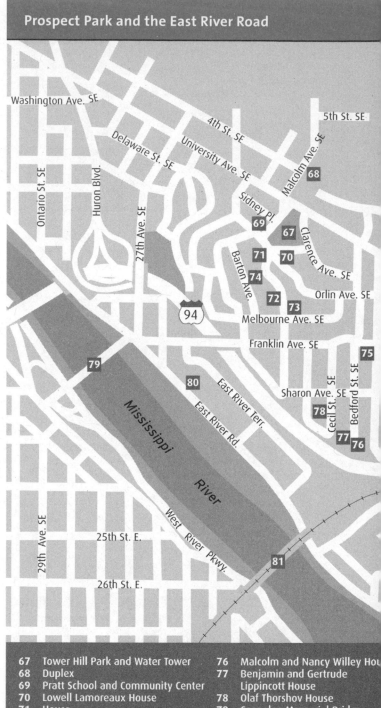

67 Tower Hill Park and Water Tower	**76** Malcolm and Nancy Willey Hou
68 Duplex	**77** Benjamin and Gertrude
69 Pratt School and Community Center	Lippincott House
70 Lowell Lamoreaux House	**78** Olaf Thorshov House
71 House	**79** Cappelen Memorial Bridge
72 Harold Deutsch House	**80** House
73 Gerald Johnson House	**81** Canadian Pacific Railroad Bridg
74 House	
75 St. Panteleimon Russian	
Orthodox Church	

1 Nicollet Island Park and Pavilion (William Brothers Boiler Works) N *L*

40 Power St.

shelter, 1893 / renovated, Collaborative Design Group, 1988 / park, 1988

The park provides a fine view of St. Anthony Falls and the downtown skyline. Its renovated pavilion was originally built for a company that manufactured boilers.

Nicollet Island Inn

2 Nicollet Island Inn (Island Sash and Door Works) N *L*

95 Merriam St.

1893 / renovated, 1982

A remnant of the island's industrial past. The limestone structure was built just before the fire of 1893 but survived the blaze with little damage. The Minneapolis Park Board acquired the building in the 1970s, and it was later redeveloped into its current use as an inn and restaurant.

POI A Grain Belt Beer Sign N *L*

Island Ave. West

ca. 1945 / renovated, ca. 1992

A local icon in the form of an outsized, neon-lit beer cap that proclaims the frothy splendors of Grain Belt. Its placement next to DeLaSalle High School is perhaps not an ideal form of encouragement for students.

3 DeLaSalle High School N *L*

1 DeLaSalle Dr.

1922 / additions, 1959, ca. 1990s

This Catholic high school, operated by the Christian Brothers and originally for boys only, was established here in 1900.

Eastman Flats, 1948

LOST 1 *Previous buildings on DeLaSalle's site include the* **William King House,** *a Gothic Revival–style mansion built in 1874, and* **Eastman Flats,** *two large row houses constructed by William Eastman between 1871 and 1882. King's mansion was torn down in about 1920. The row houses, considered the most elegant of their day in Minneapolis, were later subdivided into cheap apartments, and the last of them was razed in 1959.*

Grove Street Flats

4 Grove Street Flats N *L*

2–16 Grove St.

Kenway and Wirth, 1877 / renovated, ca. 1982–84

The island's only surviving row house, and a good example of the French Second Empire style. Built of local limestone, it originally had eight multistory units, which were subdivided into 16 condominiums when the building was renovated. The rugged gray walls offer little in the way of ornament except for modest window hoods, but reconstructed wooden porches and a patterned mansard roof help bring the old row house to life.

5 R. M. S. Pease House N *L*

101 Island Ave. West

1864

The oldest house on the island, originally located at 814 University Ave. Southeast and moved here in 1986. It's in a simplified style that might be called frontier Greek Revival.

6 Frank Griswold House N *L*

107–9 Island Ave. West

Frederick Corser, 1891 / renovated, ca. 1976

A double house that includes a three-story tower and all the Queen Anne finery your heart could desire. Now four apartments, it was built for a lawyer whose son, also named Frank, later founded Griswold Signal Co., which made flashing signs and gates used for railroad crossings.

7 House N *L*

27 Maple Pl.

1888 / renovated, ca. 1976

One of the island's architectural delights—a cottage with French ambitions in the form of a mansard roof you'd normally expect to find on a much grander house.

Merriam Street Bridge

8 Merriam Street (Broadway Avenue) Bridge N *L*

East channel Mississippi River at Nicollet Island

King Iron Co. and Andrew Rinker (engineer), 1887 / moved here, 1987

In engineering parlance, this is a Pratt through-truss bridge, its beautiful ironwork from an age when even bridges received their share of ornament. It was originally one of four spans that made up the Broadway Avenue Bridge a mile or so upstream. After a new bridge was built, this section of the old span was floated downriver and remounted here on modern support beams.

The East Bank

This is Minneapolis's "old town," founded as part of St. Anthony in the 1840s. It began as a village of industry clustered around mills and factories that drew power from St. Anthony Falls. Sawmills built on platforms above the falls were especially abundant. Flour and paper mills, along with factories manufacturing everything from fencing to mattresses, also operated here, in some cases well into the twentieth century. However, this industrial area never achieved the concentrated might of the west side milling district, despite the presence of the Pillsbury A Mill.

The east bank was also home to a commercial district along Main Street—now largely incorporated into St. Anthony Main—as well as the site of the city's first big hotel, the Winslow House (1857). Later, the hotel was replaced by the Industrial Exposition Building (1886), where in 1892 Republican Benjamin Harrison was nominated for president of the United States.

As industry dried up, the east bank went into decline after World War II, only to undergo a revival in the late 1970s with the opening of St. Anthony Main, the Twin Cities' first foray into the "festival market" concept pioneered at Faneuil Hall in Boston. A somewhat similar development, Riverfront, soon followed. Alas, fudge and candles failed to woo the masses, and both developments eventually converted much of their retail space to office use. Today, housing is the latest hot commodity on the east bank.

9 Riverplace N *L*

Main St. Southeast and
Hennepin Ave. East

*Miller, Hanson, Westerbeck and
Bell and others, 1984 and later*

Along with St. Anthony Main to
the south, this was one of two
megaprojects that redefined the
east bank in the 1980s. It includes
three residential towers, office
space in a mix of new and historic buildings, restaurants, and a
parking ramp. Its original centerpiece was a shopping mall—food
market awash in sunlight, bou-
tiques, and taffy—a product of
festival marketplace mania, an
urban disorder of the 1980s. The
mall failed, and most of it has
been converted to offices. Other
portions of the complex include
the Brown-Ryan Livery Stable, a
limestone structure from 1880
redeveloped into offices, and
Exposition Hall (also offices), built
in 1917 as a furniture factory.

St. Anthony Main N *L*

Main St. and Second Ave.
Southeast

various architects, 1978–85

The first festival marketplace in
the Twin Cities as well as an early
historic preservation project. As
with Riverplace, the retailing
side failed, but restaurants and
offices continue to occupy the
complex, which has benefited
from a second wave of building
in the neighborhood that began
in the late 1990s. St. Anthony
Main's historic buildings include
some of the oldest in Minneapolis.

10 Pracna Restaurant N *L*

117 Main St. Southeast

*Carl F. Struck, 1890 / renovated,
Peter Hall, 1969, 1973*

A lively brick Victorian, originally
a saloon. It was the first historic
building along this part of Main
St. to be renovated. Peter Hall,
an architect-entrepreneur, converted the building into a residence in 1969, then remodeled it
into a bar and restaurant four
years later.

*Pracna Restaurant, Martin and
Morrison Blocks, and Aster Cafe*

11 Martin and Morrison Blocks N *L*

125 Main St. Southeast

1858 / renovated, 1985

This appears to be a single building, but there are in fact two separate structures here, built at the
same time, of the same materials
and identical in style. With their
delicately recessed arched windows, fine proportions, and
beautiful stonework, these buildings are unusually sophisticated
designs for their time and place.
The eastern section (four bays
wide) was constructed for John
Martin, who operated a sawmill
at St. Anthony Falls. The other
side was built for Francis Morrison, whose company built the
first Hennepin Avenue Suspension Bridge in 1855.

12 Aster Cafe (Upton Block, Union Iron Works) N *L*

125 Main St. Southeast

*Benjamin O. Cutter, 1855 /
addition, ca. 1890 / renovated,
ca. 1978*

The city's oldest commercial building, constructed of local brick for
brothers Rufus and Moses Upton,
who operated a hardware business. It was designed by pioneer
builder Benjamin Cutter in a
simple version of the Federal
Style. In 1879 the Union Iron
Works bought the building and
later constructed a rear addition.
The company occupied the
building until 1930, after which
it served as a warehouse until
it was renovated as part of
St. Anthony Main.

13 Offices and restaurants (Salisbury and Satterlee Co. Warehouse and Factory) N *L*

factory, 201–5 Main St. Southeast

Bertrand and Chamberlin, 1909

warehouse, 221 Main St. Southeast

Frederick A. Clarke, 1892 / renovated, ca. 1977

These interconnected factory and warehouse buildings form the core of St. Anthony Main, which was initially developed as a shopping, restaurant, and entertainment complex. The festival concept proved short-lived, however: by the 1990s this had become a ghost mall. It was revived by new owners who converted most of it into offices. The original factory complex here was owned by Salisbury and Satterlee Co., a manufacturer of mattresses and bed springs.

14 Pillsbury A Mill **!** N *L* ★

301 Main St. Southeast

LeRoy Buffington (with W. F. Gunn, engineer), 1881 / rebuilt, C. A. P. Turner (engineer), 1913 / additions: **grain elevators,** *Barnett and Record, 1910, 1914, 1916 /* **cleaning house** *and* **warehouse,** *1917 /* **hydroprocessing building,** *1974*

A National Historic Landmark and the greatest of all American flour mills, built for a family whose name is among the most famous in the city's history. In its peak years around 1905, the mill—divided into two identical sections—poured out nearly 3.5 million pounds of flour a day, using over 400 rollers for grinding hard spring wheat. Moving all of this machinery were two water-powered turbines. Fed by a 400-foot-long underground canal from St. Anthony Falls, the turbines could generate a combined 2,400 horsepower. Later, steam and electric power were added to the mill, but it wasn't until 1955 that the water was turned off and the turbines removed.

The leader of the Pillsbury clan, John S. Pillsbury, arrived in St. Anthony in 1855 and soon became a partner in a hardware business here. In 1869, Pillsbury, his nephews Charles and Fred, and a fourth partner bought a flour mill on the west side of the falls. Despite serving three terms as Minnesota governor in the 1870s, Pillsbury remained in the milling business, and he and his family already owned five other mills on the west bank by the time this one was built.

The Pillsbury A is the city's only architect-designed flour mill (its layout, however, was the work of engineer W. F. Gunn). Architect LeRoy Buffington's design is simple but effective. He grouped windows within shallow recesses and enlarged others beneath broad arches, set off the top floor with a belt course, and

Pillsbury A Mill, 1879

placed parapets at the center and corners of the building. Buffington also spelled out the mill's name in white marble letters set into the front facade. Only 20 or so years after it was built, the mill experienced severe structural problems when some of its limestone walls (eight feet thick in places) began to cave inward. The mill had to be closed and rebuilt from the inside out to avoid a collapse. Engineer C. A. P. Turner stabilized the mill by adding concrete buttresses, which were linked to tie rods that held up the sagging front facade.

Purchased by Archer Daniels Midland Co. in 1992, the mill continued to produce flour until 2003, when it was closed and sold to developers who plan to convert it to housing. However the old mill is reused, everyone seems to agree that one of its most prominent features—a huge illuminated rooftop sign reading "Pillsbury's Best Flour"—will stay.

15 Main Street Hydroelectric Station N L

206–10 Main St. Southeast

Stone and Webster (Boston), 1911

16 Hennepin Island Hydroelectric Plant N L

Hennepin Island near Main St. Southeast and Third Ave. Southeast

William de la Barre, 1908

17 University of Minnesota Southeast Steam Plant (Twin City Rapid Transit Co. Power Plant)

12–20 Sixth Ave. Southeast (also 600 Main St. Southeast)

Sargent and Lundy, 1903 / renovated, Foster Dunwiddie Architects, 2004

St. Anthony Falls is among the first sites in the United States where hydroelectric power was generated. The Hennepin Island plant, now owned by Xcel Energy, once provided electricity for the streetcar system and is still in use today. The large University of

Minnesota steam plant also remains in operation and was recently renovated. The Main Street Station is no longer in service.

POI B Chute's Tunnel and Cave N L

Beneath Main St. near Third Ave. Southeast

1864

In 1864, the St. Anthony Waterpower Co., led by Richard Chute, began digging a tunnel to bring waterpower to mills and factories along the east bank. After tunneling 550 feet, workers broke into a natural cave. Filling in the cave would have made it too costly to continue the project, and the tunnel was abandoned. Eventually, the cave and tunnel were closed off. In 1990, urban caver Greg Brick was able to confirm that the cave still exists, though much of its roof has collapsed.

POI C Father Hennepin Bluff Park and Pillsbury Park N L

Along Main St. between Third and Sixth Aves. Southeast

Minneapolis Park Board, ca. 1971

These parks lead down to Hennepin Island (now a peninsula) and provide a view of the Pillsbury A Mill's old tailrace tunnels. Between 1875 and 1883 there was a small resort here, beneath Fourth Ave. Southeast, known as Chalybeate Springs. Near the Stone Arch Bridge, you'll also see a river ruin: a pier from the old Tenth Avenue Bridge, razed in 1943.

POI D Sixth Avenue Stroll, bronze sculptures

Sixth Ave. Southeast between Main St. and University Ave. Southeast

Aldo Moroni, 2004

Moroni's small bronze sculptures, mounted on brick columns along Sixth Ave. Southeast, depict in his usual fanciful way 23 landmarks in the Marcy-Holmes neighborhood.

Aveda Institute, 1936

18 Aveda Institute (Cataract Temple)

101–9 Fourth St. Southeast
(also 400 Central Ave. Southeast)

George O. Huey, 1926 / renovated, ca. 1975

A "Venetian" style building (as described at the time of its opening) originally constructed for Cataract Lodge No. 2., the first Masonic Lodge in Minneapolis. The building is most notable for its creamy terra-cotta ornament, which frames the windows and also appears as rocketlike projections along the roofline. Within, the main lodge room was especially splendid, with Doric colonnades framed beneath an illuminated dome. Cataract Temple sold the building in 1945.

19 Dolly Fiterman Fine Arts (Pillsbury Library)

100 University Ave. Southeast

Charles Aldrich, 1904

Beaux-Arts bravado in a small package, offering monumental front steps, a triple-arched entry pavilion, and a rooftop balustrade. Donated to the city by the estate of John S. Pillsbury, it was the city's most lavish branch library. The Minneapolis Public Library sold the building in 1967 and relocated the southeast branch elsewhere. The building became an art gallery in the 1980s.

20 Ard Godfrey House N *L*

Richard Chute Square,
Central and University Aves.

Ard Godfrey (builder), 1849 / restored and renovated, Brooks Cavin, 1977 and later / addition (kitchen wing), 1985

The oldest documented house in the Twin Cities, originally located near Main St. and Second Ave.

Ard Godfrey House, 1924

Southeast and moved five times before finally settling here. Restored and painted its original yellow, the house is a small but chaste example of the Greek Revival style. Ard Godfrey was a Maine-born millwright who built this house two years after arriving in St. Anthony in 1847. Godfrey and his family moved to the Minnehaha Falls area in 1853, when he built a gristmill (gone) in the glen below the falls. This house was moved here in 1909 by the Hennepin County Territorial Pioneers Association. The Minneapolis Woman's Club, working with architect Brooks Cavin, restored the house in the late 1970s and operates it as a museum.

21 Lourdes Square N *L*

Second and Bank Sts. Southeast

Paul Madson and Associates, 1994

These 40 luxury townhomes, arranged as a series of row houses, were the first of their kind in the east bank area. They're well designed—traditional in feel but not literal in their historicism.

Industrial Exposition Building, 1926

LOST 2 *Lourdes Square occupies a site with a rich architectural history. The* **Winslow House Hotel,** *a five-story limestone structure,* *was built here in 1857 and served briefly as home to Macalester College before being razed in the 1880s to make way for the **Industrial Exposition Building.** Built for an industrial fair in 1886, it was also the site of the 1892 Republican National Convention. Portions of it stood until 1946, when a **Coca-Cola Bottling Plant** took over the site. That plant operated until the 1980s.*

22 Our Lady of Lourdes Catholic (First Universalist) Church N L

1 Lourdes Pl.

1857 / enlarged, 1880–83 / addition (front vestibule), ca. 1914 / interior restored, Al Berreau, 1980 and later

Surrounded now by apartment towers and townhomes, this church is an important surviving monument of the historic village of St. Anthony. It's also the city's oldest church. The front portion, Greek Revival in style, was built in 1857 for a Universalist congregation. In 1866, a new pastor—the Reverend Herman Bisbee—took over the church. A skeptic when it came to biblical miracles and Noah's ark, Bisbee was soon booted out of the Universalist fold. Without their leader, the congregation struggled and in 1877 sold the church to a French Catholic group.

Our Lady of Lourdes Catholic Church, 1936

Renamed Our Lady of Lourdes, the church was expanded to accommodate its new owners. Between 1880 and 1883, the parish added a transept and apse at the rear of the church as well as a front bell tower complete with three steeples. These additions were described as "French Provincial" in style. A front vestibule, of a more or less Classical Revival mode, was added in 1914. Within, the church is quite plain, in keeping with its modest exterior.

University of Minnesota East Bank Campus and Environs

Aside from the orderly if rather dull precinct of Northrop Mall, this gigantic campus is just the sort of sprawling muddle you'd expect of a place that has grown by fits and starts over more than 150 years. With its polyglot collection of buildings, its ad hoc interventions, and its edges that bleed off into surrounding neighborhoods, the campus is a kind of architectural confederation, loose and a bit chaotic, yet interesting by virtue of it untamed variety.

The university's earliest buildings, beginning with Old Main, were built in what is now known as the Old Campus Historic District near University and 15th avenues. Many buildings from the 1880s and 1890s still stand here. Also known as the Knoll, this part of the campus is quite pleasant, with winding streets and expansive lawns. The next big round of development occurred after Cass Gilbert won a competition to plan campus growth in 1908. Gilbert's design called for a mall extending from the old campus district south to the Mississippi. As built in the 1920s, however, Northrop Mall never reached the river. Although Gilbert sketched out future buildings as part of his plan, their actual design fell to Clarence Johnston, who'd become state architect in 1901. Between 1912 and 1930, Johnston's office designed over a dozen buildings along or near the mall, culminating in Northrop Memorial Auditorium (1929).

The Depression brought campus expansion to a halt until 1940, when Coffman Memorial Union—which closed off the mall's river link as Gilbert had envisioned it—was built. After World War II, new campus buildings appeared in just about every known architectural style. In more recent years, celebrity architects have made their mark on campus with distinctive buildings. These include Frank Gehry's ode to twisted metal, the Weisman Art Museum (1993), and Antoine Predock's peculiar McNamara Alumni Center (2000).

Northrop Mall and Northrop Auditorium

23 Northrop Mall

Cass Gilbert, 1908 / Arthur Nichols and others, ca. 1920s and later

When the university's board of regents sponsored a competition for a campus plan in 1908, the City Beautiful movement was ascendant, and architects everywhere were drawing up schemes for classically inspired malls and boulevards. Competition winner Cass Gilbert had already produced plans for a State Capitol mall in St. Paul, and it was inevitable that he would propose one for the university as well. Today, the mall—which was not built entirely in accord with Gilbert's design—remains a vital organizing feature on the East Bank campus.

Although Gilbert didn't design the mall's buildings, he had a say in their appearance. He and Clarence Johnston agreed that the buildings should be in the so-called Roman Renaissance style, should have uniform cornice heights, and should be clad in stone (the cost-conscious regents later settled for brick). The buildings ultimately designed by Johnston's firm, with his son Clarence Johnston, Jr., taking a lead role, are indeed in the specified style. However, only one—the restored Walter Library—is of the first rank; the others come across as drably institutional.

24 Northrop Auditorium

84 Church St.

Clarence H. Johnston, 1929

This monumental auditorium, which stands at the head of the mall, was envisioned by Cass Gilbert in 1908, but it wasn't until the 1920s that money was raised to build it. The death of long-time university president Cyrus Northrop in 1922 spurred construction of the auditorium, intended as a memorial both to him and to World War I veterans. Northrop's thundering Ionic portico and the lobby behind it are certainly impressive, as is the sheer size of the auditorium (its 4,800 seats were sufficient to hold the university's entire student body in 1929). The building as a whole, however, has always felt ponderous and embalmed.

POI E Site of former Northern Pacific Railroad main line

Northrop Mall, near Johnston and Morrill Halls

ca. 1887–ca. 1924

Part of the area now occupied by Northrop Mall was once crossed by a rail line just south of where Johnston and Morrill halls stand today. Built by the Northern Pacific Railroad in the 1880s, the line was relocated in 1924 to a sunken corridor north of the old campus, thereby clearing the way for construction of Northrop Auditorium and development of the mall.

Walter Library interior, 1924

25 Walter Library !

117 Pleasant St. Southeast

Clarence H. Johnston, 1925 / renovated, Stageberg Beyer Sachs, 2001

Beautifully restored and renovated, this is the best building on the mall. Behind its restrained facades you'll find a sequence of colorful rooms finished in marble, limestone, bronze, wrought iron, tile, stained glass, and polychromed plaster. Highlights include the lobby with its coffered ceiling, the Arthur Upson Room (named for the man who wrote the lyrics to "Hail Minnesota"), the skylit great hall on the second floor, and the three gorgeous reading rooms arrayed around it. As part of a renovation completed in 2001, the library's original 12-level central book stack was removed and the space infilled and enlarged to accommodate a variety of new uses.

26 Coffman Memorial Union

300 Washington Ave. Southeast

Clarence H. Johnston, Jr., 1940 / renovated, Community Planning and Design, 1976 / renovated, Ellerbe Becket, 2003

This building opened four years after a new campus plan called for placing a student union at the south end of the mall. The decision dealt a deathblow to Cass Gilbert's idea of extending the mall to the river. Be that as it may, Coffman Memorial Union (named after a university president with the improbable name of Lotus Delta Coffman) is a pleasing example of the Moderne style. The building was maimed by a dreadful remodeling job in the 1970s; much of the damage was undone by a more sensitive— and far more costly—renovation completed in 2003.

27 Malcolm Moos Health Sciences Tower and Phillips-Wangensteen Building

515, 516 Delaware St. Southeast

Architectural Collaborative, Cerny and Associates, HGA, Setter Leach and Lindstrom, 1974–76

The architectural equivalent of a Hummer, the idea apparently being to show just how big and bad a building can be. Designed for the schools of medicine, dentistry, and public health, the complex consists of two interconnected buildings that read as a single structure. Together, they constitute the supreme Twin Cities example of the Brutalist style of the 1960s and 1970s. With their crushing scale and ominously overhanging upper floors, they certainly convey a sense of the power of modern medicine, albeit in a thoroughly unpleasant way.

Frederick R. Weisman Art Museum

28 Frederick R. Weisman Art Museum !

333 East River Pkwy.

Frank Gehry and Associates (Santa Monica, CA) with MS&R Architects, 1993

The most famous work of modern architecture on campus, and a building that proved to be quite a shocker when it rose like a shimmering mirage beside the Washington Avenue Bridge. Once you get past the gyrations of the facade, however, you'll discover that the building is a good place to enjoy art. It was built for the University of Minnesota Art Museum, established in 1934 and long hidden away within the dim bowels of Northrop Auditorium. The museum wanted a new building that would give it the strong identity it had always been lacking, and architect Frank Gehry delivered the goods.

Named after its chief benefactor, the Weisman is best known for its stainless-steel facade, a jolly jumble of colliding forms that faces the Mississippi like a giant signboard, shouting out the museum's presence, especially when afternoon sunlight sets the steel aglow. Behind all the razzle-dazzle, however, there's a plain brick box. Architect Robert Venturi coined the term "decorated shed" to describe buildings that hide boxes behind elaborate facades. The Weisman could fairly be called Gehry's decorated shed, particularly if you compare it to his later designs—such as the Guggenheim Museum in Bilbao, Spain—where the entire building is treated in the free-form manner of the Weisman's facade. The Guggenheim has been criticized for overwhelming the art inside. By contrast, the far more modest Weisman offers very pleasant galleries illuminated in part by irregularly shaped skylights carved out of the roof.

29 Washington Avenue Bridge

Across Mississippi River

Sverdrup and Parcel (engineers), 1965 / renovated, 1980 and later

The only double-decker bridge in the Twin Cities, with pedestrians on the upper level and vehicles below. Intended to provide a strong link between the university's East and West Bank campuses, the bridge is utterly prosaic. As built, it was also impractical: the pedestrian deck was left open to the elements. A clumsy enclosure was added later; if anything it made the bridge look worse. Over the years, the bridge has been the unfortunate site of several suicides, including that of poet John Berryman, a university professor who jumped to his death in 1972.

McNamara Alumni Center and Gateway Plaza

30 McNamara Alumni Center and Gateway Plaza !

200 Oak St. Southeast

Antoine Predock (Albuquerque, NM) with KKE Architects, 2000 / plaza, Antoine Predock with LHB Engineers, 2000 / Art: Alumni Wall of Honor (metal sculpture), Constance DeJong, 2004

Like the Weisman Museum, this building is all about making a big, eye-catching statement. Yet whereas the Weisman manages to do so with great *brio,* here the predominant quality seems to be a kind of rockbound chill. Named after an alumnus who donated $3 million toward its cost, the center is the only work in Minnesota by New Mexico–based architect Antoine Predock, best known for naturalistic buildings that emerge like rock formations out of their desert settings.

The heart of the center, which includes two copper-clad office wings, is a hall designed to resemble a giant, granite-sheathed geode. Irregularly shaped windows penetrate this faceted mass, as do long, crisscrossing slits of glass. Inside is 85-foot-high Memorial Hall, which like the building as a whole isn't very inviting. Mounted within the hall is a processional arch salvaged from Memorial Stadium (1924), which once occupied this site. The center rises behind a plaza adorned with a long, obtrusive *Alumni Wall of Honor,* unattractively rendered in rusted steel.

LOST 3 *Memorial Stadium, long home to the University of Minnesota's football team, was built here in 1924. It was demolished in 1992, ten years after the Gophers decamped to the Metrodome in 1982. Unhappy with the plastic pallor of the Metrodome, the uni-versity won state funding in 2006 to build a new stadium just across from this site.*

31 Williams Arena (University of Minnesota Field House)

1925 University Ave. Southeast

Clarence H. Johnston, 1928 / renovated, ca. 1950 / renovated, HGA, 1993

Known as the "barn," this is one of the nation's oldest college arenas. For a time it was also the largest, seating over 18,000 fans (it now holds 14,625). Built as a field house, it originally served as a basketball arena and practice facility. It was remodeled in 1950 to accommodate hockey as well (that sport later moved to nearby Mariucci Arena [1993]) and was then renamed in honor of Henry Williams, a former university football coach. The arena was remodeled and updated in 1993.

32 Bell Museum of Natural History

10 Church St. Southeast

Clarence H. Johnston, Jr., 1940 / addition, 1967

An ivied PWA Moderne–style building. The entrance, flanked by a pair of elegant light standards, features a sculpted buffalo roaming above the doors. A variety of other creatures also lurk amid the ivy. The museum will move to a new building on the university's St. Paul campus in 2009.

33 Rapson Hall (College of Architecture and Landscape Architecture)

89 Church St. Southeast

Thorshov and Cerny, 1960 / addition and renovation, Steven Holl and others, 2002

The original portion of this building is a delicate glass and brick box that wraps around an airy central court. It's all understated and surprisingly serene. Steven Holl's addition is also subdued despite its free-form shape. Clad largely in copper, it makes

University

much use of translucent glass. The building was renamed in 2002 in honor of Ralph Rapson, longtime head of the university's

Rapson Hall

school of architecture and the most prominent Minnesota architect of his era.

34 Civil Engineering Building

500 Pillsbury Dr. Southeast

BRW Architects, 1980

Underground architecture was in vogue during the energy-anxious 1970s, and this building is among the largest of its kind in the Twin Cities. The building is organized around a sunken courtyard that helps bring natural light into its seven below-ground levels.

Old Campus Historic District (the Knoll)

The most historic portion of the campus. Landscape architect Horace Cleveland planned its curving streets (though his plan was never completely carried out). The casually sited buildings and large lawns create a relaxed atmosphere not unlike that of a small liberal arts college. The older buildings here—13 of which lie within a National Register historic district—display a wide variety of styles, but they're generally of modest size and pleasing appearance.

35 Armory N

15 Church St. Southeast

Charles Aldrich, 1896 / Art: Spanish American War Soldier (bronze statue), Theo-Ruggles-Kitson, 1906

A splendid example of the castellated style often used around 1900 for armories. The high point of architect Charles Aldrich's design is a round tower outfitted with a corbelled parapet, where

you half expect to see archers, or maybe the guys with boiling oil, preparing for an attack.

Pillsbury Hall, 1900

36 Pillsbury Hall ! N

310 Pillsbury Dr. Southeast

LeRoy Buffington with Harvey Ellis, 1889

Along with Minneapolis City Hall, this building is one of the state's outstanding examples of the Romanesque style pioneered by Boston architect H. H. Richardson. However, it's less an homage to the master than a kind of hopped-up, over-the-top salute to Richardson's work from the fantastic imagination of Harvey Ellis. The walls combine two kinds of sandstone: a beige variety from the Kettle River quarries near the city of Sandstone in east-central Minnesota and a reddish brown stone from the southern shore of Lake Superior. These stones are worked into a dazzling variety of patterns. Pillsbury Hall is also notable for its cavelike entrances, the grandest of which along Pillsbury Dr. takes the form of an arch that tapers inward by means of giant voussoirs. Around these entrances you'll find stone carving that includes, among other delights, gargoyles, a Medusa, and sea lions. The building is named after John S. Pillsbury, who donated $150,000 toward its construction. Fittingly enough, it's now home to the university's geology department.

37 Folwell Hall ! N

9 Pleasant St. Southeast

Clarence H. Johnston, 1907

An extravagant Tudor-Jacobean romance, gorgeously ornamented in terra-cotta. It shows that Clarence Johnston, many of whose later campus buildings cannot be described as scintillating, knew how to party when the opportunity presented itself. The normally tight-fisted board of regents gave Johnston a big budget for this building, which was designed to replace Old

Folwell Hall, 1910

Main after its destruction by fire in 1904. Terra-cotta in an array of tones and textures is the star of the architectural show here. It surrounds windows and doors and appears in all manner of ornamental work, from a chain-like balustrade to decorative wall panels to a row of faces that project from a frieze along the roofline. Terra-cotta finials also adorn the roof, which is itself a wonder, piling up at either end into a Tudor forest of intricately detailed chimneys, 26 in all.

38 Eddy Hall N

192 Pillsbury Dr. Southeast

LeRoy Buffington, 1886 / additions, 1903, 1966

The oldest building on campus, topped by the requisite tower.

39 Burton Hall N

178 Pillsbury Dr. Southeast

LeRoy Buffington (exterior) and Charles S. Sedgwick (interior), 1894 / Art: Governor John Pillsbury (bronze sculpture across street), Daniel Chester French, 1900

Built as the university's library, Burton Hall is the closet thing to a Greek temple you'll find on campus. A decorative frieze behind the Doric portico extols science, sculpture, architecture, painting, and literature, in that order.

40 Shevlin Hall N

164 Pillsbury Dr. Southeast

Ernest Kennedy, 1906

A gracious Renaissance Revival building that once served as a campus center for women students. Ernest Kennedy also designed the Pillsbury Gate at University and 15th Aves. Southeast.

LOST 4 *A rock-mounted plaque by Shevlin Hall marks the site of **Old Main,** the university's first building. The building was constructed in 1856, enlarged in 1875, and destroyed by fire in 1904. Not everyone seems to have mourned the loss. Maria Sanford, a faculty member who watched the fire, wrote: "I could not repress a feeling of satisfaction as I thought of the millions of cockroaches being consumed in that holocaust."*

Other buildings in the Old Campus Historic District include **Music Education (Student Christian Association) Building** (Warren H. Hayes, 1888); **Pattee Hall** (J. Walter Stevens, 1890); **Nicholson Hall** (LeRoy Buffington with Harvey Ellis, 1890 / renovated, Collaborative Design Group, 2005); **Jones Hall** (Charles Aldrich, 1901 / renovated, Stageberg Beyer Sachs, ca. 2004); **Westbrook Hall** (Frederick Corser, 1898); **Wulling Hall** (Reed and Stem, 1892); and **Child Development (Mines) Building** (Clarence H. Johnston, 1903).

41 Pedestrian (Northern Pacific Railroad) Bridge

Across Mississippi River

Frederick Cappelen, 1887 / renovated, 1917 / renovated and moved, ca. 1921–24 / converted to pedestrian/bike use, 1999

This steel-truss bridge was actually built several hundred yards downstream. It was moved in 1924 after the Northern Pacific Railroad agreed to relocate its tracks off the university campus.

Greek Letter Chapter House Historic District

This city historic district, established in 2003, includes 33 Greek letter chapter houses, mostly clustered in "fraternity row" along University Ave. between 17th Ave. and Oak St. Southeast. The houses, designed by leading Twin Cities architects, mostly date from 1910 to 1930 and form a rich body of work in the Period Revival styles popular at that time. By 1930 there were 52 fraternities and 22 sororities active at the university. Today the number of Greek chapters has dwindled to just over 30.

42 Kappa Kappa Gamma Sorority *L*

329 Tenth Ave. Southeast

Frederick Mann, 1915 / rear addition

This is home to the university's oldest sorority, chartered in 1880. Its architect, Frederick Mann, founded the university's architecture department in 1913. Here he delivered a steep-roofed stucco house reminiscent of the work of the English Arts and Crafts architect Charles Voysey.

43 Delta Upsilon Fraternity (Pi Beta Phi Sorority) *L*

1019 University Ave. Southeast

Ethel Bartholomew and Alice Parker, 1916

The only Prairie Style chapter house in the district, built for a sorority and doubly unusual in that its architects were women. Ethel Bartholomew was perhaps best known as the editor of publications such as *Construction Details* and *Keith's Magazine*. At the time this house was designed, Parker—among the state's first female architects—was working for the firm of Purcell and Elmslie, local masters of the Prairie Style. Note the Elmslie-inspired sawnwood ornament above the side entrance.

44 Phi Gamma Delta Fraternity *L*

1129 University Ave. Southeast

Carl B. Stravs, 1911

The university's strangest chapter house, designed by an architect born in Yugoslavia in a variation of the Art Nouveau style imported from Vienna. What's most striking about this three-story brick and concrete house is the way in which architect Carl Stravs took a standard symmetrical template and used it to fashion a building full of odd details: an elliptic arch on the porch, an attenuated central window, a thin cornice that floats above abstracted swags. Besides this house there are only a few other Art Nouveau–inspired buildings in the Twin

Phi Gamma Delta Fraternity

Cities, among them St. Bernard's Catholic Church (1906) in St. Paul, designed by Stravs's one-time partner, John Jager.

45 Phi Kappa Psi Fraternity *L*

1609 University Ave. Southeast

William Kenyon, 1907

Fraternity row's oldest chapter house, a dignified Georgian Revival design that looks more like the home of a banker than the sort of place you'd expect to encounter any *Animal House* hijinks.

46 Phi Sigma Kappa Fraternity *L*

317 18th Ave. Southeast

Kenneth Worthen, 1928

This house, which has a dizzyingly steep roof, looks as though it could spring from its foundations and charge across 18th Ave. were it not for an end-wall chimney checking its forward momentum. Although nominally Tudor Revival, the house's fanciful detailing and exaggerated roof suggest the Hollywood-inspired Storybook Style popular in the 1920s.

Marcy-Holmes and Como

These two neighborhoods lie within the enormous shadow of the University of Minnesota, and they've been shaped to varying degrees by its presence. Marcy-Holmes is in many ways a classic campus-edge neighborhood, indicated by the fact that only 11 percent of its 4,000 or so housing units are owner-occupied. The neighborhood, in fact, has all the elements of what might be called "studentville"—numerous apartment buildings, scores of old homes subdivided into rental units, a scattering of fraternity and sorority houses, and a small commercial area (the wonderfully named Dinkytown) that caters to students.

Still, Marcy-Holmes isn't entirely dominated by the university. The historic east bank area around St. Anthony Main falls within the neighborhood's boundaries, as does the locally designated Fifth Street Southeast Historic District, which boasts of some of the city's few remaining houses from the 1850s and 1860s. Marcy-Holmes was sliced in half in the 1960s by Interstate 35W, bringing the usual disruptions to the urban fabric but also creating a barrier against westward expansion of the university campus.

The Como (or, as it's sometimes called, Southeast Como) neighborhood lies to the east of Marcy-Holmes, wedged between Hennepin Avenue East on the north and a complex of rail yards, grain elevators, and other industries to the south. The neighborhood is primarily residential even though it's almost literally surrounded by rail and industrial uses. Its name comes from Como Avenue, which runs through the neighborhood before crossing over into St. Paul. Como has a higher percentage of owner-occupied housing (36 percent) than Marcy-Holmes, but it lacks the extensive Victorian housing stock of that community. Most of Como's houses are quite modest, including a colony of brick ramblers built near the eastern edge of the neighborhood just after World War II.

47 Tenth (Cedar) Avenue Bridge N

Across Mississippi River

Kristoffer Oustad, 1929 / renovated, Howard Needles Tammen and Bergendorf, 1976

Engineers love to classify bridges, and if you really want to know, this is a reinforced-concrete, open-spandrel, two-rib, continuous-

arch span. More importantly, it's a beautiful piece of engineering that flows across the river gorge on seven arches. Extending nearly 3,000 feet when built, it was the longest and highest of all the city's river bridges. It was also the culminating work of its designer, Norwegian-born engineer Kristoffer Oustad. The bridge was extensively renovated in 1976, when the southern approaches were shortened and a new deck installed.

48 Florence Court *L*

1000–1018 University Ave. Southeast

Jeremiah Spear (builder) and Long and Kees, 1886 / additions, 1921, 1929

An early example of what might be called a planned residential community. The complex consists of 12 brick row houses, four wood-frame houses (moved here in 1921), and a large brick house on University, all arranged around a courtyard. Given its proximity to the university, it's hardly surprising that Florence Court has been subdivided into over 40 apartments.

Dinkytown

Centered at the intersection of Fourth St. and 14th Ave. Southeast, this commercial district offers a suitably collegiate mix of shops and restaurants. The oldest buildings go back to about 1900, a time when the university was experiencing a surge in enrollment. It's uncertain how Dinkytown acquired its name, although one theory holds that the inspiration came from a small type of locomotive known as a *dinkey* that once ran on the rail line that cuts through the neighborhood.

49 Dinky Dome (Minnesota Bible College)

1501 University Ave. Southeast

1915 / renovated

Originally used as a library, this Dinkytown landmark is named after its glass dome, which crowns an atrium. Along University, there's an Ionic portico of the type you'd associate with a public building or bank. But in this case there's only a food court behind all the classical gas.

POI F Al's Breakfast

413 14th Ave. Southeast

1937 and later

Occupying part of an old alley, this legendary diner is ten feet wide, has 14 stools, closes at 1:00 PM, and features sublime buttermilk pancakes. It was opened in 1950 by Al Bergstrom, who ran it for 24 years before turning over the business to others.

50 Varsity Theater and Cafe des Artistes (University Theater)

1308 Fourth St. Southeast

1915 / remodeled and enlarged, Liebenberg and Kaplan, 1939 / later renovations

This theater opened in 1915 as the University and offered vaudeville acts as well as movies. The building you see today—with its jazzy pleated walls of Mankato-Kasota stone, glass-block windows, and gorgeous vertical sign—is a Moderne makeover. The lobby and an expanded 877-seat auditorium also received the full Moderne treatment in the redo. The Varsity survived as a movie house until 1988. It took on its most recent incarnation as a performance venue and cafe in 2005.

51 Southeast Community Library (State Capitol Credit Union)

1222 Fourth St. Southeast

Ralph Rapson, 1964 / renovated, Ralph Rapson, 1967

A crisp, convincing period piece from the 1960s by Minnesota's leading architectural modernist. It began its life as a credit union but was converted into a branch library just three years later, after the splendid old Pillsbury Library was closed. Rapson himself supervised the conversion.

52 Sigma Phi Epsilon Fraternity (B. O. Cutter–John Gilfillan House) **! N** *L*

400 Tenth Ave. Southeast

Benjamin O. Cutter, 1856 / additions, 1874, 1968

Although it's been shorn of some detail and coated with stucco, this lacy confection is a rare surviving example in the Twin Cities of the Gothic Revival "cottage" style. Virtually all the key elements of the style can be found here, including steeply pitched gables and dormers, decorative bargeboards that curl and twist like

Sigma Phi Epsilon Fraternity, 1948

climbing vines, and drip moldings above the windows. The builder and first owner, Benjamin Cutter, also designed the Upton Block that's now part of St. Anthony Main. Cutter later sold the house to John Gilfillan, who enlarged it in 1874. A lawyer by profession, Gilfillan was also a university regent and a U.S. congressman. Converted to fraternity use in 1949, the house was enlarged again in 1968, when a rear addition was built.

LOST 5 *Where the* **Pillsbury Court townhomes** *(1965) now stand at 1001–53 Fifth St. Southeast was the site of the* **John S. Pillsbury House,** *built in 1879 to the designs of LeRoy Buffington (also the architect for Pillsbury's famous A mill). From 1911 to 1960, the house served as the official residence of the university's president. It was torn down in 1964.*

53 Gamma Eta Gamma Fraternity (Reverend Joseph Wright House)

1126 Fifth St. Southeast

Babb Cook and Willard (New York), 1892

A stylistic gumbo, blending the picturesque qualities of Queen Anne—including a Moorish-inspired horseshoe-arch window above the porte cochere—with the massive stonework typical of Romanesque Revival.

54 Earle Brown House

925 Sixth St. Southeast

Ernest Kennedy, 1899

A Renaissance Revival house built for Earle Brown, who served for many years as Hennepin County sheriff and who is also credited with founding the Minnesota Highway Patrol.

55 Fred and Susan Pillsbury Snyder House

915 Sixth St. Southeast

1887

A Victorian converted long ago into the usual warren of student apartments and now looking as though it could use a rest from its labors on behalf of education. It was originally built as a wedding present for one of John S. Pillsbury's daughters, Susan, and her husband.

56 Church (Holy Trinity Episcopal Church)

316 Fourth Ave. Southeast

William Causdale, 1873 / addition, 1890 / rebuilt after fire, 1893

A lovely Gothic church constructed of gray local limestone trimmed with yellow Mankato-Kasota stone. It was built for St. Anthony's first Episcopal congregation, Holy Trinity, founded in 1848.

Fifth Street Southeast Historic District

This city-designated historic district was established in 1976 and extends along both sides of Fifth St. between Fourth and Ninth Aves. Southeast. It includes some of the city's oldest houses, many built by prominent businessmen who made their money in milling or manufacturing at St. Anthony Falls. Here, too, you'll find the First Congregational Church (1888), an impressive monument in the Richardsonian Romanesque style.

57 Octavius Broughton House *L*

511 Fourth Ave. Southeast

1859

This little gem is among the oldest homes in the historic district. Its sidelighted door, mock corner pilasters, return eaves, and frieze band are all classic Greek Revival elements. The house, which has a rear addition, was built for Octavius Broughton, a millwright. In 1901 the house was moved a short distance and placed on a new stone foundation.

58 Frank Stetson House *L*

323 Fifth St. Southeast

ca. 1892

A strange Victorian house. Its mansard roof evokes the French Second Empire style, but the house itself seems too small and plain to be wearing such a fancy hat. Then again, considering that the original owner's name was Stetson, maybe the big hat was inevitable.

Woodbury Fisk House, 1965

59 Woodbury Fisk House ! N *L*

424 Fifth St. Southeast

1869

A full-blooded and generally well-preserved example of the Italianate Villa style. The L-shaped brick house, which includes a rear addition, displays all the usual Italianate goodies: a decorated porch with arched openings, ornate cast-iron window hoods, and a cornice supported by pairs of scrolled brackets set between carved wooden panels. The house was built for Woodbury Fisk, a New Hampshire native who arrived in St. Anthony in 1855 with two friends, Thomas Andrews and John S. Pillsbury. Fisk started out in the hardware

business with Pillsbury and by 1869 had prospered sufficiently to build this house on a lot that originally extended for a full block along Fifth. Not long after moving here with his family, Fisk took up a new line of work— flour milling—and for several years was in partnership with Pillsbury.

60 John E. Lockwood House *L*

501 Fifth St. Southeast

Orff and Joralemon, 1893

This house, among the largest on Fifth St., was more handsome before stuccoers had their way with it. It originally came with clapboard siding, a side porch topped by a balustraded balcony, and small loggia (now filled in) over the front porch. As it stands today, the house's outstanding feature is the broad Palladian window in the front gable. The house was built for John Lockwood, who founded the Union Iron Works nearby on Main St.

61 Andrews Condominiums (Thomas Andrews House) *L*

527 Fifth St. Southeast

1869 / addition (at 505 Sixth Ave. Southeast), 1903 / renovated, 1999

Thomas Andrews began his career in St. Anthony when he opened a dry goods store on Main St. in 1855. He eventually became involved in real estate and politics. This wood-frame house, which once sported a cupola, is a good example of the foursquare, symmetrical variant of the Italianate style often built in frontier communities. A rear addition built in 1903 was occupied by one of Andrews's daughters until 1961. The house is now divided into two condominiums.

62 William Kimball (later Horatio and Charlotte Van Cleve) House N *L*

601–3 Fifth St. Southeast

1858 / addition (porch), ca. 1900 / renovated, 1988

Although it was built for a furniture manufacturer named William Kimball, this house is chiefly associated with its second owners—Horatio and Charlotte Van Cleve. He was known for his military exploits, serving as colonel and later as a general in the Civil War. She was a suffrage advocate, the first woman elected to the Minneapolis School Board, and the mother of 12 children. She was also a social reformer who in 1875 founded an organization to help "erring women," of which there appears to have been no shortage at the time. Their house, renovated into condominiums in the 1980s, is a Greek Revival–Italianate hybrid.

First Congregational Church, 1890

63 First Congregational Church **N** *L*

500 Eighth Ave. Southeast (or 801 Fifth St. Southeast)

Warren H. Hayes, 1888

This congregation was established in 1851, holding services in a small wood-frame structure. A larger church was built in 1874 but burned down 12 years later. Architect Warren Hayes then designed this fine brownstone church. Its most striking feature is the corner tower, which features a cagelike belfry with unusually slender columns. Overall, the church has the verticality you'd expect of the Gothic, combined with the kind of rock-bound heft of the Romanesque Revival style. Within, the church follows the so-called Akron Plan, which Hayes introduced to the Twin Cities. In accord with this scheme, the square auditorium has raked

seating that curves around a corner pulpit.

Donald Cattanach House

64 Donald Cattanach House *L*

1031 13th Ave. Southeast

Donald Cattanach, 1893

A cottage right out of a fairy tale, built largely of randomly laid blocks of local limestone. Stone construction was normally used only for large houses because of its expense, and this cottage is a rarity in Minneapolis. Donald Cattanach was a mason, and it's likely he built the house himself. Note the checkerboard pattern in the gable and the fine stonework around the big window.

65 Quinn Violins

1081 21st Ave. Southeast

ca. 1930s

A slick Moderne building with unusual, slightly projecting glass-block windows that curve around the corners.

66 Double bungalows

23rd and 24th Aves. Southeast between Elm St. and Fairmount Ave.

ca. 1948–50

A colony of at least a dozen double bungalows. What's unusual is that they're all faced in brick as opposed to the far more typical wood-sided or stucco finish.

POI G Grain elevators

South of Elm St. and Kasota Ave. near 25th Ave. Southeast

A huge grain elevator complex developed here beginning in the

1870s, drawn by the central location and access to rail lines. Most of the concrete and steel elevators that remain date to the early 1900s. The University of Minnesota demolished two elevators in 2006 to make way for campus expansion, and it's probable that others will soon vanish as development plans advance.

Prospect Park and East River Road

With its woodsy hills, twisty streets, and tweedy population of academics, Prospect Park has always seemed a bit out of place amid the great Minneapolis gridiron. Many streets swirl around Tower Hill, a monument to the last glacier that swept into the Twin Cities 14,000 years ago. The water tower (1914) atop this steep hill is the community's most visible and cherished landmark.

Like other Twin Cities neighborhoods that began as genteel suburbs, Prospect Park attracted developers because of its proximity to rail (and, later, streetcar) lines and its scenic terrain. The first streets were platted in 1884, and houses began to appear not long after. Development moved slowly at first, in part because electric streetcar service (along University Avenue) didn't arrive until the 1890s, while public utilities weren't available until after 1900. Although it's thought of primarily as a residential enclave, Prospect Park's boundaries also encompass parts of the rail, grain elevator, and industrial corridor north of University Avenue.

A significant threat to the neighborhood occurred in the late 1950s, when plans were unveiled for Interstate 94 between Minneapolis and St. Paul. The proposed route, just south of Tower Hill, would have required the demolition of over 200 homes. Residents fought the plan and eventually forced highway engineers to settle on a less destructive route. Even so, more than 100 neighborhood homes were ultimately lost to the freeway.

Architecturally, Prospect Park is of interest primarily because of its varied housing stock, which ranges from mid-1880s Victorians to a surprising number of early modernist homes. The neighborhood's most celebrated work is the Malcolm and Nancy Willey House (1934), by Frank Lloyd Wright. Directly across the street is another modern home of note: the Lippincott House (1940), designed by Winston and Elizabeth Close. Two blocks from these houses you'll also find the dainty and delightful St. Panteleimon Russian Orthodox Church (ca. 1906).

67 Tower Hill Park and Water Tower ! N *L*

55 Malcolm Ave. Southeast

Minneapolis Park Board, 1906 / **water tower,** *Frederick Cappelen, 1914 / renovated, Minneapolis Building and Maintenance Dept., 1998*

Tower Hill Park Water Tower

Perhaps the most romantic structure in Minneapolis. The hill on which the tower stands was acquired by the city's park board in 1906, and just in the nick of time, since a similar hill to the south had already been chewed away for its sand and gravel. The tower itself was built to enclose a standpipe needed to improve water pressure in Prospect Park. City engineer Frederick Cappelen took up the challenge of designing a tower that would be beautiful and practical. It is fair to say that he succeeded on both counts.

The 107-foot-high, poured-concrete tower rises from its base to an octagonal observation platform framed by circling arches. Hovering over the observation deck is the tower's signature feature: a steep, wide-brimmed witch's-hat roof clad in green tile. The tower became obsolete for water storage in 1952 and was damaged three years later by a lightning strike. The city's water department then decided it would be a marvelous idea to tear down the tower. Fortunately, neighborhood residents got wind of the plan and were able to save the tower from destruction.

68 Duplex (Samuel and Emily Eustis House)

3107 Fourth St. Southeast

1865 / remodelings and additions

The oldest house in Prospect Park, built as a farm home well before the main residential portion of the community was platted around Tower Hill. Samuel and Emily Eustis, whose holdings extended well north of University Ave., farmed until the 1880s, when they subdivided the property. The house itself has been extensively remodeled, and few original features are visible.

69 Pratt School and Community Center (Elementary School)

66 Malcolm Ave. Southeast

Edward S. Stebbins, 1898 / additions, 1906, 1926 / renovated, Close Associates (Gar Hargens), 1999

The city's oldest public school building still being used, in part at least, for its original purpose. The school's 1898 portion, sandwiched between additions, includes a cupola.

70 Lowell Lamoreaux House

39 Seymour Ave.

Lowell Lamoreaux, 1886

A Shingle Style house with an unusual granite porch and a truncated tower.

71 House

66 Seymour Ave.

Edwin Ludwig, 1916

One of the neighborhood's finest houses. It's essentially an Arts and Crafts foursquare, but some of the detailing—such as the banded soffits—suggests the Prairie Style. The house's arched side entry, which resembles an old-fashioned porte cochere, is an unusual touch.

72 Harold Deutsch House

90 Seymour Ave.

Winston and Elizabeth Close, 1951

An early modern house built for the chairman of the University of Minnesota's history department. The house is deliberately plain in the manner of much of the Closes' work.

73 Gerald Johnson House

103 Seymour Ave.

ca. 1903 / renovated and enlarged, Gerald Johnson, 1969

Shed roofs—all the craze for a time in the 1960s and 1970s—are a dead giveaway as to the era of this house (a rebuilding of an older home) and the garage-studio in front of it.

74 House

63 Barton Ave.

Lowell Lamoreaux, 1906

A large house in the Swiss Chalet variant of the Arts and Crafts style. There's another, smaller house of this type a few blocks away on Cecil St.

75 St. Panteleimon Russian Orthodox Church

2210 Franklin Ave. Southeast

ca. 1906 / remodeled, ca. 1950s and later

This tiny church was built around 1906 for a Lutheran congregation. Originally on Washington Ave. Southeast, it was moved to a site in Prospect Park in 1909 and later served as a Baptist church until 1956, when it was moved a second time to this site after being purchased by St. Panteleimon's.

Malcolm and Nancy Willey House

76 Malcolm and Nancy Willey House ! N L

255 Bedford St. Southeast

Frank Lloyd Wright, 1934

In June 1932, Nancy Willey—whose husband, Malcolm, was an administrator at the University of Minnesota—sent a letter to Frank Lloyd Wright. "I want to build a house in Minneapolis for about $8,000," she wrote. "What do you think are the chances of my being able to have a 'creation of art?'" Wright, then 65 years old and desperate for work, replied: "Nothing is trivial because it is not big. And if I can be of service to you neither the distance nor the 'smallness' of the proposal would prevent me from giving you what help an architect could give you."

Two years later, the Willeys moved into their "creation of art," which Wright named "Gardenwall." It's a long, low house

Willey House interior

built of red brick and cypress wood, set on a wooded lot with what used to be a panoramic view of the Mississippi River gorge before Interstate 94 ruined the scene in the 1960s. Despite its modest size (about 1,200 square feet) and equally modest price tag (it cost only $10,000), the house turned out to be among

the most important of Wright's career. Its significance lay in the fact that it was in many ways a prototype of his so-called Usonian houses, which were intended to be high style but relatively inexpensive homes for the masses. Wright ultimately designed scores of such houses in the 1940s and 1950s.

What might be called the Wright experience begins here with an elaborate entry sequence that takes you up brick steps to a sheltered walkway and then to an all-but-hidden front door. Just past the entrance is one of the house's most dramatic features: a cantilevered trellis hovering above a brick patio. Inside, Wright works his usual magic. Ceilings rise and fall, light filters in from unexpected places, and spaces flow effortlessly into one another. The living room, which opens out to the patio via French doors, includes Wright's signature hearth. A dining area and a small kitchen are located to one side of the living room, while on the other side a narrow corridor with built-in shelves leads to two bedrooms, a den, and a bathroom.

The Willeys sold the house in 1963 to another family, who later sold it to a Wright aficionado from Wisconsin. For 30 years or so, the house was occupied only periodically, which led to problems. Wright's houses tend to be like Italian sports cars: they're beautiful to behold but very touchy—and they require careful maintenance. The Willey House was in need of major repairs by the time new owners acquired it in 2002. Restoration work is now under way.

77 Benjamin and Gertrude Lippincott House

252 Bedford St. Southeast

Winston and Elizabeth Close, 1940

Located across the street from the Willey House, this buttoned-down residence lacks the dynamism of Wright's design. Still, it was perhaps the first house in the Twin Cities to embrace the early modernist credo of strict functionalism, which also entailed the rejection of ornament and historic styles (not to mention gabled roofs). The house, basically a series of boxes, presents a drab facade to the street but opens up with strips of windows on the south side to take in the river view, now obscured by the interstate. Benjamin Lippincott was a political science professor at the University of Minnesota; his wife, Gertrude, was a dancer and dance teacher.

78 Olaf Thorshov House

208 Cecil St. Southeast

Olaf Thorshov, 1912

A nifty house designed by Minneapolis architect Olaf Thorshov as his own residence. The house bears some resemblance to a Swiss chalet or perhaps something from the mountains of Norway, where Thorshov was born.

79 Cappelen Memorial (Franklin Avenue) Bridge ! N *L*

Across Mississippi River

Frederick Cappelen and Kristoffer Oustad, 1923 / renovated, Howard Needles Tammen and Bergendorf (Bernard Rottinghaus), 1971

The concrete-arch bridges that span the Mississippi River between downtown Minneapolis and the Ford Dam seldom attract much notice, yet they really are an exceptional body of work, among the finest of their kind in the United States. The Cappelen Memorial Bridge is especially

elegant, crossing the river in a graceful 400-foot span that was the longest concrete arch in the

Cappelen Memorial Bridge

world when completed in 1923. The bridge, which replaced an earlier span at Franklin Ave., was the final work of Minneapolis city engineer Frederick Cappelen, who died two years before the bridge opened. The bridge was renovated in 1971, when the deck was rebuilt and half of the original spandrels (the vertical supports linking the deck to the arch below) were removed.

80 House

1509 East River Pkwy.

1955

A fieldstone and redwood house from the 1950s with an upthrust roof and large front windows.

81 Canadian Pacific (Milwaukee Road) Railroad Bridge

Across Mississippi River north of Lake St.

American Bridge Co., 1902

This span is of a type known in engineering parlance as a pin-connected Baltimore deck truss. It was built for the old Milwaukee Road's "Short Line" connecting St. Paul and Minneapolis.

Cedar-Riverside

1   O. Meredith Wilson Library
2   Carlson School of Management
3   Hubert H. Humphrey Center
4   Blegen Hall
5   Walter F. Mondale Hall
6   Elmer L. Andersen Library
7   Ted Mann Concert Hall
8   Rarig Center
9   Regis Center for Art
10 Barbara Barker Center for Dance
11 University of Minnesota Medical Center, Fairview
12 Augsburg College
13 Murphy Place
14 James G. Lindell Library
15 Old Main
16 John Widstrom Tenement
17 Apartments
18 Riverside Plaza
19 Cedar-Riverside Light Rail Station

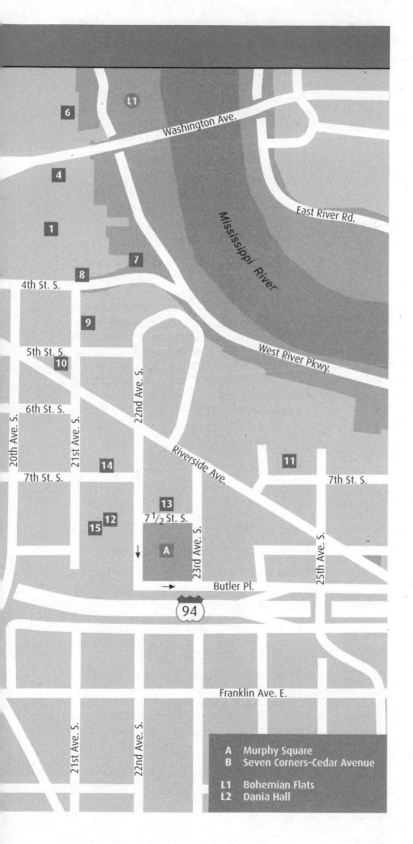

Cedar-Riverside

Washington Ave.

East River Rd.

Mississippi River

West River Pkwy.

4th St. S.

5th St. S.

6th St. S.

Riverside Ave.

7th St. S.

7th St. S.

7 1/2 St. S.

Butler Pl.

20th Ave. S.

21st Ave. S.

22nd Ave. S.

23rd Ave. S.

25th Ave. S.

Franklin Ave. E.

21st Ave. S.

22nd Ave. S.

94

A   Murphy Square
B   Seven Corners–Cedar Avenue

L1   Bohemian Flats
L2   Dania Hall

Cedar-Riverside

As with other working-class districts around the downtown core, this old immigrant neighborhood did not age gracefully. Its housing stock—never the best to begin with—gradually grew decrepit, industry faded away, and by the 1950s the population had dipped to just over 8,000. In the 1960s, with the "counterculture" in full swing, the neighborhood took on a bohemian air as many university students moved in, drawn by cheap housing. At one point, half of the neighborhood's residents were aged 18 to 24.

Yet even as the counterculture took root, a series of events began to reshape the neighborhood. The first occurred in the early 1960s when the University of Minnesota established its West Bank campus here on a site that eventually grew to over 50 acres. At about the same time, two new interstate highways—94 and 35W—plowed along the edges of Cedar-Riverside, leveling everything in their paths. The construction of Cedar Square West (now Riverside Plaza) between 1968 and 1973 rearranged yet another big chunk of the neighborhood.

From an architectural standpoint, the neighborhood in its rebuilt state showcases some of the strengths—and all too many of the weaknesses—of urban planning and design in the 1960s. The West Bank campus, for example, was laid out with great care by a platoon of planners and architects, yet it's always seemed cold and uninviting, in part because so many of its early buildings are absolute dullards. Later campus buildings such as the Carlson School of Management (1998) are considerably better. And while the buildings that form Riverside Plaza are boldly designed, the development as a whole has always had the feel of a place apart—*in* the city but not *of* it. Still, Cedar-Riverside remains a fascinating corner of the city, if only because it demonstrates both the opportunities and the perils of urban renewal.

University of Minnesota West Bank Campus

Pietro Belluschi, Lawrence Anderson, Dan Kiley, Winston Close, with others, ca. 1960 / revised, Hodne-Stageberg Partners, ca. 1970

It took a committee of architects, landscape architects, and planners to design the West Bank campus, but nothing memorable came out of this exercise in groupthink. As befitting the anti-authoritarian spirit of the 1960s, the campus plan isn't hierarchical. Instead, "space flows freely and dynamically around the buildings," as one university publication put it. This sort of arrangement—buildings posed like giant sculptures in expanses of space—has long been a primal fantasy of architectural modernism even though it's almost always a bad idea. Here, the open space includes plazas, pathways, and carefully boxed-in lawns.

The earliest West Bank buildings—including Heller and Blegen Halls (1963, 1964) and the Social Sciences Building (1963)—were arranged as a group north of the Wilson Library (1967), which seems to have been intended as the campus's centerpiece. Unfortunately, these foundation buildings are banal. Numerous buildings have been added to the campus since the 1960s, and while some are quite good, the campus as a whole simply isn't very attractive or interesting. It's hard to see what could be done now to make it much better short of tearing everything down and starting over.

1 O. Meredith Wilson Library

309 19th Ave. South

Cerny Associates, 1967 / renovated, 2005

A brick box that makes no attempt to achieve the sort of architectural presence you'd expect of a major

O. Meredith Wilson Library

university's central library. The interior is equally pedestrian.

2 Carlson School of Management

321 19th Ave. South

Ellerbe Becket, 1998

Designed for the university's business school, this glass and brick building conveys an appropriately corporate image, looking as though it might have migrated here from a suburban office park. More or less triangular in shape, the building opens out toward the center of the campus by means of a long, curving glass wall. Within, there's a lozenge-shaped atrium.

3 Hubert H. Humphrey Center

301 19th Ave. South

Leonard Parker Associates, ca. 1990

The chief feature of this building is an atrium that serves, among other things, as a place where the center's resident gurus can enjoy casual—and presumably stimulating—encounters with their fellow deep thinkers.

4 Blegen Hall

269 19th Ave. South

Setter Leach and Lindstrom, 1964

Another dull building but with one unexpected touch: abstract brick ornamental panels that burst out from the walls and are now covered with wire, presumably to keep the pigeons at bay.

5 Walter F. Mondale Hall

229 19th Ave. South

Parker Klein Associates, 1978 / addition, Leonard Parker Associates, 2001

The interlocking, stepped-down brick volumes of this building create an interesting play of light and shadow. An addition was completed in 2001, after which the building was named in honor of former vice president Walter Mondale.

6 Elmer L. Andersen Library

222 21st Ave. South

Stageberg Beyer Sachs, 2000

This building's most impressive feature lies deep underground in the form of two huge caverns excavated out of shale and sandstone. These chambers, which lie behind an arched portal visible along the river bluffs, can readily be kept at the optimal temperature and humidity for storing documents, film, and other artifacts. All told, some 1.5 million items are stored here.

Bohemian Flats, 1890

LOST 1 *The portal of Andersen Library looks out over a riverfront park once known as* **Bohemian Flats.** *In 1900 over 1,200 people lived on the flats, many in small wood-frame houses arranged along dirt streets. Despite its name, the flats actually had more Slovakians than Czechs in its ethnic potpourri. The city eventually decided to build a barge terminal on the flats, and in 1931 most of the remaining residents were evicted. However, a few diehards remained until 1963, when the last house was demolished.*

West Bank Arts Quarter

Five buildings along the southern edge of the West Bank campus form what has been designated as the university's Arts Quarter. The overall quality of the buildings, constructed between 1971 and 2003, is quite high.

7 Ted Mann Concert Hall

2128 Fourth St. South

HGA (Kurt Green), 1993

A nicely designed hall that provides flexible stage and orchestra arrangements for a variety of musical and theatrical performances. The 1,250-seat auditorium adheres to the classic shoebox shape of traditional European halls, although the details are modern. The building also features a three-story-high lobby with a curving glass wall that overlooks the Mississippi River.

Rarig Center, 1975

8 Rarig Center !

330 21st Ave. South

Ralph Rapson and Associates, 1971

The strongest architectural statement on the West Bank campus. Home to the university's theater department as well as radio and television studios, Rarig is one of Ralph Rapson's most important works and the best example in the Twin Cities of the style called Brutalism (the name derives from *beton brut,* the French term for raw concrete). Like most Brutalist buildings, Rarig has a rather menacing air, and when you venture inside you half expect to find the leaders of the Evil Empire gathered somewhere in the three-story-high atrium, plotting the demise of Luke Skywalker. But if you take time to wander around a bit, you can appreciate the consistency and skill with which the building is put together. Part of what makes Rarig so interesting is that it accommodates an unusually complex array of spaces—

including four theaters, studios, and offices—all of which can be "read" by one means or another on the building's intricate facades.

9 Regis Center for Art

405 21st Ave. South

MS&R Architects, 2003

This center, which consists of two sections connected via a skyway across 21st Ave., goes off in all different design directions. There's techno-chic stuff, oddly angled walls, and even hints of 1930s classicism. The idea, say the architects, was to create a "collage" that would "gather the disparate neighboring buildings into a unified Arts Quarter." But in trying to relate to everything around it, the building ends up confused about itself.

Barbara Barker Center for Dance

10 Barbara Barker Center for Dance

500 21st Ave. South

HGA (Joan Sorrano), 1999

This curvaceous building is intended to convey via abstract forms a sense of the movement of dance. The building certainly does just that, but it's so minimally detailed (in glass and stucco) that after you've absorbed the essential conceit, there isn't much else to draw your eye. Inside, a bright lobby links the two sections of the building, which houses studios, classrooms, and offices.

11 University of Minnesota Medical Center, Fairview

2450 Riverside Ave.

various architects, including John W. Wheeler and Lang and Raugland, 1917 and later

A sprawling (is there any other kind?) medical complex with

buildings of varying vintages piled up every which way and linked by a maze of skyways. In the middle of it all are two historic hospitals—Fairview and St. Mary's. The old portion of St. Mary's, designed by St. Paul architect John Wheeler, is still the most pleasant building of the lot.

12 Augsburg College

This liberal arts college grew out of a seminary founded in Marshall, WI, in 1869. The seminary, the first established by Norwegian Lutherans in the United States, moved to Minneapolis in 1872. It later branched off into three sections—a preparatory school, a theological seminary, and a collegiate training school for Lutheran ministers. The preparatory school closed in 1933, and the theological seminary was merged into Luther Seminary in St. Paul in the 1960s. Today, Augsburg is the largest private college in Minneapolis, enrolling about 3,000 students.

The campus occupies a wedge of blocks between Riverside Ave. and Interstate 94. It includes a quadrangle behind Old Main but is otherwise rather hard-edged and not especially appealing. Most buildings are of the brickbox variety that Lutherans seem to favor.

POI A Murphy Square

801 22nd Ave. South

1857

Donated to the city in 1857 by Edward Murphy, this is Minneapolis's oldest park. Judging by its lack of amenities, it must also be one of the least appreciated.

13 Murphy Place

2222 7½ St. South

J. Calder Peeps, 1964 / addition

A delicate, pavilionlike building marred by a graceless addition. In many ways it appears to be a smaller version of Rapson Hall on the University of Minnesota's East Bank campus.

14 James G. Lindell Library

Seventh St. and 22nd Ave. South

BWBR Architects, 1998

The most pleasing of Augsburg's newer buildings, this well-designed library offers ample natural light within.

Old Main, Augsburg College

15 Old Main (Augsburg Seminary) N *L*

725 21st Ave. South

Omeyer and Thori, 1901

When it opened in 1901 as part of Augsburg Seminary, this brick building was known as New Main. At that time it stood alone, but it's now crowded by newer buildings and is well away from the center of the campus, which has expanded to the north and east. A portico flanked by polished granite columns provides a suitably dignified entrance to the building, which also makes liberal use of terra-cotta ornament, especially in the arches above the first-floor windows.

16 John Widstrom Tenement *L*

617–21 19th Ave. South

1886

A tenement of a type once common in Cedar-Riverside. The bracketed cornice is Italianate, but other features, like the incised keystones over the windows, are Eastlake in character.

17 Apartments (Holy Rosary Seminary)

1819 Fifth St. South

Edward P. Bassford, 1879

A brick Italianate house with a gabled front pavilion and the usual window hoods. The home was built for Holy Rosary Church, once located on this block.

Dania Hall, ca. 1900

LOST 2 *A vacant lot at 427 Cedar Ave. marks the site of historic* **Dania Hall,** *built in 1886 by a benevolent organization serving Danish immigrants and the last surviving Scandinavian ethnic hall of its type in the United States until it was destroyed by fire in February 2000. Its loss to the neighborhood was incalculable.*

Riverside Plaza

18 Riverside Plaza (Cedar Square West Apartments) !

Fourth St. South and Cedar Ave.

Ralph Rapson and Associates, 1973

Depending on your point of view, this development is either a brave attempt at creating a progressive way of living or a monstrosity that demonstrates the hubris of modern architecture. Originally known as Cedar Square West, the project was the brainchild of a team that included developers Gloria Segal and Keith Heller along with architect Ralph Rapson. It came to fruition during the time of the federally backed New Town movement (which produced the community of Jonathan just west of the Twin Cities). Cedar Square West was unique, however, in that it was the nation's first urban New Town (or New Town–In Town, as the government called it).

The complex encompasses the equivalent of eight square blocks and contains 1,300 apartments in 11 buildings that range in height from four to 40 stories. It was intended to be far larger. The ultimate plan envisioned four other projects of similar size, all interconnected to form a 100-acre complex that would have turned Cedar-Riverside into Manhattan on the Mississippi. Neighborhood opposition and financial problems ultimately killed this grandiose scheme. It's easy to enumerate the faults of the complex—from cramped apartments to a confusing layout at street level—but Rapson's overall design, which makes distinctive use of colored panels, is characteristically strong. Still, you can't help but feel here the dark side of classic architectural modernism—its tendency toward megalomania, its belief that society can be rigorously engineered, its rejection of the lessons of the past. At the same time, Cedar Square West speaks to modernism's deep strain of idealism. The developers specified a variety of apartment types because they believed the complex could become home to all manner of people—a dream of diversity that was never achieved.

Plagued by financial difficulties from the start, Cedar Square West fell into bankruptcy in the 1980s. The City of Minneapolis later sold it for just $15 million to new owners, who renamed it Riverside Plaza. Today, many residents are immigrants, including a large number of Somalis.

19 Cedar-Riverside Light Rail Station

Near Sixth St. and 15th Ave. South

Julie Snow Architects, 2004 / Art: Thomas Rose, Dick Elliot, Aldo Moroni, and Janet Zweig

A glass canopy etched with star constellations and pavers that use Somali textile patterns are among the features of this station.

POI B Seven Corners–Cedar Avenue

Various buildings and streets, ca. 1880s and later

For many years this intersection—where Second St. South converged with Cedar, Washington, and Fifteenth Aves.—lived up to its name. Today, however, there are only four corners here, largely because of changes made in the 1960s to accommodate development of the university's West Bank campus. The area along Cedar just to the south of Seven Corners contains much of what remains of the neighborhood's historic commercial building stock. Here you'll find a jumble of businesses behind storefronts that have been remodeled with a refreshing disregard for the stultifying canons of good taste. How long this funky mojo will persist is anyone's guess.

4

Longfellow, Nokomis, & Fort Snelling

Overview

This area along and to the west of the Mississippi River gorge takes in some of the most scenic and historic ground in the Twin Cities as well as two of its busiest places: Minneapolis–St. Paul International Airport and the Mall of America. Within Minneapolis are the Longfellow and Nokomis neighborhoods, which include such natural attractions as Minnehaha Park and its falls along with three lakes—Nokomis, Hiawatha, and Diamond. Farther south, just beyond the city's borders, Fort Snelling stands at the confluence of the Minnesota and Mississippi rivers. The fort and nearby village of Mendota are the oldest local outposts of European American settlement in the Twin Cites, and both have buildings of great historic importance.

The Longfellow neighborhood, best known as a place where the bungalows roam, lies between the green ribbon of the Mississippi and a gritty rail corridor along Hiawatha Avenue to the west. Although Longfellow is dominated by bungalows, it offers other architecture of interest, beginning with Christ Lutheran Church (1949). Designed by Eliel Saarinen and his son, Eero, this brick church is among the city's architectural masterpieces. The Minnesota Veterans Home (1887) and the Milwaukee Avenue Historic District are also of note here.

Elsewhere in Longfellow, high- and mid-rise apartments cluster near Interstate 94, while Franklin Avenue and Lake Street form major commercial strips. Along the southern reaches of West River Parkway, there's an intriguing area originally developed for institutional uses, some of which remain. Industry is concentrated in the northern part of the neighborhood, known as Seward, and along Hiawatha Avenue, which follows an old Milwaukee Road line (built in about 1870) that angles through the street grid. Grain elevators from the early 1900s tower over this corridor, which is also used by the new Hiawatha Light Rail Line.

With its three lakes and large parks, and with Minnehaha Creek meandering through it, the almost exclusively residential Nokomis neighborhood is better known for its natural than its architectural attractions. Only one building in Nokomis, an old fire station, is individually designated by the city as historic, and much of the neighborhood consists of block upon block of tract housing. However, the neighborhood does have a historic district, Nokomis Knoll, where you'll find more than 75 well-preserved Period Revival–style homes from the 1920s and 1930s.

Just to the southeast, Fort Snelling is where the Twin Cities began. The first agent of transformation was Lieutenant Zebulon Pike, who in 1805 negotiated a treaty with the Dakota Indians by which the U.S. government obtained, for the usual pittance, 100,000 acres of land encompassing much of present-day Minneapolis as well as portions of the southern suburbs and St. Paul. This land grant included a bluff overlooking the Mississippi and Minnesota rivers that would soon become the site of Fort Snelling. Established in the 1820s as part of a plan to secure the nation's northwest frontier, the outpost was named after its second commander, Colonel Josiah Snelling. Today, much of the fort is a historic site.

Across the Minnesota River from the fort is Mendota, the state's oldest community, established in the 1820s. Befitting its age, the village is the site of Minnesota's oldest house, built in the 1830s for fur trader and later Minnesota governor Henry Sibley. Mendota is also home to the historic Church of St. Peter, which dates to 1853.

Longfellow

About 60 percent of this neighborhood's homes are bungalows built between 1910 and 1930. Most are small—you won't find any Pasadena-style high-art bungalows here—and were built from standard plans. Even so, the houses display a range of styles within the broad bungalow format. The earlier bungalows tend to be in the Arts and Crafts style, while those from the 1920s often wear Period Revival attire, the English Cottage look being especially popular.

Longfellow isn't entirely given over to bungalows. Seward, the neighborhood's oldest and most northerly section, has many late nineteenth-century homes in the blocks south of Franklin. Although Seward was subjected to urban renewal beginning in the 1960s, residents fought hard to maintain its architectural legacy. Seward's undisputed gem is the Milwaukee Avenue Historic District, a unique collection of mostly brick working-class houses from the 1880s and 1890s. Most of Longfellow's largest houses, mainly from the 1920s, are on West River Parkway. There's also an enclave of modernist houses from the 1950s and 1960s along and near the southern end of Edmund Boulevard, which parallels the parkway.

Lying at Longfellow's southern tip is Minnehaha Park, home to the famous waterfall. Said to be the most photographed spot in the Twin Cities, the falls pours into a glen that's long been a favorite locale for adventuresome children. On a high wedge of land between the glen and the Mississippi gorge you'll find another fascinating place—the Minnesota Veterans Home, a campus of more than 20 buildings that occupies one of the Twin Cities' most spectacular sites.

Lake Street light rail station

1 Hiawatha Line Light Rail Stations

Along Hiawatha Ave. between Franklin Ave. and 54th St. East

Franklin Avenue Station, Barbour LaDouceur Architects / Art: Seitu Jones, Dick Elliot, Michael Flechtner, Janet Zweig / Lake Street Station, Julie Snow Architects / Art: Thomas Rose, Joann Verburg, Janet Zweig / 38th Street Station, MS&R Architects / Art: Karen Wirth, Dick Elliot, Cliff Garten, Deborah Mersky, Janet Zweig / 46th Street Station, MS&R Architects / Art: Karen Wirth, Dick Elliot, Cliff Garten, Joann Verburg, Janet Zweig / 50th Street (Minnehaha Park) Station, MS&R Architects / Art: Karen Wirth, Greg

LeFevre, Deborah Mersky, Joann Verburg, Janet Zweig / Veterans Administration Medical Center Station (near 54th St. East and Minnehaha Ave.) Cuningham Group / Art: Brad Kaspari, Dick Elliot, Janet Lofquist, Janet Zweig

The Hiawatha Line, which opened in 2004, runs along Longfellow's western border. Six of the light rail line's 17 stations are located on this stretch of track. The stations offer a variety of architectural approaches to the task of providing shelter, and for the most part they do so with considerable flair. All of the stations also feature artwork specific to their sites. The 300-foot-long Lake Street station is the largest of the group and displays architect Julie Snow's characteristically elegant glass detailing. Residential development has already occurred near the new line in scattered locations, but it could take many years before the grain elevators and industrial buildings along the east side of Hiawatha give way to new uses.

Longfellow

1   Hiawatha Line Light Rail Stations
2   Twenty-First Avenue Lofts
3   House
4   Milwaukee Avenue Historic District
5   Perkins-Russell Cottage
6   Apartments
7   Industrial and warehouse building
8   Brackett Park Community Center
9   House
10 Christ Lutheran Church
11 Simmons Manor Apartments
12 Riverview Theater
13 "Insulite" house
14 House
15 Dowling Urban Environmental School
16 Ray and Kay Price House
17 Frederick Lange House
18 R and R Automotive
19 Hiawatha Elementary School
20 Becketwood Cooperative Apartments
21 Robert F. Jones House Interpretive
    Center
22 Minnehaha Railroad Depot
23 John H. Stevens House
24 Minnesota Veterans Home
25 Minneapolis Veterans Administration
    Medical Center

A   Orfield Laboratories
B   Riverside parks and parkway
C   The Martin Property
D   Minnehaha Historic District,
    Minnehaha Park
E   Camp Coldwater

L1 Minneapolis-Moline Co.
L2 Lutheran Children's Friend Society
    Orphanage

Franklin Ave. E.

Cedar Ave. S.

Lake St.

38th St. E.

42nd St. E.

Lyndale Ave. S.

Portland Ave. S.

Park Ave. S.

35W

46th St. E.

Cedar Ave. S.

Minnehaha Pkwy.

LOST 1 *The shopping mall north-west of Lake St. and 26th Ave. South was once the site of* **Minneapolis-Moline Co.,** *which made tractors and other farm equipment. After a long decline, the plant closed in 1972, and all 15 buildings on the site were demolished. Incidentally, the Target Store here was the first ever built in an inner-city neighborhood.*

2 Twenty-First Avenue Lofts

2012–24 21st Ave. South

DJR Architecture, 2003

Five colorful townhomes and two loft apartments organized around a courtyard.

3 House

2201 21st Ave. South

1978

An earth-sheltered house set in a crater dug out of a small corner lot. The landscaping and other features of the design imbue the house with an air of mystery.

4 Milwaukee Avenue Historic District ! N *L*

Milwaukee Ave. between Franklin Ave. and 24th St. East

William Ragan (builder), 1883 and later / renovated, various architects, 1970s

In 1883 a developer and builder named William Ragan platted a two-block stretch of what was then known as 22½ Ave. into narrow quarter lots. Over the next decade, several dozen small brick-veneer houses of similar appearance were built, and they ultimately created a working-class enclave that was striking by virtue of its architectural consistency. Most of the early residents along Milwaukee Ave., as it was renamed in 1906, were Scandinavian immigrants.

By the 1970s, many of the old houses had taken on a rather decrepit air. Meanwhile, the city's housing and redevelopment authority was eyeing much of western Seward, including Milwaukee Ave., for clearance. Residents fought the idea, arguing that the avenue was a unique historic resource that merited renovation. The residents—bless them—won the battle, and in 1974 the avenue was designated as a historic district. As part of the restoration plan, Milwaukee Ave. was turned into a pedestrian mall while about 30 original homes (two-thirds of which are between Franklin Ave. and 22nd St. East) were renovated. New infill housing was also added.

5 Perkins-Russell Cottage

2103 23rd Ave. South

1873

One of the neighborhood's oldest houses, this charming Italianate cottage has a perfectly

Milwaukee Avenue Historic District

Perkins-Russell Cottage

symmetrical facade. Note how the arched door transom duplicates the window hoods.

6 Apartments (John Nordstrom Store) *L*

2110 24th Ave. South

Elwood S. Corser, 1883

A wood-frame Italianate store building, converted into housing.

POI A Orfield Laboratories (Sound 80 Studios)

2709 25th St. East

1970

A building with a rich audio history. It was originally home to Sound 80 Studios, which in the late 1970s made what are believed to be the first ever *digital* recordings (of classical and jazz music) released commercially. The building, now owned by Orfield Laboratories, has also become known for the sound of silence. The Orfield firm—which works in sound engineering, lighting, and other fields—maintains a so-called anechoic chamber here that is certified by the *Guinness Book of World Records* as the "world's quietest room."

7 Industrial and warehouse building (Shasta Beverage Co.)

3530 28th St. East

Walter M. Covy, 1946

A Moderne-style industrial building. Its centerpiece is a curved corner entry pavilion featuring a two-story wall of glass brick.

8 Brackett Park Community Center

2728 39th Ave. South

Bentz/Thompson/Rietow Architects, ca. 2004

This whimsical building's deep red walls culminate in a low cylinder topped by a witch's-hat roof. It all has the feel of a child-sized castle presided over by a most benign king.

POI B Riverside parks and parkway

Minneapolis Park Board, 1880s and later

The Mississippi River gorge, which extends from St. Anthony Falls to Fort Snelling, forms the eastern border of the Longfellow neighborhood. Landscape architect Horace Cleveland proposed the system of parks and parkways here in 1883. West River Pkwy. itself dates to the early 1900s. The Winchell Trail, which runs along the blufftop, was built in the 1930s under the auspices of the federal Works Progress Administration. Today, the gorge remains one of the jewels of the Minneapolis and St. Paul park systems.

Lake Street–Marshall Avenue Bridge

(see under Powderhorn)

9 House

3124 44th Ave. South

ca. 1970s

A geodesic dome home that rises above a three-car garage. Think of it as the counterculture and the consumer culture living in perfect harmony.

10 Christ Lutheran Church *! N L*

3244 34th Ave. South

Eliel Saarinen, 1949 / addition, Eero Saarinen, 1962 / Art: sculptured stone panels (front of church), William M. McVey, 1949

This early modernist church has been acknowledged as a masterpiece from the day it was built.

Longfellow

It is, however, a very subtle masterpiece that takes some effort to appreciate fully. Designed by

Christ Lutheran Church

Finnish architect Eliel Saarinen, the church has a Scandinavian personality—an outer calm that, when you look more closely, hints at deep emotions beneath the surface.

The Christ Lutheran congregation built this church in part to save money after discovering that a traditional Gothic Revival church would be too costly. In 1946 a new pastor, Reverend William A. Buege, learned of Saarinen's work from a friend and contacted the architect, then president of Cranbrook Academy of Art near Detroit, MI. The pastor convinced Saarinen to take on the job. By this time Saarinen had already designed a pioneering modern church—First Christian (1942) in Columbus, IN—that served as a model for Christ Lutheran.

At first glance, Christ Lutheran appears to be a simple oblong box of brick and stone with a

Christ Lutheran Church interior, 1949

corner tower. In fact, the side walls aren't parallel and neither are those at the front and rear. This slight skewing adds a note of quiet dynamism to the design and also improves acoustics. The only exterior ornament consists of carved stone panels adorning the front wall. Within, the nave's ceiling slants to one side, the north wall undulates like rippling water, and the detailing throughout is chaste and elegant. The chancel (altar area) is particularly fine, with light pouring in from a concealed south window.

Speaking at the church's dedication in 1949, Saarinen said that "if a building is honest, the architecture is religious." That seems as good a summation as any of his achievement here. Christ Lutheran was Saarinen's last building; he died in 1950 at age 77. Attached to the church is an education wing designed by Eliel's son, Eero. The wing, organized around a courtyard, nicely complements the church. As with the father, so with the son: the addition was among Eero's last commissions. He died at age 51 a year before the education wing opened in 1962.

Christ Lutheran proved to be highly influential, inspiring many similar brick churches in the 1950s and 1960s. A number of these were designed by the Minneapolis firm of Hills, Gilbertson and Hayes, which worked on the church with Saarinen.

11 Simmons Manor Apartments (Simmons Elementary School)

3800 Minnehaha Ave.

Edward S. Stebbins, 1905 / additions, Edward S. Stebbins, 1910, 1914 / renovated, ca. 1980s

This is among the oldest school buildings in the city. It's also one of four historic Minneapolis schools (Bremer, Madison, and Whittier are the others) that have been converted to housing.

12 Riverview Theater

3800 42nd Ave. South

Liebenberg and Kaplan, 1948 / renovated, Liebenberg and Kaplan, 1956

A fine early modern movie theater, the last of its kind still operating in the Twin Cities. Faced with competition from television, theater owners Sidney and William Volk sought to bring back something of the glamour of the 1920s movie palaces. Just three years after the Riverview opened, the Volks built their masterpiece: the Terrace Theater

Riverview Theater

(closed) in Robbinsdale. The Riverview features a fine lobby, remodeled in 1956, as well as snazzy restrooms. The auditorium offers an early example of stadium-style seating.

13 "Insulite" house

3518 45th Ave. South

Insulite Co., 1936

A Moderne-style house built by a company to showcase its brand of fiberboard insulation.

LOST 2 *The modern houses near Edmund Blvd. and 36th St. East occupy the site of the* **Lutheran Children's Friend Society Orphanage,** *constructed in 1924 and razed in 1968. The house at 3624 Edmund was built for the orphanage's superintendent.*

14 House

3750 Edmund Blvd.

People's Home Construction Co., 1937

A Moderne-style brick house. Hoping to break out of the Depression, homebuilders in the late 1930s constructed many "spec" houses like this one in novel materials or styles.

POI C The Martin Property

South of 38th St. East between West River Pkwy. and 46th Ave. South

1850s and later

In 1857 a large area along the river south of 38th St. East came into the possession of banker

Richard Martin, an orphan with physical disabilities, including a deformed spine. Upon his death, Martin willed 90 acres of his land for use as a new home for Sheltering Arms Orphanage. In 1923, the orphanage in turn sold part of the property to Henry Eustis, a lawyer and one-time mayor of Minneapolis. Eustis also had a disability—he required crutches because of a childhood accident—and upon his death he gave half of his land to the Minneapolis School District and the other half to the University of Minnesota. The school district built Michael Dowling School in 1924, and the university eventually sold its property, which was then developed for housing along streets bearing the names of former university presidents (such as Folwell and Northrop).

Dowling Urban Environmental School, 1924

15 Dowling Urban Environmental School (Michael Dowling School)

3900 West River Pkwy.

Bureau of Buildings (Edward Enger, supervising architect), 1924 / additions, 1936, 1961, and later

This Tudor Revival–style school on an 18-acre campus consists of a series of long, low brick volumes that resemble a group of houses strung together. Two additions have enlarged the original building. Built for handicapped children, the school is named after Michael Dowling, who despite losing both legs and one arm to frostbite at age 14 went on to a successful career in banking and politics. Today the school is home to an environmental learning center.

16 Ray and Kay Price House

4730 Coffey Ln.

Ralph Rapson, 1961

One of many modernist houses built on property once owned by the University of Minnesota. This International Style box has vertical redwood siding painted white.

17 Frederick Lange House

4736 Coffey Ln.

Herb Fritz, 1960

Fritz served an apprenticeship with Frank Lloyd Wright; the master's influence is evident here.

18 R and R Automotive (gas station)

4224 41st St. East

ca. 1926

The Longfellow neighborhood has some wonderful Period Revival gas stations. This is one of the cutest: a tiny English cottage with a mock thatched roof and an eyebrow window.

Hiawatha Elementary School

19 Hiawatha Elementary School

4201 42nd Ave. South

R. V. L. Haxby, 1916

A so-called California Plan school building. This approach to school design, in vogue around World War I, specified one-story buildings in which every classroom would have its own outside door. Here, the original 12 classrooms are arranged around a central court. A plan of this kind made sense for California, but in Minnesota it was hardly ideal for efficient heating. **Longfellow Elementary School** (1918), at 3017 31st St. East, is similar.

20 Becketwood Cooperative Apartments

4300 West River Pkwy.

HGA, 1986

A low-key, nicely designed housing complex on the old Sheltering Arms site. The orphanage's chapel still stands here, as does its front gate along River Pkwy. Both structures date to 1922. The main orphanage building was torn down in 1983.

Intercity (Ford) Bridge

(see under Highland Park)

Lock and Dam No. 1 (Ford Dam)

(see under Highland Park)

POI D Minnehaha Historic District, including Minnehaha Park ! N *L*

Hiawatha Ave. and Minnehaha Pkwy.

1889 / renovated, Bentz/Thompson/Rietow Architects with Sanders Wacker and Bergly (landscape architects), 1992 and later / Art: Hiawatha and Minnehaha (bronze statue on island above falls), Jacob Fjelde, 1893 (moved to park, 1912)

The city's most celebrated park, centered around a 53-foot-high waterfall (once known as Little or Brown's Falls) that was a tourist attraction before Minneapolis itself was founded. The area around the falls and its cool deep glen was a favorite picnic spot for soldiers from Fort Snelling as early as the 1820s. It also became a popular stop for steamboat excursionists after Henry Wadsworth Longfellow celebrated it as "Minnehaha Falls" in his 1855 epic, *The Song of Hiawatha*. Today, the park is in a historic district that also includes several buildings of note.

The first effort to preserve this scenic ground came in 1885, when the Minnesota Legislature authorized a state park here. However, the lawmakers never appropriated money for the project. Four years later, the Minneapolis

Bridge over Minnehaha Creek

Park Board stepped in and made a deal to acquire 120 acres that now form the heart of the park. By this time, the Milwaukee Road had already built a small depot near the falls. Park development occurred in piecemeal fashion. A small zoo was established in 1894 but later moved out of the park. A refectory building, which still stands, was constructed in 1905, after an earlier one burned down. In the 1930s, the Works Progress Administration built stone walls, steps, and bridges, many of which also remain.

In the 1990s, a series of developments reshaped the park. A new park plan approved in 1992 led to many worthwhile improvements, including renovation of the refectory building. Other projects were not so benign, however. The most drastic changes began in 1999 when Hiawatha Ave., which forms the park's western border, was rebuilt as a six-lane expressway. This work also provided a route for the Hiawatha Light Rail Line. The expressway's visual impact on the park proved to be profound despite such mitigation efforts as a "tuck and cover" tunnel that carries it beneath Minnehaha Pkwy. A long wall runs beside the highway, destroying the park's historic visual relationship with the neighborhood beyond. The park now feels in places like an isolated preserve, cut off from the life of the city, and you can't help but believe that something precious has been lost to progress.

Robert F. Jones House Interpretive Center

21 Robert F. Jones ("Longfellow") House Interpretive Center N *L*

4800 Minnehaha Ave.

1907 / renovated, Kodet Architectural Group, 1995

A two-thirds-scale replica of a Colonial-style house built in 1759 in Cambridge, MA, and once owned by Henry Wadsworth Longfellow. Originally at 4001 Minnehaha Pkwy. East, the house was built for Robert F. ("Fish") Jones. A legendary eccentric, Jones seldom ventured out in public without his top hat or his Russian wolfhounds. He built this house in Longfellow Gardens, a zoo and botanical garden he operated just outside Minnehaha Park. The gardens closed four years after Jones's death in 1934. His house then gradually fell into a state of abandonment. It was moved a block to the east and renovated in 1995 by the Minneapolis Park and Recreation Board and the Longfellow House Restoration Group. It's now an interpretive learning center.

22 Minnehaha Railroad Depot N *L*

49th St. East and Minnehaha Ave.

ca. 1875

In the early 1900s, up to 39 trains a day stopped at this picture-perfect little station on summer weekends. Known as "the princess," it was built by the Milwaukee Road to serve Minnehaha Park visitors. The depot is now a museum operated by the Minnesota Historical Society.

23 John H. Stevens House N *L*

4901 Minnehaha Ave.

1850 / renovated, 1985

This clapboard house, one of the city's oldest, was built for pioneer John Stevens near St. Anthony Falls. It had been moved twice before a Minneapolis *Tribune* reporter "rediscovered" it near downtown in 1896. The newspaper campaigned to save the house, and later that year 10,000 schoolchildren, working in relays, pulled it to Minnehaha Park. In the 1980s it was restored after being moved again—but only a few hundred feet—to its current site. It now serves as a museum.

Minnesota Veterans Home

24 Minnesota Veterans Home (Minnesota Soldiers' Home Historic District) N

5101 Minnehaha Ave.

includes 22 buildings and structures, various architects (beginning with Warren E. Dunnell) with Horace Cleveland (landscape architect), 1887 and later / renovated, Ellerbe Becket and Mac-Donald and Mack Architects, 1999

This campus, designed by Horace Cleveland, occupies a 51-acre triangle of high ground between the glen of Minnehaha Creek and the Mississippi River gorge. A steel-arch bridge completed in 1908 spans the glen and provides access to the home from Minnehaha Ave. (it can also be reached off Godfrey Pkwy.). Established in 1887, the home provides long-term care for indigent military veterans and their families.

The first eight campus buildings, in the Richardsonian Romanesque style, were constructed between 1888 and 1892 to the designs of architect Warren Dunnell. Five of these structures survive, including the towered **Administration Building** (1892), which features a cavernous arched entrance and carved sandstone ornament. The most impressive building here, known historically as the **Women's Residence,** is the work of St. Paul architect Augustus Gauger. Completed in 1905, it has a pair of magnificent two-story-high semicircular porches. Several of the campus's historic buildings were renovated in the 1990s.

POI E Camp Coldwater

East side of Hwy. 55 south of 54th St. East (reached from frontage road along east side of highway)

1820 and later

A small monument marks the site of Camp Coldwater, named after a spring that still flows. Native Americans often camped here, as did the soldiers building Fort Snelling in the 1820s. In the 1830s, Benjamin Baker built a stone house and trading post near the springs. The house was later used as a hotel until a fire destroyed it in 1859. Today, the springs are located on the site of a former U.S. Bureau of Mines research facility.

25 Minneapolis Veterans Administration Medical Center

One Veterans Dr.

MVA Group, 1987

A medical colossus that, on the outside at least, makes few welcoming gestures.

Nokomis

This neighborhood takes its name from Lake Nokomis, a 210-acre body of water that extends almost to the city's southern border. The Minneapolis Park Board acquired the lake and 195 acres of land surrounding it in 1907. Only after the lake was dredged, however, did it become the recreational and scenic attraction it is today. The development of Hiawatha Lake and Park in the 1920s provided the neighborhood with additional green space as well as a public golf course. Minnehaha Parkway, the last section of which was completed in 1935, added another amenity.

Except for a few Victorian houses near Minnehaha Park, most of the neighborhood developed, generally from north to south, after 1900. Bungalows and Period Revival "cottages" predominate, although tract houses from the 1940s and 1950s are common south of 54th Street East, an area that wasn't incorporated into Minneapolis until 1927. As late as 1950 a farm—the last in the city—operated on the site of Bossen Park. The neighborhood's finest homes cluster around Lake Nokomis and along the parkway. On the southwest side of the lake is the Nokomis Knoll Residential Historic District, which covers several square blocks. Most commercial activity is concentrated along old streetcar routes such as Chicago, Bloomington, 28th, and 34th avenues.

Among the neighborhood's many churches, two stand out: St. Helena (1940), a colorful exercise in the Italian Romanesque Revival, and Hope Lutheran (1971), designed by Ralph Rapson. Nokomis is also home to St. Mary's Cemetery, the largest Catholic burial ground in Minneapolis. Across from the cemetery is St. Joseph's Home for Children, founded in the 1880s as a Catholic orphanage for boys.

POI A Lake Nokomis and Nokomis Park

South of Minnehaha Pkwy. and Cedar Ave.

Minneapolis Park Board, 1907 and later

includes **Nokomis Community Center,** 2401 Minnehaha Pkwy. East

Hustad Pontinen Architects, 1975

Minneapolis's lakes are, to a great extent, the product of human intervention. Lake Nokomis (originally known as Lake Amelia) is a case in point. In its natural state, it was a five-foot-deep marsh. Three years after the Minneapolis Park Board bought the lake and its surrounding land in 1907, dredging began, and the marsh was transformed. Today, Nokomis reaches a maximum depth of about 35 feet, has two swimming beaches, and is also used for sailing. The park includes a low-key community center at the northern end of the lake.

POI B Minnehaha Parkway

Between Minnehaha Park and Lake Harriet

Minneapolis Park Board, 1893–1935

This scenic parkway along Minnehaha Creek forms one of the most prominent segments of the Grand Rounds National Scenic Byway that circles through virtually every part of Minneapolis. Most of the houses along the parkway date from about 1910 to the early 1930s.

POI C Hiawatha Lake, Park, and Golf Course

North of Minnehaha Pkwy. near Cedar Ave.

*Minneapolis Park Board, 1923 and later / includes **Hiawatha Lake Recreation Center,** Harry Jones, ca. 1929–32 / renovated, 1977 / **golf clubhouse,** Stravs Dorr Bersback and Chapin Architects, 1932*

The small lake and 200 acres of parkland here were even more of a reclamation project than Lake

Nokomis

A   Lake Nokomis and Nokomis Park
B   Minnehaha Parkway
C   Hiawatha Lake, Park, and Golf Course
D   Diamond Lake and Pearl Park
E   Cottages, duplexes, and bungalows

42nd St. E.

43rd St. E.

19

44th St. E.

45th St. E.

Hiawatha
Lake

46th St. E.

C

Hiawatha Ave. S.

B

Minnehaha Pkwy. E.

49th St. E.

50th St. E.

3

Lake
Nokomis

51st St. E.

1

52nd St. E.

4

2

53rd St. E.

34th Ave. S.

54th St. E.

31st Ave. S.

Woodlawn Blvd.

43rd Ave. S.

44th Ave. S.

45th Ave. S.

56th St. E.

23rd Ave. S.

5

57th St. E.

58th St. E.

62

Nokomis

1	House	**11**	House
2	House	**12**	Lustron houses
3	Dwight Demaine Dental Office	**13**	House
4	House	**14**	House
5	Wenonah Elementary School	**15**	John W. Lindstrom House
6	Hope Lutheran Church	**16**	St. Joseph's Home for Children
7	House	**17**	St. Mary's Cemetery
8	Dairy Queen	**18**	HCM Architects
9	William and Irma Dale House	**19**	St. Helena Catholic Church
10	Our Lady of Peace Church		

Nokomis. A swamp when it was purchased by the Minneapolis Park Board in 1923, it was known then as Rice Lake. The name was changed to Hiawatha two years later. Beginning in 1929, the swamp was dredged to a depth of 20 feet. Material hauled up by the dredges was used as fill to create Hiawatha Golf Course, which opened in 1934. The park includes the city's oldest recreation center, dating to about 1929, as well as a golf clubhouse built in the early 1930s.

1 House

5016 44th Ave. South

ca. 1889

One of a handful of Victorian homes that overlook Minnehaha Park. The outstanding feature is a wraparound porch that offers a primer in the joy of spindlework.

2 House

5028 Hiawatha Ave.

ca. 1875–80 / addition

A restored Italianate house with prominent hoods above the second-story windows, a bracketed cornice, and a two-story bay window. This may be the oldest home in Nokomis.

Dwight Demaine Dental Office

3 Dwight Demaine Dental Office

3319 50th St. East

ca. 1938

This little beauty looks like a refugee from Miami Beach's art deco district. Its Moderne credentials include a curving wall of glass block next to the entrance, a rounded front parapet, and a porthole window. Even a root canal might be fun amid such architectural delights.

4 House

5145 Woodlawn Blvd.

Liebenberg and Kaplan, 1931

A Tudor Revival mansion built of brick and fieldstone. It's one of the largest homes on this part of Woodlawn Blvd., which runs along a ridge overlooking Lake Nokomis.

5 Wenonah Elementary School

5625 23rd Ave. South

Thorshov and Cerny, 1952

A typical 1950s elementary school, long and low. Sprawling buildings of this kind proved costly to heat; here, the original window openings have been largely filled in with concrete block.

Hope Lutheran Church

6 Hope Lutheran Church

5728 Cedar Ave.

Ralph Rapson and Associates, 1971

Shed roofs abound in this energetic church, which displays Rapson's love for what might be called architectural action. The volumes are nicely composed, but if you're seeking serenity, this probably isn't the church for you: the message here seems to be that God is restless.

7 House

6113 Loren Dr.

1952

A brisk little 1950s house with an upthrust roofline that rises from one corner through a large stone chimney, makes an abrupt turn,

6113 Loren Dr.

and then drops straight down beside the front door.

8 Dairy Queen

6014 Portland Ave.

1957

The first Dairy Queen opened in Illinois in 1940, but it wasn't until after World War II that the chain, now based in Minneapolis, took off. This is one of the Twin Cities' oldest Dairy Queen outlets. The blue-and-white, neon-lit tilted cone sign may well be original.

9 William and Irma Dale House

340 Diamond Lake Rd. East

Carl Graffunder, 1955

Built of concrete block, this is one of a number of architect-designed houses from the 1950s in the vicinity of Diamond Lake.

POI D Diamond Lake and Pearl Park

Portland Ave. and Diamond Lake Rd. East

*Minneapolis Park Board, 1926– 36 / includes **Pearl Park Recreation Center,** Peterson Clark and Griffith, 1967 / renovated and enlarged, Bentz/Thompson/ Rietow Architects, 1995*

Diamond Lake was once linked to another body of water to the north known as Pearl Lake. After acquiring the site in 1926, the Minneapolis Park Board dredged Diamond Lake and filled in Pearl Lake. The recreation center, enlarged in the 1990s, features distinctive fan-shaped windows.

10 Our Lady of Peace Church (Catholic Church of the Resurrection)

5426 12th Ave. South

Thorshov and Cerny, 1954 / addition, Opus Architects, 1994

The original portion of this church, built for the Resurrection parish, is a severe brick box with copper accents. The church was enlarged to the east—and made considerably more inviting—in the 1990s when Resurrection and St. Kevin's parishes merged to create Our Lady of Peace.

Nokomis Knoll Residential Historic District N

Area bounded by Nokomis Pkwy. West, Bloomington Ave., 17th Ave. South, and 52nd and 54th Sts. East

various architects and builders, 1920s–40s

This National Register district, created in 1999, showcases the popular Period Revival styles of the 1920s, 1930s, and early 1940s. All the usual suspects are here— Italian and French Renaissance, Tudor, Spanish, and Colonial Revival—as well as a smattering of Craftsman foursquares and bungalows. The Tudor Revival crowd is most numerous, however.

5208 17th Ave. South

11 House N

5208 17th Ave. South

W. W. Purdy, 1929

Perhaps Nokomis Knoll's most impressive house, more or less Italian Renaissance Revival in style but with pointed Tudor arches—not what you'd expect to find on a nostalgic tour of Italy.

4916 Cedar Ave.

12 Lustron houses

4900, 4916 Cedar Ave.

Lustron Corp., 1949

A pair of prefabricated steel houses built in 1949 by the short-lived Lustron Corp. The one at 4900 has been remodeled, painted black (much to the dismay of some Lustron aficionados), and enlarged with a rear addition. The house at 4916, renovated and restored by architects Judy and Rob Grundstrom in 2000, hews more closely to its original appearance. There's another Lustron house on the east side of Lake Nokomis at 5217 31st Ave. South, plus seven others elsewhere in Minneapolis. For more on the history of Lustron homes, see pages 235–36.

13 House

820 Minnehaha Pkwy. East

1925

A near-perfect English Cottage–. Storybook house from the 1920s. There are many other fine houses of this type nearby, particularly along the 4900 blocks of Elliot, Tenth, and 11th Aves. South.

14 House

508 Minnehaha Pkwy. East

1935

An L-shaped Moderne house with a stepped-down entry. Overall, the house seems more in the spirit of the faceted art deco skyscraper style of the 1920s than the streamlined look of the 1930s.

15 John W. Lindstrom House

200 Minnehaha Pkwy. East

Lindstrom and Almars, 1912

John Lindstrom was a Swedish-born cabinetmaker who worked his way into the architectural profession in Minneapolis in the early 1900s. Between 1907 and 1916, he teamed with Joseph Almars to produce many outstanding Arts and Crafts bungalows. This house, one of several Lindstrom designed and built for himself, is a stucco bungalow with Tudor Revival elements. Lindstrom and Almars also designed the bungalow (1916) next door at 5101 Second Ave. South.

16 St. Joseph's Home for Children (Catholic Boys' Home)

1121 46th St. East

1886 and later

At the center of this campus is a four-story, Italianate-style brick building constructed in 1886 for the newly established Catholic Boys' Home, an orphanage. In the 1960s, the Boys' Home was merged with St. Joseph's Home for Children. Today, the campus consists of a half dozen or so buildings, and the home continues to provide services for troubled children and teenagers.

POI E Cottages, duplexes, and bungalows

Portland and Oakland Aves. between 43rd and 47th Sts. East

various architects, 1920s–30s

These blocks include a group of Period Revival cottages between 43rd and 44th on Portland and Oakland, a well-preserved colony of Tudor Revival duplexes on Portland between 44th and 45th, and a collection of Arts and Crafts and Period Revival bungalows on Portland between 45th and 47th. The bungalows are mainly from 1920s; the cottages and duplexes date to the 1930s.

17 St. Mary's Cemetery

4403 Chicago Ave.

1873

The city's largest Catholic cemetery, laid out with winding roads in the picturesque style favored during the late 1800s. It originally served as the burial ground for

Immaculate Conception Church (forerunner of the Basilica of St. Mary) but was taken over by the archdiocese in 1887. There isn't much showy funereal architecture here, especially compared to nearby Lakewood Cemetery, where the city's Protestant elite are buried, often amid much postmortem pomp.

18 HCM Architects (Fire Station No. 13) *L*

4201 Cedar Ave.

Collins and Kennison, 1923 / renovated, HCM Architects, 2004

The city's only bungalow-style fire station, given a domestic look so that it would blend in with the neighborhood's houses. It served as a fire station until 1980 and then as an ambulance garage. HCM Architects acquired the building in 2003 and converted it to office use.

St. Helena Catholic Church

19 St. Helena Catholic Church

3201 43rd St. East

1940 / addition, 1990 / Art: stained glass, Conrad Pickel Studio (Milwaukee), ca. 1950

This brick church, the parish's second, has a colorful tile roof, exceptional stained-glass windows, and other fine detailing. The design is said to be modeled on an eleventh-century Romanesque hall church. The stained-glass windows are among the earliest produced by Conrad Pickel Studio of Milwaukee, which was founded in 1947 and is still in business.

Nokomis

HCM Architects

Fort Snelling and Environs

1   Historic Fort Snelling
2   Visitor Center
3   Fort Snelling Veterans Memorial
    Chapel
4   Upper Post
5   Fort Snelling State Park Visitor
    Center
6   Mendota Bridge
7   Hypolite DePuis House

8   Henry Sibley House
9   Jean Baptiste Faribault House
10 Catholic Church of St. Peter
11 Minneapolis–St. Paul International
    Airport
12 Lindbergh Terminal
13 Fort Snelling National Cemetery
14 Mall of America

Fort Snelling and Environs

Old and new coexist here more dramatically than anywhere else in the Twin Cities. Historic Fort Snelling (1820s and later) stands adjacent to Minneapolis–St. Paul International Airport (1920s and later). As airplanes roar overhead, traffic zooms along the web of freeways around the old fort, some of it bound for the Mall of America (1992), just three miles or so to the west. Cross the Mendota Bridge (1926) to the community of the same name, however, and you can plunge into the past by touring the historic houses (1830s and later) that form the town's nucleus.

Much of Fort Snelling is included within a state park established in 1961. At the heart of the park is the old fort, a National Historic Landmark that includes 14 stone and wood buildings, among them a fine round tower. The entire fort, which was greatly enlarged in the 1880s and later, includes numerous other buildings, such as barracks, officers quarters, and a stone chapel built in the 1920s. A national cemetery was established near the fort in 1939.

Minneapolis–St. Paul International Airport is due west of Fort Snelling. Although the airport's perpetually expanding architectural ensemble falls considerably short of breathtaking, it includes Lindbergh Terminal (1961), a significant early modernist work in the Twin Cities. Only two miles from the airport is the building by which more people probably know the Twin Cities than any other: the Mall of America, where the world—quite literally—comes to shop. The mall's architecture isn't inspiring, but the mega complex is exceptionally well planned.

Fort Snelling ! N ★

Near intersection of Hwys. 5 and 55

1821–25 and later

Over a period of four years, in a distant wilderness, Colonel Josiah Snelling and his soldiers built a truly remarkable structure: a diamond-shaped citadel with walls of yellow limestone, barracks, officers quarters, and other buildings, all arrayed around a parade ground. Completed in 1825, the fort was in many ways Snelling's folly, more massive than required to repel an assault by Indians, yet poorly sited to repel artillery fire from an invading army. As it was, neither Indians nor armies ever attacked the fort, but Snelling was so assailed by his own officers—who spent much of their time in obscure intrigues—that he left his command in 1827 and died a year later.

As settlers poured into the region, the fort's rationale grew tenuous, and in 1858 the federal government actually sold it. The onset of the Civil War in 1861 caused the government to reconsider, however, and it reclaimed the fort. After the war, the fort took on a new role as headquarters for the U.S. Army's Department of the Dakota. In the late 1870s, the government began constructing buildings for the department in the area of the fort known as the Upper Post. Later, the army stationed cavalry, artillery, and infantry units at the fort, which also served as an induction center during World War II. It finally closed in 1946. Beginning in the 1960s, the Minnesota Historical Society reconstructed the original portion of the fort, now a historic site.

1 Historic Fort Snelling !

200 Tower Ave.

1821–25 and later / reconstructed, Minnesota Historical Society (Loren Johnson) with Brooks Cavin (consulting architect), ca. 1965–80

As built by Josiah Snelling and his successors, the walled portion of the fort included 14 buildings and four corner towers. By the time rebuilding began in 1965, only four original structures—three of them substantially modified—still stood: the round and hexagonal towers, the commandant's house, and the officers

Historic Fort Snelling

quarters. The 15-year-long reconstruction, designed to restore the fort to its 1830s look, was done with great care. The restoration team found limestone to match that of the original fort and even went so far as to use period tools whenever possible. In addition to its obvious historic value, the rebuilt fort demonstrates that Snelling and his builders possessed considerable skill as designers. The fort's walls, well-proportioned buildings, and quiet rooflines create a sturdy architectural ensemble that rests easily atop the bluffs.

2 Visitor Center

200 Tower Ave.

Bennett and Myers, 1983

One of the last big underground buildings in the Twin Cities. The architects found ways to bring natural light into the public portions of the building, but the overall design is pedestrian.

3 Fort Snelling Veterans Memorial Chapel

Hewitt and Brown, 1929

A Romanesque-style stone chapel with a 60-foot-high round tower that echoes the fort's landmark tower. The nave's stained-glass windows depict early figures in Minnesota's history.

4 Upper Post

Along Taylor Ave.

1879 and later

In 1879, the federal government undertook a building program

here to accommodate the U.S. Army's Department of the

Upper Post

Dakota. The new brick buildings included barracks, officers quarters, shops, and administrative headquarters. Other buildings were added over a period of many years. Today, 28 buildings remain in the Upper Post area. Among the most significant are the towered administration building (1879–80), three large barracks (1885), and 11 houses built as officers quarters between 1879 and 1905. Long vacant, the deteriorating buildings now form a military ghost town. In 2006, the National Trust for Historic Preservation named the Upper Post complex as one of the country's 11 most endangered historic sites. As of 2007, the Minnesota Historical Society was seeking state funds to convert one of the barracks into a museum and visitors center.

5 Fort Snelling State Park Visitor Center

Post Rd. and Hwy. 5

Thorbeck Architects, 1997

An attractive stone- and wood-clad building that draws on the historic fort for its inspiration.

Mendota Bridge

6 Mendota Bridge ! N

Hwy. 55 across Minnesota River

Walter H. Wheeler and C. A. P. Turner (engineers), 1926 / renovated, 1968 and later

Spanning over 4,100 feet, this concrete-arch bridge was the longest of its type in the world at the time of its completion in

1926. Its 13 main spans (304 feet each) spring gracefully across the forested river bottom: in the summer the bridge almost seems to be floating above a luxuriant canopy of trees. The view from the bridge's sidewalk is among the best in the Twin Cities: the skyscrapers of downtown Minneapolis and St. Paul, the walls of Fort Snelling, and the rivers and valleys that shaped the destiny of the region are all visible in one grand sweep.

Mendota

Located at the confluence of the Minnesota and Mississippi rivers (in the Dakota language, *mendota* means "meeting of waters"), this small community is the state's oldest permanent settlement. Although fur traders were active here in the eighteenth century, the community itself dates to the 1820s, when Fort Snelling was established just across the Minnesota River. Today, Mendota is best known for a historic district that includes the Henry Sibley House (ca. 1836), two other pioneer homes, and the Church of St. Peter (1853).

7 Hypolite DePuis House N

1357 Sibley Memorial Hwy. (Hwy. 13)

1854 / remodeled, 1928 and later

Used as offices for the Sibley House Historic Site, this brick house was built for a fur trader who was also Henry Sibley's private secretary.

Henry Sibley House

8 Henry Sibley House ! N

Water St.

John Mueller, ca. 1836 / addition, ca. 1843 / restored, 1910 and later

Minnesota's oldest house. Henry Sibley was just 25 years old and in charge of a fur trading post in Mendota when he hired mason John Mueller to build the house, which included a trading room. The Colonial-style house has 30-inch-thick outer walls of limestone, timber framing, and mud-plastered interior walls. Sibley, who was elected Minnesota's first state governor in 1858, moved with his family to St. Paul in 1862. The St. Paul Chapter of the Daughters of the American Revolution opened the house as a museum in 1910. It is now owned by the Minnesota Historical Society and continues to serve as a historic site.

9 Jean Baptiste Faribault House N

Water St.

John Mueller, ca. 1840 / restored, Public Works Administration, 1937

Also built by mason John Mueller, this home is more formal than the Sibley House and includes a mix of Federal and Greek Revival detailing. Jean Baptiste Faribault was a French Canadian fur trader who settled in Mendota in the 1820s. He used the house as an inn as well as his residence. The house was rehabilitated in the 1930s through the federal Public Works Administration. It's now part of the Sibley House Historic Site.

10 Catholic Church of St. Peter N

1405 Sibley Memorial Hwy. (Hwy. 13)

1853 / restored, 1978 / new church, 2005

This historic church is the oldest in continuous use in Minnesota. It replaced an earlier chapel built to serve Mendota's French Catholics. The limestone church is a simple Gothic Revival structure with a central tower. Its exterior remains relatively intact (though the steeple isn't original), but the interior has been altered. The parish completed a much larger church and social hall here in 2005, but the old church is still used for daily mass, weddings, and funerals.

11 Minneapolis–St. Paul International Airport (Wold-Chamberlain Field)

Hwy. 5 and Glumack Dr.

1920 and later

One of the nation's ten largest airports, Minneapolis–St. Paul International grew out of a small airfield established in 1920 on the site of a defunct auto racetrack. Known as Speedway Field, its name was changed in 1923 to honor pilots Ernest Wold and Cyrus Chamberlain, killed in World War I. Northwest Airlines began providing passenger service here in 1929. Like other airports, Minneapolis–St. Paul International (a name adopted in the 1940s) was enlarged during World War II. The introduction of jet airliners in the 1950s fueled additional growth. Since the completion of the main (Lindbergh) terminal in 1961, the airport has undergone an unending series of expansions to accommodate the 37 million passengers who fly in and out every year.

Lindbergh Terminal, 1962

12 Lindbergh Terminal

4300 Glumack Dr.

Thorshov and Cerny, 1961 / numerous additions and remodelings, Architectural Alliance, HGA, and others, 1980s and later

Now largely hidden behind parking ramps, this terminal as built was a fair example of heroic modernism, its design dominated by a wavelike, folded-plate concrete roof. Half of the roof was replaced during a 1980s remodeling, but the terminal still retains such original features as interior walls built of colorful glazed bricks. Overall, however, the terminal lacks the soaring presence of the best modern airport buildings. Still, its 2.8 million square feet, including four concourses that seem to stretch to infinity, are organized in a reasonably efficient way, which is all that most travelers ask for.

13 Fort Snelling National Cemetery

7601 34th Ave. South

1939 / enlarged, 1960–61

Initially used as a burial ground for soldiers from the fort, this national cemetery was formally established in 1939. More than 167,000 veterans and their family members are buried here.

14 Mall of America !

I-494 and Cedar Ave. (Hwy. 77)

Jerde Partnership (Los Angeles), KKE Architects, HGA, and others, 1992

To the world at large, the Mall of America is the Twin Cities' best-known building as well as its prime tourist attraction. Yet for all of its size and pretensions to splendor, this vast temple of consumerism offers little in the way of architectural inspiration. With its themed avenues, circling array of shops anchored by department stores, and aura of middle-brow glitz, it really is just another mall, albeit bigger than the usual sort and organized around a central atrium occupied by an amusement park. Oh yes, and don't forget the aquarium in the basement.

Still, it's worth noting that one reason for the mall's success is that its architects and planners did a virtuoso job of handling

Fort Snelling

circulation. Everything here flows smoothly, from the entrances to the flat-floored, unusually spacious parking ramps, to the connections between the ramps and the mall, to the interior concourses that feature sightlines designed to help shoppers orient themselves. In late 2006, plans were announced to expand the mall to the north with more stores, a hotel, a performing arts center, and other attractions.

Mall of America

Overview

These neighborhoods form the heart of south Minneapolis. They offer a diverse architectural environment that ranges from enormous mansions along Park Avenue and around Fair Oaks Park to crowded public apartment projects to important commercial monuments like the Sears, Roebuck Building (1928), now called Midtown Exchange, on Lake Street. Here, too, you'll find perhaps greater extremes of wealth and poverty than anywhere else in Minneapolis.

Long known as the Near South Side, Phillips acquired its current name—in honor of nineteenth-century Boston abolitionist Wendell Phillips—in the 1960s. One of the city's most densely populated neighborhoods, Phillips is also among the poorest. In the 1880s and 1890s, however, it was home to some of Minneapolis's richest families, who lived in baronial mansions along Park Avenue. The names of these mansion dwellers—Bell, Bemis, Heffelfinger, Peavey—formed a who's who of the city's milling industry, and for a time Park became the Minneapolis version of Summit Avenue in St. Paul.

To the east of Park, however, particularly near the old Milwaukee Road rail yards along Hiawatha Avenue, the neighborhood took on a different character. Here, the streets teemed with immigrants from Europe, living in small wood-frame houses and tenements. An east-west dichotomy still marks Phillips to some degree, although Park is no longer the mansion row it once was. Today, the neighborhood continues to attract immigrants—most recently Asians, Latinos, and Somalis—and it also has the city's largest population of Native Americans.

Powderhorn lies south of Phillips. Lake Street, which separates the two neighborhoods, is the main commercial thoroughfare in south Minneapolis and has several buildings of note. As officially defined by the city, Powderhorn extends west of Interstate 35W and north of Lake to take in the Lyndale and Whittier neighborhoods. However, that's always seemed a stretch, and those neighborhoods are covered in a separate section, as is Stevens Square.

With its flat terrain, Powderhorn is the city's most Cartesian landscape. The grid is close to perfect here, and only one street of any consequence, Hiawatha, deviates from the ordinal points of the compass. This triumph of regularity has a price—you long for a bend or wrinkle to dispel the grid's monotony. The neighborhood takes its name from Powderhorn Park and the small lake at its center. The park dates to about 1890, which is when the neighborhood also began to fill out; today it consists mainly of modest single-family homes.

The neighborhoods known as Whittier, Lyndale, and Stevens Square offer a primer in the complexities and contradictions of urban life. Wealth and poverty openly rub up against each other here, especially in Whittier, which is home to the Minneapolis Institute of Arts (1915 and later). A white temple of culture, the institute overlooks Washburn–Fair Oaks Park, where it's not uncommon to see people asleep on the ground in the middle of the day. Mansions built by hallowed Minneapolis names line the leafy avenues just north of the institute, while a few blocks to the east you'll find yourself on rough-looking streets that border a roaring freeway. Meanwhile, new immigrant populations, including Somalis and Latinos, have been stirred into the cosmopolitan mix here in recent years.

The Lyndale neighborhood also includes some fine housing, as well as many apartments. North of Whittier, across Franklin Avenue, is the distinctive community of Stevens Square. Instead of mansions, the developers of Stevens Square constructed apartment buildings, more than 50 in all in a 15-year span between 1910 and 1925. These brick, predominately three-story buildings form a unique architectural environment in the Twin Cities, now incorporated within the Stevens Square Historic District.

Phillips

This neighborhood saw its greatest period of development between about 1880 and 1910. New housing followed the streetcar lines as they extended south of downtown, while two east-west thoroughfares with trolley service—Franklin Avenue and Lake Street—grew into busy commercial corridors. Although single-family homes (often sub-divided into apartments) still predominate in Phillips, the neighborhood also has numerous duplexes, townhomes, and apartment buildings. Many are the product of urban renewal programs in the 1960s and 1970s.

Commercial, industrial, and institutional buildings are also prominent in Phillips. Among the most significant is the old Honeywell complex (1927 and later), which dates its beginnings to 1883 when Albert Butz invented a thermostat (he called it a "damper flapper") to control heat from furnaces. The company Butz established to manufacture his invention eventually evolved into the Minneapolis-Honeywell Regulator Co., which for years maintained its world headquarters and a large manufacturing plant at Fourth Avenue and 28th Street East (Wells Fargo Home Mortgage now occupies the complex). Another large presence in the neighborhood is Abbott-Northwestern Hospital, which opened (as Northwestern Hospital) in 1887.

For the architectural tourist, Phillips offers an eclectic array of sights. Highlights include the Gothic Revival–style Holy Rosary/Santo Rosario Catholic Church (1889); the Anson and Georgia Brooks House (ca. 1909), a rare example of Venetian Gothic in the Twin Cities; the American Swedish Institute (1908), a Chateauesque mansion built for publishing magnate Swan Turnblad; and the elegant Franklin Community Library (1914).

POI A Minneapolis Pioneers and Soldiers Memorial (Layman's) Cemetery N

2945 Cedar Ave. South

Martin Layman, 1860 and later

The oldest cemetery in Minneapolis and an oddity in that the city owns it. Burials began here in the 1850s on land owned by Martin Layman. Layman's Cemetery, as it was called, expanded twice before reaching its present size in 1886. The cemetery gradually grew decrepit, and in 1919 the city banned further burials. Various groups then rallied to save the cemetery. In 1928 the city agreed to acquire and maintain the graveyard, renamed Minneapolis Pioneers and Soldiers Memorial Cemetery. Most of the 20,000 or so dead here were buried long ago, and only about a quarter of the graves are marked. The sole building of note is a stone office that dates to 1871.

POI B Midtown Greenway (including Chicago, Milwaukee and St. Paul Railroad Grade Separation Historic District) N

grade separation, along 29th St. East and West between Hiawatha and Hennepin Aves.

Chicago, Milwaukee and St. Paul Railroad, H. C. Lothholz and C. F. Loweth (engineers), 1912–16

greenway, along 27th, 29th, and Lake Sts. between Mississippi River and France Ave.

SRF Consulting Group and others, 2000, 2004

In 1881 the Chicago, Milwaukee and St. Paul Railroad (the Milwaukee Road), completed a rail line along 29th St. The line ran at grade, with numerous street crossings. By 1910, it had become so troublesome that the city council passed an ordinance requiring that the Milwaukee Road depress the tracks between Hiawatha and Irving Aves. After an unsuccessful court challenge, the railroad

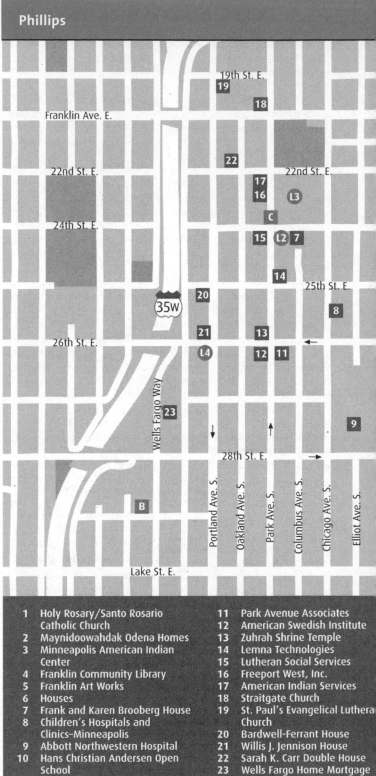

Phillips

19th St. E.

19

18

Franklin Ave. E.

22nd St. E.

22nd St. E.

22

17
16

L3

C

24th St. E.

15 **L2** **7**

14

25th St. E.

20

8

35W

21

13

26th St. E.

L4

12 **11**

Wells Fargo Way

23

9

28th St. E.

B

Portland Ave. S.
Oakland Ave. S.
Park Ave. S.
Columbus Ave. S.
Chicago Ave. S.
Elliot Ave. S.

Lake St. E.

1	Holy Rosary/Santo Rosario Catholic Church	
2	Maynidoowahdak Odena Homes	
3	Minneapolis American Indian Center	
4	Franklin Community Library	
5	Franklin Art Works	
6	Houses	
7	Frank and Karen Brooberg House	
8	Children's Hospitals and Clinics–Minneapolis	
9	Abbott Northwestern Hospital	
10	Hans Christian Andersen Open School	

11	Park Avenue Associates
12	American Swedish Institute
13	Zuhrah Shrine Temple
14	Lemna Technologies
15	Lutheran Social Services
16	Freeport West, Inc.
17	American Indian Services
18	Straitgate Church
19	St. Paul's Evangelical Lutheran Church
20	Bardwell-Ferrant House
21	Willis J. Jennison House
22	Sarah K. Carr Double House
23	Wells Fargo Home Mortgage

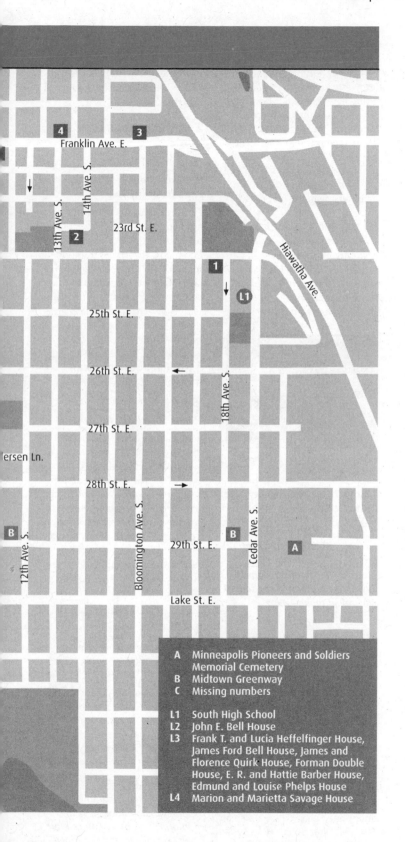

A   Minneapolis Pioneers and Soldiers
    Memorial Cemetery
B   Midtown Greenway
C   Missing numbers

L1 South High School
L2 John E. Bell House
L3 Frank T. and Lucia Heffelfinger House,
    James Ford Bell House, James and
    Florence Quirk House, Forman Double
    House, E. R. and Hattie Barber House,
    Edmund and Louise Phelps House
L4 Marion and Marietta Savage House

Phillips

undertook the so-called grade-separation project, digging a trench nearly three miles long, building 37 reinforced concrete bridges (28 of which still stand), laying new track, and shoring up adjacent buildings. Acquired by Hennepin County in 1993, the rail line was later transformed into the Midtown Greenway—a walking, biking, and skating trail. Long-range plans also envision a light rail line in the greenway.

LOST 1 *Where Little Earth of United Tribes Housing project stands at Cedar Ave. South and 24th St. East was the site of* **South High School,** *a Romanesque Revival–style building constructed in 1892. The towered building was razed in 1970.*

Holy Rosary/Santo Rosario Catholic Church

1 Holy Rosary/Santo Rosario Catholic Church

18th Ave. South and 24th St. East

Edward S. Stebbins, 1889 / rebuilt after fire, 1904 / new tower, ca. 1978 / **parish office (convent),** *Edward S. Stebbins, 1888 /* **school,** *Edward S. Stebbins, 1891*

Founded in 1878, mainly to serve Irish immigrants, Holy Rosary is the oldest Catholic parish in south Minneapolis. This church, the parish's second, was designed by architect Edward Stebbins to accommodate 2,200 worshippers. Built of sandstone, the Gothic Revival–style church features two front towers and a steep roof punctuated by rows of dormers. The nave, rebuilt after a 1904 fire, has a blue and gold vaulted ceiling, along with much statuary and stained glass. There's also an elaborate altar. Today, Holy Rosary is a bilingual parish with a large Latino membership, but it also serves immigrants from East Africa, Asia, and elsewhere. The parish office adjoining the church was designed by Stebbins as well, as was the old school at 2448 18th Ave. South.

2 Maynidoowahdak Odena Homes

1321 23rd St. East

Douglas Cardinal (Ottawa, ON) and DJR Architecture, 1998

Fourteen housing units arranged as an interconnected series of octagons with tepeelike roofs, all designed to evoke the traditional forms of a Native American village. The units were built to provide homes for Native Americans with HIV. *Maynidoowahdak odena* means "a place where ceremonies happen" in Ojibwe.

3 Minneapolis American Indian Center

1530 Franklin Ave. East

Hodne-Stageberg Partners, 1975

Minneapolis has a large Native American population, and this center was one of the first of its kind in the nation. It's an aggressive concrete and wood building organized around an angular, multilevel courtyard. Like many buildings of its period, it doesn't present an especially friendly face to the street, although there is an inviting, parklike plaza at the rear.

Franklin Community Library, 1914

4 Franklin Community Library N *L*

1314 Franklin Ave. East

Edward L. Tilton (New York) with Magney and Chapman, 1914 / addition, Johnson and Backstrom, 1937 / renovated and expanded, MS&R Architects, 2005

The city's oldest neighborhood library, one of four built in the early 1900s with funds from Andrew Carnegie. Renaissance Revival in style, the library has a lovely skylit reading room. The 2005 renovation was designed to adapt the library to modern technology while maintaining its historic integrity. A new community room was also added as part of the work.

5 Franklin Art Works (New Franklin Theater)

1021 Franklin Ave. East

Lindstrom and Almars, 1916 / renovated, 1999 and later

One of the city's oldest movie theaters, renovated by Franklin Art Works as a gallery and performance space. The arched, art-glass window displaying the theater's name is a delight.

6 Houses

2100, 2104, 2108, 2110 Tenth Ave. South

ca. 1890

Four Victorian workers' cottages, only a few blocks from the mansions of Park Ave.

7 Frank and Karen Brooberg House *L*

727 24th St. East

August Cedarstrand (builder), 1905

A Classical Revival house built for a Swedish immigrant named Frank Brooberg, who arrived in Minnesota in 1869 at age 11 and later owned a 2,000-acre farm in South Dakota. He returned to Minneapolis in 1905 and hired his brother-in-law, August Cedarstrand, to build this fine house.

8 Children's Hospital and Clinics–Minneapolis

2525 Chicago Ave. South

Ellerbe Architects, 1972 / addition, BWBR Architects, 2005

Hospital architecture tends to be like hospital food—bland—but the addition completed here in 2005 is spicier than the usual fare. Done in red, white, yellow, and blue stucco, it includes circular windows and a projecting stair tower topped by a swooping, upthrust green roof.

9 Abbott Northwestern Hospital

800 28th St. East

Long and Thorshov, 1926 / many additions / includes **Heart Hospital,** *HKS Architects (Dallas), 2005*

The product of numerous mergers, this hospital complex includes half a dozen buildings. One of the latest additions is a heart hospital designed to provide a soothing experience for patients.

10 Hans Christian Andersen Open School

1098 Andersen Ln. (near Tenth Ave. South and 27th St. East)

Bissel Belair and Green, 1975

No architectural fairy tale, this school is an all-too-real example of 1970s Brutalism, heavy on concrete and attitude. Circular wall openings and cylindrical projections do little to soften it.

Park Avenue

Lake St. to 18th St. East

As commercial development swallowed up the first generation of mansions around downtown, many wealthy residents built new homes on Park Ave. in the 1880s and later. At least 30 mansions appeared between 18th and 28th Sts. East in the so-called "golden mile." This mansion district did not remain intact for long. By 1910, half of the houses on Park north of 26th St. East had already been subdivided. Later, in the 1950s and 1960s, many mansions were razed for commercial or institutional developments. Today, this portion of Park consists of modern-era buildings interspersed among the remaining mansions, few of which still serve as residences.

11 Park Avenue Associates

2615 Park Ave. South

Martin Lindquist, 1930

This suave apartment building may well be the largest of its time in the Twin Cities. Stylistically, it's a blend of Renaissance Revival and art deco.

American Swedish Institute, 1907

12 American Swedish Institute (Swan J. Turnblad House) ! N *L*

2600 Park Ave. South

Boehme and Cordella, 1908 / addition, B. Aaron Parker and Associates, planned for 2008 / Art: exterior stone carving, Herman Schlink / wood carving, Ulrich Steiner / statuary, Albin Polasek

A seven-year-old named Sven Mansson was among more than 50,000 Swedes who in 1868–69 left their homeland to escape poverty and famine. By 1880, Mansson had changed his name to Swan Turnblad and was working in Minneapolis as a typesetter. Five years later, he became manager of a failing newspaper called the *Svenska Amerikanska Posten.* Turnblad quickly transformed the *Posten* into the nation's largest Swedish-language newspaper. By 1897 he was the newspaper's publisher and also a very rich man.

Completed in 1908, this 33-room house—where Turnblad lived with his wife and daughter—is a stylistic mélange, displaying Chateauesque and Baroque Revival elements, among others. The "Swedish Castle," as the house came to be called, offers an assortment of towers, turrets, gables, dormers, and chimneys to repel the demons of architectural boredom. Within, the house is organized around a two-story-high grand hall. Decorative details include mahogany woodwork, onyx fireplace man-

American Swedish Institute interior, 1950

tles, statuary, and a stained-glass window above the staircase that reputedly cost $27,000—enough to build a large house at the time. There are also 11 tile stoves—known as *kakelugn*—imported from Sweden. The mansion's cost was the source of much contention, and Turnblad was later sued by *Posten* stockholders, including his own brother, over alleged financial irregularities.

After his wife died in 1929, Turnblad donated the property to the Swedish community. The American Swedish Institute was formally established that year. In 1930, Turnblad moved to the apartment building across from the mansion at 2615 Park. He died there in 1933. Seven years later, the *Posten* was gone as well. The institute plans to build an addition in 2008—the house's 100th anniversary—that will include a performance hall, galleries, and a restaurant.

13 Zuhrah Shrine Temple (Charles M. Harrington House) *L*

2540 Park Ave. South

Kees and Colburn, 1902 / addition, P. M. Design, 1989

This Italian Renaissance Revival–style mansion, complete with an elaborate carriage house, was built for Charles Harrington, a grain dealer and one-time president of the Minneapolis Chamber of Commerce. The richly finished interior includes an entrance hall with mahogany paneling and wall frescoes. The house was acquired by the Zuhrah Shrine in 1929, a year after Harrington's death, and has been the organization's local headquarters ever since. A pre-

Zuhrah Shrine Temple, 1963

cast concrete auditorium added in 1989 shows the folly of trying to imitate historic styles with inferior materials.

Lemna Technologies, 1974

14 Lemna Technologies (Anson and Georgia Brooks House)

2445 Park Ave. South

Long and Long, 1907

A little piece of Venice on Park Ave., built for lumber baron Anson Brooks. This house is a rare example of the Venetian Gothic style in the Twin Cities, and it still looks striking today. With its interlaced arches, ornate parapets, and foursquare massing, the house resembles a small palace.

15 Lutheran Social Services

2414 Park Ave. South

Sovik Mathre and Associates, 1957

A dainty, arcaded, one-story brick building with a folded roof. It displays a kind of calm, rational modernism that served as a counterpoint to the more garish architectural instincts of the 1950s.

LOST 2 *Where a parking ramp for the Phillips Eye Institute now stands at Park Ave. and 24th St.*

*East was the site of the **John E. Bell House,** a wild Queen Anne–style mansion from 1885 that fell to the wrecker in 1961.*

POI C Missing numbers

Mathematically astute observers will note that the east-west streets here skip over two numbers: 21st and 23rd. Given the city's devotion to numerical order, this seems more than a little odd. Legend holds that the two numbers were omitted so that Lake St. would end up as a nice even number (it's equivalent to 30th). East of Chicago Ave., however, you will find short stretches where 21st and 23rd Sts. do indeed exist.

16 Freeport West, Inc. (George Peavey House)

2222 Park Ave. South

William Channing Whitney, 1903 / renovated, 1981

A sober Renaissance Revival mansion with an arcaded entry porch, a balustraded roof, and a porte cochere. It was built for George Peavey by Charles Haglin, best known for designing the first cylindrical concrete grain elevator (for George's father, Frank Peavey) in 1900. The experimental elevator still stands in St. Louis Park and is a National Historic Landmark.

E. R. and Hattie Barber House

LOST 3 *Lost mansions on this block include the **Frank T. and Lucia Heffelfinger House** at 2205 Park; the **James Ford Bell House,** 2215 Park; the **James and Florence Quirk House,** 2300 Park; the **Forman Double House,** 2303–5 Park; the **E. R. and Hattie Barber House,** 2313 Park; and the **Edmund and Louise Phelps House,** 2323 Park. All were built between 1880 and 1900, and all were gone by the 1970s.*

American Indian Services

17 American Indian Services (Sumner T. and Eugenie McKnight House)

2200 Park Ave. South

Bertrand and Keith, 1892

A massive house built of Lake Superior sandstone, Romanesque Revival in character but treated with something close to classical symmetry. The two corner towers with their witch's-hat roofs make for a very impressive composition. The original owner made his money in lumber and real estate. Incidentally, the mansion is said to be insulated with the manes and tails of 20,000 horses.

18 Straitgate (Park Avenue Congregational) Church

638 Franklin Ave. East

Charles S. Sedgwick, 1889

A rugged brownstone church, now owned by a Baptist congregation, that evokes the work of H. H. Richardson yet also has pointed arches and other Gothic Revival details.

Portland Avenue

18th St. East to Lake St.

Now a busy one-way street, this stretch of Portland never attracted as many mansions as Park Ave. two blocks to the east, and today it's a hodgepodge of older homes, apartments, and infills of varying quality. But Portland still has a few fine homes, particularly on the blocks immediately south of Franklin Ave. Included among them are two exceptional Victorians: the Bardwell-Ferrant House (ca. 1883) and the Willis J. Jennison House (1901).

19 St. Paul's Evangelical Lutheran (First Presbyterian) Church

1901 Portland Ave. South

Warren H. Hayes, 1889

A Romanesque Revival church in granite and brownstone. Originally built for the First Presbyterian congregation, the church has been home to St. Paul's since 1964.

Bardwell-Ferrant House

20 Bardwell-Ferrant House N *L*

2500 Portland Ave. South

ca. 1883 / remodeled, Carl F. Struck, 1890 / renovated and restored, Rolf Lokensgard, 1986

An Oriental folly by way of Norway (sort of). It was built around 1883 in the Queen Anne style for Charles Bardwell. Seven years later the house—then on its original site at 1800 Park Ave.—was purchased by Emil Ferrant, who instigated the Moorish mayhem that followed, hiring Norwegian-born architect Carl Struck to perform the makeover. Struck added two onion-domed towers and a wraparound porch with spindle-work columns, all in keeping with the Moorish Revival style briefly popular in the late 1880s. The home eventually settled into a state of genteel decay as a rooming house. In 1986, new owners converted it into four apartments.

21 Willis J. Jennison House

2546 Portland Ave. South

Edwin P. Overmire, 1901

A brick and terra-cotta house in the Chateauesque style. The front dormer, topped by a rounded pinnacle, is one of the most distinctive in the city. The house was built for the owner of a company that operated flour mills.

LOST 4 *The Marion and Marietta Savage House once stood at 2600 Portland Ave. South, now the site of the Portland Place townhomes. Marion Savage owned Dan Patch, the pacer who set a world record for the mile at the Minnesota State Fair in 1906.*

22 Sarah K. Carr Double House

616–18 22nd St. East

1891

Romanesque Revival in yellow brick, rather than the usual brownstone. The house is one of about ten rental properties on this block operated by Hope Community, Inc., a nonprofit organization founded in 1977 by three Roman Catholic nuns.

23 Wells Fargo Home Mortgage (Honeywell Heat Regulator Co. Plant and Headquarters)

2701 Wells Fargo Way

Wells Fargo Mortgage Building, *Joseph V. Vanderbilt, 1927 / **West building,** Edmund J. Prondzinski, 1940 / renovated, HGA, ca. 1978 / **North building,** RSP Architects, 2004 / Art: water park, M. Paul Friedberg, ca. 1970s / renovated, 2005*

This corporate campus served as world headquarters for the Honeywell Corp. until the 1990s, when Honeywell merged with another company and moved to New Jersey. In 2000, Wells Fargo and Co. purchased the complex

Wells Fargo Home Mortgage

and poured $175 million into renovating and expanding it. Dominating the campus is a brick building from 1927 designed by Minneapolis architect Joseph Vanderbilt. The building's 11-story tower, an amalgam of Romanesque Revival and art deco elements, has long been a neighborhood landmark. The newest addition to the campus is a sleek glass and metal building by RSP Architects. The campus also includes a renovated 1940s building, parking ramps, and a recently restored water park designed by M. Paul Friedberg, best known locally for his work at Peavey Plaza in downtown Minneapolis.

Powderhorn

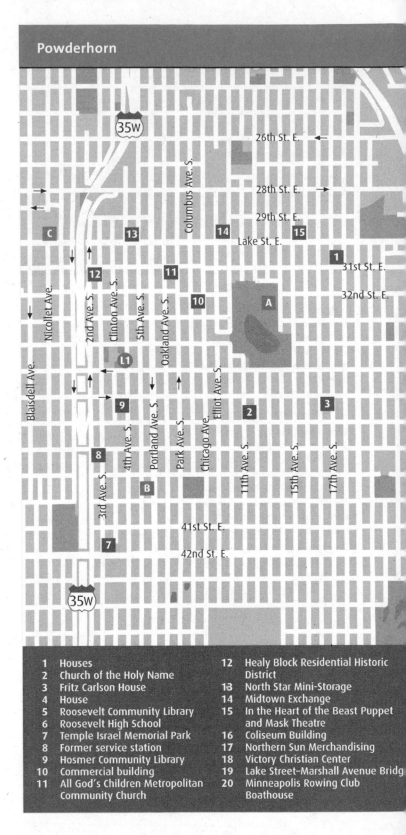

1   Houses
2   Church of the Holy Name
3   Fritz Carlson House
4   House
5   Roosevelt Community Library
6   Roosevelt High School
7   Temple Israel Memorial Park
8   Former service station
9   Hosmer Community Library
10 Commercial building
11 All God's Children Metropolitan
    Community Church

12 Healy Block Residential Historic
    District
13 North Star Mini-Storage
14 Midtown Exchange
15 In the Heart of the Beast Puppet
    and Mask Theatre
16 Coliseum Building
17 Northern Sun Merchandising
18 Victory Christian Center
19 Lake Street–Marshall Avenue Bridg
20 Minneapolis Rowing Club
    Boathouse

A   Powderhorn Park
B   Lena O. Smith House
C   Shopping center

L1   Central High School
L2   Wonderland Amusement Park
L3   First Lake Street–Marshall
       Avenue Bridge

Powderhorn

Before dredges did their work, beginning in 1904 and again in the 1920s, the lake that constitutes this neighborhood's most prominent natural feature was indeed shaped much like the horns in which soldiers once carried their gunpowder. Development of the park, which is the largest in south-central Minneapolis, helped spur residential growth here, as did the extension of streetcar lines in the 1890s.

Powderhorn's oldest homes, including a few from the 1880s, are generally located in the blocks immediately south of Lake Street. However, the bulk of the neighborhood's housing was built in the early decades of the twentieth century, and most of it isn't large or fancy. Beginning in the 1960s, there was a good deal of spot clearance in Powderhorn to make way for new housing built under a variety of urban renewal programs. For the most part, however, the neighborhood has maintained its original housing stock. Many of the neighborhood's early residents were immigrants, with Scandinavians, as usual in Minneapolis, predominating. Today, Hispanics are the fastest growing segment of Powderhorn's diverse population.

Lake Street is by far the neighborhood's busiest commercial strip, though parts of it have lost their luster over the last few decades. There are also smaller commercial areas along old streetcar routes such as Chicago, Bloomington, and Cedar avenues.

Among Powderhorn's architectural treasures is the Healy Block Residential Historic District along Second and Third avenues just south of Lake, which includes 15 ornate homes built between 1886 and 1898. Another of the neighborhood's most interesting places, though not well known, is Temple Israel Memorial Park, a Jewish cemetery that includes a fine stone gatehouse completed in 1890.

Powderhorn Park

POI A Powderhorn Park

3400 15th Ave. South

Horace Cleveland (landscape architect) and Minneapolis Park Board, 1890 and later

This 65-acre park encompasses Powderhorn Lake, a 12-acre body of water set within a natural bowl. The northern half of the lake was filled in during dredging operations in the early twentieth century. An island was also created at that time for picturesque effect. The lake's glory years were in the 1930s, when a speed skating track attracted top-flight competitors. Ken Bartholomew, one of the neighborhood's own, went on to win a silver medal at the 1948 Olympics in Switzerland. Today the park is home to an annual arts festival and a May Day pageant staged by In the Heart of the Beast Puppet and Mask Theatre.

1 Houses

3027–43 17th Ave. South

ca. 1890s

A gathering of late nineteenth-century brick "worker's cottages." Some have been stuccoed over. The two nicest are at 3031 and 3033.

2 Church of the Holy Name

3637 11th Ave. South

Cerny Associates, 1961

A brick box topped by a copper roof that flares up at either side like angel wings. Nearby is the old parish school, a Collegiate Gothic building from 1923, now known as Risen Christ School.

3 Fritz Carlson House

3612 17th Ave. South

Purcell and Elmslie, 1917

This lovely little house is among the last in Minneapolis designed by William Purcell and George Elmslie. It was built as a wedding gift for their building foreman. Despite its modest size and budget, the house is by no means ordinary. It features an open-plan first floor organized around a central fireplace and a number of fine details such as custom-designed light fixtures.

3547 27th Ave. South

4 House

3547 27th Ave. South

1906

If you were handing out awards for the cutest cottages in the Twin Cities, this tiny gem, which doesn't look to be more than ten feet wide, would certainly be in the running. The two overscaled front porch windows make the home seem larger than it is.

5 Roosevelt Community Library N *L*

4026 28th Ave. South

Jerome Paul Jackson, 1927 / renovated, 2007

This one-story neighborhood library is vaguely Classical in style and resembles a small brick industrial building of the period.

6 Roosevelt High School

4029 28th Ave. South

Bureau of Buildings (Edward Enger, supervising architect), 1922 / additions, 1950 and later

A Collegiate Gothic–style high school with several additions.

Temple Israel Memorial Park

7 Temple Israel Memorial Park (Montefiore Cemetery) *L*

4153 Third Ave. South

*1876 and later / **chapel and gatehouse,** Septimus J. Bowler, 1894*

The oldest Jewish cemetery in Minneapolis. It dates to 1876, two years before the founding of the city's first synagogue, Temple Israel (originally known as Shaarai Tof). The cemetery's most significant work of architecture is a gatehouse and chapel along Third Ave. Constructed of red brick and Lake Superior sandstone, it features an arched drive-through, a tower topped by a bell-shaped roof, and a pair of horseshoe-arch windows.

POI B Lena O. Smith House N *L*

3905 Fifth Ave. South

1912

A typical Classical Revival house, notable as the home of the Twin Cities' first black female lawyer, Lena O. Smith. After her admission to the bar in 1927, Smith became active in civil rights issues and was a founder of the Minneapolis Urban League. She practiced law in Minneapolis until her death in 1966.

8 Former service station

3800 Third Ave. South

1931

A gas station in the English Cottage style. It's one of a dozen or so such stations from the 1920s and 1930s that survive in south Minneapolis.

9 Hosmer Community Library N L

347 36th St. East

Henry D. Whifield (New York), 1916 / renovated and enlarged, MS&R Architects, 1997 / Art: art-glass window, Michael Pilla, 1997

A Collegiate Gothic–style branch library that once matched up perfectly with the old Central High School. It features polygonal towers flanking the main entrance, a crenellated parapet, and profuse terra-cotta trim. A well-designed rear addition was completed in 1997. The building is named after James K. Hosmer, who headed the Minneapolis Public Library from 1892 to 1904.

Central High School, 1930

LOST 1 *Where Richard R. Green Central Park Community School now stands at Fourth Ave. South and 34th St. East was the site of* **Central High School,** *an impressive Collegiate Gothic–style building constructed in 1913. The red brick building served students until 1982, when it was closed and then demolished.*

3200 Chicago Ave.

10 Commercial building (Modern Cleaners)

3200 Chicago Ave.

ca. 1909 / remodeled, ca. 1940s

An old brick commercial building turned into a giant sign by a dry cleaning outfit in the 1940s. The cleaners are gone, but the sign—

rendered in an orange, lime green, black, and white color scheme that can be called anything except unobtrusive—lives on in all of its Moderne glory.

11 All God's Children Metropolitan Community Church (Fourth Church of Christ Scientist)

3100 Park Ave. South

Clyde Smith, 1929

A brick church that, like several others in the Twin Cities, takes its inspiration from Roman classicism. It was originally built for a Christian Science congregation.

Bennett-McBride House

12 Healy Block Residential Historic District N L

3101–45 Second Ave. South and 3116–24 Third Ave. South

Theron P. Healy (builder), 1886–98

Bennett-McBride House, 3116 Third Ave. South

Theron P. Healy, 1891

This historic district overlooks a high sound barrier bordering Interstate 35W and lacks the cachet a more pleasing location would give it. Nonetheless, its collection of Victorian houses is among the finest in Minneapolis. The houses are the work of Theron P. Healy, who arrived in Minneapolis from Canada in the mid-1880s and began designing, building, and financing houses. All told, Healy built 14 homes on the block bounded by Second and Third Aves. South and 31st and 32nd Sts. East. Another nine on the west side of Second Ave. were razed for the interstate.

The Healy-designed homes here are believed to be the largest group of nineteenth-century houses by the same builder on any block in Minneapolis. Although Healy had no formal architectural training, his houses—almost all in the Queen Anne style—are accomplished designs. They typically offer bays, balconies, and porches along with richly patterned surfaces and no shortage of gingerbread. Among the best is the Bennett-McBride House on Third. Built for a lumberman, the house sports a dazzling variety of turned, sawn, and beaded ornament.

East Lake Street
from Nicollet Avenue to the Mississippi River

This bustling, jangly, and in places less than savory street has been an important thoroughfare since the 1880s. Like Manhattan's east-west streets, Lake runs against the grain of the city, and it probably has more stoplights per mile than any Minneapolis street outside the downtown area.

Lake established itself as a major street after the first Lake Street–Marshall Avenue Bridge was built across the Mississippi River in 1888. The opening of the Marshall-Lake interurban streetcar line in 1906 assured that Lake would see extensive commercial development. Many of the commercial buildings on the street date to the early decades of the twentieth century and are typically no more than two or three stories high.

By the time the trolleys stopped running in 1954, Lake had already become an auto-oriented street, with car dealerships among its most prominent businesses. In 1955, what boosters claimed to be the longest strip of fluorescent street lights in the world gave Lake a new—if visually harsh—appearance. It wasn't long, however, before Lake started to fade despite the fluorescent glow. East Lake in particular began a decline in the 1960s that was to continue for years. When the street's iconic building, the giant Sears, Roebuck Retail and Mail Order Center, closed in 1994, East Lake seemed to have reached a nadir.

In recent years, the street has begun a comeback, fueled in part by new businesses owned by Hispanics, Somalis, and other immigrants. The reopening of the Sears building as an office, shopping, and residential complex in 2005 promises further revitalization. Meanwhile, the street itself is in the process of a $31 million makeover scheduled for completion in 2008.

POI C Shopping center

Lake St. East at Nicollet Ave.

1978

To entice development, the city in 1978 vacated Nicollet Ave. between 29th St. East and Lake to make way for a shopping center. One of Lake's vital intersections was thereby destroyed. Not surprisingly, the city has had second thoughts about this dunderheaded scheme. So far, however, proposals to remove the shopping center and reestablish the intersection haven't panned out.

13 North Star Mini-Storage (Boyd Transfer and Storage Warehouse)

400–410 Lake St. East

Long and Long (Lowell Lamoreaux), 1902 / later additions

A seven-story brick warehouse that stands out on this portion of Lake. It has varying floor heights and what appears to be a nine-story addition to the rear. The building's widely spaced windows are arranged symmetrically and rise above a base with mild Classical Revival detailing.

Midtown Exchange, 1945

14 Midtown Exchange (Sears, Roebuck Retail and Mail Order Center) ! N *L*

900–930 Lake St. East

*Nimmons Carr and Wright (Chicago), 1928 / additions, 1929, 1964 (demolished), 1979 / renovated, Collaborative Design Group and others, 2005 / **Allina Commons** (offices), Perkins+Will / **Chicago Lofts** (housing), ESG Architects / **townhomes,** Urban-Works Architecture / **Sheraton Hotel,** ESG Architects / **Global Marketplace** (shops), Shea Architects*

Lake Street's dominant work of architecture, a 1.2-million-square-foot behemoth that was once one of nine regional catalog centers operated by Sears. Forty homes were razed to make way for the $5 million building, which took less than a year to construct and required no public subsidies. The building is clad in brick but has a concrete-frame skeleton suitable for heavy loads. Its general style is art deco, evident in the stepped-back massing, faceted wall planes, and carved ornament around the tower entrance. Consisting mostly of loft-style warehouse space for Sears's catalog operation, the building included a large retail store along Lake.

After Sears left in 1994, the building remained vacant for a decade amid fears it would meet the same fate as Montgomery Ward's old St. Paul catalog center, razed in 1995. Instead, the Sears building was finally trans-

formed in 2005 into a multi-use complex known as Midtown Exchange. A team of architects and builders led by the Collaborative Design Group did a first-class job of restoring and renovating the building in what was the largest project of its kind in the city's history. The building includes corporate offices for Allina Health Systems, more than 300 apartments and condominiums (among them a penthouse atop the tower), and a marketplace geared for small ethnic businesses. A parking ramp wrapped by townhomes, a Sheraton Hotel, and a new transit station were also built as part of the project.

In the Heart of the Beast Puppet and Mask Theatre

15 In the Heart of the Beast Puppet and Mask (Avalon) Theatre i

1500 Lake St. East

Ekman Holm and Co., 1924 / remodeled and enlarged, Perry Crosier, 1937 / renovated, Vincent James Associates, 1997

As it appears today, this Moderne-style theater—notable for its striated walls of Mankato-Kasota stone, glass-block window, and jazzy corner marquee—dates to 1937. The building was not entirely new, however. A theater built in 1924 occupied part of the site, and Crosier expanded that building and wrapped it with a new facade to create the Avalon. The Avalon served a dreary stint as a porno house before Heart of the Beast came to the rescue in 1988. The theater has been remodeled to accommodate stage performances.

16 Coliseum Building

2700 Lake St. East

1917 / renovated, Sjoquist Architects, 2002

A dignified, crisply ornamented brick commercial building that was long home to Freeman's Department Store, which closed in 1975 after nearly 60 years in business on the ground floor.

17 Northern Sun Merchandising (East Lake Branch Library) N *L*

2916 Lake St. East

Jerome Paul Jackson, 1924

A former branch library with a hint of Tudor Revival styling.

LOST 2 *In 1905, as the Selby Ave.– Lake St. streetcar line neared completion,* **Wonderland Amusement Park** *opened on a 20-acre site on the south side of Lake between 31st and 33rd Aves. South. Perhaps the park's most popular attraction was its so-called infantorium, a small hospital where visitors could observe premature babies in incubators, then a novelty. Wonderland Park never proved to be a great hit with the public, closing in 1911. Today, all traces of the park are gone except for the infantorium, which was converted into an apartment building that still stands at 3101 31st Ave. South.*

18 Victory Christian Center (El Lago Theater)

3500 Lake St. East

Ekman Holm and Co., 1927

A brick, stone, terra-cotta, and tile fantasy from the 1920s, ren-

dered in an exotic mix of Baroque Classicism and Moorish Revival. The theater has been a church since the 1970s.

19 Lake Street–Marshall Avenue Bridge

Across Mississippi River

Howard Needles Tammen and Bergendorf (engineers), 1992

The newest of the concrete-arch spans that cross the Mississippi in the Twin Cities, and probably the last, since other types of bridges are now more economical to build.

LOST 3 *The* **First Lake Street– Marshall Avenue Bridge** *was also an arched span but was constructed of wrought iron. It was completed in 1888 and later enlarged for streetcar traffic. The bridge was pronounced a "foolish extravagance" by the Minneapolis Tribune, whose editors perhaps feared it would only encourage people to visit St. Paul. A spindly span that looked as though it might have come out of a kit, the bridge stood for a century before being razed.*

20 Minneapolis Rowing Club Boathouse

Off West River Pkwy. beneath Lake Street–Marshall Avenue Bridge

Vincent James Associates, 2001

A wood- and copper-clad building that sports a hyperbolic paraboloid roof—a shape inspired by the movement of an oar through water.

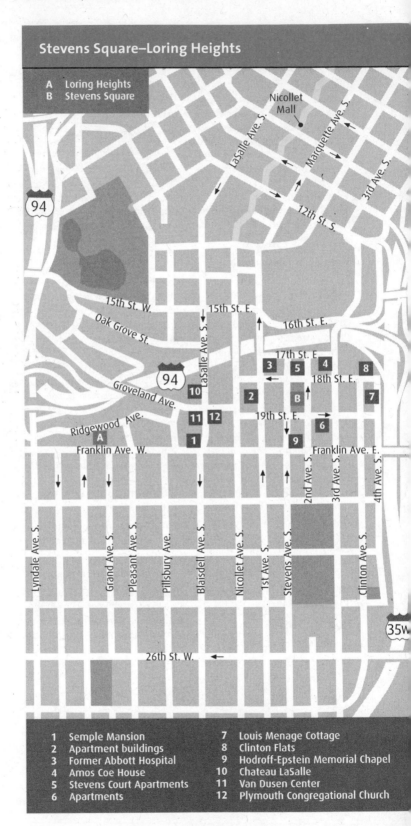

Stevens Square–Loring Heights

A   Loring Heights
B   Stevens Square

Nicollet Mall

LaSalle Ave. S.
Marquette Ave. S.
3rd Ave. S.

12th St. S.

15th St. W.
15th St. E.
Oak Grove St.
16th St. E.
17th St. E.
LaSalle Ave. S.
3   **5**   **4**   **8**
Groveland Ave.
10   18th St. E.
2   **B**   **7**
11   **12**   19th St. E.
Ridgewood Ave.   **6**
A   **1**   **9**
Franklin Ave. W.   Franklin Ave. E.

Lyndale Ave. S.
Grand Ave. S.
Pleasant Ave. S.
Pillsbury Ave.
Blaisdell Ave. S.
Nicollet Ave. S.
1st Ave. S.
Stevens Ave. S.
2nd Ave. S.
3rd Ave. S.
4th Ave. S.
Clinton Ave. S.

35W

26th St. W.

1	Semple Mansion	**7**	Louis Menage Cottage
2	Apartment buildings	**8**	Clinton Flats
3	Former Abbott Hospital	**9**	Hodroff-Epstein Memorial Chapel
4	Amos Coe House	**10**	Chateau LaSalle
5	Stevens Court Apartments	**11**	Van Dusen Center
6	Apartments	**12**	Plymouth Congregational Church

Stevens Square–Loring Heights

The northern part of this neighborhood—the hilly area around Ridgewood and Groveland avenues known as Loring Heights—began filling in with homes in the 1880s. It remains a prime residential district today, even though it was rudely bisected by Interstate 94 in the 1960s. Many of the old houses here have been replaced by apartments and condominiums, but two superb mansions—the Newell and Van Dusen (1888, 1893) houses—still stand along LaSalle Avenue.

Just south of Loring Heights is Stevens Square, and its history is a different story. Most of the land here was once owned by Richard Mendenhall, a New England–born Quaker who reached Minneapolis in 1856, and by his brother-in-law, Nathan Hill. The men seem to have felt no urgent need to develop their holdings, even though the area had been platted in the 1850s. Mendenhall, whose interests included banking and horticulture, apparently liked the idea of owning a piece of country in the city; for many years he maintained a greenhouse on his land.

After Mendenhall's death in 1906, however, everything changed. His heirs—and Hill's as well—quickly cashed in on their valuable property. They first persuaded the Minneapolis Park Board to establish a park—now Stevens Square—in the center of the area, then turned the real estate men loose to create a high-density, apartment-house environment of a kind the Twin Cities had never seen before.

Although the interstate now severs Stevens Square from its historic connection to downtown, the neighborhood has come down through the years virtually intact. Its sturdy stock of apartments still lines nicely landscaped streets, and many of the buildings have been renovated. In recent years, a handful of new condominium complexes have been wedged into available sites, but with their lightweight construction they seem as insubstantial as a passing breeze compared to the weighty brick buildings of old that still define this neighborhood.

POI A Loring Heights

The area along Ridgewood Ave. was platted in 1881 as part of Loring Heights and is located on the south side of the glacial ridge also known as Lowry Hill. Most of Ridgewood was once lined with large houses, although apartment buildings also appeared early on. By the 1960s, when Interstate 94 was built directly to the north, apartment buildings replaced many of the older houses along the avenue. More recently, new condominiums have also sprung up here.

1 Semple Mansion (Ann and Frank Semple House) N

100–104 Franklin Ave. West

Long and Long, 1901

Located on the same block as the Newell and Van Dusen houses, this Beaux-Arts mansion demonstrates how architectural style

Semple Mansion, 1954

shifted around 1900 toward Renaissance classicism and away from Victorian picturesqueness. The main facade on Franklin features a balustraded entry porch with Ionic columns, a lavishly detailed Palladian window, and a rounded bay. Within, the reception hall has mahogany paneling, a hardwood floor inlaid with marble, and a frescoed ceiling. There's also a 1,000-square-foot living room and, for the cotillion crowd, a ballroom.

The first owner, Frank Semple, was a partner in Janney, Semple and Co., a large wholesale hardware firm. The house remained a private residence until 1935, after which there were a series of owners, including the Franklin National Bank. In 2005 new owners began restoring the mansion, which is now used for special events and also contains office space. Another Beaux-Arts mansion, the **John DeLaittre House** (ca. 1900–ca. 1960), once stood next door on the site now occupied by the Minnesota Church Center.

Stevens Square Historic District N *L*

Along First, Stevens, Second, and Third Aves. South between 17th St. East and Franklin Ave.

various architects, 1912 and later

This nationally and locally designated historic district encompasses all or part of ten blocks surrounding Stevens Square Park. Aside from the old Abbott Hospital complex and a few houses, the significant buildings here are apartments, and they follow a standard pattern. Built of brick, most are three and a half stories high, with 12 to 24 units. They usually offer a decorated front in one style or another, Renaissance Revival being perhaps the most popular.

2 Apartment buildings N *L*

1812, 1820 First Ave. South

Alexander Rose, 1924

Two of most ornate buildings in the district, their facades done up in a Mediterranean-Moorish Revival blend.

3 Former Abbott Hospital N *L*

1711–25 First Ave. South

William Channing Whitney, 1910 / additions, 1919 (Janney Building) and later

Abbott Hospital for Women was founded in 1902 by Dr. Amos Abbott, a gynecologist. Among his patients was Kate Dunwoody, whose millionaire husband, William, paid for this Classical Revival–style building. Abbott merged with Northwestern Hospital in 1970, and these buildings are now vacant.

4 Amos Coe House N *L*

1700 Third Ave. South

1884 / carriage house, 1887

This pleasing brick house, mainly Eastlake in style, was built for a Minneapolis real estate dealer. It's now subdivided into three apartments.

POI B Stevens Square N *L*

Stevens Ave. and 18th St. East

Minneapolis Park Board, 1904 and later

This pleasant green square was designed to attract development to this area, and it proved to be a success. It was named after Minneapolis pioneer John Stevens in 1908.

Stevens Court Apartments

5 Stevens Court Apartments N *L*

128–32 18th St. East

W. P. Holtgren (builder), 1912

A U-shaped, 41-unit building that was the first to overlook Stevens Square. Its Renaissance Revival styling set the tone for many buildings that followed.

6 Apartments N *L*

209 19th St. East

Charles A. Anderson (builder), 1917 / renovated, Close Associates (Gar Hargens), ca. 1980s

An old apartment building given an ingenious new plan in the 1980s when the apartments were reconfigured into two-level units oriented crossways rather than lengthwise along a central corridor. One level of each apartment extends the full width of the building while the other is shorter.

This interlocking arrangement follows a scheme first used by the architect Le Corbusier at his Unite d'Habitation, an apartment complex in Marseilles built just after World War II.

Louis Menage Cottage

7 Louis Menage Cottage *L*

1808–10 Fourth Ave. South

1878 / renovated, ca. 1984

A rare Gothic Revival "cottage." Its steep gables, pointed arch windows, and board-and-batten siding are hallmarks of the style. The house was built by real estate developer Louis Menage, best known as the man behind the lost Metropolitan Building. Originally at 715 14th St. East, the house was moved here by the city in 1983, then renovated. It now contains two apartments.

8 Clinton Flats

326–36 18th St. East

Carl F. Struck, 1889

This red brick building, trimmed with sandstone quoins around the windows and doors, is one of the few row houses in Stevens Square. Across 18th St. is another row house of similar vintage.

9 Hodroff-Epstein Memorial Chapel (Edwin Hewitt House) **N** *L*

126 Franklin Ave. East

Edwin Hewitt, 1906 / addition, ca. 1930s

Architect Edwin Hewitt was adept at working in a variety of styles, as this house—designed for himself and his family—demonstrates. Here, he blended Arts and Crafts with Tudor Revival elements to produce a very inviting home. The first story is clad in two-toned, striated brickwork of the sort Frank

Hodroff-Epstein Memorial Chapel, 1974

Lloyd Wright used for his early Prairie Style houses. The upper stories are stucco with wood trim. Note the carved dragons stationed at the ends of brackets protruding from the front gables. Interior features include glazed tile floors as well as tiled mantels designed by Hewitt himself. The house has been used since the 1930s as a funeral home.

Chateau LaSalle

10 Chateau LaSalle (McKnight-Newell House) **N** *L*

1818 LaSalle Ave.

Charles S. Sedgwick, 1888

A Romanesque Revival hunk and one of the grand houses of the city. The exterior of rusticated Lake Superior sandstone includes a terrace, an entrance porch formed by a flattened Syrian arch, carved ornamental panels, and a crested dormer atop the roof's peak. It's all quite imposing, although some features, such as a Flemish-inspired front gable, are more picturesque than those you'd find in the work of the Romanesque Revival style's founding father, H. H. Richardson.

Inside, the house is a lush Victorian extravaganza with oak and sycamore woodwork, light fixtures designed by Tiffany Studios, and even an allegorical figure or two loitering amid gold-leaf scrollwork. Although the house was built for lumber and real estate tycoon Summer T. Mc-Knight, he sold it almost immediately to George Newell, founder of the food wholesaling firm that became SuperValu. The house now contains six apartments and three offices.

Van Dusen Center, 1894

11 Van Dusen Center (George and Nancy Van Dusen House) ! N *L*

1900 LaSalle Ave.

Orff and Joralemon, 1893 / addition, 1961 / renovated and restored, Bob Poehling, David Sabaka, and others, 1997

The most romantic pile in Minneapolis, a rough-cut Chateauesque fantasy in pink stone teeming with towers, pinnacles, tourelles, parapets, gables, and dormers, not to mention seven chimneys. Built for a grain merchant and his family, the house has walls of Sioux quartzite, an ultra-hard stone from southwestern Minnesota. Because this stone was so difficult to work, the house has little carving, and some pinnacles are so coarsely finished that they resemble cairns left by some lost tribe of builders. A rear carriage house is as rockbound and romantic as the mansion itself. Within, architect Edgar Joralemon rummaged through historic styles to produce one grand room after another. Oak and maple paneling (some

elaborately carved), marble, mosaic tiling, beveled and stained glass, and parquet floors all contribute to a Victorian aura of deep-toned luxury.

The man who built this unlikely castle, George Van Dusen, hailed from New York State. He invented a system for hoisting grain into elevators and was a wealthy man by the time he settled in Minneapolis in 1887. After Van Dusen died in 1928, descendants remained here until 1937. The house then served for over two decades as a secretarial school, receiving a stucco addition in 1961. By 1994 the mansion was vacant and in danger of demolition. Fortunately, new owners stepped in at the last minute and restored the house, which is now used for meetings, weddings, and other events and also has apartments. In 2006, the owners auctioned off the house on E-Bay for over $3.5 million.

12 Plymouth Congregational Church

1900 Nicollet Ave.

Shepley Rutan and Coolidge (Boston), 1908 / additions, 1940s and later

A Gothic Revival church built of dark St. Cloud granite with limestone trim. Designed by H. H. Richardson's successor firm in Boston, it's modeled on an earlier church in Massachusetts. The spacious sanctuary features an impressive hammer-beam roof. Plymouth was organized in 1857 and occupied three other churches before this one, including a rugged stone building constructed in 1875 at Eighth St. and Nicollet Ave. That property eventually proved so valuable that the church sold it for more than $200,000, which covered virtually the entire cost of this building.

Whittier-Lyndale

Named after John Greenleaf Whittier, a poet much read in his day, this neighborhood is most familiar to visitors as the home of the Minneapolis Institute of Arts and the mansions that cluster around it. The neighborhood began attracting wealth in the 1850s when Dorilus Morrison built an estate where the art institute now stands. It was not until the 1880s, however, that mansion building began in earnest here. The most spectacular of them all was the giant house built for William Washburn (1884) on the site of the park that bears his name. Other chieftains of industry, including members of the Pillsbury family, also found the area to their liking and built homes just to the north of Washburn's mansion.

Today, much of the area around the art institute's campus, which includes the Children's Theatre (1974) as well as the Minneapolis College of Art and Design (1974), is protected within a historic district. Among the district's notable mansions are the Alfred F. Pillsbury House (1903), the Charles S. Pillsbury House (1914), the Edward C. Gale House (1912), and the George H. Christian House (1919), now the Hennepin History Museum. Apartment buildings and smaller homes—not all of them beautifully preserved—mingle amid the mansions, most of which are now used for institutional or commercial purposes. Whittier's complement of buildings also includes such notable churches as St. Stephen's Catholic (1891) and Calvary Baptist (1889). Whittier School (1997) is the neighborhood's outstanding modern building.

The Lyndale neighborhood's housing stock is generally more modest, and somewhat newer, than Whittier's. There are no great mansions in Lyndale, but you will find the superb Charles Backus House (1915), a small Prairie Style beauty designed by Purcell and Elmslie, as well as Purcell's wonderful Redeemer Baptist Church (1910). And just south of Lake Street off Nicollet is the sporting equivalent of sacred ground, for it was here that the Minneapolis Millers played for nearly 60 years at Nicollet Baseball Park (1896, gone).

Washburn–Fair Oaks Historic District

There are actually two overlapping historic districts here. A large city-designated district extends from Franklin Ave. to 26th St. East and from First to Fourth Aves. South, taking in all or part of more than 20 square blocks. A much smaller National Register District encompasses seven mansions along and near 22nd St. East north of Fair Oaks Park.

St. Stephen's Catholic Church

1 Windsor Apartments *L*

2001–11 Third Ave. South

Louis Bersback, 1923

The largest of the neighborhood's historic apartment buildings. Its 109 units are arranged in an H-shaped plan that allows for a courtyard along Third Ave., where there's an entry pavilion.

2 St. Stephen's Catholic Church N *L*

2211 Clinton Ave.

Frederick Corser, 1891 / Art: stained-glass windows (in transepts), Tiffany Studios, 1892

Long known for its social work, St. Stephen's parish was organized in 1884 and built this Romanesque Revival–style

Whittier-Lyndale

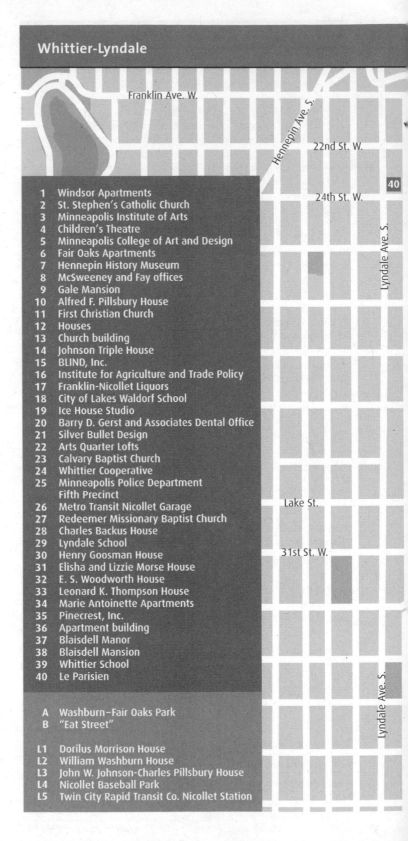

1   Windsor Apartments
2   St. Stephen's Catholic Church
3   Minneapolis Institute of Arts
4   Children's Theatre
5   Minneapolis College of Art and Design
6   Fair Oaks Apartments
7   Hennepin History Museum
8   McSweeney and Fay offices
9   Gale Mansion
10 Alfred F. Pillsbury House
11 First Christian Church
12 Houses
13 Church building
14 Johnson Triple House
15 BLIND, Inc.
16 Institute for Agriculture and Trade Policy
17 Franklin-Nicollet Liquors
18 City of Lakes Waldorf School
19 Ice House Studio
20 Barry D. Gerst and Associates Dental Office
21 Silver Bullet Design
22 Arts Quarter Lofts
23 Calvary Baptist Church
24 Whittier Cooperative
25 Minneapolis Police Department
    Fifth Precinct
26 Metro Transit Nicollet Garage
27 Redeemer Missionary Baptist Church
28 Charles Backus House
29 Lyndale School
30 Henry Goosman House
31 Elisha and Lizzie Morse House
32 E. S. Woodworth House
33 Leonard K. Thompson House
34 Marie Antoinette Apartments
35 Pinecrest, Inc.
36 Apartment building
37 Blaisdell Manor
38 Blaisdell Mansion
39 Whittier School
40 Le Parisien

A   Washburn–Fair Oaks Park
B   "Eat Street"

L1 Dorilus Morrison House
L2 William Washburn House
L3 John W. Johnson-Charles Pillsbury House
L4 Nicollet Baseball Park
L5 Twin City Rapid Transit Co. Nicollet Station

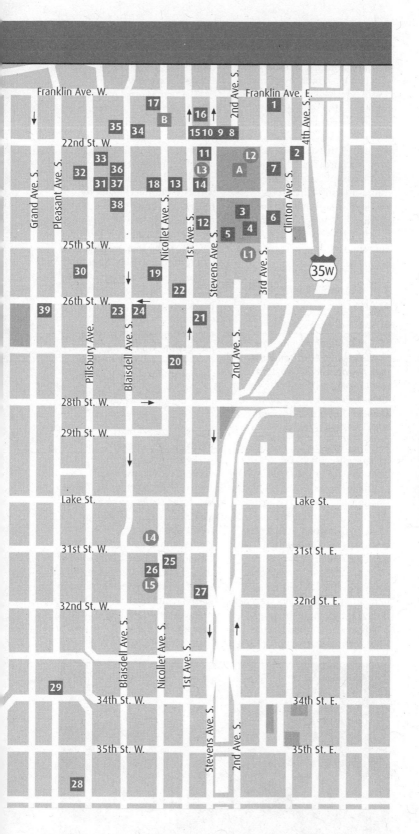

church, its second, seven years later. Constructed largely of rock-faced sandstone, the church is a neighborhood landmark by virtue of its 150-foot-high corner tower, which culminates in a copper-clad spire. The church features a pair of arched entrances beneath a rose window, while high transepts extend out from the north and south sides. Each transept contains three round-arched, stained-glass windows designed by Tiffany Studios of New York. Within, the church has been remodeled but retains its original hammer-beam ceiling.

3 Minneapolis Institute of Arts ! *L*

2400 Third Ave. South

McKim Mead and White, 1915 / addition (Julia Morrison Building), Hewitt and Brown, 1916 / addition, Kenzo Tange with Parker Klein Associates, 1974 / addition, Michael Graves and Associates with RSP Architects, 2006

The origins of the art institute go back to 1883, when some of the city's leading citizens founded the Minneapolis Society of Fine Arts. Under the leadership of architect Edwin Hewitt and flour magnate William Dunwoody, the society began to raise money for a museum and art school after Clinton Morrison agreed to donate his family's old estate here. In 1911, the society staged a design competition for a new building. The winner was the New York firm of McKim, Mead

and White, which had launched a new wave of Classical Revival architecture in the United States with its design for the Boston Public Library in 1887.

The firm's initial proposal called for a series of colonnaded buildings, oriented around courtyards, that would have taken up more than two square blocks. A city plan prepared in 1910 also envisioned a Parisian-style boulevard (never built) linking the museum to downtown. As it turned out, there wasn't enough money for the gigantic building envisioned by McKim, Mead and White, and only about a seventh of their original design was ever completed. Still, what did get built is impressive. Clad in Vermont marble, the historic portion of the museum forms a great white wall along 24th St. At its center is an Ionic entrance portico that has few local peers as a statement of the classical ideal. Within, the lobbies, galleries, and halls offer parquet floors, Botticelli marble, and much elegant detailing.

By the 1970s, the museum was bursting at the seams, and Japanese architect Kenzo Tange was hired to design an addition, as well as a new building for the Minneapolis College of Art and Design and a playhouse for the Children's Theatre Company. For the art institute, Tange created a series of pristine volumes clad in glazed white brick with dark metal accents. He also provided a new entrance along Third Ave. South. Tange's two large wings

Minneapolis Institute of Arts, 1920

grip the original museum like giant brick pincers, and they've been criticized for overwhelming McKim, Mead and White's work. Even so, Tange's addition is essentially classical in spirit, and it's worn well. That said, it's also true that the addition, with its aura of modernist solemnity, generates few architectural sparks.

In 2006, the institute acquired another major addition, designed by postmodern guru Michael Graves. It includes 27 new galleries and a reception hall, among other features, all organized around a three-story-high rotunda. The exterior displays Graves's fondness for abstracted classicism, in the form of walls with inset panels that hold dowel-like columns. It's all Graves being Graves, but given how static and airless the design seems, you have to believe that the institute went in the wrong direction here and that a livelier, more contemporary addition would have worked much better.

LOST 1 *The art institute stands on the site of the* **Dorilus Morrison House.** *Built in 1858 and known as "Villa Rosa," the towered Italianate house was the first home in this neighborhood. Morrison was a Maine-born lumberman who became a businessman in Minneapolis as well as the city's first mayor. The house was razed in 1911.*

4 Children's Theatre

2400 Third Ave. South

Kenzo Tange with Parker Klein Associates, 1974 / addition, Michael Graves and Associates with RSP Architects, 2005

The Children's Theatre Company, established in 1965, has been part of the art institute campus since 1974, when Tange designed a 746-seat theater here. The theater works well enough but isn't a memorable space. Michael Graves's 2005 addition follows the panel-and-dowel theme of his work for the art institute. It includes a 275-seat theater and a drum-shaped rotunda that holds a tower built from century-old

recycled timbers. The tower has no structural function—it's essentially a big sculpture—and it

Children's Theatre

might have been more impressive had it been built *outside* the theater, as a public artwork. Still, Graves's addition brings some welcome pizzazz to the theater. The rotunda and adjoining spaces are slathered in color, and there's also a spiral-like pattern worked into the floor. In a complex of buildings starved for life and color, Graves provides some of both here, and even if adults may find the addition too cutesy, kids appear to love it.

5 Minneapolis College of Art and Design

2501 Stevens Ave.

Kenzo Tange with Parker Klein Associates, 1974 / additions, 1995, 2000

Founded in 1886 as the Minneapolis School for Fine Arts, this college was once located in the Julia Morrison Building, an addition to the art institute completed in 1916. Like the institute itself, the college eventually outgrew its quarters, and in 1974 it moved into this building south of the museum. Connected via skyway to the art institute, the building is of a piece with Tange's work for the museum—impeccably detailed but rather dull. Long a branch of the art institute, the college became an independent institution in 1988 and now enrolls more than 700 students.

6 Fair Oaks Apartments *L*

2415 Third Ave. South

Perry Crosier, 1940

Set amid beautifully landscaped grounds, these buildings form

Whittier-Lyndale

the best example in the Twin Cities of so-called garden apartments. The complex consists of six brick buildings that are in

Fair Oaks Apartments

either a U or a squared-S shape, a layout that leaves room for interlinked courtyards and walkways. Colonial Revival in style, the ivied buildings are simple but elegant, with carefully detailed entrances. The one- and two-bedroom apartments are arranged so that there are no more than six to each exterior entrance, and many of the apartments have both front and back doors.

POI A Washburn–Fair Oaks Park *L*

Third Ave. South and 24th St. East

Minneapolis Park Board, 1924 and later

A simple green square fronted by mansions, a church, and, on its south side, the Minneapolis Institute of Arts. It was once the estate of William Washburn.

William Washburn House, 1886

LOST 2 *The* **William Washburn House ("Fairoaks")** *was among the grandest of all Twin Cities mansions but stood for only 40 years. Trained as a lawyer, Washburn arrived in Minneapolis in 1857, got in on the ground floor of the milling business at St. Anthony Falls, became a very wealthy man, and served in the U.S. House of Representatives and as a U.S. senator. In 1884, he built a huge stone mansion here amid grounds that included a pond and a stream crossed by a rustic bridge. Washburn lived on the estate until his death in 1912. The property then went to the Minneapolis Park Board, which found the mansion too costly to maintain; in 1924, it fell to the wrecker.*

7 Hennepin History Museum (George H. and Leonora Christian House) *L*

2303 Third Ave. South

Hewitt and Brown, 1919 / Art: ironwork, Samuel Yellin, ca. 1919

Home to the Hennepin County Historical Society, this mansion was the last to be built in the neighborhood. It's a straitlaced house that resembles a Collegiate Gothic school building, though it mixes in Renaissance Revival elements such as a balustraded roof. The interior features cypress floors, carved fireplace mantles, and ornamental ironwork by the Philadelphia master Samuel Yellin. The house was built for George H. Christian and designed by the firm of Hewitt and Brown, each of whose partners was married to one of Christian's nieces.

As the manager of the Washburn-Crosby milling complex in the 1860s, Christian played a key role in perfecting the "new process," as it was known, that allowed Minneapolis millers to make pure white flour from hard spring wheat. His efforts made him rich, and he retired in 1875. Nearly 80 years old when he began building this house, Christian did not live to see it completed. However, his daughter-in-law, Carolyn McKnight Christian, lived here until the 1950s.

8 McSweeney and Fay offices (Eugene Merrill House) N *L*

2116 Second Ave. South

William Channing Whitney, 1884

The oldest mansion on the park, built of rusticated red sandstone and dominated by a polygonal tower. Its style falls in the broad territory of Chateauesque. The house was built for John S. Bradstreet, who for many years was Minneapolis's decorator for the well-to-do. For reasons unknown, Bradstreet never occupied the house, and in 1887 it was acquired by a lawyer and banker named Eugene Merrill.

Gale Mansion, 1974

9 Gale Mansion (American Association of University Women's Clubhouse, originally Edward C. Gale House) N L

2115 Stevens Ave. South

Ernest Kennedy, 1912 / addition, 1962

Beaux-Arts mansions can easily seem overbearing (witness the nearby Semple House), but that's not the case here. This elegant, subtly asymmetrical Renaissance Revival house keeps everything at a human scale. The wrought-iron balconies, the intimate colonnade and veranda along 22nd St. East, and the ornament all convey a sense of quiet graciousness, as do the rooms within. Edward Gale was the son of pioneer Minneapolis real estate dealer Samuel Gale, while his wife Sara (known as Sadie) was the only daughter of John S. Pillsbury of milling renown. The Gales lived here until they died, both in 1943. The American Association of University Women now uses the mansion as a clubhouse and also for a variety of special events.

10 Alfred F. Pillsbury House N L

116 22nd St. East

Ernest Kennedy, 1903

One of many Pillsbury houses in this neighborhood. Tudor Revival in style and executed in rock-faced local limestone, it has a

dense, craggy presence that still impresses today. Alfred F. Pillsbury was the only son of John S. Pillsbury, a founder of the family

Alfred F. Pillsbury House, 1910

flour milling empire. Alfred Pillsbury was more interested in art than business, and over his long life he amassed a collection of Chinese jades that are now on display at the Minneapolis Institute of Arts.

11 First Christian Church L

2201 First Ave. South

Thorshov and Cerny, 1954 / addition, Cerny Associates, 1964

A modernist brick church modeled on Eliel Saarinen's Christ Lutheran Church (1949) in the Longfellow neighborhood. Like Saarinen's masterpiece, this church has a long brick nave with seating that extends into the low-roofed side aisles, a canted ceiling, and a side-lighted sanctuary. However, the tower here is at the rear, whereas Christ Lutheran's tower is at the front.

LOST 3 *This site was once occupied by the* **John W. Johnson–Charles Pillsbury House,** *a twin-gabled stone mansion built in 1883 and razed in 1937. The house was built for John W. Johnson, who soon sold it to Charles A. Pillsbury. After Pillsbury died in 1899, his twin sons (John S. and Charles S. Pillsbury) supposedly flipped a coin for the property. John won, and Charles later built a mansion of his own just across 22nd St. East.*

12 Houses L

2400–2600 Stevens Ave.

1880s and later

Here, across from the Minneapolis Institute of Arts, you'll find a group of restored Victorian houses. Three of the prettiest, Eastlake–Queen Anne in style and dating to the 1880s, are at 2416, 2418, and 2536 Stevens. The house at 2404 Stevens was designed by architect Edward Stebbins in 1879 as his own home and was moved from the Loring Park area in 1982.

13 Church building (Christian Science Church) *L*

4–10 24th St. East

Solon Beman (Chicago), 1914

A Beaux-Arts church, quite plain except for a pedimented Ionic entrance porch. It was built for a Christian Science congregation and conveys a sense of clarity and rationalism. The church is one of only two buildings in the Twin Cities designed by Chicago architect Solon Beman.

Johnson Triple House

14 Johnson Triple House *L*

106–8 24th St. East and 2319 First Ave. South

Harry Jones, 1890

This Romanesque-Gothic brick and sandstone triple house displays Harry Jones at the top of his game, dishing out one delightful detail after another. Check out the three tiny lancet windows above the entrance to 108 24th St. East, the marvelous witch's-hat roof (a Jones specialty) that caps the corner tower, and the exquisite stonework of the front porches.

15 BLIND, Inc. (Charles S. Pillsbury House) *N L*

100 22nd St. East

Hewitt and Brown, 1914

Another miller's mansion, built for a son of one of the Pillsbury

Co.'s founders, Charles A. Pillsbury. The Tudor Revival–style house features a polygonal conservatory, bas-relief carvings, and a pair of stone lions who guard the entrance gate. Its sumptuous interiors were the work of antiques dealer Charles Duveen, known as "Charles of London," his talents apparently being so extraordinary that no one could mistake him for any other Charles in the English capital. Duveen filled the house with old-world treasures—leaded glass, fireplace mantles, oak paneling, and furniture—all extracted from historic English castles, churches, and guildhalls. Charles S. Pillsbury lived here until his death in 1939. The house has been owned since 1993 by an organization that provides training programs for the blind.

16 Institute for Agriculture and Trade Policy (Caroline Crosby House) *N L*

2105 First Ave. South

William Channing Whitney, 1906

A brick Georgian Revival house designed by Minneapolis's premier society architect of the early twentieth century. Caroline Crosby was the daughter of John Crosby, cofounder of the Washburn-Crosby milling colossus, and devoted much of her life to charitable work.

POI B "Eat Street" (Nicollet Avenue)

A 17-block stretch of Nicollet Ave. from the edge of downtown to 29th St. East has been formally designated by the city as "Eat Street" because of its mix of restaurants. More than 50 in all, they offer a range of cuisines as well as an architectural goulash that's American to the core.

17 Franklin-Nicollet Liquors

2012 Nicollet Ave.

1962

This garish liquor emporium from the 1960s presents plenty of visual evidence that good taste, thank heaven, was the last thing on the mind of the architect (if indeed there was one).

18 City of Lakes Waldorf School (Hardware Mutual Insurance Co. Building)

2344 Nicollet Ave. South

Magney and Tusler, 1923

A well-detailed Renaissance Revival–style building that originally served as the offices of a company founded in Minneapolis in 1900 to provide fire insurance for hardware dealers.

19 Ice House Studio (Cedar Lake Ice and Fuel Co.)

2540 Nicollet Ave. (along alley)

ca. 1900

A massive, windowless brick box that was used to store blocks of ice in the days before every home had a refrigerator. It's now a sound studio.

20 Barry D. Gerst and Associates Dental Office

2701 Nicollet Ave.

1948

You could write a book on dental offices of the post–World War II era (whether anyone would read it is another matter). Dentists of the time sought a modern look, and brick offices like this one sprang up all across the Twin Cities. Many are still performing their drill-and-fill duties.

Silver Bullet Design

21 Silver Bullet Design (Despatch Laundry Building) *L*

2611 First Ave. South

Louis B. Bershack, 1929 / renovated, 1981

Laundry with an Islamic twist. This enchanting storefront—which includes pointed arches, decorative mosaic tiles, and a half dome attached to the front parapet—is perhaps the city's most exotic small commercial building. It was designed as a come-hither storefront for the Despatch Laundry Co. The company's plant here also included a building to the north along 26th St. East.

22 Arts Quarter Lofts

10 26th St. East

2006

Clad in brick and metal, this building features apartments with interlocking two-level floor plans.

Calvary Baptist Church, 1953

23 Calvary Baptist Church

2608 Blaisdell Ave.

Warren H. Hayes, 1889 / addition (sanctuary), Harry Jones, 1902 / addition (parish house), Harry Jones, 1928

One of Whittier's landmark churches. The oldest portion, by architect Warren Hayes, is a Romanesque Revival–style chapel dating to 1889. Now a fellowship hall, it forms the northwest portion of the church along 28th St. West. Hayes also envisioned an addition to the east, facing Blaisdell, that would provide a 1,200-seat sanctuary. This addition, however, wasn't built until 1902, three years after Hayes's death. Harry Jones, a Calvary member, oversaw construction of this part of the church, which includes a chunky tower. The auditorium itself has a domed ceiling and the usual radial seating. Jones also designed a connecting parish house in 1928.

24 Whittier Cooperative (Whittier School)

2609 Blaisdell Ave.

Walter S. Pardee, 1883 / 1888 / additions, 1903, 1910, 1923 / renovated, ca. 1980

The oldest public school building in Minneapolis. It opened in 1883 and has multiple additions in a mix of styles, all done in yellow brick. It was converted to cooperative apartments in the 1980s.

LOST 4 *A plaque in front of the Wells Fargo Bank at 3030 Nicollet Ave. marks the site of* **Nicollet Baseball Park.** *Built in 1896 for the minor league Minneapolis Millers and upgraded in 1913, the park had only 8,500 seats, although 15,000 fans could jam in for big games. The park was known for its short right-field fence, only 280 feet from home plate. Following the 1955 season, the park was torn down, and the Millers moved to Metropolitan Stadium (also gone) in Bloomington.*

25 Minneapolis Police Department Fifth Precinct

3101 Nicollet Ave. South

Julie Snow Architects, 1998

An elegant police station that manages to convey notions of transparency and security at the same time. As with Snow's other buildings, what you admire is not only the clarity of the basic forms but also the quality of the detailing, achieved here with largely off-the-shelf materials.

26 Metro Transit Nicollet Garage

10 32nd St. West (also 3106 Nicollet Ave.)

HGA, 1990

A large concrete-block bus garage that sports ridiculous fake gables on one side.

LOST 5 *The* **Twin City Rapid Transit Co. Nicollet Station,** *built in 1912 to store and service streetcars, once stood here. Most of the station's buildings were razed in 1954.*

Redeemer Missionary Baptist Church, 1973

27 Redeemer Missionary Baptist (Stewart Memorial Presbyterian) Church ! N *L*

116 32nd St. East

Purcell and Feick, 1910 / addition, 1915 / renovated and restored, MacDonald and Mack Architects, 2000

A superb Prairie Style church— one of only a handful of its kind in the country. With its flat roof, broad eaves, lack of a bell tower, and disregard of traditional stylistic cues, the church must have seemed shockingly unorthodox when it opened in 1910. Its basic form was inspired by the mother of all Prairie churches: Frank Lloyd Wright's Unity Temple (1906) in Oak Park, IL.

William Purcell designed the church just before he went into partnership with George Elmslie and while engineer George Feick was still part of the firm. Faced in brick and stucco, the original portion of the church is organ-

Redeemer Missionary Baptist Church interior, 1973

ized around a cubic auditorium lighted by a wall of east-facing, green-tinted windows. A narrower section with a deep balcony extends to the south. The auditorium has a modest decorative program that consists largely of wood strips that form geometric patterns. Purcell also planned a Sunday school wing to the west of the auditorium. However, another firm was hired to design the classroom addition, completed in 1915.

Stewart Presbyterian Church, named after the Reverend David Stewart, was an offshoot of First Presbyterian Church in Minneapolis. Redeemer Missionary Baptist Church bought the property, which had become run-down, in 1988. The church then raised over $2 million for a restoration and renovation expertly supervised by MacDonald and Mack Architects.

Charles Backus House

28 Charles Backus House ! *L*

212 36th St. West

Purcell and Elmslie, 1915

The American Foursquare as high art. It was built for piano tuner Charles Backus, whose work took him one day to William Purcell's own house (1913) near Lake of the Isles. Backus was enchanted by what he saw and asked Purcell to design a house for him. There was just one catch: it had to cost no more than $3,000—average for a house at the time. Backus got his wish. At a final cost of $2,992, Purcell and his partner George Elmslie designed a stucco box that sports such Prairie Style features as bands of casement windows, a trellised entryway, carefully applied wood trim, and the usual wide eaves. Inside, Purcell and Elmslie performed wonders, creating a dynamic open plan that makes the house seem much larger than it is. They also designed built-in shelving and benches as well as a special place for Backus's piano near the front door.

29 Lyndale School

312 34th St. West

1972

A two-story, nearly circular red brick school with concrete window hoods that resemble starched white bonnets. Like so much from the 1970s, the school can best be described as weird.

30 Henry Goosman House

2532 Pillsbury Ave.

Purcell and Feick, 1909

One of Purcell's earliest Minneapolis houses, a bungalow with hints of the Prairie Style in the deep overhanging eaves and the diamond-shaped window tucked under the front gable.

Elisha and Lizzie Morse House

31 Elisha and Lizzie Morse House N *L*

2325–27 Pillsbury Ave.

1874 / renovated and restored, Roark Kramer Roscoe Design, 1993

Known as the "cupola house," this delightful example of the Italian Villa style was restored after being moved in 1991 from its original site at 2402 Fourth Ave. South. Clad in clapboard siding that imitates cut stone, the house is most notable for its cupola, which features shallow arches that hover over paired windows. The porches are later additions. Now condominiums, the house was built for grocer Elisha Morse, Jr., and his family as a country home.

32 E. S. Woodworth House

2222 Pillsbury Ave.

William S. Kenyon, 1906

A home inspired by the work of Chicago architect George Maher, who around 1900 grafted Prairie elements to the Renaissance Revival style to produce a distinctive housing type.

33 Leonard K. Thompson House

2215 Pillsbury Ave.

Harry Jones, 1903 / remodeled, Harry Jones, ca. 1915

A vivid Colonial Revival house. With its front-facing pedimented gable and two-story Ionic pilasters, the house also evokes the earlier Greek Revival style, albeit on a much enlarged scale.

34 Marie Antoinette Apartments

26–30 22nd St. West

Carleton W. Farnham, 1939

A charming Moderne apartment building with black vitrolite glass around the entrances.

35 Pinecrest, Inc. (John P. and Nelle Snyder House)

2118 Blaisdell Ave.

Ernest Kennedy, 1913 / addition, ca. 1960s

Many large houses line Blaisdell Ave., named after a pioneer farm family. This brick and stone Renaissance Revival mansion was built for John Pillsbury Snyder and his wife, Nelle, who were most fortunate souls. A year earlier, as newlyweds, the wealthy young couple had been aboard the *Titanic* when it sank on April 14, 1912. Both were eventually rescued from Lifeboat No. 7.

36 Apartment building

2312 Blaisdell Ave.

1963

An apartment building jazzed up with decorative brickwork in an interlaced hexagonal pattern.

37 Blaisdell Manor (Bovey House)

2322 Blaisdell Ave.

Ernest Kennedy, 1915

This Georgian Revival house is among several in the neighborhood built by descendants of lumberman Charles Bovey, who also platted a northern Minnesota town bearing his name. The house was once owned by the inventors of Lavoris mouthwash, an early product designed to combat the horror of halitosis. These days, the house is used for weddings and other events.

38 Blaisdell Mansion (Matthew McDonald House)

2400 Blaisdell Ave.

1903

A sumptuous Beaux-Arts house, now used for offices. Built of brick, it has a wealth of terracotta trim—at the entrance, around windows, along the roof, and atop boldly scaled dormers.

Whittier School

39 Whittier School !

315 26th St. West

Kodet Architectural Group, 1997

The finest public school building of its time in the Twin Cities. Long and high, the building calls to mind a ship that's somehow beached itself on the plains of south Minneapolis. Built largely of reddish orange brick, the school has a Scandinavian feel, and the ghosts of Alvar Aalto and Eliel Saarinen, two great Finnish modernists, lurk in the architectural shadows. Part of what makes the design exceptional is that the building manages to be both monumental and inviting. The monumentality comes from its powerful massing, which sends a message that education is important. Other features—the school's asymmetrical pitched roof, chimneylike stair towers, and patterned brickwork—make it welcoming to children. Parking is neatly tucked under the building. Inside, most classrooms are placed along a central hallway in traditional fashion.

40 Le Parisien

2301 Lyndale Ave. South

Miller Hanson Partners, 2007

French fakery featuring 13 steep-roofed apartments with outside access to all units, a courtyard, and shops on the ground floor. Although it's supposedly modeled on apartments in Paris, the real inspiration here is the Storybook Style of the 1920s, which came from California.

6 Southwest

Overview

Lake Harriet—named after the wife of Colonel Henry Leavenworth, first commandant of Fort Snelling—lies at the heart of this neighborhood, which also takes in the southern shores of Lake Calhoun. The area around these two large lakes and others to the north forms the city's premier residential district, a magical meeting of land and water that endows Minneapolis with its unique urban identity. The architectural environment to the east of Lake Harriet is especially rich and includes an outstanding collection of Prairie Style houses by the Minneapolis firm of Purcell and Elmslie.

Settlement here began well before the city itself was founded. In 1829, Indian agent Lawrence Taliaferro established a village at the southeast corner of Lake Calhoun on the present site of Lakewood Cemetery. Originally known as Cloud Man's Village after the local Dakota chief, it was later renamed Eatonville in honor of a U.S. secretary of war. Missionary brothers Samuel and Gideon Pond were also early arrivals, building a cabin near Lake Calhoun in 1834. A year later, Reverend Jedediah Stevens established a mission at Lake Harriet. These tiny settlements, all located on the Fort Snelling military reservation, soon vanished, largely because of continuing warfare between the Dakota and the Ojibwe.

Even after the military land was opened for settlement in 1855, it took a while for development around the lakes to begin in earnest. The man who more than any other led the way was Colonel (a self-imposed title) William King. A newspaperman, a land speculator, a visionary, and, judging by his financial adventures, something of a slick operator, King began buying up huge chunks of land around Lake Harriet and Lake Calhoun in 1870. He also helped found Lakewood Cemetery in 1871.

Within the span of a few years, King established the expansive Lyndale Farms, at what is today 38th Street and Bryant Avenue South, built a grand pavilion on the east side of Lake Calhoun, and promptly went bankrupt, though he later reclaimed much of his fortune. He also donated Lake Harriet and surrounding land to the Minneapolis Park Board in 1885, his most extraordinary legacy. Kings Highway, a portion of Dupont Avenue South, is named after him.

As always in the Twin Cities in the nineteenth century, it was public transit that ultimately drove development here. A rail line connected Lake Calhoun to downtown as early as 1879. It was soon replaced by streetcars, which reached the western side of Lake Harriet in 1891 and also extended south along Hennepin and Bryant avenues.

Southwest remains among the city's most desirable places to live, a situation that is unlikely to change judging by the number of costly new homes that in recent years seem to have filled in every available lot, no matter how compact. Because the neighborhood is so heavily residential, it has few large architectural monuments. There is, however, no shortage of fine homes and churches, most dating from the first three decades of the twentieth century.

Among the neighborhood's architectural gems are Harry Jones's Byzantine-inspired chapel (1910) at Lakewood Cemetery; Church of the Incarnation (1918), designed by Emmanuel Masqueray; the Charles and Grace Parker House (1913), one of Purcell and Elmslie's best designs; the Kirby Snyder House (1915), an odd Prairie-Classical amalgam; the Washburn Park Water Tower (1932); the Museum of Russian Art (formerly a church), a Spanish fantasy from 1936; and the Lake Harriet Band Shell (1986), perhaps the most beloved work of postmodern architecture in the Twin Cities.

Around Lake Harriet

Living by one of Minneapolis's lakes wasn't always considered desirable, which seems hard to believe given the premium now placed on lakeshore property. In their natural state, however, the lakes had marshy shorelines that were prime breeding grounds for mosquitoes and other pests. Before 1880, only a few homes, most qualifying as country estates, were built around the lakes.

All of that began to change once the Minneapolis Park Board dredged the lakes, filled in much of the marshland, and constructed parkways. Harriet was not as heavily dredged as some of the other lakes, however, and much of the work was along the northern shore, where a marsh was turned into Lyndale Park. By 1886 the park board had built a dirt road around Harriet, making it the first city lake to be ringed by a parkway. Despite this improvement, residential development was retarded by the lake's relative distance from early streetcar lines. This was especially true of the eastern and southern shores, and it wasn't until automobiles arrived in the early twentieth century that houses started to appear all around Harriet.

Although some new mansions have sprung up in recent years, most of the big houses that circle the lake date from about 1910 to 1935—the great age of Period Revival architecture. Tudor, Norman, Colonial, and Classical are among the revived styles on display. Most of these houses were designed by local architects, and while there are no masterpieces among them, they display the fine craftsmanship and lively pictorial imagination typical of Period Revival design.

POI A Lake Harriet parks and parkways

Minneapolis Park Board, 1880s and later

At 344 acres, Harriet is the second largest of the city's lakes. Insulated by Lyndale Park and Lakewood Cemetery on its north side, Harriet has wooded, steeply banked shores that give it a more "natural" feel than nearby Lake Calhoun. It was known to the Dakota people as *Mde Unma*, or simply "the other lake," a reference to its relationship to Lake Calhoun. Like most Minneapolis lakes, it occupies an old channel of the Mississippi River.

The lake remained largely undeveloped until the 1880s. Among those attracted to its wild beauty was Henry David Thoreau, who visited the area in 1861, a year before his death. In 1880, the Minneapolis, Lyndale and Lake Calhoun Railway (known as the Motor Line) reached the lake's west shore. The railway built a pavilion to attract visitors but never made a profit and abandoned its line in 1886. Five years later, the Twin City Rapid Transit Co. began streetcar serv-ice to the lake along the old Motor Line route. By this time, the Minneapolis Park Board had acquired the lake. After constructing Lake Harriet Pkwy., the board built a picnic pavilion and bandstand on the west shore. Today, the lake remains one of the city's most popular attractions.

1 Women's and Men's Restrooms *L*

Near Lake Harriet Pkwy. West and 42nd St.

Harry Jones, 1891

These small Shingle Style restrooms are the oldest public buildings at Lake Harriet. Their style influenced the design of the nearby band shell and refectory.

2 Lake Harriet Band Shell and Refectory !

4135 Lake Harriet Pkwy. West

Bentz/Thompson/Rietow Architects, 1986 / renovated, 2004

These marvelous buildings will remind you that at its best postmodernism was an effort to re-infuse architecture with a sense of beauty, memory, and continuity. Both buildings, which play on the

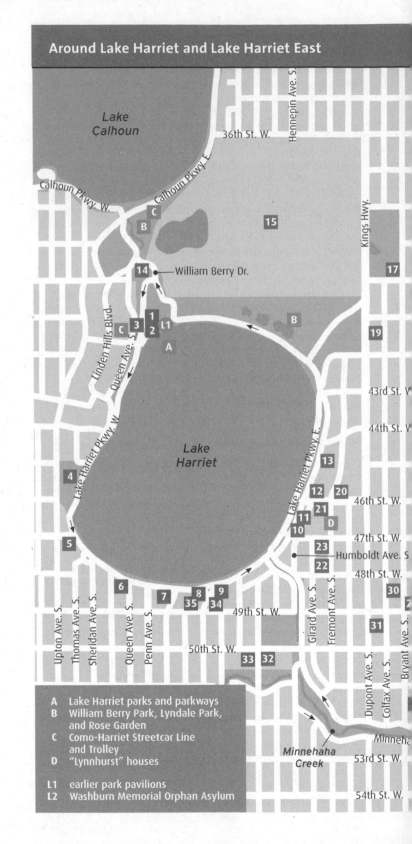

Around Lake Harriet and Lake Harriet East

Lake Calhoun

36th St. W.

Calhoun Pkwy. W.

Calhoun Pkwy. E.

Hennepin Ave. S.

C

B

15

Kings Hwy.

17

14 — William Berry Dr.

Linden Hills Blvd.

C

3

1

2

L1

A

B

19

Queen Ave. S.

43rd St. W

44th St. W

Lake Harriet Pkwy. W.

Lake
Harriet

Lake Harriet Pkwy. E.

13

4

12   20

21

11

D

46th St. W.

10

5

47th St. W.

23 — Humboldt Ave. S

22

48th St. W.

30

Upton Ave. S.

Thomas Ave. S.

Sheridan Ave. S.

Queen Ave. S.

Penn Ave. S.

6

7

8

35

9

34

49th St. W.

Girard Ave. S.

Fremont Ave. S.

31

Dupont Ave. S.

Colfax Ave. S.

Bryant Ave. S.

50th St. W.

33   32

Minnehaha
Creek

Minneha

53rd St. W.

54th St. W.

A Lake Harriet parks and parkways
B William Berry Park, Lyndale Park,
       and Rose Garden
C Como-Harriet Streetcar Line
       and Trolley
D "Lynnhurst" houses

L1 earlier park pavilions
L2 Washburn Memorial Orphan Asylum

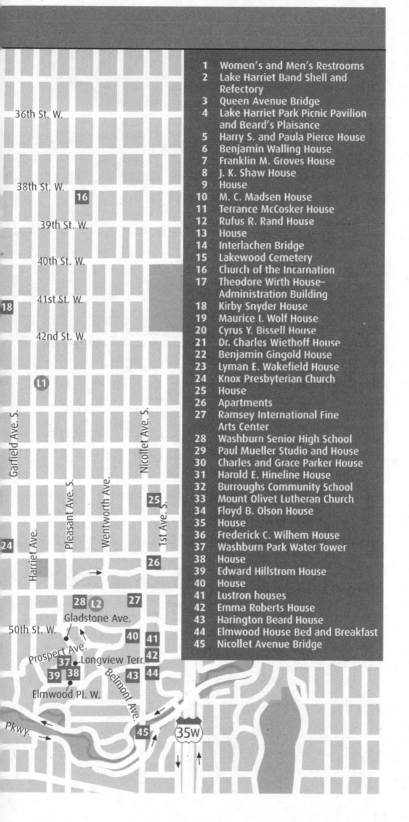

1   Women's and Men's Restrooms
2   Lake Harriet Band Shell and Refectory
3   Queen Avenue Bridge
4   Lake Harriet Park Picnic Pavilion and Beard's Plaisance
5   Harry S. and Paula Pierce House
6   Benjamin Walling House
7   Franklin M. Groves House
8   J. K. Shaw House
9   House
10 M. C. Madsen House
11 Terrance McCosker House
12 Rufus R. Rand House
13 House
14 Interlachen Bridge
15 Lakewood Cemetery
16 Church of the Incarnation
17 Theodore Wirth House–Administration Building
18 Kirby Snyder House
19 Maurice I. Wolf House
20 Cyrus Y. Bissell House
21 Dr. Charles Wiethoff House
22 Benjamin Gingold House
23 Lyman E. Wakefield House
24 Knox Presbyterian Church
25 House
26 Apartments
27 Ramsey International Fine Arts Center
28 Washburn Senior High School
29 Paul Mueller Studio and House
30 Charles and Grace Parker House
31 Harold E. Hineline House
32 Burroughs Community School
33 Mount Olivet Lutheran Church
34 Floyd B. Olson House
35 House
36 Frederick C. Wilhem House
37 Washburn Park Water Tower
38 House
39 Edward Hillstrom House
40 House
41 Lustron houses
42 Emma Roberts House
43 Harington Beard House
44 Elmwood House Bed and Breakfast
45 Nicollet Avenue Bridge

Southwest

South of Minnehaha Creek and West of Lake Harriet

Lake Calhoun

36th St. W.

Calhoun Pkwy.

Calhoun Pkwy. E.

I

38th St. W.

H

39th St. W.

France Ave. S.

Xerxes Ave. S.

40th St. W.

William Berry Dr.

78

79   77

Linden Hills Blvd.

80   42nd St. W.

76

Queen Ave. S.

42nd St. W.

73

43rd St. W.   74 75

69

72 L3 G

Lake Harriet Pkwy. W.

44th St. W.   71

York Ave. S.

Washburn Ave. S.

Lake Harriet

70

46th St. W.

67

47th St. W.

68

48th St. W.

Ewing Ave. S.

Upton Ave. S.

Thomas Ave. S.

65
64   66

49th St. W.

Zenith Ave. S.

Xerxes Ave. S.

Vincent Ave. S.

Sheridan Ave. S.

Queen Ave. S.

Penn Ave. S.

50th St. W.

63

52nd St. W.

62

France Ave. S.

61   53rd St. W.   58   54

59   56 57   F

60   55   Cromwell Ct.

54th St. W.   Minnehaha Creek

53   56th St. W.

E   Red Cedar Lane
F   Streetcar right-of-way
G   Cottage City
H   Infill houses

L3   Frank and Ottalie Fletcher House

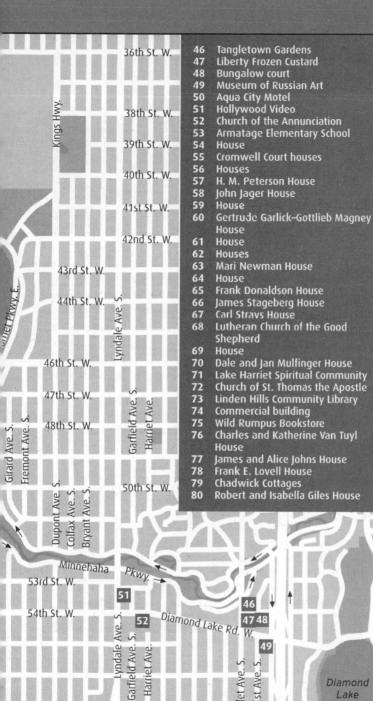

46 Tangletown Gardens
47 Liberty Frozen Custard
48 Bungalow court
49 Museum of Russian Art
50 Aqua City Motel
51 Hollywood Video
52 Church of the Annunciation
53 Armatage Elementary School
54 House
55 Cromwell Court houses
56 Houses
57 H. M. Peterson House
58 John Jager House
59 House
60 Gertrude Garlick–Gottlieb Magney House
61 House
62 Houses
63 Mari Newman House
64 House
65 Frank Donaldson House
66 James Stageberg House
67 Carl Stravs House
68 Lutheran Church of the Good Shepherd
69 House
70 Dale and Jan Mulfinger House
71 Lake Harriet Spiritual Community
72 Church of St. Thomas the Apostle
73 Linden Hills Community Library
74 Commercial building
75 Wild Rumpus Bookstore
76 Charles and Katherine Van Tuyl House
77 James and Alice Johns House
78 Frank E. Lovell House
79 Chadwick Cottages
80 Robert and Isabella Giles House

Southwest

Lake Harriet Band Shell and Refectory

site's history (there were three earlier pavilions here), also show that architecture can be flat-out fun. Since its completion in 1986, the band shell has become a civic icon. Clad in shingles, it features a flared arch rising above a steel truss, with steep-roofed towers to either side. Although it's a sophisticated design, the band shell feels as natural as a child's drawing, and it captures the essence of summery delight. The adjacent refectory—a miniature castle with six delicate towers that shoot skyward as festively as Fourth of July fireworks—is just as good.

LOST 1 *Three earlier pavilions occupied this site; all came to disastrous ends. In 1888 the Minneapolis Street Railway Co. erected the **first pavilion** near Queen Ave. South and 42nd St. West. It burned down in July 1891. The **second pavilion,** designed by Harry Jones, was a pagodalike wooden structure along the lakeshore where the refectory now stands. It stood 12 years before it, too, burned. Jones designed a **third pavilion** on the same spot in 1904. Classical Revival in style, it extended out over the lake to shelter a swimming area. In July 1925, the pavilion's roof collapsed in a windstorm, killing a woman and her young daughter who were huddled with others inside.*

3 Queen Avenue Bridge **N**

Lake Harriet Blvd. West at Queen Ave. South over streetcar tracks

Charles Shepley (engineer), 1905

An early reinforced concrete bridge now listed on the National Register of Historic Places.

4 Lake Harriet Park Picnic Pavilion **L** and Beard's Plaisance

4525 Upton Ave. South

Harry Jones, 1904

This pagodalike picnic pavilion is nestled in a grove of trees at Beard's Plaisance, which is named after Henry Beard, a real estate developer who donated land for a park here in 1888.

Harry S. and Paula Pierce House

5 Harry S. and Paula Pierce House

4700 Lake Harriet Pkwy. West

Bertrand and Chamberlin, 1910

A taste of Vienna on Lake Harriet. This distinctive house mixes Prairie Style elements, such as the grouped corner windows on the second floor, with Art Nouveau features that appear to be drawn from the contemporaneous

Viennese Secession movement in Austria. Secessionist details include segmental arch windows and the tilework arranged in geometric patterns. The house's most unusual feature is a second-story frieze that depicts knights and maidens in a forest scene.

6 Benjamin Walling House *L*

4850 Lake Harriet Pkwy. West

Magney and Tusler, 1930

An exquisitely detailed brick house that melds Tudor Revival with the English Arts and Crafts style of the 1890s.

7 Franklin M. Groves House *L*

4885 Lake Harriet Pkwy. East

Carleton W. Farnham, 1928 / addition, 1936

Perhaps the most secretive house on the lake, this Mediterranean mansion would be at home in Beverly Hills. Set on a steep, lushly landscaped lot, the house has the feel of a romantic hideaway, rising in a series of stucco-clad, tile-roofed volumes that culminate in a cupola. A garage and caretaker's apartment were added to the house in the 1930s. The first owner, Franklin Groves, was part of a family of builders. Along with his father, S. J. Groves, and two brothers, he formed a company in 1908 that specialized in excavating basements. Under Franklin Groves's leadership, the company eventually grew into one of the nation's largest construction firms.

J. K. Shaw House

8 J. K. Shaw House

4861 Lake Harriet Blvd. East

Frederick Mann, 1928

A full-dress exercise in Tudor Revival that rambles handsomely across its outsized corner lot.

4855 Lake Harriet Pkwy. East

9 House

4855 Lake Harriet Pkwy. East

Charles Stinson, 2002

Architect Charles Stinson designs houses that draw on Frank Lloyd Wright's Prairie Style and the International Style of the 1920s and 1930s. By now, he's settled so comfortably into what might be called the Stinson Style that his multilayered houses are instantly recognizable.

M. C. Madsen House

10 M. C. Madsen House

4637 Lake Harriet Pkwy. East

Albert Van Dyck, 1923 / enlarged and remodeled, ca. 1990s

The smooth stucco surfaces, blocky massing, and generally sparse ornament of the Spanish Revival houses of the 1920s often gave them a protomodern appearance. That's the case here, where a modern-era addition blends in beautifully with the original portion of the house.

11 Terrance McCosker House

4615 Lake Harriet Blvd. East

Purcell and Feick, 1909

One of William Purcell's early Craftsman-Prairie houses, with a gabled roof and banded windows on the second floor. Within, Purcell created an open-floor plan modeled on Frank Lloyd Wright's design for "A Fireproof House for $5,000," published in 1907 in the *Ladies' Home Journal*. Originally clad in wood siding and shingles, the house has been modified over the years in ways that have not enhanced its appearance.

12 Rufus R. Rand House

4551 Lake Harriet Pkwy. East

Ernest Kennedy, 1916 / remodeled, ca. 1990s

A rather severe Beaux-Arts mansion with a concave curve at the corner, where ornament frames the front door. The house's original stone walls have been stuccoed over.

13 House

4427 Lake Harriet Pkwy. East

D. C. Bennett, 1923

This Spanish-Mediterranean concoction, posed atop a high lot, includes balustraded terraces.

POI B William Berry Park, Lyndale Park, and Rose Garden

William Berry Park, Berry Dr. and Richfield Rd.

Minneapolis Park Board, 1890 and later

Lyndale Park, including **Rose Garden** and **Peace Garden,** 42nd St. West and Dupont Ave. South (Kings Hwy.)

Minneapolis Park Board, 1891, 1908, 1929, 1983, and later

The 100 or so acres of parkland and gardens between Lake Harriet and Lake Calhoun were acquired in 1890–91. The western portion is named in honor of William Berry, the city park system's first superintendent. Lyndale Park, to the east, is renowned for its rose garden, begun in 1907 by another park superintendent, Theodore Wirth. There's also a peace garden built from an abandoned rock garden unearthed by, of all things, a tornado in 1981. The garden includes

stones from the sites of the atomic blasts that devastated Hiroshima and Nagasaki, Japan, in 1945. The park is also home to the Roberts Bird Sanctuary, named after Thomas S. Roberts, a physician and ornithologist who in 1932 authored an 840-page opus, *The Birds of Minnesota.*

14 Interlachen Bridge N

William Berry Dr.
over streetcar tracks

William S. Hewett (builder), 1900

The oldest reinforced concrete bridge in Minnesota, with a veneer of stone. It was built using a system patented in 1894 by a Swiss engineer.

POI C Como-Harriet Streetcar Line and Trolley N L

Between Lake Harriet and Lake Calhoun

Twin City Rapid Transit Co., 1891 and later / track restored, Minnesota Transportation Museum, 1971–77

Rail operations here date to 1880, when the Motor Line was built between Lake Calhoun and Lake Harriet. Streetcars replaced the steam-powered trains in 1891. Seven years later, the route was expanded to become the Como-Harriet interurban line. The trolleys stopped running in 1954. In 1971 the Minnesota Transportation Museum began rebuilding a mile-long segment of track, much of it following the historic right-of-way here. In 1989 museum members also built a replica of the original Linden Hills streetcar station at 42nd St. and Queen Ave. South. During summer months, the Minnesota Streetcar Museum (an offshoot of the Transportation Museum) operates two historic wooden streetcars along the restored track.

Lakewood Cemetery

Lake Calhoun

35th St. W.

Hennepin Ave. S.

36th St. W.

k

j

i

c

b

a

d

Kings Hwy.

h

f

g

e

Lake Harriet Pkwy. E.

Lake Harriet

Rose Way Rd.

42nd St. W.

Kings Hwy.

a Lakewood Cemetery Memorial
   Chapel
b Mausoleum-Columbarium
c Walker Family Monument
d Hubert H. Humphrey Monument
e Rocheleau Monument
f Lowry-Goodrich Mausoleum
g Floyd B. Olson Monument
h Emil Oberhoffer Monument
i Pillsbury Monument
j Flour Mill Explosion Monument
k Wellstone Memorial

Southwest

East of Lake Harriet

This part of Minneapolis—which includes the East Harriet, Kingfield, Tangletown, and Lynnhurst neighborhoods—offers a clear demonstration of how wealth is drawn to water like a dowsing rod. Near Lake Harriet and along Minnehaha Creek you'll encounter block after block of elegant houses ranging from 1880s Victorians to the latest modernist designs. As you venture farther away from the lake, however, the homes become smaller, with bungalows predominating.

The East Harriet and Lynnhurst neighborhoods have an especially good stock of homes from the early twentieth century. Included among them are four Prairie Style houses designed by William Purcell and George Elmslie, along with numerous Arts and Crafts, Period Revival, and early modern designs. Many of the best houses are located along Colfax, Dupont, Emerson, and Fremont Avenues, which run just to the east of Lake Harriet. East Harriet is also home to Lakewood Cemetery, the Twin Cities' preeminent burial ground, established in 1871.

South of 46th Street is Tangletown, so named because its streets meander along wooded hills above Minnehaha Creek in defiance of the standard gridiron. Two large public schools—Washburn (1925) and Ramsey (1931)—are located here, partly on land once occupied by an orphanage. Period Revival houses are common along Tangletown's picturesque streets, but the neighborhood also has some notable Victorians—among them architect Harry Jones's own home (1888)—as well as the city's largest colony of Lustron metal houses (1949) along Nicollet Avenue. There are also a number of modernist houses from the 1950s here, mostly near the creek.

15 Lakewood Cemetery

36th St. West and Hennepin Ave.

Charles W. Folsom, Adolph Strauch, and R. M. Copeland, 1871 and later

In 1871, William King proposed the establishment of a cemetery away from what he called "the encroachments of the city." Other local nabobs were drafted to help with the planning, and before long a search committee agreed to buy 130 acres of rolling land between Lakes Calhoun and Harriet for $21,000. The seller of this property, conveniently enough, was King himself.

Fifteen of Minneapolis's leading businessmen then formed what soon became known as the Lakewood Cemetery Association. By this time, so-called "garden" cemeteries, as opposed to crowded old church burial grounds, had become fashionable in the United States. Hoping to create a parklike setting for their new cemetery, which included a pond, Lakewood's trustees hired a team that included Charles W. Folsom, Adolph Strauch, and R. M. Copeland to design the grounds.

Folsom was superintendent of Mount Auburn Cemetery in Cambridge, MA, while Strauch was a gardener known for his role in creating Cincinnati's Spring Grove Cemetery.

With its winding roadways and carefully crafted "natural" look, Lakewood remains the Twin Cities' finest Victorian cemetery-park. It's also chock-full of monuments and mausoleums built by prominent Minneapolis families. Here, too, are the graves of Civil War soldiers, members of Minneapolis's early Chinese community, and political leaders such as Floyd B. Olson, Hubert Humphrey, and Paul Wellstone. The cemetery's architectural jewel is a Byzantine Revival–style chapel renowned for its radiant mosaics.

a Lakewood Cemetery Memorial Chapel ! N i

Near cemetery entrance off 36th St. West

Harry Jones, 1910 (interior by Charles Lamb, New York) / renovated, 1987 / restored, Brooks Borge Skiles (Jim Miller), 1998

Lakewood's trustees began planning a new chapel in 1904, but it wasn't until 1908 that Harry

Lakewood Cemetery Memorial Chapel

Jones won the commission by proposing a domed building modeled on Hagia Sophia in Istanbul, built in AD 537 by the Byzantine emperor Justinian I. Jones's mini-version of the famed church features a 65-foot-high granite dome rising above a drum ringed with 24 stained-glass windows that indicate the time of day and season based on where light shines in. Four smaller domes rise from the corners of the chapel, which is entered through bronze doors lodged within a deep arch.

Step inside and you enter a shimmering world of tesserae—ten million tiny pieces of marble, colored stone, and glass fused

Lakewood Cemetery Memorial Chapel interior

with metal to form mosaics that cover virtually every surface of the interior. Italian artists assembled the mosaics, then traveled to Minneapolis in 1909 to install them. Designed by Charles Lamb of New York and his wife, Ella Condie Lamb, the mosaics include 12 Art Nouveau–style angels who circle the dome. Dressed in gowns of various colors, the angels are said to represent everything from the 12 tribes of Israel to the 12 apostles of Christ. Another four female figures adorn the pendentives supporting the dome.

Extensive restoration work was performed on the chapel in 1987 and again in 1998. Fittingly, Harry Jones's own funeral was held here on September 25, 1935. He was 76 when he died.

b Mausoleum-Columbarium

Near cemetery entrance off 36th St. West

Harley Ellington Corwin and Stirton (Detroit), 1967

A luxuriously appointed building, clad in granite and featuring 24 stained-glass windows designed by the Willet Studios of Philadelphia.

c Walker Family Monument

Near cemetery entrance off 36th St. West

1927

Among those buried here is Thomas Walker, founder of the Walker Art Center.

d Hubert H. Humphrey Monument

Section 51

1978

A simple stone memorial marks the burial place of Minnesota's most famous politician, who served as mayor of Minneapolis, as a U.S. senator, and as vice president of the United States.

e Rocheleau Monument

Section 23

1907

The tallest of Lakewood's monuments, built by Minneapolis businessman Louis Rocheleau in memory of his wife, Charlotte, who died at age 37.

f Lowry-Goodrich Mausoleum

Section 27

1900

A replica of the Parthenon.

g Floyd B. Olson Monument

Section 18

1936

A monument to Minnesota's first Farmer-Labor Party governor, who died in office at age 44.

h Emil Oberhoffer Monument

Section 44

1933

An obelisk with carved musical notes commemorating the first conductor of the Minneapolis (now Minnesota) Symphony Orchestra.

i Pillsbury Monument

Section 2

1901

A draped female figure stands atop a pedestal in this monument to the milling family. There's also a sheaf of wheat carved into the base.

Flour Mill Explosion Monument

j Flour Mill Explosion Monument

Section 1-D

1885

This obelisk commemorates 18 workers killed in the explosion of the Washburn A Mill in 1878.

k Wellstone Memorial

Section 1-D

U.S. Senator Paul Wellstone and his wife, Sheila, are buried here beside a simple boulder memorial. The Wellstones died in a plane crash in 2002.

Church of the Incarnation, 1920

16 Church of the Incarnation

3801 Pleasant Ave. South

Emmanuel Masqueray (completed by Slifer Abrahamson and Lundie), 1918

The last and largest Catholic parish church designed by Emmanuel Masqueray before his death in 1917. Italian Romanesque in style, the church includes a 150-foot-high bell tower visible throughout the neighborhood. Masqueray by this time had already designed two giant Beaux-Arts churches—the St. Paul Cathedral (1915) and the Basilica of St. Mary (1914)—and here he couldn't quite shake off his taste for heavy classical forms, such as the massive lintel above the triple entry doors. Following Masqueray's death, three of his draftsmen—Edwin Lundie, Frank Abrahamson, and Fred Slifer—completed his commissions, and it's likely they handled the finish work here. Incarnation's richly decorated interior consists of a broad ached nave, transepts, and a sanctuary outfitted with a marble baldachin over the altar. Murals, stained glass, and statuary complete an impressive ornamental program.

17 Theodore Wirth House–Administration Building N L

3954 Bryant Ave. South

Lowell Lamoreaux, 1910

This Colonial-Mission Revival house was once the home and office of Theodore Wirth. Born in Switzerland in 1863, Wirth immigrated to the United States and later became superintendent of parks in Hartford, CT. Recruited by Charles Loring, Wirth agreed to come to Minneapolis to head its park system in 1906, but only if the park board would build a residence for him and his family—evidence that executive perks have been around for a long time. Wirth moved to California after his retirement and died there in 1949. He and his wife are buried at Lakewood Cemetery. The house is still owned by the Minneapolis Park and Recreation Board.

Kirby Snyder House

18 Kirby Snyder House

4101 Lyndale Ave. South

Kirby T. Snyder, 1915

Although not quite up to the standards of Frank Lloyd Wright or Purcell and Elmslie, this house presents many familiar Prairie elements: bands of casement windows with geometric decorative patterns, overhanging eaves, a low-slung roof, and blocky, asymmetrical massing. Inside, however, the house develops a split personality on the first floor, portions of which feature deluxe details that are closer in spirit to Beaux-Arts Classicism than the Prairie Style. Snyder, who mainly designed schools and churches during his career, later moved on to California.

19 Maurice I. Wolf House

4109 Dupont Ave. South

Purcell Feick and Elmslie, ca. 1912–17

Although designed in 1912, this house wasn't built for another five years or so. The final product didn't please William Purcell, who pronounced it "a pretty disappointing building." Be that as it may, the house shows how Purcell and Elmslie, laboring with a tight budget, managed to produce a variant of the usual Craftsman foursquare. They did so by carefully framing the windows, adding some of their distinctive beam-and-pendant ornament, and placing the entrance to one side. Maurice Wolf, a businessman, supervised construction of the house himself.

20 Cyrus Y. Bissell House

4545 Fremont Ave. South

Cyrus Bissell, 1930

A scenic sprawl of a house, Tudor-Norman Revival in style with a round tower rising above the front door. The house's slate roof seems to fall every which way, and the stonework and stucco details are all expertly handled. Bissell, a partner in the Minneapolis architectural firm of Haxby Bissell and Stebbins, designed this home for himself and his family.

21 Dr. Charles Wiethoff House

4609 Humboldt Ave. South

Purcell and Elmslie, 1917

One of the last of Purcell and Elmslie's Minneapolis houses, closer in form to a Craftsman chalet—or perhaps even a front-gabled Colonial Revival home—than the typical Prairie Style design. Clad in cedar siding and stucco, the house has many elegant details such as leaded-glass windows, globed light fixtures, and an arched fireplace—all the work of George Elmslie. The house, built for a physician, includes a flat-roofed garage designed by the architects.

22 Benjamin Gingold House

4745 Girard Ave. South

Benjamin Gingold, 1958

A striking modernist house, finished in white stucco, that thrusts forward on its hilly lot with a two-story wall of windows extending over a mezzanine and garage. Off to one side, a winding staircase leads to the front door, located beside a round tower that looks a bit like a silo

Benjamin Gingold House

but in fact holds a spiral staircase. The interior is organized around a living room ringed by balconies.

Lyman E. Wakefield House

23 Lyman E. Wakefield House *L*

4700 Fremont Ave. South

Purcell Feick and Elmslie, 1912

Like most architects, Purcell and Elmslie often had to work with a limited budget, as was the case here. Lyman Wakefield was a banker and, according to William Purcell, a close man with a dollar. "His interest," Purcell wrote, "was wholly 'how much house for how little money.' From the first we were obliged to make a box of it, and then the struggle began." As it turned out, the architects produced more than a mere "box" for their client. Although the house is indeed quite plain, it displays many deft touches, including a distinctive attic dormer, an upstairs sleeping porch subtly accented by horizontal strips of wood, and a side stair bay with leaded glass.

POI D "Lynnhurst" houses

4600 block Fremont Ave. South

various architects, 1893 and later

Most of the 11 houses along either side of Fremont here stem

from a plan undertaken in 1893 by Charles Loring, known as the father of the Minneapolis park system but also a partner in the Minneapolis Street Railway Co. Loring gave lots to young married men who worked for him on the condition that they build houses costing at least $3,000. His goal was to jump-start growth in the area, known as Lynnhurst, but the depression of 1893 sank the real estate market, and further development came slowly. Today, the big Victorian houses here form a most pleasant ensemble. Two of the most interesting, at 4601 and 4629 Fremont, are attributed to Harry Jones.

24 Knox Presbyterian Church

4747 Lyndale Ave. South

Harry Jones, 1920 / additions, 1954 (new sanctuary), 1959, 1980s

Gothic Revival in white stone.

25 House

4629 Nicollet Ave.

1910

A Colonial Revival "cottage" with overscaled porch columns and oval windows to either side of the perfectly centered front door.

26 Apartments

4815 Nicollet Ave. South

Perry Crosier, 1931

The southerly portions of Nicollet Ave. present a feast of Period Revival apartment architecture, and this Spanish-Moorish extravaganza is among the most colorful of the lot. Its architectural paraphernalia includes twisted columns, inset balustrades, and wrought-iron balconies.

27 Ramsey International Fine Arts Center

1 49th St. West

Bureau of Buildings (Edward Enger, supervising architect), 1931

28 Washburn Senior High School

201 49th St. West

Bureau of Buildings (Edward Enger, supervising architect), 1925

A pair of large school buildings, both built in a rather dry, flat version of the Classical Revival.

LOST 2 *Where these schools stand was once the site of the **Washburn Memorial Orphan Asylum,** built in 1886 with a $375,000 bequest from milling magnate Cadwallader Washburn. The towered, three-story brick building was set amid 45 acres. The institution accepted orphans and so-called half-orphans up to 14 years old. As foster care became more popular, the orphanage's population dwindled, and it had only 11 residents when it closed in 1929 (by which time much of the grounds had been sold off). A successor organization, the Washburn Child Guidance Center, continues to operate.*

Paul Mueller House

29 Paul Mueller Studio and House

studio, 4845 Bryant Ave. South

Purcell Feick and Elmslie, 1911

house, 4844 Aldrich Ave. South

Paul Mueller, 1913

These properties, on high wooded lots, sit back to back. Both were built for Paul Mueller, a landscape architect. After his marriage, Mueller hired Purcell and Elmslie to design a studio for his new practice. Clad in horizontal board-and-batten siding, the studio isn't one of the firm's major works. Still, it's skillfully done, with a polygonal bay at one end atop a tuck-under garage.

Purcell and Elmslie also planned a house for Mueller, but he ultimately decided to build his own. Although Purcell later dismissed Mueller's house as "ordinary," it is in fact unusual. Built of timber framing in the old English manner, the house has board-and-batten siding, rows of casement windows, and a limestone base punctured by a deep-set entrance arch. Mueller later moved to Chicago; this house remains his sole work of architecture in the Twin Cities.

Charles and Grace Parker House

30 Charles and Grace Parker House ! N L

4829 Colfax Ave. South

Purcell Feick and Elmslie, 1913

One of Purcell and Elmslie's greatest houses. The broad gabled roof, carefully grouped windows, side porch, and meticulously worked entry sequence are classic features of the firm's work. The entrance, behind a brick-walled front terrace, includes a gorgeous fretsawn arch and frieze above the door. Beams and a pair of pendants extend to either side. Elmslie, a master ornamentalist, also designed leaded-glass windows for the house. Inside, the house has the usual open plan and includes many built-ins as well as a large brick fireplace.

Charles Parker worked for a wholesale fruit company before becoming co-owner of an auto parts firm. He built this house after he married his partner's daughter, Grace Robertson. The couple stayed in the house for only six years before selling it. The house has been extensively restored by later owners.

31 Harold E. Hineline House

4920 Dupont Ave. South

Purcell Feick and Elmslie, 1910

A two-story stucco box brought to life by the placement of the windows, the side porch (originally open), and such lovely details as the sawn-wood ornaments (restored) that project from the small roof above the front entrance. Within, the house has a typical Prairie Style open plan pinwheeling around a central hearth. The first owner, Harold Hineline, was a bookkeeper.

Burroughs Community School

32 Burroughs Community School

1601 50th St. West

Kodet Architectural Group, 2003

Tall and narrow, this school consists of two sections, one of which is angled to follow the line of nearby Minnehaha Creek. The lower stories are clad in red brick, with blue green metal above.

33 Mount Olivet Lutheran Church

5025 Knox Ave. South

Hugo Haeuser (Milwaukee), 1949 / later additions

With 13,000 members, Mount Olivet is the world's largest Lutheran congregation. Founded in 1920, the congregation grew rapidly after World War II, leading to the construction of this stone church, which follows English Gothic models. The long nave, beneath a beamed ceiling, has stained-glass windows in deep blue and red hues.

34 Floyd B. Olson House N *L*

1914 49th St. West

1922

This house is listed on the National Register of Historic Places because of its association with Floyd B. Olson, one of Minnesota's most extraordinary politicians. Yet the house itself is quite interesting. Most bungalows feature Arts and Crafts or Tudor Revival detailing, but here a pair of classically inspired consoles support an arched roof over the entrance porch. A driving force behind the Farmer-Labor Party, Olson won election three times as governor, beginning in 1930. He was poised to run for the U.S. Senate when he died of pancreatic cancer in 1936.

35 House

2006 49th St. West

Architects Small House Service Bureau, 1923

Just after World War I, Minneapolis architect Edwin Brown, then in partnership with Edwin Hewitt, created the Architects Small House Service Bureau. It eventually became national in scope, providing architect-designed plans for small, generally inexpensive homes. This brick Colonial Revival house is a representative example of the bureau's work.

Frederick C. Wilhem House

36 Frederick C. Wilhem House

5140 Aldrich Ave. South

S. B. Appleton, 1924

A Spanish-Moorish confection with arabesques framing the front door, a tall bay window beneath a fanciful copper half dome, and an arcaded side porch with twisted columns. Like so much Period Revival architecture, the house conveys a sense of the theatrical and the fantastic.

Tangletown

This hilly neighborhood's origins go back to 1886, when William Washburn and 20 or so other investors bought 200 acres of farmland along Minnehaha Creek near 50th St. and Nicollet Ave. Their idea was to create a residential enclave for the well-to-do to be known as Washburn Park. Landscape architect Horace Cleveland planned large lots and winding streets that followed the hills and ravines around the creek. Most of the area was still countryside, although an orphanage had just been built nearby with a bequest from Cadwallader Washburn (William's brother).

Washburn Park was not an immediate success, however. By 1893, when a deep depression took hold, only nine homes had been built. Eventually, Washburn and other investors sold their property to a real estate firm, which in 1909 replatted the development, altering parts of Cleveland's original design, especially east of Nicollet. In its rearranged form, Washburn Park finally began to fill out. Development continued through the boom years of the 1920s. Today, Tangletown's elegantly appointed houses remain much in demand.

37 Washburn Park Water Tower N *L*

401 Prospect Ave.

Harry Jones and William S. Hewett (engineer), 1932 / renovated, 2002 / Art: concrete sculptures (eagles and guardsmen), John Karl Daniels

The only one of the city's three historic water towers that's still in use, and also a most curious design. It's one of the last works of Tangletown resident Harry Jones, who cast it in a style somewhere out of Medieval Europe by way of art deco. The tower comes with its own protective service—an octet of 18-foot-high "guardians of health" encircling the base. These concrete sculptures are the work of another neighborhood resident, John K. Daniels, who added a like number of eagles above. The tower's

Washburn Park Water Tower

1.35-million-gallon concrete tank provides water to the neighborhood between May and October.

38 House

35 Highview Pl.

Jacobson and Jacobson, 1930

A very large and handsomely detailed Period Revival house, in a style that can best be described as French Provincial–Norman Revival–And Other Stuff.

39 Edward Hillstrom House

348 Elmwood Pl. West

Edward Hillstrom, 1961

A boxy two-story house from the 1960s. It has lots of glass, a side entry, patterned concrete walls, and what look to be terra-cotta panels used as ornament.

40 House (Washburn Orphanage superintendent's residence)

5000 Nicollet Ave.

Harry Jones, 1903

An Arts and Crafts house with Medieval overtones, built for Charles Faulkner, who was superintendent of the Washburn Orphanage from 1903 to 1920. It's now a private residence.

41 Lustron houses

5009, 5015, 5021, 5027, 5047, 5055 Nicollet Ave.

Lustron Corp. (Morris Beckman, architect), 1949

Southwest

The largest colony of Lustrons in Minnesota. The Lustron Corp. was established in 1946 by Carl Strandlund, an engineer and

Lustron house

industrialist from Chicago. His dream was to produce an all-steel prefabricated house that could be shipped to anywhere and assembled at a modest cost. By the late 1940s, Lustrons began rolling off the assembly line. The standard one-story model (designed by architect Morris Beckman) was only about 1,000 square feet but included two bedrooms, a bathroom, a living room, a small dining area, a galley-style kitchen, and a utility room. The houses were built on concrete slabs and came in seven pastel colors.

Problems plagued Lustron from the start. The houses ended up costing about $10,000 ($3,000 more than Strandlund had estimated), on-site assembly took longer than expected, and the company's plant couldn't turn out enough houses a day to be cost efficient. By 1950, the company was in trouble, and it abruptly failed when a federal agency called in a large loan. During its brief existence, Lustron produced around 2,500 houses, 29 of which were shipped to Minnesota. The six houses here are in varying condition, but they've generally worn well.

42 Emma Roberts House

14 51st St. East

Edwin Hewitt, 1913 / Art: ceramic tiles, Ernest Batchelder (Pasadena, CA) and Moravian Pottery and Tile Works (Doylestown, PA)

Mary Emma Roberts, who preferred to use her middle name, was a high school art teacher who helped found the Handicraft Guild of Minneapolis in 1904 and later served as its president. This

house features decorative tiles worked into its stucco walls. One of the tilemakers, California-based Ernest Batchelder, taught classes for the Handicraft Guild between 1905 and 1909.

Harington Beard House

43 Harington Beard House ("Sunnyside") *L*

5100 Nicollet Ave.

Harry Jones, 1888 / addition, 1908

One of Harry Jones's most pleasing designs—a grab bag of Shingle Style, Dutch Colonial Revival, and Queen Anne elements. As built, the house had clapboard siding rather than stucco covering the first story. The first owner, Harington Beard, dubbed it "Sunnyside," a name etched into a glass panel on the front door. Beard himself was an interesting character. Born in England, he moved with his family to the United States as a child. In 1885, at age 23, he established a downtown Minneapolis store that included the city's first gallery offering artwork for sale. Beard operated the gallery until 1938, two years before his death. The gallery remains in business under the ownership of one of Beard's descendants.

44 Elmwood House Bed and Breakfast (Harry Jones House) **! N** *L*

5101 Nicollet Ave.

Harry Jones, 1888

Along with the Beard House across Nicollet Ave., this is one of the two oldest homes in Tangletown. Early photographs show the house standing in a thick forest beside Nicollet, which in the 1880s was still a dirt road.

Elmwood House Bed and Breakfast

A lively Shingle–Norman Revival mix, the house sports two round towers crowned by conic hats, and it has the air of a jaunty castle in the woods. Jones, who designed at least six other homes in Tangletown as well as its landmark water tower, lived here with his wife, Bertha, and their three children until his death in 1935.

45 Nicollet Avenue Bridge

Over Minnehaha Creek

Kristoffer Oustad and N. W. Elsberg (engineers), 1923 / renovated, 2002

A long concrete-arch structure, best seen from the creek below. Brick and concrete gateposts, installed in 2002, display the Tangletown neighborhood's logo.

South of Minnehaha Creek

Much of this part of Minneapolis, which forms the city's southwest corner, was developed after World War II and so looks considerably different from the area around Lake Harriet. There are three officially designated neighborhoods here—Armatage, Kenny, and Windom. All are heavily residential, although Windom has a commercial-industrial district along its southern edge. The terrain is generally flat, which means that the standard Minneapolis gridiron prevails. A small body of water—Grass Lake—interrupts the grid just west of Lyndale Avenue.

Cape Cod bungalows, ramblers, and ranch houses are common in all three neighborhoods. Earlier Period Revival homes can be found in the blocks closest to Minnehaha Creek as well as in sections of Windom, which tends to have an older housing stock than its neighbors to the west.

Although the overall architectural environment here isn't especially impressive, a few buildings stand out. The Museum of Russian Art (1936), formerly a church, is an excellent example of the Spanish Revival style. The nearby Church of the Annunciation (1962) is impressive as well. There are also some classic 1950s-style school buildings here, including Armatage Elementary School (1952). Architect-designed modernist houses from the same period show up on a number of streets near Minnehaha Creek, such as Cromwell Court. Along Lyndale you'll find one of the Twin Cities' last 1950s center-court, drive-up motels—the Aqua City.

46 Tangletown Gardens (Pure Oil Co.)

5353 Nicollet Ave.

1940 / renovated, Scott Endres and Dean Engelmann, 2003

47 Liberty Frozen Custard (Standard Oil Co.)

5401 Nicollet Ave.

1961 / renovated, KKE Architects, 2004

Two old gas stations with new lives. Tangletown Gardens is a station of the English Cottage type, complete with a cupola and a blue tile roof. Liberty Frozen Custard, a flat-roofed building clad in porcelain enamel steel panels, is a stock design once used by the Standard Oil Co.

48 Bungalow court

17–27 54th St. East

1928

Possibly the only Colonial Revival–style bungalow court in the Twin Cities.

Museum of Russian Art

49 Museum of Russian Art (Mayflower Congregational Church)

5500 Stevens Ave. South

Bard and Vanderbilt, 1936 / renovated, Julie Snow Architects, 2005

What could be more American than a museum devoted to Russian art located in an old Spanish-style church? The building, originally home to Mayflower Congregational Church, is one of the finest Spanish Revival designs in the Twin Cities, featuring an explosion of baroque-inspired stone ornament around its east window. Mayflower moved across Diamond Lake Rd.

to a new church in 1975. In 2004, the old church was acquired by art collector Raymond E. Johnson, whose specialty is Russian art. Minneapolis architect Julie Snow was hired to transform the old church–funeral home into a museum. She did so with impeccable results. Besides restoring much of the church's exterior, Snow and her team added an elevator tower (clad in terracotta), created a courtyard, and refashioned the interior into a gallery that includes a new mezzanine.

50 Aqua City Motel

5739 Lyndale Ave. South

Rodger Patch, 1954 / addition, 1968

This 38-unit motel with what looks to be its original sign is an example of a vanishing building type. So-called center-court motels could once be found all around the fringes of Minneapolis and St. Paul, but most have now been done in by redevelopment and the proliferation of chains.

51 Hollywood Video (Boulevard Theater)

5315 Lyndale Ave. South

Perry Crosier, 1933, 1939 / remodeled, 1978 and later

One of two identical theater-restaurants (the other is in West St. Paul) built in the 1930s. Traces of the theater's Moderne styling can still be seen in the curved windows along the north side. The dinner-and-a-movie format was a new twist when the Boulevard opened but has since been tried elsewhere. The theater closed in 1997.

52 Church of the Annunciation

509 54th St. West

Patch and Erickson, 1962 / Art: The Annunciation, sculpture (in front of church), Foster Wiley, Jr., 1995

Built of Mankato-Kasota stone, the main body of this church is a high, oblong box set beneath a low-pitched roof. Stained-glass windows rise above the main doors, while off to one side there's a tower that has the feel of an Italian campanile. Annunciation parish was founded in 1922. An adjacent parish school did double duty as a church until this building was completed.

53 Armatage Elementary School

2501 56th St. West

Magney Tusler and Setter with Perkins and Will (Chicago), 1952 / additions, 1954, 1956

If you grew up in a newer part of the city or in a suburb in the 1950s, there's a good chance you attended a school much like this one. The firm of Perkins and Will, which consulted in the design of Armatage, produced the prototype for this kind of one-story building: Crow Island School (1940) in Winnetka, IL. Designed with Eliel and Eero Saarinen, Crow Island features long brick classroom wings with bands of windows. Armatage follows this by now familiar format, as does nearby **Kenny School**

(built in 1954 and located at 5720 Emerson Ave. South).

54 House

2318 53rd St. West

James Stageberg, 1968

A wood-sided International Style house. Several other high-quality modernist houses are located along this side of 53rd St.

2602 Cromwell Ct.

55 Cromwell Court houses

2602, 2604, 2606, 2808 Cromwell Ct.

Carl Graffunder (2604 and 2606) and Stowell Leach (2808), 1951–52

Another of Minnehaha Creek's early modernist enclaves. The most interesting house, at 2602, consists of two flat-roofed volumes (house and garage) connected by a breezeway.

West of Lake Harriet

Two neighborhoods—Linden Hills and Fulton—take in the area west of Lake Harriet. Linden Hills extends as far north as Lake Calhoun, while Fulton reaches south to Minnehaha Creek. Both neighborhoods are among the city's most stable and attractive residential precincts.

Parts of Linden Hills, including the so-called Cottage City addition along the southwest side of Lake Calhoun, were platted as early as the 1880s, which was also when the Motor Line route reached Lake Harriet at 42nd Street West and Queen Avenue South. Extensive development didn't begin for another decade. A company formed by some of the city's leading real estate men—including Thomas Lowry, William King, and Louis Menage—finally started to attract home builders to Linden Hills in 1894, but only after providing free lots to the first 20 of them.

The majority of homes in Linden Hills date to the early decades of the twentieth century, as do many of the buildings that form a small commercial district around 43rd Street West and Upton Avenue South, where there was once a streetcar loop. Architecture of note here includes one of the most mysterious properties in Minneapolis: the Robert and Isabella Giles House (1908), which commands a wooded hilltop and which, like a rare bird, is very hard to spot.

Like Linden Hills, the Fulton neighborhood has a good stock of Period Revival houses dating to between about 1910 and the early 1930s. However, you'll also find occasional outcroppings of modernist homes from the 1950s and later, especially along Minnehaha Creek. Fulton's greatest treasure may well be Red Cedar Lane, a glorious little street laid out in 1904 by John Jager and a place where trees upstage the man-made architecture.

Southwest

56 Houses

5309, 5312, 5315, 5319 Upton Ave. South

Purcell and Strauel, 1929–33

These four speculative houses were designed by William Purcell, living at the time in Portland, OR, and minus his old partner, George Elmslie. By the late 1920s, the Prairie Style was no longer in vogue, so Purcell—working with draftsman Frederick Strauel—dressed his designs in Period Revival attire. Even so, you can find traces of Purcell's Prairie Style roots in these houses, particularly the one at 5315 Upton.

Red Cedar Lane

POI E Red Cedar Lane

Off Upton Ave. South between 52nd and 53rd Sts.

John Jager, 1904 and later

It would be hard to find a more beautiful street in the Twin Cities than this narrow cul-de-sac created over a century ago on a hill above Minnehaha Creek. The man behind it was John Jager, who was born in what is today Slovenia and educated in Vienna before emigrating to Minneapolis in 1902. A planner and architect, Jager also built his own house here. The plantings along the street include not only red cedars but, behind them, towering white pines.

57 H. M. Peterson House

3 Red Cedar Ln.

William Purcell, 1928

A variant of the English Cottage type and an interesting design from what might be called Purcell's post-Prairie career. The house's wood-shake roof curls up like a wave over the front

door, which features a surprising pointed arch. The first owner was a real estate developer who also hired Purcell to design nine speculative houses nearby, including four on Russell Ave.

58 John Jager House

6 Red Cedar Ln.

John Jager, 1904 / later additions and renovations

As designed and built by John Jager, this was a rather spartan house rising from a wide boulder base to a smaller second floor with an open, south-facing porch. Over the years the house has been enlarged, stuccoed over on its upper floors, and modified in other ways. Jager, who lived here until his death in 1959, had a varied career. He designed the superb St. Bernard's Church in St. Paul (1906), prepared a city plan for Minneapolis, worked as an engineer for the architectural firm of Hewitt and Brown, and later maintained a vast archives, now at the University of Minnesota, documenting the work of William Purcell and George Elmslie. Despite his achievements, Jager died a bitter man, believing his work had never been properly appreciated.

59 House

5312 Vincent Ave. South

Purcell and Strauel, 1928

Another "spec" house designed by William Purcell and his former draftsman. Here the style is Colonial Revival, albeit of a very abstract kind.

60 Gertrude Garlick–Gottlieb Magney House

5329 Washburn Ave. South

Magney and Tusler, 1922

From the front, this sedate English Cottage–style house doesn't appear exceptional. Walk around back (off Brookwood Terr.), however, and you'll find a series of brick garden walls that include a round gazebo with a conical roof. Resembling a miniature castle, the gazebo adds a note of romance to the architectural proceedings. As it turns out, romance was also in the air. Two years after this house was built, owner Gertrude Garlick and architect Gottlieb Magney married.

61 House

5250 Washburn Ave. South

1912 and later

The eye-catcher here—best seen from the alley—is a fantastic chimney made from bricks, stone, pipes, ducts, a metal ladder, chains, cinder blocks, sewer tiles, and other scrap materials.

62 Houses

10, 16, 20, 30 Russell Ct.

various architects, 1951–65

One of several outposts of post–World War II modernist architecture along Minnehaha Creek. The most interesting house—at 30 Russell Ct., built in 1953 and designed by Benjamin Gingold—steps downhill to the creek and has a secluded rear terrace.

Mari Newman House

63 Mari Newman House

5117 Penn Ave. South

1915 / renovated, Mari Newman, ca. 1988 and later

Architecture and art merge in this eccentric folk house. Self-taught artist Mari Newman grew up in the house—a standard bungalow—and in the 1980s began to transform it. Her boldest gesture was to paint the house in an array of colors and then decorate it with fields of flowers and circles. A revolving collection of art objects—many of the "found" variety—adorn the front yard.

64 House

4831 Sheridan Ave. South

Louis Bersback, 1927

A Period Revival house that hovers, like a piece of atonal music, somewhere between the usual stylistic keys. The projecting entrance, with its brick quoins and split pediment, has a kind of baroque bravado, but other details suggest everything from French Provincial to Tudor Revival.

Frank Donaldson House, 1925

65 Frank Donaldson House

4807 Sheridan Ave. South

Stebbins Haxby and Bissell, 1931

Just uphill from Lake Harriet, this stone house has a Tudor arch at the front door but few other Tudor Revival details. Overall, it evokes the quietly picturesque work of English Arts and Crafts architects such as Charles Voysey, and it's very nicely done.

James Stageberg House

66 James Stageberg House

4820 Penn Ave. South

James Stageberg, 1981

Built by the architect as his own residence, this fanciful green and purple house is one of the more colorful specimens from the postmodern era in the Twin Cities.

67 Carl Stravs House

4649 York Ave. South

Carl B. Stravs, 1929

This cubic, shingle-clad house built by and for architect Carl Stravs offers one unusual feature: an angular split window that follows the line of the staircase inside. A similar window is at the Phi Gamma Delta fraternity house Stravs designed at the University of Minnesota in 1911.

68 Lutheran Church of the Good Shepherd

4801 France Ave. South (or 4800 Ewing Ave. South)

Hills Gilbertson and Hayes, 1950 / Art: relief sculpture (front of church), 1950

An early modernist church in the brick box mode. The building is quite stark except for some stained glass and a huge relief sculpture of a shepherd and lamb that's pinned to the front facade. One of the architects, Victor Gilbertson, had worked with Eliel Saarinen on Christ Lutheran Church just a year or so earlier, and the influence of that seminal design is clearly evident here.

69 House

3514 Motor Pl.

ca. 1890

Motor Pl. takes its name from the Motor Line railroad (later converted to streetcar use) that once ran just to the south along its route between downtown Minneapolis and Lake Minnetonka. This festively painted Victorian was moved here.

70 Dale and Jan Mulfinger House

4529 Washburn Ave. South

Dale Mulfinger, 1996

Architect Dale Mulfinger and his firm have specialized in designing houses that evoke the warm, woodsy feel of the Arts and Crafts era. This house, deep red in color, is long and narrow, with a front-facing gable and vertical board-and-batten siding.

71 Lake Harriet Spiritual Community (Lake Harriet Methodist Episcopal Church)

4401 Upton Ave. South

Fulton and Butler (Uniontown, PA), 1916

A domed Classical Revival church that calls to mind small county courthouses built at this time. Its original occupants, a Methodist congregation, moved to a new church in the 1950s.

POI F Streetcar right-of-way

Parking lot between buildings at 4312 and 4316 Upton Ave. South

Streetcars in the Twin Cities sometimes operated on private rights-of-way in the middle of blocks. This parking lot was once just such a right-of-way. Tracks here were first built in 1882 by the Minneapolis, Lyndale and Minnetonka Railway. From this point, the right-of-way—taken over by streetcars in the 1890s—continued just north of 44th St. West to the city limits and beyond.

72 Church of St. Thomas the Apostle

2914 44th St. West

Joseph V. Vanderbilt, 1927 / additions, 1955, 1996

An Italian Romanesque Revival–style church designed by architect Joseph Vanderbilt, who was also a member of the parish. There were plans to build a grander church to the east along Upton Ave., after which this building was to become an auditorium for the parish school. The Depression and World War II intervened, however, and the big church never materialized.

LOST 3 *A remarkable home and garden once stood along 44th St. West in what is now the St. Thomas Church parking lot. The Frank and Ottalie Fletcher House was built in about 1900 by an insurance agent and his wife. The grounds included a Japanese garden with a pond, winding pathways, and cedar trees sheltering a*

Buddha. The Fletchers sold their home and garden to St. Thomas in

Frank and Ottalie Fletcher House, 1902

1923. After serving as the parish's rectory, the house was demolished in 1940, and the high-maintenance garden went with it.

73 Linden Hills Community Library N L

2900 43rd St. West

Bard and Vanderbilt, 1931 / restored and enlarged, Leonard Parker Associates, 2002

Although this library's Tudor Revival styling is conventional, inside you'll find a series of gracious reading rooms, including one with a fireplace.

2726–32 43rd St. West, detail

74 Commercial building

2726–32 43rd St. West

Downs and Eads, 1915

A Prairie Style commercial building with vigorous terra-cotta ornament in the manner of Louis Sullivan and George Elmslie. It was originally built as a telephone exchange.

75 Wild Rumpus Bookstore (Lake Harriet Commercial Club)

2718–20 43rd St. West

Downs and Eads, 1911 / remodeled, Bowers Bryan and Feidt, 1992

This brick Classical Revival building was originally home to a club. The children's bookstore

within, designed in 1992, is a delight, featuring many whimsical touches.

76 Charles and Katherine Van Tuyl House

4236 Queen Ave. South

Harry Jones, 1897 and later

Set on a hill above terraced walls, this brick and stucco Tudor Revival mansion was built for Charles Van Tuyl, who was in the insurance business. Van Tuyl acquired lots to the rear along Linden Hills Blvd. and gradually created a mini-estate outfitted with stables, a tennis court, and a greenhouse. In 1933, a new owner, U.S. Senator Thomas D. Schall, moved in. A Republican, Schall was also the first blind man elected to the U.S. House of Representatives and to the U.S. Senate. Schall, who'd lost his sight in an accident as a young man, had nearly completed his second senate term in late 1935 when he was struck and killed by a car in Washington, DC.

77 James and Alice Johns House

4000 Linden Hills Blvd.

Orff and Joralemon, 1894

One of the first houses built in this part of Linden Hills, on a lot that the neighborhood's developers provided free of charge. The original owner was in the grain business.

Frank E. Lovell House

78 Frank E. Lovell House

2504 40th St. West

Lowell Lamoreaux, 1906

A wonderful Swiss Chalet–style house. Balconies sheltered under deep overhanging eaves extend all the way around the house, which also has a terrace offering views of Lake Harriet.

POI G Cottage City

Area bounded by Richfield Rd., Xerxes Ave. South, Calhoun Pkwy. West, and 40th St. West

This area on the south side of Lake Calhoun was platted in 1882–83 by developer Louis Menage as Cottage City. The plat specified lots 25 feet wide, compared to the norm of 40 feet. Menage hoped small lots would attract people wanting to build summer lake cottages. Development was slow, however, and most of the early homes that survive here weren't built until after 1900. As Cottage City filled out, lots were often combined, but some narrow lots remain, mostly along Thomas, Vincent, and Upton Aves. The old "cottages" themselves are scattered here and there, usually in remodeled form. There's an especially good group on the 3800 block of Thomas.

79 Chadwick Cottages *L*

2617 40th St. West

Loren Chadwick (builder), 1902 / enlarged and combined, 1972

Perhaps the best remaining example of what Cottage City's small homes once looked like. One of the three identical cottages built here in 1902 was removed in 1929, but the other two stayed put. In 1972, new owners merged the pair by connecting them with an addition at the rear.

Robert and Isabella Giles House

80 Robert and Isabella Giles House

4106 Vincent Ave. South

Jager and Stravs, 1908

One of the city's most secretive houses, set atop a wooded hill hidden away within an otherwise ordinary residential block. The house is as unusual as its site. Architects John Jager and Carl Stravs were born in the Austro-Hungarian Empire and were trained by leaders of the Viennese Secessionist movement, an early branch of modernism. The house's curving eaves, blue brick accents, and exotic Art Nouveau details make it a one-of-a-kind production. It was built for Robert Tait Giles, an artist who founded his own stained-glass company in Minneapolis, and his wife, Isabella.

POI H Infill houses

3600 block Zenith Ave. South

various architects, ca. 2000 and later

This block has several McMansions akin to those found elsewhere around the Minneapolis lakes. Some of these infill homes result from teardowns, in which perfectly good houses are

Chadwick Cottages, 1983

destroyed to make way for fancier properties. This phenomenon isn't new: the first big wave of teardowns in the Twin Cities occurred in the 1880s along ritzy streets like Summit Ave. in St. Paul. What's different now is that out-sized new houses are often being wedged into modest lots, and the effect is like squeezing an SUV into a tiny parking space: it can be done, but seldom gracefully.

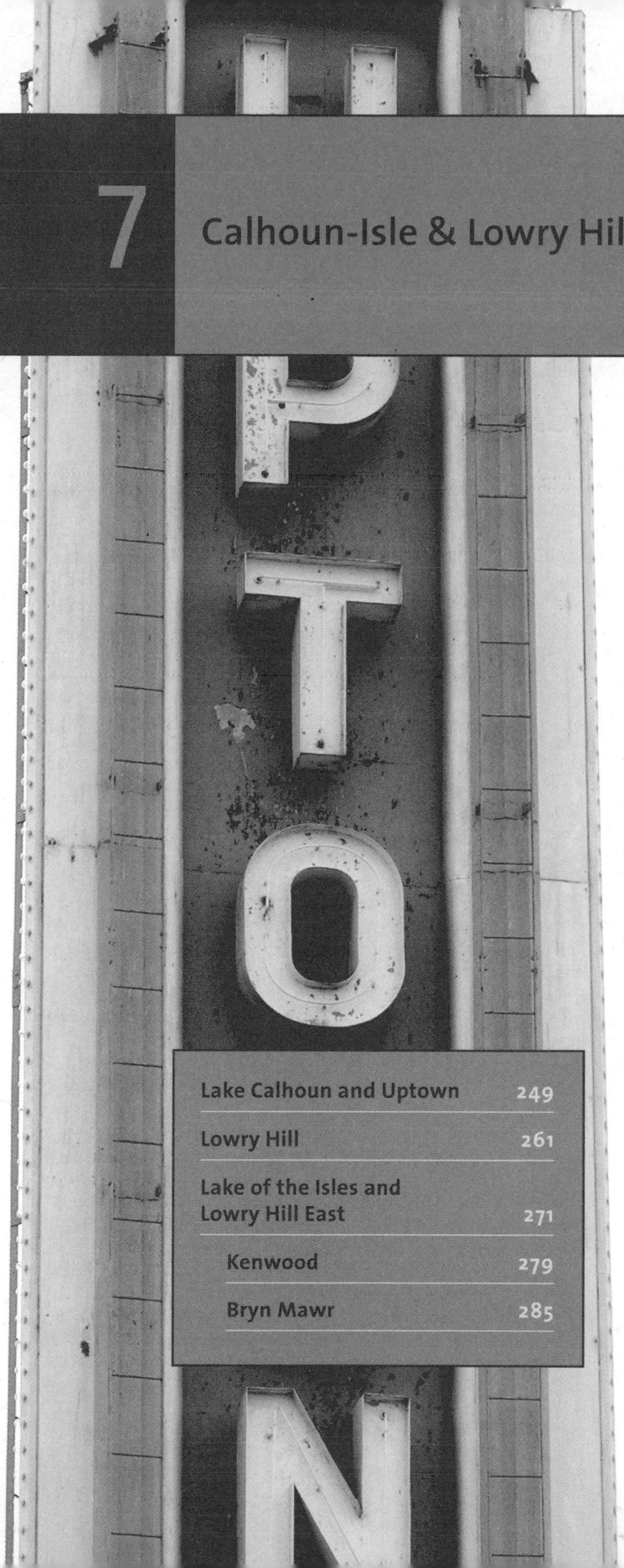

7 Calhoun-Isle & Lowry Hill

Overview

Known as the Lake District, this remarkable area is the image Minneapolis strives to present to the world. Four lakes—Calhoun, Isles, Cedar, and Brownie—form an interconnected chain here, encircled by parks and parkways. By one estimate more than 5.5 million people a year visit the lakes to walk, jog, bike, skate, swim, or simply enjoy the scenery. Around this glacial gift of water lies a world of sumptuous homes, manicured lawns, and gracious curving streets. These neighborhoods have been prime residential territory for at least a century and show no signs of losing their popularity.

At the edges of Calhoun-Isle, just north and west of the lakes, you'll find two other neighborhoods—Lowry Hill and Bryn Mawr—that offer their own distinct charms. Lowry Hill, a steep glacial ridge lined with mansions that overlook downtown, is Minneapolis's version of Summit Avenue in St. Paul, albeit on a smaller scale. Farther west is Bryn Mawr, a pleasant residential enclave near Bassett's Creek.

Despite their natural appeal, the lakes didn't come prepackaged with amenities. It wasn't until the Minneapolis Park Board had undertaken its work of dredging and shoreline stabilization, which lasted well into the twentieth century, that the lakes began to attract wealthy home builders. This explains why most of the oldest homes in Calhoun-Isle are actually well away from water's edge.

The first landowners here were farmers and speculators, both of whom arrived in droves once most of what is now Minneapolis was thrown open to settlement in the 1850s. The largest property owner was William King, who amassed 1,400 acres along the eastern side of Lake Calhoun. He built a house, barn, and other buildings on what became known as Lyndale Farmstead. By the late 1870s, as rail and horsecar lines penetrated into the Lake District, King and at least two competitors built short-lived resort hotels on Lake Calhoun. Another hotel, the Oak Grove House, appeared on Cedar Lake.

Everyone knew that the district would one day attract fine homes, and development soon started spilling south from downtown, following a horsecar line that ran on Lyndale Avenue and the so-called Motor Line along Hennepin Avenue. The Wedge neighborhood between Lyndale and Hennepin saw some of the earliest housing, as did Lowry Hill. The introduction of streetcar service in 1890 spurred development, especially in Kenwood, where many pre-1900 homes survive. However, the big houses overlooking the lakes usually date from about 1910 to 1930.

Although it's primarily residential, the Lake District includes one of the city's most important commercial hubs: the ultra-trendy (by Minneapolis standards) Uptown area, centered around the intersection of Lake Street and Hennepin Avenue. Calhoun-Isle is also home to one of the city's most important cultural institutions—the Walker Art Center and Minneapolis Sculpture Garden (1971 and later), located on a pivotal site at Hennepin and Lyndale, where downtown meets the northern flank of Lowry Hill.

Architecturally, the glory of the Lake District is its stock of superb houses. These include the Frank Long House (1894), a sterling example of the Richardsonian Romanesque style; Chicago architect George Maher's intriguing Winton House (1910) on Lowry Hill; four Prairie houses designed by William Purcell and George Elmslie, including the incomparable Purcell-Cutts House (1913); a late and lovely work from Frank Lloyd Wright, the Neils House (1951) on Cedar Lake; and the rigorously modern Kenneth and Judy Dayton House (1997).

Lake Calhoun and Uptown

This is the most varied portion of the Calhoun-Isle neighborhood. Here you'll find the city's largest lake, a broad mix of homes and apartments, an old rail and industrial corridor that's attracted much new development, and, of course, the Uptown district with its conglomeration of shops, restaurants, and theaters.

At the center of it all is Lake Calhoun. While the city's other lakes are ensconced in exclusively residential neighborhoods, Calhoun is bordered on the north by Lake Street, a heavily traveled thoroughfare. Commercial buildings and residential towers as high as 20 stories loom over this end of the lake. It's quieter along the southern and western shores, where expensive homes drink in the scenery.

Just to the east of the lake is the thriving Uptown area, where the look ranges from chic to punk and the action goes on well into the night. What might be called the modern era of Uptown's development began in the early 1980s when the Calhoun Square shopping mall opened at Hennepin and Lake. More recently, scores of new condominiums and apartments have added to Uptown's vitality—and traffic. The Calhoun-Uptown area also had an industrial zone at one time along the old Milwaukee Road tracks—today's Midtown Greenway—paralleling 29th Street. Among the former factories that still stand here is the Buzza Co. Building (1907 and later).

The residential neighborhoods to the east of Lake Calhoun are generally quite modest. Here, early twentieth-century houses and walk-up apartment buildings predominate. The western side of the lake, near the city limits, has some larger homes, including the Goodfellow House (1930), now a museum. Much of this choice area is taken up by the Minikahda Country Club (1898), the city's oldest golf course.

POI A Lake Calhoun parks and parkway

Minneapolis Park Board, 1886 and later

Named in 1817 after U.S. secretary of war John C. Calhoun (who authorized construction of Fort Snelling), this 422-acre lake was known to the Dakota as *Mde Medoza* (Lake of the Loons). The first year-round settlement, on the eastern shore, was Cloud Man's Village, established in 1828. Brothers Samuel and Gideon Pond built a cabin nearby six years later. Both the village and the cabin were gone by 1840. The lake area remained largely unpopulated until the 1870s, when resort hotels sprang up. Later, at least two companies began harvesting ice from the lake and built sheds along the northern shore that stood until 1909. For the most part, however, the lake was undeveloped when the Minneapolis Park Board began acquiring land around it in 1886. By 1909, the board had control of the entire lake and 89 acres of shoreland, for a cost of just $127,000.

Although a naturally deep lake, Calhoun's original shoreline was marshy, and today's parkways and beaches were made possible by dredging undertaken between 1911 and 1915 and again in the 1920s. All told, the park board's dredging crews removed more than a million cubic yards of material and redeposited it along the shore. A channel linking Calhoun to Lake of the Isles was completed in 1911. Over the next several years, the park board dug canals connecting Isles to Cedar and Cedar to Brownie, creating the chain of lakes as they're known today.

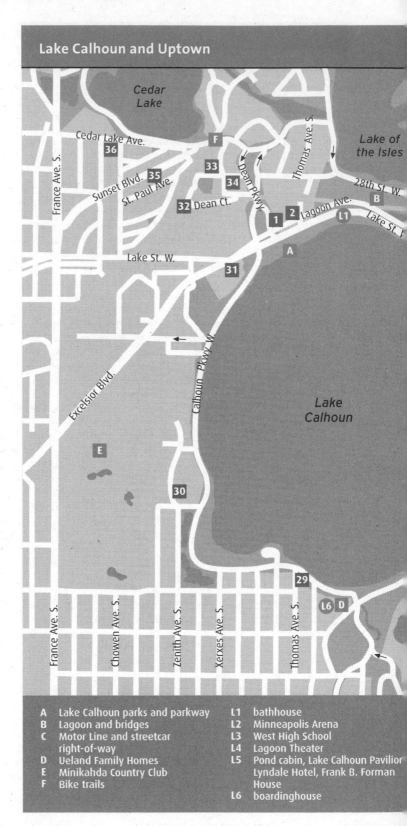

Lake Calhoun and Uptown

A   Lake Calhoun parks and parkway
B   Lagoon and bridges
C   Motor Line and streetcar
    right-of-way
D   Ueland Family Homes
E   Minikahda Country Club
F   Bike trails

L1   bathhouse
L2   Minneapolis Arena
L3   West High School
L4   Lagoon Theater
L5   Pond cabin, Lake Calhoun Pavilion
     Lyndale Hotel, Frank B. Forman
     House
L6   boardinghouse

26th St. W.

Hennepin Ave. S.

Lake of the Isles Pkwy.

28th St. W.

29th St. W.

Lagoon Ave.

Lake St. W.

James Ave. S.

Irving Ave. S.

Humboldt Ave. S.

Hennepin Ave. S.

Fremont Ave. S.

Dupont Ave. S.

Lyndale Ave. S.

31st St. W.

32nd St. W.

33rd St. W.

34th St. W.

35th St. W.

Calhoun Pkwy. E.

Holmes Ave. S.

Girard Ave. S.

Emerson Ave. S.

Colfax Ave. S.

Aldrich Ave. S.

Bryant Ave. S.

Lyndale Ave. S.

36th St. W.

1	Vintage Apartments	19	Joyce Memorial Methodist Church
2	Calhoun Beach Club Apartments	20	Houses
3	Edgewater Condominiums	21	Calhoun Park Terrace
4	Condominiums	22	Castle Jeweler
5	Moorish Mansion Apartments	23	First Universalist Church
6	Lehmann Education Center	24	Apartment building
7	Crowell Block	25	Hennepin Aristocrat Apartments
8	Track 29 Lofts	26	House
9	Midtown Lofts	27	House
10	Mozaic Condominiums	28	St. Mary's Greek Orthodox Church
11	Granada Apartments	29	House
12	Commercial building	30	The Bakken Library and Museum
13	Uptown Transit Station	31	Lake Calhoun Executive Center
14	Walker Community Library	32	3141 Dean Court
15	Old Walker Branch Library	33	George and Frances Reid House
16	Uptown Theatre	34	Duplexes
17	Calhoun Square	35	NowHaus01
18	Suburban World Theatre	36	Aaron and Naomi Friedell House

Vintage Apartments, 1963

1 Vintage Apartments (Calhoun Beach Club) N

2925 Dean Pkwy.

Charles W. Nicol (Chicago) with Magney and Tusler, 1928–46 / renovated, 1977 / renovated, ESG Architects, 2002

In the early 1920s, businessman Harry S. Goldie conceived of the idea for a swank club and residential building overlooking Lake Calhoun. By 1928 he'd raised enough money to begin construction of this Renaissance Revival–style building, which at the time was the tallest outside the downtown core. Goldie's timing proved poor, however. The stock market crashed just as the building neared completion in 1929, and it stood vacant until after World War II. When it finally opened in 1946, the building consisted of ground-floor commercial space, club facilities (including a pool, gymnasium, and ballroom) on the lower three floors, and apartments and one floor of hotel rooms above. In 2002, the building was extensively renovated; it now includes 57 luxury apartments as well as a health club, retail space, and meeting rooms.

2 Calhoun Beach Club Apartments

2900 Thomas Ave. South

KKE Architects, 1999

This 12-story apartment complex just to the east of the Calhoun Beach Club is an example of what might be called the Beau Brummel Style: a flashy architectural dandy clad in such thin material you have to wonder how long it will be before it begins to look threadbare.

LOST 1 *The north shore of Lake Calhoun was once the site of a large* **bathhouse.** *Built in 1912, it was a Spanish-Moorish concoction with a twin-towered central pavilion flanked by large changing rooms. These were open to the sky, thereby affording residents who moved into the upper floors of the Calhoun Beach Club an interesting view. It didn't last for long: four years after the club opened in 1946, the bathhouse was demolished.*

Bridge over lagoon at Lake St.

POI B Lagoon and bridges

Lagoon between Lake Calhoun and Lake of the Isles

Minneapolis Park Board, 1911

Bridges at Lake St. and Lake of the Isles Pkwy.

Cowles and Chapman, 1911

The isthmus between Lake Calhoun and Lake of the Isles was once a swampy lowland. Partially filled in by the construction of railroad tracks in the 1880s, it assumed its present configuration in 1911, when the Minneapolis Park Board completed the channel and small lagoon that connect the two lakes. This work was part of a project that also entailed dredging and reshaping Lake of the Isles. To span the new channel here, and another that would link Isles to Cedar Lake, new bridges were required. The park board held a design competition for these structures. William Cowles and Cecil B. Chapman of Minneapolis won, and their classically inspired concrete-arch bridges are still in service today. The bridge at Lake St. features an elliptical arch faced in granite. Other bridges are clad in limestone and include balustrades and ornamental keystones.

3 Edgewater Condominiums

1805 Lake St. West

ESG Architects, 2006

A chunky six-story condominium building that would have looked better had it been taller and thinner. But residents in most Twin Cities' neighborhoods have become averse to height, making slender residential towers all but impossible to build outside of downtown areas.

4 Condominiums

3033 Calhoun Pkwy. East

Richard F. Zenisek, 1973

An angular building sheathed in wood. The sawtooth profile assures that each apartment has a good view of the lake.

5 Moorish Mansion Apartments *L*

3028 James Ave. South

Carl J. Bard, 1929

Apartment buildings from the 1920s offer a salmagundi of styles, the more exotic the better. Here the look is Islamic Revival, done with considerable flair.

Uptown

Area centering around Lake St. West and Hennepin Ave.

Although there's no official Minneapolis neighborhood called "Uptown," the area around Lake St. and Hennepin Ave. has been known by this name since at least the 1920s. Once a major streetcar transfer point, the intersection is now at the center of what might be called Minneapolis's *other* downtown—home to shops, clubs, restaurants, and theaters, along with a growing number of apartments and condominiums. Commercial development surged here in the early 1900s after the city rescinded an earlier designation of Hennepin Ave. as a parkway south of downtown. By the 1920s several hundred businesses were operating near Hennepin and Lake. The opening of Calhoun Square shopping mall in 1983 helped revitalize the neighborhood, which is now among the busiest places in the Twin Cities.

Buzza Co. Building, 1920

6 Lehmann Education Center (Buzza Co. Building)

1006 Lake St. West

1907 / additions, Magney and Tusler, 1923–27 / renovated, 1971 and later

This brick and concrete industrial building, mildly Classical Revival in style, is among the largest structures in Uptown. The oldest portion dates to 1907. It was purchased in 1923 and greatly expanded by the Buzza Co., once the nation's second-largest maker of greeting cards and calendars. The company's namesake and founder, George Buzza, was a commercial artist who branched out into the card business in 1909. Buzza brought in talented artists to design his cards and hired popular poet Edgar Guest, among others, to endow them with memorable sentiments.

The company grew rapidly and enlarged this building three times in the 1920s. Most of it was loft space, but the upper floors once included elegant offices and showrooms furnished with Italian antiques. The company merged with a New York firm in 1928 to become the Buzza-Clark Co., but its fortunes sank during the Great Depression. It went out of business in 1942, when the federal government acquired the building. The government sold it in 1971 to the Minneapolis Public Schools, which uses it as an education center.

7 Crowell Block *L*

614 Lake St. West

Joralemon and Ferrin, 1888 / renovated, Dovolis Johnson and Ruggieri, 1990

A Richardsonian Romanesque building that features rusticated sandstone facades, bay and arched windows, and a heavy stone parapet. With its broad windows and narrow piers, the building has a more open, cellular look than is typical of the Richardsonian style. Frank Crowell, after whom the building is named, was a real estate developer.

8 Track 29 Lofts

Aldrich and Bryant Aves. South north of 29th St. West

2006

9 Midtown Lofts

Bryant and Colfax Aves. South north of 29th St. West

ESG Architects, 2004

These projects are part of a plan to create an "urban village" here with nearly 200 units of housing. The stucco-, brick-, and metal-clad apartments and townhomes built so far eschew nostalgia and should be hip enough to attract the Uptown crowd.

LOST 2 *Where Uptown Rainbow Foods stands at 1104 Lagoon Ave. was from 1920 to 1965 the site of the* **Minneapolis Arena.** *Never much to look at, the 5,000-seat arena was used primarily for hockey and ice events but also did occasional duty as a ballroom. The Ice Follies, founded by three Minneapolis men, got its start at the arena in the 1930s.*

10 Mozaic Condominiums

1320 Lagoon Ave.

BKV Group, 2007

An office, retail, and residential complex organized around a plaza is planned for this site.

Granada Apartments, 1968

11 Granada Apartments

1456 Lagoon Ave.

Carl J. Bard, 1929

It's said that the Islamic look of many buildings in the 1920s was influenced by the popularity of silent film star Rudolph Valentino, who did several turns as a sheik during his brief career. Be that as it may, this apartment building does a nice Spanish-Moorish turn of its own. The loveliest feature is an arcaded front courtyard.

12 Commercial building

2748–56 Hennepin Ave.

Jenson and Foss, 1927

A charming little building dominated by arched windows with circling bricks laid in such a way that they almost look wedged into place. There's also plenty of stone and terra-cotta trim, not to mention spiral pinnacles along the roofline.

LOST 3 *The Kenwood Isles Condominiums at 1425 28th St. West occupy the site of* **West High School.** *The school, built in 1907, was a sturdy Classical Revival design featuring large arched entries to either side of a pedimented central pavilion. The school closed its doors in 1982 and was demolished two years later.*

13 Uptown Transit Station

Hennepin Ave. at 29th St. over Midtown Greenway

LSA Design, 2001

A zippy brick, glass, and steel transit station with a cable-supported roof and a clock tower.

14 Walker Community Library

2880 Hennepin Ave. South

Myers and Bennett and BRW Architects, 1981 / renovated, Bonestroo, Rosene, Anderlik and Associates, 2004

A library for bookworms who like to burrow. The two main floors are set below grade and overlook a sunken courtyard. An entry pavilion with a large "library" sign pops up on Hennepin to let you know there's a building somewhere below. The problem with underground buildings is that they don't make much of a statement, and as of 2006 proposals were being considered to replace this library with one that would have a more visible presence in the community.

15 Old Walker Branch Library *L*

2901 Hennepin Ave. South

Jerome Paul Jackson, 1911 / remodeled, 1984

A Classical Revival building constructed of light brown Roman brick with limestone trim. It was last used as a library in 1980, just before its replacement opened across the street.

Uptown Theatre

16 Uptown Theatre *i*

2906 Hennepin Ave.

Liebenberg and Kaplan, 1939 / remodeled, 1968 / Art: murals, Gustave Krollman, 1939

The city's last single-screen movie theater, and a fine example of the Moderne style. The theater, which has survived by showing art films and the like, features Mankato-Kasota stone

walls punctuated by an exclamation point in the form of a 50-foot-high vertical sign. Originally topped by a searchlight, the sign is a dramatic presence along Hennepin. Also accenting the theater's facades are two bas-relief sculptures framed within circles. Inside, the lobby has been compromised by remodeling, but the auditorium retains two murals, the best of which depicts bare-breasted maidens pouring water from one city lake to another. Compare this artistic delight to what passes for decoration in movie houses today, and you'll understand why people love old theaters.

LOST 4 *The first movie house here was the **Lagoon Theater,** which opened in 1913 and included a second-floor dance hall. The theater was remodeled and renamed the Uptown in 1929 but was demolished ten years later after a fire.*

17 Calhoun Square

3001 Hennepin Ave. West (at Lake St.)

*Paul Pink and Associates, 1983 / incorporates older buildings, including the **Geanakoplos Building,** Adam Lansing Dorr, 1917 / addition, ca. 2007*

A classic redevelopment project from the early 1980s, a time when significant tax credits were available and there was renewed public interest in historic preservation. This atrium-style indoor shopping mall, built from a group of old buildings, isn't especially impressive as a design, but it played a critical role in launching a new wave of development in Uptown. As of 2007, developers were planning an addition with apartments and retail space.

18 Suburban World (Granada) Theatre *i*

3022 Hennepin Ave.

Liebenberg and Kaplan, 1928 / remodeled, 1954, 1966

Originally the Granada, this old movie house—now used mainly for live performances and special events—is the last operating "atmospheric" theater in the Twin

Suburban World Theatre

Cities. Invented by St. Louis architect John Eberson in the early 1920s, this type of theater was designed to convey a sense of being outside at night in a romantic setting. Eberson wrote: "We visualize and dream a magnificent amphitheater, an Italian garden, a Persian court, a Spanish patio, or a mystic Egyptian templeyard, all canopied by a soft moonlight sky." For the Granada, architects Liebenberg and Kaplan opted for the Spanish patio. Balconies, balustrades, and arched doorways rise along the auditorium walls, while stars and drifting clouds animate the ceiling. The theater's lobby and entrances have been remodeled, but much of the front facade, decorated in a style known as Spanish Churrigueresque Revival, remains intact.

19 Joyce Memorial Methodist Church

1219 31st St. West

Downs and Eads, 1907

Established in 1886, this church was renamed in 1905 after a Methodist bishop, Isaac Joyce, who fell dead while delivering a fire-and-brimstone sermon. The church is a thoroughgoing example of the California Mission look, complete with a three-stage tower, sculpted parapets, and tile roofs.

20 Houses

3136, 3140, 3142 Colfax Ave. South

ca. 1883–85

Three working-class homes that must have been all but identical originally. The L shape and narrow front profile are characteristic of vernacular housing in the 1880s.

21 Calhoun Park Terrace

3013–23 Aldrich Ave. South

1888

One of the Lake District's few row houses. The style is a blend of Queen Anne and Romanesque Revival. There's another row house a few blocks away, at 3310–20 Humboldt Ave. South.

Castle Jeweler

22 Castle Jeweler (White Castle Building No. 8) N *L*

3252 Lyndale Ave. South

L. W. Ray, 1936

The oldest home of little square hamburgers in the Twin Cities, now selling gems instead of gut bombs. The White Castle chain, founded in Kansas in 1921, had by the 1930s become such a large operation that it maintained its own fabricating plant, where this 840-square-foot porcelain-steel building was made. It's one of only a half dozen or so White Castle buildings of this type left in the United States. The building was erected in 1936 at 616 Washington Ave. Southeast and later relocated to 329 Central Ave. Southeast. White Castle closed the restaurant in 1983. Preservationists working with the city saved the structure from demolition and moved it here.

23 First Universalist Church (Adath Jeshurun Synagogue) *L*

3400 Dupont Ave. South

Liebenberg and Kaplan, 1927 / additions, Liebenberg and Kaplan, 1954 and later

This Renaissance Revival–style building was constructed for Adath Jeshurun, founded in 1884 by immigrants from Eastern Europe and said to be the oldest Conservative Jewish congregation west of Chicago. Adath Jeshurun moved to a new synagogue in suburban Minnetonka in the early 1990s and sold this building to the First Universalist Church.

24 Apartment building

3452 Emerson Ave. South

1969

Mansard roofs of ridiculous size sprouted like bad hairdos on many apartment buildings in the 1960s and 1970s. Here's a classic, done in a screaming blue so you can't miss it.

Hennepin Aristocrat Apartments

25 Hennepin Aristocrat Apartments

3332 Hennepin Ave.

Liebenberg and Kaplan, 1961

The architectural equivalent of a loud sport coat—the kind, say, a car salesman might have worn in the days of tail fins and V-8s. High-toned 1960s modernists of the less-is-more school must have been appalled by the building's multicolored brick facade, which also offers gaudy grill-like panels made from patterned concrete blocks. But if you enjoy the sweet aroma of kitsch when it wafts your way, then you will adore this building.

POI C Motor Line and streetcar right-of-way

Alley in block bounded by 32nd and 34th Sts., Irving Ave. South, and Calhoun Pkwy. East

1879 and later

Go down this long alley and you'll discover that most of the garages on the west side are set farther back than you'd expect them to be. The reason for this anomaly is that the alley occupies part of what was once a 33-foot-wide private right-of-way, used first by the Minneapolis, Lyndale and Lake Calhoun Railway (the Motor Line) and later by streetcars. When the streetcar era ended in the 1950s, the tracks were removed and the right-of-way vacated.

26 House

3247 Calhoun Pkwy. East

ca. 1900

Most of the older houses on Lake Calhoun are along the eastern shore. This one has a side tower and concrete block walls with a sandstone-like veneer laid up in an interlocking pattern.

27 House

3424 Humboldt Ave. South

1946

A two-story Moderne box with rose-colored concrete trim.

St. Mary's Greek Orthodox Church

28 St. Mary's Greek Orthodox Church

3450 Irving Ave. South

Thorshov and Cerny, 1957 / addition, Chris Kamagais, 2001

Occupying a historic site overlooking Lake Calhoun, this church blends traditional and modern elements. The Greek cross shape and a golden dome are common features of Orthodox churches, but here they're combined with crisply detailed brickwork and a glass-walled entry typical of 1950s modernism. An events center was added in 2001.

Frank B. Forman House, 1953

LOST 5 *St. Mary's stands on a site with a long history of buildings. In the courtyard, a plaque commemorates the* **Pond cabin,** *built by Samuel and Gideon Pond in 1834. The next occupant of note was William King, whose 1,400-acre Lyndale Farm included this site. In 1879, King built his* **Lake Calhoun Pavilion** *here. Later, real estate developer Louis Menage took over the pavilion and renamed it the* **Lyndale Hotel.** *In an era of cigar smoking and oil lamps, wooden hotels were notoriously prone to combustion, and the Lyndale burned down in 1888. The site then remained vacant until 1901, when the* **Frank B. Forman House** *appeared. Forman, who founded a glass and paint company, built the 20-room mansion for himself and his wife. He died in 1912, but his wife lived in the house until her death in 1949. The house was demolished six years later.*

POI D Ueland Family Homes

Calhoun Pkwy. West and Richfield Rd.

1890 and later

In 1890, Andreas and Clara Ueland built a 16-room Colonial Revival house on a site wedged between Calhoun Pkwy. and Richfield Rd. He was a Norwegian immigrant who became a probate court judge. She was a teacher and suffrage advocate. Their eight children included three Nordicly

named sons—Sigurd, Rolf, and Arnulf—who in the 1920s built the houses at 3832, 3846, and 3850 Richfield Rd. One of the couple's daughters, Brenda Ueland, was a talented writer who produced articles for leading magazines, later worked for the *Minneapolis Times,* and in 1939 wrote an autobiography entitled *Me.* The Andreas and Clara Ueland House was torn down in 1953. Condominiums and townhomes at 3810 and 3830–32 Calhoun Pkwy. West now occupy the site. Brenda Ueland continued to live nearby until her death, at age 93, in 1985.

LOST 6 *Before Andreas and Clara Ueland built their home here, the property was the site of a* **boardinghouse** *operated by a certain Mrs. Elizabeth Hamilton. It's not clear when the establishment was built, but it is known that Henry David Thoreau, author of* Walden, *stayed at Mrs. Hamilton's during his visit to the Lake District in June 1861.*

29 House

3766 Calhoun Pkwy. West

ca. 1860s and later

Portions of this house, which shows traces of the Greek Revival style, may date to the 1860s. If so, it's the oldest house on Lake Calhoun.

The Bakken Library and Museum

30 The Bakken Library and Museum (William Goodfellow House, "West Winds")

3537 Zenith Ave. South

Carl Gage, 1930 / addition, MS&R Architects, 1998

Focusing on the role of electricity and magnetism in medicine, this museum occupies a house built—

so it's said—for love. The story goes that William Goodfellow constructed the 15-room mansion, called "West Winds," to impress a woman he hoped to marry. The mansion's stone, stucco, and half-timbered exterior is fairly conventional Tudor Revival, but the interior is lavish. It includes a great hall, wood-carving executed by Italian craftsmen, and 11 bathrooms. Alas, Goodfellow's building campaign didn't win over the woman of his dreams, and he died in 1944, presumably unrequited. The house was sold in 1976 to the Bakken. The museum and library were established by Earl Bakken, cofounder of Medtronic Corp., a Twin Cities–based company known for its cardiac pacemakers. A seamless addition nearly doubled the size of the museum in 1998. The museum's large grounds include a garden designed by Michael Swingley.

POI E Minikahda Country Club

Includes *clubhouse*, 3205 Excelsior Blvd.

Long and Long, 1899, 1902 / numerous additions / renovated, Partners and Sirny, 1995

Established in 1898 on a bluff overlooking Lake Calhoun, this is the city's oldest golf course. The Classical Revival–style clubhouse dates to 1899 but has several additions. In 1916, the U.S. Open golf tournament was held here—the only "major" ever played in Minneapolis.

31 Lake Calhoun Executive Center (American Hardware Mutual Building)

3033 Excelsior Blvd.

1955 / remodeled, 1988

A 1950s office building that received a complete face-lift in the 1980s and now looks as though it would be perfectly at home in a suburban office park.

32 3141 Dean Court (grain elevators)

3141 Dean Ct.

McKenzie-Hague Co., 1915–28 / renovated, Brantingham Architects, 1982–85

This is the first—and so far the only—example in the Twin Cities of concrete grain silos being converted into housing. It wasn't done with much panache, however, and instead of celebrating the historic silos, the architects did their best to cover them up.

33 George and Frances Reid House

3114 28th St. West

Molly Reid (Los Angeles), 2004

A colorful house, clearly under the influence of Frank Gehry and other California modernists. Built for the architect's parents, the house has sculpted volumes, an eclectic mix of cladding materials, eccentric window shapes, and an angular metal roof, all set behind a brick screen formed by portions of an old commercial storefront that once occupied the site.

34 Duplexes

2801, 2805 Xerxes Ave. South

Perry Crosier, 1936

A pair of stuccoed duplexes with corner windows, stepped-down staircases, and projecting balconies. Not as exciting as, say, Miami Beach's tropical deco, but pretty jazzy for Minnesota.

POI F Bike trails

Various rail corridors

An outstanding feature of the Lake District is the system of trails that thread through the neighborhood along old rail corridors. The Cedar Lake Trail, established in 1995, follows a former Great Northern right-of-way. The Kenilworth Trail, which cuts between Cedar Lake and Lake of the Isles, is built along an old Chicago and Northwestern route. It connects to yet another rail corridor trail—the Midtown Greenway—that follows a former Milwaukee Road line.

NowHaus01

35 NowHaus01

3440 St. Paul Ave.

1952 / rebuilt, Locus Architecture (Wynne Yelland and Paul Neseth), 2004

This house, built up from a 1950s rambler, garnered reams of publicity when it appeared on an otherwise ordinary residential block. It employs novel materials such as siding made from billboard vinyl, and it's also full of trendy design features. Overall, the house is a bit much, but if not for young architects exploring new ideas, the world of design would be very dull indeed.

36 Aaron and Naomi Friedell House *L*

2700 Chowen Ave. South

Norman R. Johnson, 1940

An interesting Moderne-style house. Aaron Friedell was a physician who helped develop the first health maintenance organization in the Twin Cities. His wife, Naomi, was a sculptor. It appears both worked closely with St. Paul architect Norman Johnson in designing the house.

Lowry Hill

The elevation known as Lowry Hill was once called the Devil's Backbone, a fanciful name often applied to steep-sided ridges. Unlike Old Nick's presumably gnarled spine, the hill once had two crests, which were leveled out in the 1880s. Because of its height and its proximity to the Lake District, the hill was identified early on as a prime spot for mansion building.

Lowry Hill was in fact the first portion of the Lake District to be platted. Soon-to-be transit kingpin Thomas Lowry, a lawyer who'd arrived in Minneapolis in 1867, was among the real estate men who prepared the plat in 1872. Two years later, Lowry built the first mansion on the hill, which later took his name. It wasn't until the 1880s, however, that other homes began to appear on Mount Curve—Minneapolis's version of Summit Avenue—and other winding streets atop the hill. The more typical gridiron of streets along the southern reaches of the hill generally saw development a bit later, with most of the houses dating from between 1890 and 1910. Today, mansions still line Mount Curve and other streets in Lowry Hill. Quite a few are early to mid-twentieth-century replacements of Victorian-era homes. More recently, infill properties—mainly condominiums—have been shoehorned into just about every available lot.

While most of Lowry Hill is residential, its northern flank is dominated by the Walker Art Center, which built its first museum on the site in 1927 after its founder, Thomas Walker, acquired the Lowry mansion. In 1963 the Guthrie Theater also located here, next to the Walker, but Ralph Rapson's seminal building was demolished in 2006 to make way for an eventual expansion of the Walker's sculpture garden.

1 Dunwoody College of Technology

818 Dunwoody Blvd.

Hewitt and Brown, ca. 1917, 1925, and later

A pleasant group of brick buildings with Classical Revival details. Originally known as the Dunwoody Institute and now a two-year technical college, it was founded in 1914 with a $3 million bequest from businessman William H. Dunwoody, who once owned a mansion nearby.

2 301 Kenwood Parkway

301 Kenwood Pkwy.

ESG Architects, 2003

At a time when an epidemic of nostalgia afflicted most new apartment architecture in the Twin Cities, this mid-rise condominium building came across as a breath of fresh modernist air. Floor-to-ceiling windows alternating with balconies give the building an open feel and also provide residents with views of the Walker Art Center and downtown Minneapolis.

3 Walker Art Center and Minneapolis Sculpture Garden !

1750 Hennepin Ave.

Edward Larrabee Barnes (New York), 1971 and later / addition, Herzog and de Meuron (Switzerland) with HGA, 2005 / sculpture garden, Edward Larrabee Barnes, 1988 / addition, Desvigne-Dalnoky (France), ca. 2007

The Walker and its adjoining sculpture garden occupy a crucial transition point where downtown merges into the hilly terrain of the Lake District. Loring Park, three large churches, and two interstate highways converge here, as do Hennepin and Lyndale Aves. The Walker stands in the middle of it all as a highly visible emblem of modernism—in both its art and its architecture.

The evolution of the Walker began when lumberman, entrepreneur, and art collector Thomas

Lowry Hill

1   Dunwoody College of Technology
2   301 Kenwood Parkway
3   Walker Art Center and Minneapolis
    Sculpture Garden
4   Kodet Architectural Group
5   Groveland Gallery
6   John Lind House
7   Kenwood Gables Apartments
8   First Unitarian Society
9   A. D. Arundel House
10 Charles Martin House
11 Charles and Helen Winton House
12 A. R. Rogers House
13 Lester R. and Josephine Brooks House
14 House
15 Lawrence S. Donaldson House
16 House
17 House
18 House
19 Elizabeth Quinlan House
20 John F. Calhoun House
21 House
22 House
23 E. E. Atkinson House

A   Thomas Lowry Park
B   Early twentieth-century houses

L1 Thomas Lowry House, first Walker
    Art Museum, George Daggett House,
    North American Life and Casualty
    Insurance Co., Tyrone Guthrie
    Theater, Parade Stadium,
    Minneapolis Armory, Armory
    Gardens
L2 Edmund Walton House
L3 William and Kate Dunwoody House

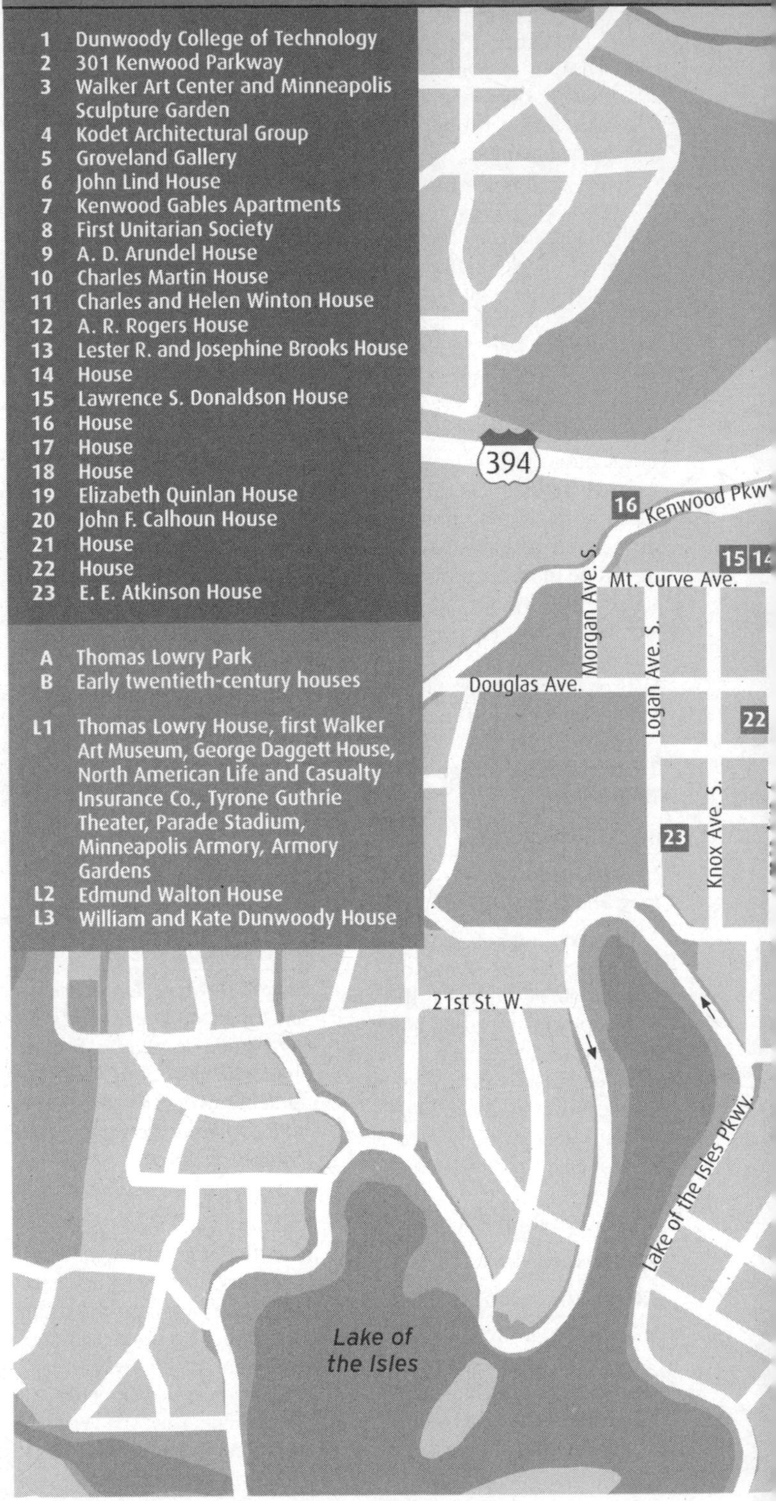

394

16 Kenwood Pkwy

15 14

Morgan Ave. S.

Logan Ave. S.

Mt. Curve Ave.

Douglas Ave.

22

Knox Ave. S.

23

21st St. W.

Lake of the Isles Pkwy

Lake of
the Isles

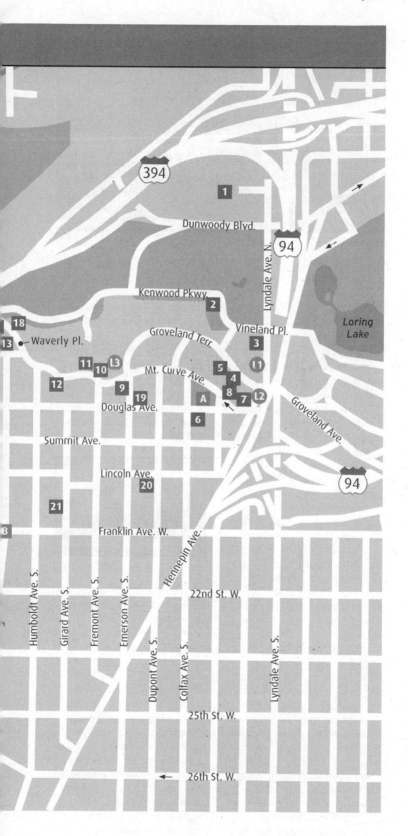

Walker Art Center

Walker bought the old Lowry mansion. Walker immediately laid plans for a new building to house his art. Located next to his home, the museum opened in 1927. It eventually proved too small and was replaced in 1971 by the purple brick building that now forms the northern half of the Walker complex.

The 1971 building was designed by Edward Larrabee Barnes, who studied under such Bauhaus luminaries as Walter Gropius and Marcel Breuer, and it's in the minimalist mode of high modernism. Organized into carefully proportioned volumes, the building has always seemed like a distant father figure—admirable for its disciplined strength but hard to love. It works well, however. Galleries pinwheel around a central core, each a half level above or below the next, allowing museumgoers to follow a clear path.

In 2005, the Walker opened a 130,000-square-foot addition along Hennepin. Designed by the Swiss architectural duo of Jacques Herzog and Pierre de Meuron, the irregularly shaped addition is a playful lump perforated with odd-shaped windows and clad in embossed aluminum mesh panels that, unfortunately, are the color of dirty snow, not an ideal hue in Minnesota. The addition—which includes a lobby, galleries, a museum shop, a restaurant, a theater, offices, and parking—encountered prob-

lems ranging from cost overruns to acoustic flaws. Its meandering plan has also proved confusing to some visitors. Despite these imperfections, the addition is great fun, a sort of architectural exploratorium where wonder and surprise are part of the design strategy. It will set you to thinking about the possibilities of architecture, and that alone makes it a must-see Twin Cities building.

Minneapolis Sculpture Garden

The Walker's other key component is the 11-acre Minneapolis Sculpture Garden, which opened in 1988 and was built in cooperation with the Minneapolis Park and Recreation Board. Most visitors, of course, are interested in the garden's sculpture, the signature piece being Claes Oldenburg and Coosje van Bruggen's *Spoonbridge and Cherry.* Yet the underlying architecture is equally good. Barnes laid out much of the garden as a grid with wide walkways (or *allees,* as they're called) defined by low walls and hedges. This understated arrangement works well, allowing the architecture to serve as a straight man to the art. Barnes also designed the **Sage and John Cowles Conservatory,** the garden's most prominent structure. A four-acre addition to the garden, designed by French landscape architect Michel Desvigne, is scheduled to be built in 2008 on the former site of the Guthrie Theater.

Lewis Gillette House, 1912

LOST 1 *Befitting its pivotal location, the site occupied by the Walker and its sculpture garden has an exceptionally complex building history. The oldest architectural ghost here is the* **Thomas Lowry House,** *built in 1874 about where the new Walker addition now stands. The house, part of a four-acre estate, was acquired by Thomas Walker and then razed after he built the* **first Walker Art Museum** *in 1927. An odd Venetian–Byzantine Revival affair that later received a slick Moderne makeover, it was torn down in 1969 to make way for Barnes's new and much larger building.*

Meanwhile, a grand mansion had been built in 1898 on what is today the south end of the Walker's property. The **George Daggett House,** *at 40 Groveland Terr., was a castellated fantasy known as "Eldor Court." It was later purchased and enlarged by Lewis Gillette. Rising above walls, terraces, and gardens, the house resembled a baronial estate minus, of course, the peasants. A vast Moorish-style ballroom was among its wonders. The house was gone by 1947, when the* **North American Life and Casualty Insurance Co. (later Allianz)** *built a corporate headquarters on the site. Allianz moved to the suburbs in 2001, and its building was razed for the Walker's addition.*

The most renowned lost building on the Walker site is the **Tyrone**

Tyrone Guthrie Theater, 1966

Guthrie Theater. *Designed by Ralph Rapson and completed in 1963, the theater was a high point of architectural modernism in the Twin Cities. Its innovative thrust stage was set in a colorful, brilliantly configured auditorium. Unfortunately, the theater was built on the cheap—the screen across the front facade, for example, was made of plywood—and later "improvements" did away with other original features. After the Guthrie announced plans to build a new theater complex, preservationists mounted an unsuccessful campaign to save Rapson's building. The new Guthrie opened in 2006.*

The site of the sculpture garden, directly north of the Walker, also has an interesting history. It's part of the historic Parade Ground, once used for military drills. The park board began buying land here in 1893 and eventually owned 66 acres, much of which was developed into an athletic complex. In 1951, **Parade Stadium,** *seating 17,000 people, was built west of the area now occupied by the sculpture garden. The stadium was demolished in about 1990 and replaced by multi-use athletic facilities.*

Although much of the Parade was swampy, the city decided that the western portion of it near Lyndale and Hennepin Aves. would be a good site for a new **Minneapolis Armory,** *completed in 1907. Near this massive building, the park board established* **Armory Gardens,** *which became popular with the public. The armory, on the other hand, proved to be a disaster. It sank into the boggy soil and by 1929 was reported to be in danger of "immediate collapse." Four years later, it was dynamited, having stood for just 26 years.*

4 Kodet Architectural Group (William Nott House) *L*

15 Groveland Terr.

Long and Kees, 1894

Winding along the northern flanks of Lowry Hill, Groveland Terr. became a favored site for large houses in the 1890s, due largely to the efforts of Thomas Lowry, who replatted the area to accommodate mansions. The streetcar magnate also hired the firm of Long and Kees to design two houses here: this one, purchased by industrialist William Nott, and a larger mansion (gone) next door for department store owner William Donaldson. Built of rough-faced stone, the Nott House shows Long and Kees moving away from the Richardsonian Romanesque style, which they'd employed so skillfully for their Minneapolis City Hall (1889–1906), toward a more subdued classical manner. The mansion is now home to an architectural firm.

5 Groveland Gallery (Frank Long House) ! *L*

25 Groveland Terr.

Long and Kees, 1894 / addition, 1913

A superb example of how the Richardsonian Romanesque style could be pared down to produce a bold, sculptural work of architecture almost modern in character. Built of rough-faced granite, the house is dominated by a steep mountain of a roof that drops down 30 feet to an inset porch. Two dormers and a projecting tower with a conical cap provide the only interruptions in the tile roof's precipitous descent. The roof shelters two side gables rising above stark walls punctured by irregular window openings. There's not a superfluous gesture anywhere.

The house's decisive style reflects the personality of its original owner, architect Franklin Long. A partner in what in its day was the city's most successful architectural firm, Long was not a man haunted by doubt. "The longer I live," he once wrote, "the more I am certain that the great difference between men, between the feeble and the powerful . . . is energy, invincible determination, a purpose once fixed, and then death or victory." Spoken like a true Victorian. Long died in 1912, and a year later his house received its only major addition, when the entry porch was extended to the east by enclosing what had originally been a walled terrace.

Groveland Gallery, 1948

POI A Thomas Lowry (Douglas) Park

Douglas and Colfax Aves. South

Minneapolis Park Board, ca. 1919 / renovated, Damon Farber Associates, 1995

An urbane little park with brick paths, a grape arbor, a tumbling watercourse with seven pools, and benches ideal for whiling away time in unproductive fashion.

6 John Lind House *L*

1775 Colfax Ave. South

William Channing Whitney, 1905

A red brick Georgian Revival house most notable as the one-time home of John Lind, who in 1898, running as a Democrat, became the first non-Republican in 40 years to be elected governor of Minnesota. Lind lost his bid for reelection in 1900 and then acted out every politician's dream. After delivering a farewell address, he walked to the offices of the *St. Paul Dispatch*, a frequent critic of his administration, and punched the managing editor in the nose. Those were the days.

7 Kenwood Gables Apartments

700 Douglas Ave.

KKE Architects, 1989

At 12 stories, this is the tallest apartment tower in the Lowry Hill neighborhood. It's crowned by several small gables of the type that were affixed like cheap party hats to all manner of buildings during the salad days of postmodernism.

LOST 2 *This was once the site of the* **Edmund Walton House ("Grey Court"),** *one of the loveliest nineteenth-century homes on Lowry Hill. Built in 1893, the house offered a fetching blend of Medieval and Shingle Style elements. It fell to the wrecker in 1959.*

Mount Curve Avenue

This winding street at the crest of Lowry Hill is where you'll find most of the neighborhood's larger mansions. As with Summit Ave. in St. Paul, you wish the blufftop side of the street had been preserved as parkland. The lots overlooking downtown were too desirable, however, and mansions started appearing by 1880. A substantial number of these early mansions have been demolished, and most of the homes atop the hill today date from the early 1900s and later. The mansions offer all the usual flavors along with some exotic blends, making Mount Curve a good place to see the evolution of housing styles through the twentieth century.

8 First Unitarian Society

900 Mount Curve Ave.

Roy Thorshov, 1951

An early modernist church in a subdued version of the International Style. A long, covered walkway extends across the front facade, which has windows above the entrance but is otherwise a plain brick box. The rear portion of the building, which occupies the site of the old William Donaldson House (1893–1933), has ribbons of windows that provide views of the city.

LOST 3 *The modern townhomes at 1200–22 Mount Curve Ave. occupy the site of the* **William and Kate Dunwoody House.** *Built in 1905, the brick Tudor Revival mansion was suitably impressive; even better was its beautifully landscaped yard surrounded by balustrades. The house came down in 1967.*

9 A. D. Arundel House

1203 Mount Curve Ave.

James McLeod, 1895

Set at an angle on its corner lot, this two-story brick house features a curving front portico with wings flaring off to either side. Classical Revival designs tend to be quite staid, but here the architect injected some welcome zip into the proceedings.

Charles Martin House, 1950

10 Charles Martin House N L

1300 Mount Curve Ave.

William Channing Whitney, 1904

Built largely of brick and set behind a wrought-iron fence, this house is essentially an updated version of a Renaissance palace. It offers a full range of classical paraphernalia: molded window surrounds, dentils, cornices, pediments, quoins, and a balustraded entry porch. Interior features include a monumental staircase, mosaic tile floors, and Italian marble hearths. Much of Lowry Hill is dusted with flour money, and this house is no exception. It was built for Charles Martin, who was secretary and treasurer of the Washburn Crosby Co., which later evolved into General Mills. Across the street at 1315 Mount Curve is the **J. T. Wyman House** (1909), which is also in the Renaissance Revival style but is more compact and less ornate than the Martin House.

Charles and Helen Winton House

11 Charles and Helen Winton House !

1324 Mount Curve Ave.

George Maher, 1910

The only known work in the Twin Cities by George Maher, a Chicago architect whose style defies easy categorization. Like many of his houses, this one combines classical monumentality with a mixed bag of details: Prairie Style art-glass windows, an enframed front door modeled on the work of Louis Sullivan, pedestal lanterns that evoke Viennese Secessionist architecture. The house also features a four-story-high garage and servant's apartment built into the side of the hill. Maher also produced three significant buildings in Winona, MN, including an administrative and manufacturing complex for the Watkins Co. (1911–13). Prone to bouts of depression and never really satisfied that he'd managed to forge his own style, Maher committed suicide in 1926.

12 A. R. Rogers House

1415 Mount Curve Ave.

William Channing Whitney, 1906, 1910

Lowry Hill's very own stone castle, a Tudor Revival estate complete with walls, gates, and a crenellated tower. All that's missing is a moat.

Lester R. and Josephine Brooks House, 1930

13 Lester R. and Josephine Brooks House !

1600 Mount Curve Ave.

Hewitt and Brown, 1905 and later

Along with the Winton House to the east and the Donaldson House a few doors to the west, this home is one of three mansions on Mount Curve that offer a Prairie–Arts and Crafts–Renaissance Revival amalgam. The most distinctive feature here is a Sullivanesque ornamental frieze that runs the entire length of the front facade. Plaques of similar design are affixed near the recessed front door, which opens onto a terrace. Above are three windows divided by colonettes and framed by a drip molding that steps down and around the doorway. Architect Edwin Hewitt pulls off the stylistic blend here with great aplomb. The house was built for Josephine Brooks, whose husband, Lester, had died in 1902 after a career in banking, lumbering, and milling.

14 House

1700 Mount Curve Ave.

Bliss and Campbell, 1960

A one-story brick house with transom windows, exposed roof beams, and a side-entry garage. The house was designed for maximum privacy; even the front door is hidden from the street.

Lawrence S. Donaldson House

15 Lawrence S. Donaldson House

1712 Mount Curve Ave.

Kees and Colburn, 1907

Lawrence S. Donaldson, who with his brother William founded a Minneapolis department store, built this house just up the hill from William's mansion on Groveland Terr. At first glance the house appears to be a conventional Renaissance Revival exercise. Look more closely, however, and you'll see its diverse origins. The terra-cotta ornament, as well as the railings on the terrace, derive their intertwining forms from Louis Sullivan (who was building his famous bank in Owatonna, MN, at the time). The casement windows in the front dormer are more Prairie Style, while the curved porch roof resembles a Beaux-Arts theater marquee. Somehow, it all works.

16 House

1118 Kenwood Pkwy.

Mark Mack (California), 2000

A stucco house in a style that might be called California Modern. Because it's set on a narrow lot, the house unfolds itself from front to back in a series of irregular volumes that suggest an interesting floor plan within. Mack also designed the condominiums at 1124–28 Kenwood.

1521 Waverly Pl.

17 House

1521 Waverly Pl.

1996

A sleek house clad in stainless steel. This stylish house is among many modern infills on Lowry Hill that make no attempt to disguise their modernity, and one of the pleasures of the neighborhood is the lively architectural interplay between old and new.

18 House

1520 Waverly Pl.

Horty Elving and Associates, 1970

If you substituted brick for this house's wood and metal sheathing and eliminated most of the windows, you'd have a small-scale version of the 1971 Walker Art Center building down the hill. Like the Walker, this house adheres to a cool, severe brand of modernism.

19 Elizabeth Quinlan House

1711 Emerson Ave. South

Frederick Ackerman (New York), 1924

This suave Italian Renaissance Revival house might be thought of as architect Frederick Ackerman's trial run for his Young Quinlan Building completed just two years later downtown. Clothier Elizabeth Quinlan was the client behind both buildings, and here—as in her store—she opted for a kind of understated historicism that, before art deco swept all before it, represented the height of architectural fashion in the 1920s.

20 John F. Calhoun House

1900 Dupont Ave. South

1896

A rigorously symmetrical Classical Revival house. The semicircular portico is echoed by an arched pediment atop the central dormer.

21 House

1912 Girard Ave. South

Bertrand and Keith, 1894

This house's brownstone entry arch is in the Richardsonian Romanesque manner, but other elements fall within the realm of late Queen Anne.

POI B Early twentieth-century houses

ca. 1750–2100 Irving Ave. South (from Douglas Ave. to 22nd St. West)

various architects, ca. 1895–ca. 1915

Much of southern Lowry Hill was built up in the early 1900s after streetcar service had been extended down Douglas Ave. These four blocks along Irving Ave. offer a representative collection of homes from this period, mostly in one version or another of Classical, Colonial, or Georgian Revival. Among the houses of note are those at 1766 Irving,

1800 block of Irving Ave. South

built in 1901 and featuring a cross-gabled gambrel roof and a semicircular front porch; 1790 Irving, which dates from 1907 and sports a giant Corinthian portico; 1800 Irving, a Queen Anne–Colonial Revival mix from about 1900; and 1937 Irving, which was built in 1901 and has a curving wraparound porch.

22 House

1778 James Ave. South

1926

One of Lowry Hill's best Period Revival houses. With its gentle undulations, calm lines, and ivied stucco walls, this house has an English Arts and Crafts feel, although the way the roof swirls down over the front door is pure 1920s architectural theater.

23 E. E. Atkinson House

1901 Logan Ave. South

Albert Van Dyck, 1914

A brick Beaux-Arts mansion that would be right at home on Mount Curve. Note the fine terra-cotta ornament, the elaborate carriage house, and the terrace that looks out over Kenwood Park.

Lake of the Isles and Lowry Hill East

There are two distinct neighborhoods here, and their differences point to the role of water, parks, and mass transportation in molding Minneapolis. The area around Lake of the Isles and immediately to the east is a residential gold coast and has been from the time the lake was created by dredging around 1910. In its natural state, Lake of the Isles was a swamp, and its ragged shores attracted few home builders. Once the modern lake emerged out of the mire, however, mansions bloomed all around it like luxuriant flowers. Among them was the grandiose Charles Gates Mansion (1913). Although the Gates house is long gone, many other big houses still line Lake of the Isles Parkway, and it remains among the city's most prestigious addresses.

Just to the east of the lake, extending to Hennepin Avenue, the blocks filled in with slightly smaller houses. There are many Arts and Crafts–era houses here, as well as two of Purcell and Elmslie's most magnificent Prairie Style homes: the Edward L. Powers House (1911) on 26th Street West and the Purcell-Cutts House (1913) on Lake Place.

Farther east of the lake, between two busy commercial corridors—Hennepin and Lyndale avenues—you'll find a more varied housing stock in the neighborhood officially known as Lowry Hill East but more commonly referred to as the Wedge. Heavy traffic surges around and through this neighborhood, which has a more frenetic feel than the area around Lake of the Isles. The Wedge includes a mix of Victorian-era houses, new upscale condominiums, and modest working-class homes. Among the most notable historic homes here is the John G. and Minnie Gluek House (1902) on Bryant Avenue South.

POI A Lake of the Isles parks and parkway

Minneapolis Park Board, 1889–93, 1907–11

This lake, with its long northern finger and pair of wooded islands, is essentially a man-made creation. Originally, it was a marsh interspersed with four small islands. The first reshaping occurred in the early 1880s, when two islands were removed to make way for a rail line. Later in the decade, the Minneapolis Park Board acquired the entire lake, then undertook four years of dredging to stabilize the shoreline so that a parkway could be built. It required yet another bout of dredging, between 1907 and 1911, before the lake took on its present appearance. The Kenilworth Lagoon, through which Isles connects to Cedar Lake, was completed in 1913. All of the fill around the lake deteriorated over the years, and since 2001 the Minneapolis Park and Recreation Board has spent more than $5 million on a long-term shoreline reclamation project.

The mansions around the lake mostly date from between 1900 and 1930, with those along the east shore tending to be a bit older than those on the western side. New houses spring up whenever a site becomes available, and some of these are of high quality as well.

1 George C. Stiles House

2801 Lake of the Isles Pkwy. East

Harry Jones, 1910

At first glance this appears to be a formal Beaux-Arts house, and it's certainly in that territory. But the Egyptian capitals on the porch columns are an odd touch, while the plainness of the overall detailing owes something to the Arts and Crafts sensibility of the time.

2 George B. Clifford Jr. House

2601 Lake of the Isles Pkwy. East

Ernest Kennedy, 1931

A Tudor Revival house dolled up in stone, stucco, and half-timbering. With its quaint tower and unreal ordering of parts, it could do

Lake of the Isles and Lowry Hill East

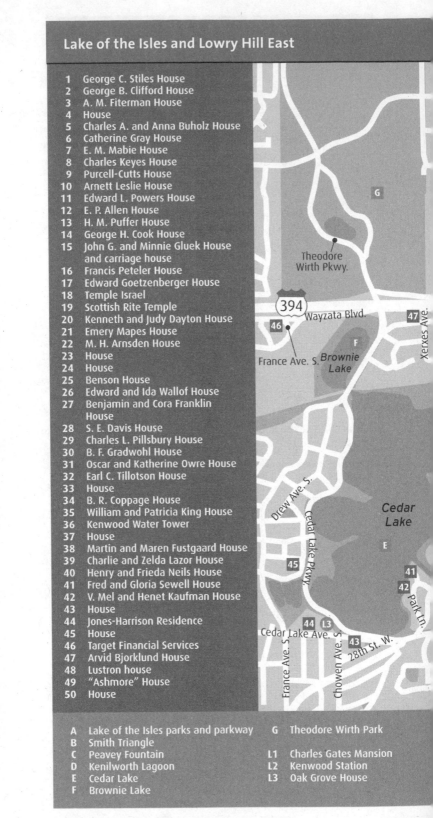

1   George C. Stiles House
2   George B. Clifford House
3   A. M. Fiterman House
4   House
5   Charles A. and Anna Buholz House
6   Catherine Gray House
7   E. M. Mabie House
8   Charles Keyes House
9   Purcell-Cutts House
10 Arnett Leslie House
11 Edward L. Powers House
12 E. P. Allen House
13 H. M. Puffer House
14 George H. Cook House
15 John G. and Minnie Gluek House
    and carriage house
16 Francis Peteler House
17 Edward Goetzenberger House
18 Temple Israel
19 Scottish Rite Temple
20 Kenneth and Judy Dayton House
21 Emery Mapes House
22 M. H. Arnsden House
23 House
24 House
25 Benson House
26 Edward and Ida Wallof House
27 Benjamin and Cora Franklin
    House
28 S. E. Davis House
29 Charles L. Pillsbury House
30 B. F. Gradwohl House
31 Oscar and Katherine Owre House
32 Earl C. Tillotson House
33 House
34 B. R. Coppage House
35 William and Patricia King House
36 Kenwood Water Tower
37 House
38 Martin and Maren Fustgaard House
39 Charlie and Zelda Lazor House
40 Henry and Frieda Neils House
41 Fred and Gloria Sewell House
42 V. Mel and Henet Kaufman House
43 House
44 Jones-Harrison Residence
45 House
46 Target Financial Services
47 Arvid Bjorklund House
48 Lustron house
49 "Ashmore" House
50 House

A   Lake of the Isles parks and parkway
B   Smith Triangle
C   Peavey Fountain
D   Kenilworth Lagoon
E   Cedar Lake
F   Brownie Lake

G   Theodore Wirth Park

L1 Charles Gates Mansion
L2 Kenwood Station
L3 Oak Grove House

double duty as a set for *Robin Hood* or some other costume romance. The original owner was a son of one of the founders of the Cream of Wheat Co.

A. M. Fiterman House

3 A. M. Fiterman House

2525 Lake of the Isles Pkwy. East

Edwin Lundie, 1953

One of Edwin Lundie's typically elegant houses, in the Cape Cod variant of Colonial Revival. The house, built of brick with a fading coat of white paint that creates a mottled effect, is large and complex in plan. Even so, it looks modest on the outside, where Lundie assembled the volumes in such a way that the house resembles a small village of buildings.

Charles Gates Mansion, 1916

LOST 1 *The houses at 2505 and 2525 Lake of the Isles Pkwy. East occupy the site of the* **Charles Gates Mansion.** *The Renaissance Revival–style mansion was built in 1913 for the son of John W. ("Bet-a-Million") Gates, who made a fortune in barbed wire, railroading, and oil. Charles G. Gates seems to have inherited his father's flamboyance gene. After marrying, Gates announced plans to build a "cottage" on Lake of the Isles. Coming in at 38,000 square feet (larger than James J. Hill's mansion in St. Paul), the house was a stone palace outfitted with the best of everything money could buy, including what is reputed to have been the nation's first home air-conditioning system. Unfortunately for Gates, money couldn't buy him a reliable appendix, and*

he died, apparently of complications from surgery, before his mansion was completed.

A St. Paul physician, Dr. Dwight Brooks, later bought the house but never lived in it. Once the Great Depression set in, there were no buyers for such a costly property, and the mansion was demolished in 1933. Much of its interior was salvaged, including a marble staircase later installed in the Burbank-Livingston-Griggs House in St. Paul.

4 House

2505 Lake of the Isles Pkwy. East

1958

A large, long, modernist house clad in fieldstone—a favorite material of architects in the 1950s. The house looks to have much fine detailing.

Charles A. and Anna Buholz House, 1974

5 Charles A. and Anna Buholz House

2427 Lake of the Isles Pkwy. East

Frederick Soper, 1911

Minneapolis's very own Mediterranean villa, and quite a showstopper. Mounted on a high corner lot above a series of gates, staircases, walls, and terraces, the L-shaped house is coated in gleaming white stucco and includes a curving veranda that poses beneath a fanlike pergola.

6 Catherine Gray House

2409 Lake of the Isles Pkwy. East

Purcell and Feick, 1908 / additions, 1918 and later

This house was one of William Purcell's first projects, done before George Elmslie became his partner (though Elmslie helped with the design). Purcell planned the house for himself but later named it for his grandmother, who came from Chicago in 1907 to live with him. Prairie

Style features here include high brick corner piers, a shallow hipped roof, and bands of case-

Catherine Gray House

ment windows. Originally, the house had a one-story entry pavilion on its north side, where there's now an addition. In 2004, Minnesota Public Radio acquired the house from a longtime supporter, refurbished it, and sold it for more than $1.5 million as part of a fundraising campaign.

7 E. M. Mabie House

2405 Lake of the Isles Pkwy. East

Francis W. Fitzpatrick (Duluth), 1887

One of the oldest houses on the lake, built before the first round of dredging started in 1889. The house is a Queen Anne–Shingle mix and has been extensively renovated.

8 Charles Keyes House *L*

2225 Lake of the Isles Pkwy. East

Adam Lansing Dorr, 1904

An Arts and Crafts foursquare in which Victorian vestiges, such as a polygonal bay above the porch, still linger.

9 Purcell-Cutts House ! N *L*

2328 Lake Pl.

Purcell and Elmslie, 1913 / restored and renovated, MacDonald and Mack Architects, 1990

In 1911, three years after his marriage to Edna Summy, William Purcell began to think about creating a house for his family, which included a recently adopted infant son. Although Purcell's partnership with George Elmslie had produced few lucrative commissions, he had family money and was able to spend $14,000, a goodly sum at the time, to build this exquisite house near Lake of the Isles. Purcell's aim was to cre-

Purcell-Cutts House, 1965

ate a house for what he called "modern American family life" (which in his case later included divorce). The result was this Prairie Style masterpiece.

Dubbed by Elmslie as "the Little Joker," the house isn't large, but it's gorgeously designed down to the last detail. Set well back on its lot to catch views of the lake, the house from the outside presents a series of rectilinear volumes, one of which juts out toward the sidewalk and ends in an array of tall art-glass windows. Rows of smaller art-glass windows flow across the second story, where stencil patterns in the stucco walls create a frieze beneath an extremely low-pitched roof. The main entry is off to one side beneath an inset porch. Here you'll find a projecting beam that culminates in a swirl of Elmslie's characteristic sawn-wood ornament as well as stained-glass windows adorned with this message: "Peek a Boo."

Purcell-Cutts House interior

Within, the house has an intricate array of spaces on five levels. At the heart of the design is a spatial procession that extends along an axis from a sunken living room in front, up half a level to a dining room with a prowlike projection, and then out to a rear porch. A tent ceiling unifies the living and dining rooms, which open to an entry hall on a level midway between them. The upstairs includes two bedrooms, the largest of which can be subdivided by screens.

Although the plan is ingenious, what sets this house apart is the quality of its details. Elmslie's gifts as an ornamentalist are fully evident here, in art-glass windows, stencilwork, desks and chairs, light fixtures, and other furnishings. The main fireplace is particularly fine. Gold- and glass-flecked mortar glitters between the hearth's Roman bricks, while, above, a mural by artist Charles Livingston Bull emerges from an arched framework of wood strips.

Purcell and his family did not stay here for long. Lacking commissions, the firm of Purcell and Elmslie was all but defunct by 1918, when Purcell moved from Minneapolis and put the house up for sale. It was purchased by Anson Cutts, Sr., a railroad traffic manager, and his wife, Edna, a singer who gave private concerts at the house. Their only son, Anson Cutts, Jr.—a painter, writer, and critic—moved back to the house in the 1960s to care for his ailing mother. Upon his death in 1985, he bequeathed the house to the Minneapolis Institute of Arts, which undertook an extensive restoration. In 1990 the house, occupied by art institute staff, was opened to limited public tours, and it remains one of the glories of the city.

10 Arnett Leslie House

2424 Lake Pl.

Long, Lamoreaux and Long, 1917

An L-shaped Arts and Crafts–Prairie house with a centralized formal entry and broadly proportioned windows that derive from the work of George Maher. The first owner was president of the Leslie Paper Co. and in 1930 cofounded the Ampersand Club,

an organization devoted to fine printing and the book arts that remains active today.

Edward L. Powers House

11 Edward L. Powers House !

1635 26th St. West

Purcell Feick and Elmslie, 1911

Although not as well known as the Purcell-Cutts House two blocks away, this home is of comparable quality and ranks among Purcell and Elmslie's finest works. Clad in stucco above brick, it has an unusual plan in which the living room is at the rear so as to capture what were once good views of Lake of the Isles. To accommodate this unorthodox layout, the main entry is well back to one side. The house's polygonal front bay echoes a semicircular bay off the living room, a feature the architects also used at their Decker House (1912, razed) at Lake Minnetonka.

This home is also among the most richly adorned of Purcell and Elmslie's residential works, despite the fact that they had to do some major redesigning to cut costs. Elmslie had just joined the firm when the commission came in, and he poured out a wealth of ornament in sawn wood, stencils, glass, and terra-cotta, including a magnificent plaque over the main fireplace.

Edward L. Powers was a vice president of the Butler Brothers Co., which a few years earlier had constructed a superb warehouse designed by Harry Jones in downtown Minneapolis. Perhaps Powers's familiarity with that building sharpened his appetite for good architecture. Purcell described Powers and his wife as "people of fine intelligence and very appreciative of our methods and results." He also wrote, years later, that "this Powers House is a distinguished piece of work, and it still stands fresh and interesting, truly contemporary with the most thoughtful buildings of today." Purcell wasn't always a reliable guide to his own architecture, but in this case it would be hard to disagree with him.

12 E. P. Allen House

2425 Humboldt Ave. South

1914

One of the nicest of the neighborhood's Mission Revival houses. A triple-arched porch dominates the design.

13 H. M. Puffer House

1414 24th St. West

Dorr and Dorr, 1911

A bungalow placed on a corner lot so that its broad side serves as the front. The composition of the three gables gives the house a restful, gracious quality.

14 George H. Cook House

2400 Bryant Ave. South

Keith Co., 1902

The 2400 block of Bryant features an array of Colonial Revival houses built between about 1900 and 1910. This house includes an outsized split pediment above the front porch.

15 John G. and Minnie Gluek House and carriage house N L

2447 Bryant Ave. South

William Kenyon, 1902 / carriage house, Boehme and Cordella, 1902

Occupying three city lots, this beautiful Georgian Revival house was built for a son of Gottlieb Gluek, who founded the Minneapolis brewery that bore his name. The house, sheathed entirely in white clapboard, includes a balustraded front porch that extends northward to form a port cochere. Architect William Kenyon took great care in composing the major elevations, which offer Palladian windows,

elegant split pediments, and other fine details. Equal care was lavished on the carriage house, which the Glueks hired the firm

John G. and Minnie Gluek House

of Boehme and Cordella, rather than Kenyon, to design. John Gluek and his wife, Minnie, enjoyed their house for only a few years. Both were killed in 1908 when their car struck a train near Lake Minnetonka.

16 Francis Peteler House

2726 Dupont Ave. South

1887 / remodeled, ca. 1920s

This house has a Spanish Revival stucco facade, but it was originally Italianate, as evidenced by the vestigial cupola on the roof. The man who built the house, Francis Peteler, invented a railroad dump car that brought him a tidy fortune.

17 Edward Goetzenberger House

2621 Emerson Ave. South

Purcell and Feick, 1910

One of Purcell's early pre-Elmslie designs. The house is a two-story box with a gable roof and a rather crowded arrangement of windows around the front door. Goetzenberger was a sheet metal worker who'd become acquainted with Purcell while employed on an earlier project.

POI B Smith Triangle

24th St. West and Hennepin Ave. / Art: Thomas Lowry Monument (bronze and stone sculptures), Karl Bitter, 1915

This monument to streetcar tycoon Thomas Lowry was originally at the south end of the "Bottleneck" at Lyndale and Hennepin Aves. Construction of Interstate

94 drastically altered the intersection, and the monument—which consists of a bronze statue of Lowry set before a stone wall with carved figures—was moved here in about 1970.

Temple Israel interior, 1964

18 Temple Israel

2324 Emerson Ave. South

*Liebenberg and Kaplan, 1928 / addition, **Rabbi Max Shapiro Education Building,** 1955 / addition, Bentz/Thompson/ Rietow Architects, 1987*

Initially known as Shaarai Tov (Gates of Goodness) and organized in 1878, this is the oldest Jewish congregation in Minneapolis. The congregation, which became Temple Israel in 1920, occupied several other buildings before constructing this Classical Revival–style synagogue. Symbolic elements are worked into the design, including the five front doors that represent the books of the Torah. The sanctuary is renowned for its acoustics. Architect Jack Liebenberg used tiles made from sugar beet stalks to modulate the sound.

19 Scottish Rite Temple (Fowler Methodist Episcopal Church) N i

2011 Dupont Ave. South

Warren H. Hayes, 1894 / Harry Jones, 1907 / remodeled, Bertrand and Chamberlin, 1916

Constructed of ultra-hard quartzite from southwestern Minnesota with red sandstone trim, this Romanesque Revival–style building features two massive towers, an arcaded entry porch, and a 24-foot-diameter rose window. The oldest portion is a rear chapel designed by Warren Hayes and built for the Fowler Methodist congregation in 1894. By the time the congregation was able to

Scottish Rite Temple, 1974

complete the church in the early 1900s, Hayes had died, and Harry Jones took over the work.

In 1915, the Fowler congregation merged with Hennepin Avenue Methodist Church and sold this building to the Scottish Rite Temple, a Masonic organization. Although the church's vaulted auditorium was modified in 1916 to accommodate Masonic rituals, it retains many of its original features, including an extensive stained-glass program. In May 1931, what's said to have been the largest funeral in Minneapolis history was held here for local daredevil and stunt pilot Charles "Speed" Holman, who died when his plane crashed during a performance in Omaha, NE.

Kenneth and Judy Dayton House

20 Kenneth and Judy Dayton House

1719 Franklin Ave. West

Vincent James Associates and Hargreaves Associates (landscape architects), 1997 / Art: glass and sliding panels, James Carpenter Design Associates (New York)

A temple of high modernism in teak, stone, glass, and steel. Its owners, from the Dayton's Department Store family, acquired two older houses here near the north end of Lake of the Isles, then razed them to make way for this home. Set amid precisely landscaped grounds, the L-shaped, two-story house is clad in Indiana limestone with teak framing around the windows. Its two wings partially enclose a motor court and a sculpted lawn, creating the sense of a private compound. The house's floor-to-ceiling windows, chaste detailing, insistent rectilinearity, and aura of deluxe understatement call to mind one of Ludwig Mies van der Rohe's modernist pavilions. Within, the house includes sliding panels and glass designed by artist James Carpenter.

21 Emery Mapes House

2218 Lake of the Isles Pkwy. West

Harry Jones, 1915

One of the biggest mansions on the lake, this brick Renaissance Revival palace includes a second-floor terrace that extends for almost the entire length of the house. It was built for Emery Mapes, a founder of the Cream of Wheat Co. in 1893. Mapes devised advertising campaigns that made the cereal—milled from coarse wheat middlings—into a national brand.

M. H. Arnsden House, 1974

22 M. H. Arnsden House

2388 Lake of the Isles Pkwy. West

Liebenberg Kaplan and Martin, 1922

A Cotswold Cottage house in full regalia, complete with a wood shake roof that curls down over the eaves in imitation of thatching. Quite a few houses of this type were built in the 1920s, but this may well be the largest example in Minneapolis.

23 House

2424 Lake of the Isles Pkwy. West

Carl Gage, 1929

The 1920s English Cottage look boiled down to a kind of pictorial minimalism. What little elaboration there is focuses on the windows, which are framed by brick quoins but are so flat that they almost look as though they were glued onto the stucco walls.

Kenwood

Occupying the hilly ground between Lake of the Isles and Cedar Lake, Kenwood has long been one of the city's most charming residential enclaves. The neighborhood, which extends north along Kenwood Parkway to the flanks of Lowry Hill, has a reclusive quality, in part because it's buffered on all sides by either water or railroad corridors (many of which are now trails). The streets that wind through Kenwood were laid out in 1880, and by the early 1890s more than 30 homes had already been built. Rail lines spurred initial development, and there was a small station that served commuters. In 1890, a streetcar line was extended to 21st Street West and Penn Avenue. The commercial area at this intersection is a legacy of the streetcar era.

In addition to its founding stock of Victorians, Kenwood offers houses in the usual variety of styles, ranging from neoclassical to Prairie (including two designed by Purcell and Elmslie) to Period Revival. Modern infills have appeared here and there, mainly along the edges of the neighborhood, since the 1950s. Among them is Frank Lloyd Wright's beautiful Neils House (1951) on Cedar Lake. However, Kenwood's best-known property is probably the so-called "Mary Tyler Moore" House (1892), the exterior of which was depicted as part of the comedienne's long-running television show.

24 House

2421 Russell Ave. South

1907 / rebuilt, Hugh G. S. Peacock, 1967

An old house turned into a prominent example of the shed-roof style that was imported into the Twin Cities from California in the 1960s and 1970s.

25 Benson House

2700 Kenilworth Pl.

Sarah Susanka, 1994

Architect Sarah Susanka scored a popular hit with her 1998 book *The Not So Big House.* This, by contrast, is a not-so-little house that strives for a sort of Prairie Revival look but comes across as a bland box with lots of windows.

Edward and Ida Wallof House, 1890

26 Edward and Ida Wallof House

2200 Sheridan Ave. South

Harry Jones, 1891 / addition, 2006

Among the oldest—and most frequently photographed— houses in Kenwood. A Queen Anne–Shingle Style mix, the house includes a sweeping stone porch and a broad shingled arch above the Palladian window in the front gable. It was built for Edward G. Wallof and his wife, Ida. Edward, who founded a machine tool company, lived here with his extended family, including a brother named William. Considered something of a ne'er-do-well, William was handy with a camera, and he took scores of photographs of his family as well as many scenes of early life in Kenwood. His photographs are now in the collections of the Minneapolis Public Library.

LOST 2 *One of William Wallof's photo subjects was* **Kenwood Station,** *at 21st St. West and Thomas Ave. The station, which sported a cupola, was built in the 1870s by the Minneapolis and St. Louis Railroad. Later used as a house, it was razed in the 1970s.*

Benjamin and Cora Franklin House

27 Benjamin and Cora Franklin House *L*

2405 22nd St. West

1915

A rare local example of the Viennese Secession style, one of modernism's many early variants. The flat-roofed stucco and brick house consists of a high central block flanked by one-story wings. The wings and the upper portion of the main block have casement windows separated by thin piers. Decorating each pier is a glazed tile set beneath an inset band of stucco that descends from the eaves—a subtle touch that gives each tile the look of a pendant. A two-story house with similar tile detailing is located nearby at 2215 Sheridan Ave. South. Its architect is also unknown.

28 S. E. Davis ("Mary Tyler Moore") House

2104 Kenwood Pkwy.

Edward S. Stebbins, 1892 / renovated, 2006

A Queen Anne house that became a local icon by virtue of its association with the popular *Mary Tyler Moore Show,* which aired on network television from 1970 to 1977. An exterior shot of the house identified it as the location of Moore's apartment. Had this been true, she would have been living beyond her means as a producer for a bargain-basement television station.

29 Charles L. Pillsbury House

2216 Newton Ave. South

Carl B. Stravs, 1910

Another peculiar house from architect Carl Stravs. Among the curiosities here are dormers with oddly clipped roofs and trapezoidal windows around the front door. The first owner was an electrical engineer who later became an executive vice president of Munsingwear, Inc.

30 B. F. Gradwohl House

2621 Newton Ave. South

Albert Van Dyck, 1918

A three-story Renaissance Revival house that makes for an interesting comparison with the Owre house next door.

Oscar and Katherine Owre House

31 Oscar and Katherine Owre House N L

2625 Newton Ave. South

Purcell Feick and Elmslie, 1912 / restored, MacDonald and Mack Architects, 1996

This Purcell and Elmslie house is a stuccoed cube with a notch in one corner for the front door. Bands of casement windows punch through the smooth walls beneath a low-pitched roof. Extending out from this compact volume are a porch in front and what was originally a maid's room to the rear. Within, the open plan is organized around a fireplace that divides the living and dining rooms. Budget limitations kept ornament to a minimum.

The house was built for Dr. Oscar Owre, a surgeon, and his wife, Katherine. William Purcell later wrote, "Oscar was scared to death that his building was going to cost him more than he could afford, and had been told by all his friends that every building

operation carried on by an architect was loaded with heartbreaking extras which would spoil all his fun, if not ruin him financially." Purcell managed to assuage the doctor's fears, and the house cost $17,275, which was under budget. Katherine Owre, incidentally, was a daughter of reformer Jacob Riis, whose book *How the Other Half Lives* painted a grim picture of New York City's slums.

32 Earl C. Tillotson House

2316 Oliver Ave. South

Purcell Feick and Elmslie, 1912

An obtrusive front porch mars the appearance of this house, which is among several Purcell and Elmslie designed with high gable roofs. According to Purcell, the house went through the budget wringer a number of times, and it shows. This is not one of the firm's choicer designs.

POI C Peavey Fountain

Kenwood Pkwy. at Lake of the Isles Pkwy. West

1891

A fountain dedicated to dead horses. Frank Peavey gave the fountain to the city in 1891, with the idea that horses could use it to quench their thirst. After World War I, the fountain was rededicated to honor horses from the 151st Field Artillery killed in action.

2000 Kenwood Pkwy.

33 House

2000 Kenwood Pkwy.

McLeod and Lamoreaux, 1899

One of Kenwood's delights. This house is a late Victorian take on French Gothic, as evidenced by *fleur-de-lis* adorning the front bay, pointed arch windows, and an exceptionally tall, steep roof punctuated by two charming mini-dormers. The large carriage house is equally picturesque.

34 B. R. Coppage House

1912 Queen Ave. South

Harry Jones, 1891

A castlelike house, presided over by a corner tower wearing a witch's-hat roof. The house has lost its original porch as well as its clapboard siding, now covered by stucco.

35 William and Patricia King House

1941 Penn Ave. South

Close Associates, 1952

Winton and Elizabeth Close specialized in low-key but very carefully designed houses that strove for a high degree of functionalism. This house bears some similarity to Frank Lloyd Wright's Usonian homes of the same period.

36 Kenwood Water Tower *L*

1724 Kenwood Pkwy.

Frederick Cappelen (engineer), 1910

At 110 feet, this octagonal brick water tower, vaguely Medieval in appearance, is Kenwood's tallest structure. In the late 1970s there was a proposal to convert the tower, which hasn't been used to store water since 1954, into condominiums. The scheme failed, however, and the tower is now designated as a local landmark.

37 House

1908 Kenwood Pkwy.

Walter J. Keith, ca. 1900

A stone, brick, shingle, and stucco house that merrily combines various Tudor Revival and Arts and Crafts motifs with a sort of French Gothic tower.

38 Martin and Maren Fustgaard House

2512 Franklin Ave. West

Martin Fustgaard, 2003

If Prince ever decides to make a sequel to *Purple Rain*, here's just the house he needs. Sporting a color scheme that's heavy on purple, violet, and fuchsia, this whimsical stucco house prompted one unhappy neighbor to tell a newspaper, "I've got Disneyland across the street." Well, not exactly. The house—a scenic affair with a tower, a busy roofline, and an ornamental program that includes a sun, a moon, and a star—is actually rooted in the Storybook Style of the 1920s. That style wasn't Walt Disney's doing, but it did come out of Hollywood.

Charlie and Zelda Lazor House

39 Charlie and Zelda Lazor ("Flatpak") House

2024 Thomas Ave. South

Lazor Office (Charlie Lazor), 2004

Modern architects have long been infatuated with modular and prefabricated housing designed to supplant the standard "stick-built" home, which uses a structural system—known as balloon or platform framing—that's now well over 150 years old. From Buckminster Fuller's geodesic domes to Frank Lloyd Wright's Usonians to the all-metal Lustrons built after World War II, these dreams of a sort of house-in-a-kit have never made much headway in the marketplace.

This house, designed by and for Minneapolis architect Charlie Lazor, is a recent entry in the modular movement. Its name derives from the fact that it's built largely of wood, steel, and glass panels that can be shipped in so-called flat packs. The panels can be combined in different ways to produce a variety of designs. Here, the results are truly elegant, without any of the clunkiness that usually afflicts modular housing. Whether the Flatpak house can find a niche in the housing market remains to be seen, but this prototype makes you hope that it will.

POI D Kenilworth Lagoon

Between Lake of the Isles and Cedar Lake

Minneapolis Park Board, 1913

This is the longest of the three canals built between 1911 and 1917 to link four Minneapolis lakes. The water level in Cedar dropped by six feet when this canal opened.

40 Henry and Frieda Neils House ! *L*

2801 Burnham Blvd.

Frank Lloyd Wright, 1951

This gorgeous house, one of only two in Minneapolis designed by Frank Lloyd Wright, shows how even an architect as supremely gifted as Wright could benefit from close collaboration with his clients. Wright's talents—a fabulous eye, an uncanny command of scale, an almost mystical feel for materials, and a highly refined spatial sensibility—are all on display here. Yet the house's distinctive marble walls were first suggested by Henry and Frieda Neils, both of whom were exceptionally knowledgeable about architecture. At the time the house was built, Henry was the retired president of the Flour City Ornamental Iron Co. Frieda was the artistically minded daughter of the iron company's founder and also an admirer of Wright's work.

In 1949, the couple began making plans for a new home overlooking Cedar Lake on property adjoining their existing home at 2815 Burnham Blvd. Believing Wright could give them just the house they wanted, the couple journeyed to the great architect's Wisconsin estate to meet with him. At some point they showed him a picture of their 1920s "Mediterranean" house. Wright agreed that they needed a new home and suggested—probably facetiously, though you never could tell with him—that they should "burn the old one down."

The Neilses didn't follow that incendiary bit of advice, but they did hire Wright. In many ways this house is typical of the so-called Usonian designs that Wright developed in the 1930s. It's L shaped, has just one story, uses a limited palette of materials, and is planned in a way that separates what Wright called "active" and "quiet" zones. The house's main "active" area is its living room, which features a 17-foot-high vaulted ceiling and offers lake views across a walled terrace. The long wing that extends into a triple carport holds the quiet area, devoted to bedrooms and a gallery connecting to the front door, which in typical Wrightian fashion is well hidden.

The house is the only one Wright ever built with marble walls. The colored and textured walls, which taper as they rise, consist of small blocks of "cull" marble left over from other building projects. Henry Neils, who was a trustee of a marble company, had acquired the stone at a good price and convinced Wright to use it. However, when the walls were finally completed, neither Wright nor his clients liked the overall color. Wright dispatched one of his students to supervise a process by which some blocks were stained to create just the right color effects.

The house's aluminum windows, made by Neils's company,

Henry and Frieda Neils House

are also unique in Wright's residential work, since he generally preferred wooden frames. Neils's connection to a lumber company owned by his father resulted in another atypical feature: interior paneling made of western larch as opposed to the cypress or redwood Wright usually preferred. The house, impeccably maintained, is still owned by members of the Neils family.

41 Fred and Gloria Sewell House

16 Park Ln.

Charles Stinson, 2001

A stone, wood, and stucco house in Stinson's signature layered style. The L-shaped house is nicely sited on its narrow lot to exploit lake views.

42 V. Mel and Henet Kaufman House *L*

20 Park Ln.

James Brunet, 1936

A significant early work of modernist architecture in the Twin Cities. The house's ribbonlike arrangement of windows, smooth stucco walls, and boxy massing (though there are some curves to the rear) are all drawn from the modernist vocabulary, as is the flat roof. Salesman V. Mel Kaufman and his wife had visited the 1933 Century of Progress Exposition in Chicago, where futuristic design was on display, and it convinced them to build a modern house of their own.

POI E Cedar Lake

Minneapolis Park Board, 1908 and later

With its bays and wooded points, Cedar appears to be the "wildest" of the Minneapolis lakes. Yet it's actually the product of much manipulation by railways, road builders, and dredgers. The first railway line cut along the lake's eastern shore in 1867, and two other lines soon followed. Dredging began in the early 1900s as the Minneapolis Park Board filled in marshlands to create a more stable shoreline. In 1991 the board substantially expanded its holdings here with the purchase of 28 acres on the northeast side of the lake formerly occupied by the Minneapolis and St. Louis Railroad shops. Cedar's southeastern side, however, remains unique among the city's lakes in that private lots come close to the shore, with no intervening parkway. Most of the housing around Cedar dates from the automobile age—1920 and later—largely because streetcar lines never came close enough to the lake to provide convenient service.

43 House

3523 Cedar Lake Ave.

1973

The streets around Cedar Lake have quite a few architect-designed modern houses. This one features multiple levels, lots of glass and concrete, and an inset tower with finlike projections.

44 Jones-Harrison Residence

3700 Cedar Lake Ave.

1959 and later

A residential complex for the elderly, founded in 1888 and occupying one of the oldest building sites on Cedar Lake.

Oak Grove House, 1870

LOST 3 *This was the site of the **Oak Grove House,** a resort hotel in the shape of an octagon built in 1870. Its original owners—Reverend Ebenezer Scott and his wife, Gertrude—sold the property in the 1880s to Edward Jones. Later, Jones's mother-in-law, Jane T. Harrison, left a bequest to establish a home for women in the old hotel, which stood until 1892, when it was replaced by a larger building.*

Bryn Mawr

This neighborhood is north of Kenwood and curls around to take in the western shore of Cedar Lake. It has a secluded feel because of its well-defined borders: Theodore Wirth Park to the west, Bassett's Creek to the north, and rail lines, trails, and Interstate 394 to the south and east. As with other Minneapolis neighborhoods, Bryn Mawr grew with mass transit. Horsecars were operating on Glenwood Avenue at the northern fringes of the neighborhood as early as 1886, but it wasn't until 1892 that streetcars reached into the heart of Bryn Mawr, along Laurel Avenue, where you'll find some of the neighborhood's oldest homes.

Most of Bryn Mawr's housing dates to the early 1900s. The houses aren't generally as fancy as those in Kenwood. Even so, Bryn Mawr has a little bit of everything, including Victorians, bungalows, plenty of Period Revival homes, a smattering of flat-roofed modernist dwellings from the 1950s, and even an all-metal Lustron house. Bryn Mawr's major architectural monument is the Target Financial Services building (1954), located just south of Interstate 394.

45 House

2500 Cedar Shore Dr.

1961

A sprawling one-story house in the manner of Frank Lloyd Wright. Clad in Mankato-Kasota stone, the house has broad overhanging eaves, long ribbons of windows, and other Wrightian features. At the rear there's a sunken courtyard bordered by a stone wall.

POI F Brownie Lake

Named after a settler's daughter, this ten-acre lake was once larger. Portions were filled in by railroad and highway construction in the late 1800s. The lake shrank to its present size in 1917, when it was connected to Cedar Lake by a channel, causing the water level to drop by nine feet.

POI G Theodore Wirth (Glenwood) Park

Minneapolis Park Board, 1889 and later

Wirth Park Chalet, 500 Wirth Pkwy.

Magney and Tusler, 1923

Eloise Butler Wildflower Garden

Eloise Butler, ca. 1907 and later

Encompassing nearly 700 acres, much of it in suburban Golden Valley, this is the largest park in the Minneapolis system. The park board began acquiring land here in 1889 and made its largest

purchase in 1909. Once known as Glenwood Park, it was renamed in honor of longtime parks superintendent Theodore Wirth. Wirth Lake, Birch Pond, Bassett's Creek, the Eloise Butler Wildflower Garden, and two golf courses are among the attractions. The park's best building is the Wirth Chalet, which combines a golf clubhouse on the lower level with a rental hall above. The rustic-style hall, set behind a terrace, has a vaulted ceiling and the requisite stone fireplace.

Target Financial Services

46 Target Financial Services (Prudential Building)

3701 Wayzata Blvd.

Magney Tusler and Setter, 1954

A solid example of 1950s corporate architecture, built as a regional office for the Prudential Insurance Co. The offices are grouped into three wings, ranging from four to eight stories, that splay off a central ten-story core. Clad in Mankato-Kasota limestone, these wings have slightly projecting square windows that march across the facades with military precision, conveying an image of corporate rationalism and modernity. By contrast, the central core and an auditorium wing have few windows and are sheathed in pink granite. The building occupies a 30-acre site that was once part of Theodore Wirth Park. The park board sold the property to Prudential and used the proceeds to buy additional shoreland around Cedar Lake. The land sale sparked a legal challenge that was ultimately settled in the board's favor by the Minnesota Supreme Court.

47 Arvid Bjorklund House

1204 Cedar Lake Rd.

1927

A split-level house in a style that might be called Mediterranean Moderne. There's a similar house just a few doors down at 1224 Cedar Lake Rd.

48 Lustron house

2436 Mount View Ave.

Lustron Corp., 1949

Of the ten metal Lustron houses in Minneapolis, this is the only one not located in the far southern parts of the city. The garage around back is also partly encased in metal panels.

49 "Ashmore" house

424 Oliver Ave. South

Sears, Roebuck and Co., 1917

A fine mail-order bungalow supplied by Sears, Roebuck and Co., which from 1908 to 1940 manufactured and sold about 100,000 houses-in-a-kit. This home is a rare example of the "Ashmore" model, only three of which are known to have been built in the

United States. Sears sold the "Ashmore" between 1916 and 1922 at a cost ranging from

"Ashmore" house

$1,600 to $3,600, depending on level of finish. The materials for the house, which includes a fieldstone chimney, were shipped by rail to Minneapolis in two boxcars. The first owners presumably hired a contractor to build the house, which features paneled living and dining rooms and built-in oak cabinetry. Other Sears houses can be found in the Twin Cities, though the exact number isn't known.

2006 Laurel Ave.

50 House

2006 Laurel Ave.

1888

A Queen Anne–Shingle Style amalgam and the grandest of Bryn Mawr's Victorians. The front tower with its steep polygonal roof is echoed by small dormers that poke up to either side. There's also a large 1903 house, Colonial Revival in style, across the street at 2007 Laurel.

8

North Side

Overview

The North Side has never been a glamorous part of Minneapolis. It has no lake district or scenic river gorge to recommend it, and it is literally on the other side of the tracks, separated from downtown Minneapolis by the city's oldest rail corridor, along Third Avenue North, built in the late 1860s. Although the North Side still has pleasant residential areas, in recent decades it has become associated with high rates of violence and crime. These problems have been especially pronounced in the heart of the neighborhood, between West Broadway and Dowling avenues, and the unfortunate reality is that it is now the roughest part of the Twin Cities.

It was not always so. For much of its history, the North Side was a traditional working-class neighborhood. Parts of it were indeed poor, but there were also many blocks of well-built and well-maintained houses, a vibrant commercial district along West Broadway Avenue, and a solid industrial base. The first settlers arrived in the 1850s, concentrating near the Mississippi River just above downtown. Sawmills, lumberyards, factories, and railroads quickly spread up the west bank. By the 1870s, houses, churches, commercial buildings, and saloons (lots of them) occupied the area around this industrial district as far north as Plymouth Avenue, where a bridge was built across the river in 1874. A year later, horsecars begun running up Washington Avenue; they reached Plymouth by 1876, and the service was soon extended to West Broadway.

The North Side saw its most intense period of development between 1880 and the 1920s, when streetcars connected much of the neighborhood to downtown. Developers platted numerous subdivisions bearing the usual euphonious names, and these were gradually built up with single-family homes and a smattering of apartments. A variety of ethnic and immigrant groups were drawn to the neighborhood during these years. Germans and Scandinavians led the way, but the North Side also had sizable black and Jewish communities as early as 1900.

For the most part, the North Side's housing stock is unpretentious. Vernacular Victorians, modest bungalows, and standard Period Revival homes predominate. Ramblers, ranch houses, and split-levels are common farther north in portions of Camden that weren't developed until after World War II. However, the North Side has a few pockets of exceptional homes, including a group of elaborate Queen Annes around 16th and Dupont avenues. There's also an especially nice collection of Period Revival houses in the Homewood area just north of Olson Memorial Highway near the western city limits.

Large portions of the North Side, particularly south of Broadway, have been transformed by urban renewal, beginning in the 1930s and continuing to the present day. In one project alone, north of Glenwood Avenue, more than 600 old homes and other buildings were cleared away in the 1950s and replaced by apartments and new industrial uses. Most of the new housing wasn't very good, but neither was what it replaced.

Although it probably doesn't attract many architectural tourists, the North Side has some wonderful buildings both old and new. These include an outstanding group of early concrete-block houses (1885) along Third and Fourth Streets North; the Young House (1888), a Queen Anne gem; the old North Branch Public Library (1894); International Market Square (1904–15), long the home of Munsingwear and one of the city's largest industrial buildings; Disciples Ministry Church (1927), a Byzantine Revival–style building that was originally a synagogue; and Jordan Park School (1999), a strong example of modern school architecture.

Near North

This neighborhood takes in the area from Bassett's Creek to Lowry Avenue. West Broadway cuts through the neighborhood and forms a divide of sorts. South of Broadway, the diverse architectural environment has been the scene of much urban renewal. To the north, single-family housing predominates, except for industrial areas along the river.

The lower portion of Near North around Olson Highway as far west as Penn Avenue is largely the product of modern-era interventions. Once a notorious slum, it's seen several rounds of urban renewal, with varied results. The Heritage Park housing development (2002 and later) is the most recent effort to create a new community here. Farther to the west, you'll find a small surprise: the Homewood neighborhood, which has an abundance of Period Revival houses from the 1920s and 1930s. There are also impressive churches in this vicinity, including three built as synagogues by the Jewish community that flourished here for years. Many Jewish-owned businesses once operated along Plymouth Avenue, but the last of them closed after a riot in 1967.

The area between Plymouth and Broadway is equally mixed. At 18th and Lyndale avenues is Lynpark—an in-city suburb with cul-de-sacs and homes that date to the 1970s. Just a few blocks to the west, however, stately Victorians line parts of Dupont, Emerson, and Fremont avenues. There are also handsome houses around North Commons Park. Among the important institutional presences here is Ascension Catholic Church (1902).

North of Broadway you'll find mostly early twentieth-century houses, in varying states of repair, along with modern infills. There were never many big houses here, but the neighborhood at one time may have had more corner groceries per square mile than any other part of the city. Today, most of the stores are gone or converted to apartments, and the deep connection to place that they once helped to create now seems a distant dream in this troubled part of Minneapolis.

POI A Bassett's Creek

In its natural state, this 12-mile-long creek, named after pioneer Joel Bassett, flowed through a valley from Medicine Lake to the Mississippi River just above Nicollet Island. By 1900, however, much of the valley had become a rail corridor and an informal dump. After a 1913 flood, the city diverted the last mile and a half of the creek, from about Lyndale Ave. to the river, into a tunnel. In 1992, the creek was redirected through a new tunnel.

1 ConAgra (Fruen) Mill

301 Thomas Ave. North

1915, 1917, 1928 and later

Now vacant, this towering concrete mill and elevator complex once produced rolled oats. The first gristmill here, powered by Bassett's Creek, was built in the 1870s. It was later operated by William H. Fruen, who in 1884 discovered the nearby spring from which the Glenwood-Inglewood Co. (now part of Deep Rock Water Co.) still draws its bottled water.

2 Ripley Gardens (Ripley Memorial Hospital) N L

300 Queen Ave. North

1910, 1916 / renovated, LHB Architects, 2007

This 60-unit housing complex, which includes both old and modern buildings, is named after Dr. Martha Ripley, a Vermont native who decided at age 37 to become a doctor, moved with her family to Minneapolis, and in 1886 founded a maternity hospital that ultimately settled here.

Near North

1   ConAgra Mill
2   Ripley Gardens
3   International Market Square
4   Heritage Park Housing Development
5   Sumner Community Library
6   Wayman African Methodist Episcopal
    Church
7   W. L. Hathaway House
8   St. John's Missionary Baptist Church
9   Disciples Ministry Church
10 Houses
11 H. L. Gitelman House
12 Carl Graffunder House
13 Houses
14 Plymouth Avenue Bridge
15 Lynpark Housing Development
16 F. S. Stevens House
17 Neighborhood Housing Services
18 Case-Lang House
19 John Lohmar House
20 Ascension Catholic Church
21 Splawn's Okinawan Karate Kobudo
22 House
23 House
24 North Community High School
25 Capri Theater
26 Upper Midwest American Indian
    Center
27 Friedman's Department Store
28 Broadway Avenue Bridge
29 Northwind Lofts
30 Castle Townhomes
31 Houses
32 Andrew Oleson House
33 Nellie Stone Johnson School
34 Giving in Grace Christian Center
35 Baker-Emerson House
36 Jerry Gamble Boys and Girls Club
    of the Twin Cities
37 St. Olaf Lutheran Church
38 Jordan Park School for Extended
    Learning
39 Church of St. Anne

A   Bassett's Creek
B   Homewood
C   Interstate 94
D   Old Highland
E   North Commons Park
F   Forest Heights Addition
G   Farview Park

L1 Sumner Field Housing Project,
    Glenwood Homes
L2 St. Joseph's Catholic Church
L3 First and second North High Schools
L4 First and second Broadway Avenue
    bridges
L5 Farview Park tower

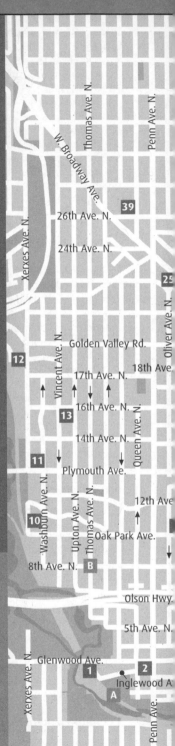

Her ashes are entombed in the cornerstone of the hospital, which operated until 1956. The historic portion of the complex consists of the hospital (1916), a nurses' residence (1910), and a boulder-walled cottage (1910) known as the "babies' bungalow" that once served as an isolation ward for sick infants. Townhouses and two new apartment buildings were added to the complex in 2007.

3 International Market Square (Northwestern Knitting Co., later Munsingwear Corp.) N L

275–90 Market St.

Bertrand and Chamberlin with C. A. P. Turner (engineer), 1904–15 / renovated, Kaplan McLaughlin Diaz (San Francisco) with Winsor/Faricy Architects, 1985 / renovated, ESG Architects, 2005

In the 1880s, George D. Munsing made a breakthrough in the realm of intimate apparel. It was a time when most people wore woolen underwear during the winter and suffered itching and skin irritation as a result. Munsing, who was superintendent of the Rochester Knitting Works in New York, found a way to interlace silk threads with wool to create a warm and comfortable fabric. He and two partners moved to Minneapolis, where they established the Northwest-ern Knitting Co. to make their "itchless" underwear. The business flourished, and by 1890 the company had built its first factory on this site. A year later Munsing introduced another stellar invention: the one-piece "union" suit. This item proved so popular that the company, which in 1919 changed its name to Munsingwear, eventually became the world's largest manufacturer of underwear.

Between 1904 and 1915, the company constructed five brick and concrete buildings here, creating a 650,000-square-foot complex that employed up to 2,000 workers, including many young women. The five- to eight-story factory buildings feature long rows of windows and are very plain. Perhaps the most intriguing feature within the complex, which was mostly loft space as built, is a double-helix staircase that separated workers going up from those coming down. The oldest of the build-ings—along Glenwood Ave.—is the city's first entirely reinforced concrete structure. Engineer C. A. P. Turner, who devised the framing system, went on to patent a widely used type of concrete column shaped like a mushroom at the top.

Munsingwear closed the factory in 1981. Four years later, the buildings were reborn as Inter-national Market Square—home to offices, shops, and over 100

International Market Square

showrooms for home and office products. Its centerpiece is a five-story atrium created by roofing over an old courtyard where rail tracks once ran. In 2005, portions of the complex were rehabilitated once again, this time as 96 loft apartments.

Heritage Park Housing Development

4 Heritage Park Housing Development

Area roughly bounded by Lyndale, Emerson, Third, and 10th Aves. North

ESG Architects, LHB Architects, Bauknight Associates, and others, 2002 and later

This 145-acre development, on the site of two demolished public housing projects, came about as part of the settlement of a lawsuit alleging that the city had illegally concentrated minorities in public housing. A consent decree opened the way to $117 million in federal funding to help replace the old housing here. Slated for completion in 2009, Heritage Park is expected to cost about $250 million, making it the most expensive project of its kind in the city's history. Its 900 housing units will include single-family homes, townhouses, duplexes, and apartments, all set amid parks, ponds, and winding streets. The laudable goal is to create a vibrant mixed-income residential community in what was once widely perceived as a dumping ground for the poor.

Unfortunately, the architecture is a huge disappointment. The overall design follows a master plan intended to ensure that the low-income housing isn't stigmatized by looking inferior to everything else. On that score, the plan succeeds. Trouble is, nothing here looks very good. All

the housing is designed to reflect historic Minneapolis building styles labeled under such categories as "Victorian," "Classic," "Craftsman," and "European Romantic." The single-family homes, with their appliqués of nostalgia, are relatively innocuous versions of what you'll find in the suburbs. The multi-unit buildings, however, look like second-rate Period Revival houses on steroids. It's sad to think that this is the best Minneapolis could do for such a significant project.

Sumner Field Housing Project, 1946

LOST 1 *In 1938, the* **Sumner Field Housing Project**—*the first government-built and -operated housing development in the Twin Cities—opened here at about the same time Sixth Ave. North was widened to become Olson Hwy. Sumner Field consisted of 44 two-story row houses and four three-story apartment buildings in a park-like setting. Many of the early residents were black, and at least one—Prince—went on to fame. Another urban renewal project,* **Glenwood Homes,** *was later built just to the south of Sumner Field. The remains of both projects were razed to make way for Heritage Park.*

5 Sumner Community Library N i

611 Van White Memorial Blvd.

Cecil B. Chapman, 1915 / additions, 1927, 1939 / renovated and enlarged, KKE Architects, 2005

A lovely neighborhood library. The original Tudor Revival portion of the building is L shaped and includes a tower with an inset arched entry. Within, the main reading room has a timber-beam ceiling and a fireplace. The library was renovated and enlarged in 2005 by KKE Architects, which designed an addition featuring a metal-clad, barrel-vaulted roof.

6 Wayman African Methodist Episcopal Church

1221 Seventh Ave. North

Henry E. Gerrish, 1967

A flamboyant little modernist church with 16 sides and a roof that pinches in as it rises to form a tall proboscis-like central steeple.

7 W. L. Hathaway House

624 James Ave. North

Charles S. Sedgwick, 1888

There are a handful of Victorians in the blocks just north of Olson Hwy., and this is the finest of the lot. It's now largely covered with asbestos siding, but what appears to be a restored section at the rear gives a sense of how the house looked in its original cladding of clapboard and shingles.

8 St. John's Missionary Baptist Church (Sharei Zedeck Synagogue) *L*

1119 Morgan Ave. North

Frenzel and Bernstein, 1937 / addition, 1943

At least four synagogues were built in Near North in the 1920s and 1930s. All were theaterlike brick boxes. This one was built for Sharei Zedeck Orthodox congregation, founded by Lithuanian immigrants. The Moderne-style building is adorned with cast-stone menorahs in the arches above the doors. Sharei Zedeck merged with another congregation and moved to the suburbs in the 1960s, after which St. John's Missionary Baptist Church bought the building.

9 Disciples Ministry Church (Mikro Kodesh Synagogue) *L*

1000 Oliver Ave. North

Septimus J. Bowler, 1927 / addition, 1949

The largest and most ornate of the neighborhood's former synagogues. Byzantine Revival in style, the building has patterned brickwork, domed stair towers, arched entry doors reached via a high staircase, and a rounded central parapet. It was built for

Disciples Ministry Church, 1937

Mikro Kodesh, an Orthodox congregation established in 1890 and originally called Anshei Russia. For a time, Mikro Kodesh was the largest Orthodox Jewish congregation in the Upper Midwest. During the 1950s and 1960s, however, thousands of Jews left the North Side, and Mikro Kodesh merged with another congregation in 1969. The Disciples Ministry Church has owned the building since about 1980.

POI B Homewood

Area north of Olson Hwy. and west of Penn Ave.

1908 and later

This 80-acre subdivision was platted in 1908 with the idea of attracting an upper middle-class clientele. The development included large lots, especially near Wirth Park, as well as 26 stone pillars placed at intersections to serve as street signs; many still stand. Homewood also came with unsavory restrictive covenants (long since overturned) that were aimed at keeping out blacks and Jews. Today, you'll find some of the North Side's largest houses here.

10 Houses

1015, 1025, 1035, 1045 Washburn Ave. North

Liebenberg and Kaplan, 1921–38

The closest thing to a mansion district on the North Side. These four brick houses, mostly designed in some version of French

Provincial Revival, stand on huge lots that extend all the way

1035 Washburn Ave. North

between Washburn and Xerxes Aves. All the houses have views of Wirth Park to the west.

11 H. L. Gitelman House

1305 Washburn Ave. North

ca. 1942

This Moderne house has a stepped-up glass-block window and a rounded canopy over the front door. A smaller Moderne home, from 1938, is just around the corner at 1300 Xerxes Ave. North.

12 Carl Graffunder House

1719 Xerxes Ave. North

Carl Graffunder, 1950

Carl Graffunder, an early local modernist, built this woodsy house as his own residence.

13 Houses

1520, 1526 Vincent Ave. North

1933–35

Two Storybook Style houses. The one at 1526 Vincent has an especially colorful entrance, while 1520 offers fine detailing in brick and stone. Nearby, on the 1400–1600 blocks of Upton, Vincent, and Washburn Aves. you'll find many similar houses that were advertised in their day as "English cottages."

Plymouth Avenue

The first bridge linking the North Side to Northeast Minneapolis was built at Plymouth Ave. in 1874. Before long, a commercial hub grew around the intersection of Plymouth and Washington Aves. Later, Jewish-owned businesses flourished farther west along Plymouth. This com-

mercial district was already in decline, however, by the time of the 1967 riots, after which the last of the Jewish businesses closed. Apartments, parking lots, parks, and industrial plants have since replaced many of the old buildings on Plymouth, and today there's little commercial activity.

14 Plymouth Avenue Bridge

Across Mississippi River

Van Doren–Hazard-Stallings (engineers), 1983

A concrete box girder bridge that will not overwhelm you with its beauty. There were two earlier bridges here.

POI C Interstate 94

From I-394 to north city limits

Minnesota Department of Transportation, 1981

Although land acquisition began in the 1950s, the last portion of Interstate 94 through the North Side wasn't completed until 1981. Many commercial, industrial, and institutional buildings were lost to the freeway, as were more than 100 houses. Today the interstate serves as a kind of divide between largely industrial areas along the river and residential districts to the west.

St. Joseph's Catholic Church, 1974

LOST 2 *The most notable building demolished to make way for the North Side segment of Interstate 94 was* **St. Joseph's Catholic Church,** *at 1127 Fourth St. North. Built in 1887, it was a twin-towered Romanesque Revival church that served a German parish founded in 1870. The towers blew off in a 1967 storm. The church came down in 1976.*

Lynpark houses

15 Lynpark Housing Development

Area bounded by Plymouth, Aldrich, and 18th Aves. North and I-94

1973 and later

It's interesting to compare this development, which includes market-rate and subsidized housing, with Heritage Park a mile or so to the south. Aside from the well-designed **Boardwalk Condominiums** (1982) near Plymouth Ave., Lynpark offers no eye-catching architecture. Instead, it was clearly designed to be an in-city suburb. Everything about it—from its winding streets and cul-de-sacs to its split-level, ranch, and other "suburban" houses, more than 100 in all—reinforces its identity as a modern insertion into the fabric of the city. Today, it would be hard to build a project like this in Minneapolis. Perhaps that's just as well, although it's by no means clear that Heritage Park represents a vast aesthetic improvement over what you see here.

POI D Old Highland

Area bounded by Aldrich, James, Plymouth, and West Broadway Aves.

1860s and later

This part of the North Side, platted in the 1860s, was named Highland because it's a bit above the level of downtown. Although homes were built here in the 1870s, the major development push began in the 1880s. Most of the North Side's big Victorian houses are in this neighborhood.

16 F. S. Stevens House

1425 Dupont Ave. North

Theron P. Healy (builder), 1884

One of at least two large Queen Anne houses built in this neighborhood by Theron Healy. He also worked extensively in south Minneapolis, where a historic district bears his name.

Neighborhood Housing Services

17 Neighborhood Housing Services (John Young House)

1501 Dupont Ave. North

1888

Perhaps the neighborhood's most spectacular Victorian. Among its many lively details are horseshoe arches that frame a second-story porch.

Case-Lang House

18 Case-Lang House *L*

1508 Dupont Ave. North

ca. 1865 / additions, ca. 1874, ca. 1885, ca. 1914–17 / renovated, 1981

Moved here in 1981 from its original location six blocks away, this is one of the oldest houses on the North Side. It was built in the late 1860s for Emanuel Case, who arrived in the village of St. Anthony in 1851, operated a store, and then moved across the river and claimed a tract of land here. Case farmed portions of his land until his death in 1871 but subdivided other sections for development. As built, his house was a Greek Revival–Italianate mix. Later owners, including John Lang, added to the house, which was meticulously restored by new owners in the 1980s.

19 John Lohmar House N *L*

1514 Dupont Ave. North

Peter Jeub, 1898

Local merchants, many of German ancestry, were among those who built big houses in Highland. This one belonged to John Lohmar, who was in the millinery business, and it's a beauty. Although it looks very Victorian with its shingled walls, gingerbread woodwork, and twin conical spires, the house's overall symmetry and sense of restraint suggest the calming influence of the Classical Revival styles that were rapidly gaining popularity in the late 1890s.

Ascension Catholic Church

20 Ascension Catholic Church

1723 Bryant Ave. North

1902

Founded in 1890 primarily to serve Irish families, this parish includes the North Side's oldest Catholic church. Gothic Revival in style, the twin-towered brick church has a fine interior that features stained glass, statuary,

and an altar made of Carrara marble and Mexican onyx. Besides the usual school, convent, and rectory, the parish complex includes the **Ascension Club.** Built in 1922, the club provided a gymnasium, a bowling alley, a swimming pool, and meeting rooms. Today, the parish has shrunk to a fraction of its former size but still operates its parochial school. There's also a charter school called Ascension Academy based in the club building.

Splawn's Okinawan Karate Kobudo

21 Splawn's Okinawan Karate Kobudo (North Branch Public Library) N *L*

1834 Emerson Ave. North

Frederick Corser, 1894 / addition, 1914

This brick and brownstone mini-castle, now given over to the martial arts, is the Twin Cities' oldest surviving public library building. With its slender tower, stepped front gable, and basket-handle arched entrance, the building resides in the general vicinity of the Chateauesque style. When it opened, it was said to be the nation's first branch library designed as an "open-shelf" facility, which meant patrons could browse for books themselves rather than relying on librarians to retrieve them. A new and underwhelming North Side library was built in 1971 on Lowry Ave.

LOST 3 *A running field and track at 18th and Fremont Aves. North occupies the site of the **first North High School,** built in 1886 and destroyed by fire in 1913, and the **second North High School,** completed in 1914 and razed in the early 1970s.*

Near North

22 House

1427 Fremont Ave. North

C. C. Johnson (builder), 1897

A towered Victorian that sports an unusual front porch in the form of a half oval.

23 House

1607 Emerson Ave. North

Theron P. Healy (builder), ca. 1890

A Queen Anne house with a wraparound porch on the first floor and a curving corner porch above. Note also the horseshoe-arched window—a type much used by Victorian designers.

24 North Community High School

1500 James Ave. North

Larson and McLaren, 1973

The 1970s wasn't a golden age for school buildings. This one, a series of brick boxes arranged around a courtyard spanned by bridges, isn't as oppressive as some other schools of the time, but its inwardness doesn't allow it to connect well with the community at large.

POI E North Commons Park

1801 James Ave. North

Minneapolis Park Board, 1909 and later / includes Ruth R. Hawkins Community Recreation Center, 1973

A large expanse of greenery that includes the city's only outdoor water park.

West Broadway Avenue

Once known as 20th Ave. North and Crystal Lake Rd., West Broadway took its present name in about 1920. It follows an old trail, which accounts for its curving route as it swings to the northwest. In its prime, West Broadway was a bustling commercial street lined with numerous small businesses, from clothing and hardware stores to banks, movie theaters (three), and restaurants. In the 1960s, the street began a long decline. Strip malls and big-box retail stores built in the 1980s did little to improve its bedraggled appearance. In 2006 the city announced plans to restore West Broadway's old luster. Whether this will entail more malls and their large parking lots remains to be seen.

25 Capri (Paradise) Theater

2027 West Broadway Ave.

Buechner and Orth?, 1925 (theater opened in 1931)

West Broadway's only surviving theater, now home to a dance company. Its "atmospheric" auditorium has mock battlements along the walls. Movies were last shown here in the 1960s.

POI F Forest Heights Addition

Northwest of West Broadway and Humboldt Aves.

Nutter and Plummer (engineers), 1883 and later

In 1883, brothers Harlow and Samuel Gale, along with a partner, platted this addition just north of where West Broadway makes its big bend. An engineering firm was hired to lay out the curving streets, which split in places to form small parks. Horsecar and soon streetcar service were close at hand, and by the late 1880s a few homes had already been built here. However, most houses in the addition date to the early twentieth century and are generally of modest size.

26 Upper Midwest American Indian Center (Plymouth Lodge Masonic Building)

1035 West Broadway Ave. (also 1912 Emerson Ave. North)

Downs and Eads, 1922

A sturdy old Masonic hall, Classical Revival in style.

27 Friedman's Department Store (Gatzemeier Building)

400 West Broadway Ave.

1894

This store, which occupies the ground floor of a three-story brick commercial building, has been in the family for over a century. Another longtime business—**Brix Grocery and Meats,** established in 1893—stands a few blocks up the street at 917 West Broadway.

28 Broadway Avenue Bridge

Across Mississippi River

Van Doren–Hazard-Stallings (engineers), 1987

A straightforward steel girder bridge with two predecessors.

LOST 4 *The **first bridge** here, a wooden structure, was built in about 1857 but succumbed to a flood just two years later. The **second bridge,** completed in 1887, stood until 1985, when it was dismantled. However, one section was salvaged and later floated downriver to Nicollet Island, where it now forms a span to the east bank.*

29 Northwind Lofts (Bardwell-Robinson Millwork Factory)

2400 Second St. North

ca. 1885 and later / renovated, ca. 2000

One of the oldest industrial buildings left on the North Side. It's now office condominiums.

30 Castle Townhomes *L*

300–14½ 26th Ave. North (also 2605–7 Third St. North)

William D. Kimball, 1885

31 Houses *L*

2611, 2617, 2619, 2705, 2727, 2831 Third St. North and 2826, 2828 Fourth St. North

S. Littlefield or Lemuel Jepson, 1885–86

The largest and oldest collection of concrete-block houses in the Twin Cities. Precast concrete blocks, a low-cost way to imitate stone, were made as early as the 1860s but weren't widely used until the early 1900s. The build

ings here—eight two-story homes and an 11-unit row house—were built by developer William N. Holway to promote his concrete-block company. All of the houses

2617 and 2619 Third St. North

are constructed of bevel-edged blocks that resemble cut stone. The most handsome houses are the two at 2617 and 2619 Third St. North. Originally identical, these houses still maintain the natural color of the concrete. They also feature quoining in the form of pointed, projecting corner blocks: the effect is similar to log construction. The two-story row house, now dubbed Castle Townhomes, is built of somewhat larger blocks than those used for the individual homes. Its design is very simple, with a patterned cornice providing the only ornamental note.

POI G Farview Park

26th and Lyndale Aves. North

Minneapolis Park Board, 1883 and later / Art: Circle of Vision (sculpture), Norman Andersen and Katherine Schaefer, 2004

The name says it all: a hill here provides a view of the downtown skyline. Initially known by the much less descriptive name of Third Ward Park, this is also the oldest park on the North Side.

LOST 5 *Around 1890, the hill here was crowned with a sandstone **tower** perhaps 30 feet high. The Gothic-style tower contained a winding staircase that led up to a lookout platform. Long thought by neighborhood children to be haunted, the tower was torn down in the 1960s. The park's Circle of*

Farview Park tower, 1930

Vision *sculpture is inspired by the tower.*

32 Andrew Oleson House

2635 Lyndale Ave. North

ca. 1890

A refurbished Victorian with a multicolored paint job that highlights its variety of wall textures. The band of circular windows on the bell-roofed tower is a distinctive touch. This house probably stood alone, overlooking the park, at the time it was built.

33 Nellie Stone Johnson School

807 27th Ave. North

Kodet Architectural Group, 2001

A Y-shaped brick-, glass-, and metal-clad building, angled on its large site to accommodate a variety of athletic fields. The school's namesake, businesswoman Nellie Stone Johnson, was the first black person to be elected to citywide office, winning a seat on the library board in 1945.

34 Giving in Grace Christian Center (Victory Temple)

2401 Aldrich Ave. North

1939

This barrel-vaulted Moderne building resembles a small-scale version of an arena.

35 Baker-Emerson House *L*

2215 Dupont Ave. North

1883

The west side of Dupont between 22nd and 23rd Aves. North has five sizable houses, all set well

back on their lots. This Victorian, the largest and oldest of the group, has a wraparound front porch, a sunburst motif in the front gable, and stickwork trim.

Baker-Emerson House

It was built for George Baker, who owned a dry goods store. On a Sunday in March 1890, Baker attended services at the nearby Fourth Baptist Church, returned home, and killed himself; his suicide drew much coverage from the local press. Among later owners of the property was Carey Emerson, a merchandise broker.

36 Jerry Gamble Boys and Girls Club of the Twin Cities

2410 Irving Ave. North

Cerny and Associates, 1968

Fun with geometry. Back in the 1960s, architects loved to play around with bold forms, and here you have a variety of circles, ovals, and other curving elements that combine to create an undeniably interesting, if rather odd, building.

37 St. Olaf Lutheran Church

2901 Emerson Ave. North

1911

Brick Gothic Revival with a central tower. The church is home to one of the neighborhood's oldest congregations, which has been worshipping here since 1911.

38 Jordan Park School for Extended Learning

1501 30th Ave. North

Kodet Architectural Group, 1999

Like several of the Kodet Group's other schools, this one has a long, high spine that links to a series of wings. The building's colorful tile, brick, and metal exterior includes chimney-like

Jordan Park School for Extended Learning

projections that provide a visual signature for the wings containing classrooms.

39 Church of St. Anne

2627 Queen Ave. North

Slifer and Cone, 1949

St. Anne's is one of the city's oldest Catholic parishes, founded in 1884 (as St. Clotilde's) to serve French Canadians. The parish moved here in 1922 and dedicated this church in 1949. It's one of the last Italian Romanesque–style stone churches built in the Twin Cities. It's also among the last works of St. Paul architect Frederick Slifer, who apprenticed under Emmanuel Masqueray, architect of the St. Paul Cathedral. The church includes an

Church of St. Anne

arched central doorway, a circular window, carvings that represent the four evangelists, and a bell tower. Within, the church is basilican in style and features a half-domed sanctuary, much fine marble- and bronzework, numerous stained-glass windows, and a mosaic of St. Anne, installed in 1958 above the altar.

Camden

This neighborhood, which includes all of Minneapolis north of Lowry Avenue, grew around the mouth of Shingle Creek. Pioneers John W. Dow and John C. Bohanon claimed large sections of land here in 1852. A shingle mill, from which the creek took its name, opened a few years later. By 1887, when Camden became part of Minneapolis, sawmills, brickyards, and other industries extended along the riverfront. The Soo Line (now part of the Canadian Pacific Railroad) built tracks to serve these industries and also established its Humboldt Yards north of 46th Avenue.

Much of the early housing in Camden (supposedly named by a Methodist minister who hailed from Camden, NJ) was close to these industrial areas. A streetcar line reached 42nd and Lyndale by 1890, spurring development of a commercial district there. Other lines soon stretched along Emerson and Penn avenues, strewing new houses in their wake. The Minneapolis Park Board assured that there would be a green centerpiece for the neighborhood by acquiring land along Shingle Creek in 1908 for what became Webber Park. Victory Memorial Drive (now officially a parkway) added a long green edge to the neighborhood when it opened in 1921.

Although Camden has scenic areas around Webber Park as well as some of the city's highest hills southeast of Lyndale and Dowling avenues, its housing stock is almost entirely of the working-class variety. In the northern part of the neighborhood, many homes date to the 1950s and are indistinguishable from those in adjoining suburbs. Notable buildings in Camden include the Bremer Way Apartments (1887 and later), the Lawrence and Mary Fournier House (1910), and Maranatha Christian Academy (built in 1950 as St. Austin's School). Just across the border in Robbinsdale is the marvelous Terrace Theater (1951).

Bremer Way Condominiums

1 Bremer Way Condominiums (Fredrika Bremer School) N *L*

1214 Lowry Ave. North
(3232 Fremont Ave. North)

Walter S. Pardee, 1887 / additions, Edward S. Stebbins, 1897, 1910 / addition, Stebbins and Haxby, 1916 / remodeled and enlarged, 1985

One of four remaining nineteenth-century school buildings in Minneapolis. Named after a Swedish author who visited Minnesota in 1850, the yellow brick building is Romanesque Revival in style. Its towers, arched entry porches, and aura of castellated romance must have seemed quite fantastic to early generations of students. The school was converted to condominiums in the 1980s, when a new apartment building was also constructed to the north.

2 Lowry Avenue Bridge

Across Mississippi River

*City of Minneapolis, 1958
(piers, 1905)*

This is the only vehicular bridge across the Mississippi River in the Twin Cities that has a metal superstructure, called a through-truss, above the deck. It incorporates piers and abutments from a 1905 span, one of two earlier bridges here.

3 Cityview Community School

3350 Fourth St. North

Smiley Glotter and Nyberg, 1999

One of Camden's newer schools, situated on a high hill. The brick school has two wings with barrel-vaulted metal roofs, and the design as a whole is dignified without being overweening.

Lawrence and Mary Fournier House

4 Lawrence and Mary Fournier House N *L*

3505 Sheridan Ave. North

Lawrence Fournier, 1910

This lovely bungalow, an Arts and Crafts–Prairie blend, was designed and built by Lawrence Fournier, an architectural drafts-man, with his wife, Mary, an artist. Fournier worked for several local architectural firms, including Purcell and Elmslie. Although this house would seem to show their influence, Fournier actually built it two years before hiring on with them. The cobble-stone and stucco house, which occupies a triple lot, has pitched roofs with shed dormers, exposed rafters, and other typical bunga-low features. However, some details—most notably the case-ment windows that wrap around one corner—are inspired by the work of Frank Lloyd Wright and other Prairie architects. Within, the house has an open plan on the main floor.

LOST 1 *The most peculiar church ever built in the Twin Cities was once at 3800 Washburn Ave. North. The* **first St. Austin Catholic Church,** *completed in 1939, was built around laminated timber trusses formed into steep parabolic arches, and it looked like a cross between an airplane hangar and something from the fertile imagi-nation of the Catalan architect Antoni Gaudi. Designed by the Minneapolis firm of Bard and Vanderbilt, the white stucco church was modeled on an exposition building St. Austin's first pastor had seen in Brno, Czechoslovakia,*

First St. Austin Catholic Church, 1951

in the 1920s. The building was demolished in 1963 after St. Austin moved into a new church a few blocks away.

5 Maranatha Christian Academy (St. Austin's School)

4021 Thomas Ave. North

1950

Originally built for St. Austin's, this Moderne-style school, clad in white stucco, consists of a series of two-story volumes. Long ribbons of windows, par-tially infilled with glass brick, provide horizontal emphasis, but there's also one nod to vertical-ity—a four-story tower. Overall, the school bears a resemblance to several buildings from the same period at the state fair-grounds.

6 St. Austin Catholic Church

4047 Thomas Ave. North

1963

A long, high church clad in golden limestone. It has side aisles extending out from the main walls, clerestory windows, and a cupola that brings light down into the sanctuary.

7 Crystal Lake Cemetery

3816 Penn Ave. North

F. L. Stearns, 1886 and later / includes **chapel,** *1928*

The oldest portion of this ceme-tery was platted in 1886. Designed by a civil engineer named F. L. Stearns, Crystal Lake is a Victo-rian garden-style cemetery,

Camden

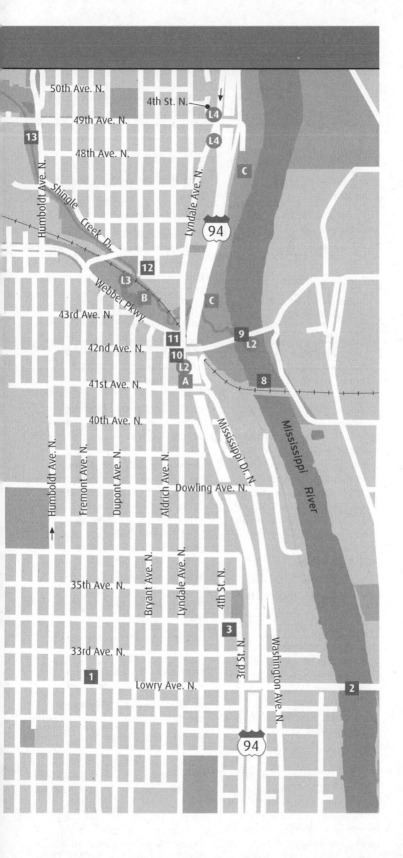

offering the usual winding roads and parklike expanses. The cemetery, which was expanded to 150 acres in 1911, has never served a particularly wealthy clientele, and it has few of the grand funereal monuments you'll find at, say, Lakewood Cemetery. The cemetery's Gothic Revival chapel dates to 1928.

8 Canadian Pacific (Soo Line) Bridge

Near 41st Ave. North across Mississippi River

Soo Line Railroad, 1905

9 Camden Bridge

42nd Ave. North across Mississippi River

Jacus Associates (engineers), 1977

The Camden Bridge is a steel-plate girder span painted royal blue. The much older railroad bridge just to the south is of a type known as a Warren deck truss.

LOST 2 *The* **first Camden Bridge** *was built in 1913. Work on its approaches claimed one of Camden's Victorian monuments: the* **Hotel Lyndale.** *Built in 1888, the towered hotel was located near a small Soo Line passenger station at 41st and Lyndale Aves. North.*

POI A Camden Neighborhood Gateway

41st and Lyndale Aves. North

Zoran Mojsilov (artist), 1996

The major work in this wedge-shaped sculpture garden consists of rocks orbiting a metal framework, representing Camden's seven neighborhoods.

10 Commercial building (Camden Park State Bank)

4171 Lyndale Ave. North

Septimus J. Bowler, 1910

This is the most prominent building in a small commercial area at what used to be a six-cornered intersection where Lyndale, Washington, and 42nd Aves. North and Webber Pkwy. came together.

11 Camden Physicians

4209 Webber Pkwy.

1997

The large letters spelling out this clinic's name were salvaged from the marquee of the Camden Theater, which was located here from about 1925 until its demolition in the 1990s.

POI B Webber (Camden) Park

4400 Dupont Ave. North

Minneapolis Park Board, 1908 and later / includes **Webber Park Community Library,** *1980 / Art: Lumberman (statue near Webber Pond), Charles Brodin, 1990*

This park includes an outdoor pool, a pond, and a branch library. It was renamed in 1939 in honor of Charles C. and Mary Webber, who financed the popular "baths" once located here.

LOST 3 *The* **Camden (Webber) Baths,** *a* **field house,** *and a* **library** *were built here in 1910 as a memorial to the Webbers' 11-year son, who died in 1907. Some accounts say the boy drowned; others attribute his death to meningitis. The baths, a large swimming pool with open-air changing rooms, were a great summer attraction in a part of the city without natural lakes. All three structures donated by the Webbers are gone.*

POI C North Mississippi Regional Park

Along Mississippi River between 41st and 53rd Aves. North

Hennepin County and Minneapolis Park and Recreation Board

includes **Carl W. Kroening Interpretive Center,** 4900 Mississippi Ct.

Partners and Sirny, 2002

A narrow, mile-long riverfront park that includes an inviting, well-designed interpretive center.

LOST 4 *The land occupied by the regional park was once home to brickyards, quarries, institutional buildings, and public housing. The*

Minneapolis Workhouse, *a gloomy brick structure, opened east of Lyndale Ave. near 51st Ave. North*

Minneapolis Workhouse, 1902

around 1886. Just west of the workhouse, the city in 1908 built ***Hopewell Hospital*** *to care for tuberculosis patients. Renamed* ***Parkview,*** *it later served as a public charity hospital. The park also includes the site of the* ***Mississippi Courts Apartments,*** *a flood-prone public housing complex built in 1949 and demolished in the 1980s.*

12 House (Kinnard-Haines Manufacturing Co.) *L*

826 44th Ave. North

Adam Lansing Dorr, 1902

This brick building, now a residence, once served as the offices of a company that manufactured agricultural equipment. The company's plant, razed in about 1940, was directly across Bryant Ave. in what is now Shingle Creek Park. Founded by Owen B. Kinnard and his father-in-law, Albert Haines, the company was known for its Flour City Road Tractor. Intense competition in the tractor business and the onset of the Great Depression led to the company's demise in 1929.

13 Humboldt Avenue Greenway

4600–5300 Humboldt Ave. North

2001 and later

An ambitious project by the City of Minneapolis, Hennepin County, and other agencies to remake what had become a scruffy area of tiny post–World War II houses, apartments, and commercial buildings. The old properties were replaced by new single-family homes, townhomes, and apartments done in the nostalgic styles that the public seems to prefer.

14 Archer Daniels Midland (Soo Line Terminal) Elevator

2125 49th Ave. North

1923–25

Camden's mightiest building, a colossal pile of concrete silos crowned by a brick head house.

Victory Memorial Drive, 1945

POI D Victory Memorial Drive Historic District *L*

Along Victory Memorial Pkwy. from Lowry Ave. North to Webber Park

1921 / Art: Abraham Lincoln (statue), near 44th and Xerxes Aves. North, 1930

This 2.8-mile-long drive is in effect a linear park with a street down the middle. Making an L as it runs from Lowry Ave. at the western city limits to Webber Pkwy., the parkway forms a key link in the city's Grand Rounds. Planned as the Glenwood-Camden Pkwy. in 1910 but not built until 1921, it became a memorial to the 528 servicemen from Hennepin County who died in World War I. A tree and an in-ground plaque honor each of the dead. There's also a memorial and flagpole, as well as a statue of Abraham Lincoln, where the parkway turns near 44th and Xerxes Aves. North. Homes from the 1920s and 1930s line the streets paralleling the parkway.

15 Terrace Theater

3508 France Ave. North

Liebenberg and Kaplan, 1951

The early 1950s were a prosperous time for the movie industry—an age of color-drenched costume dramas, blond goddesses, Cinerama, and huge audiences. The

Terrace Theater, 1950s

Terrace Theater, now boarded up, is a remnant of this privileged era and the last true movie palace built in the Twin Cities. Located just past the city limits in Robbinsdale, the Terrace was built, at a cost of $1 million, by brothers William and Sidney Volk, who owned several other local movie houses.

On the outside, the Terrace features a brick and glass tower crowned by a pair of signs and slanted lobby windows set between stone piers. Within, the expansive lobby—a modernist fantasy in stone, brick, glass, and metal—included a smoking lounge and a television room (to keep youngsters entertained while waiting for the big-screen show). The 1,300-seat auditorium provided stadium-style seating and remained intact until it was partitioned into three screens in 1988. The Terrace finally closed in 1999 and was still vacant as of 2007.

9

Downtown St. Paul

Overview

Compared to its glitzy, skyscraper-laden competitor a few miles to the west, downtown St. Paul seems small and rather provincial. Its site, hemmed in by the Mississippi River and a ring of hills and steep bluffs, has always felt constricted, especially compared to the broad plain of downtown Minneapolis. Yet the site offered at least two key advantages for settlers who began drifting downriver from Fort Snelling in the 1830s. First, most of it was high enough above the river to be safe from flooding. Equally important, there were two steamboat landings (the so-called Lower Landing at the foot of Jackson Street and the Upper Landing at Chestnut Street) that could be reached with relative ease from the bluffs above. Geography in downtown St. Paul's case was indeed destiny, both for better and for worse.

Today, under even the most expansive definition of its boundaries, downtown St. Paul encompasses little more than a square mile, making it less than half the size of downtown Minneapolis. St. Paul's civic and business leaders recognized the problems posed by this compact site. Early in the twentieth century they went so far as to propose a plan for rerouting the Mississippi closer to the West Side bluffs, thereby creating more land for downtown growth. The plan never won federal approval.

For many years, downtown St. Paul also had a somewhat claustrophobic feel because of its narrow, crooked, and often confusing streets, which pioneer newspaper editor James Goodhue memorably described as the product of "a survey without measurement, a plan without method." The street system became especially bizarre near Seven Corners, where Sixth and Ninth originally followed a parallel course but were only a block apart. (If you're wondering what happened to Seventh and Eighth, well, it's a long story.) Over the years, streets have been widened, straightened, or even eliminated, and downtown St. Paul is now a model of clarity compared to what it once was. Even so, navigation can still prove perplexing to visitors from such exotic locales as Minneapolis.

Four distinct divisions characterize downtown St. Paul, which like Minneapolis features an extensive skyway system. In the center, naturally enough, is the commercial core, which extends back from the river bluffs between roughly St. Peter and Jackson streets. Office and government buildings dominate. To the west of St. Peter, where the downtown grid takes a sharp turn, is the Rice Park area, once more commonly known as Uppertown. Most of the city's cultural attractions, including the Ordway Center for the Performing Arts (1985) and the Science Museum of Minnesota (2000), are located here. East of Jackson Street is Lowertown, the city's historic warehouse district. As in Minneapolis, most of the old warehouses have been converted to apartments or offices. To the north, on a series of hills, is the State Capitol area, presided over by Cass Gilbert's magnificent white marble palace.

Although St. Paulites speak often and fondly of their city's devotion to historic preservation, this supposed trait is not overwhelmingly evident in the downtown core. Like Minneapolis and many other American cities, St. Paul embarked on an orgy of urban renewal in the 1960s, and over the following two decades much of downtown was utterly transformed. During the course of this upheaval, some of the city's most important nineteenth-century monuments were wantonly destroyed. Smaller Victorian-era commercial and institutional buildings also fell one by one, as did virtually all of downtown's remaining houses. With a few exceptions, the new buildings that rose from the ruins were mediocre at best and appallingly bad at worst.

Today, most of downtown St. Paul is a sleepy sort of place: only during the noon hour—when workers emerge from their cubicles and roam the skyways in search of food—does it have something like the pace and crackle of urban life. Part of the problem is that very little retail activity remains (only one department store, now owned by Macy's, lingers in the commercial district). Downtown's night life is also considerably less than scintillating, although the Seven Corners area does heat up on nights when the Minnesota Wild hockey team plays at the Xcel Energy Center (2000).

One positive trend has been the construction of a good deal of new and renovated housing, particularly in Lowertown. Downtown riverfront development has also moved forward with such projects as the hugely popular—but architecturally uninspiring—Science Museum. The area around the historic Union Depot (1923) in Lowertown is also being championed as a future site for development along the river. However, St. Paul's peculiar geography—most of the downtown riverfront is a narrow floodplain lodged beneath steep cliffs with railroad tracks and a highway running down the middle of it—will make development at water's edge very difficult.

Despite its dowdy image, downtown St. Paul offers much of architectural interest, beginning with its extraordinary collection of major public buildings. Landmark Center (1892–1902), the Minnesota State Capitol (1905), the St. Paul Public Library and Hill Reference Library (1917), and the St. Paul City Hall–Ramsey County Courthouse (1932) are nationally significant works of architecture, as is the immense St. Paul Cathedral (1915), which lords over all of downtown from the nearby heights of Summit Avenue.

Downtown St. Paul can also boast of two lovely little squares—Rice Park and Mears Park—as well as the Lowertown Historic District, home to over two dozen late nineteenth- and early twentieth-century brick warehouses, many of them of very high quality. Just to the west of Lowertown, along Robert Street, you'll find an outstanding group of late nineteenth-century office buildings, most notably the Pioneer Building (1889), which still has its original light court and open-cage elevators. Also of interest are such historic churches as Assumption Catholic (1874), First Baptist (1875), Central Presbyterian (1889), and St. Louis Catholic (1910). A pair of theaters—the Fitzgerald (1910) and the closed Orpheum (1916)—is all that remains of what was once a sizable entertainment district clustered around Seventh and Wabasha streets.

When it comes to modern architecture, downtown St. Paul is mostly meat and potatoes, although the quality of new buildings has improved since the drab days of the 1960s and 1970s. Still, you won't run across many examples of the sort of "starchitecture" that Minneapolis has long pursued. Two of downtown's finest modern buildings—Benjamin Thompson's visually pleasing but acoustically challenged Ordway Center and William Pedersen's headquarters building (1991) for St. Paul Travelers Insurance Companies—are the work of native sons who went on to national prominence. But most of downtown's modern buildings, including the delightful Minnesota Children's Museum (1995) by Vincent James and Julie Snow, are the work of local architects.

St. Paul Central Core

1   Kellogg Mall Park
2   Wabasha Street Bridge
3   Robert Street Bridge
4   Downtown Skyway System
4A   First skyway bridge
5   Lowry Square Apartments
6   St. Paul Building
7   Ecolab Building
8   Ecolab Center and Plaza
9   Wells Fargo Place
10   Minnesota Children's Museum
11   Fitzpatrick Building
12   World Trade Center Parking Ramp
13   Fitzgerald Theater and Fitzgerald Condominiums
14   McNally Smith College of Music and
     History Theatre
15   Public Safety Building and Penfield Apartments
16   Rossmor Building
17   Church of St. Louis King of France
18   Central Presbyterian Church
19   Exchange Building
20   Minnesota Public Radio
21   Securian Center
22   Golden Rule Building
23   USB Plaza, Bremer Tower, Town Square Shopping
     Center and Park, City Center Hotel
24   Fifth Street Center
25   Pioneer Press Building
26   Downtown University Club
27   Minnesota Building
28   First National Bank Building
29   Pioneer Building
30   Endicott Building
31   Empire Building
32   Ramsey County Government Center East
33   Paul and Sheila Wellstone Elementary School

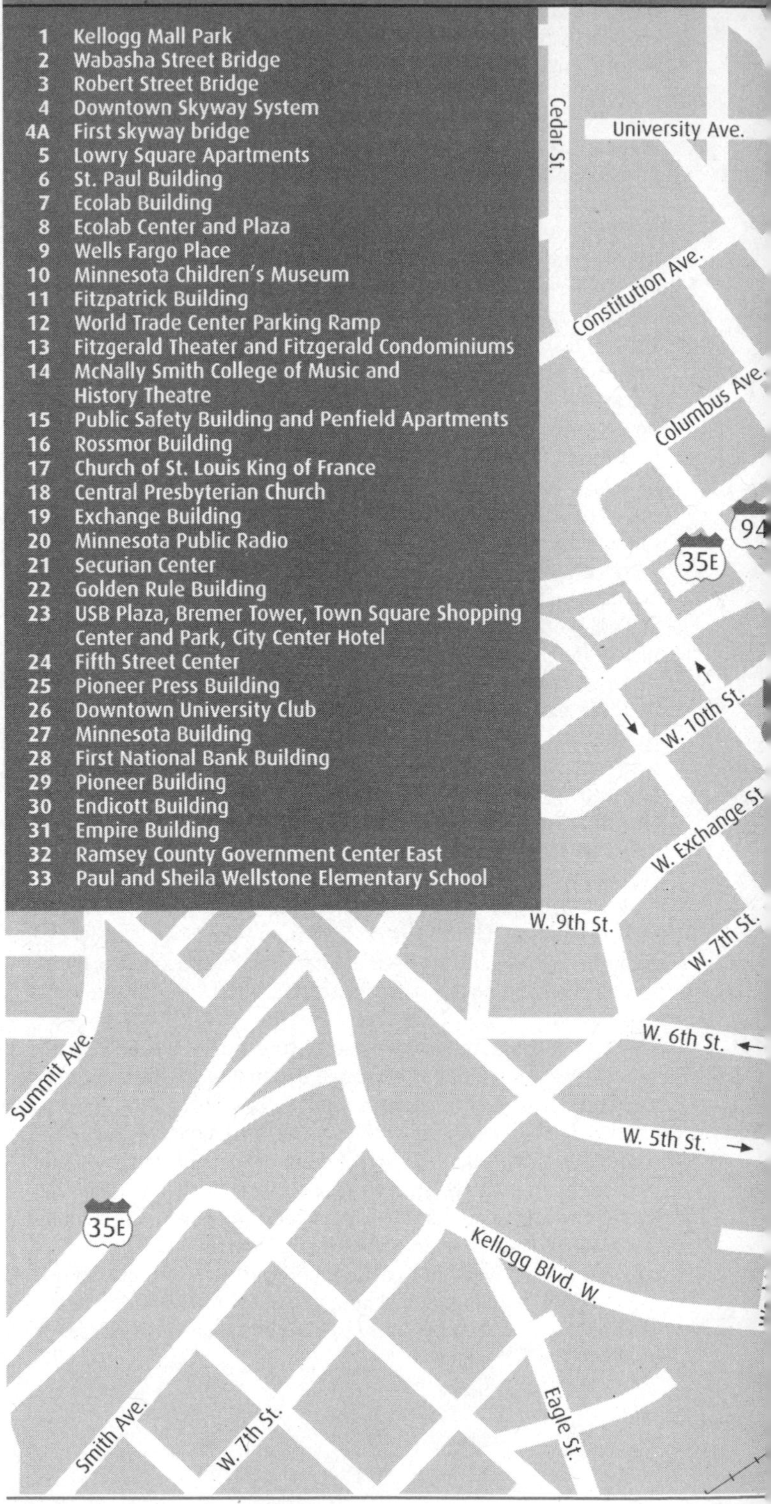

Cedar St.

University Ave.

Constitution Ave.

Columbus Ave.

94

35E

W. 10th St.

W. Exchange St.

W. 9th St.

W. 7th St.

W. 6th St.

W. 5th St.

Summit Ave.

35E

Kellogg Blvd. W.

Smith Ave.

W. 7th St.

Eagle St.

A	Remains of U.S. Quartermaster's Department Building	L1	Chapel of St. Paul
B	Remnants of Hotel Spalding	L2	State Capitols
C	Skyway and stone heads	L3	First Central High School
		L4	Ryan Hotel
		L5	New York Life Building
		L6	St. Paul City Hall and Ramsey County Courthouse
		L7	Globe Building

The Central Core

Most of downtown's central core—an area bounded by the Mississippi River bluffs, Interstate 94, and St. Peter and Jackson streets— is part of the city's first plat, St. Paul Proper, surveyed in 1847 by brothers Ira and Benjamin Brunson. As plats go, there is nothing remarkable about it. The Brunsons laid out a standard gridiron, with numbered east-west streets running parallel to the river. The plat featured small blocks (about 300 feet square on average) and 60-foot-wide streets (tight by midwestern standards) and left no room for alleys, which would have been helpful. There was also no provision for parks, riverfront promenades, or other public amenities. It was, in short, a plat made mainly with the business of real estate speculation in mind.

As St. Paul began a period of spectacular growth in the 1880s, St. Paul Proper—originally the site of many small homes—quickly filled with commercial, retail, and industrial buildings. Among these were such prominent monuments as the Ryan Hotel (1885), the Globe Building (built in 1887 and designed by E. Townsend Mix, best known for his magnificent Metropolitan Building in Minneapolis), and the step-gabled New York Life Building (1889), one of the most distinctive skyscrapers of its era. Interspersed among these landmarks were scores of modest two- to six-story commercial buildings, usually clad in brick or stone and dating to 1900 or earlier.

Beginning in the late 1920s, the widening of Third Street to create Kellogg Boulevard removed many old buildings, but otherwise change came slowly to the central core through the first half of the twentieth century, largely because the city's stodgy growth rate did little to stimulate new development. As late as 1960, a visitor to this part of downtown would have found a virtual museum of nineteenth- and early twentieth-century commercial architecture. To be sure, it wasn't particularly pretty or quaint (many of the old buildings had been remodeled from the 1930s onward), and some blocks were downright shabby. Still, the downtown core in those days remained an undeniably *interesting* place, with the comfortably lived-in feel of a favorite old couch. It also functioned as a kind of anti-Minneapolis: a slow-paced, history-rich alternative to the Mill City's bustle and hustle.

Like almost all other American cities, however, St. Paul couldn't resist the urge to modernize, and by the early 1960s a great transformation of the central core began. An ambitious plan known as the Capital Centre project, backed by city government and the business community, served as the blueprint for redevelopment. The plan called for an array of new office towers and plazas, mostly along Fifth and Sixth streets, and it also introduced the mixed blessing of skyways to the downtown scene.

Over the next 20 years, the plan was carried out with ruthless enthusiasm. Numerous old buildings—among them some of the city's very best—came down, and new structures rose in their place, sometimes after a delay of many years. It all might have been worthwhile had the new work been of high quality, but that was seldom the case. The upheaval also had a devastating effect on the downtown retail trade. More than 200 stores left, and efforts to rebuild this lost retail base have proved futile.

Despite the damage done by years of urban renewal, this part of downtown has retained a number of important historic buildings, most notably the Pioneer-Endicott complex (1889–91) at Fourth and Robert streets. There are also some excellent modern buildings such as the Minnesota Children's Museum (1995). Overall, however, a walk through the central core provides a discouraging object lesson in how *not* to remake a city, best of intentions or no.

Wabasha Street Bridge

1 Kellogg Mall Park

South side of Kellogg Blvd. between Wabasha and Robert Sts.

1932 / rebuilt, St. Paul Parks Department (Tim Agness and Jody Martinez), 1991 / Art: fountains, sculptures, terra-cotta plaques, Cliff Garten, 1991

This park atop the downtown river bluffs was created as part of St. Paul's first big urban renewal project. Between 1929 and 1936, the city widened old Third St. and renamed it in honor of Frank B. Kellogg, a St. Paul lawyer who served as U.S. secretary of state in the 1920s and later won a Nobel Peace Prize. Forty-three buildings, some dating to the 1860s, were demolished to make way for the new boulevard and mall, obliterating what might be thought of as St. Paul's original "old town." The park in its current guise dates to 1991. Its adornments include terra-cotta plaques depicting the inelegant puss of Pig's Eye Parrant, the whiskey-dealing reprobate who was among the city's founders. Below the mall, incidentally, is Second St. (originally Bench), which in earlier days provided a way up the bluff from the Lower Landing at the foot of Jackson St.

LOST 1 *Near the Robert St. end of the park a plaque marks the approximate site of the first **Chapel of St. Paul,** a log church built by Father Lucien Galtier in 1841. The city later took its name from this small structure.*

2 Wabasha Street Bridge

Across Mississippi River between downtown and the West Side

TKDA, James Carpenter and Associates (New York), and others, 1998 (opened)–2001 (overlooks completed)

The first bridge here opened in 1859; at that time, only two other bridges—the Hennepin Avenue Suspension Bridge (1855) in Minneapolis and a railroad bridge (1856) at Rock Island, IL—spanned the Mississippi. The original bridge was replaced by a steel span that stood until 1995, when it was knocked down to make way for a modern replacement. New York artist James Carpenter was selected to design the new bridge and produced a spectacular proposal for a cable-stay structure with a V-shaped central mast. His design touched off heated debate. One critic likened it to "Madonna's bra"; others rightly praised it as a dazzling work. In the end, cost concerns doomed the design, and the city settled for a concrete girder span with split roadways (best seen from below). The bridge's many amenities include overlooks set behind weird, obtrusive metal cages, custom-designed railings and lights, pylons with flags, and an elaborate staircase that leads down to Raspberry Island.

Great Western Lift Bridge and Robert Street Bridge

3 Robert Street Bridge N

Across Mississippi River between downtown and the West Side

Toltz, King and Day, 1926 / renovated and restored, TKDA, 1989

The first bridge here opened in 1886 and served until the early 1920s, when a higher bridge was required to accommodate a raised railroad platform at St. Paul Union Depot. Designed by Toltz, King and Day of St. Paul, the bridge is of a type known as a "rainbow arch," so named because the arches of the main span rise above the roadway like, well, rainbows. This form was dictated by the demands of the site: the bridge's roadway needed to reach Kellogg Mall at grade but also had to clear the elevated tracks of the adjacent Great Western Lift Bridge (1913) and be high enough to permit the passage of riverboats. The bridge, which has art deco touches, was rebuilt in 1989 by the same firm, now known as TKDA, that had designed it 65 years earlier.

POI A Remains of U.S. Quartermaster's Department Building

Beneath Kellogg Mall near Robert St.

George Wirth, 1884

Buried here are the foundation walls and ground floor of the old U.S. Quartermaster's Building, which helped supply the armies that battled Native Americans on the northern plains. The building was largely destroyed in the late 1920s when work began on Kellogg Mall. Its stone walls were uncovered, documented, and then reburied during the 1989 bridge reconstruction.

4 Downtown Skyway System

About 50 bridges, connecting more than 30 blocks

HGA (standard design), 1967 and later

Look along Fourth and Wabasha Sts. and you'll see at least ten of the 50 or so bridges that make up St. Paul's downtown skyway system. The first bridge (between the Pioneer Building and the Burger Federal Building) opened in 1967. From the start the system differed in two key respects from the one in Minneapolis. Almost all of St. Paul's bridges look alike—the standard bridge is a steel truss painted dark brown and infilled with glass—whereas Minneapolis's come in an array of styles. Not everyone likes this uniform design, but its neutrality means that the standard bridge can be punched into almost any kind of building without creating too much architectural discord. St. Paul also differs from Minneapolis in that its skyway system is publicly maintained, much as streets would be, making for relatively consistent hours of operation from one end to the other.

It's also an unfortunate truth that St. Paul has suffered more from the negative impact of skyways than has its larger twin. In Minneapolis, the Nicollet Mall provides an outdoor pedestrian spine through the heart of downtown, and the emergence of the old warehouse district as an entertainment venue has also brought people back to the sidewalks. Downtown St. Paul, however, has become almost completely internalized because of its reliance on skyways and the web of building corridors that connect them. The streets, meanwhile, have largely gone dead. Although city design guidelines call for resuscitating street life, it's hard to see how this could happen without a reworking of the entire skyway system and its relationship to the world outside.

Sixth St. skyway, 1975

5 Lowry Square Apartments (Lowry Hotel)

345 North Wabasha St.

*Lambert Bassindale, 1927 / addition, Ellerbe Architects, 1930 / includes **ballroom,** Werner Wittkamp, ca. 1935 / Art: relief sculptures, John B. Garatti, 1930*

This formerly first-class brick hotel was converted to apartments in the 1970s. To the north on Wabasha St. is an addition that once housed the Lowry Lounge, an art deco ballroom. A relief panel on the lounge building depicts a pair of thinly clad Greek gods, Bacchus and Persephone, who are playing music and seem to be having a wonderful time of it.

St. Paul Building

6 St. Paul (Germania Bank) Building N *L*

6 West Fifth St. (at Wabasha St.)

J. Walter Stevens, 1889 / renovated, Wold Architects, 1989

Often overlooked even by locals, this building showcases the deep-toned beauty of reddish brown Lake Superior sandstone. The stone is easily carved, as evidenced by the fanciful ornament that decorates much of the eight-story office building. Note especially the intricately carved column capitals and the rich patternwork on the upper floors. It was once thought that Harvey Ellis, an itinerant draftsman famed for his romantic renderings, had a hand in the building's design, but that does not appear to be the case. Inside, the building has been modernized: the original second-floor banking hall is long gone.

7 Ecolab Building (Northern States Power Co.)

360 North Wabasha St.

Ellerbe Architects, 1932 / Art: Light, Heat and Power (bronze relief over main entrance), John B. Garatti

This art deco building was initially envisioned as a taller structure, but the Depression intervened and only six stories were built. Above the main entrance is a relief sculpture extolling the wonders of electricity.

8 Ecolab Center (Osborn Building) and Plaza

370 North Wabasha St.

Bergstedt Wahlberg and Wold, 1968 / Art: Skygate (stainless-steel sculpture in front plaza), R. M. Fischer, 2000 / Above, Above (welded steel sculpture in rear plaza), Alexander Liberman, 1972

The best skyscraper of its era in St. Paul. The materials—polished granite, stainless steel, and glass—project an image of cleanliness in keeping with Ecolab's business as a supplier of sanitation products

Ecolab Center

and services. Situated on a templelike podium above the downward slope of Fifth St., the building is in the classic modern manner of Chicago architect Ludwig Mies van der Rohe. Inside, the glass-enclosed lobby may well be the purest Miesian space in the Twin Cities. Behind the building, above Cedar St., is downtown's finest plaza. It features sinuous black granite benches and a colorful abstract sculpture by Alexander Liberman that serves as a perfect foil to the resolutely rectilinear building.

9 Wells Fargo Place (Minnesota World Trade Center)

Wabasha St. and Seventh Pl.

WZMH Group with Winsor/Faricy Architects, 1987

This skyscraper's V-shaped glass top is certainly distinctive, resembling a giant cobra poised to strike at the heart of the city. Overall, however, its architecture is far more conventional than dangerously *avant-garde.* The building was originally home to the Minnesota World Trade Center, intended to become a vibrant hub of internationalism in St. Paul. The idea never took off, however, and today the building functions as a standard office tower. An indoor shopping mall was included in the project, but it failed and has largely been converted to office space.

10 Minnesota Children's Museum !

10 West Seventh St. (at Wabasha St.)

James/Snow Architects with Architectural Alliance, 1995

The best of St. Paul's modern museum buildings and an object lesson in how to fit a new building into a historic environment without succumbing to architectural nostalgia. With its colorful exterior, porthole windows, and vaguely boatlike shape, the building floats like a jolly pirate ship in downtown's sea of sober gray, brown, and beige buildings. Yet its volumes are so carefully modulated that the museum doesn't seem at all obtrusive, perfectly playing off against historic neighbors like the Orpheum Theater and the Coney Island buildings. Despite a tight site, the museum also includes a lovely little garden

Minnesota Children's Museum

along St. Peter St., protected by a tall iron fence ornamented with fanciful animal heads.

A suitably playful lobby and a series of well-designed spaces showcase the museum's knack for mounting entertaining, instructive exhibits. But if you step inside, be on the alert for gangs of roving toddlers.

11 Fitzpatrick Building (Wabasha Hotel) N

465–67 North Wabasha St.

Clarence H. Johnston (Thomas Fitzpatrick, builder), 1890

The Fitzpatrick is among the few small Victorian-era commercial buildings left in the central core. It originally housed shops, offices, and apartments.

12 World Trade Center Parking Ramp

477 Cedar St.

1987 / enlarged, HGA, 1998

Created by enlarging a nondescript ramp from the 1980s, this colorful structure, which neatly complements the Children's Museum across the street, is a stepchild of all those garish metal facades that were tacked onto old buildings in the 1950s. More importantly, it's great fun.

POI B Remnants of Hotel Spalding

Wabasha St. between Seventh and Exchange Sts.

ca. 1890

A sandstone column next to the south wall of the Fitzgerald Condominiums is all that remains of the Hotel Spalding, located for 80 years at the corner of Ninth (now Seventh) and Wabasha Sts.

Fitzgerald Theater and Fitzgerald Condominiums

13 Fitzgerald (Shubert) Theater and Fitzgerald Condominiums (Shubert Building)

Theater, 10 East Exchange St.

Marshall and Fox (Chicago), 1910 / remodeled, ca. 1933 / remodeled and restored, Miller, Hanson, Westerbeck and Bell, 1986

Condominiums, 484–96 North Wabasha St.

Buechner and Orth, 1910 / renovated, Collaborative Design Group, 2005

Home to Garrison Keillor's *Prairie Home Companion* radio show, this double-balconied theater (originally called the Shubert and later the World) was built as a playhouse, though it also hosted vaudeville and was later adapted to showing movies. Its severe gray neoclassical facade conveys a sense of refinement. Restored in 1986, it now serves as an intimate venue for a variety of shows and concerts in addition to Keillor's weekly extravaganza. The attached commercial and now condominium building features boldly colored facades of glazed terra-cotta with supersized pilasters of a kind seen nowhere else downtown.

14 McNally Smith College of Music and History Theatre (Minnesota Arts and Science Center)

30 East Tenth St.

Ellerbe Associates, 1964

17 West Exchange St.

HGA, 1980

A formal type of architectural modernism that emerged in the 1960s was frequently applied to museums, usually with lackluster results, as is the case here. At Wabasha and Exchange Sts., a newer part of the complex, built in 1980 to provide additional exhibit space for what by then was known as the Science Museum of Minnesota, somehow manages to be even duller than this building.

LOST 2 *This block was the site of both the first and the second state* *capitols. The **first State Capitol** was built in 1853 and burned down in 1881. The **second State Capitol,** a gawky Victorian affair with a 200-foot-high central tower, opened in 1883 but proved so inadequate that planning began just ten years later for the current capitol, completed in 1905. The second capitol wasn't demolished until 1938.*

15 Public Safety Building and Penfield Apartments (proposed)

100 East 11th St.

***Public Safety Building,** St. Paul City Architect (Frank X. Tewes), 1930 / **Apartments,** Humphreys and Partners Architects, 2008*

The neoclassical Public Safety Building, once St. Paul's police and fire headquarters, now stands vacant, but plans call for incorporating it into a new 33-story apartment tower to be built on the site.

LOST 3 *St. Paul's **first Central High School,** a towered Victorian Gothic pile, opened on this block in 1883. It was razed in 1929 to make way for the Public Safety Building.*

16 Rossmor Building (Foot, Schulze and Co.)

500 North Robert St.

Kees and Colburn, 1916 / renovated, Collaborative Design Group, 2004

As many as 1,000 people once worked in this brick-clad, concrete-frame building, which began life as a shoe factory operated by Foot, Schulze and Co. Like many old warehouses, it was later populated by small businesses and artists seeking inexpensive studio and living space. In 2004, it was converted to condominiums.

17 Church of St. Louis King of France

506 Cedar St.

Emmanuel Masqueray, 1910

This parish was founded in 1868 by St. Paul's French Catholics,

Church of St. Louis King of France, 1964

who built their first church that year. A second church, located at Wabasha and Exchange Sts. (the Fitzgerald Theater site), served until the dedication of this lovely Renaissance Revival–style brick church. Architect Emmanuel Masqueray, best known for the St. Paul Cathedral, called this church his "little gem."

Extensively renovated in the late 1990s, St. Louis has a gracious, barrel-vaulted interior, one of the city's handsomest Renaissance-inspired spaces. Note also the large round window with its "telephone dial" pattern, a Masqueray trademark, in the north transept. At the rear, along Tenth St., a small chapel includes a replica of the Grotto of Our Lady of Lourdes.

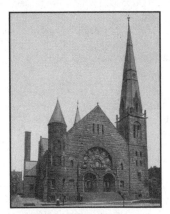

Central Presbyterian Church, 1908

18 Central Presbyterian Church N *L*

500 Cedar St.

Warren H. Hayes, 1889

Central Presbyterian, founded in 1852, built its first church here two years later and enlarged it in the 1870s. Still, it proved too small for the fast-growing congregation and was replaced in 1889 by this burly brownstone church, one of the city's outstanding examples of Romanesque Revival architecture. The arched entrances—a hallmark of the style—sport an abundance of carved floral and geometric motifs. The skylit interior, somewhat modified over the years, originally followed the so-called Akron plan, with seating curved around a pulpit at one corner of the sanctuary.

19 Exchange Building (St. Agatha's Conservatory) N L

26 East Exchange St.

John W. Wheeler, 1910, 1914

This building was known to generations of St. Paulites as St. Agatha's Conservatory of Music and Arts, founded by the Sisters of St. Joseph of Carondelet in 1884. Besides serving as a private academy for children of well-heeled Catholic families, it functioned as a citywide convent for nuns teaching in parishes that couldn't afford their own convents. As many as 100 nuns lived here during peak years. St. Agatha's closed in 1962, and the building was later sold to a private developer; it's now used for offices. The building has two features unique in downtown St. Paul: a double staircase leading up to the main entrance on Exchange St. and a covered rooftop garden (now enclosed), where nuns once enjoyed summer breezes high above the temptations of the city.

20 Minnesota Public Radio

480 Cedar St.

ca. 1966 / remodeled, Leonard Parker Associates, 1980 / addition, HGA, 2005

The dark brick corner building is a mildly postmodern makeover of an earlier structure. The glassy addition to the north tries to add a little pizzazz to the proceedings but, like public radio itself, may be too quietly tasteful for its own good.

Securian Center, 400 Building

21 Securian Center (Minnesota Mutual Life Insurance buildings)

400 Building, 400 North Robert St.

BWBR Architects, 1981

401 Building, 401 North Robert St.

Architectural Alliance, 2000

The taller and older of these two buildings, 400 Robert, is very large, very gray, and very uninviting. It also thumbs its nose at its surroundings by standing askew from the street grid and by presenting nothing except blank walls and tinted glass at street level. Across the street, the company did considerably better with a second building, completed in 2000. Instead of presenting itself as a monolith, 401 Robert offers a variety of forms and, compared to its hulking predecessor, is much more attentive to what goes on at street level. The best part is a section along Sixth St. that uses double-storied, deeply inset windows to convey a sense of heft and volume reminiscent of the old Lowertown warehouses just down the street.

LOST 4 *400 Robert occupies the site of what many people consider to be downtown St. Paul's greatest lost building: the **Ryan Hotel,** a Victorian Gothic extravaganza that opened in 1885. The seven-story* *hotel was demolished in 1962, the same year Minneapolis lost its*

Ryan Hotel, ca. 1900

equally beloved Metropolitan Building.

22 Golden Rule (Department Store) Building

85 East Seventh Pl.

Clarence H. Johnston, 1915 (incorporated older buildings on site) / renovated, BWBR Architects, 1985

Although the Golden Rule Department Store is long gone, this sturdy Classical Revival–style building has found a second life as offices. Note the eagles posted at regular intervals beneath the ornate cornice. Across Robert St. is the old Emporium Department Store, sheathed in a modern blue glass skin and now known as the Metro Square Building.

23 Town Square

UBS Plaza, 444 Cedar St.

SOM (Chicago), 1980

Bremer Tower, 445 Minnesota St.

SOM, 1980

Town Square Shopping Center and Park, 445 Minnesota St.

SOM, 1980

City Center Hotel, 411 Minnesota St.

BWBR Architects, 1980

Intended as a new city center, this megablock complex—which includes a largely moribund shopping mall, two office towers, a hotel, and a glass-roofed park—

is one of downtown's biggest architectural duds. Like its equally wretched cousin, City Center (1983) in downtown Minneapolis, it's a clumsy gray hulk sheathed in precast concrete panels that seem to have been selected with maximum ugliness in mind. The indoor park, now closed, was botched from the start. Located one level above the shopping mall instead of being integrated into it, the park became a hard-to-police space that provided too many opportunities for mischief amid the shrubbery. The hotel didn't fare much better. Its triangular metal roof was built with a solar heating system designed to provide all the hotel's hot water. However, like pretty much everything else connected with this misbegotten complex, the system never worked.

Fifth Street Center

24 Fifth Street Center

55 East Fifth St.

Grover Diamond Associates, 1971

This office tower, originally home to a bank, offers one outstanding feature in the form of an elegant banking hall (vacant as of 2007) on the skyway level. The multiblock parking ramp to the rear, along Sixth St., is another story. An architectural atrocity in raw concrete and Cor-Ten steel, it is the ugliest object in all of downtown. It's especially depressing when you consider that one of St. Paul's finest old skyscrapers was destroyed to make way for this dreck.

New York Life Building, ca. 1900

LOST 5 *The **New York Life Building** stood at the southwest corner of Sixth and Minnesota Sts. from 1889 until 1967. A superb bronze eagle above the main entrance was spared from destruction and is now located at Lookout Park on Summit Ave.*

25 Pioneer Press Building (Minnesota Mutual Life Insurance Co.)

345 Cedar St.

Ellerbe Associates, 1955 / renovated, ca. 1980

When this building opened as the new home of Minnesota Mutual Life Insurance Co. (now Securian) in 1955, it was the first major office structure to be built downtown since the early 1930s. A lackluster building with a slightly Nordic cast, it features the long-banded windows and spare utilitarian look favored by advocates of the so-called International Style of modernism.

LOST 6 *Virtually all of this block was once taken up by the first combined **St. Paul City Hall** and **Ramsey County Courthouse,** completed in 1889. The building was torn down in 1933 after the present city hall–courthouse opened. The **first Ramsey County Jail** was also located on the northeast corner of this block, from 1858 to about 1900.*

26 Downtown University Club (St. Paul Athletic Club)

340 Cedar St.

Allen H. Stem with Beaver Wade Day Associates, 1918 / additions, Ellerbe Associates, ca. 1960 and later / Art: ornamental plaster, Brioschi-Minuti Co., 1918

This building teetered at the brink of extinction in the 1980s after the St. Paul Athletic Club fell into debt and disbanded, but it's found a new life as home to the Downtown University Club, a fitness center, and offices. The complex interior includes gymnasiums, banquet and meeting rooms, restaurants, a swimming pool, and, on the upper floors, small guest rooms now converted to office space. The club's two-story-high lobby is well worth a look: it includes a baronial fireplace, ornate plasterwork, and unusual terra-cotta railings on the balconies.

Globe Building, ca. 1902

LOST 7 *Where the Degree of Honor Building stands at 325 Cedar St. was from 1887 to 1959 the site of the ten-story **Globe Building,** an early skyscraper. Originally home to the long-gone St. Paul Daily Globe newspaper, the building was designed by E. Townsend Mix, who also produced the Metropolitan Building in Minneapolis.*

27 Minnesota Building

42–48 East Fourth St.

Charles A. Hausler, 1930

Mild art deco. The delicately detailed entrances on Fourth and Cedar Sts., which include a version of the state seal in terracotta, are very urbane.

First National Bank Building

28 First National Bank Building

First Farmers and Merchants Bank Building, Fourth and Robert Sts.

Jarvis Hunt (Chicago), 1916

First National Bank and First Trust Co., 332 Minnesota St.

Graham Anderson Probst and White (Chicago), 1931 / addition, Haarstick Lundgren and Associates, 1971 / Art: St. Paul Sculptural Complex (metal sculpture), George Sugarman, 1971

Although the First National Bank is no more, this complex still bears its name. The 32-story First National Bank Building was St. Paul's tallest skyscraper until the 1980s. Designed in a sedate, classically inspired version of art deco, the building lacks the jazziness usually associated with this style. However, it does offer downtown's largest sign, a ten-story-high, three-sided number "1" that flashes through the night. The Robert St. side of the complex includes the old First Farmers and Merchants Bank Building,

which at 16 stories was St. Paul's tallest skyscraper when it opened in 1916. Clad in glazed white brick, it's a fine example of the dignified Beaux-Arts commercial style that prevailed in the early twentieth century. As built, it included a grand second-floor lobby (gone) that was one of the finest banking halls in the state.

POI C Skyway and stone heads

Fourth St. between Robert and Minnesota Sts.

Look to the north here and you'll see the Twin Cities' highest skyway between the First Farmers and Merchants and First National Bank buildings. It was built in 1931 to link the upper stories of the buildings. On the other side of the street, adorning part of Kellogg Square, is St. Paul's very own theater of redheads— sculpted sandstone giants rescued from the old **Germania Life (later Guardian) Building,** constructed on this site in 1889 and razed in 1970.

29 Pioneer (Press) Building ! N

336 North Robert St.

Solon Beman (Chicago), 1889 / addition (top four stories), 1909 / renovated, TKDA, 1983

30 Endicott Building N L

350 North Robert St. and 141 East Fourth St.

Gilbert and Taylor, 1890 / addition (142 East Fifth St.), 1910

31 Empire (Manhattan) Building N

360 North Robert St.

Clarence H. Johnston, 1891 / remodeled, ca. 1960 and later

This trio forms the finest ensemble of late nineteenth-century office buildings in the Twin Cities. Dominating the threesome is the Pioneer Building, which at 12 stories was the city's tallest skyscraper when it opened in

1889. Four stories were added in 1909. It was originally built for the *Pioneer Press* newspaper; a bulletin board where the latest

Pioneer Building, Endicott-Midwest Building, and Empire Building

Pioneer Building light court

news was once posted can still be seen at the corner of the building.

With its arched entryway surrounded by massive blocks of granite, the Pioneer Building was meant to convey a sense of power and permanence. Although its brick and stone facades offer a mix of Romanesque and Classical Revival elements, the building is in the no-nonsense tradition of Chicago skyscrapers of the period. Inside, much of the building bears the faux-historic look of a 1980s remodeling. However, its 16-story-high "light court" (a kind of atrium) remains largely intact. A pair of modified open-cage elevators (still run by operators) flanks a spiral staircase that climbs to the top floor, where the dizzying view down into the light court remains one of St. Paul's great architectural experiences.

The five-story, L-shaped Endicott Building wraps around the Pioneer Building. Designed by

Cass Gilbert, it's a suave essay in the Italian Palazzo style. Within, you'll find a long arcade with a colorful barrel-vaulted glass ceiling. Also of note is the Fourth St. lobby, which features fine stonework and an arcaded staircase.

The Empire Building, by Gilbert's longtime friend and sometime competitor Clarence Johnston, has suffered more than its neighbors from insensitive remodeling. The ground floor—originally done in a Renaissance Revival style with rusticated stonework and an arched entrance—received an ugly makeover in about 1960. However, renovation of the building's interior began in 2006.

32 Ramsey County Government Center East (Farwell, Ozmun and Kirk Co.)

150–60 Kellogg Blvd. East

Louis Lockwood, 1905 / remodeled, Winsor/Faricy Architects, 1992–95

This strapping brick warehouse, built for the wholesaler behind the OK Hardware chain, is one of the Twin Cities' earliest examples of concrete-frame construction. The faux-classical features pasted on the building in the 1990s seem as inappropriate as lace frills on a football uniform.

33 Paul and Sheila Wellstone Elementary School (YWCA)

65 Kellogg Blvd. East

ca. 1910 / renovated and enlarged, Grover Diamond Associates, 1961 / renovated, 1988

This building's structural bones date to the early twentieth century, when it was a food processing plant. In 1961 it was rebuilt to serve as the downtown branch of the St. Paul YWCA. The 1960s work includes a handsome brick screen around the base of the building, an elevated entry porch, and a folded concrete roof with unusual abstract ornament beneath the folds. The building was remodeled once again in the 1980s, and it's now a public school.

Rice Park and Environs

1 Rice Park
2 Landmark Center
3 St. Paul Hotel
4 Qwest Buildings
5 RiverCentre Connection
6 St. Paul Central Library and James J. Hill Reference Library
7 Ordway Center for the Performing Arts
8 317 on Rice Park
9 Science Museum of Minnesota
10 St. Paul RiverCentre, Roy Wilkins Auditorium, Xcel Energy Center
11 Minnesota History Center
12 Colonnade Apartments
13 Catholic Charities Building
14 Father Emmett Cashman Building
15 Assumption Catholic Church
16 Mickey's Diner
17 Coney Island Restaurant buildings
18 Seventh Place Mall
19 Orpheum Theatre
20 St. Paul Travelers Insurance Companies Headquarters
21 Hamm Building
22 Hamm Plaza
23 Lawson Commons
24 The Lowry
25 Wold Architects
26 St. Paul City Hall and Ramsey County Courthouse
27 Former Ramsey County Adult Detention Center and Plaza
28 Ramsey County Government Center West, Minnesota Museum of American Art

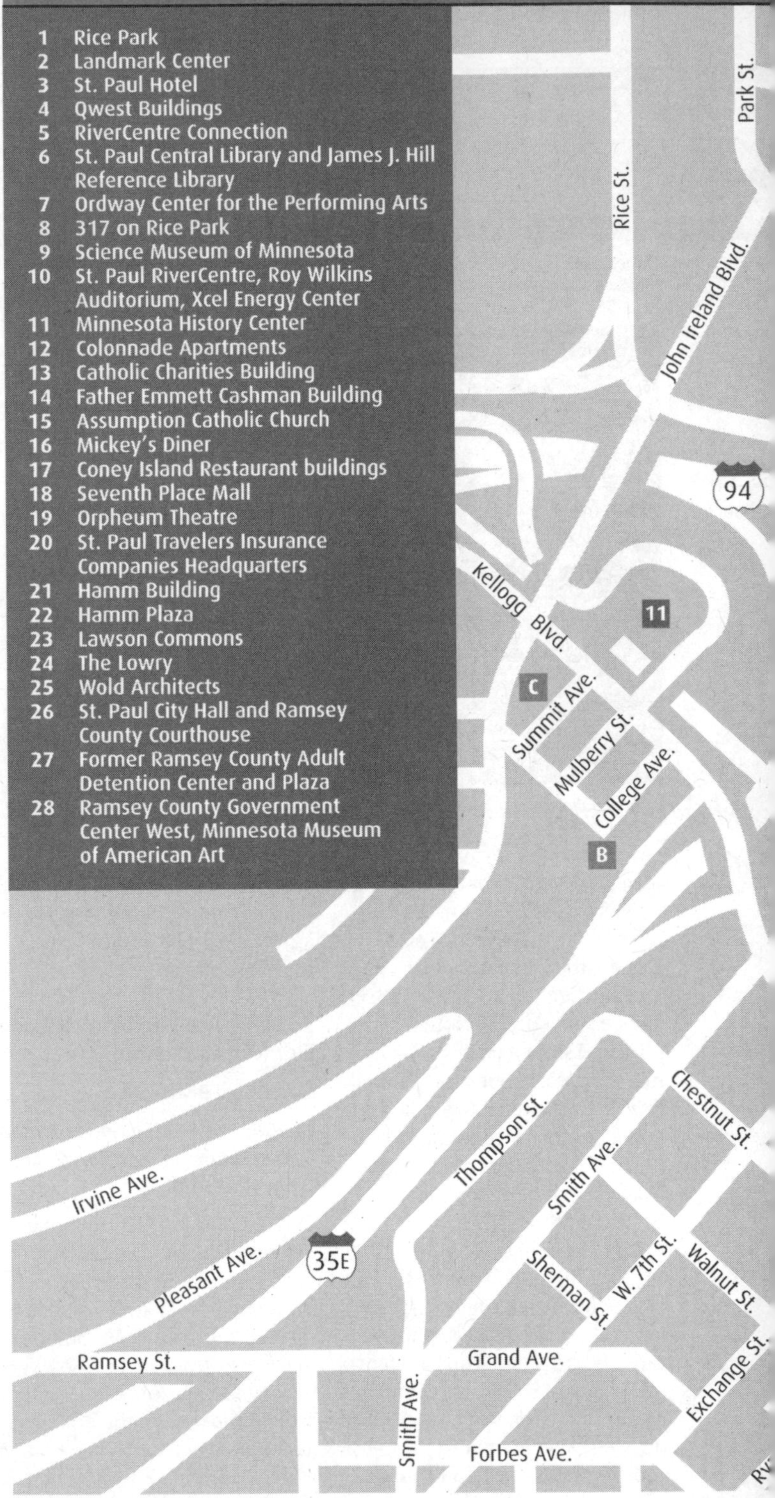

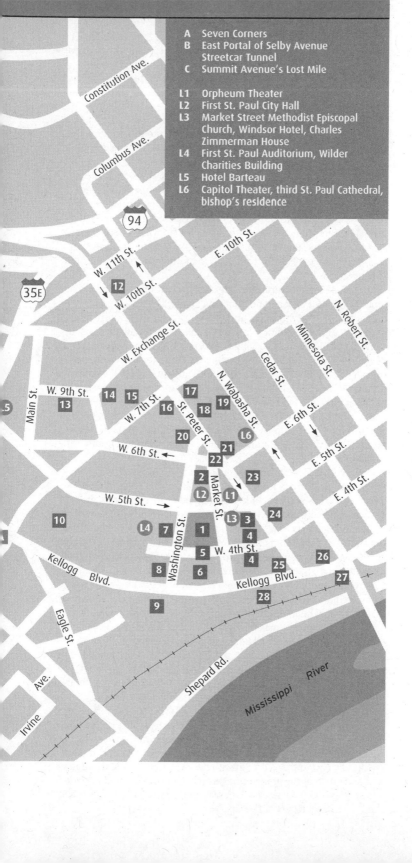

A   Seven Corners
B   East Portal of Selby Avenue
    Streetcar Tunnel
C   Summit Avenue's Lost Mile

L1   Orpheum Theater
L2   First St. Paul City Hall
L3   Market Street Methodist Episcopal
     Church, Windsor Hotel, Charles
     Zimmerman House
L4   First St. Paul Auditorium, Wilder
     Charities Building
L5   Hotel Barteau
L6   Capitol Theater, third St. Paul Cathedral,
     bishop's residence

Rice Park and Environs

This part of downtown was platted in 1849 by John Irvine and Henry Rice, pioneer businessmen and civic leaders (Rice later served as Minnesota's first U.S. senator). Like almost everyone else in the city's early days, the two men speculated extensively in real estate. They also seem to have been mischief-makers at heart, given the peculiarities of their plat, which added a distinctive if troublesome twist to the city's street system. In an apparent effort to follow the line of the river bluffs, Rice and Irvine laid out their modified grid at a 45-degree angle to that of St. Paul Proper's 1847 plat to the east, thereby creating the decisive turn that occurs at St. Peter Street. This turn—one of the sharpest in any American gridiron city—produced an intriguing arrangement of streets, most notably the tangle at Seven Corners.

Over the years, many of these enchanting irregularities have been eliminated by street widenings, highway construction, and the development of such multiblock projects as RiverCentre (1998) and the St. Paul Travelers headquarters complex (1991). As a result, the Rice Park area, despite its reputation as a haven for historic architecture, is actually the least historic section of downtown in terms of its street pattern.

The area's architectural character has also changed markedly over time. Today, Rice Park and neighboring Landmark Plaza are at the heart of St. Paul's cultural life and provide an elegant setting for some of the city's finest buildings. It was not always so. Small houses and commercial buildings of varying quality ringed the park through much of the nineteenth century. The original St. Paul City Hall (1854) was the only public building facing the park until 1892, when the south portion of the Federal Building (now Landmark Center) opened. Then, between 1900 and 1920, several significant new buildings appeared on or near the park, including the first St. Paul Auditorium (1907), the St. Paul Hotel (1910), the Wilder Charities Building (1913), the Minnesota Club (1915), the Hamm Building (1920), and, most notably, the St. Paul Public Library and Hill Reference Library (1917).

Even with this handsome array of buildings, Rice Park wasn't quite the picture-postcard place it is today. As late as the 1950s, the park's architectural ensemble included, among other incongruities, an auto service garage on a portion of the site where the Ordway Center for the Performing Arts now stands. Not until the late 1970s restoration of Landmark Center and the 1985 opening of the Ordway did the park cement its iconic status as downtown's visual and cultural centerpiece.

Unfortunately, much of the area between the park and Seven Corners to the west has not been treated as kindly by time. This precinct was once home to a haphazard assortment of commercial, industrial, and residential buildings that formed a classic example of what is today the holy grail of urban planners—a genuine mixed-use neighborhood. Although the area began to decline as early as the 1950s, the period of greatest devastation occurred in the 1960s, when entire blocks were cleared for the construction of Interstates 35E and 94. So complete was this work of urban rearrangement that few old buildings survived and entire streets such as Auditorium vanished.

The completion of Xcel Energy Center in 2000 and the return of professional hockey to the Twin Cities injected new life into the Seven Corners area, where a strip of small shops, restaurants, and taverns has become downtown's most vibrant commercial corridor (though technically part of the West Seventh neighborhood). Still, the area east and north of the arena remains an urban void devoted to parking lots and fast one-way streets. One day, perhaps, it will become what it should be—a vital part of the city.

Rice Park

1 Rice Park !

Bounded by Fourth, Fifth, Market, and Washington Sts.

1849 / plaza and fountain, HGA, 1965 / modified, ca. 2002 / Art: The Source (statue), Alonzo Hauser, 1965 / F. Scott Fitzgerald (bronze statue), Michael Price, 1996

This civilized little park, with its distinctive trapezoidal shape, was—along with Irvine and Smith Parks—one of three public squares created in 1849 by early city developers. It was an informal place in the beginning. Local women sometimes hung their laundry out to dry while grazing animals trimmed the grass. There was also a public market here for a time, from which Market St. derives its name.

Development of the park began in 1872 when the city put in a fountain (cost: $964) and a wooden bandstand. In 1883, the city made further improvements, including installation of St. Paul's first electric streetlights, in advance of a mammoth celebration marking completion of the Northern Pacific Railroad's line to the West Coast. Chester A. Arthur was among the celebrants and became the first of several U.S. presidents to orate in the park. In 1898, the park was upgraded again with new walkways, benches, and plantings. Except for removal of the fountain in 1925, the park changed little over the next half century.

In 1965 Rice Park took on a new look. A circular plaza and fountain were installed, as was Alonzo Hauser's fetching statue. The plaza has always seemed a bit too big for such a small park, although as originally built it was broken up into a series of concentric rings created by steps leading down to the fountain. This feature was eliminated in a 2002 remodeling, and the plaza now seems larger than ever. Still, the plaza and fountain work well enough as a gathering place, and on summer afternoons the park is crowded with brown baggers eating lunch and soaking up the sun. The park's best season may be winter, when holiday lights twinkle in the trees and winter carnival ice sculptures gleam in the cold light.

Just northeast of the park is **Landmark Plaza** (2003), where you'll find three bronze sculptures of characters from the "Peanuts" comic strip. Charles Schulz, creator of the classic comic, was raised in St. Paul.

LOST 1 *The **Orpheum** (later **President**) **Theater,** a vaudeville house built in 1906 and later converted to a movie theater, once stood on the site of Landmark Plaza. It was demolished in 1939.*

Landmark Center

2 Landmark Center (U.S. Post Office and Federal Courts Building) ! N *L*

75 West Fifth St.

Supervising architect of the U.S. Treasury (Willoughby J. Edbrooke and others), 1892–1902 / renovated and restored, Brooks Cavin, Stahl/Bennett, Winsor/Faricy Architects, 1972–78

St. Paul's very own castle, with a fairy tale of a story behind it. Declared surplus property by the federal government in 1969, the building was a week away from possible demolition when it was saved by a coalition of city and county government officials, civic leaders, and private citizens, led by the redoubtable Betty Musser. Next came years of painstaking restoration and renovation as the building was fitted out for its new life as home to arts and cultural groups. Its rebirth as Landmark Center in 1978 was the first great triumph of historic preservation in St. Paul.

The building is well worth the extraordinary effort that went into saving it. Constructed in two stages—the southern part, with a tower overlooking Rice Park, came first, followed several years later by the northern section and its even more massive tower—Landmark Center is one of a number of magnificent Romanesque-Chateauesque–style courthouses and post offices built by the federal government in the 1890s. It's also a remarkably appealing work of public architecture, with none of the rather oppressive heaviness of Minneapolis City Hall (1889–1906), a contemporaneous exercise in the Romanesque Revival style. Instead of that build-

Landmark Center interior

ing's raw display of civic power, Landmark Center offers a cheery array of tourelles, arcades, and gables, all rendered in smooth blocks of St. Cloud granite. The result is pure architectural romance—not a quality usually associated with federal buildings.

Within, the building is organized around a large skylit atrium, the Elizabeth Willert Musser Cortile. Offices and old courtrooms ring this six-story-high space, one of the most dramatic in St. Paul. Don't miss seeing the third- and fourth-floor courtrooms, which display Victorian design at its most exuberant. Perhaps the finest is the Sanborn Room, which showcases carved white Vermont marble beneath a stained-glass skylight. The courtrooms also have a rich history that includes the trials of notorious gangsters like Alvin "Creepy" Karpis in the 1930s.

LOST 2 *The **first St. Paul City Hall** occupied the southern part of this block from 1854 to 1890, when it was razed to make way for what is now Landmark Center.*

3 St. Paul Hotel

350 Market St.

*Reed and Stem, 1910 / renovated, HGA, 1983 / addition (**St. Paul Grill**), HGA, 1990*

Occupying an irregularly shaped block at the turn of the downtown grid, this grand old hotel is the last of its kind in the Twin

Cities. It was financed by 3M magnate Lucius P. Ordway, who contributed $1 million to the project. The hotel's rather plain stone base and glazed-brick middle stories are crowned by a grandiose cornice that makes the entire design seem top-heavy. Closed in 1979, the hotel was rescued from oblivion four years later by new owners. As part of its 1983 renovation, the hotel was reoriented toward Rice Park: its main entrance had been at Fifth and St. Peter Sts. The St. Paul Grill, a popular eating spot with a clubby atmosphere, was added in 1990.

LOST 3 *Lost buildings here include the **Market Street Methodist Episcopal Church** (1849–1927), the **Windsor Hotel** (1878–1910), and the **Charles Zimmerman House** (1887–1924), a Moorish-style townhome built for a pioneer St. Paul photographer.*

4 Qwest Buildings

70 West Fourth St.

Clarence H. Johnston, Jr., 1937 / additions, Ellerbe Associates, 1968, 1977

The oldest of these three interconnected buildings is an art deco gem constructed for the Tri-State Telephone Co. It's clad in two beautiful Minnesota stones: swirling morton gneiss at the base and golden Mankato-Kasota limestone above. Inside the Fourth St. entrance is a handsome lobby now used as a telephone museum. The additions to the east of the original building add little except bulk to the proceedings; the newer of the two, an overweening purple brick monolith, is particularly unpleasant.

5 RiverCentre Connection (tunnel)

Beneath Fourth St. between St. Peter and Washington Sts.

Architectural Alliance and CNA Engineers, 2002

This tunnel, linked to the skyway system, was built to provide an indoor passage between downtown hotels and RiverCentre, mainly for conventiongoers reluctant to face the brute terrors of Minnesota winter. A tunnel was dug because a skyway link would have required impaling either the library or Landmark Center with bridges or building a glass and steel trestle around Rice Park, any of which would have raised a mighty stink in history-conscious St. Paul.

St. Paul Central Library and James J. Hill Reference Library

6 St. Paul Central Library and James J. Hill Reference Library ! N *L*

80–90 West Fourth St.

Electus Litchfield, 1917 / Central Library restored and renovated, MS&R Architects, 2002

One of the city's—and the state's—great Beaux-Arts monuments. Rising behind a balustrade along the southern side of Rice Park, the building projects an air of cultured dignity, and it's probably what most people think a library *should* look like. Yet it is very much a product of its time— an era from roughly 1895 to 1925

James J. Hill Reference Library interior, 1920

in which classicism (in this case, of the Northern Italian Renaissance variety) served as the dominant language of American public architecture.

The architect, East Coast blue blood Electus Litchfield, got the job because his father was an associate of James J. Hill, who bankrolled the project. Even so, Litchfield came with excellent credentials, including a stint with Carriere and Hastings, architects of the magnificent New York Public Library (1911). Litchfield's task here was to design a building that would seamlessly combine two institutions—the St. Paul Central Library and the privately endowed Hill Reference Library—and he succeeded brilliantly. Arched doorways reached by staircases at either end of the Fourth St. facade express this duality.

The building's refined exterior of pink Tennessee marble is matched by its elegant interior. The Central Library's main reading room is a high point: light pours through large arched windows while overhead hand-painted ceiling beams (some sporting Litchfield's monogram, EDL) add dashes of color. Other major rooms are equally graceful. A grand staircase winds through the building, providing views of the Mississippi. Much of the interior is finished in Kettle River sandstone from a quarry once owned in part by Hill himself.

The Central Library was designed for a "closed" system in which books were kept in stacks and delivered to patrons on request. This arrangement proved inefficient as publicly accessible shelving came into favor, and numerous modifications had to be made, including the addition of stacks to the main reading room. Many of these intrusive changes were undone when the library was restored and renovated between 2000 and 2002. Workers repainted original ornament, converted old stacks into reading rooms, created a new entry sequence, added a mezzanine in the main reading room, and built a new children's room,

which incorporates a puppet theater designed in the 1940s by the St. Paul architect-artist team of Magnus and Elsa Jemne. Today the Central Library looks—and works—as well as it ever has.

The James J. Hill Reference Library, founded and endowed by its namesake to provide business information, occupies the building's east wing. At its heart is a superbly proportioned reading room that conveys a remarkable sense of serenity, and there is no lovelier place in the Twin Cities to spend an afternoon lost in reading or research. With its sturdy classical columns, old-fashioned book alcoves, glass-floored balconies, and long reading tables lit by shaded lamps, the room has changed little since its opening in 1917. The only defect is a lack of natural light, lost when the original skylight was covered in the 1970s. If and when the skylight is restored, the reading room will enjoy a radiant rebirth.

7 Ordway Center for the Performing Arts !

345 Washington St.

Benjamin Thompson and Associates, 1985

Built during the height of the postmodern era, when architectural pastiches sprouted like gaudy hothouse flowers, the Ordway is refreshingly understated. Its architect, St. Paul native Benjamin Thompson, used a limited palette of traditional materials—hand-molded brick, copper, stone, and wood—to craft an enduring work. Inside, Thompson created the feel of an old-fashioned opera house, with a broad lobby, a sweeping staircase, and a large but intimate 1,900-seat auditorium. The Ordway's acoustics have never been as successful as its architectural design. Critics—and there are legions—contend the auditorium is a better place to see than hear the St. Paul Chamber Orchestra, which regularly plays at the Ordway, as do touring Broadway shows.

Ordway Center for the Performing Arts

Still, the Ordway ranks among the best of downtown St. Paul's modern-era buildings, and it's hard now to imagine what Rice Park would look like without it. The building is named in honor of Lucius P. Ordway, whose granddaughter, Sally Ordway Irvine, contributed a third of its $45 million construction cost.

LOST 4 *Previous buildings at this site include the **first St. Paul Auditorium** (later known as **Stem Hall**), built in 1907 and razed in 1982, and the **Wilder Charities Building**, which stood from 1913 to about 1984.*

8 317 on Rice Park (Minnesota Club)

317 Washington St.

Clarence H. Johnston, 1915

Originally built for the tony Minnesota Club (founded in 1869) but now used as offices for the Minnesota Wild hockey team, this gracious structure conveys an Edwardian sense of elegance. Today, hip young executives populate the building, but if you step inside the old clubrooms you can still smell the plush aroma of old money. Legend holds that a secret tunnel once connected the club to a brothel down the hill run by famed madam Nina Clifford. Alas, modern excavations have yet to uncover any evidence of this supposed passageway to sin.

Science Museum of Minnesota

9 Science Museum of Minnesota

120 Kellogg Blvd. West

*Ellerbe Becket, 2000 / includes **Science House**, Barbour LaDouceur Architects, 2003 / Art: Iguana (sculpture), Nick Swearer, 1978*

Occupying a splendid site on the bluffs above the Mississippi River, this museum ought to have shouted its presence as one of the city's most important cultural attractions. Instead, it's a curiously uneventful work of architecture, polite as a gathering of Minnesota Lutherans and not much interested in standing out from the crowd.

A smidge of visual drama occurs along Kellogg Blvd., where a wall of windows thrusts up from the main entrance. Inside, the museum offers a large if not striking lobby, the inevitable Omnitheater, and a series of galleries and education spaces. A winding staircase distributes visitors to six levels while offering views of the river; there's also an outdoor staircase on the east side of the building. Balconies provide museumgoers with a chance to enjoy the scenery on pleasant days. The multilevel layout can be confusing, in part because visitors start at the top and work their way down, but the building's biggest shortcoming is a failure of imagination.

A small river-level park called the Big Back Yard lies below the museum, and here you'll find the Science House, a small but spunky metal-clad structure designed to show how a building can generate all of its own energy needs, even in Minnesota's extreme climate.

10 St. Paul RiverCentre

Roy Wilkins Auditorium,
Fifth St. west of Washington St.

St. Paul City Architect
(Charles A. Bassford with
Clarence Wigington), 1932 /
renovated, 1986

RiverCentre,
175 Kellogg Blvd. West

HGA, 1998

Xcel Energy Center,
199 Kellogg Blvd. West

HOK Sports Facilities Group, 2000

A convention complex that, to borrow a phrase from Chicago architect Daniel Burnham, fails to "stir the blood." The main facade along Kellogg Blvd. is especially unattractive. It's dominated by a massive second-story overhang—the architectural equivalent of a beer belly—that throws the whole design off-kilter. The Xcel Energy Center, home to the Minnesota Wild hockey team, is a more successful design. Although the arena's brick-and-glass exterior is as clunky as the rest of the complex, inside you'll find one of the nation's best venues for hockey. The oldest part of River-Centre is Roy Wilkins Auditorium, named after a civil rights leader raised in St. Paul. The Wilkins, a rather plain example of the normally exuberant art deco style, was largely designed by Clarence Wigington, the nation's first black municipal architect.

POI A Seven Corners

Kellogg Blvd. and Seventh and Eagle Sts. (note: buildings west of Kellogg on Seventh are listed under the West Seventh neighborhood)

In a 1927 story, F. Scott Fitzgerald wrote of "a vague part of town, broken by its climb into triangles and odd shapes—there are names like Seven Corners—and I don't believe a dozen people could draw an accurate map of it." That probably remains true today, although Seven Corners has changed greatly since the 1920s. The original intersection brought together Third (now Kellogg Blvd.), Fourth, Seventh, Main, and Eagle Sts. Today, there are only five corners—Fourth and Main were removed from the mix due to various street realignments in the 1970s—and the intersection no longer offers the splendid sense of befuddlement it once did.

POI B East Portal of Selby Avenue Streetcar Tunnel

College Ave. near Old Kellogg Blvd.

Charles Shepley, 1907

This old tunnel's lower portal can be seen from Kellogg Blvd. just north of Seven Corners. The tunnel made it possible for electric streetcars to reach the top of the hill on their own power. Before the tunnel was dug, trolleys required the help of a clumsy, time-consuming counterweight system to negotiate the steep grade. The 1,500-foot-long tunnel emerged in the middle of Selby Ave. near the St. Paul Cathedral. It remained in use until the last streetcar ran on July 11, 1953; the tunnel was filled in a few years later.

POI C Summit Avenue's Lost Mile

Between Kellogg Blvd. and Old Kellogg Blvd. east of John Ireland Blvd.

Before freeways, the Minnesota History Center, and other forms of progress, Summit Ave. continued another mile or so to the east of here. Descending a long slope into downtown, Summit finally ended at today's intersection of Robert St. and Columbus Ave. Apartments and two nineteenth-century houses are now all that remain along this vestigial stretch of Summit.

Minnesota History Center

11 Minnesota History Center

345 Kellogg Blvd. West

HGA, 1992 / Art: glass etchings, Brit Bunkley, 1993 / Charm Bracelet (inlays in rotunda floor), James Casebere, 1993 / Minnesota Profiles (stone and terra-cotta columns in plaza), Andrew Leicester, 1995

Home to the Minnesota Historical Society, the History Center is the most important state building of its time. It includes exhibit halls, classrooms, an auditorium, a restaurant, two museum stores, offices, and a large amount of underground work space. Built largely from materials of the old order—granite, limestone, copper, and oak—the History Center is the last Twin Cities public building that might invite comparison with Beaux-Arts monuments such as the State Capitol. Wags dubbed the building "fortress history"; indeed, it suggests a great stone keep where the treasures of the past will be safe for the ages.

Yet in some ways the History Center seems at odds with itself, as though it can't decide whether to be classical (as in the monumental facade along John Ireland Blvd.) or picturesque (as in the odd tower that dominates the building's east side). Mixed messages also abide within. Wide corridors with vaulted oak ceilings invoke the Beaux-Arts era, but the overall layout of the L-shaped building doesn't support this grand conceit. The main entrance, for example, takes you down a hallway and into a rotunda, where you'd expect to be swept into the building via a grand staircase. Instead, the stairs are all but hidden off to the side. The biggest disappointment is the library, which should be the true heart of the building. Instead, it's a very ordinary room that does nothing to convey its importance as a central repository of the state's past.

LOST 5 *Before land was cleared in the 1960s for the Interstate 94–35E interchange, a neighborhood of old apartments, mansions, and institutional buildings extended from the site of the History Center east to St. Peter St. By 1970 virtually the entire neighborhood was gone. Among the prominent architectural casualties was the* **Hotel Barteau (Piedmont Apartments),** *a six-story Victorian that held down the now vanished corner of Ninth St. and Smith Ave. from 1889 to 1969.*

12 Colonnade (Palazzo) Apartments

532–44 St. Peter St.

Hodgson and Stem, 1889 / renovated, ca. 1899

One of four large apartment hotels built in St. Paul in the late 1880s, this building features a two-level central arcade recessed between projecting wings. It received a minor face-lift in 1899 when balconies and small window pediments were added. By 1955, the Colonnade (then known as the Willard) was limping along as a faded old apartment hotel when disaster struck. Fire raced through the upper floors, killing a maid who'd gone up in an elevator to warn residents. After the fire, the two upper floors were amputated, none too gently, leaving the abridged four-story building visible today.

13 Catholic Charities (Junior Pioneer Association) Building

192 West Ninth St.

Mark Fitzpatrick, 1909

The last of its breed downtown—a small building with a classically colonnaded porch. Its out-of-the-way location probably saved it from the wreckers, although it has lost some original features.

14 Father Emmett Cashman Building (Assumption School) N *L*

68 West Exchange St.

ca. 1861–64

Predating Assumption Church is this small stone building, Italianate in style and originally home to Assumption School.

Assumption Catholic Church, 1964

15 Assumption Catholic Church ! N *L*

51 West Seventh St.

Eduard Riedel, 1874 / Art: clock faces and other motifs in towers, Philip Larson, 1981

St. Paul's oldest functioning church structure and a nationally significant example of the nineteenth-century revival style variously known as Romanesque, Lombard, or even the "Round Style." Built of the gray, heavily stratified Platteville limestone that underlies much of downtown, Assumption seems to have been in the city forever, its distinctive multistage towers poking up in old photographs that otherwise depict nothing but long-vanished buildings.

Assumption parish is even older than the church, dating to 1854, when St. Paul's German settlers, many tracing their roots to Catholic Bavaria, persuaded the diocese that they needed a church of their own. The first church was finished in 1856 but proved too small. By 1869, the parish was ready to begin building the present church, using plans that came directly from the Old Country via a Munich architect named Eduard Riedel. He modeled Assumption on Munich's Ludwigskirche (1844), which had twin towers and was inspired by the Romanesque architecture of the early Middle Ages. Assumption, however, is far more austere than the Munich church. Inside, Assumption features vaulted ceilings presiding over a three-aisled basilican plan that includes the usual complement of statuary and stained glass. The wooden cross to the left of the altar is particularly intriguing. It was dug up in 1955 by children playing on a vacant lot near the State Capitol. Detective work revealed that the cross, dating to 1871, had been discarded by a parish trustee after he'd made a copy of it. Suitably enough, the cross was resurrected on Good Friday and returned to the church in time for Easter.

Mickey's Diner

16 Mickey's Diner N *L*

36 West Seventh St.

Jerry O'Mahony Co., 1937–39

St. Paul's beloved greasy spoon. Although some think Mickey's is a converted railroad car, in fact it was constructed as a diner in 1937 by the Jerry O'Mahony Co. of Bayonne, NJ, which began building lunch wagons in 1913 and later graduated to full-scale diners. Shipped to St. Paul in pieces, Mickey's was assembled on site and opened for business in 1939. The best time to experience Mickey's is in the wee hours of the morning, when nighthawks, seeking coffee and omelets, form a scene straight out of an Edward Hopper painting.

17 Coney Island Restaurant buildings (Vater Rhein Hotel, Gebhard Eck Hotel and Saloon) *L*

444–48 St. Peter St.

Weisen and Fischer, 1858 / Augustus Gauger, 1884 / renovated, MacDonald and Mack Architects, ca. 2001

The smaller of these two buildings is the oldest structure surviving on its original site in either downtown St. Paul or downtown Minneapolis. It dates to 1858 and served as the state arsenal from 1865 to 1880. The Coney Island Restaurant opened in 1923 but has been closed for over a decade. Nonetheless, the owners continue to insist that they will reopen it someday.

18 Seventh Place Mall

Seventh Pl. between St. Peter and Wabasha Sts.

Sanders Associates with St. Paul Planning and Economic Development Department, 1984

This mall, announced by an arch at St. Peter St., is a remnant of historic Seventh St., whose duties have now largely been taken over by what used to be Eighth St. but is now called Seventh St. Meanwhile, Seventh St. was renamed Seventh Pl. Everyone clear on that?

19 Orpheum (New Palace) Theatre and Seventh Place Apartments (St. Francis Hotel)

17 West Seventh Pl.

Buechner and Orth, 1916 / later remodelings

The Orpheum, originally called the New Palace, was downtown's largest theater, seating 2,300 when it opened in 1916 as a vaudeville and movie house. It was built as part of a complex that included the 215-room St. Francis Hotel, now apartments. The theater's auditorium once offered colorful testimony to the plasterer's art, but the grand space has been dimmed by remodelings and years of deterioration. Largely vacant since 1984, the Orpheum's future remains cloudy.

St. Paul Travelers Insurance Companies Headquarters

20 St. Paul Travelers Insurance Companies (St. Paul Companies) Headquarters

385 Washington St.

*Kohn Pedersen Fox (New York) with Architectural Alliance, 1991 / includes **St. Paul Travelers South Building**, Childs and Smith, 1961 / addition, Ellerbe Associates, 1981 / renovation, Kohn Pedersen Fox, 1992*

Downtown's most notable corporate palace, designed by St. Paul native William Pedersen in his postmodernist period for a company with roots in the city that go back to the 1850s. The complex is well and expensively done in St. Cloud granite and Mankato-Kasota stone, but the main tower looks rather chubby—a common problem in a corporate era that demands buildings with large floorplates. The design's most intriguing feature is a metal-clad entry pavilion at Sixth St. Here you'll find a vigorous lobby decorated with metal strips in the geometric manner of Frank Lloyd Wright. Had the St. Paul Companies (which became St. Paul Travelers in 2004) waited another five years for a new building, it might have gotten something livelier from Pedersen, who cut his teeth as a modernist and never seemed at home in the postmodernist camp.

Hamm Building, 1920

21 Hamm Building N

408 St. Peter St.

Toltz, King and Day with Roy Child Jones, 1920 / restored, Oertel Architects and ESG Architects, 1998

This office building was supposed to be a department store for Mannheimer Brothers, once a prominent St. Paul retailer. After the steel frame was completed in 1915, however, construction suddenly stopped for reasons that are unclear. The metal skeleton stood like a giant abstract sculpture in the heart of downtown until 1919, when William Hamm of the brewing family stepped forward to complete the building as an office structure. Recently restored, the building is unique in the Twin Cities because all three of its street facades are sheathed entirely in terra-cotta. Featuring classical and Renaissance motifs, the terra-cotta was manufactured by a Chicago company in a distinctive finish called "pulsichrome." The company was so proud of its work that it advertised the Hamm Building as "a new era in terra cotta finishes."

The building's basement once included a bowling alley and recreation center that also served as a popular gambling den in the 1920s. The bowling alley is gone, as are the building's golden canvas awnings, which used to sprout every spring but were removed after suffering wind damage. Inside, there's an attractive lobby

off St. Peter St. that's vaulted with Gustavino tile.

LOST 6 *The northeast corner of the Hamm Building along the Seventh Place Mall once contained the* **Capitol (Paramount) Theater,** *built in 1920 as the Twin Cities' first motion picture palace. Its exterior featured a flamboyant tango of Spanish-influenced ornament, while the ornate auditorium within seated well over 2,000. The theater was demolished in 1965. A portion of the cavernous space it once occupied is now home to the Park Square Theater.*

Third St. Paul Cathedral and bishop's residence, 1860

Before the Hamm Building appeared, its site was occupied by the **third St. Paul Cathedral,** *built in 1858. More impressive architecturally was the* **bishop's residence,** *completed next door along Sixth St. in 1860. The Italian Villa–style mansion cost $15,000 and was probably the most lavish home of its time in St. Paul. Like the old cathedral, it was demolished in 1914.*

22 Hamm Plaza

Sixth and St. Peter Sts.

William Pedersen and Jackie Ferrara (artist), 1992

A small plaza so crowded with artsy "features" that it doesn't work well as a place for people.

23 Lawson Commons

380 St. Peter St.

BWBR Architects, 2000

Many modern buildings that try to look historic fall flat on their fake pilasters, but this one doesn't because its St. Paul–based architects clearly had a feel for the rhythms and nuances of the older buildings nearby. The building is unmistakably modern, as the curving glass penthouse demonstrates, yet its brick facades fit comfortably with the historic surroundings. The art deco–inspired parking ramp and retail building along Wabasha St. is also well done.

24 The Lowry (Lowry Medical Arts Building)

350 St. Peter St.

Kees and Colburn, 1912 / renovated, Collaborative Design Group, 2005

This brick office building, long home to doctors and dentists, took on new life in 2005 when 135 condominium apartments were carved out of its upper ten floors. The conversion yielded surprisingly bright and spacious apartments, all with the building's original terrazzo floors intact. Outside, the building's glazed-brick exterior is fairly plain, but it does offer bursts of terra-cotta ornament, including clusters of grapes, overscaled heads, and other classically inspired motifs.

of the old Women's City Club. It later became home to the Minnesota Museum of Art before Wold Architects bought and renovated it in 1999.

Sheathed in Mankato-Kasota stone and polished black granite that steps up around the main entrance, the building has a delicacy rarely seen in institutional architecture yet also holds down its corner site with convincing authority. The equally deft interior offers a sinuous central staircase, an auditorium decorated with gold leaf, a top-floor room— once used as a restaurant—that provides sweeping river views, and inlaid floor patterns and other decorative designs by Elsa Jemne, best known for her Depression-era murals.

St. Paul City Hall and Ramsey County Courthouse

Wold Architects, 1935

25 Wold Architects (Women's City Club, Jemne Building) N *L*

305 St. Peter St.

Magnus Jemne, 1931 / renovation, Wold Architects, 1999 / Art: inlaid floors and other decorative features, Elsa Jemne, 1931

Is there a lovelier small building in the Twin Cities than this jewel from Magnus and Elsa Jemne? A sophisticated work that skillfully mixes the zigzag and streamlined phases of art deco, it was built for the well-heeled membership

26 St. Paul City Hall and Ramsey County Courthouse ! N *L*

15 Kellogg Blvd. West

Holabird and Root (Chicago) with Ellerbe Architects, 1932 / addition and renovation, Wold Architects and others, 1992 / Art: exterior relief sculptures, Lee Lawrie, 1931 / Vision of Peace (onyx statue), Carl Milles, 1936 / bronze elevator doors, Albert Stewart, 1931 / murals, John Norton, 1931 / etched glass mural, Christopher Cosma and Denis Amses, 1991

St. Paul City Hall interior

This remarkable public building, a masterpiece of American art deco, is the result of both brilliant design and fortuitous timing. Built at a cost of $4 million to replace the old city hall–courthouse a block away, it was financed as part of a city bond issue approved in 1928. By the time construction actually began in 1931, however, the cost of materials and labor had plunged as the Great Depression gripped the nation. Gifted with a virtually unlimited budget, the architectural team—led by Holabird and Root of Chicago—was able to specify only the finest in materials and equipment for the new building.

Stylistically, the building combines two types of art deco—the early perpendicular style, with its facets and setbacks, and the later streamlined phase, visible in its many curved interior details. Holabird and Root had already shown its mastery of art deco in the Chicago Board of Trade Building (1930), to which the city hall–courthouse bears considerable resemblance.

With its stepped-up massing, wide piers of Indiana limestone, and dark vertical window bands, the building is all business on the outside and might pass for a commercial skyscraper. Exterior ornament is largely confined to unobtrusive bas-relief sculptures around the entrances. Unfortunately, the city defaced the building's Fourth St.

facade by ramming a skyway through it.

Inside, business gives way to pure architectural pleasure, beginning with the War Memorial Concourse, dedicated to Ramsey County soldiers who died in World War I. The concourse features pillars of black Belgian marble inscribed with the soldiers' names, dramatic bronze light wands, a mirrored ceiling, and, as its centerpiece, a 36-foot-tall statue of an Indian leader carved out of white Mexican onyx. Originally known as the *Indian God of Peace*, the statue was politically corrected in the 1990s to become the *Vision of Peace*. To courthouse denizens, however, the big fellow will always be known as "Onyx John." St. Paul architect Thomas Ellerbe brought in Swedish sculptor Carl Milles to design the statue, which was installed in 1936 and still exerts a kind of hushed magic: schoolchildren on tour grow quiet and even adults find themselves whispering in the presence of the great onyx god, who rotates on his mirrored base. It's theater, but of a very powerful and moving kind.

There's much else of note in the building, from the Kellogg Blvd. lobby with its gold-leaf ceiling and bronze elevator doors to the third-floor city council chambers adorned with murals by Chicago artist John Norton to the richly paneled courtrooms on the upper floors. Fine details abound throughout, including custom-designed bronze and glass light fixtures, 25 different types of wood, and 14 varieties of stone. Hardware, signs, and furniture were designed with equal care.

In 1992, a team led by Wold Architects of St. Paul completed a $48 million renovation, restoration, and expansion of the building. Three stories that mimic the original building were added at Fourth and St. Peter Sts., where the Ramsey County Jail (1903–80) once stood. The architects also created neodeco interiors, including courtrooms, offices, and a basement concourse. If you find your way to the basement, don't miss the Glass Mural Commons, which offers a narrated sound-and-light show devoted to the history of the city and county.

27 Former Ramsey County Adult Detention Center and Plaza

12–14 Kellogg Blvd. West

Wold Association and Gruzen Associates, 1980 / Art: Sky *(sculpture on rooftop plaza), Georgette Sosin, 1981*

A jail built into the river bluffs. It's now closed and awaiting possible redevelopment or demolition. The large cell windows, it's said, allowed inmates to "moon" passing boaters if the spirit so moved them.

28 Ramsey County Government Center West, including Minnesota Museum of American Art (West Publishing Co.)

50 Kellogg Blvd. West

various architects including J. Walter Stevens (1886) and Reed and Stem (1911), ca. 1886 and later / renovated (new facade), ca. 1940s / remodeled, ca. 1990s

Home for many years to the West Publishing Co., this six-building complex is a big architectural dullard, which is most unfortunate given its prime site overlooking the river. In 2004, the Minnesota Museum of American Art moved into the complex's western end, and it may eventually expand its quarters there. Meanwhile, various plans have been floated to convert all or part of the complex to housing, retail, and cultural uses and perhaps even add space; as of 2007, however, nothing had happened.

Lowertown

1 Mears Park
2 Galtier Plaza
3 Park Square Court
4 Konantz Saddlery Co. Building
5 Koehler and Hinrichs Co. Building
6 River Park Lofts
7 Gilbert Building
8 East Seventh Street historic
   commercial row:
   Bonnie Jean Bungalows
   Heritage House Apartments
   Constans Block
   O'Connor Block
9 Walsh Building
10 First Baptist Church
11 Wacouta Commons area
12 Apartments
13 St. Paul Farmers' Market
14 Lowertown Commons
15 Northern Warehouse Artists'
    Cooperative
16 Tilsner Artists' Cooperative
17 Great Northern Lofts
18 Main U.S. Post Office
19 Brooks Building
20 180 East Fifth
21 Mears Park Centre: Fairbanks-
    Morse Co. Building, Powers Dry
    Goods Co. Building
22 Straus Apartments
23 Union Depot Place
24 American House Apartments
25 Parkside Apartments
26 Cosmopolitan Apartments

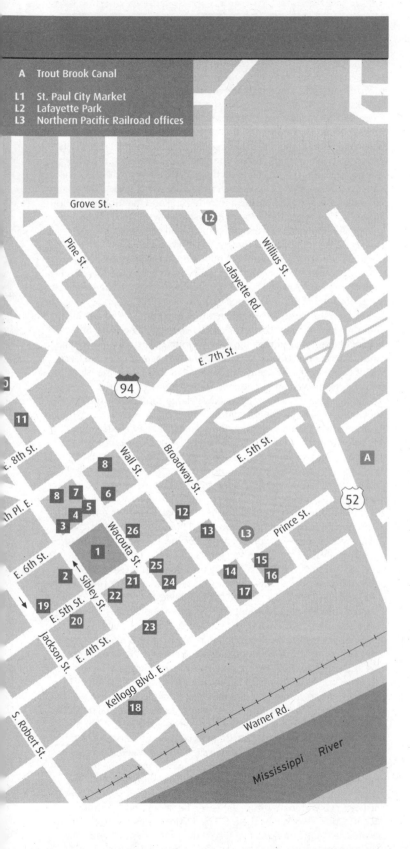

A Trout Brook Canal

L1 St. Paul City Market
L2 Lafayette Park
L3 Northern Pacific Railroad offices

Lowertown

As its name indicates, Lowertown lies below the blufftop plateau occupied by the rest of downtown St. Paul. Its name also derives from its proximity to the Lower Landing on the Mississippi River at the foot of Jackson Street. This landing was the city's main docking point in steamboat days, and a commercial and warehousing district inevitably grew up around it. Geography also abetted Lowertown's growth once railroads arrived in the 1860s. Early rail lines negotiated St. Paul's hilly terrain via two natural corridors: the Mississippi River and the wide valley of Trout Brook, which enters the river at Lowertown's eastern edge. Because of its location at this critical juncture, Lowertown was perfectly positioned to become a warehousing and manufacturing district as St. Paul began its period of explosive growth in the 1880s.

In its natural state, Lowertown actually had some high ground—a hill that rose 50 feet above the present level of Mears Park. Known as Baptist Hill after a small church built atop it, this prominence was gradually carved away beginning in the 1870s to accommodate development and to provide fill for the rail lines being built though the boggy bottoms of the Trout Brook valley.

Before warehouses and manufacturing buildings spread northward from the river, much of Lowertown was occupied by housing. Some of St. Paul's largest mansions could once be found here along Eighth and Ninth streets and in the old Lafayette Park area near today's intersection of Grove Street and Lafayette Road. All of these early mansions are gone, swallowed up by commercial development and the ever-expanding railroads, which chewed away large chunks of historic Lowertown in the early twentieth century.

The historic warehouses that dominate Lowertown today represent two distinct eras of building. The older generation dates from the 1880s to about 1905 and consists of massive brick bearing wall structures typically constructed with interior frames of iron, steel, or timber. While many of these buildings survive, others were superseded early in the twentieth century by the second generation, new "daylight" warehouses built with concrete frames that permitted large windows.

Like many another old warehouse and manufacturing district, Lowertown by the 1960s was deep into decline as businesses moved elsewhere. By the 1970s, however, artists and other intrepid urbanites began to infiltrate the district, setting up studios and residences in the old warehouses. During this time Lowertown had a rather funky air to it—a little bit of SoHo transferred to the Midwest.

More formal redevelopment soon followed. Industrialist Norman Mears began to stir the pot in the early 1970s, but the creation of the quasi-public Lowertown Redevelopment Corp. in 1978 really spurred redevelopment. The designation of the Lowertown Historic District in 1983 also proved crucial. Before long, one old warehouse after another was being converted to office or housing use as part of a strategy to create an "urban village." New construction included Galtier Plaza (1986), a huge multi-use project that proved to be a financial debacle.

Despite its successes, Lowertown has never achieved the vibrancy of Minneapolis's warehouse district. In its cleaned-up, carefully restored state, Lowertown has always seemed slightly embalmed. This quality is evident in the district's newer buildings, which tend to be timid brick boxes. Still, Lowertown continues to grow, with new and redeveloped housing now filling in the area north of East Seventh Street. The key to Lowertown's future, however, lies along the riverfront—now effectively blocked by the U.S. Post Office complex (1934) and the elevated rail platform that once served the Union Depot. When new development reaches the river, as it inevitably will, Lowertown may finally burst fully to life.

Mears Park

1 Mears (Smith) Park ! N *L*

Bounded by Fifth, Sixth, Sibley, and Wacouta Sts.

1849, 1880s, and later / rebuilt, William Sanders, 1973 / rebuilt, Brad Goldberg and Don Ganje, 1992

One of the Twin Cities' nicest urban squares, though it took nearly 150 years for the park to take on its current form. Originally named after Robert A. Smith, an otherwise obscure speculator who donated the site to the city in 1849, the park wasn't developed until the 1880s, after Baptist Hill had been leveled. For many years it was a standard urban square with a central fountain from which sidewalks radiated to each corner. In 1973, a new design encased much of the park in brickwork, which promptly began to crumble. The park's name was also changed at this time to honor Norman Mears. The "brickyard," as it was popularly known, reached such a state of disrepair that the park was in need of complete rebuilding by the late 1980s.

The new park, designed by Dallas artist Brad Goldberg and St. Paul Parks landscape architect Don Ganje, proved to be a local wonder. Seamlessly mixing formal and informal elements, the park—with its rushing stream, rough-cut stone benches, generous plantings, and bandstand—is the finest modern-era design of any kind in Lowertown, a most pleasant place to while away a summer afternoon doing nothing in particular.

Galtier Plaza

2 Galtier Plaza *L*

175 East Fifth St., 380 Jackson St.

Miller, Hanson, Westerbeck and Bell, 1986 / incorporates facades (on Sibley St.) of **Bishop Block,** *Asher Bassford (builder), ca. 1883, and* **J. P. Allen Building,** *J. Walter Stevens, 1888 / also includes* **YMCA,** *Miller, Hanson, Westerbeck and Bell, 1985*

When it opened in 1986, this mixed-use complex promised to be the complete downtown package, a dolled-up postmodern Babylon amid the sober old warehouses of Lowertown. The idea was to provide living, shopping, working, eating, drinking, and recreating opportunities under one large (and, as it turned out, quite leaky) roof. The complex included two towers with condominiums and rental apartments, a new home for the downtown YMCA, and a block-long, skylit atrium with shopping and offices. Two old brick building facades were even incorporated into the mix as part of the "contextualism" so popular at the time.

A chimera spun of hope and some very creative financing, Galtier Plaza didn't shine for long. Instead, it quickly became a sinkhole into which money and reputations drained away, until a buyer finally snapped up much of it at a fire-sale price. Today, the nicely designed apartments and condominiums have kept the place going. Meanwhile, the once colorful mall, converted largely to office use, has been painted a penitential white as if to atone for its initial excesses.

Park Square Court

3 Park Square Court (Noyes Brothers and Cutler Co.) N *L*

215–25 East Sixth St., 400 Sibley St.

J. Walter Stevens, 1886 / 1889 / 1906 / renovated, ca. 1971–73 / renovated, Miller, Hanson, Westerbeck and Bell, BWBR Architects, 1982 and later

This is the largest in a block-long row of buildings—all designed by architect J. Walter Stevens—that form the north wall of Mears Park. Built for a drug and medical supply wholesaler, it's Richardsonian Romanesque in style, with sweeping ground-floor arches and tight Victorian brickwork. Unfortunately, the building's original double-hung windows were replaced with inappropriate single-pane glass during a 1970s remodeling.

4 Konantz Saddlery Co. Building N *L*

235 East Sixth St.

J. Walter Stevens, 1893 / renovated, ca. 1980s

5 Koehler and Hinrichs Co. Building N *L*

237 East Sixth St.

J. Walter Stevens, 1891 / renovated, ca. 1980s

These warehouses beautifully complement the Noyes Brothers and Cutler Building next door. Koehler and Hinrichs Co. was an eclectic wholesaling firm whose line of goods included "high-class bar outfits" and "fancy groceries." Today both buildings are used for offices and shops.

6 River Park Lofts (George Sommers Co.) N *L*

245 East Sixth St.

J. Walter Stevens, 1905 / renovated, ca. 1970s / renovated, MS&R Architects, 2006

includes **apartments** (St. Paul Fire Station No. 2, later No. 4), 412 Wacouta St.

St. Paul City Architect (Charles A. Hausler), 1872 / addition, Edward P. Bassford, 1885 / new facade, St. Paul City Architect (Charles A. Hausler), 1921 / renovated, MS&R Architects, 2006

The Sommers Co. building is the last of six warehouses that Stevens designed around Mears Park. The company dealt in toys, notions, and "cheap counter supplies." In the 1970s, the structure was converted to office use and renamed the Lowertown Business Center after being bought by the now defunct Control Data Corp. The building has since been converted to condominiums, as has an old fire station next door.

7 Gilbert Building (T. L. Blood Warehouse) N *L*

413 Wacouta St.

Cass Gilbert, 1894 / renovated, ca. 1980s

Another of Gilbert's attractive warehouse buildings, this time in a Renaissance Revival mood. The building was renovated in the 1980s for office use.

East Seventh Street historic commercial row

8 East Seventh Street historic commercial row N L

South side of East Seventh St. between Sibley and Wall Sts.

Bonnie Jean Bungalows (J. H. Weed store and flats), 212 East Seventh St.

Denslow W. Millard, 1884 / renovated, 2006

Heritage House Apartments, 218 East Seventh St.

A. D. Hinsdale, 1882 / renovated, ca. 1990

Constans Block (Hotel Economy), 224–40 East Seventh St.

Augustus Gauger, 1884

Commercial blocks, 246–56 East Seventh St.

A. D. Hinsdale, 1882 / Omeyer and Thori, 1889 / renovated, 2006

O'Connor Block, 264–66 East Seventh St.

Emil Ulrici, 1887

Although not all of these old commercial buildings have found a sympathetic new use—part of Butwinick's Building, for example, is used to park cars—they provide a good sense of what much of this part of Lowertown once looked like. Taken together, they form one of the last great rows of 1880s commercial buildings in St. Paul. They've survived in part because when Seventh was widened in the 1930s all the rebuilding occurred on the other side of the street. It's instructive to compare the ornate facades of these buildings against the much more sparsely detailed, albeit openly nostalgic, apartments across the street.

9 Walsh Building N L

189–91 East Seventh St.

Edward P. Bassford, 1888

A lovely little Victorian building. Note, for example, the intricate detail around the arched second-floor windows.

LOST 1 *The site of the Embassy Suites Hotel at Tenth and Jackson Sts. was home to the* **St. Paul City Market** *from 1902 to 1981. At its zenith in the 1930s and 1940s, the market covered four square blocks, offered 682 stalls, and served as a regional center for the produce trade. The* **Produce Exchange Building** *(now apartments) and the* **Eisenberg Fruit Co.** *at Tenth and Jackson Sts. are remnants of the market-related businesses that once dominated here. The market was torn down in 1981 and relocated to a new, smaller site in Lowertown.*

10 First Baptist Church ! N L

499 Wacouta St.

William Boyington (Chicago) with Monroe and Romaine Sheire, 1875 / additions, Milton Bergstedt, 1950s and later / new steeple, Milton Bergstedt, 1967 / Art: copper doors, Hillis Arnold, 1971

A historic limestone church, built for what is now Minnesota's oldest Baptist congregation, founded in 1847 when pioneer teacher Harriet Bishop established a Sunday school. The first church was on Baptist Hill (now Mears Park); this church—the third—was dedicated in 1875. Designed by Chicago architect William Boyington in conjunction with local master builders Monroe and Romaine Sheire, the Gothic Revival church features a corner tower and a large stained-glass window above the entrance. The original steeple, much taller (and handsomer) than the current one, as well as a triple-arched entrance porch were removed in 1945: their weight threatened to collapse part of the church built on an old creek bed.

Inside, the sanctuary's ceiling is supported by five black walnut hammer beams rising from ornate

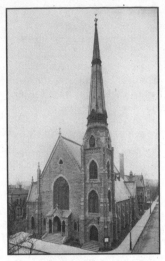

First Baptist Church, 1925

brackets. The fine stained-glass windows reflect the congregation's early wealth; its membership included some of St. Paul's business elite, many of whom resided nearby.

Wacouta Commons area

11 Wacouta Commons area

Area northeast of East Seventh and Sibley Sts.

*Wacouta Commons Park, ca. 2005 / **Sibley Park Apartments,** Paul Madson and Associates and KKE Architects, 2002 / **Essex on the Park Town Homes and Apartments,** Paul Madson and Associates, 2002 / **Sibley Court Apartments,** KKE Architects, 2003 / **Dakota on the Park Town Homes and Apartments,** LHB Architects and Engineers, 2003 / **Ninth Street Lofts** (Workforce Center of St. Paul), 1909 / renovated, ESG Architects, 2004 / **Printer's Row Condominiums,** ESG Architects, 2005*

For much of the modern era, this portion of Lowertown consisted largely of old warehouse and industrial buildings interspersed with parking lots. After many fits and starts, development dollars finally started pouring into the area in the late 1990s; since then it has filled with new and renovated housing. A new park called Wacouta Commons Park serves as the centerpiece.

While the brick-clad buildings surrounding the park are decent examples of their kind, they embody the mistaken notion that buildings must look "old" to fit within historic districts. They're also much too restrained for their own good. Lowertown has long needed a jolt of architectural caffeine, but the buildings around Wacouta are strictly decaf.

LOST 2 *Across the Interstate 94– 35E junction from the Wacouta Park neighborhood is an industrial area that was once St. Paul's mansion district, organized around* **Lafayette Park** *(a vanished square near present-day Lafayette Rd. and Grove St.). In the 1860s and 1870s, merchant princes such as James J. Hill, Amherst Wilder, and Horace Thompson built estates here. Industrial development driven by nearby rail tracks soon made the area less desirable, however, and in the 1880s the moneyed class began to leave for, in most cases, Summit Ave. By 1920, new rail lines and freight houses had taken up much of the land south of Grove and only scattered housing remained. Today, there is none.*

12 Apartments (Crane-Ordway Building) N *L*

281–87 East Fifth St.

Reed and Stem, 1904 / renovated, Cermak Rhoades Architects, 2006

Converted into over 60 units of affordable housing in 2006, this chunky brick warehouse was built for the Crane and Ordway Co., which manufactured valves and fittings used for steam engines and other industrial equipment. Company president Lucius P. Ordway later secured control of another business, an up-and-coming firm known as the Minnesota Mining and Manufacturing Co. (now 3M). It did very well for him.

13 St. Paul Farmers' Market N *L*

Fifth and Wall Sts.

Nemeth Associates, 1982 / enlarged and remodeled, Krech, O'Brien, Mueller and Wass, 2004

The Farmers' Market is one of Lowertown's success stories and a very popular place during summer weekends, even though it's always seemed cramped on this site. A 2004 remodeling resulted in a new roof, more stalls, and a much-improved color scheme.

14 Lowertown Commons (St. Paul Rubber Co.) N *L*

300 East Fourth St.

1905 / renovated, Bower Lewis Thrower Architects (Philadelphia), 1987

Building close to the river here has always posed foundation problems: the ground in parts of Lowertown is little more than casual fill. This warehouse had settled so badly on its southern side that it had to be substantially rebuilt before its conversion to apartments in the 1980s. Inside, there's an atrium created by tearing out walls and floors and exposing a portion of the building's structural frame.

15 Northern Warehouse Artists' Cooperative (Northern Pacific Railroad Warehouse) N *L*

308 Prince St.

Northern Pacific Railroad (in-house architect), 1908 / renovated, 1990

The largest remnant of the Northern Pacific Railroad headquarters complex that once clustered around Prince and Broadway Sts. This warehouse is historic for another reason: it was the first development completed by Artspace, a Twin Cities–based nonprofit corporation that has since become a leading developer of art-related projects nationwide. Working with the City of St. Paul and other public and private partners, Artspace converted the old warehouse into 52 studio-

housing units, some as large as 2,000 square feet.

LOST 3 *The site of the former Gillette Co. plant just to the north was for many years the headquarters of the* **Northern Pacific Railroad,** *which built its central offices at Broadway and Prince Sts. in 1883 and enlarged them with an elegant addition designed by Cass Gilbert in 1896. Both buildings were demolished in 1929 when the railroad constructed new tracks and a freight house on the site. These in turn gave way to the* **Gillette Co. plant,** *which was vacant as of 2007.*

POI A Trout Brook Canal

Fourth St. beneath and east of Lafayette Freeway (Hwy. 52) Bridge

George Wilson (engineer), 1891–94

Venture east past Broadway along Fifth St., then jog south to Fourth, and you'll encounter an old stone canal that carries Trout Brook beneath the railroad tracks east of Lowertown. The canal leads to a tunnel through which the brook then flows into Phalen Creek, also diverted underground here long ago. Trains still use the Trout Brook corridor to climb out of the Mississippi River Valley, but the number of tracks in use today is only a fraction of what it once was.

Tilsner Artists' Cooperative

16 Tilsner Artists' Cooperative (FOK Warehouse) N *L*

300 Broadway St.

Edward P. Bassford, 1894 / renovated, 1993

With its gorgeous orange brickwork and stately proportions, this Romanesque Revival–style building stands out from the Lowertown crowd. Perhaps

Bassford's best surviving work in St. Paul, it was built as a warehouse for the giant hardware wholesaling firm of Farwell, Ozmun and Kirk (FOK) and was later occupied by the Tilsner Box Co. In 1993, Artspace and various partners renovated the building into 66 "live-work units," as they're called, organized around two seven-story-high atriums that bring in natural light.

17 Great Northern (Railway Headquarters) Lofts ! N L

281–99 Kellogg Blvd. East

James Brodie, 1888 / two stories added, James Brodie, 1900 / renovated, Cermak Rhoades Architects, 2003

Architecturally and historically, one of Lowertown's most significant buildings. Now consisting of 53 luxurious condominiums, the building was once the headquarters of the Great Northern Railway and its chief executive James J. Hill, who ran his railroad empire from a second-floor office. Like Hill, the building is rock solid and all business, and with its overscaled stone entrance on Kellogg and massive brick walls, it has the rather forbidding look of a Florentine palace.

Hill and his in-house architect, James Brodie, were obsessed by the Chicago fire of 1871 and took unusual steps to make the building fireproof. Instead of the typical iron or timber frame, the building has solid exterior and interior masonry walls (three feet thick in places), with steel beams supporting arched brick or clay ceilings. The building's massiveness turned out to be nearly its undoing. Pilings driven into the Lowertown muck failed at one corner, causing the building to settle by as much as two feet.

A year before his death in 1916, Hill moved his headquarters to a new building at 180 East Fifth St. This building was then used for record storage and other purposes. It sat vacant for 30 years before its conversion into condominiums. The $30 million renovation included foundation repairs as well as restoration of some original features, among them an impressive wrought-iron staircase in the main lobby. The building's open courtyard, reached via an arched carriageway off Wall St., was also preserved.

18 Main U.S. Post Office

180 Kellogg Blvd. East

Holabird and Root (Chicago) with Lambert Bassindale, 1934 / renovated and enlarged, Ellerbe Associates and Brooks Cavin, 1964

This large, rather grim art deco building may not be around for much longer: the Postal Service plans to relocate its main St. Paul post office to suburban Eagan by 2009. The move would open up this prime riverfront site for new development.

Great Northern Lofts

Brooks Building

19 Brooks Building (Merchants National Bank) N *L*

366–68 Jackson St.

Edward P. Bassford, 1892 / renovated, ca. 1985

A richly ornamented Richardsonian Romanesque building, originally home to Merchants National Bank. It makes excellent use of the easily carved Lake Superior sandstone widely used by Twin Cities architects in the 1880s and 1890s. The small, partially restored lobby is worth a look, but the original banking hall is gone.

180 East Fifth

20 180 East Fifth (Railroad and Bank Building) N *L*

176–80 East Fifth St.

Charles S. Frost (Chicago), 1916 / renovated, HGA, 1987

With a million square feet of floor space, this office building was the Twin Cities' largest until completion of the IDS Center in Minneapolis in 1973. Known as the "Railroad and Bank Building," it housed the central offices of James J. Hill's Great Northern and the Northern Pacific railroads as well as the First National Bank of St. Paul. The latter occupied a skylit banking hall at the bottom of the open light court in the building's center. Like Hill's office building on Kellogg Blvd., this one offers few architectural frills, although classical details can be found on the lower floors and at the cornice. It's said that the building was originally divided by a wall separating the two railroad operations, the only interior connection a door in Hill's office.

When the building was renovated for office use in 1987, the old banking hall was given a fashionable mauve and teal color scheme. What seemed like a good idea at the time in retrospect was a bit like dressing a burly laborer in drag.

21 Mears Park Centre N *L*

Fairbanks-Morse Co. Building, 220 East Fifth St.

J. Walter Stevens, 1895 / renovated, Winsor/Faricy Architects, 1988

Powers Dry Goods Co. Building, 230–36 East Fifth St.

J. Walter Stevens, 1892 / renovated, Winsor/Faricy Architects, 1988

Two sturdy warehouses, now used for offices. The Fairbanks-Morse Building is the more interesting of the two, offering a Renaissance Revival facade that is rather ornate by Lowertown's utilitarian standards.

22 Straus Apartments (Noyes Brothers and Cutter Co. Building) N *L*

350–64 Sibley St.

1879 / additions (including fifth floor), 1900 / renovated, KKE Architects, 2003

The oldest commercial building in Lowertown, constructed for John Wann, a St. Paul businessman who hailed from Northern Ireland. Its first occupant was Noyes Brothers and Cutler Co., a large wholesaling firm that later moved to the north side of Mears Park. The four-story building originally included a bracketed cornice, a shallow central pediment, and other ornamental details. These features have disappeared, but the building retains its prominent window hoods—a signature element of the Italianate style. Used for many years by the Straus Knitting Co., the building suffered a number of unsympathetic remodelings before being renovated for use as apartments in 2003.

Union Depot Place, 1924

23 Union Depot Place (including Union Depot Lofts) ! N *L*

214 East Fourth St.

Charles S. Frost (Chicago), 1923 / renovated, Rafferty Rafferty Mikutowski Associates, 1983 / renovated, James Dayton Design, 2006

St. Paul's first Union Depot opened in 1881 directly below this one, at the foot of Sibley St., along the riverfront. Damaged by fire in 1884, it was rebuilt and survived until 1913, when it burned to the ground. After some haggling among the railroads, work on this mighty depot—a sober Beaux-Arts building with a monumental Doric colonnade— began in 1917. The depot was only part of a $15 million project that included construction of a concrete rail platform to lift tracks 17 feet above the flood-prone Mississippi. (This platform in turn required construction of a new, higher Robert Street Bridge and rebuilding of the adjacent Chicago and Great Western Railroad Lift Bridge.) To make room for the depot, the railroads cleared away several blocks of historic buildings.

The depot has two distinct sections. At the front is the main building, or head house, organized around a skylit lobby finished in polished marble and Mankato-Kasota stone. The skylights have been closed over; today's lobby is thus much darker than the original. To the rear, extending across Kellogg Blvd., is a long barrel-vaulted concourse now closed to the public. The concourse offers one especially fetching detail in the form of a terra-cotta frieze depicting the history of transportation across the Upper Midwest. In the depot's glory years, as many as 20,000 passengers a day poured through the concourse, which led to 21 sets of tracks used by seven railroads. Trains—up to 140 daily— arrived and departed at all hours.

The last train pulled out in 1971. The old building was renovated by a hopeful developer in 1983 but never enjoyed much financial success. Beginning in 2005 the upper floors of the head house were converted into 33 condominium units. Ambitious plans for returning local and regional rail service to the depot are afoot. Meanwhile, the concourse, owned by the U.S. Postal Service, remains vacant.

24 American House Apartments (Western Supply Co. Warehouse) N *L*

352 Wacouta St.

Cass Gilbert, 1895 / renovated, Rafferty Rafferty Tollefson Lindeke Architects, 1986

Like the old shoe factory (now Parkside Apartments) next door, this building was commissioned by members of the Gotzian family. Designed by Cass Gilbert, it's a lovely little brick building that draws its inspiration from the Italian Renaissance. It served as a company outlet store but was later rented to other businesses. Now used for housing, the building was for many years known to St. Paulites as home of the American Beauty Macaroni Co.

Parkside Apartments

25 Parkside Apartments (Gotzian Shoe Co.) N *L*

242–50 East Fifth St.

Cass Gilbert, 1892 / 1905 / reno-vated, Bower Lewis Thrower Architects (Philadelphia), 1986

Includes **J. H. Mahler Co. Building,** 258–60 East Fifth St.

1883

The Parkside was originally home to a shoe company founded by German immigrant Conrad Gotz-ian. A shoemaker by trade, Gotz-ian arrived in St. Paul in the 1850s and at the time of his death in 1887 had built a shoe manufactur-ing and wholesale business em-ploying more than 450 workers. Gotzian's heirs planned this build-ing, one of three surviving works in Lowertown by Cass Gilbert.

Although Gilbert is best known for his palatial State Capitol, he was an excellent designer of warehouses and other industrial buildings because of his sure sense of proportions and his skill-ful handling of large volumes. Here, he used windows grouped within broad recessed arches to create an especially pleasing struc-ture reminiscent of the Chicago

work of such architectural mas-ters as H. H. Richardson and John Wellborn Root, Jr. Considered purely as a designed object, this may be Lowertown's best building.

Included in the renovated Parkside complex is the old J. H. Mahler Co. Building, originally home to a carriage dealer. The cast-iron columns on the ground floor were made by the Wash-ington Foundry in St. Paul.

26 Cosmopolitan Apart-ments (Finch, Van Slyck and McConville Co.) N *L*

366 Wacouta St.

James F. Denson (Chicago) with C. A. P. Turner, 1911 / 1915 / addi-tion, Clarence H. Johnston, 1923 / renovated, Bower Lewis Thrower Architects (Philadelphia), 1986

Although this warehouse was built only a few years after Som-mers Co. across Sixth St., it repre-sents a giant leap forward in technology. The Sommers build-ing relied on a time-honored sys-tem known as "mill construc-tion," consisting of outer brick bearing walls tied to an interior frame of heavy timber. This warehouse, erected for a large dry-goods wholesaler, was built of reinforced concrete using a slab-and-column system patented by Minneapolis engi-neer C. A. P. Turner. The concrete frame offered many advantages for warehouse construction: tremendous strength, virtual invulnerability to fire, large free-span spaces, and room for many windows to bring in daylight for workers.

State Capitol Area

Until the 1890s, when work began on the present State Capitol, this part of St. Paul was a curious mix of splendor and squalor. The splendor: a row of mansions that crowned the hills along University and Sherburne avenues north of downtown. Among them was the magnificent John Merriam House (1887), a brownstone fantasy that may have been the finest of all nineteenth-century mansions in St. Paul. Yet just to the east of the mansion district, in what is now the Mount Airy Housing Development, a tangle of short, steep streets and battered old houses formed a tough neighborhood sometimes called the "Badlands." To the south of University, where the Capitol Mall spreads out today, was a mixed commercial-residential zone that wasn't as impoverished as the Badlands but wasn't one of the city's garden spots either.

Today, virtually all traces of these old neighborhoods are gone, largely as a result of two far-reaching decisions in city planning made half a century apart. The first came in 1893, when it was decided to build a new State Capitol on the so-called "Wabasha Street site"—a tract of land on what was then the northern fringes of downtown St. Paul. This decision had two significant consequences. First, it separated the center of state government from the center of St. Paul (the first two capitols had been located at Tenth and Wabasha streets not far from the downtown core). The northward move of the capitol also doomed the hilltop mansions, which gave way one by one to the inevitable expansion of government offices. The process was slow, however, and the last of the great houses stood until the 1960s.

The second critical development in this area's history occurred in the 1940s. At that time, the capitol still lacked a formal setting, having only a small, oddly shaped patch of open lawn in front of it. Over the years there had been many proposals for a grand mall, including several (in 1903, 1909, and 1931) from the building's architect, Cass Gilbert. But it wasn't until 1944 that plans for a true mall finally began to move forward. In that year, a team consisting of Clarence H. Johnston, Jr., Edward Nelson, and Arthur Nichols prepared a design for the St. Paul City Planning Board that envisioned something very close to the current fan-shaped mall. The three planners also surmised, correctly, that a proposed federal highway (now Interstate 94–35E) would be routed south of the mall rather than to the north of the capitol building.

The 1944 plan, slightly modified a year later, was carried out in the early 1950s. The new mall was a huge project that required sweeping away dozens of old buildings and completely reordering the historic streetscape around the capitol. Four new government structures—the Veterans Service Building, the State Transportation Department, the Centennial Office Building, and a National Guard Armory—were also built around the mall in the 1950s and early 1960s.

A decade later, the transformation of the capitol area continued with construction of the interstate highway south of the mall. This rude trench filled with rushing traffic only reinforced the sense of separation between the capitol area and downtown. In the 1980s, efforts were made to undo some of the damage by redesigning a section of the freeway near the capitol to incorporate classically inspired bridges, walls, railings, lampposts, and other features. There was also a grand plan to rebuild the mall in a more formal neoclassical manner, but it fizzled for lack of money. The 1990s and early years of the twenty-first century saw another boom in state construction around the mall and just south of the interstate along 10th and 11th streets. These recent buildings range in style from tepid exercises in faux classicism to more energetic modernist works. Overall, however, most of these newer works represent a missed opportunity to complement Gilbert's brilliant capitol building with modern architecture of real distinction.

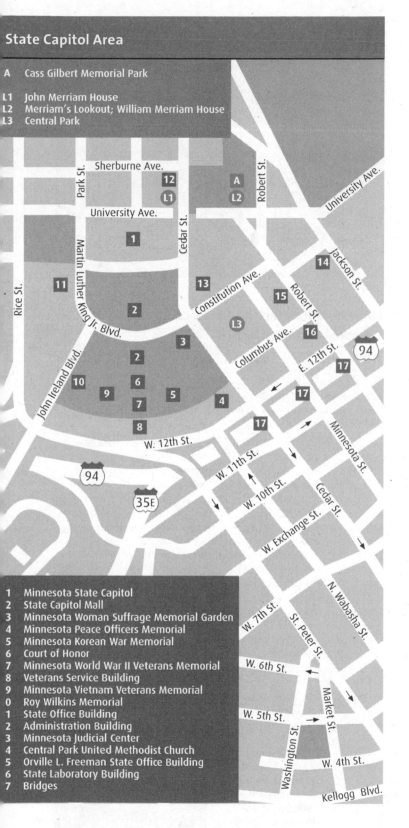

State Capitol Area

A   Cass Gilbert Memorial Park

L1   John Merriam House
L2   Merriam's Lookout; William Merriam House
L3   Central Park

State Capitol Area

Minnesota State Capitol

1 Minnesota State Capitol ! N

75 Rev. Dr. Martin Luther King Jr. Blvd.

Cass Gilbert, 1905 / restoration, Miller Dunwiddie Architects, 1983 and later / Art: Quadriga *(sculpture), Daniel Chester French and Edward Potter, 1906*

This gleaming marble palace has become such a familiar Minnesota icon that it's easy to take the building for granted, especially in view of its obvious similarities to other big public buildings (including numerous state capitols) of the time. Yet it really is an exceptional work in any number of respects, beginning with the fact that its now famous architect, Cass Gilbert, was just 35 years old when he won a design competition for the building in 1895. That age is still very young in a profession where mastery tends to come late in life. Fortunately, Gilbert was wise beyond his years, and he produced for the people of Minnesota a remarkably rich and sophisticated work of architecture.

Gilbert was able to do so not just because he knew his pediments and pilasters but because he was so skilled at the fundamentals of architecture. The capitol showcases all of Gilbert's strengths—his sure command of form and proportion, his careful handling of materials, his talent as an ornamentalist, his ability to orchestrate a "total design" with a team of artists and craftsmen, even his sense of humor, evident in such whimsical details as the gophers and loons that inhabit the capitol's decorative bronzework.

The mere fact that Gilbert was able to get the building he wanted testifies to his force of will—an essential character trait for any ambitious architect. Large works of public architecture almost always generate controversy, and the capitol was no exception. One of the biggest brouhahas centered on Gilbert's desire to dress the capitol in snowy white marble from

Minnesota State Capitol rotunda

Georgia. Minnesota's quarrymen thought such a lucrative contract should stay within the state. In the end, Gilbert got his marble after agreeing to build the capitol's base of St. Cloud granite and to use other Minnesota stone inside the building.

The capitol has one other quality seldom remarked on. Although it's large and sumptuous in the usual Beaux-Arts manner, it's not as relentlessly overwhelming as some other state capitols of the period—Wisconsin's, say, or Pennsylvania's. In other words, Gilbert's building seems to be just the right size— big enough to show off the majesty of the state but not so large as to seem, well, swollenheaded in a very unMinnesotan way. Gilbert struck close to a perfect balance here—no small accomplishment.

Like other major public buildings of its era, the capitol is chock-full of art in the form of paintings, sculpture, and all manner of hortatory inscriptions designed to encourage noble thinking. Much of this high-minded art seems quaint today, but it adds considerably to the building's charm. The one piece of art that has something like an architectural function is the famous *Quadriga,* officially entitled *The Progress of the State,* sculpted by Daniel Chester French and Edward Potter. Positioned at the base of the dome, these muscular horses add a note of vital,

golden energy to Gilbert's otherwise classically serene building.

Over the years, the capitol suffered from its share of inept remodelings and benign neglect, but in the 1980s, under the leadership of Governor Rudy Perpich, the state finally began to treat the building with the respect it deserves. Most major spaces have been restored, and a carefully developed preservation plan now guides all renovation work. Gilbert undoubtedly would be pleased.

Because the capitol is so large and so packed with architectural detail, it's best seen by taking one of the regularly scheduled tours or by wandering around yourself with the aid of a book such as Thomas O'Sullivan's excellent *North Star Statehouse: An Armchair Guide to the Minnesota State Capitol.*

2 State Capitol Mall

Area bounded by Rev. Dr. Martin Luther King Jr. Blvd., Cedar St., 12th St., and John Ireland Blvd.

Clarence H. Johnston, Jr., Edward Nelson, Morrell and Nichols (George Nason), 1950–54 and later

Something like the mall as it exists today was envisioned as far back as 1902, when Cass Gilbert drew the first of his many plans for such a project. Gilbert's modest sketch blossomed over time into more grandiose schemes. His last plan in 1931 proposed a vast mall that would have

State Capitol Mall

marched down from the capitol like one of Baron Haussmann's famous Parisian boulevards, circled around a war memorial column near today's Interstate 94–35E corridor, sliced through Seven Corners and Irvine Park, and crossed the Mississippi River on a new bridge before terminating in a traffic circle atop the West Side bluffs at Smith Ave. A wonderful dream, but it had no hope of becoming reality in those dark financial days.

The mall that finally was built after World War II has always been a disappointment. For all of its size, it's not especially grand, and except for a few special occasions it receives little public use. Size, in fact, is part of its problem: big and diffuse, it bleeds past the edges of the state buildings that make a futile effort to define and contain it.

Over the years, various proposals to remake the mall have come and gone. Chicago architect Helmut Jahn produced a brilliant scheme in the 1970s to build parking and new office space beneath the mall, where a system of tunnels connecting the capitol and other buildings was already in place. In the 1980s the state conducted a competition to redesign the mall. The winning entry called for a classically inspired series of plazas, gardens, and walls. But this decidedly Gilbertian dream, like Jahn's proposal, failed for lack of financing.

In the 1990s, the mall began to take on a new dimension as home to memorials honoring significant people and events. Five were built between 1992 and 2000 and more are in the works. While they're generally well designed, these commemorative spaces have given the mall an increasingly funereal feel at a time when what it really needs is more liveliness and less embalmed solemnity.

In keeping with its status as Minnesota's formal front yard, the mall also offers a variety of public art, mostly of the heroic sculptural variety.

3 Minnesota Woman Suffrage Memorial Garden ("The Garden of Time")

Rev. Dr. Martin Luther King Jr. Blvd. and Cedar St.

Art: Loom *(Ralph Nelson and Raveevarn Choksombatchi), 2000*

A pleasant green place at the northeast corner of the mall that includes a timeline of the suffrage movement incorporated into a metal trellis.

4 Minnesota Peace Officers Memorial

Near 12th and Wabasha Sts.

Ankeny Kell Architects (Fred Richter), 1995

A classically inspired memorial honoring law enforcement officers who died in the line of duty.

5 Minnesota Korean War Memorial

East of Court of Honor near center of mall

Bob Kost and Dean Olson with Art Norby, 1998

Statuary and stone markers list the names of 700 Minnesotans who died in the Korean War.

6 Court of Honor

North of Veterans Service Building

Johnston, Nelson, and Nichols, 1951

A semicircular plaza with plaques describing Minnesotans' service in the nation's wars.

7 Minnesota World War II Veterans Memorial

Between Veterans Service Building and capitol

Craig Amundsen and Ben Sporer, Bryan D. Carlson and Myklebust-Sears, ca. 2006

An oval-shaped plaza with etched-glass panels narrating Minnesotans' role in World War II.

Veterans Service Building

8 Veterans Service Building

20 West 12th St.

Brooks Cavin, 1954 / 1973 / Art: Promise of Youth (statue), Alonzo Hauser, 1958

The best post–World War II work of architecture on the mall and one of the city's first truly modern buildings of note. It has been criticized for standing square in the middle of Cass Gilbert's grand vista; however, by the time the building was planned, Gilbert's dream of a mighty boulevard marching south from the mall was long since dead. A fairer criticism might be that the Veterans Building, with its bridgelike structure and rather quiet presence, isn't monumental enough to effectively terminate the north-south axis that connects it visually to the capitol.

9 Minnesota Vietnam Veterans Memorial (*Lakefront DMZ*)

West of Court of Honor

Nina Ackerberg, Jake Castillo, Rich Laffin, and Stanton Sears, 1992

A sunken plaza featuring a map of Minnesota and a granite wall incised with the names of soldiers killed or missing in Vietnam. The design was clearly influenced by Maya Lin's celebrated Vietnam Memorial in Washington, DC.

10 Roy Wilkins Memorial (*Spiral for Justice*)

Along John Ireland Blvd.

Curtis Patterson, 1995

The mall's most peculiar memorial, using copper-clad walls, pyramids, and other exotic elements

to celebrate the achievements of Roy Wilkins, a civil rights leader raised in St. Paul. The effect, however, is vaguely unsettling: knowing nothing of the memorial's true purpose, visitors might think they have wandered into the open-air temple of a religious cult.

11 State Office Building

100 Rev. Dr. Martin Luther King Jr. Blvd.

Clarence H. Johnston, 1932 / remodeled and top floor added, Leo Lundgren Architects, 1986 / parking ramp, BWBR Architects, 1988

Not a great building, but, like Johnston's earlier Historical Society on the other side of the mall, its restrained classicism nicely complements the State Capitol. The building was revamped and a seventh floor added in the 1980s, when the parking ramp to the rear was also built.

12 Administration Building

50 Sherburne Ave.

Ellerbe Associates, 1966

A marble-clad bureaucratic box from the 1960s, notable less for its own pompous presence than for what it replaced.

John Merriam House, ca. 1895

LOST 1 *This was the site of the* **John Merriam House,** *completed in 1887 and a nationally significant example of the Richardsonian Romanesque style. The St. Paul Institute (ancestor of today's Science Museum of Minnesota) bought the house in 1927. After the museum moved away in 1964, the state acquired the house and promptly demolished it to make way for the Administration Building.*

POI A Cass Gilbert Memorial Park

Sherburne Ave. east of Cedar St.

ca. 1970s

An outthrust concrete overlook is the main feature of this park, which occupies some of the most intriguing ground in St. Paul.

LOST 2 *Mansions once lined the hilltop here along Sherburne Ave., which ended in a cul-de-sac known as **Merriam's Lookout.** Set above a curving stone wall reached by a staircase, the lookout was a favorite vantage point. The top of the wall can still be seen near the edge of the hill, while parts of the staircase are visible along Robert St. below. A nearby stone wall along Cedar St. was part of the estate of William Merriam (John's son, and governor of Minnesota from 1889 to 1893). The **William Merriam House,** built in 1882, stood east of Cedar and was among the neighborhood's earliest mansions.*

13 Minnesota Judicial Center (Minnesota Historical Society) N

25 Rev. Dr. Martin Luther King Jr. Blvd. (at Cedar St.)

*Clarence H. Johnston, 1918 / addition and renovation, Leonard Parker Associates, 1989 / includes **East Capitol Plaza,** Richard Fleischner, 1990 / Art: Falling Water (skylight), Pat Benning and Michael Pilla, 1995*

The original part of this building, initially home to the state historical society, is a solid if less than scintillating exercise in the heavy-duty classicism common to American public buildings of the era. Though it served well enough as a sober gray foil to the State Capitol, the building was significantly improved in 1989 when an addition housing judicial chambers and other court-related offices was constructed to the north and east of the original, which was remodeled to accommodate new court- and hearing rooms.

The addition is one of the high points of postmodern design in Minnesota. Especially notable is the north wing, the working quarters of the state's supreme court justices and other appellate judges. Arranged around a semicircle, the offices overlook a plaza designed by artist Richard Fleischner and the capitol itself (where the supreme court still hears cases). This visual relationship is beautifully worked out, as is the addition as a whole.

14 Central Park United Methodist Church

639 Jackson St.

Haarstick and Lundgren, ca. 1960

This is home to St. Paul's oldest Protestant congregation, founded in 1848 as Market Street Methodist Church. In the 1880s, the congregation built a large church near Central Park but lost it to freeway construction in the 1960s. The most distinctive feature of this rather odd stone-and-brick structure is a rounded meeting room in front that calls to mind a Pullman car.

15 Orville L. Freeman State Office Building

625 North Robert St.

HGA and Pickard Chilton, 2005

16 State Laboratory Building (Minnesota Departments of Agriculture and Health)

601 North Robert St.

HGA with CUH2A (Princeton, NJ), 2005

Minnesota Judicial Center

With its bold play of vertical and horizontal elements and the spatial complexity of its facade, the Freeman Building has a Ralph Rapson–like swagger to it. Although purists may shudder, it's refreshing to see a major building in the capitol complex that isn't content to be just another deferential box. The laboratory building next door isn't as strong a design.

17 Bridges

Cedar, Minnesota, Robert, and other downtown streets across Interstate 94–35E

David Mayernik and Tom Rajkovich with HGA, 1987–92

The classically inspired bridges, walls, and railings along the interstate corridor were built to complement the State Capitol and its surroundings. The cast-stone detailing tends to be crude, and, while the state deserves credit for its good intentions, the bridges and other structures— gatehouses, obelisks, and the like—aren't convincing as classical designs.

LOST 3 *A parking ramp behind the Centennial Office Building at 658 Cedar St. occupies the site of Central Park, once a beautiful little urban square. The park, dating from 1884, was home to the first three St. Paul Winter Carnival ice palaces, built in 1886, 1887, and 1888. The park was little more than a vacant lot by the time the ramp was built in 1974.*

Ice Palace, 1886

Overview

Although this large section of the city is known collectively as the East Side, it actually consists of several distinct neighborhoods. Overlooking downtown on a series of terraced hills is Dayton's Bluff. Home to a large historic preservation district, the neighborhood is rich with Victorian-era architecture ranging from hilltop mansions to working-class cottages. However, the housing here tends to be more modest than in St. Paul's other great repository of Victoriana: the Historic Hill District. Dayton's Bluff is also a neighborhood in transition, where elegantly restored homes stand next to properties that look as though their best days are long gone. The neighborhood's contrasts give it an edge—wealth and poverty are often in close proximity—but they are also part of what makes it a fascinating place.

Dayton's Bluff didn't develop in a big way until the early 1880s, when the Seventh Street Improvement Project made the neighborhood easier to reach. At a cost of $1 million, the city widened East Seventh from downtown to the top of the bluffs and also reduced its once daunting grade. The project was completed in 1884, after which horsecars (soon replaced by cable cars and then streetcars) were able to climb the long hill. Three years later, the first Third Street Bridge opened, providing more access to the neighborhood, and the boom was on. Between 1882 and 1892, nearly 400 buildings were constructed in Dayton's Bluff; many still stand today.

North and east of Dayton's Bluff is Payne-Phalen. In almost every respect, from its people to its topography to its architecture, this neighborhood is one of the most diverse in the Twin Cities. For much of its history, however, Payne-Phalen was a proudly insular part of St. Paul, possessing the same sense of self-containment and ethnic cohesion as Northeast Minneapolis. Large industries—including 3M, Seeger-Whirlpool, and the Hamm's Brewery (officially in the Dayton's Bluff neighborhood but strongly linked to Payne Avenue)—once employed thousands of people here in a neighborhood that was solidly working class and overwhelmingly white. Things began to change in the 1980s as industries downsized or closed. At the same time, a new generation of immigrants, many of them Asian or Latino, started flowing into the neighborhood, which is now home to people from all corners of the world.

Named after its main commercial thoroughfare and the deep lake that forms its northeastern boundary, Payne-Phalen is also home to a rich body of architecture, ranging from pioneer-era houses to splashy Victorians to early twentieth-century works in various Period Revival styles. There are also some respectable examples of modernism. The best way to get a feel for the neighborhood is to drive—or, better yet, bike or walk—up Payne Avenue, which offers a wonderful array of small commercial buildings, many dating to the late nineteenth century. Near Payne Avenue you'll also find Swede Hollow, one of the Twin Cities' most curious places.

Farther out on the East Side are three neighborhoods that tend to be viewed by many people as the architectural equivalent of flyover land. Known as the Greater East Side, Battle Creek, and Highwood Hills, these neighborhoods have few prominent monuments, and much of their architecture consists of tract housing. Even so, it would be a mistake to overlook this part of St. Paul, which offers some wonderful pockets of Victorian-era housing, such as the small Burlington Heights enclave along Point Douglas Road. There are several impressive homes from the modern era as well. Portions of an important nineteenth-century industrial site—the old St. Paul Harvester Works (1875 and later)—survive near Case Avenue and Hazel Street. You'll also find some of the Twin Cities' most spectacular topography in the little-known Highwood Hills neighborhood.

Dayton's Bluff

Dayton's Bluff has three distinct sections. North of Interstate 94 is the Dayton's Bluff Historic District, which takes in all or part of more than 30 square blocks in the traditional heart of the neighborhood. Rising above Trout Brook–Phalen Creek valley, this area offers superb vistas of downtown St. Paul and the Mississippi River Valley. Views usually attract money, and that was the case in the early days here: beginning in the 1850s, some of St. Paul's wealthiest men built country estates along the blufftops. Among them were such local luminaries as Lyman Dayton, a real estate speculator after whom the neighborhood is named; P. H. Kelley, a grocer; John Keller, a grain dealer; and Gustave Muench, a lumberman. All of these pre-1880s mansions are gone except for Muench's house (ca. 1869), which survives in modified form. The dominant institutional presence is Metropolitan State University, which occupies what was once the site of the A. W. Mayall Mansion and later St. John's Hospital.

On the north side of East Seventh Street is the small but intriguing neighborhood known as Upper Swede Hollow. Theodore Hamm, one of Dayton's Bluff's many German settlers, lived here in a mansion (1887, gone) overlooking his brewery. Large houses built by his descendants can still be seen above the hollow, especially along Greenbrier Street. East Seventh continues to serve as Dayton's Bluff's major commercial corridor. 3M Corp. still maintains an office complex here but will soon close the last of its manufacturing operations. Other historic industries have also faded away.

To the south of Interstate 94 is Mounds Park, a residential enclave that seems to lead a secret life, known only to locals. The neighborhood takes its name from a blufftop park with a much-compromised set of American Indian burial mounds. Its hilly streets are lined with homes ensconced in leafy hideaways. Among them is one of the city's great Victorians, the towering Giesen-Hauser House (1891).

Dayton's Bluff Historic District

Area roughly bounded by Swede Hollow, Mounds Blvd., I-94, and Hope and Arcade Sts.

1992

Much of Dayton's Bluff falls within the boundaries of this local heritage preservation district, established in 1992. The district encompasses a varied stock of buildings, but houses—mostly dating to the 1880s and 1890s—are the chief attraction. The oldest and grandest homes are in the western part of the district on the hillsides above downtown, where a good many towered Victorians poke up their heads to take in the view. The creation of this historic district was controversial in part because of fears that design guidelines would drive up renovation costs and force out poorer residents. Although gentrification has occurred, it's been sporadic: for every lavishly restored house you see here you are likely to see another much in need of attention.

Dayton's Bluff

A   Upper Swede Hollow Park
B   Lyman Dayton burial site
C   Warren Burger's Boyhood Home
D   Harry Blackmun's Boyhood Home
E   Building No. 20
F   DNR Fish Hatchery
G   Bruce Vento Nature Sanctuary and Carver's Cave

L1   Theodore Hamm Mansion

1   First Lutheran Church
2   Linz-Bergmeier House
3   William and Marie Hamm House
4   Otto and Marie Hamm Muller House
5   Peter and Emma Classen House
6   Henry and Hilda Defiel House
7   Eichenwald Row
8   Michael and Rose Walter House
9   Andrew Hoban House
10   Arthur and Elsa Koenig House
11   Peter and Louisa John House
12   House
13   Charles Tracy House
14   Max and Amilia Toltz House
15   Adolph and Anna Muench House
16   Muench-Heinemann House
17   Apartments
18   Jacob Petter House
19   Condominiums
20   Frederick Reinecker Houses
21   Dayton's Bluff Elementary School
22   Ecclesia Condominiums
23   Euclid View Apartments
24   Condominiums
25   Metropolitan State Universit
26   New Main
27   Stutzman Block
28   HealthEast Care Center
29   Commercial building
30   Sacred Heart Catholic Churc
31   Bethlehem Lutheran Church
32   3M, Corp., complex
33   Office building
34   Charles and Marguerite
      Messerli House
35   "Triangle" house
36   Henry Gray House
37   William and Harriet
      Wakefield House
38   Wolkoff Building
39   Mounds Park
40   McLean Terrace
41   Giesen-Hauser House
42   Glennis Ter Wisscha–James
      Lano House
43   Mounds Park Residence

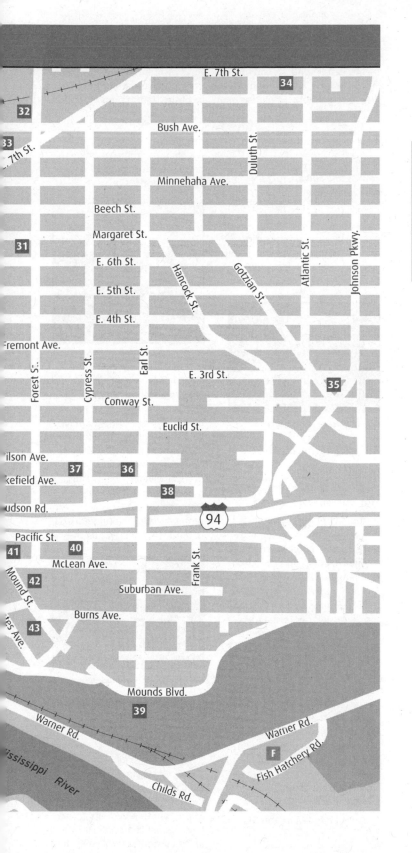

North of East Seventh Street (Upper Swede Hollow)

This area is separated from the rest of the Dayton's Bluff Historic District by East Seventh St. and forms a distinct community of its own above Swede Hollow. You'll find many pattern book Victorian houses here as well as larger homes built for members of the Hamm brewing family.

1 First Lutheran Church *L*

463 Maria Ave.

Edwins and Edwins, 1917 / addition, 1964

As its name attests, this is St. Paul's—and Minnesota's— oldest Lutheran congregation, founded in 1854 by Swedish immigrants. The church is standard Gothic Revival, done in brick.

Linz-Bergmeier House, 1915

2 Linz-Bergmeier House *L*

614 Fountain Pl.

1885 / additions and remodelings, 1891, 1916, and later

A stunning photograph taken around 1915 shows a magnificent terraced yard here, adorned with fountains, pools, and gardens dropping down to Swede Hollow. The home and its grounds were built by Francis Linz. His daughter, Clara, and her husband, Fredrick W. Bergmeier, later took over the property. Fredrick was publisher of *Volkszeitung*, a German-language daily newspaper in St. Paul. Clara succeeded him after his death in 1905. Their house is now something of an architectural mishmash, while the yard appears to have been largely reclaimed by nature.

POI A Upper Swede Hollow Park

Greenbrier and Margaret Sts.

1973

A pleasant little park with a staircase leading down into the mysterious hollow. Here, too, is a plaque commemorating one of St. Paul's most famous vanished houses.

Theodore Hamm Mansion, 1888

LOST 1 *This park was the site of the* **Theodore Hamm Mansion,** *a commanding stone and brick pile built in 1887. Posing in baronial majesty atop Swede Hollow, the mansion was the largest of what ultimately became a small colony of Hamm family and employee homes along or near Greenbrier St. The mansion, later used as a nursing home, was vacant by the time a youthful arsonist burned it to the ground in 1954.*

William and Marie Hamm House

3 William and Marie Hamm House *! L*

668 Greenbrier St.

Allen H. Stem, 1892

Theodore Hamm's only son, William, built this Classical Revival–style house for his bride, Marie Scheffer. With its corner bays, robust central dormer, and arched entrance flanked by delicate pilasters, the house is among the most sophisticated in the neighborhood. After hard service as a rooming house, it was purchased in 1976 by a couple who have been restoring it ever since.

4 Otto and Marie Hamm Muller House *L*

672 Greenbrier St.

Augustus Gauger, 1891

While William Hamm next door opted for the latest in classical styling, two other family members—William's sister, Marie, and her husband, Otto Muller—stayed with the old-time Queen Anne when they built this house. Much modified before being restored, the house includes a prominent corner tower capped with a bell-shaped roof.

5 Peter and Emma Classen House *L*

680 Greenbrier St.

Edward P. Bassford, 1887

A much-remodeled house—now used as a group home—in which a number of styles coexist, not always peacefully. It was built for Peter Classen, who worked at

Hamm's Brewery and whose wife, Emma, was the sister of their next-door neighbor, Otto Muller.

Henry and Hilda Defiel House

6 Henry and Hilda Defiel House *L*

732 Margaret St.

Hermann Kretz, 1891

A mix of rigor and romanticism. The main mass of the house is quite subdued, its forms outlined by long bands of precisely detailed ornament. By contrast, the house's pointy-headed tower, from which a pair of semicircular dormers erupt like giant ears, is pure Victorian romance. Henry Defiel made his money in ice and was later involved in real estate and oil refining.

South of East Seventh Street

This is the main portion of the Dayton's Bluff Historic District. The most elaborate houses, not surprisingly, are often located on hilltops or at corners.

7 Eichenwald Row *L*

393–99 Eichenwald St.

Andrew Hoban (builder), 1892

A well-dressed Victorian row house, merrily mixing all manner of styles under the general banner of Queen Anne. Eichenwald St. was platted in 1877 by John Keller, who named it after his birthplace in Germany and who built a large estate here (gone) in 1871.

8 Michael and Rose Walter House *L*

770 East Sixth St.

1880

An exceptionally well-preserved Italianate house that includes a

bracketed front porch and a decorative bargeboard hovering over a small bull's-eye window in the front gable.

Andrew Hoban House

9 Andrew Hoban House *L*

762 East Sixth St.

Andrew Hoban (builder), 1889

Although this house falls within the broad realm of a Colonial

Revival foursquare, it fairly hums with idiosyncratic touches such as the oversized limestone voussoirs that envelop two first-floor windows like a lush head of hair. Other unusual features include long sticklike brackets that support the northeast corner of the roof, boldly framed second-story corner windows, and, on the west side, a shingled attic dormer that morphs into an oriel window below.

Arthur and Elsa Koenig House

10 Arthur and Elsa Koenig (Koenig-Osgood) House *L*

757 East Sixth St.

1879

Although this vigorous Italianate house has lost its corner tower and part of its wraparound porch, it still offers many exuberant details, such as the attenuated columns and ornate brackets found on the remaining porches. Arthur and Elsa Koenig were from Austria. Arthur served as local agent for a Milwaukee brewery. Benjamin Osgood, president of a St. Paul company that manufactured boxes, later bought the property.

11 Peter and Louisa John House *L*

373 Maple St.

Buechner and Orth, 1906

The last of Dayton's Bluff's turn-of-the-century mansions, built for Peter John, a grocery store and saloon owner who later became a foreman at the Hamm's Brewery. John had the good sense to marry one of brewing tycoon Theodore Hamm's five daughters, Louisa. Occupying a corner lot, the house is a stately exercise in Colonial Revival. Its

features include a wraparound porch built on a limestone base, corner pilasters sporting lion's head capitals, and much stained glass.

12 House

393 Bates Ave.

Elmer H. Justus, 1929

This faux adobe house stands out as a true oddity. Its symmetry is not a typical feature of Spanish-inspired houses, while some of its detailing—such as the tiny pent roofs that hang like eyebrows above the side windows—is mighty peculiar.

13 Charles Tracy House *L*

358 Bates Ave.

ca. 1860, 1878

One of the oldest houses in Dayton's Bluff, moved here from an adjoining lot in 1887 by its first owner of record, a bookkeeper named Charles Tracy. The house, which originally had a balustraded front porch, is Greek Revival in style.

Max and Amilia Toltz House

14 Max and Amilia Toltz House *L*

352 Bates Ave.

Max Toltz, 1902

Max Toltz was born in Germany and trained as an engineer in Berlin. He became chief engineer of the Great Northern Railway before forming his own architectural and engineering firm (now known as TKDA) in 1910. This sturdy Arts and Crafts house, its first floor built of rough-faced sandstone, possesses the convincing heft of an engineer's work. Although the front porch conveys a strong sense of the

Arts and Crafts style with its heavy beams and brackets, the house also has Tudor and Colonial Revival characteristics. The shingled carriage house to the rear is an original feature of the property.

Adolph and Anna Muench House

15 Adolph and Anna Muench House N *L*

653 East Fifth St.

Emil Ulrici, 1884

Overlooking downtown at the western edge of Dayton's Bluff, this Queen Anne house is among the best surviving works of architect Emil Ulrici, who designed homes for some of St. Paul's leading German American families. The house's octagonal tower, its pointed roof harboring a small pediment, is particularly striking. Ulrici designed the house for Adolph Muench and his family after their first home, on the same site, burned down. Born in Germany, Muench became president of the company that published the *Volkszeitung* newspaper. Other members of the family owned homes nearby, including Adolph's brother, Gustave, who lived across the street.

16 Muench-Heinemann House *L*

334 Mounds Blvd. (also 652 East Fifth St.)

ca. 1869 and later

This considerably modified house, built for Gustave Muench and later owned by Maria Heinemann, is the only remaining property on Mounds Blvd. that faces downtown in the manner

of the neighborhood's early mansions. It's Italianate in style, although modern siding and the

Muench-Heinemann House

addition of a neoclassical porch have altered its character. The house's big front yard was chewed away by the construction of Mounds Blvd. and Interstate 94, and it takes an act of imagination to envision what it looked like long ago, when it crowned green, wooded blufftops.

POI B Lyman Dayton burial site

After his death in 1865, Lyman Dayton was buried here between Fifth and Sixth Sts. Four years later, when Gustave Muench built his house, he was not enchanted by the prospect of a corpse buried in his front yard. As a result, Dayton's remains were relocated to Oakland Cemetery.

17 Apartments (Tandy Row) *L*

668–74 East Fourth St.

John Coxhead, 1888

A row house that achieves a kind of willful asymmetry by means of its oddly grouped windows. The design is further enlivened by a roof-mounted canopy that looks like a giant oven hood poised to suck up anyone who ventures onto the porch below.

18 Jacob Petter House *L*

338 Maple St.

1887

A cottage with delicate Eastlake detailing. Especially delightful is the overscaled front window topped by a decidedly underscaled pediment.

754–58 Fourth St. East

19 Condominiums (St. Peter's Protestant Episcopal Church) *L*

754–58 East Fourth St.

Willcox and Johnston, 1888 / addition, Clarence H. Johnston, 1905 / renovated, ca. 1970s

This little stone beauty, built as an Episcopal church, was converted to condominiums in the 1970s. One of the few nineteenth-century church buildings left in Dayton's Bluff, its walls are constructed of gray Platteville limestone embellished with reddish brown Lake Superior sandstone—an unusual combination. The church's pointed arch windows are Gothic, but its overall feel is more in keeping with the small Shingle Style churches of the period.

20 Frederick Reinecker Houses *L*

700, 702 East Third St.

Frederick Reinecker, 1882–83

These houses were constructed a year or so apart by master builder Frederick Reinecker. The older of the two, at 702 East Third St., is mostly Italianate; the newer one is Queen Anne.

POI C Warren Burger's Boyhood Home *L*

695 Conway St.

1884

POI D Harry Blackmun's Boyhood Home

847 East Fourth St.

1906

The odds of two prominent U.S. Supreme Court justices being raised in houses just blocks apart must be long indeed, but it happened here. Warren Burger was the high court's chief justice from 1969 until his retirement in 1986. His colleague, Harry Blackmun, served from 1970 to 1994 and is best remembered as the author of the 1973 *Roe v. Wade* opinion that legalized abortion.

21 Dayton's Bluff Elementary School

262 Bates Ave.

Freerks Sperl and Flynn, 1975 / addition, ca. 2000

Although it's elegantly composed, this school—with its slit windows and unyielding walls of purple brick—looks like a maximum-security prison for children. A colorful addition on the north side is more inviting.

22 Ecclesia Condominiums (Holman United Methodist Church) *L*

243 Bates Ave.

Boehme and Cordella, 1904 / addition, ca. 1960s

Built as a Methodist church, this is an Arts and Crafts gem with Shingle Style roots. The building has the informal, welcoming air of a small country church. Its corner tower, crowned by a flaring spire with four dainty dormers, could charm even the sourest of nonbelievers. After the Holman congregation left to merge with another church, the building was converted into condominiums.

23 Euclid View Apartments *L*

234–38 Bates Ave.

Hermann Kretz, 1894

An apartment building mounted on a high, terraced site. Arched windows and entrances on the ground floor evoke Romanesque Revival, but on the whole this isn't a building of strong stylistic persuasion. It originally contained 12 apartments but was later subdivided into 24.

223 Bates Ave.

24 Condominiums (William Schornstein Saloon and Grocery) N *L*

223 Bates Ave. (also 707 Wilson Ave.)

Augustus Gauger, 1884

When it was constructed for German immigrant William Schornstein, this building occupied a prime site a block from Hastings (later Hudson) Rd., a heavily traveled route now superseded by Interstate 94. The building is an elusive blend of Italianate, French Second Empire, Eastlake, and Queen Anne features. It included a grocery store with a saloon at the back, family apartments on the second floor, and a meeting hall in the attic, which is punctured by a profusion of dormers. An ornate balcony once extended over the cast-iron storefront facing Wilson Ave. Schornstein operated his businesses here until 1910, after which son Otto took over for another decade.

Central Dayton's Bluff

East Seventh Street

This street still follows the grade established by the improvement project of 1883–84 that carried it across Trout Brook valley and Swede Hollow and then up the bluffs. One of only two cable car lines ever built in the Twin Cities operated here, extending from downtown to a power plant at Duluth St. The cable cars debuted in 1889 but were replaced just four years later by electric trolleys. Today, Seventh is a blend of commercial, residential, institutional, and industrial uses, and it remains Dayton's Bluff's main artery.

25 Metropolitan State University

700 East Seventh St.

Dayton's Bluff's major institutional presence. Local financier Ferdinand Willius built a country estate here in about 1870, but the site's longest tenant was St. John's Hospital. The hospital occupied Willius's mansion from 1910 until 1918, when it constructed its own buildings, some of which form part of the university's compact campus.

New Main, Metropolitan State University

26 New Main

Bentz/Thompson/Rietow Architects, 1992

The campus's signature building. Long, narrow, and bridgelike, it has pavilions at either end connected by walls of fritted glass. Within, there's a large hall. Like the campus as a whole, the building could use a little more color, but it does succeed in giving the university an architectural identity it had previously lacked.

27 Stutzman Block *L*

725–33 East Seventh St.

Augustus Gauger, 1885 / 1889 / renovated, Cermak Rhoades Architects, 2001

A Victorian constructed in two phases, the corner tower coming after the rest. Carefully restored (it had been covered with stucco for many years), the building is home to the Swede Hollow Cafe and other businesses. The builder's name, W. F. Stutzman, adorns a rooftop pediment.

28 HealthEast Care Center *L*

753 East Seventh St.

Clarence H. Johnston, 1916

This property, wedged between Seventh St. and Swede Hollow, was once the site of a mighty stone mansion erected by A. W. Mayall in 1881. The mansion was torn down in 1915 to make way for a new building operated by an institution with an unblinkingly candid name: the Home for the Friendless. Later known as the Protestant Home, it's now a care center for the elderly.

29 Commercial building

798–804 Margaret St.

1895

There should be a meat market here because this is a prime example of how to butcher a historic building (which, in fact, was originally a grocery). Fortunately, the dirty deeds done on the ground floor do not extend to the upper portion, where a tile roof sports three charming dormers that look as though they might have come from a French chateau (albeit a very small one).

30 Sacred Heart Catholic Church

840 East Sixth St.

Ellerbe Architects, 1949

Sacred Heart parish was established in 1881, but this church, occupying a prominent hilltop site at Sixth and Arcade Sts., is from the modern era. Like a number of Catholic churches built in the Twin Cities after World War II, it offers an updated, simplified version of the Romanesque Revival style. Inside, there's a long nave with arcaded aisles and clerestory windows.

Bethlehem Lutheran Church, 1964

31 Bethlehem Lutheran Church

655–61 Forest St.

Emmanuel Masqueray, 1914 / addition, 1957 / Art: stained-glass windows, Gaytee Studios, ca. 1940s

A little brick church designed by the architect best known for his work on a vastly larger scale at the St. Paul Cathedral. Instead of baroque grandeur, Masqueray opted here for a crisp, somewhat abstracted version of Gothic Revival, evident in the triangles that hover over the side entrance, rise above the nave windows, and define steep dormers in the bell tower. The school addition to the south isn't sympathetic, but it's pretty much what you'd expect for the 1950s.

32 3M Corp. complex

900 Bush Ave. and surrounding area

various architects, ca. 1914 and later

Founded in 1902 in Two Harbors, MN, the company that would eventually become 3M moved in 1910 to St. Paul, where it built this 40-acre office-industrial complex. Lucius Ordway, William L. McKnight, and Archibald Bush—names that still resonate in the Twin Cities philanthropic community—were among the businessmen who built the company into an industrial colossus. In late 2006, 3M, which has been based at a campus in Maplewood since the 1960s, announced that it intends to sell all of its property here except for two office buildings. It's likely that most of the factory buildings—where tape,

900 Bush Ave.

sandpaper, and abrasive products were once made—will eventually be demolished, bringing to an end an important chapter in St. Paul's industrial history.

33 Office building

900 Bush Ave.

Toltz, King and Day with Albert Kahn Associates (Detroit), 1941 / addition, ca. 1950s

A significant St. Paul building that is often missed, in part because it's now all but hidden behind a bland seven-story addition along Seventh St. This building is also low-key, but its restrained mix of Moderne and classical styling is elegantly done. Until 3M moved to new headquarters in Maplewood in 1962, this was the company's corporate office. Like many high-style buildings of the period, its classicism is stripped to the bare bones. The design team included the St. Paul firm of Toltz, King and Day as well as the Detroit-based Albert Kahn Associates. Kahn is best known today for his industrial architecture, including the Ford Motor Company's assembly plant (1925) in St. Paul.

POI E Building No. 20 (Minerals Building)

881 Bush Ave.

ca. 1928

The interest here is primarily historical. On February 8, 1951, a thunderous butane gas explosion tore through this building, killing 15 workers and injuring 54 others.

It remains the deadliest Industrial accident in St. Paul's history.

34 Charles and Marguerite Messerli House *L*

1216 East Seventh St.

Augustus Gauger, 1886

This brick Italianate house was built for a couple who immigrated to St. Paul from the Alsace-Lorraine region along the German-French border. It's a very late example of the Italianate style, which had generally petered out by the mid-1880s.

35 "Triangle" house

1250 East Third St.

Bill Fasbender (builder), 2004

A lesson in following the letter of the law. When neighbors successfully challenged Fasbender's request for a zoning variance that would allow him to build a standard rectilinear house on a triangular lot, he didn't give up. Instead, he went back to the drawing board and produced this oddity, which meets all setback requirements by mimicking the lot's shape. Fasbender's geometric one-upmanship didn't please the neighbors, but the house is certainly an eye catcher.

36 Henry Gray House

1044 Wilson Ave.

Gilbert and Taylor, 1887

Though hardly one of Cass Gilbert's more celebrated achievements, this considerably altered home—the architect's only work in Dayton's Bluff—is still better than anything else in the vicinity. Like all good Shingle Style houses, it's more disciplined than its Queen Anne contemporaries. Here, Gilbert uses tall, steep side gables to give the house a monumental feel despite its relatively modest size.

37 William and Harriet Wakefield House

963 Wakefield Ave.

1860 and later

Here, in heavily remodeled form, is one of Dayton's Bluff's oldest houses, built for a couple who migrated to St. Paul from Rhode Island in 1856. The house has lost many of its original Italianate details, including eaves brackets and corner pilasters. Note that it's slightly angled on its lot—a

sure sign that it preceded street development in the neighborhood. In fact, the house was once part of a large estate that included a small pond. The Wakefields named their estate "What Cheer Lawn," and both lived to ripe old ages in the house, William dying in 1906 and Harriet in 1915. Wakefield Ave. was named in their honor in 1902.

38 Wolkoff Building

1075 Hudson Rd.

1942

A Moderne structure that originally served as the offices of Dr. Hyman Wolkoff, a physician. Note the circular window—a common feature of the Moderne style, which drew much of its inspiration from the streamlined look of ships (think portholes).

Mounds Park

This charming little neighborhood isn't well known to outsiders, and its residents are undoubtedly content to maintain this discreet state of affairs. The neighborhood's eponymous park is its major public attraction, but the surrounding streets also offer much of interest.

39 Mounds Park

Mounds Blvd. and Earl St.

1892 and later / **pavilion,** Charles A. Hausler with Percy Dwight Bentley, *1916* / **aerial beacon,** *1929*

Occupying a blufftop site above the Mississippi, this park is home to the oldest works of architec-

ture in the Twin Cities: earthen burial mounds built 1,500 to 2,000 years ago by the people known as the Hopewell culture. Much later, the Dakota Indians also made burials here. A park was proposed in the 1860s, but the city didn't begin acquiring land until the 1890s. The park's

Mounds Park pavilion

six mounds are all that remain, in compromised form, out of 37 that once dotted the bluffs. Relic hunters and would-be archaeologists dug up some of the larger mounds; others were destroyed by road building and related development.

Besides the mounds, the park includes two notable structures. At the end of Earl St. is a brick Prairie Style pavilion built in 1916. It's a rarity because almost all of the other Prairie Style works in the Twin Cities are either houses or small commercial structures. The park's other architectural curiosity is a 110-foot-high steel tower constructed in 1929 as an aerial beacon designed to guide aircraft flying between the Twin Cities and Chicago. The beacon, refurbished in the 1990s, still does its nightly flash dance even though electronic guidance systems have made it obsolete. It's thought to be the only beacon of its kind still operating in the United States.

POI F Department of Natural Resources (Willow Brook) Fish Hatchery

1200 Warner Rd.

1878 and later

This state hatchery, Minnesota's first, opened in 1878, using the spring-fed waters of a brook that tumbled down from Mounds Park. At its height, the facility included three ponds for hatching brook trout and walleyed pike. With its beautiful grounds at the base of the river bluffs, the hatchery became a popular local tourist attraction in the 1880s and 1890s. Today, the old grounds have been bisected by Warner Rd. and the hatching operation is conducted indoors.

POI G Bruce Vento Nature Sanctuary and Carver's Cave

Off Commercial St. beneath Mounds Blvd.

In the sandstone bluffs beneath Mounds Blvd. near Cherry St. are the remains of Carver's Cave, long one of the most famous

natural attractions in the Twin Cities. The cave is named after English explorer Jonathan Carver, who first described it in 1766. It was, of course, already well known to the local Dakota Indians, who called it *Wakan Tipi* (house of spirits) and carved animal figures into the soft sandstone walls. Inside was a spring-fed pond in a chamber that extended back about 130 feet. Around 1870, part of the cave was destroyed by railroad construction, which also blocked the entrance with debris. Over the years, various expeditions—formal and informal—have revisited the cave, which is now sealed. The cave is within the boundaries of a nature sanctuary created in 2002; there are plans to develop it as an interpretive site.

40 McLean Terrace (Mound Park School)

998 Pacific St.
(also 995 McLean Ave.)

Buechner and Jacobson, 1901 / addition, Buechner and Orth, 1910 / addition, St. Paul City Architect (Charles A. Bassford), ca. 1930s / renovated, Roark Kramer Roscoe Design, 1987

Now apartments, this is among the oldest surviving public school buildings in St. Paul, designed in the popular Romanesque Revival style of the 1890s.

41 Giesen-Hauser House ! N

827 Mound St.

Albert Zschocke, 1891

One of St. Paul's great houses, situated on a one-acre hilltop lot just south of Interstate 94. It was built for Peter and Mary Giesen, a remarkable couple who were among the most successful of Dayton's Bluff's German immigrants. Peter was a bookbinder whose fortune was assured in 1876 when his firm secured a contract to bind law books for St. Paul's West Publishing Co. Mary Dreis Giesen was his equal in business, founding a highly successful theatrical costuming firm in 1872.

Giesen-Hauser House

Architect Albert Zschocke, also German born, was a meteor who flashed across the local architectural scene in the 1880s, dying at age 33 in 1892. This house, the largest surviving example of his residential work, blends Queen Anne and Romanesque Revival elements. The tower, with its arcaded belfry beneath a steep octagonal roof, is one of the city's most romantic. Other features include a wraparound porch, a one-story turret supporting a balustraded brick balcony, and a pair of dormers that peep out from the roof like the watchful eyes of a child.

The Giesens sold the house in 1907. The next owner, Eric Hauser, was a railroad contractor who also had a hand in building New York City's subways. After the Hauser family sold the house in 1944, it was cut into apartments but is now again a single-family dwelling.

42 Glennis Ter Wisscha–James Lano House

865 Mound St.

John Howe (from his plans), 1995

A hilltop house designed by John Howe, who served for 25 years as Frank Lloyd Wright's chief draftsman before establishing his own practice in the Twin Cities in 1967. Most of his commissions were in the suburbs; this is his only work in St. Paul. Not surprisingly, Howe's designs have a distinct Wrightian quality. This house, clad in redwood siding, is of modest size and features an octagonal living room bathed in natural light.

43 Mounds Park Residence (Smith-Davidson-Scheffer House)

908 Mound St.

ca. 1850s / enlarged, 1886 / later remodelings

This nursing home is what remains of the historic Smith-Davidson-Scheffer House, named after its most prominent owners. It was built around 1856 as a country estate. In 1886, a new owner—steamboat tycoon William Davidson (known as "Commodore")—greatly enlarged the house and surrounded it with porches decorated in a gaudy Victorian style called Steamboat Gothic. Later, when it became a nursing home, the mansion was stripped of its riverboat finery. Modern houses at 50, 54, 60, and 64 Bates now occupy the lower portion of the old mansion property.

Payne-Phalen

The oldest section of this neighborhood, located between Swede Hollow and the nearby Trout Brook valley, is a fascinating enclave known as Railroad Island. Its name is aptly descriptive: the neighborhood is all but surrounded by a web of tracks. With its steep hills, small houses, and narrow streets, the neighborhood has the tight, gritty feel of an old Pennsylvania railroad town. In the early days of St. Paul, mansions dotted the hillsides here. By the 1860s, however, Swedish, Irish, and Italian immigrants began pouring into the neighborhood, and it took on the working-class character that it maintains to this day. The neighborhood includes an important pre–Civil War home—the Benjamin Brunson House (1855).

North of Railroad Island, to either side of Payne, is another hilly grid of streets lined with a mixed housing stock, mostly dating from between about 1885 and 1920. Architecturally, this area is not especially well documented, but it offers much of interest. A number of streets—Case, York, Geranium, and Jessamine avenues in particular—have intriguing pockets of Victoriana, and there are also some fine old churches. Two architectural treasures are the Olaf Lee House (1905), a delightful mix of Craftsman and Swiss chalet elements, and the Italianate-style Jacob Hinkel House (1872).

Farther north and east, near Lake Phalen, the neighborhood takes on a more modern character. Here you'll find the usual assortment of bungalows and Period Revival houses from the 1920s and 1930s, along with Levittown-style Cape Cods, ramblers, and ranch houses built in the 1950s and later. Phalen Park, most of which is devoted to a golf course, provides a large green backdrop for some of this housing. Located at the edge of the park is one of Payne-Phalen's architectural jewels—the delightful, Spanish-flavored Minnesota Humanities Commission building (1925), formerly Gillette Children's Hospital.

POI A Phalen Park

Arcade St. and Wheelock Pkwy.

1899 and later

This park, which like its namesake lake extends north into suburban Maplewood, opened in 1899 and includes a golf course as well as St. Paul's only public beach. The deep lake once provided drinking water for the city and is the source of Phalen Creek, now largely diverted underground.

POI B Ice Palace Plaque

Island in channel between Phalen and Round lakes

A plaque marks the site of the 1986 St. Paul Winter Carnival Centennial Ice Palace, which attracted an estimated one million visitors during its brief existence. The palace was at that time the largest built in St. Paul since before World War II. Designed by Karl Ermanis of Ellerbe Architects, the palace was an elegant arrangement of slender, gravity-defying towers, the highest reaching over 128 feet. Most aficionados of ice construction regard this palace as the greatest of the modern era in St. Paul, unrivaled for its beauty and daring.

Ice Palace, 1986

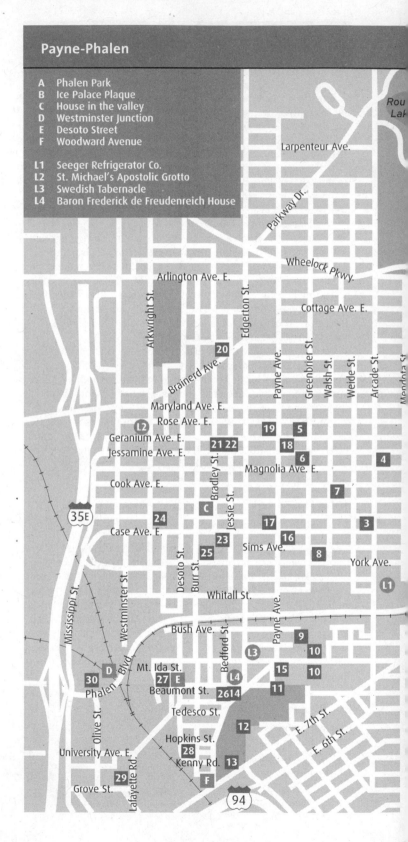

Payne-Phalen

A   Phalen Park
B   Ice Palace Plaque
C   House in the valley
D   Westminster Junction
E   Desoto Street
F   Woodward Avenue

L1   Seeger Refrigerator Co.
L2   St. Michael's Apostolic Grotto
L3   Swedish Tabernacle
L4   Baron Frederick de Freudenreich House

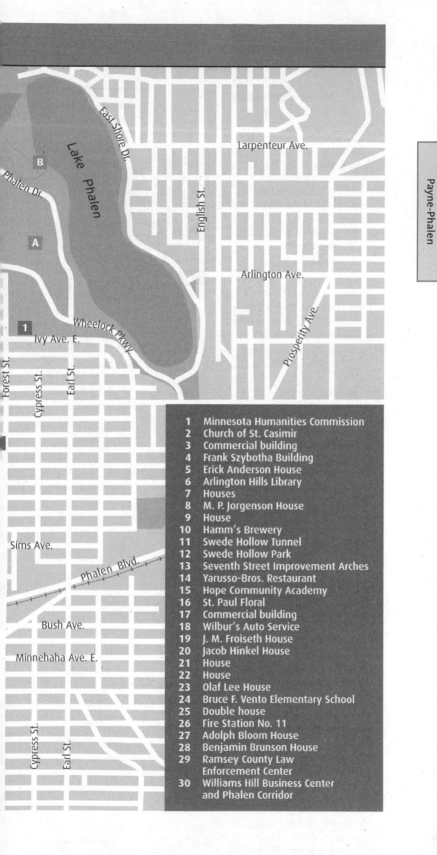

Larpenteur Ave.

East Shore Dr.

Lake Phalen

Phalen Dr.

English St.

Arlington Ave.

Prosperity Ave.

Wheelock Pkwy.

Ivy Ave. E.

Forest St.

Cypress St.

Earl St.

Sims Ave.

Phalen Blvd.

Bush Ave.

Minnehaha Ave. E.

Cypress St.

Earl St.

1   Minnesota Humanities Commission
2   Church of St. Casimir
3   Commercial building
4   Frank Szybotha Building
5   Erick Anderson House
6   Arlington Hills Library
7   Houses
8   M. P. Jorgenson House
9   House
10   Hamm's Brewery
11   Swede Hollow Tunnel
12   Swede Hollow Park
13   Seventh Street Improvement Arches
14   Yarusso-Bros. Restaurant
15   Hope Community Academy
16   St. Paul Floral
17   Commercial building
18   Wilbur's Auto Service
19   J. M. Froiseth House
20   Jacob Hinkel House
21   House
22   House
23   Olaf Lee House
24   Bruce F. Vento Elementary School
25   Double house
26   Fire Station No. 11
27   Adolph Bloom House
28   Benjamin Brunson House
29   Ramsey County Law
     Enforcement Center
30   Williams Hill Business Center
     and Phalen Corridor

Minnesota Humanities Commission

1 Minnesota Humanities Commission (Michael J. Dowling Memorial Hall) *L*

987 Ivy Ave. East

Clarence H. Johnston, 1925 / renovated and restored, Finn Daniels Architects, 1996 / Art: carved tiles, Henry C. Mercer / plaster sculptures, Brioschi-Minuti Co.?

This captivating building is all that remains of the former Gillette Children's Hospital campus, most of which was razed in 1979 after Gillette relocated to Regions Hospital in downtown St. Paul. Founded in 1897, Gillette moved here in 1911 to a campus that ultimately consisted of ten low-slung, Spanish Revival–style buildings.

Dowling Memorial Hall is named for Michael J. Dowling, a state legislator who lost his hands and feet to frostbite and became an advocate for disabled children. Designed as an education wing, the building features a beautiful arched entryway and bright interior spaces adorned with whimsical details, including carved tiles from Moravian Pottery of Pennsylvania and plaster sculptures probably by the Brioschi-Minuti Co. of St. Paul. The building as a whole is light, spacious, and cheerful, quite unlike any hospital or school of recent vintage. Despite its significance, the building stood vacant for nearly two decades until it was renovated in 1996 to serve as administrative offices and a conference center for the Humanities Commission.

2 Church of St. Casimir **N** *L*

937 Jessamine Ave. East

Boehme and Cordella, 1904 / renovated (interior) Haarstick Lundgren and Associates, 1956

A twin-towered Renaissance Revival–style church built for a parish established by Polish immigrants in 1892. As built, the

Church of St. Casimir

church displayed a more Eastern European character, its towers topped by traditional onion domes, which were later replaced by the present egg-shaped domes. Within, the church features a barrel-vaulted ceiling rising from elegant Corinthian columns that project out into the nave. Minneapolis architect Victor Cordella, who designed the church, was a native of Poland. The old parish school, built next door in 1924, is also a strong design.

Arcade Street

East Seventh St. to Larpenteur Ave.

Like nearby Payne Ave., portions of Arcade St. developed as a commercial corridor with the arrival of streetcars in the late nineteenth century. The trolleys ran as far north as Case Ave. before turning east. The most significant complex of buildings along Arcade—the old Seeger Refrigerator Co. manufacturing plant—is gone, and today the street is home to a mix of modest commercial buildings and residences.

LOST 1 *The Seeger Square Shopping Mall at Arcade and Wells Sts. occupies the site of the* **Seeger Refrigerator Co.** *At its height, the Seeger* *plant sprawled over 14 acres, employed up to 5,000 people, and manufactured one in every ten of the nation's refrigerators, many of which were marketed under the Cold Spot label by Sears, Roebuck. Absorbed by the Whirlpool Corp. in the 1950s, Seeger continued to produce refrigerators and freezers until the plant closed in 1984. It was then demolished to make way for the shopping mall and other redevelopment.*

3 Commercial building

965 Arcade St.

1921

A one-story building that displays a passing resemblance to some of the small-town banks designed by Prairie Style architects such as William Purcell and George Elmslie.

4 Frank Szybotha Building

1110 Arcade St.

1919

The original owner operated a grocery store here and lived upstairs, a common arrangement at the time.

Erick Anderson House

5 Erick Anderson House

671 Geranium Ave. East

1896

A rarity: a worker's cottage built largely of stone. Anderson was a mason and obviously decided to display his skills here. The first floor consists of an irregular mix of rock-faced and smooth sandstone blocks, beautifully put together. The second story is brick, but its windows have stone sills and lintels.

6 Arlington Hills Library N *L*

1105 Greenbrier St.

St. Paul City Architect (Charles A. Hausler), 1916

One of three classically inspired neighborhood libraries constructed by the City of St. Paul in 1916–17 (the other two, also designed by then city architect Charles Hausler, are the Riverview and St. Anthony Park branches). Andrew Carnegie financed all three libraries, among the last to be built under a program sponsored by the steel titan, who died in 1919. With its Ionic pilasters, arches, simple parapet, and strict symmetry, the library is an excellent example of how even small public buildings of this period could achieve a monumental effect.

7 Houses

746, 748, 754, 756, 762 Cook Ave. East

1883–88

A group of pattern book Queen Annes with angled corner towers, likely all the work of the same builder.

8 M. P. Jorgenson House

718 Sims Ave. East

Omeyer and Thori, 1888

A brick house that combines a hodgepodge of styles—Queen Anne, Classical Revival, Romanesque Revival, Eastlake, Italianate, and heaven knows what else.

9 House

656 Bush Ave.

1880

Hidden away on a dead-end street just east of Payne Ave., this small, mildly Italianate house appears to be one of the best preserved of its era in the neighborhood.

Hamm's Brewery, 1946

10 Hamm's Brewery !

707 Minnehaha Ave. East

*ca. 1860s / **brew house**, August Maritzen (Chicago), 1894 / 1901 / ca. 1950s*

A largely vacant East Side industrial colossus with an uncertain future, in part because old breweries are inherently difficult to reuse but also because the Hamm's complex has lost much of its historic appearance to modern remodelings. Lacking the Victorian curb appeal of other old breweries, such as the Grain Belt in Minneapolis or the Schmidt in St. Paul, the Hamm's complex will be a challenge to redevelop.

Founded in 1864 by Theodore Hamm, the brewery was operated by his descendants for over a century. It was not only the largest brewery in St. Paul but one of the five largest in the country by the 1950s. Like many other regional brewers, Hamm's fell on hard times in the 1960s, and the company was sold. Several owners followed until the last one, Stroh Brewing Co. of Detroit, closed the brewery for good in 1997.

At its frothy zenith, the brewery included about 40 buildings.

It's believed that the complex's oldest surviving structure (damaged by fire in 2005) is a stone-walled carpentry shop from the 1860s. Unfortunately, the brewery's centerpiece—a domed brew house built in 1894—has been extensively modernized, although some of its original walls with their arched windows still stand. Parts of the old brewery are now used for warehousing, but the future of the complex as a whole is by no means assured.

11 Swede Hollow Tunnel

Beaumont St. near Drewry Ln.

ca. 1880s

For well over 100 years, the major access point into Swede Hollow was this short tunnel, which made it possible for wagons to negotiate the otherwise steep descent from Payne Ave. The tunnel is still used today, although it's now just as easy to enter the hollow from the bike trail that begins at Payne and East Seventh.

12 Swede Hollow Park

East of Payne Ave. between East Seventh St. and Minnehaha Ave.

This precipitous ravine, a small green gash steeped in history and legend, is among the most mysterious places in the Twin Cities. It seems a world away

Swede Hollow, 1910

from the city around it, even more so than the equally deep but more frequently visited glen of Minnehaha Creek in Minneapolis. Although it's a quiet, almost wild place now, Swede Hollow was for many years a unique residential neighborhood, home to a succession of immigrants who built houses by the fast-flowing waters of Phalen Creek. As late as 1905, fully 1,000 people were living in the hollow.

One of St. Paul's pioneer residents, an unpleasant and apparently murderous ex-soldier named Edward Phelan, was the hollow's first settler in 1841. In its pristine state, the little valley would have offered wood for heat, fresh water, and protection from fierce winter winds. What it never did offer, however, was easy access to water and sewer lines as the city grew around it. Without such services, it attracted some of the city's poorest immigrants—Swedes, Poles, Italians, and Mexicans. Families continued to live here until the 1950s, when the city cleared everybody out. Old housing foundations are all that remain of this unusual neighborhood.

The hollow also attracted industry. Several gristmills were operating by the 1850s along Phalen Creek, known in its early days as Mill Creek. Later, what was to become Hamm's Brewery located at the northern end of the hollow near Minnehaha Ave. By 1865, railroad tracks had also been built through the valley, which provided a relatively easy grade up from the Mississippi River.

After the city evicted the last 14 families from the hollow in 1956, it became a hobo jungle and dumping ground. In the 1970s, local residents and the St. Paul Garden Club began working with the city to turn the derelict valley into a park. Today, a bike and walking trail follows the old railroad grade and a portion of Phalen Creek—long confined to tunnels—has been reopened. Plans are in the works to further improve the park and to connect it to the Mississippi River corridor via a new trail.

13 Seventh Street Improvement Arches ! N ▲

East Seventh St. across Swede Hollow

William A. Truesdell, 1884

This double-arched stone bridge is one of the most astonishing structures in the Twin Cities. What makes it so extraordinary is its use of the so-called helicoidal or spiral method of construction—a sophisticated and mathematically challenging form of arch design invented in 1828 by an English architect.

William Truesdell, the 38-year-old engineer in charge of the project, decided to build helicoidal arches here because he was faced with a difficult problem: Seventh St. crossed the railroad tracks at a 63-degree angle, necessitating an oblique design, a tricky proposition when the material is stone. Truesdell had to use stone for the bridge because it carried a tremendous amount of weight—not only Seventh St. itself but also a thick layer of fill required as part of the street's regrading. Because of the angled crossing, however, standard arch construction would have dictated the use of precisely cut stone blocks of many different shapes.

"The cost of such a work would have been beyond all consideration," Truesdell later wrote. The spiral method, by contrast, had one signal advantage: almost all

Seventh Street Improvement Arches

of the blocks of Mankato-Kasota limestone used for the double arch could be cut in the same shape, saving both time and money. Truesdell, whose hobby was mathematics, was up to the task, and so St. Paul acquired one of the few bridges of its kind in the United States. In 2000, the arches were designated a Historic Engineering Landmark by the American Society of Civil Engineers. The arches aren't visible from above on Seventh but can be readily seen along the Bruce Vento Regional Trail, accessible at Seventh and Payne.

Payne Avenue

This street is named after Rice Payne, a real estate speculator who spent a short time in St. Paul in the 1850s before returning to Virginia and later serving as a Confederate officer during the Civil War. Historically, the avenue is best known for its role in the life of the East Side's early Scandinavian and Italian immigrant communities. In fact, it was once said that if you couldn't speak Swedish you'd have trouble doing business on Payne. Of late, the ethnic mix has changed markedly—fluency in Spanish or Hmong is likely to be of more linguistic help than Swedish.

Payne's eclectic mix of buildings offers a chronological cross section of architecture in St. Paul. The lower portion near Swede Hollow has the oldest stock of buildings, including some houses, and an Italian flavor provided by such longtime establishments as Yarusso-Bros. Restaurant (1933). From Minnehaha Ave. north to Maryland Ave., Payne developed as an almost exclusively commercial street in the 1880s after a horsecar line was built. Trolleys replaced the horsecars just a few years later, in 1891.

14 Yarusso-Bros. Restaurant

635 Payne Ave.

Kopp and Lee (builder), 1933

A Payne Ave. institution, founded in 1933 by Francesco and Dora Yarusso, Italian immigrants who lived for a time in Swede Hollow just across the street. Still in the Yarusso family, the restaurant also is home to St. Paul's oldest bocce ball courts and has a small version of the Statue of Liberty mounted on the roof.

15 Hope Community Academy (Hamm's Brewery Offices)

720 Payne Ave.

Clarence H. Johnston, Jr., 1937 / addition, ca. 1947 / addition, ATS & R Architects, 2006

A rather buttoned-down variant of art deco sometimes called PWA Moderne, built as offices for Hamm's Brewery. Before wings were added in the 1940s and again in 2006, the building presented a symmetrical front; its original portion still conveys a sense of classical formality. Hope Community Academy, a Hmong charter school, took over the building in 2000.

16 St. Paul Floral

960 Payne Ave.

James Forsyth (builder), 1886

With its mansard roof, gabled dormers, and ornate oriel window on the north side, this charmer—altered at street level—looks like something you might find in Europe.

17 Commercial building (Payne Avenue State Bank)

961–63 Payne Ave.

William Linley Alban, 1922 / renovated, 2006

The avenue's most impressive work of commercial architecture, originally built as a bank. Its prominent corner location,

monumental Ionic columns, and tall first floor with plate-glass windows are all typical of banks built in the early twentieth century. Renovation of the formerly vacant building began in 2006; it will become home to a credit union and offices.

18 Wilbur's Auto Service

1138 Payne Ave. North

J. F. and L. A. Cramer (builders), 1925

Gas came with a touch of sun-drenched California at this old service station now used by an auto repair business. Beautifully kept, the building is one of the avenue's gems.

19 J. M. Froiseth House

1153 Payne Ave.

J. M. Froiseth, 1889

Froiseth, a builder, produced this delightful small home that features an arched entrance and subtle brick detailing.

Jacob Hinkel House

20 Jacob Hinkel House ! N

531 Brainerd Ave.

1872

This restored house, which sits on a generous lot, is a beautiful example of the Italian Villa (also known as Italianate) style. It's the only wood-frame Italianate house in St. Paul that still sports a cupola, albeit a reconstructed one. Other Italianate elements include tall arched windows, thin porch columns, bracketed eaves, and a shallow central gable. Houses of this type were popularized by Andrew Jackson Downing and other American tastemakers around 1850 as a romantic counter-reaction to the chaste Greek Revival style.

The home (original cost: $8,000) was built as a country estate by Jacob Hinkel, who made his money in railroading and by cutting ice from local lakes. Hinkel apparently spent too much in pursuit of his domestic dream, however: buffeted by the depression of 1873, he defaulted on his payments and lost the house in 1876. The house then went through the usual vicissitudes of ownership and various remodelings until 1970, when it was purchased by a couple who undertook the restoration visible today.

St. Michael's Apostolic Grotto, 1935

LOST 2 *Behind an ordinary house at 376 Rose Ave. East there was once a remarkable work of folk architecture:* **St. Michael's Apostolic Grotto,** *hand built in the early 1930s by Gabriel Pizzuti, who wanted to be a priest but married instead. Using stone, concrete, and salvage items, Pizzuti fashioned a unique testimony to his faith that included an 18-by-12-foot chapel and two towers. The grotto gradually fell into disrepair after Pizzuti's death in 1981 and was demolished seven years later.*

21 House

525 Jessamine Ave. East
Fred U. Hand (builder), 1888

A curvaceous Shingle Style house that crowns one of the neighborhood's many hills. Now extensively modified, the house must have been quite a beauty in its day.

543 Jessamine Ave. East

22 House

543 Jessamine Ave. East
James Acklin (builder), 1888

Even more impressive than its hilltop neighbor to the east, this brick Queen Anne features a hefty side tower sporting a polygonal roof, a wraparound porch, and a front bay with sandstone lintels over the windows. There are also mysterious details, such as two stone globes resembling oversized bowling balls mounted atop a pair of tall piers to either side of the front bay. Another odd piece of stonework, a finial in the shape of an urn (or perhaps an inverted bowling pin), crowns the tower roof.

Olaf Lee House

23 Olaf Lee House N

955 Jessie St.
Clarence H. Johnston, 1905

You might feel an urge to yodel when you pass by this house, which evokes a chalet in the Alps with such features as overhanging eaves supported by wooden brackets, zigzag half-timbering, a jerkinhead roof, and an attic balcony adorned with a slat-style balustrade. Although its alpine aura makes this house a rarity in St. Paul, it does fit within the period's broader Craftsman esthetic. It was built for Olaf Lee, a pharmacist who owned two neighborhood drugstores. How he came to hire an architect of Johnston's caliber is unknown, as is his reason for wanting a chalet-style house. In any event, Lee must have liked his Swiss fantasy: he lived here with his family until his death in 1937.

POI C House in the valley

1011 Bradley St.

1889

The hill here is so steep that Bradley St. couldn't be extended through this block, leaving a small pocket of woods. Down in this valley there's a house, visible in winter but hidden once the foliage comes out. Such forested hideaways are scattered all throughout the East Side, and they are one of the reasons St. Paul has always seemed a more mysterious city than Minneapolis.

24 Bruce F. Vento (East Consolidated) Elementary School

409 Case Ave. East

Freerks Sperl and Flynn, 1971 / addition, Cuningham Group, 2002

This Brutalist exercise in brick and concrete—named after a longtime St. Paul congressman—was originally known as East Consolidated, and it does indeed have the look of something large, bureaucratic, and punitive. Arranged in one-story sections that step down a hillside, the school is not the least bit inviting. Even so, it's a strong and consistent design, which is more than can be said for most of the city's other public schools of this period. A curvy addition built on the south side of the school in the 1990s manages to soften up the tough-guy appearance of the original.

25 Double house

904–6 Burr St.

John H. Coxhead, 1889

A Romanesque Revival double house with a steep front gable rising above an intricately shingled arch. There's also an exotic onion-dome roof, complete with finial, atop the corner turret.

POI D Westminster Junction

Near Westminster St., south of Whitall St.

1860s and later

This complex railroad junction, best seen from the Phalen Blvd. bridge east of Mississippi St., is an important historic site. Three railroads, all following the grade of Trout Brook valley up from the Mississippi River, once intersected here in a maze of tunnels, walls, and bridges. As late as the 1930s, 1,000 or more freight cars and nearly 100 passenger trains passed through the junction on an average day. In the 1880s, the Northern Pacific Railroad, seeking a way through the already clogged corridor, built four stone tunnels, the longest more than 1,000 feet, to accommodate its freight and passenger traffic. A keystone reading "1885" is visible on the south portal of the long tunnel. The junction, still in use today, is not as busy as it used to be.

LOST 3 *The nondescript apartment building at 579 Minnehaha Ave. East stands on the site of the* **Swedish Tabernacle.** *Designed by Queen Anne masters Didrik Omeyer and Martin Thori in a style known only to them, the church—completed in 1904—featured two towers separated by a rounded gable vaguely baroque in character. It was demolished in 1963.*

LOST 4 *Near what used to be 547 Beaumont St., modern homes occupy a hilltop that for over 140 years was the site of the* **Baron Frederick de Freudenreich House.** *The baron (an honorary title) was a Swiss immigrant, and his house—built in 1854—presented a* *unique style that might be called Alpine Greek Revival. Described as "a gentleman of culture, taste,*

Baron Frederick de Freudenreich House, 1905

refinement and education," Freudenreich died in 1872. The house, later occupied by pioneer photographer Edward Bromley, stood until the mid-1990s, when it was torn down despite protests from preservationists.

26 Fire Station No. 11

676 Bedford St.

Havelock E. Hand, 1890

Now a fire department mainte-nance shop, this is one of St. Paul's few surviving nineteenth-century fire stations. The Romanesque Revival building has been modified: paint covers its brick and stone walls and the original arched entries are now squared off.

POI E Desoto Street

Minnehaha Ave. East to Tedesco St.

This alleylike street, which lacks the usual side boulevard of grass, is one of the narrowest in St. Paul, resembling something you might see in Boston or even Europe (though the old houses, some of which date as far back as the 1870s, are unmistakably American). The right-of-way is so tight that there wasn't room to put power poles on the sidewalk, so they stand in the street.

27 Adolph Bloom House

416 Mount Ida St.

1890

A Queen Anne funhouse that fairly shouts for attention. Despite its asbestos siding, the

Adolph Bloom House

house has retained much of its original and highly exuberant detail. Features worth noting are the bell-roofed corner tower with second-story porch, the Moorish-style arched window on the second floor, and the dormer that projects from the peak of the roof. Little is known about original owner Adolph Bloom, but judging by this house you'd have to guess that he wasn't a timid man.

POI F Woodward Avenue

Payne Ave. just north of East Seventh St.

Woodward Ave. is a vestigial street that once extended well to the west. It leads to nowhere in particular these days, but in the last half of the nineteenth cen-tury it was lined with mansions. What drew the wealthy to this area was the once pristine Trout Brook valley. In the 1870s and 1880s, however, the valley was transformed into a busy rail cor-ridor, and the neighborhood quickly lost its residential cachet. Most of the mansions were gone by the early 1900s.

28 Benjamin Brunson House N *L*

485 Kenny Rd.

Benjamin Brunson (builder), 1855 / renovated and restored, Design for Preservation, 2000

One of the best preserved of St. Paul's pre–Civil War houses and a rare surviving example in Minnesota of the Federal Style, a

Benjamin Brunson House, 1896

Colonial variation popular along the eastern seaboard from about 1780 to 1820. The Brunson House, basically a two-story brick box with a rear appendage, is a much-simplified provincial version of the style. Nicely restored, the house seems out of place amid the warehouses and other commercial buildings that predominate in this part of Railroad Island. When Benjamin Brunson built the house, however, the area was still largely rural, and he must have enjoyed fine views of Trout Brook valley just to the west.

Brunson and his brother, Ira, are best known to history as surveyors. They are credited with making the first land survey of St. Paul in 1847, the same year Benjamin arrived in the city. Benjamin Brunson did the survey work for many early city plats, among them the neighborhood around his house, known to this day as Brunson's Addition.

29 Ramsey County Law Enforcement Center

425 Grove St.

Wold Architects, 2003

A large new jail and sheriff's office that's quite varied stylistically but seems to draw some of its inspiration from the early Prairie Style bank and commercial buildings of Frank Lloyd Wright. It certainly doesn't look as forbidding as most jails, and it's downright sunny compared to the rather grim "public safety facility" (i.e., jail) that opened in downtown Minneapolis in 2001.

30 Williams Hill Business Center and Phalen Corridor

Phalen Blvd. near Mississippi St.

1998 and later

This industrial park is part of the Phalen Corridor Initiative, a plan to redevelop about 100 acres of old and often polluted industrial land along a new road named Phalen Blvd. Completed in 2005, the boulevard begins at Interstate 35E, follows rail lines that skirt the northern edge of Swede Hollow, and ends at Maryland Ave. Its construction obliterated at least one historic structure of note: a superb stone wall, built in 1892, that used to divide a portion of Wells St.

Williams Hill Business Center lies at the western end of the boulevard. It takes its name from a high hill that was once dotted with houses, some built before the Civil War. The houses were all gone by the 1970s, after which the historic hill was mined for its sand and gravel until it, too, disappeared.

Payne-Phalen

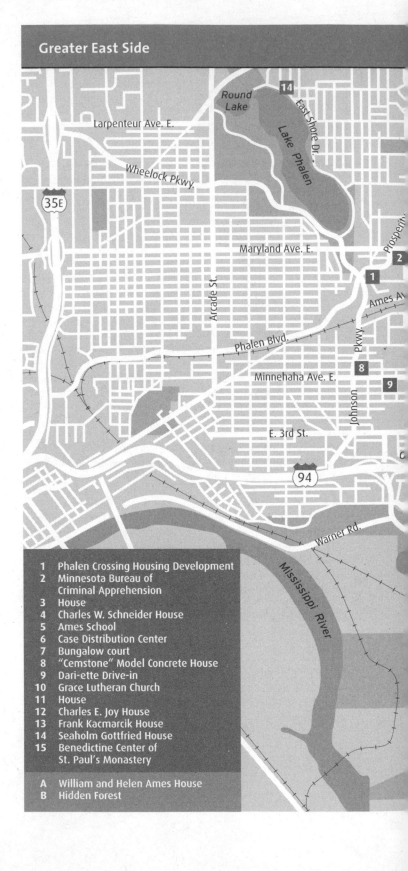

Greater East Side

1 Phalen Crossing Housing Development
2 Minnesota Bureau of
   Criminal Apprehension
3 House
4 Charles W. Schneider House
5 Ames School
6 Case Distribution Center
7 Bungalow court
8 "Cemstone" Model Concrete House
9 Dari-ette Drive-in
10 Grace Lutheran Church
11 House
12 Charles E. Joy House
13 Frank Kacmarcik House
14 Seaholm Gottfried House
15 Benedictine Center of
   St. Paul's Monastery

A William and Helen Ames House
B Hidden Forest

Greater East Side

These neighborhoods are for the most part quite new compared to other sections of St. Paul, and much of the housing stock is post–World War II. The area north of Minnehaha Avenue comprises the Greater East Side. Industry and railroads arrived here by the 1870s, when some small houses were also built. In 1885 William Ames platted a rail commuter suburb here called Hazel Park. It never flourished, however, and only a few houses from its early days remain. Among them is the superb Charles W. Schneider House (1890). Across the border in Maplewood is another architectural surprise—the stark and powerful St. Paul's Monastery (1965).

South of the Greater East Side is Battle Creek, much of which wasn't developed until the 1960s. The neighborhood's eponymous creek is its major landscape feature. Set within a green corridor of parks, the stream tumbles through a rocky glen before emptying into the Mississippi. Above the creek, modern houses occupy wooded lots reached by short streets that often end in cul-de-sacs. The feeling is very suburban even though downtown St. Paul is just two miles away.

The sense of being in a suburb in the city is even more pronounced in Highwood Hills. No other neighborhood in St. Paul or Minneapolis feels so remote and isolated, which is remarkable considering how close it is to downtown. Highwood Hills also offers dramatic terrain. Its steep streets wind up ravines to wooded hilltops where houses perch on large lots overlooking the Mississippi River Valley. Here you'll find the exquisite Frank Kacmarcik House (1962), the only Twin Cities work by Marcel Breuer, the Hungarian-born architect best known in Minnesota for his Abbey Church at St. John's University. Highwood Hills' oldest homes lie below the bluffs in Burlington Heights, founded in the 1880s as a commuter suburb, much like Hazel Park. It, too, failed to flourish, and only a dozen or so houses were ever built. Most of them, including the wonderful Charles E. Joy House (1888), can be seen today along Point Douglas Road, which parallels Highway 61.

Greater East Side

1 Phalen Crossing Housing Development

Johnson Pkwy. and Phalen Blvd.

Pope Associates, 2004 and later

One of the largest housing developments ever built on the East Side. Almost 300 units in a variety of forms spread across a 14-acre site once occupied by a 1960s-vintage shopping mall. The project includes new roads, new landscaping, and a restored pond. It's hard to argue with the effort here, but the vaguely nostalgic housing offers little of architectural interest.

2 Minnesota Bureau of Criminal Apprehension

1430 Maryland Ave. East

Leonard Parker Associates, 2003 / Art: Prints-Passages (sculpture), Jon Isherwood

This new state building overlooks the Phalen Crossing development. With its long, carefully framed bands of windows, it seems to draw inspiration from the so-called Corporate International style of the 1950s. Clad largely in brick, the building is divided into wings separated by a courtyard plaza, home to Jon Isherwood's fanciful rock sculpture of a fingerprint pattern.

POI A William and Helen Ames House

1667 Ames Ave.

ca. 1883

The interest here is chiefly historical. William L. Ames, Jr., built
this now considerably modified
house in about 1883, a few years
before he began developing Hazel
Park. The house's unusually large
lot indicates that it predates
other houses in the development.
The small rail station that once
served Hazel Park was located
near this house.

3 House

993 Flandrau St.

1890

One of the original Hazel Park
houses, closer to the Stick Style
than anything else. A more elaborate Stick Style house from 1887
stood just up the street at 1007
Flandrau but was replaced in
recent years by a nondescript
modern home.

4 Charles W. Schneider House ! N *L*

1750 Ames Pl.

Allen H. Stem, 1890

A Shingle Style beauty built for
a bookkeeper at the St. Paul Pioneer Press and one of a handful of
late nineteenth-century homes
that formed the nucleus of Hazel
Park. This house's boulder base,
shingle-clad second story, and
polygonal tower are all signature
Shingle Style elements; here
they're combined in a way that
manages to strike a romantic
pose without compromising the
overall discipline of the design.
Architect Allen Stem designed
several other exquisite Shingle
Style homes in St. Paul, including
the William Horne House (1889)
in the Crocus Hill neighborhood.

5 Ames School

1760 Ames Pl.

*St. Paul City Architect (Charles A.
Hausler), 1915 / additions, 1923
and later*

One of the more monumental
of St. Paul's public school buildings, with a pair of ornate entries
set between colossal paired brick
columns. It's one of the earliest
designs of Charles Hausler, St.
Paul's first city architect, who
served in that position from 1914
until 1922. The school was named
after William L. Ames, Sr., an
East Side settler who owned a
large farm in the area. Ames's
son later developed the surrounding Hazel Park area.

Charles W. Schneider House, 1983

6 Case Distribution Center (Walter A. Wood Harvester Co.)

1921 Case Ave.

Edward. P. Bassford, ca. 1892 and later

One of the oldest industrial sites on the East Side: its history goes back to about 1875, when the St. Paul Harvester Co. built a plant here to make farm machinery. The Walter A. Wood Harvester Co. took over the site in 1891 and constructed the large brick industrial buildings still visible today. The Wood Co.—which manufactured binders, mowers, and something called a horse hay rake—survived only two years before going under in the depression of 1893. Later used for making twine and manufacturing guns during World War II, the brick buildings were acquired in the 1960s by 3M. A warehouse complex now operates on the site.

7 Bungalow court

1842–58 Reaney Ave.

G. A. Moshier, 1928

Three double bungalows, of no strong style, arranged around a grassy courtyard. Bungalow courts were most commonly built in California, though a handful appeared in St. Paul and Minneapolis in the 1920s. This is the only one of its kind on the East Side.

"Cemstone" Model Concrete House, 1937

8 "Cemstone" Model Concrete House

1345 Minnehaha Ave. East

Cemstone Products Co., 1937 / remodeled, 1950s and later

In 1937, 200 people paid a dime each to tour this home, which no longer looks as radically new as it did in those days. Before its appearance was altered, however, it was indeed unusual. All concrete, it was built as a "concept house" by the Cemstone Products Co., founded in 1927 a few blocks east on Minnehaha Ave., where the company still maintains a plant. Concept houses—designed to show off new technologies and new building materials—were popular in the 1930s.

As originally designed, the Moderne-style house was loosely modeled on one featured at the 1933–34 Century of Progress Exposition in Chicago. The design included a rounded corner balcony (still visible), blocky massing, and, shockingly, a flat roof. Alas, these distinctive qualities failed to impress later owners, who installed new siding and put a gable on the roof, among other "improvements."

Battle Creek

9 Dari-ette Drive-in

1440 Minnehaha Ave. East

Mike Fida (builder), 1951

One of the last drive-ins of its era in St. Paul, built before the great American roadside was McDonaldized. The stucco building is plain as can be, but the wonderful neon sign belongs in a museum if, God forbid, the place ever closes.

Dari-ette Drive-in

POI B Hidden Forest

Block bounded by White Bear Ave., Hazel, Third, and Fifth Sts.

This part of the East Side contains a number of oversized blocks, unique in the Twin Cities, in which houses occupy deep lots around the perimeter of a thick forest (which here holds a storm retention pond). The effect is peculiar: you're in the city, yet the houses and yards seem to have been carved out of a mysterious wilderness lying just beyond the reach of civilization.

10 Grace Lutheran Church

1730 Old Hudson Rd.

Gauger and Associates, 1962 / addition, ca. 1990s

An unusual church with folded concrete walls influenced by the nearly contemporaneous work of Marcel Breuer at St. John's University. What really sets this church apart, however, is its clock tower—an angular, tapering affair topped by an upthrust roof from which a large, inwardly tilted cross dangles as though suspended from a crane. The effect is truly odd; the whole composition has the otherworldly feel of something out of German expressionism.

Highwood Hills

11 House

482 Point Douglas Rd. South

Charles E. Joy, 1895

This historic Burlington Heights house, a mix of the Queen Anne and Shingle styles, is attributed to Charles Joy, although it's not as nice as his own home a few blocks away.

Charles Joy House

12 Charles E. Joy House

882 Point Douglas Rd. South

Charles E. Joy, 1888

Architect Charles Joy was best known in his day as the designer of the two most glorious of all St. Paul Winter Carnival ice palaces—the second (1887) and the third (1888). Joy also designed houses, including his own and several others in the Burlington Heights development. This house is the most impressive of the small group of Victorians along and near Point Douglas Rd. Although the house has been

altered, it retains its outstanding feature: an arched stone entryway.

Frank Kacmarcik House

13 Frank Kacmarcik House !

2065 Wildview Ave.

Marcel Breuer, 1962

One of St. Paul's few high-art modern houses, beautifully sited atop a bluff overlooking the Mississippi. Not surprisingly, the house has ties to architect Marcel Breuer's most renowned work in Minnesota—the buildings, including the Abbey Church (1961), he designed at St. John's University. Frank Kacmarcik taught art and design at St. John's, where he later became a monk and was also a noted liturgical consultant.

Low-keyed and surprisingly intimate, the house is arranged in the form of an irregular L around a modest courtyard, and it's oriented so that every major room ends in a wall of glass offering views of the river valley.

Like most of Breuer's work, the house employs a limited palette of materials, including concrete block walls, tile floors, and cypress wood ceilings. With its rather chilly devotion to a certain kind of architectural modernism, the house isn't to everyone's taste. Still, its aura of monkish severity is part of its appeal. Implicit in its subdued design is the idea that architecture should nourish the spirit as well as the body.

Maplewood

14 Seaholm Gottfried House

1800 East Shore Dr.

1948

A Moderne house built just after World War II. Its most prominent feature is a rounded staircase tower with glass-block windows. The house's flat-roofed modernity apparently didn't have broad appeal: it was two years before Seaholm Gottfried, an assistant signals superintendent for the Great Northern Railway, bought the property.

15 Benedictine Center of St. Paul's Monastery (St. Paul's Priory) !

2675 Larpenteur Ave. East

Val Michelson, 1965

This monastic complex, which creates powerful visual poetry out of concrete, may be the finest building of its era in the Twin Cities. The only contemporaneous local structure of comparable architectural significance was Ralph Rapson's Guthrie Theater (1963). But unlike the Guthrie (now gone), a much-visited landmark in the heart of Minneapolis, the monastery occupies a rather out-of-the-way site in suburban Maplewood.

It was designed as a home for Benedictine nuns in the Twin Cities by architect Val Michelson, who had worked on another great Benedictine project: the Abbey Church at St. John's University. With its rugged yet sensuous concrete work and boldly scaled elements, the monastery is a bravura display of heroic modernism that consists of three interconnected elements—a six-story residence hall, a central section with administrative offices, and a wing that houses a chapel, dining rooms, and a kitchen beneath a folded concrete roof. Superbly detailed, it was built by the same contractor, McGough Construction, that worked on St. John's Abbey Church, and its concrete is of a quality rarely seen before or since in the Twin Cities. Home to a dwindling community of nuns, the monastery faces an uncertain future, in part because it can't easily be adapted to some new use. It merits preservation at all costs.

Benedictine Center of St. Paul's Monastery

Overview

Although the West Side and West Seventh neighborhoods face each other across the Mississippi River and carry the same geographical prefix, they are by no means alike. The West Side's distinctive qualities begin with its name, long a source of bafflement to those unfamiliar with the peculiar geography of St. Paul. The trouble is that the neighborhood actually lies *south* of downtown. Yet because it's the only part of the city located on what is, in the broadest sense, the western side of the river, the name has stuck for over a century despite occasional misguided efforts to change it.

Separated as it is from the rest of St. Paul, the West Side has always seemed like a small community of its own. In fact, for a time it was chartered as the city of West St. Paul, then part of Dakota County. This occurred after the first Wabasha Street Bridge opened in 1859, but the West Side's state of independence proved short-lived, and in 1874 it was annexed by St. Paul. Although the West Side was among the first parts of St. Paul to be settled, almost all of its oldest houses, especially those built along the river flats, are long gone. However, you will find a nice collection of Victorians here, mainly atop the neighborhood's high bluffs.

The West Side's topography is among the most dramatic in St. Paul, rising abruptly from the flats along the river in a series of cliffs and wooded bluffs incised with precipitous ravines. Because of its rugged terrain, the West Side has a highly irregular street grid. Blocks come in an assortment of sizes, and there are frequent dead ends where streets encounter hills or other natural obstacles. The housing stock is equally unpredictable. Homes of different sizes, styles, and ages often coexist—for the most part peacefully—on the same block, and there's little of the "tract" look found in some of St. Paul's newer neighborhoods.

Across the river, the West Seventh neighborhood is named after the prominent street, also known as Fort Road, that slices through it on a long diagonal. Extending from the western edge of downtown at Seven Corners to the Interstate 35E bridge across the Mississippi River, West Seventh takes in some of the most historic ground in St. Paul and contains many of the city's oldest homes. Part of its appeal to early settlers was topographical. The neighborhood occupies an almost perfectly level plateau between the Mississippi and its steep bluffs yet is high enough above the river to be safe from the threat of floods.

Settlers began trickling into the area in the 1830s, in some cases after being booted out of the Fort Snelling military reservation just upriver. Among these pioneers was the legendary "Pig's Eye" Parrant, who dispensed whiskey and trouble from Fountain Cave, long lost beneath Shepard Road. Many European immigrants arrived later in the nineteenth century, but no ethnic group dominated.

Because its settlement dates back so far, West Seventh has more pre–Civil War houses—at least two dozen—than anywhere else in St. Paul. The Irvine Park Historic District, a charming residential enclave within the shadow of downtown, has an especially large complement of these very senior architectural citizens, including what is thought to be the oldest home in St. Paul, the Charles Symonds House (1850). Other antebellum houses can be found to the west of Irvine Park in the Uppertown area, along streets such as Banfil, Goodhue, and Michigan. It's estimated that as many as 150 of the neighborhood's older houses were moved to their current locations at one time or another as commercial expansion forced them out of areas closer to downtown.

West Seventh's most monumental building is the towering old Schmidt Brewery (1901 and later). Now vacant and awaiting redevelopment, the brewery once employed hundreds of local men but fell on hard times and was last used as an ethanol plant, an operation that quite literally raised a big stink.

West Side

The West Side's landscape of valley and blufftop divides the neighborhood into three sections. Below the bluffs is the area known historically as the West Side flats, which in its natural state was pure floodplain, subject to annual inundations. For this reason, the flats attracted mostly poor immigrants—Germans and Irish, followed by East European Jews and Mexican Americans. Little of the historic flats community remains today. Following a disastrous flood in 1952, the city cleared much of the flats to create Riverview Industrial Park, which is bookended by Harriet Island Park on the west and the Downtown St. Paul Airport to the east.

To the south of the flats, past the railroad tracks that parallel Eaton Street, there's a slightly higher area not subject to flooding. Here you'll find the heart of St. Paul's Latino community around the intersection of State and Cesar Chavez streets. Above the bluff line, on hills that climb up from the river valley, is the largely residential Upper West Side. The opening of the first Smith Avenue High Bridge in 1889 was a key impetus to development here, particularly in the Cherokee Park area.

Despite the superb views it offers, the West Side never developed anything like the mansion district along Summit Avenue. Even so, the area along and to the south of Prospect Boulevard can boast of at least a dozen first-class Victorians, including the Heimbach House (ca. 1885) on Delos Street, the Dearing House (1886) on George Street, and the Villaume House (1893) on Isabel Street. However, the bulk of the West Side's housing is quite modest, even where the views are most fetching. Other important neighborhood monuments include the Riverview Library (1916), the Rau-Strong House (1883), and the Wabasha Street Caves, once home to the Castle Royal Nightclub (1933).

POI A West Side Flats

Area roughly bounded by the Mississippi River, Concord and South Wabasha Sts., and Plato Blvd.

A complete urban world once existed here—homes, churches and synagogues, schools and stores—along with large industries such as the Towle Co. (makers of the original Log Cabin syrup) and American Hoist and Derrick Co. There were also brewers who dug caves in the sandstone bluffs to cool their beer. Other manmade caves were used to grow mushrooms and to age cheese. Another became home to the legendary Castle Royal.

In the 1960s the creation of Riverview Industrial Park, which included construction of levees, forever altered the flats. Scores of homes and other buildings were knocked down to make way for industrial and commercial buildings set within a subur-banized landscape of lawns and parking lots. Even so, a few significant historic structures remain on and around the flats, including the Harriet Island pavilion (1941), the Minnesota Boat Club (1910) on Raspberry Island, the Colorado Street Bridge (1888), and the tower of St. Michael's Church (1882), better known by its Spanish name, Torre de San Miguel.

1 Harriet Island Park

South Wabasha and Water Sts.

1900 / rebuilt, Wallace Roberts and Todd (Philadelphia) and St. Paul Division of Parks and Recreation, 2000

Despite its name, this riverfront park isn't an island. It was, however, just that when it was purchased in 1900 by Dr. Justus Ohage, then St. Paul's public health officer. Ohage outfitted the island with a bathhouse, playground, zoo, and other attractions before donating it to

West Side

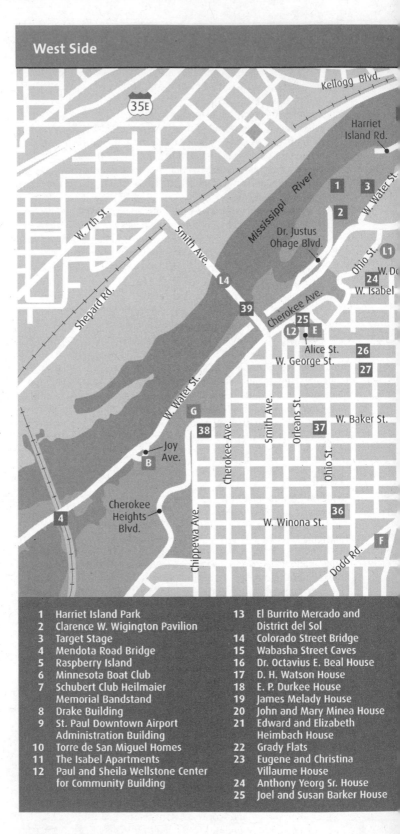

1   Harriet Island Park
2   Clarence W. Wigington Pavilion
3   Target Stage
4   Mendota Road Bridge
5   Raspberry Island
6   Minnesota Boat Club
7   Schubert Club Heilmaier Memorial Bandstand
8   Drake Building
9   St. Paul Downtown Airport Administration Building
10 Torre de San Miguel Homes
11 The Isabel Apartments
12 Paul and Sheila Wellstone Center for Community Building

13 El Burrito Mercado and District del Sol
14 Colorado Street Bridge
15 Wabasha Street Caves
16 Dr. Octavius E. Beal House
17 D. H. Watson House
18 E. P. Durkee House
19 James Melady House
20 John and Mary Minea House
21 Edward and Elizabeth Heimbach House
22 Grady Flats
23 Eugene and Christina Villaume House
24 Anthony Yeorg Sr. House
25 Joel and Susan Barker House

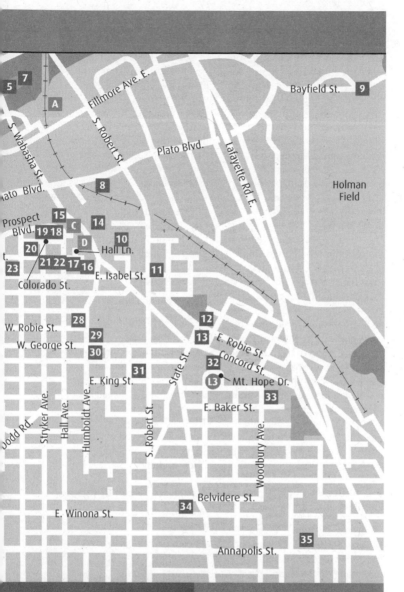

West Side

the city. The baths were a success, drawing as many as 25,000 people on hot summer days, but had to be closed for good in 1919 when the Mississippi became too polluted for swimming. The park, prone to flooding, also proved hard to maintain, and in 1949 the narrow channel on the island's south side was filled in. Another change came in 1964 when a levee was completed to provide flood protection for Riverview Industrial Park. The levee was later raised an additional four feet.

After languishing for years, the park was rebuilt in the late 1990s as part of St. Paul's riverfront renewal effort. Improvements included a riverwalk, an enlarged public dock, and a new pedestrian gateway along with two significant architectural projects: renovation of the park's 1941 pavilion and construction of a bandstand. River craft that dock at the park include the University of Minnesota Centennial Showboat and a 1940s-vintage towboat that has been renovated into a bed and breakfast called the Covington Inn.

2 Clarence W. Wigington Pavilion

200 Dr. Justus Ohage Blvd.

St. Paul City Architect (Charles A. Bassford with Clarence Wigington), 1941 / restored, Rafferty Rafferty Tollefson, 2000

Built under the auspices of the federal Works Progress Administration, this pavilion is Moderne in style but has a vaguely traditional feel. Its designer and namesake, Clarence Wigington, was the nation's first black municipal architect; he worked as a draftsman and later as chief designer for the St. Paul City Architect's Office from 1915 until 1949. The pavilion is also of interest because the Mankato-Kasota stone used in its construction was salvaged from the old St. Paul City Hall–Ramsey County Courthouse, built in 1889 and demolished in 1933.

3 Target Stage

Harriet Island Park

Michael Graves and Associates, 2001

Graves built his reputation as a postmodern theorist and architect but has become better known of late as a designer of household items for Target Corp. This bandstand, which looks like a pair of oil derricks in search of some crude, is not one of his finer moments.

4 Mendota Road Bridge N

Water St. over outlet from Pickerel Lake

St. Paul City Engineer, 1894

A tiny stone bridge that has somehow survived the march of progress.

Clarence W. Wigington Pavilion

POI B Site of Twin City Brick Co. and Mystic Caverns

Water St. near Joy Ave.

The Twin City Brick Co. operated here from 1889 to the 1970s; the site is now a favorite spot for fossil hunters. Among the many caves in the vicinity was Mystic Caverns, which in the 1930s served as a nightclub that attracted the usual contingent of gangsters as well as the legendary fan dancer Sally Rand. The joint closed in 1934 after the owners were convicted of gambling offenses, and the cave itself is no longer accessible.

5 Raspberry Island (Navy Island)

Mississippi River beneath Wabasha Street Bridge

Connected to Harriet Island Park by a small bridge is Raspberry Island, once known as Navy Island. The island, which can also be reached by a staircase from the Wabasha Street Bridge, took its present shape in 1948 when the U.S. Navy built a reserve training facility on the eastern side. The navy left in 1968. The western portion of the island has been owned since 1872 by the Minnesota Boat Club. Today, Raspberry Island is home to the historic Minnesota Boat Club Boathouse and a band shell built for the Schubert Club of St. Paul.

6 Minnesota Boat Club N *L*

Raspberry Island
(1 South Wabasha St.)

George H. Carsley, 1910

Founded in 1870, the Minnesota Boat Club is the state's oldest athletic organization. This building is the club's second on the island, replacing a wooden structure erected in 1885. The boathouse, done in the Spanish Revival style, contains storage on the main level for rowing shells and other equipment. The upper floor was originally used as a meeting and dining room. A survivor of many floods, the boathouse continues to serve as the club's headquarters.

7 Schubert Club Heilmaier Memorial Bandstand

Raspberry Island

James Carpenter Design Associates, 2002

The most poetic object on St. Paul's riverfront, a sensuous sweep of laminated glass and stainless steel that, in Carpenter's words, "float[s] like a volume of light on the Mississippi River." Technically, the saddle-shaped roof is a hyperbolic paraboloid, but you don't have to be a mathematician to appreciate its elegance. The $2 million structure was built largely with private funds raised by the Schubert Club of St. Paul. Carpenter, a New York–based designer best known for his work with glass, was no stranger to St. Paul when he received this commission. Earlier, he'd won a competition to design the new Wabasha Street Bridge that soars above Raspberry Island, but the spectacular cable-stay bridge he proposed was never built.

West Side

Schubert Club Heilmaier Memorial Bandstand

8 Drake Building (Drake Marble Co.)

60 Plato Blvd. East

1909 / renovated, MS&R Architects, 2002

A sleek makeover of an early twentieth-century concrete-frame industrial building into offices. The architects refaced the exterior with corrugated metal in sassy colors, added a stair and elevator tower, and topped it all with a bold sign. The result is a crisp, clean design that calls to mind the work of the German Bauhaus.

Torre de San Miguel

9 St. Paul Downtown Airport (Holman Field) Administration Building **N**

644 Bayfield St.

St. Paul City Architect (Charles A. Bassford with Clarence Wigington), 1941

This Moderne-style terminal, built of limestone, would fit nicely into an Indiana Jones movie, especially if an old Ford Tri-Motor were parked at the gate. The interior highlight is a large floor mosaic depicting North America. The airport was established in 1926 and later named after Charles "Speed" Holman, Northwest Airline's first pilot. Holman died in 1931 at age 33 when his plane crashed during a stunt performance in Omaha, NE.

10 Torre de San Miguel Homes

58 Wood St. (between Wabasha and Robert Sts. south of Plato Blvd.)

St. Paul Housing Authority, 1968 / enlarged, Fishman and Associates, ca. 1980 / reno-vated, ca. 1990s / includes **St. Michael's Catholic Church tower**, *1882*

An unremarkable modern hous-ing project except for the church tower after which it's named. The bell tower, Italian in charac-ter, is all that remains of the old St. Michael's Catholic Church,

demolished in 1970. The tower is the flats' oldest surviving work of architecture.

11 The Isabel Apartments

109–19 East Isabel St.

Louis Lockwood, 1904

One of the West Side's few row houses. To the rear is a 150-year-old cottonwood tree said to be one of the largest in Ram-sey County.

12 Paul and Sheila Wellstone Center for Community Building

179 East Robie St.

BWBR Architects, 2005

A nicely designed new home for Neighborhood House, a historic West Side institution founded in 1900 by Mount Zion Temple as a settlement house for immi-grants. The building is named after two of Neighborhood House's longtime supporters—former U.S. Senator Paul Well-stone and his wife, Sheila, who along with six other persons died in a plane crash in 2002.

13 El Burrito Mercado and District del Sol

175 Cesar Chavez (formerly Concord) St.

ca. 1950s / renovated, ca. 1990s

At least a third of the West Side's residents are Hispanic, and here at the intersection of State and

Cesar Chavez Sts. is one of the city's most colorful (literally) commercial districts, where Spanish-themed shop fronts and restaurants abound. El Burrito Mercado, located in a building that originally housed a furniture store, features festive colors and swirling stuccowork in the manner of a Mexican market. Next door is La Placita, a small plaza that always attracts a crowd during the summer months. Throughout this area, known as the District del Sol, you'll also find murals and other forms of public artwork.

Colorado Street Bridge

14 Colorado Street Bridge N

East side of South Wabasha St. about three blocks south of Plato Blvd.

Andreas Munster, 1888

A historic masonry bridge built to carry Colorado St. across Starkey St. but now used only by pedestrians. Like the Seventh Street Improvement Arches, this bridge required a tricky angled crossing. Assistant city engineer Andreas Munster decided against the spiral technique used for the Seventh Street arches. Instead, he designed alternating stone and brick courses that run the length of the arch rather than in the traditional crosswise manner. Munster's design was daring: as a precaution he left wooden centering beneath the arch for a year after the bridge opened.

POI C Channel Street (Hall Avenue) Steps and Wabasha Street Retaining Wall

Steps, South Wabasha St. near Wabasha Street Caves

City of St. Paul, 1916

Wall, Wabasha St.

City of St. Paul Department of Public Works and Seitu Jones (artist), 2005

The tallest of St. Paul's 90 or so public staircases, this iron and wood tower reaches Hall Ave. on the blufftops after a climb of 191 steps. The stairs take their official name from a street that once ran here. Next to the stair tower is an undulating concrete retaining wall that doubles as an art object. It features a decorative steel railing and the word for *home* inscribed in 12 languages.

Wabasha Street Caves, 1933

15 Wabasha Street Caves (Castle Royal Nightclub)

215 South Wabasha St.

ca. 1890s / converted to nightclub, Myrtus Wright, 1933 / renovated, 1975 and later

St. Paul's most celebrated underground establishment, once home to the Castle Royal Nightclub. The caves—a series of interconnected tunnels excavated out of St. Peter sandstone in the nineteenth century—were mined for silica and later used to grow mushrooms. In 1933, William Lehman, son-in-law to the caves' first owner, turned them into a nightclub. Lehman hired architect Myrtus Wright to design a castlelike brick facade over the entrances. Inside, the club had two bars and fixtures scavenged from the demolished Charles Gates Mansion in Minneapolis.

Modestly billed as the "World's Most Gorgeous Underground Nite Club," the Castle Royal quickly became one of the city's hot spots. Stories, some of them no doubt embroidered, tell of gangsters, gun molls, and other disreputable characters frolicking to the music of bandleaders like Cab Calloway and Harry James. By 1940, however, the club was losing money and closed. Today, the caves are rented out for a variety of special events and tours are available.

16 Dr. Octavius E. Beal House

23 West Isabel St.

1891

This brick Queen Anne was built for a physician whose office was nearby on South Wabasha St. The house poses romantically atop a steep hill, its round tower craning for a view over the trees. It has been restored to single-family use.

17 D. H. Watson House and barn

402 Hall Ave.

Gilbert and Taylor, 1886

A very early design from Cass Gilbert and possibly the first produced during his partnership with James Knox Taylor. The house at first glance seems ordinary, but the overall composition—especially the way in which the hipped front dormer hovers above an oriel window—shows how Gilbert could wring something distinctive out of even the simplest project. The Shingle Style barn was moved to a new position on the lot in 2004 and is being restored, as is the house itself.

POI D Hall Lane

East of Hall Ave. near Prospect Blvd.

A secretive little street of the type that abounds in St. Paul. No wider than an alley, it serves a handful of houses perched atop the cliffs here.

18 E. P. Durkee House and carriage house

58 Prospect Blvd. West

ca. 1875

This mansarded French Second Empire pile is one of the oldest houses on the West Side, with a commanding view of downtown and the river valley. The house has been remodeled several times, and none of the undertakings, including the most recent one, has been especially kind to it.

19 James Melady House

361 Stryker Ave.

ca. 1885

Another remodeled French Second Empire house. Public records suggest a construction date of 1885, but it could be earlier. The original owner, James Melady, was in the paper business.

John and Mary Minea House

20 John and Mary Minea House

382 Winslow Ave.

Albert Zschocke, 1886

This imposing twin-towered house was designed for one of brewer Martin Brueggemann's daughters, Mary, after her marriage to John Minea, who owned a grocery store. The house is awash in busy details. Perhaps the tastiest bit of eye candy is a small, off-center front gable with a bull's-eye window framed by an ornate terra-cotta panel depicting a pair of cornucopias. Alas, the riches flowed for only a decade before the Mineas lost the house to foreclosure in 1896.

21 Edward and Elizabeth Heimbach House and carriage house

64 West Delos St.

ca. 1885

An exceptional house, animated by fine detailing in brick and stone. Stylistically, it's a Victorian grab bag, mixing Italianate, East-lake, and Queen Anne with fearless flair. The octagonal tower crowned by a domed roof is unusual, as is the brick banding that wraps around the second story like a taut chain. The carriage house, a miniature mansion in its own right, is one of the most delightful buildings of its kind in St. Paul. The house was built for

Anthony Yeorg Sr. House

Edward and Elizabeth Heimbach House, 1983

Edward Heimbach, a shoe retailer, and his wife, Elizabeth, who was a daughter of St. Paul brewer Martin Brueggemann.

22 Grady Flats

46–52 West Delos St.

Emil Strassburger, 1891

A renovated row house with delicate porches and plenty of hoopla along the roofline, where finials, turrets, and parapets do their part in the never-ending fight against dullness.

23 Eugene and Christina Villaume House

123 West Isabel St.

1895

Eugene Villaume was a French-born cabinetmaker who, with his brother, Victor, established a box and lumber company on the West Side in 1882. Not surprisingly, this house—Queen Anne in character but moving toward Colonial Revival—has superb interior woodwork. In the 1930s, an order of Catholic nuns bought the house for use as a convent. It's now a single-family home and has been restored.

24 Anthony Yeorg Sr. House N

215 West Isabel St.

Monroe Sheire, 1875

Yeorg was St. Paul's first and one of its most successful brewers. He arrived in St. Paul from Germany in 1848 and established a brewery near downtown. He built a new brewery on the West Side in 1871 and then constructed this house on the bluffs directly above. The house is basically a wooden box with a mansard roof and therefore qualifies as French Second Empire in style. The house next door to the west at 197 Isabel was built for Yeorg's son in 1882.

LOST 1 *A rock-walled glen near the bottom of twisty Ohio St. just south of Plato Blvd. was once the site of* **Yeorg's Brewery,** *which operated at this location from about 1871 until 1952. The brewery complex included a mile-long tunnel system where beer was kept cool. The brewery's product was, in fact, advertised as "cave-aged" beer.*

POI E Alice Park

31 Alice St.

1879

A small oval of greenery surrounded by houses. It has the feel of a private hideaway, though the park and street are both public.

LOST 2 *The River Ridge Condominiums at 334 Cherokee Ave., just east of the High Bridge, occupy the site of the* **Adolph Rosen House,** *a stone mansion built in 1899 for Adolph Rosen and his second wife, Anna. Rosen was a Swedish immi-*

West Side

grant who founded a highly successful fur business on the West Side flats. Both Rosen and his wife

Adolph Rosen House, 1902

died in 1930, and the house later served as a nursing home before being demolished in 1961.

25 Joel and Susan Barker House

354 Cherokee Ave.

SALA Architects (Kelly Davis), 2006

A neo–Prairie Style house with a spectacular view.

Samuel Dearing House

26 Samuel Dearing House

241 West George St.

Augustus Gauger, 1886

One of the West Side's most splendid houses, combining Queen Anne and Italianate features. Its signature element is a bold circle of brick that frames a pair of second-floor windows. The house was built by Samuel Dearing, who operated a dairy farm before plunging into real estate. He subdivided his farm into lots and built this house to showcase his development. Unfortunately, Dearing's "palatial home necessitated his bankruptcy," as one newspaper put it, when he fell into debt following

the depression of 1893. He tried to sell the house via a lottery— at two dollars a ticket—but even this creative scheme didn't work, and the house was ultimately auctioned off. Later, it was cut up into five apartments, but it's now once again a single-family home.

27 Charles Haas House

214 West George St.

1889

A very large house, not especially coherent in design but impressive nonetheless. Its finest feature is a beautiful front porch that bows out slightly, a gesture repeated by the attic windows in the gable above. Charles Haas was president of the South St. Paul Livestock Exchange and also served as the Ramsey County registrar of deeds.

28 St. Matthew's Catholic School N *L*

7 West Robie St.
(also 497 Humboldt Ave.)

John Fischer, 1902 / additions, 1925, 1928

One of the oldest school buildings still in use in St. Paul. The school's vaguely Gothic appearance made it a rather retro design at a time when classically inspired buildings were more fashionable. St. Matthew's Parish was founded in 1886 to serve the West Side's German immigrants. The parish built a fine church in 1887, but it burned down in 1968. The current church—a boxy brick structure completed in 1970— isn't particularly appealing.

29 Riverview Library N *L*

1 East George St.

St. Paul City Architect (Charles A. Hausler), 1916 / renovated, City of St. Paul Department of Public Design Works, 1989

A stately brick library, and one of the West Side's finest buildings. Like other small public buildings of the Beaux-Arts era, it conveys a sense of order, calmness, and tradition—three qualities that never go out of style. The large arched windows don't leave a lot

Riverview Library

of room inside for bookshelves, but they do bring in copious light, making for a most pleasant place to while away an hour or two with a book in hand. Riverview is one of three neighborhood libraries built in St. Paul in 1916 and largely financed by steel magnate and philanthropist Andrew Carnegie.

30 Rau-Strong House N *L*

2 East George St.

Adam Rau, 1883

A well-preserved example of a small nineteenth-century urban estate, complete with a stone carriage house. Now sporting a festive yellow and brown paint job, the house—a mélange of styles but more Italianate than

anything else—was built by Adam Rau, a stone cutter. Rau used limestone blocks from a quarry he operated just across George St. on the site of Riverview Library and the Humboldt Apartments. The home's walls, which Rau covered with stucco, are two feet thick and feature brush-hammered quoins at the corners. Rau sold the house in 1886 to Ossian Strong, who worked for one of the big Lowertown wholesalers. In a typical West Side story, the house remained in the Strong family until 1986, when it was purchased by the present owners, who have spent two decades restoring it.

31 Brick houses

87, 89–91, 103 East King St.

Henry Lange (builder), 1885–89

The older parts of St. Paul and Minneapolis are dotted with small brick homes from the late nineteenth century. These four are exceptional by virtue of their dazzling brickwork. Note, for example, the elaborate infilled arch above a trio of second-story windows at 87 East King St. Only a master mason, which Lange was, could have created work of this quality.

Rau-Strong House, 1975

Peter and Julie Eigenfeld House

32 Peter and Julie Eigenfeld House

219 Mount Hope Dr.

Close Associates (Gar Hargens),
2000

Working on a modest lot and within a tight budget, architect Gar Hargens created a colorful, compact house that takes full advantage of the site's extraordinary views with a rooftop overlook reached via a spiral staircase. The house has the bright, playful feel of something out of sunny southern California. Riverview Hospital once occupied this site.

Paul Martin House, 1888

LOST 3 *A number of impressive homes can still be found on Prescott St., which runs along the blufftops here. However, the grandest of them all, the **Paul Martin House,** is gone. Built in 1887 at 225 Prescott, the house had an extraordinary four-story-high corner tower. In 1909 the house became the **St. Paul German Hospital,** which later evolved into **Riverview Hospital.** The hospital, enlarged in the 1950s and 1960s, was closed in 1980 and*

demolished. Modern houses now occupy the old hospital site.

33 William Bredenhagen House

634 Woodbury St.

1891

A large brick Queen Anne. Its unusually complex polygonal tower has angular brick columns that thrust up past the roofline. The house's wooden cupola and rooftop balcony are modern additions.

34 John B. and Nina Schmidt House

182 East Belvidere St.

1889

A Victorian romantically sited on a deep, heavily wooded hillside lot. The L-shaped house, adorned with much turned and sawn wood ornament, is generally Eastlake in character.

35 Riverview Cemetery

340 East Annapolis St.

1875

This little-known cemetery occupies one of the prettiest spots in the Twin Cities, high atop the wooded river bluffs that fall away toward South St. Paul. The cemetery, established as a burial ground for German Lutherans, includes a small wooden chapel built in about 1893.

POI F Forty Acres

Area bounded by Annapolis, Charlton, Sidney, and Bidwell Sts.

A 40-acre peninsula of West St. Paul (and Dakota County) that juts into the West Side. When St. Paul prepared to annex the West Side in 1874, this quarter section was owned by Philip Crowley, the West St. Paul superintendent of schools who in 1870 had built a home on the property. The school post required him to be a West St. Paul resident. Rather than move, Crowley arranged to have his property exempted from annexation.

Ironically, he lost his job in the next election, but the 40 acres remain as testimony to his machinations, as does his house, located at 763 Dodd Rd.

George Hosmer House

36 George Hosmer (later Ernest Hummel) House

808 Ohio St.

Albert Zschocke, 1889

A beautifully preserved Shingle Style house built for a West Side banker. The home's second owner, Ernest Hummel, was a jeweler who in 1895 invented the "telediagraph," a machine that made it possible to transmit images via telegraph. The device was first used in 1898 by a New York newspaper. Later that year, during the Spanish-American War, Hummel's machine sent out a picture of the first gun fired at the battle of Manila Bay in the Philippines.

37 Workshop and residence (Fire Station No. 21)

643 Ohio St.

1910

One of many old fire stations in the Twin Cities that's been adapted to a new use. It was closed in 1943 and later sold to a Veterans of Foreign Wars post. In 1950 the St. Paul Turners Gymnastic Society bought the building and used it as a clubhouse. The current owners live on the upper floor and use the garage below as a custom boat building shop.

38 Richard and Martha Dykman House

673 Delaware Ave.

Richard Dykman, 1978

A boxlike two-story house, clad in cedar. It was the winner in a design competition for infill housing sponsored by the City of St. Paul.

POI G Cherokee Park

Baker St. and Chippewa Ave.

1903 and later

These high, oak-strewn river bluffs were long recognized as a potential park. In 1903 the city's park board began acquiring the site with funds donated by James J. Hill and others. The park, used for a time as a tourist campground, wasn't fully developed until 1924.

39 Smith Avenue High Bridge !

Across Mississippi River

Strgar Roscoe Fausch (engineers), 1987

The longest, highest, and most spectacular of the 20 highway bridges that cross the Mississippi River on its winding course through St. Paul and Minneapolis. Rising at a four percent grade as it climbs toward the West Side bluffs, the half-mile-long bridge leaps over the river via a central arch that spans 520 feet. With its elegant and evocative steel arch, tied together with tensioned cables beneath the bridge deck, the bridge has become one of the city's modern landmarks. It could have been even better, however, had the engineers paid more attention to the design of its tall concrete piers, which seem heavy and graceless compared to the arch.

Smith Avenue High Bridge

LOST 4 *The **first High Bridge** opened in 1889. A spidery maze of bents, braces, towers, and trusses, it was basically a wrought-iron bridge in a kit, fabricated by the Keystone Bridge Co. of Pittsburgh. It arrived in St. Paul in one million pieces, along with what must have been the instruction manual from hell—a 388-page how-to guide for* the aspiring bridge builder. The bridge lasted for a remarkable 106 years. Part of it had to be rebuilt, however, after being knocked down by a tornado in 1904. The bridge was finally demolished in 1985. Ornate railings from the old bridge were salvaged and can be seen at the scenic overlooks near both ends of today's High Bridge.

First High Bridge damaged by tornado, 1904

West Seventh

West Seventh—which consists of several smaller neighborhoods, including Uppertown, the West End, and Irvine Park—is best known for its many historic homes. Among the largest is the Alexander Ramsey House (1872), an excellent example of the French Second Empire style. Two other notable mansions—the Christopher Stahlmann House (1874) and the towered William Banholzer House (1885)—were built for families in the brewing business, long an important source of neighborhood jobs. West Seventh also has its share of apartments and row houses, the most significant being Lauer Flats (1887) on Western Avenue.

In addition to the Schmidt Brewery, West Seventh has a number of historic industrial buildings, among which is the old Omaha Iron and Brass Foundry (1890) on Armstrong Avenue. The Chicago, St. Paul, Minneapolis and Omaha Railroad also maintained its shops here for many years, but no traces of the roundhouse and other structures survive.

Although West Seventh retains much historic texture, it has seen extensive redevelopment. The sprawling Ancker (originally City and County) Hospital complex (1888 and later) on Colborne Street was demolished in the 1960s and replaced by a headquarters building for the St. Paul Public Schools. Also gone is the old Italian neighborhood known as the Upper Levee, once located on the river flats near Chestnut Street. Today the site has blossomed with more than 500 townhomes, condominiums, and apartments. Another, even larger development called Victoria Park is being built at Otto and West Seventh streets on a site formerly occupied by oil tanks. With these two mega-developments, the West Seventh neighborhood—among the oldest in St. Paul—has become one of the newest as well.

Uppertown and the West End

Neither Uppertown nor the West End is an officially designated neighborhood, but both names are commonly used to describe portions of the West Seventh community. Uppertown, which derives its name from the historic Upper Landing at the foot of Chestnut Street, roughly takes in the area to either side of West Seventh Street from Irvine Park to St. Clair Avenue. Beyond that is the West End, not to be confused (though it sometimes is) with the West Side across the river.

Always a working-class neighborhood, Uppertown was settled by transplanted Yankees as well as later waves of immigrants, including Bohemians, Germans, Austrians, Irish, and Poles. Over the years, many of the neighborhood's small to mid-sized houses have been altered in ways that would hardly satisfy preservation purists. Asbestos, aluminum, and vinyl siding are no strangers here, nor is chain-link fencing. Yet much of Uppertown's appeal stems from its honest history of remodeling, and it has nothing of the preserved-in-formaldehyde look that can afflict formally designated historic districts.

The West End's houses tend to be newer and larger than those in Uppertown, with late Victorians, turn-of-the-century foursquares, and bungalows all in evidence. However, there are areas of older housing, including a row of small working-class homes along Butternut Avenue.

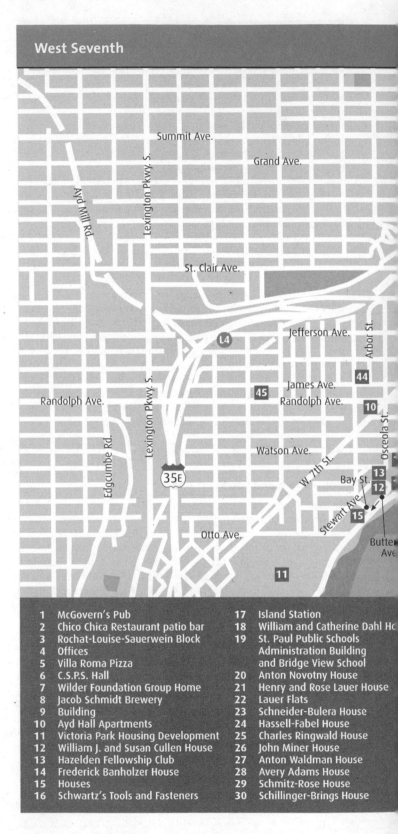

West Seventh

West Seventh

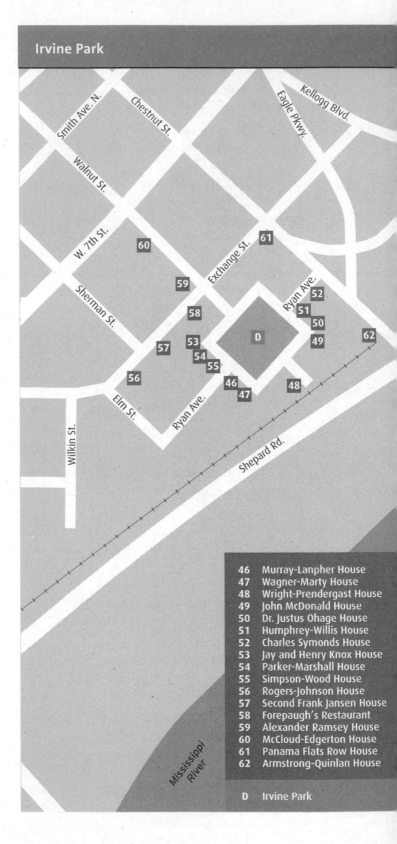

Irvine Park

46   Murray-Lanpher House
47   Wagner-Marty House
48   Wright-Prendergast House
49   John McDonald House
50   Dr. Justus Ohage House
51   Humphrey-Willis House
52   Charles Symonds House
53   Jay and Henry Knox House
54   Parker-Marshall House
55   Simpson-Wood House
56   Rogers-Johnson House
57   Second Frank Jansen House
58   Forepaugh's Restaurant
59   Alexander Ramsey House
60   McCloud-Edgerton House
61   Panama Flats Row House
62   Armstrong-Quinlan House

D   Irvine Park

West Seventh Street

Seven Corners to
Mississippi River Blvd.

West Seventh, also known as Fort Rd., is one of the city's oldest streets, providing a link between downtown St. Paul and Fort Snelling. Its present course was established in the 1850s (before then, an early version ran closer to the blufftops). The freeway of its day, West Seventh had to be cut through existing subdivisions, leaving a fractured pattern of blocks in its wake.

By 1891, streetcar lines extended the full length of West Seventh, bringing commercial development with them. Today, the street is almost entirely commercial in the Seven Corners area, where there's a lively collection of bars, restaurants, antique shops, and other businesses. Farther to the south and west, West Seventh becomes a less upscale version of Grand Ave., with houses and apartments interspersed among small business blocks. Although it could use sprucing up in places, the street has a pleasantly old-fashioned air to it, and it remains a vital artery.

1 McGovern's Pub (Smith Block)

225 West Seventh St.

Edward P. Bassford, 1888

Robert A. Smith, mayor of St. Paul from 1887 to 1902 and for whom nearby Smith Ave. is named, erected this Romanesque Revival–style brick building. The cast panels above the second-floor windows depict the mythical horse Pegasus while those above the third show a woman's face against a background of scrolls and garlands.

2 Chico Chica Restaurant patio bar (Justus Ramsey House) **N** *L*

242 West Seventh St.

ca. 1857

This tiny Greek Revival cottage, with stone walls two feet thick, was built as a rental property by Justus Ramsey. He was the brother and business partner of

Chico Chica Restaurant patio bar

Alexander Ramsey, Minnesota's first territorial governor, whose considerably more spacious stone home is a block away. The property went through many owners before being purchased by an antiques dealer in the 1930s. It is now what must surely be the most historic patio bar in Minnesota.

Rochat-Louise-Sauerwein Block

3 Rochat-Louise-Sauerwein Block **N** *L*

261–77 West Seventh St.

Rochat Building, William H. Castner, 1885 / Louise Building, Edward P. Bassford, 1885 / Sauerwein Building, Hermann Kretz, 1895

It's a rarity in the Twin Cities to find three nicely renovated Victorian commercial buildings in a row, as is the case here. The Rochat Block, the prettiest of the trio, was commissioned by a Swiss-born watchmaker named George Rochat. The Louise was built by William G. Robertson and named after his wife and daughter. The Sauerwein Block, which once had a large Odd Fellows lodge hall on its top floor, was constructed for a saloonkeeper named John Sauerwein.

4 Offices (originally houses)

William Gronewald Townhouse,
555 West Seventh St.

William Gronewald, 1891

Joseph Walla House,
557 West Seventh St.

1884

William Gronewald House,
561 West Seventh St.

1871

Two of these three houses were moved here in 1977 and renovated for use as offices. The most interesting is the tall, Queen Anne–style townhouse at 555 West Seventh St. that has a large rounded window on the top floor.

5 Villa Roma Pizza

603 West Seventh St.

ca. 1906

This isn't a prefabricated diner made to look like a railroad car but is in fact an old wooden day coach, possibly built by the Pullman Co. It served as a tavern near the stockyards in South St. Paul before being moved here in 1946.

C.S.P.S. Hall

6 C.S.P.S. Hall N *L*

383–85 Michigan St.
(605 West Seventh St.)

Emil Ulrici, 1887 / enlarged, Raymond P. Pavlecka, 1917

This well-kept club building was constructed for the Czech-Slovak Protective Society. Founded in St. Louis in 1854, the society's chief purpose was to provide insurance and death benefits for Czech immigrants. The St. Paul lodge, which dates to 1876, is the twelfth oldest in the nation. The building's lower floor has always been commercial space. Upstairs is a large, beautifully simple hall

that seems to have miraculously eluded the march of time. In 1893 Czech composer Antonín Dvořák was feted in the hall during a visit to Minnesota. Today, the hall continues to be used for a variety of events and is also home to Sokol, a Czech gymnastic society.

Wilder Foundation Group Home

7 Wilder Foundation Group Home (Christopher Stahlmann House)

855 West Seventh St.

1874 / front porch, ca. 1907

This stone mansion was built for Christopher Stahlmann, a Bavarian immigrant who established the first brewery across the street on the Schmidt site in 1855. Known as Stahlmann's Cave Brewery, it was the state's largest by the 1870s, producing 10,000 barrels a year. Stahlmann's mansion reflected his success. Built of local Platteville limestone, it's a brawny example of the Italianate style, although the small windows in the frieze are a Greek Revival carryover. The wood-frame house next door at 877 West Seventh was built for Stahlmann's son in the 1870s.

Stahlmann died of tuberculosis in 1887. Within a decade his three sons succumbed to the same disease and the brewery went bankrupt. Jacob Schmidt took over the brewery in 1900 and lived in the mansion until his death in 1911. His daughter, Maria, and her husband, Adolph Bremer, then moved into the house. After their son, Edward, was kidnapped in 1934, the Bremers built a tunnel beneath Seventh St., connecting their home to the brewery. It was sealed in 1956 after the Bremers donated the mansion to the Wilder Foundation.

8 Jacob Schmidt Brewery !

882 West Seventh St.

Bernard Barthel (Chicago), 1901 /
numerous additions

A vacant St. Paul industrial land-mark, once among the nation's largest breweries and worthy of preservation at all costs. Jacob Schmidt, a German-born brew-master, set up shop here in 1900 after fire destroyed his Dayton's Bluff brewery. He built next to the historic Stahlmann site, which already included springs for water and an enormous system of stor-age caves described as "a perfect labyrinth of rooms and cellars." Schmidt, however, introduced mechanical refrigeration for his beer and never made extensive use of the caves.

Schmidt's new brewery was designed by German-trained Bernard Barthel, one of several Chicago architects who made breweries their specialty. Today, the brewery remains the finest and most intact of Barthel's numerous projects in the Upper Midwest. As with the Twin Cities' other surviving nineteenth-century breweries—Hamm's on St. Paul's East Side and Grain Belt in Northeast Minneapolis—the Schmidt Brewery is a campus of buildings constructed over many years. At its center is the towering, castlelike brew house, the first portion of which was built in 1901 around malt houses origi-nally used by Stahlmann's Brew-ery. Sporting festive red-and-white arches, the building proclaims the Schmidt name in lettering atop the tower. A ban-ner of more recent vintage advertises Landmark Beer, brewed here for a short time in the 1990s.

Among the many additions to the brewery, the best date to the 1930s–40s, when an art deco office structure was built along Seventh and the bottling house was enlarged in the same style. Four stories were also added to the brew house, but so seamlessly

Jacob Schmidt Brewery

that they look to be part of Barthel's original design. The office building basement contains a re-created German rathskeller with stone walls and a painting depicting Schmidt, Adolph Bremer, and his brother, Otto.

Jacob Schmidt died in 1911. Son-in-law Adolph Bremer took over the brewery, which remained in local hands until 1955. Outside owners operated the brewery until 1992, when it was purchased by local investors and rechristened the Minnesota Brewing Co. The company failed, and in 2000 part of the brewery became an ethanol plant, an olfactory disaster that drenched the neighborhood in obnoxious odors. The plant went bankrupt in 2004, and the brewery now awaits a new life.

9 Building (Stahlmann Brewery Livery Stable)

363 Webster St.

1881 / addition, 1885

Though no longer part of the Schmidt complex, this building just across West Seventh St. is the oldest of the many structures once associated with the brewery. Built of limestone blocks, it first served as a livery stable for the Stahlmann Brewery and was subsequently integrated into a large group of buildings that served as Schmidt's shipping warehouse.

10 Ayd Hall Apartments

1033–35 West Seventh St.

Bergmann and Fischer, 1887

One of the largest of West Seventh's Victorian-era buildings, constructed for commercial and apartment use by Leonard Ayd, a son of pioneer St. Paul miller John Ayd. The ground floor has a cast-iron storefront made by Crown Iron Works of Minneapolis.

11 Victoria Park Housing Development

Otto Ave. between Shepard Rd. and West Seventh St.

2006 and later

This 66-acre site, once the domain of a fuel tank farm, will eventually have up to 850 new homes and apartments, making it the largest residential project in St. Paul's history.

12 William J. and Susan Cullen House

698 Stewart Ave.

Joseph W. Smyth (builder), 1862

The stone building you see here today is what remains of a mansion completed in 1862 for William Cullen, then superintendent of Indian Affairs in Minnesota. Offering a view of the river and surrounded by large grounds, the mansion included an ornate cupola that was swept away by a tornado in the 1860s. In about 1872 Cullen and his wife sold the property to the Protestant Orphan Asylum. Later, a VFW post occupied the building, which at some point lost its mansard roof and its second story. As of 2007, the property appeared to be undergoing renovation.

Hazelden Fellowship Club

13 Hazelden Fellowship Club (William Banholzer House)

680 Stewart Ave.

C. Edward Dressel, 1885

Perhaps the most impressive of all the beer baron mansions in the West Seventh neighborhood. Its original owner, William Banholzer, took over a small brewery from his father in the late 1870s. Located near present-day Drake St. and Shepard Rd., the brewery quickly grew, producing 12,000 barrels a year of

"North Mississippi Beer" by the mid-1880s.

Banholzer built this house in a late, abstracted version of the French Second Empire style, with a high-hatted tower that presides over the neighborhood. Banholzer died at age 48 in 1897, and the brewery was soon gone as well. The house, by a certain historical irony, was taken over by the Hazelden Fellowship Club in 1953 and now serves as a home for people being treated for drug and alcohol addiction.

14 Frederick Banholzer House

681 Butternut Ave.

Havelock E. Hand, 1889 / rebuilt, ca. 1940

Frederick Banholzer, William's father, purchased what was to become the family brewery in 1871. This house, which overlooked the brewery and a beer garden known as Banholzer's Park, was originally Victorian in character but was given a Colonial Revival makeover in about 1940.

15 Houses

Butternut Ave. between Sumac St. and Otto Ave.

ca. 1880s and later

This two-block-long avenue features a nice gathering of small Victorian working-class houses along its north side. The lineup includes brick cottages, simple wood-frame houses, and a sort of mini Italianate–Queen Anne style home with a picturesque tower (at 771 Butternut). A number of houses have been restored; others patiently await that day. It's likely that some of the original occupants were employees of the Banholzer Brewery.

16 Schwartz's Tools and Fasteners (Omaha Iron and Brass Foundry)

626 Armstrong Ave.

1890

A long stone structure built for a foundry that did business with the railroad shops nearby. Today,

it's one of only a few stone industrial buildings left in St. Paul.

LOST 1 *The triangle of land bounded by Drake St., Randolph Ave., and Shepard Rd. was once the site of a group of buildings, including a brick roundhouse, that formed the* **Chicago, St. Paul, Minneapolis and Omaha Railroad Shops.** *Built beginning in 1882, the shops employed as many as 1,000 workers. The last building—part of the roundhouse—came down in a 1998 windstorm, though the shops themselves closed in the 1950s.*

17 Island Station

380 Randolph Ave.
(formerly 484 Shepard Rd.)

Toltz, King and Day, 1924

An old coal-burning power plant built for the St. Paul Gas and Electric Co. It was shut down in 1975 and later became entangled in a dispute between the city and a potential developer. A new developer acquired the property in 2004, but plans to convert the plant to condominiums and to construct new townhouses on the 11-acre site have so far fizzled.

Fountain Cave, 1875

POI A Fountain Cave historic marker

Off Shepard Rd. near Randolph Ave.

Fountain Cave was one of two natural sandstone caverns—the other was Carver's Cave—once found along the Mississippi River in St. Paul. Whiskey dealer Pierre "Pig's Eye" Parrant set up shop near Fountain Cave in 1838. The cave, from which a small stream issued, was reached via a canyon-like ravine and was said to be 1,000 feet long. Development gradually polluted the creek and closed off the cave. Its last remnants were destroyed in 1960 by construction of Shepard Rd.

18 William and Catherine Dahl House

508 Jefferson Ave.

1857

Built for an English immigrant, this house was originally located at 136 13th St. just north of downtown. The State of Minnesota bought the property in 1972, but it wasn't until 1998 that a new state building—for the Minnesota Department of Revenue—began going up on the site. Preservationists then convinced the state to move the original portion of the house (which had acquired a couple of additions) here. The house was restored to its 1850s configuration by the West Seventh/Fort Road Federation and is once again a private home.

19 St. Paul Public Schools Administration Building and Bridge View School

360 Colborne St.

HGA, 1973

A pair of connected buildings that display the boxy brick look favored in the 1970s.

City and County Hospital, 1900

LOST 2 *This site was once occupied by* **City and County Hospital,** *renamed* **Ancker Hospital** *in 1923 after its longtime superintendent, Dr. Arthur B. Ancker. Established in 1874 in an old mansion, the hospital moved into a new building in 1889. The building, a grand Victorian exercise in the picturesque, featured a procession of sculpted gables that marched along to either side of a central tower. Although it might have found a new use in more enlightened times, the entire hospital complex was demolished in the late 1960s after the new St. Paul–Ramsey (now Regions) Hospital opened in downtown St. Paul.*

20 Anton Novotny House

321 Colborne St.

1880

An unusual house with a low ground floor of local limestone beneath an upper floor of brick. The house's odd configuration stems from the fact that it was built before the city established a final grade for Colborne St. Unsure as to street's ultimate level, Anton Novotny, a shoemaker, hedged his bets by building the ground floor as a sort of elevated basement.

21 Henry and Rose Lauer House

376 St. Clair Ave.

1882 / addition, Mark Fitzpatrick, 1904

Originally located nearby on Richmond St., this house—now lovingly restored—began its life as a one-and-a-half-story, wood-frame dwelling. Henry Lauer and his wife bought the house in 1887 and moved it to this site, from which Henry could oversee construction of Lauer Flats. The house was also refaced in brick at this time. A full second story and a stone porch were added in 1904.

22 Lauer Flats ! N *L*

228–40½ Western Ave. South

William H. Castner, 1887

A stately row house, unique in St. Paul by virtue of its chaste, classically inspired style and its exterior of buttery Mankato-Kasota stone. Bracketed balconies with ornamental iron railings are the boldest feature of the facade. Other elements—including slightly projecting bays, window surrounds, and pilasters—are handled with great subtlety. On the north side, there are even false windows designed to maintain the overall symmetry of the design. The row house is named after its builders and first owners, brothers Henry and Charles

Lauer Flats, 1964

Lauer. Stonecutters from Alsace-Lorraine, they settled in St. Paul in about 1880 and opened a business near the Upper Landing. They built the row house as a rental property.

Lauer Flats originally had 14 two-story units, an arrangement expressed by its paired front doors. By the early 1970s the building had fallen into utter disrepair. The availability of tax credits after 1976 finally spurred renovation, and Lauer Flats was converted to condominiums in 1979. It remains one of St. Paul's most important works of nineteenth-century architecture.

23 Schneider-Bulera House

365 Michigan St.

ca. 1857–58

For a time this wood-frame house was thought to be the oldest in St. Paul, possibly dating to the 1840s. Recent evidence suggests, however, that it was built about a decade later. The house was moved here sometime in the 1860s. Like an amazing number of houses in St. Paul, this one stayed in the same family for many years: 118, to be exact. Franz and Barbara Schneider, Austrian immigrants, moved into the house in 1869, and their descendants finally sold it in 1987.

24 Hassell-Fabel House

273 Goodhue St.

1856 and later

John Hassell built a Greek Revival cottage here in 1856. Shoemaker

Phillip Fabel bought the property in 1870 and added a wing to the west, creating the house's unusual profile. Fabel lived in the house until his death in 1921, but the shoe store he established nearby on West Seventh St. remained in business until the 1980s.

Charles Ringwald House

25 Charles Ringwald House

266 Goodrich Ave.

1874

A Greek Revival–Italianate cottage small in size but big in the charm department. It was not always so: photographs from the 1980s show a house mugged by modern-era remodelings. All that work has since been undone, however, and the little house has been restored to its original state of grace. The home's first owner, Charles Ringwald, was a cigar maker.

John Miner House

26 John Miner House

256 Goodrich Ave.

ca. 1877

One of the neighborhood's most beautifully restored homes, with everything you could want from a modest Italianate house of its era. The original owner's résumé included stints as a policeman and candy maker, two trades not usually thought to have much in common.

27 Anton Waldman House

445 Smith Ave. North

ca. 1860

This is among five early stone houses that survive in the West Seventh neighborhood. Note the S-shaped iron braces on the side walls. Connected to a rod that runs the length of the house, the braces help keep the walls from bowing out. Anton Waldman, the original owner, was a German immigrant who operated a flour and feed store on West Seventh St.

28 Avery Adams House

454 Smith Ave. North

Avery Adams (builder), 1854

One of the neighborhood's oldest homes outside of the Irvine Park Historic District, this brick cottage with Greek Revival features was built by a brick mason from Massachusetts who also worked on the first Minnesota State Capitol. A year after this house was completed, Adams and his wife left St. Paul during a cholera epidemic and settled in Steele County.

POI B North High Bridge Park

Off Smith Ave. at north end of High Bridge

1987 and later / Art: The Watcher (stone and iron sculpture), Zoran Mojsilov, 1995 / Green Chair, Joel Sisson, 2002 / Community Gate, Craig David, 2004

A small park with stone sculptures and benches, one of the oversized Adirondack chairs that are scattered around the Twin Cities, and a baptismal gate salvaged from a local church.

29 Schmitz-Rose House

182 Goodrich Ave.

Edward P. Bassford, 1887

A restored Queen Anne that, in 1995, was used in the filming of

a dog of a movie called *Feeling Minnesota* that featured such Hollywood luminaries as Keanu Reeves and Cameron Diaz.

Schillinger-Brings House

30 Schillinger-Brings House

178 Goodrich Ave.

1859

The largest of West Seventh's contingent of stone houses, moved here from 314 Smith Ave. North in 1989. It was built for (and probably by) a Swiss-born stonemason named John Schillinger. Joseph Brings, a barrel maker, was its second occupant. The house has a modern addition to the rear and reconstructed porches.

31 Gardner Row House

89–97 Leech St.

Hermann Kretz, 1891

A spicy stylistic gumbo that includes three split pediments perched on the roof like giant birds primed for flight. The open, spindly porches are also original. The row house, restored in 1978, was built by Elizabeth Gardner, who lived close at hand on McBoal St.

32 Gardner-Tracy House

192 McBoal St.

H. Sackville Treherne, 1886

Is there a more British sounding name than H. Sackville Treherne? An architect and engineer, Treherne in fact served as a British vice counsel from about 1884 to 1888. He designed this large home for Jason Gardner, a New

Yorker who migrated to St. Paul in the 1860s. For many years the house was owned, suitably enough, by an English couple named Timothy and Matilda Tracy and their descendants. The house has been extensively restored by its current owners.

33 O'Brien-Diderich House

194 McBoal St.

1877

A straightforward Italianate house restored with great care after being subdivided into apartments for almost 90 years. The front porch is a modern reconstruction, faithfully done. The original owners were Patrick and Fannie O'Brien, who raised six children here.

Martin Weber House

34 Martin Weber House

202 McBoal St.

Jacob Amos and Christian Rhinehardt (stone masons), 1867 / restored, 1989

A small home made from blocks of limestone probably quarried on site when the basement was excavated. Greek Revival in style, it was built for a German immigrant and stayed in the family for many years, sprouting a series of casual additions along the way.

35 Nathan Myrick Double House

103–5 Wilkin St.

Charles Wallingford, 1886

Although shorn of its front porch, this remains an impressive Romanesque Revival double house. Myrick was a St. Paul pioneer (and before that, the founder of La Crosse, WI) who made his living as an Indian trader until his business was

wiped out during the Dakota War of 1862. He later became involved in mining and other endeavors.

POI C Chicago, Milwaukee, St. Paul and Pacific Railroad (Milwaukee Road) "Short Line"

Along Mississippi River cliffs west of Chestnut St.

1879 and later

The rail line that climbs the cliffs here is said to be among the steepest in the Midwest, rising 230 feet in its first five miles. The project, which required construction of massive stone walls, was one of the great engineering feats of nineteenth-century St. Paul. The Milwaukee Road built this "short line" between St. Paul and Minneapolis to shave a few miles from the standard intercity route through Trout Brook valley. The tracks are now used by the Canadian Pacific Railroad.

36 St. Paul Municipal Grain Terminal (Equity Cooperative) Head House and Sack House **N**

Shepard Rd. and Chestnut St.

George M. Shepard, John W. Kelsey, and Walter F. Schulz (engineers), 1931

These two buildings—a tall concrete grain elevator and an adjoining sack house—are all that remain of the old St. Paul Municipal Grain Terminal. The terminal, designed to transfer grain from railroad cars to barges, once connected to a flour mill and elevator complex built by the farmer-owned Equity Cooperative Exchange. The idea was to provide a means of shipping grain other than through Minneapolis, where such giant firms as Cargill controlled the trade. The terminal complex gradually grew obsolete, and most of the structures were demolished in 1989. Current plans call for renovating the buildings into a restaurant and interpretive center.

"Little Italy," 1908

LOST 3 *Much lore surrounds the community known as* **"Little Italy"** *that once flourished on the Upper Levee Flats along the Mississippi west of Chestnut St. The flats were settled in the nineteenth century by a mixed lot of squatters, mainly poor immigrants. Displaying the usual sensitivity of the era, a newspaper in 1886 described these newcomers as suffering from "stinted intellects, depraved habits, and a lawless disposition."*

By 1900, immigrants from two small towns in southern Italy established themselves here and built up a community of tidy homes that survived for 60 years despite numerous inundations. A particularly bad flood in 1952 finally convinced the city to clear the flats. The last houses were demolished in 1960, after which the city—in a move that cannot be described as visionary—turned over the site to a scrap yard. By 1990, however, the flats were once again cleared, paving the way for development of new housing and parks.

37 Upper Landing Development

Shepard Rd. west of Chestnut St.

KKE Architects and ESG Architects, 2003 and later

Here on the old flood-washed flats of the former Little Italy is one of the largest housing developments in St. Paul's history, carefully protected by design guidelines from any threat of architectural inspiration. The project's seven housing blocks contain more than 600 townhomes, condominiums, and rental apartments. Arranged with all the charm of military barracks, the brick-, stucco-, and metal-clad buildings could have

gone anywhere. Looking at this uninspiring development, you have to wonder whether the city should ditch its "new urbanist" guidelines in favor of a design process open to a broader range of possibilities. Although the architecture here leaves much to be desired, the city did its usual first-class job of laying out new parks, trails, and other public amenities as part of the development.

Ramsey Professional Building, 1964

38 Ramsey Professional Building (German Presbyterian Bethlehem Church) N *L*

311 Ramsey St.

Gilbert and Taylor, 1890

A blithe fairy tale of a church, said to have been inspired by Swiss mountain chapels. With its rustic stonework, sweeping front staircase, delicately steepled tower, and timbered porch, it's not only a charming design but also an appropriate one for its site at the base of Ramsey Hill—the closet thing to the Alps you'll find in St. Paul. The church was built for a German-speaking congregation whose minister, the Reverend Nicholas Bolt, was born in Switzerland and perhaps implanted alpine thoughts in Gilbert's head. The congregation disbanded during the anti-German hysteria of World War I, and the church building later served as a clubhouse, a funeral home, and a dance studio before being converted to offices.

39 Kraus-Anderson Construction Co. (Hope Engine Co. No. 3)

1 Leech St.

Charles Hoffman, 1872

This Italianate-style fire hall, now doing mundane duty as a warehouse, is St. Paul's oldest public building. Constructed for a volunteer engine company organized in 1868, it became a city-operated fire station after 1877 and remained so for 102 years. The building originally had a bell tower as well as an arched doorway, which was squared off in 1924.

40 Anton and Karolina Jurka House

16 Douglas St.

1882

A tiny Greek Revival house with "shotgun" additions to the rear. From 1882 to 1900 it was the home of Anton Jurka and his family. Jurka was a Czech immigrant who became the first music teacher for the St. Paul public school system. The couple's daughter, who later went by the name Blanch Yurka, won fame as a stage actress and also starred in a number of movies.

James C. Burbank Row House

41 James C. Burbank Row House

277–83 Goodrich Ave.

1874 / renovated, ca. 1990s, 2006

Possibly the oldest row house in St. Paul, built by entrepreneur James C. Burbank, who is better known for his magnificent stone mansion at 432 Summit Ave. Burbank constructed this three-unit row house for members of his family, including his elderly parents and a widowed sister. The row house, which mixes Italianate and Gothic Revival elements, is now condominiums.

42 Christian Rhinehardt House

383 Goodhue St.

ca. 1855 / additions, ca. 1869, 1875

This Greek Revival house began its life as a small shop located somewhere near downtown before being moved here in 1869. The new owner, stonemason Christian Rhinehardt, enlarged the house twice over the next six years. Donald Empson, author of one of the handiest of all St. Paul history books, *The Street Where You Live*, began restoring the house in 1992. A subsequent owner completed the work.

Charles A. Hausler House, 1974

43 Charles A. Hausler House

526 Grace St.

Charles A. Hausler, 1917

An exquisite Prairie Style house in an unglamorous locale near the "Short Line" tracks. Charles Hausler was St. Paul's city architect from 1914 to 1922 and an admirer of Frank Lloyd Wright. This house's wide eaves, heavy corner piers, and banded windows all derive from Wright's bag of tricks, yet Hausler managed to combine these elements in a way distinctly his own. The house was originally at 1734 West Seventh St. In 1960, as Seventh became more commercial, Hausler agreed to sell the house to a friend with the provision that it be moved to a new location.

West Seventh

44 John Lauer House

449 Arbor St.

Charles A. Hausler, 1914

A brick house built for a son of Henry Lauer, one of two brothers who founded the firm behind Lauer Flats. The distinctive column capitals, stained-glass transoms, and compact massing are all very much in the spirit of the Chicago architect Louis Sullivan. This house's architect, Charles Hausler, worked briefly for Sullivan and clearly learned some lessons from the master.

45 John Keintz House

877 Randolph Ave.

John Keintz (builder), ca. 1885 / 1898

A rare beauty. When Keintz, a mason, rebuilt this house in 1898 he created a two-tone effect by using brick trim around windows and doors as a counterpoint to the stone walls. More typically, it was done the other way around—stone accenting brick. Note also the tree motif worked into the front gable, along with the date of the house.

Ayd Mill, 1889

LOST 4 *In 1860 John Ayd, a German immigrant, built a **stone house** and **gristmill** where Interstate 35E now crosses Jefferson Ave. To power his mill, Ayd dammed Cascade Creek, which flowed through a valley and then tumbled over a waterfall (near today's Bridge View School) before emptying into the Mississippi. In 1879 the Milwaukee Road built its "Short Line" along the creek, cutting off the mill's water supply. The mill was already a ruin by the time it was demolished in the early 1890s. Ayd's house, at 987 Jefferson, stood until 1966, when it was razed for the interstate. Today, Ayd Mill Rd. follows the old valley of Cascade Creek, long since diverted underground.*

Irvine Park

The Irvine Park neighborhood, where you'll find some of the oldest houses in St. Paul, is not quite what it seems. Platted in 1849 by John Irvine and Henry Rice, the neighborhood at first appears to be a miracle of history—a collection of historic homes within shouting distance of downtown that has somehow remained largely intact for over 150 years. To be sure, there are houses here that still stand on their original sites, and the little park itself—the only New England–style square in the Twin Cities—is indeed a survivor from another time.

But the neighborhood as a whole can best be described as a historic reconstruction, initiated in the 1970s by a determined band of residents who worked with the St. Paul Housing and Redevelopment Authority and other agencies to transform what had become a very blighted part of the city. A restoration plan guided the transformation. Although some buildings were razed, many historic homes were restored. Several houses—either from within the neighborhood or from other locales—were moved onto vacant lots. New infill houses were also designed to complement the neighborhood's historic character. Much of Irvine Park was added to the National Register of Historic Places in 1973 and is also a city-designated historic district.

Irvine Park

POI D Irvine Park **N** *L*

Walnut St. and Ryan Ave.

1849 and later / renovated,
William Sanders, 1978

This public square, laid out so that streets extend from the center of each side, was initially little more than a patch of open ground used to graze livestock. The city began to develop the park in 1872, the year in which it was named after pioneer John Irvine. A fountain was installed in 1881, but beyond that very little was done to improve the park. By the 1970s, when the neighborhood's renaissance began, the fountain was long gone and the park as a whole was in disrepair. That soon changed: in 1978 a new fountain replicating the original was installed in the center of the park, which was also landscaped to more closely resemble its nineteenth-century appearance. Today, the park continues to serve its traditional role as the neighborhood's green centerpiece.

46 Murray-Lanpher House **N** *L*

35 Irvine Pk.

Edward P. Bassford, 1886

Irvine Park's grand Victorian dame, restored in the 1970s after enduring many years as an asphalt-sided hulk cut up into numerous sleeping rooms. This is probably what most people have in mind when they dream of a Queen Anne house.

47 Wagner-Marty House **N** *L*

38 Irvine Pk.

ca. 1858

This lot's complex history provides a perfect example of how Irvine Park was re-created. The Greek Revival house you see today was built in the 1850s in what is now suburban Woodbury. It was moved here in the early 1980s after a house transplanted to this site in 1979 (from St. Paul's East Side) burned down. Before all of this happened, there were at least two other houses here.

Wright-Prendergast House

48 Wright-Prendergast House **N** *L*

223 Walnut St.

1851 / 1860 / remodeled,
Mark Fitzpatrick, 1907

A Greek Revival house that took on far grander aspirations when its second owners, James and Anna Prendergast, hired architect Mark Fitzpatrick to add some neoclassical heft to the main facade. Fitzpatrick obliged with a monumental Ionic portico crowned by an ornate pediment. It's not quite Tara, but it'll do for St. Paul. Descendants of the Prendergasts still live in the house.

49 John McDonald House **N** *L*

56 Irvine Pk.

1873

The front of this Italianate house has so much going on that it looks downright crowded. Now condominiums, it was moved from Smith Ave. in 1978 and restored. Legend holds that it's the only house in St. Paul history to receive a parking ticket, issued by an eagle-eyed enforcement agent when the structure was left in the street overnight during its move.

Dr. Justus Ohage House, 1936

50 Dr. Justus Ohage House N *L*

59 Irvine Pk.

Emil Ulrici, 1889

There's a decidedly Germanic feel to this Romanesque Revival house, built of cream-colored brick and supposedly designed to resemble the childhood home of Ohage's wife, Augusta, in St. Louis. She had little time to enjoy her new home, however, dying at age 34 just weeks after the house was finished. Notable features include a polygonal corner tower worthy of a small church and a porte cochere made of cast iron.

Its owner was more remarkable than the house. After his wife's premature death, Ohage raised their five children, established St. Paul's public health service, equipped the public baths at Harriet Island before donating them to the city, and also found time to perform the first successful gall bladder operation in the United States, in 1886.

51 Humphrey-Willis House N *L*

240 Ryan Ave.

1851 / addition, 1885

The original portion of this house is a perfectly symmetrical version

of a hip-roofed Georgian house, shrunk to cottage size.

52 Charles Symonds House N *L*

234 Ryan Ave.

1850

This simple box of a house is thought to be the oldest in St. Paul. It was built by Charles Symonds, a Scotsman and former sea captain who'd wandered far from salt water. Originally across the street and just to the east, the house was moved to this location by a new owner in 1913. The front porches were rebuilt in 1975 when the house was converted into a duplex.

53 Jay and Henry Knox House N *L*

26 Irvine Pk.

1860

Built by brothers who were bankers, this is Irvine Park's only Gothic Revival house and one of the few left in the Twin Cities. The vertical board-and-batten siding, a hallmark of the style, was discovered beneath a stucco overlay when new owners began restoring the house in the 1970s.

Parker-Marshall House

54 Parker-Marshall House N *L*

30 Irvine Pk.

1852

This side-hall Greek Revival house, the oldest on the park, was originally at 35 Irvine Pk. In 1883 it was moved to an adjoining lot. It took another short trip in 1976 when it was moved to this site. Past residents include William Marshall, governor of Minnesota from 1866 to 1870.

55 Simpson-Wood House N *L*

32 Irvine Pk.

ca. 1853 / addition, ca. 1865

A simple Federal Style house. It stood on Sherman St. before being moved in 1978.

56 Rogers-Johnson House N *L*

306 South Exchange St.

Augustus Gauger, 1881

Another stylistic combo, built by William Dice Rogers, who years earlier had gained notoriety in St. Paul when he paid a visit to his neighbor's wife while neglecting to wear pants. Rogers's apparel problems apparently continued: his second wife divorced him on grounds of infidelity.

57 Second Frank Jansen House N *L*

278–80 Sherman St.

1911

Only in St. Paul would you find a house that carries an address on a nonexistent street. When it was built by the busy Frank Jansen, the house was indeed on Sherman. However, portions of the street were vacated in the 1970s. Despite this irksome fact, the house retained its address.

58 Forepaugh's Restaurant (Joseph Forepaugh House) N *L*

276 South Exchange St.

1870 / enlarged, Abraham M. Radcliffe, ca. 1880 / renovated, 1976

One of Irvine Park's best-known attractions, this house-turned-restaurant was built by dry goods dealer Joseph Forepaugh, who made enough money supplying troops during the Civil War to retire at age 34. Parts of the mansion, including the front half of the mansard roof and the porte cochere, are modern reconstructions.

59 Alexander Ramsey House ! N *L*

265 South Exchange St.

Monroe Sheire, 1872

This hefty stone house is the best surviving example in the Twin Cities of the French Second Empire style. It was built for Alexander Ramsey, Minnesota's

Alexander Ramsey House

West Seventh

first territorial and second state governor. His first house, on the same site, was more modest. In 1857 he and his wife, Anna, moved it across Walnut St. with the intention of building a much larger new home here. But it wasn't until 1868—by which time Ramsey was a member of the U.S. Senate—that work finally began on this house. When it was finally finished in 1872, the Ramseys threw a party for laborers who had worked on it, even providing ten gallons of beer to keep things lively.

Built of blocks of local limestone, the house offers a catalog of French Second Empire features, including a mansard roof, paired eaves brackets, window hoods (a holdover from the related Italianate style), and a front porch with delicate columns and fretwork. Architect Monroe Sheire was an early master builder who designed mansions for St. Paul's elite.

Ramsey's descendants lived in the house until the 1960s, when they willed the mansion and its original furnishings to the Minnesota Historical Society, which restored it inside and out and opened it as a house museum. The house's large grounds have also remained intact, although the carriage house is a modern reconstruction of the original.

60 McCloud-Edgerton House N L

311 Walnut St.

ca. 1867

An unusual one-story house with Greek Revival and Italianate features. Built as a duplex, it was moved here from 240 West Seventh St. in 1916.

61 Panama Flats Row House (Stoddart Block) N L

226–34 South Exchange St.

George and Frank Orff, 1886

Originally known as the Stoddart Block, this Queen Anne–style row house was renamed Panama Flats in 1907 by owners who were apparently enthralled by the Panama Canal, then under construction. The building was rehabilitated into condominiums in 1979.

Armstrong-Quinlan House

62 Armstrong-Quinlan House N L

225 Eagle Pkwy.

Edward P. Bassford, 1886 / renovated, 2006

A 10,000-square-foot double house, originally located at 233–35 West Fifth St. in downtown St. Paul. It was built as a rental property by John M. Armstrong. Architect Edward P. Bassford gave it the full Victorian treatment, layering the front facade with arches, pediments, turrets, finials, and other flourishes. Later converted into a nursing home, the house was purchased by the state in 1988 for possible use as an arts high school. That idea never materialized, however, and the house stood vacant for 13 years while a blizzard of studies, plans, reports, and proposals piled up around it. In 2001 the house was moved at a cost of $2 million to its current site, where the Historic Irvine Park Association and the West Seventh/Fort Road Federation turned it into upscale condominiums.

12

Summit Avenue, the Historic Hill District, & Summit-University

Overview

Ramsey Hill, Summit Hill, Crocus Hill, Cathedral Hill, and St. Anthony Hill are all names that have been applied at one time or another to neighborhoods in this large section of St. Paul, which perhaps explains why it is often simply called the Hill District. Whatever the name, it is an extraordinary place. Extending back from the high bluffs overlooking downtown, the neighborhood offers one of the nation's great displays of Victorian-era housing. At the center of it all, literally and metaphorically, is Summit Avenue, a boulevard of dreams that remains the pride of the city.

The Hill District, which was added to the National Register of Historic Places in 1976, actually encompasses two neighborhoods. South of Summit and extending along the bluffs to Lexington Parkway is Summit Hill, popularly known as Crocus Hill. This is a gold-plated residential precinct, its long blocks lined with large, well-kept houses, generally built between about 1890 and 1920. Here, too, is Grand Avenue, where homes, apartments, and businesses have been stirred together to create a lively and urbane street.

North of Summit is Ramsey Hill, much of which is in a local historic district as well as the larger National Register district. Victorian houses of every size, shape, and style populate the streets of Ramsey Hill, which includes the lower—and most spectacular—stretch of Summit. Here you'll find such architectural monuments as the St. Paul Cathedral (1915), the James J. Hill House (1891), and Laurel Terrace (1887).

Officially, Ramsey Hill is part of a larger neighborhood known as Summit-University, which extends north to University Avenue and west to Lexington. The heart of St. Paul's black community is in this neighborhood, although many residents were uprooted in the 1960s by construction of Interstate 94, which obliterated historic Rondo Avenue.

The history of Summit Avenue and the Hill District goes back to the earliest days of the city. Mansions appeared on the crest of Summit by the 1850s; early settlers also built homes farther out along nearby streets. The neighborhood didn't begin to fill in until after the Civil War, but even then development was hampered by the lack of ready transportation to the downtown area.

The Hill District's biggest growth spurt came in the 1880s, abetted by the provision of city water service in 1884 and the completion of a cable car line along Selby Avenue in 1887. Three years later, St. Paul's first streetcars began operating on Grand. With its high elevation, proximity to downtown, and relatively level terrain suitable for home building, the Hill District became *the* place to live in St. Paul. Development came a bit later to much of the Summit Hill area, in part because of its distance from the Selby cable car line, but once trolleys began running on Grand, Summit Hill also saw new home construction.

Much of the Hill District began to decline in the 1930s. Old mansions became down-at-heels rooming houses; some homes stood vacant for years. Even so, the district's stock of historic properties remained more or less intact, in part because of geography. The bluffs separating the Hill District from downtown St. Paul formed a natural barrier against commercial sprawl. St. Paul's less than dynamic economy also minimized development pressure.

In the late 1960s and early 1970s a great turnaround began in the Hill District. Young couples discovered the neighborhood's Victorian homes—which could be bought for the proverbial song—and began restoring them. Neighborhood associations and nonprofit developers like Old Town Restorations, Inc., spurred preservation efforts and also built new infill housing in cooperation with an alphabet soup of city, state, and federal agencies. Today, just as in the nineteenth century, the Hill District is one of St. Paul's most desirable places to live.

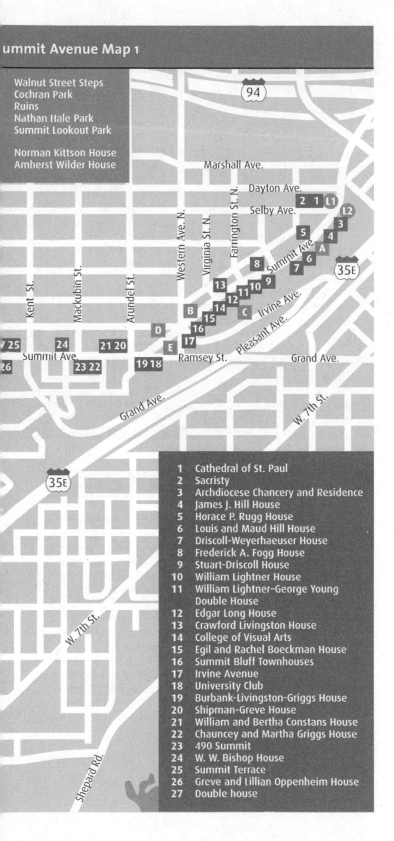

ummit Avenue Map 1

Walnut Street Steps
Cochran Park
Ruins
Nathan Hale Park
Summit Lookout Park

Norman Kittson House
Amherst Wilder House

1   Cathedral of St. Paul
2   Sacristy
3   Archdiocese Chancery and Residence
4   James J. Hill House
5   Horace P. Rugg House
6   Louis and Maud Hill House
7   Driscoll-Weyerhaeuser House
8   Frederick A. Fogg House
9   Stuart-Driscoll House
10 William Lightner House
11 William Lightner–George Young
    Double House
12 Edgar Long House
13 Crawford Livingston House
14 College of Visual Arts
15 Egil and Rachel Boeckman House
16 Summit Bluff Townhouses
17 Irvine Avenue
18 University Club
19 Burbank-Livingston-Griggs House
20 Shipman-Greve House
21 William and Bertha Constans House
22 Chauncey and Martha Griggs House
23 490 Summit
24 W. W. Bishop House
25 Summit Terrace
26 Greve and Lillian Oppenheim House
27 Double house

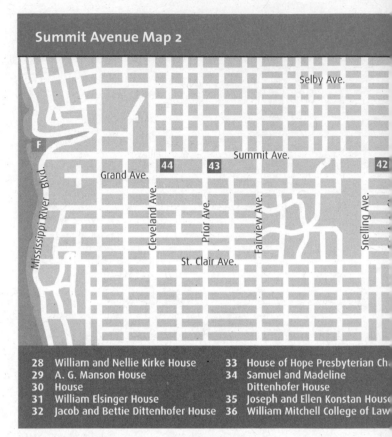

Summit Avenue Map 2

Summit Avenue

Summit Avenue is St. Paul's most renowned street, a mansion row that extends for nearly five miles through the western half of the city. It is literally ground zero for much of its course, serving as the divider between north and south street addresses. It plays an equally essential role in what might be called the city's sense of self. St. Paulites take great pride in the avenue, and its very name conjures up images of huge houses, monumental churches, wide green lawns, and a refined and gracious way of life.

Historian Ernest Sandeen pronounced Summit "the best preserved American example of the Victorian monumental residential boulevard," and it is hard to dispute that judgment. Still, Summit has over the years had its critics. F. Scott Fitzgerald, who grew up haunted by its luxurious shadow, famously called Summit "a museum of American architectural failures." It's far from that, but it is true that while a few of Summit's mansions rank among the best American houses of their

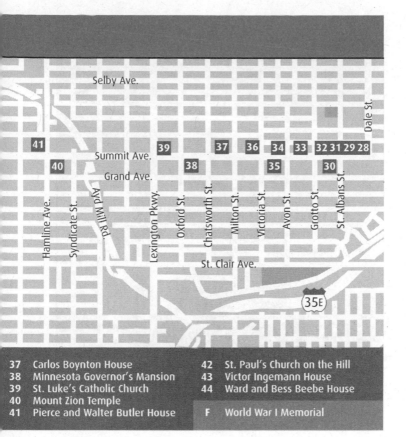

time, the vast majority are not architectural masterpieces. Nor are most of them dramatically different from those that can be found in other large cities in the United States.

Yet as Sandeen understood so well, what counts on Summit is less the individual excellence of its homes than its totality as a preserved environment. In his book *St. Paul's Historic Summit Avenue*, first published in 1978, Sandeen found that of the 440 houses built on Summit up to that time, 373 survived—a truly remarkable number. A scattering of new homes and condominiums has appeared along the avenue since 1978, but little if anything has come down. Today, all of Summit falls within local and national historic districts.

Summit is also exceptional because of the way it's integrated into the life of St. Paul. Wealth in most places tends to hide away behind walls, gates, hedges, and even armed guards. By contrast, Summit's big houses, posing forthrightly behind their broad lawns, are there for all to see and enjoy. As a result, St. Paulites view Summit not as an exclusive enclave of the rich but as a four-and-a-half-mile-long public promenade with some wonderful architectural scenery.

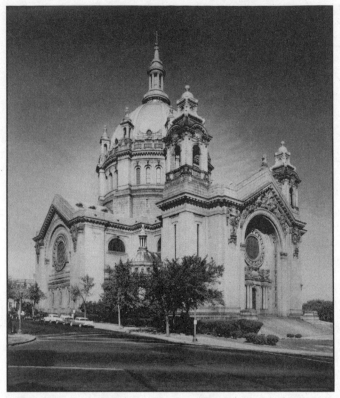

Cathedral of St. Paul, 1950

1 Cathedral of St. Paul ! N L

201 Summit Ave.
(also 239 Selby Ave.)

Emmanuel Masqueray, 1915 / interior, Maginnis and Walsh (Boston), 1925–31 / renovation, Foster Dunwiddie Architects, 2003 / Notable art: altar canopy, Whitney Warren, 1924 / "Te Deum" and "Magnificat" (bronze grilles), Albert H. Atkins, 1926 / "The Resurrection," "The Beatitudes," and "The Jesuit Martyrs" (stained-glass rose windows), Charles Connick, 1932, 1940

It's possible to think of St. Paul without this vast church of gray granite, but just barely. From its incomparable site on St. Anthony Hill, the cathedral is—along with the nearby State Capitol—one of the city's defining monuments, its dome visible from almost every corner of St. Paul. Despite its grandeur, the cathedral has been criticized as something like the SUV of churches, too large and top-heavy for its own good. F. Scott Fitzgerald, for example, likened it to "a big white bulldog

on its haunches," and he wasn't being complimentary. The cathedral does convey a sense of aggressive purpose, and its muscular architecture seems as much an expression of power as it is of faith. But step inside, and whatever doubts you may have are overwhelmed by the cathedral's mighty reality. *Awe* is a word seldom used in architectural discourse anymore, but it applies here. The sweep of space beneath the dome simply has no equal in the Twin Cities.

This cathedral is actually St. Paul's fourth; the first three, beginning with the log chapel built by Father Lucien Galtier in 1841, were all downtown and are now gone. It owes its existence to a pair of extraordinary men: Archbishop John Ireland, who presided over the St. Paul–Minneapolis Archdiocese from 1888 to 1918, and French-born architect Emmanuel Masqueray, who trained at the prestigious École des Beaux-Arts in Paris. Ireland was visiting the St. Louis World's Fair in May 1904 when he was introduced to Masqueray, the fair's chief designer. Less than a year later, Masqueray moved to St. Paul and began to design the cathedral.

Following a symmetrical Greek cross plan, the cathedral mixes Renaissance and Baroque Revival elements in a way very much Masqueray's own. As a result, the church is anything but "pure" in its style or its proportions: the 306-foot-high dome, for example, has always seemed like a giant head on a body not quite large enough to support it. Among the cathedral's most distinctive elements are three huge "telephone dial" rose windows—a Masqueray trademark.

Although the cathedral was dedicated in 1915 after eight years of construction, its interior of whitewashed brick walls was still quite stark. Another 25 years were required to substantially complete it. Masqueray died in 1917, Ireland a year later, and in 1923 the Boston firm of Maginnis and Walsh was called in to take charge of the project and also to design two new buildings—a rectory and sacristy—at the rear of the cathedral.

Inside the cathedral, finishing work proceeded through the 1930s. The brick walls were clad with Mankato-Kasota limestone over a marble base while artists provided stained-glass windows and sculptures. Among the outstanding artworks is a monumental baldachin, or altar canopy, by New York architect Whitney Warren (for whom Masqueray once worked). Equally impressive

Cathedral of St. Paul, interior

are the bronze grilles by Albert H. Atkins installed between the sanctuary and the ambulatory and the rose windows designed by Charles Connick. The interior was largely complete by 1940 except for decoration of the inner dome, which wasn't undertaken until the 1950s.

Beginning in 2001, the cathedral's exterior was repaired and restored at a cost of $32 million (about 20 times the original construction price). Workers sheathed the dome and roof in 100,000 square feet of new copper, cleaned and tuckpointed the Rockville granite facades, repaired windows, and upgraded mechanical and electrical systems. The project was finished in 2003, and the cathedral now looks as mighty and magnificent as it ever has.

2 Sacristy *L*

Maginnis and Walsh, 1925 / Art: angel (sculpture atop dome), Ernest Pellegrini, 1925

An elegant building that complements the cathedral while making a small statement of its own. Linked to the rear of the cathedral, the sacristy is in the form of a domed octagon, atop which an angel sculpted by New York artist Ernest Pellegrini poses in prayer. The rectory next door at 239 Selby Ave. was also designed by Maginnis and Walsh and dates to 1924.

LOST 1 *Before the cathedral was built, this site was occupied by the **Norman Kittson House,** a towering mansion completed in 1884. Kittson, a millionaire businessman, didn't enjoy his home for long; he died in 1888. The mansion had become a boardinghouse by the time the archdiocese bought it for $52,000 in 1904. It was razed a year later.*

3 Archdiocese Chancery and Residence *N L*

226–30 Summit Ave.

Cerny and Associates, 1963

A nicely crafted complex that displays the highly formal brand of modernism popular in the 1960s. Unfortunately, the one-story

chancery is out of sync with the historic two- and three-story homes on this part of the avenue.

Amherst Wilder House, 1895

LOST 2 *Among Summit Avenue's 60 or so lost mansions, the finest was the **Amherst Wilder House,** built in 1887 where the chancery now stands. Wilder, whose fortune continues to finance good works in St. Paul, lived in the house until his death in 1894. Like the James J. Hill House, the Wilder mansion was later owned by the archdiocese. Instead of being preserved, however, it was torn down in 1959—a great loss to the city.*

4 James J. Hill House ! *N L*

240 Summit Ave.

Peabody, Stearns and Furber (Boston), Irving and Casson (Boston), James Brodie, 1891

A stone hunk of a house that perfectly expresses the power and strength of its original owner, who roared through life like a locomotive but who also believed in building things to last. Hill's first St. Paul mansion, constructed in 1878, was a French Second Empire affair in Lowertown. By the mid-1880s, however, Summit Ave. had become the place to be.

Hill selected Peabody, Stearns and Furber of Boston as his architects. They designed a mansion of reddish Massachusetts sandstone that, at 36,000 square feet, is still St. Paul's largest private home. Stylistically, the mansion is an example of the bulked-up Romanesque Revival style pioneered by H. H. Richardson. The project didn't proceed smoothly. Hill battled the architects, who in 1889 overrode his orders regarding some stonework. Big mistake. Hill fired them and hired another

James J. Hill House

firm—along with his in-house architect, James Brodie—to finish the project.

The mansion seems rather forbidding, in part because its lively reddish brown walls were blackened over the years by coal smoke (the restored porte cochere shows the stone's original color). While *warmth* and *charm* aren't words you'd use to describe the mansion, it's actually quite inviting inside. Many of the main rooms feature gorgeously carved woodwork, executed by German-born craftsman John Kirchmayer. The house also has a lovely skylit art gallery, while to the rear are a series of open porches that provide views across the city.

Hill died in the house in 1916 and left no will despite a fortune estimated at about $20 billion in today's dollars. His wife, Mary, died in 1921, after which four of Hill's daughters donated the house to the archdiocese. The Minnesota Historical Society acquired the mansion in 1978; it's now a house museum open for tours and other events.

POI A Walnut Street Steps

Between Summit and
Irvine Aves.

ca. 1901

Walnut was once a platted street here, though the terrain was so steep that the right-of-way could accommodate foot traffic only by means of a stairway. When James J. Hill's son, Louis, decided in 1901 to build a house next

door, Hill petitioned to vacate the street. Hill got his wish, but not before the city required him to build a new staircase on the old right-of-way that would be forever open to the public. The stairs, bordered by a massive sandstone wall, remain in use today.

Horace P. Rugg House, 1891

5 Horace P. Rugg House N *L*

251 Summit Ave.

Hodgson and Stem, 1887

Mixing Romanesque and Renaissance Revival elements, this house is among the most original and sophisticated designs on Summit. Its walls of long Roman bricks, which rise above a sandstone base, are arranged in alternating bands of color that gradually dissolve into a single field as they reach the third floor. The entry porch is embellished with much stone carving, including six caryatids in different poses. Built for a Lowertown wholesaler who dealt in pumps and plumbing supplies, the house is now subdivided into condominiums.

Summit Avenue

Louis and Maud Hill House

6 Louis and Maud Hill House N *L*

260 Summit Ave.

Clarence H. Johnston, 1903 / front addition, Charles S. Frost, 1913 / restored, Close Associates (Gar Hargens), 2004–5

This might be called the *other* Hill House, and it's impressive in its own right. Louis Hill, James J. Hill's second son, commissioned the red brick Georgian Revival house before his marriage to Maud Van Courtland Taylor in 1901. In 1913 a large addition was placed across the front of the house, obscuring the 1903 facade (although the original front portico was reinstalled). The addition included four guest rooms and a second-floor ballroom. After Louis Hill's death in 1948, the house was purchased by a Roman Catholic educational guild, which in 1961 sold it to the Daughters of the Heart of Mary for use as a Catholic retreat center. The present owners have restored it, beautifully, to a single-family home.

7 Driscoll-Weyerhaeuser House N *L*

266 Summit Ave.

William H. Willcox, 1884

An early Queen Anne house with many of the usual bells and whistles—a slender round tower, decorative chimneys, and lots of busy brick- and stonework. Its first owner, Frederick Driscoll, was general manager of the *St. Paul Pioneer Press*. In 1900 the house was purchased by lumber baron Frederick Weyerhaeuser, the only man on Summit even richer than James J. Hill. The entry porch and porte cochere are not original.

8 Frederick A. Fogg House N *L*

285 Summit Ave.

Allen H. Stem, 1899

Colonial Revival treated in an unusually monumental way. Note the distinctive transoms over the windows and the elegance with which the front door's sidelights merge into a double arch above. Frederick Fogg was a director of the St. Paul Fire and Marine Insurance Co. (now St. Paul Travelers) and later served as superintendent of Ramsey County Schools.

9 Stuart-Driscoll House N *L*

312 Summit Ave.

1858 / additions, 1910, 1918

Summit's oldest house, an Italian Villa–style mansion with much Classical Revival updating. Built for lumber dealer David Stuart, the house once sported a cupola and a balustraded front terrace. Among later owners was Herman Haupt, a West Point–trained engineer who moved to St. Paul in 1881 to become general manager of the Northern Pacific Railroad. The three-story rear addition was built in 1918 by Arthur Driscoll, who owned the house from 1901 to 1949.

William Lightner House, 1973

10 William Lightner House ! N *L*

318 Summit Ave.

Cass Gilbert, 1893 / renovated and restored, Thomas Blanck, 2006

Cass Gilbert at the top of his form, and one of Summit's greatest houses. It's the last and best of a trio of Gilbert-designed mansions that form a row along the avenue's bluff side. At a time when Richardsonian Romanesque was already giving way to Classical Revival, Gilbert here combined the two into one taut yet monumental package. The sandstone entry arch is a Richardsonian trademark, as are the squat columns with Byzantine capitals that screen a row of windows above. But the rest of the front facade, built of rough-faced quartzite, has the symmetry and calm lines of classical architecture. The house was built for William Lightner, a lawyer who earlier had commissioned Gilbert and his then partner, James Knox Taylor, to design the double house next door. Once subdivided into seven apartments, the house was recently restored as a single-family home.

11 William Lightner–George Young Double House N L

322–24 Summit Ave.

Gilbert and Taylor, 1888 / renovated, JLG Architects, 2006

Although undeniably imposing, this double house—now three condominiums—isn't as crisp and masterful as the Lightner house next door. The western half has a formal, Renaissance Revival character; the eastern side tends more toward the informalities of Queen Anne and even has a shingled side gable. William Lightner built this house with his law partner, George Young.

12 Edgar Long House N L

332 Summit Ave.

Gilbert and Taylor, 1889

A broad, towered brick and stone house in the general realm of Romanesque Revival. The tower and central gable display fine floral carvings. Within the open front porch, small stained-glass windows line up beside arched double entry doors. The bricked-in wing above the tuck-under garage was originally an open porte cochere. Edgar Long was in the railroad and building construction businesses.

13 Crawford Livingston House N L

339 Summit Ave.

Cass Gilbert, 1898

Another of Gilbert's exercises in what might be called picturesque symmetry. Here, the arcaded loggia evokes the Venetian Renaissance while the central dormer above strikes a medieval pose with its steeply pitched roof and Gothic bargeboards. These romantic elements are reined in by strict overall symmetry, however. Now divided into five condominiums, the house was originally owned by Crawford Livingston, Jr., whose business interests included utilities and railroads.

14 College of Visual Arts (Watson P. Davidson House) N L

344 Summit Ave.

Thomas Holyoke, 1915

The details are Tudor Revival but the near-perfect symmetry of the facade is Beaux-Arts. The original owner was president of a prominent St. Paul real estate firm. The College of Visual Arts has occupied the house since 1961.

15 Egil and Rachel Boeckman House N L

366 Summit Ave.

David Adler and Robert Work (Chicago), 1928

In the 1920s, a Shingle Style house here was torn down. Dr. Egil Boeckman and his wife, Rachel (a daughter of James J. Hill), bought the property and then built a new house in the fashionable Georgian Revival mode. A hefty split pediment over the entry is one of many impressive details.

POI B Cochran Park N L

Summit and Western Aves.

1924 / shelter, Holyoke and Jemne, 1926 / Art: The Indian Hunter (statue), Paul Manship, 1927

This park was donated to the city by Emilie Cochran in memory of her husband, Thomas, an investment banker. The site had been an informal children's playground before the park was built.

Summit Bluff Townhouses

16 Summit Bluff Townhouses N *L*

376–78 Summit Ave.

Bentz/Thompson/Rietow Architects, 1982, 1986

The best of Summit's modern-era housing. These townhomes feature a series of layered front gables sharply outlined by white trim. The gables call to mind the avenue's traditional architecture but in an abstracted way that is unmistakably modern. Later infill housing on the avenue has generally opted for a more literal-minded, and far less successful, sort of historicism.

17 Irvine Avenue

Bluffs below Summit Ave. from near Ramsey St. to Walnut St. steps

This alleylike street plunges downhill here before dividing into two levels as it clings to the steep face of the bluffs below Summit. Old carriage houses (some renovated), newer homes, and even a ruin or two can be found along Irvine, which in the summer when the foliage is lush has the feel of a secret world all but unknown to the city around it.

POI C Ruins

Irvine Ave. beneath 332 Summit Ave.

About the closest thing to an old-world ruin in the Twin Cities. These picturesque stone remains

were once a large carriage house on the Edgar Long estate.

POI D Nathan Hale Park

Summit and Portland Aves., ca. 1900

Art: Nathan Hale *(statue), William Partridge, 1907*

The Revolutionary War patriot whose only regret was that he had too few lives to give for his country is memorialized here.

POI E Summit Lookout Park N *L*

Summit Ave. and Ramsey St.

ca. 1887 / Art: New York Life Eagle *(bronze sculpture), Augustus and Louis St. Gaudens, ca. 1889*

This small park with sweeping views of the city was from the 1860s until the 1880s home to a hotel known as Carpenter's Lookout. Today, its chief occupant is a magnificent bronze eagle sculpted by brothers Augustus and Louis St. Gaudens and originally mounted over the entrance of the New York Life Building (1889–1967) downtown. Public Art St. Paul led the effort to relocate the eagle, which was restored and installed here in 2004. The park's other outstanding feature is a huge limestone retaining wall along Ramsey St. hill that dates to the nineteenth century.

18 University Club N *L*

420 Summit Ave.

Reed and Stem, 1913

A gracious Tudor Revival club building. The dining room is open to the public and offers some of the best views in the city. Formed in 1904 as the St. Paul Club by wealthy young men from the neighborhood, the name was changed in 1910 when a new rule required members to be attending college at the time they joined.

Burbank-Livingston-Griggs House, 1880

19 Burbank-Livingston-Griggs House ! N *L*

432 Summit Ave.

Otis Wheelock (Chicago), 1863 / remodeled, Clarence H. Johnston, 1884, 1895 / addition, Allen H. Stem, 1925 / interior remodeled, Magnus Jemne, 1930, Edwin Lundie, 1930–33

This romantic limestone pile is the finest surviving mansion of its era in the Twin Cities. It's also a museum of local design, its interior worked and reworked over the years by some of St. Paul's leading architects. The home's builder was James C. Burbank, a Vermonter who migrated to St. Paul in 1850 and made a fortune by establishing a fleet of packet boats and operating stagecoach lines. In 1863, when Summit was a dusty carriage trail, he spent $22,000 (a phenomenal sum in those days) to erect this country estate. The house is a primer in the high-style Italianate of the 1860s. Its irregular massing, bracketed cornices with pendants, and tall arched windows framed by voussoirs convey a sense of the picturesque, as does the cupola crowned by an ornate finial.

After Burbank's death, a succession of owners hired prominent St. Paul architects to enlarge, renovate, and redecorate the house. In 1884, Clarence Johnston created a magnificent new front stair hall and also added the triple-arched window to the right of the front door for short-term owner George Finch. Eleven years later, Johnston updated the house's porches in the latest neoclassical style. In 1925, Allen Stem—working for the home's then owner, Crawford Livingston—designed a two-story addition to the rear. Livingston's daughter, Mary, and her husband, Theodore Griggs, later hired Magnus Jemne and then Edwin Lundie to undertake a series of interior renovations in various period styles. The house, owned by the University Club next door, is currently used as a residence.

Shipman-Greve House, 1885

20 Shipman-Greve House N *L*

445 Summit Ave.

LeRoy Buffington, 1882, 1884 / addition, ca. 1920s

This may be St. Paul's first Queen Anne–style house, and it remains one of the best, beautifully crafted in stone, wood, brick, and stucco. Although it shows an array of influences—the porch, for example, has a distinctly Chinese feel—the house is more restrained than the rambling, towered, gingerbread-laden extravaganzas usually classified as Queen Anne. Instead, it evokes the quietly picturesque, Tudor-tinged work of English Arts and Crafts architects like Richard Norman Shaw. The house was commissioned for an obscure businessman, Henry Shipman, who sold it before it was completed to real estate broker Herman Greve.

21 William and Bertha Constans House N *L*

465 Summit Ave.

Augustus Gauger, 1886 / remodeled, ca. 1920s, ca. 1969

William Constans, who arrived from France in 1850 and whose business enterprises included a wholesale brewery supply firm, built this house in the 1880s in the Queen Anne style. A subsequent owner, Walter Hill (one of James J.'s sons), gave the house an extensive Georgian Revival makeover in the 1920s. It was during this time that the house acquired its most curious element—an oblong projection atop the roof that has been likened to a coffin because of its shape and the swags that create the appearance of handles. So far as is known, however, no funeral is pending.

Chauncey and Martha Griggs House and 490 Summit

22 Chauncey and Martha Griggs House N *L*

476 Summit Ave.

Clarence H. Johnston, 1885

23 490 Summit (Addison G. Foster House) N *L*

490 Summit Ave.

Clarence H. Johnston, 1884

These complementary mansions were designed for business partners by Clarence Johnston in the first year of his practice. The Foster House—now used for weddings, receptions, and other events—is an energetic assembly of pieces that don't quite add up to a convincing whole. The Griggs House is a better design, more disciplined and monumental than its neighbor. Unfortunately, a large attic skylight added in 1939, when the house was being used as an art school, tends to undercut Johnston's overall design. Chauncey Griggs and Addison Foster were partners in a lumber and coal business.

24 W. W. Bishop House N *L*

513 Summit Ave.

Wirth and Haas, 1887

One of the few wood-frame Queen Anne houses on this part of Summit. It has a polygonal tower and a front gable that seems to be Flemish in inspira-

tion. W. W. Bishop was a real estate agent about whom little is known. Donald Ogden Stewart, the screenwriter of such classic films as *Dinner at Eight* (1933) and the *Prisoner of Zenda* (1937), once lived here.

Summit Terrace, 1891

25 Summit Terrace N *L*

587–601 Summit Ave.

Willcox and Johnston, 1889

A brownstone row house that leaves no Victorian style unaccounted for, although the general flavor is Romanesque Revival. Architecture does not explain why Summit Terrace is a National Historic Landmark, however. Its notoriety derives from its association with F. Scott Fitzgerald. The writer's parents, Edward and Mollie, moved to 593 Summit in 1914 when Fitzgerald was a student at Princeton University. In 1918 they relocated to the unit at 599 Summit, where in July and August 1919 Fitzgerald rewrote the manuscript that became his first novel. Accepted by Scribner's in mid-September, just days before Fitzgerald's 23rd birthday, and published in 1920, *This Side of Paradise* sold 50,000 copies and propelled its author to instant fame.

26 Greve and Lillian Oppenheim House N *L*

590 Summit Ave.

Ellerbe and Round, 1913

One of two notable Prairie Style houses on Summit, not up to the standards of Frank Lloyd Wright but competently done. The French doors in the projecting front bay are unusual for a home of this kind. Franklin Ellerbe and Olin Round designed one other Prairie Style building of note—a bank in Mankato that also dates to 1913. Greve Oppenheim was a real estate investor.

27 Double house N *L*

603–5 Summit Ave.

1987

This house touched off a brouhaha when it was built because its pink stucco was considered far too gaudy by Summit's guardians of good taste. It is now boringly neutral in color.

28 William and Nellie Kirke House N *L*

629 Summit Ave.

Clarence H. Johnston, 1896

A happy collision between a small French chateau and something out of merry old England. Among the noteworthy details is a pair of exquisite front doors. William Kirke was in the insurance and real estate businesses.

29 A. G. Manson House N *L*

649 Summit Ave.

1874

In 1919 John Kessler and Thomas Maguire acquired this French Second Empire house for use as a funeral parlor. Corpse-averse neighbors then prevailed on the city council to pass an ordinance forbidding funeral homes in residential areas. Kessler and Maguire opened their mortuary anyway and were promptly arrested for this, ah, grave offense. The case went to the Minnesota Supreme Court, which sided with the city and thereby preserved Summit for the living.

30 House N *L*

696 Summit Ave.

Alladin Improvement Co., 1963

Modern infill at its most unfathomably stupid. This small house was inserted here as someone's idea of a suitable addition to Summit Ave. Blame it on the bad karma of the 1960s.

31 William Elsinger House N *L*

701 Summit Ave.

Clarence H. Johnston, 1898

Jacob and Bettie Dittenhofer House and William Elsinger House

32 Jacob and Bettie Dittenhofer House N *L*

705 Summit Ave.

Cass Gilbert, 1898 / remodeled, Clarence H. Johnston, 1913

A pair of houses built in the same year and designed by St. Paul's two leading architects. Both houses are constructed of Mankato-Kasota stone, feature Medieval-inspired details, and are foursquare in form. Yet their effects are quite different. Gilbert, ever the classicist, gave the Dittenhofer House a symmetrical front facade. Johnston clung to a more picturesque Victorian manner, evident in the Elsinger House's corner tower and the off-center bay and dormer above the porch. As with other decisively paired houses on Summit, these were built for families who knew each other well. William Elsinger and Jacob Dittenhofer were partners in the Golden Rule Department Store in downtown St. Paul. They were also brothers-in law: Bettie Dittenhofer was Elsinger's sister.

33 House of Hope Presbyterian Church N *L*

797 Summit Ave.

Cram Goodhue and Ferguson (Boston), 1914 / addition, Harold E. Wagner, 1959 / Art: stained-glass windows, Charles Connick and others

House of Hope is among the oldest Protestant congregations in St. Paul, founded in 1855, and this "correct" if not especially scintillating church is one of Summit Ave.'s major monuments. With its attendant buildings, the church forms perhaps the most sophisticated example

House of Hope Presbyterian Church, 1918

of the Gothic Revival style in St. Paul. The original portions of the complex were designed by the firm of Ralph Adams Cram, a leading American church architect whose work includes the Cathedral of St. John the Divine in New York City.

Here, Cram chose his favored late English Gothic style, setting a steeply roofed nave in front of a pinnacled bell tower. Exterior detailing is chaste in keeping with Cram's desire to achieve a quiet effect. The intimate sanctuary features floor tiles from Pewabic Pottery of Detroit, a timber-beamed ceiling, and stained-glass windows designed by various artists, including Charles Connick, whose work also graces the St. Paul Cathedral. To the east of the main church is an education wing added in 1959. A chapel, offices, library, and other rooms are also incorporated into the church complex, which surrounds an inner courtyard known as a garth.

34 Samuel and Madeline Dittenhofer House N *L*

807 Summit Ave.

Clarence H. Johnston, 1908, 1911

Clarence Johnston designed 38 houses on Summit, and this one is surely among his best. It's a bold, powerful, and very long (81 feet) house, distinguished by an enormous eastern gable that plunges down to the first floor. Department store magnate Jacob Dittenhofer built the house as a wedding present for his son,

Samuel and Madeline Dittenhofer House

Samuel, and his bride, Madeline Lang. The Dittenhofers lived here until 1936, when they went off to Europe. Finding Europe to their liking, they never returned to St. Paul, and the house stood vacant until Madeline donated it to the Christian Brothers in 1966. The brothers sold the house in 1999, and it is now once again a single-family home.

35 Joseph and Ellen Konstan House N *L*

828 Summit Ave

SALA Architects, 2002

An expensive attempt, done with considerable skill, to reproduce the "old look" of Summit in a new Colonial Revival house. Trouble is, this house and other recent nostalgic infills can't compete with the avenue's elaborately detailed historic homes on their own terms.

36 William Mitchell College of Law N *L*

875 Summit Ave.

*Ellerbe and Co., 1931 / addition, 1957 / addition (**Warren E. Burger Library**), Winsor/Faricy Architects, 1990 / addition, Perkins and Will (Chicago), 2005*

The oldest part of this complex, along Portland Ave., was originally St. Luke's School and later became Our Lady of Peace Catholic High School. William Mitchell bought the Romanesque-style building in 1976 and has expanded it twice since then. The Warren E. Burger Library, which faces directly on Summit, is named after a William Mitchell graduate who was chief justice of the U.S. Supreme Court from 1969 to 1986.

37 Carlos Boynton House N *L*

955 Summit Ave.

Clarence H. Johnston, 1904

A Tudor Revival house with baroque elements such as the semicircular pediment above one of the dormers. The ornament that dances around the roof is some of the finest on Summit.

Minnesota Governor's Mansion, 1912

38 Minnesota Governor's Mansion (Horace and Clotilde Irvine House) N *L*

1006 Summit Ave.

William Channing Whitney, 1912 / Art: Man-Nam (sculpture), Paul Granlund, 1970 (located in yard west of mansion)

A standard (albeit very large) Tudor Revival exercise in red brick and stone. It was built for lumberman Horace Irvine and his wife, Clotilde. In 1965, their daughters donated the house to the state for use as a governor's mansion and guesthouse. The house has a contentious history. Governor Rudy Perpich complained in the 1980s that the roof leaked. Another colorful governor, Jesse Ventura, refused to live here after his 1998 election and shut down the mansion in a dispute with the state legislature over security costs. Despite these contretemps, the mansion—officially known as the Minnesota State Ceremonial Building—remains in use and is open for public tours.

St. Luke's Catholic Church

39 St. Luke's Catholic Church N *L*

1079 Summit Ave.

Comes, Perry McMullen (Pittsburgh) with Slifer and Abrahamson, 1925

One of the city's outstanding parish churches, a free interpretation of French and Italian Romanesque. The Summit Ave. facade has elaborately carved portals, the largest of which depicts Christ and various saints, conveniently identified in carved panels for those unschooled in hagiology. Above the main portal is a spectacular rose window set within a patterned frame. Inside, a coffered, barrel-vaulted ceiling rises over the long nave, which has arcaded side aisles. The church once had lavish mural work, but most of it was painted over in the 1980s.

Emmanuel Masqueray was the first choice for designing the church; however, after his premature death in 1917 the project went to John T. Comes of Pittsburgh. Comes also died at a relatively young age, in 1922, and the church was finished by others, including Frederick Slifer and Frank Abrahamson, two of Masqueray's former draftsmen.

Mount Zion Temple, 1958

40 Mount Zion Temple ! N *L*

1300 Summit Ave.

Erich Mendelsohn with Bergstedt and Hirsch, 1955 / renovated and restored, Bentz/Thompson/ Rietow Architects, 1997–2003

Home to St. Paul's oldest Jewish congregation, founded in 1856, this synagogue is the most striking modern-era building on Summit. It's also the last work of Erich Mendelsohn, a pioneer modernist who first gained attention for architectural sketches he produced while in the German army during World War I. He immigrated to the United States in 1941 and designed several other synagogues before receiving the commission for Mount Zion in 1950. Mendelsohn died suddenly in 1953, before the temple was finished, and St. Paul architect Milton Bergstedt completed the work.

Two boxlike, copper-clad volumes—housing the sanctuary and a small chapel—dominate the composition, rising dramatically above the main mass of the brick building, which includes a long education wing. These simple cubic forms were adopted after Mendelsohn's original design—featuring two tall volumes formed by bold triangular arches arranged in the manner of accordion pleats—proved too costly to build. Mendelsohn described the sanctuary and chapel, which have serenely elegant interiors, as "point and counterpoint," and they do indeed establish an architectural dialogue. The temple was expertly renovated by Bentz/Thompson/ Rietow Architects between 1997 and 2003.

41 Pierce and Walter Butler House N *L*

1345–47 Summit Ave.

Clarence H. Johnston, 1895

With its picturesque stepped and curved gables, this brick double house is one of Summit's more exotic specimens of architectural theater. It's done up in a late phase of the Tudor style sometimes called Jacobean Revival. Walter Butler was a founder of the Butler Brothers contracting firm. At the time this double house was built, his brother, Pierce, was the Ramsey County attorney. In 1922 Pierce was appointed to the U.S. Supreme Court; he remained a justice until his death in 1939.

42 St. Paul's Church on the Hill N *L*

1524 Summit Ave.

Emmanuel Masqueray, 1913 / additions, 1922 and later

This limestone church, built for Minnesota's second-oldest Episcopal congregation, is in the English Gothic Revival style that Masqueray preferred for Protestant churches. The copper-clad spire is especially fine. Within, you'll find an altar, woodwork, and stained glass, including two Tiffany windows, all salvaged from the congregation's first church, built in 1858 in Lowertown.

Macalester College

1600 Summit Ave.
(see under Macalester-Groveland)

43 Victor Ingemann House N *L*

1936 Summit Ave.

Ingemann and Co., 1912

A Tudor Revival house that features intricate brickwork laid up in a mason's holiday of patterns, including a broad herringbone band that wraps around the second story. The ornate bargeboards over the front porch, said to have been carved in Denmark, are also a delight. The builder of this unusually well-detailed house was himself a contractor. Victor Ingemann and his brother, George, started their business in 1884 and went on to construct hundreds of houses and other buildings in the Twin Cities. Victor's son, William, became a prominent St. Paul architect.

University of St. Thomas

2115 Summit Ave.
*(see under Merriam Park–
Lexington-Hamline)*

44 Ward and Bess Beebe House N *L*

2022 Summit Ave.

Purcell Feick and Elmslie, 1912

Purcell and Elmslie's only house in St. Paul. It's one of their high-gabled houses that draws on elements from English Arts and Crafts design. Even so, the house's recessed entrance, banded windows, wide eaves, and open floor plan are all Prairie Style trademarks. This wasn't a big-budget house, so it lacks the art-

glass windows often found in Purcell and Elmslie's work. However, there's a fretsawn orna-

Ward and Bess Beebe House, 1964

ment, in one of Elmslie's characteristically intricate patterns, adjoining the main entrance. The house was built for Dr. Ward Beebe, a bacteriologist, and his wife, Bess, as a wedding present from her parents.

St. Paul Seminary

2260 Summit Ave.
(see under Macalester-Groveland)

POI F World War I Memorial

Western end of Summit Ave.

Holyoke, Jemne, and Davis, 1922

A granite shaft erected by the Daughters of the American Revolution in honor of the St. Paul and Ramsey County servicemen who died in World War I.

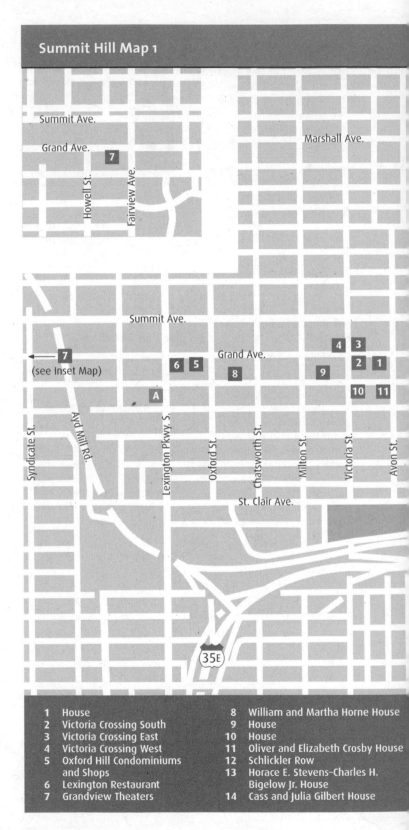

Summit Hill Map 1

1 House	8 William and Martha Horne House
2 Victoria Crossing South	9 House
3 Victoria Crossing East	10 House
4 Victoria Crossing West	11 Oliver and Elizabeth Crosby House
5 Oxford Hill Condominiums	12 Schlickler Row
and Shops	13 Horace E. Stevens–Charles H.
6 Lexington Restaurant	Bigelow Jr. House
7 Grandview Theaters	14 Cass and Julia Gilbert House

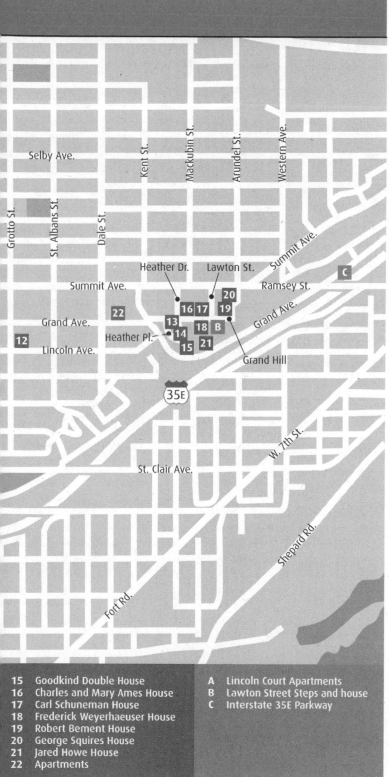

Selby Ave.

Kent St.

Mackubin St.

Arundel St.

Western Ave.

Grotto St.

St. Albans St.

Dale St.

Heather Dr.   Lawton St.

Summit Ave.

Summit Ave.

Ramsey St.

C

22

Grand Ave.

16 **17**

20

19

13

18 **B**

12

Heather Pl.

14

Grand Ave.

Lincoln Ave.

15 **21**

Grand Hill

35E

W. 7th St.

St. Clair Ave.

Shepard Rd.

Fort Rd.

Summit Hill

15 Goodkind Double House	**A** Lincoln Court Apartments
16 Charles and Mary Ames House	**B** Lawton Street Steps and house
17 Carl Schuneman House	**C** Interstate 35E Parkway
18 Frederick Weyerhaeuser House	
19 Robert Bement House	
20 George Squires House	
21 Jared Howe House	
22 Apartments	

Summit Hill Map 2

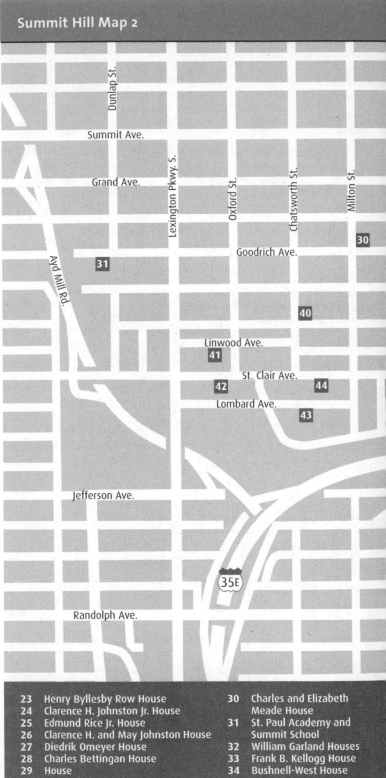

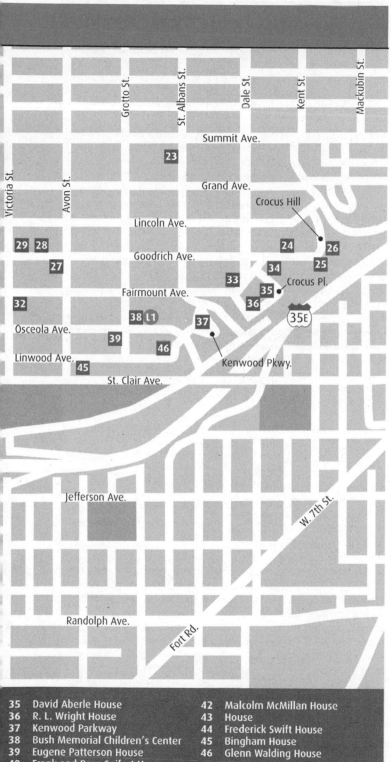

35	David Aberle House	42	Malcolm McMillan House
36	R. L. Wright House	43	House
37	Kenwood Parkway	44	Frederick Swift House
38	Bush Memorial Children's Center	45	Bingham House
39	Eugene Patterson House	46	Glenn Walding House
40	Frank and Rosa Seifert House		
41	Bungalows	L1	Visitation School and Convent

Summit Hill

This pleasant, well-kept neighborhood is almost exclusively residential, except for Grand Avenue, and it's one of St. Paul's showpieces. Popularly known as Crocus Hill, the neighborhood consists of block upon block of late nineteenth- and early twentieth-century houses, in many cases designed by leading St. Paul architects. Some of the finest homes are located along the curving, secluded streets that weave around the blufftops above Interstate 35E. Virtually all of the neighborhood is included in the federal Historic Hill District. The houses along Grand Hill, Heather Place, and Summit Court are also within the city preservation district of the same name.

As with most of the Twin Cities, Summit Hill developed in tandem with mass transportation. Horsecars began operating on Grand Avenue as early as 1872, spurring growth in the eastern part of the neighborhood. But it wasn't until the arrival of electric trolleys in 1890 that the real housing boom began here. Many of Summit Hill's larger homes were built between 1890 and 1910, when various Classical Revival styles flourished. As a result, the neighborhood has a more sedate feel than Ramsey Hill to the north, where Queen Anne reigns. In the western portions of Summit Hill, past Victoria Street, the housing stock tends to be newer, much of it dating to between 1910 and 1930.

Among the neighborhood's outstanding works of architecture are the Frank B. Kellogg House (1890), a National Historic Landmark on Fairmount Avenue; the Goodkind Double House (1910) at 5–7 Heather Place; the Frank and Rosa Seifert House (1914), a Prairie School gem at 975 Osceola Avenue; and the Edwin Lundie–designed Aberle House (1927) at 54 Crocus Place.

Grand Avenue

West of Dale Street

Grand Ave. was platted in 1871 and began as a residential street. The arrival of electric streetcars in 1890 touched off a long process of development by which Grand—now a vibrant blend of commercial and residential uses—took on its current form. Grand's best building stock dates to the 1920s, when auto dealers flocked to the avenue and built handsome garages and showrooms. Many of the avenue's three-story brick apartment buildings are also from the 1920s.

Like other older commercial strips in St. Paul, Grand declined in the 1950s. But a renaissance fueled by gentrification of the Historic Hill District in the 1970s turned everything around. Zoning changes also helped preserve the avenue's mix of housing and businesses. Architecturally, Grand is not especially remarkable, although its many small brick buildings tend to be of higher quality than those found on other commercial streets in the Twin Cities.

1 House (Peter Denzer Home and Studio)

814 Grand Ave.

1905 / addition, Peter Denzer, 1980

The simple front addition to an old house drew the wrath of the local architectural police, who deemed it awful. "Committed by supposedly artistic individuals, it is a serious crime," thundered the editor of a neighborhood newspaper. In truth, the addition's hand-built flavor adds some character to Grand, which has few architectural surprises. Nothing like Denzer's handiwork will ever appear again on the avenue: zoning rules were quickly changed to ban additions of its kind.

2 Victoria Crossing South (Byers-Patro Motor Co.)

850 Grand Ave.

John Alden, 1927 / renovated, ca. 1982

3 Victoria Crossing East (Bingham and Norton Co.)

851–57 Grand Ave.

Beaver Wade Day, 1915 / renovated, ca. 1980

4 Victoria Crossing West (Tilden Brothers Produce Co., Grand Avenue State Bank, Berry Chevrolet Co.)

861–67 Grand Ave. and 35 South Victoria St.

John Alden, 1922–23 / renovated, Jim Wengler, ca. 1974

Three of the four renovated buildings at this intersection were once auto dealerships. The building at 850 Grand, home to the popular Cafe Latté, is the most sophisticated of the three, its decorative motifs suggesting the art deco style to come. Ornament of a different sort adorns the old Chevrolet dealership that's part of Victoria Crossing West. Here you'll find three white terra-cotta cartouches in a circle-and-tab design done in the intricate style of Louis Sullivan. These were a stock item made by the Midland Terra Cotta Co. of Chicago.

5 Oxford Hill Condominiums and Shops

1060 Grand Ave.

ESG Architects, 2005

Nostalgia in brick and cast-stone, though nicely done of its kind. There are 36 apartments above the ground-floor shops.

Lexington Restaurant

6 Lexington Restaurant

1096 Grand Ave.

1911 / renovated, Werner Wittkamp, ca. 1955

This old-line restaurant offers one of the avenue's liveliest facades, a collection of pediments, pilasters, cornices, arches, keystones, and shutters pasted like oversized Post-it notes to the smooth brick walls. Their message seems to be, "I've got class." Maybe so, but the design's perilous proximity to pure fifties kitsch is what makes it so much fun.

7 Grandview Theaters

1830 Grand Ave.

Myrtus Wright, 1933, 1937 (addition)

One of St. Paul's two remaining art deco movie theaters (the other, also designed by Wright, is the Highland). The main part of the theater opened in 1933. A one-story section to the east was added four years later. The Grandview's exuberant design includes porthole windows, glass columns above the marquee, and striped brickwork. New owners renovated the interior in the 1980s and converted the balcony into a second screen.

POI A Lincoln Court Apartments

93–95 Lexington Pkwy. South

J. Walter Stevens, 1921

This building is most notable for what happened in a third-floor hallway on March 31, 1934, when John Dillinger (using the evocative alias of Carl Hellman) and his companion, Evelyn Frechette, engaged in a furious gun battle with lawmen. Despite the proverbial hail of bullets, Dillinger and Frechette escaped and no one was hurt. Less than three months later, Dillinger was shot dead by FBI agents outside a Chicago movie theater.

8 William and Martha Horne House ! N

993 Lincoln Ave.

Allen H. Stem, 1889

Perhaps the most fetching Shingle Style house in the Twin Cities. Wrapped in a taut skin of dark shingles, the house's bays, projections, balconies, and curving corners enliven the overall design, as do windows of all shapes and sizes. The large bowed window to the right of the entry porch is especially fine (and, with

William and Martha Horne House

84 panes, no doubt a chore to clean). Note also the exquisite little dormer roosting midway up the catslide roof over the entry porch. The home's first owner, William Horne, was vice president of a firm that manufactured tinware.

9 House N

899 Lincoln Ave.

ca. 1910

The Spanish Mission Revival style, which summons up images of sun-kissed adobe walls and Zorro lurking in the shadows, found its way to the Twin Cities just after 1900. This broad brick house is a good local example of the style despite a tacky addition to one side and other misadventures in remodeling. The dominant design element is a central dormer sculpted in the approved Mission manner and punctured by quatrefoil windows. A large garage on the property also sports a dormer as well a superb brick arch above the doors.

10 House (Babies Home of St. Paul) N

846 Lincoln Ave.

1880

An unusually old house for this area and one with quite a history. In 1891 a group of women bought the property and turned it into the Babies Home of St. Paul, a refuge for impoverished, abandoned, and orphaned infants, of which there was no shortage at the time. It's not known how

long the Babies Home was here, but city directories indicate it was gone by no later than 1932.

11 Oliver and Elizabeth Crosby House N

804 Lincoln Ave.

Clarence H. Johnston, 1900 and later

Oliver Crosby, who cofounded the American Hoist and Derrick Co., is best remembered for Stonebridge, a later mansion he built in the Macalester-Groveland neighborhood. Still, this four-square stone house, newly restored, is impressive in its own right. Except for the lacy Gothic bargeboards decorating the attic dormers, the house isn't strongly styled. Instead, it conveys a sense of solid utilitarianism, which must have made it appealing to an engineer like Crosby.

12 Schlickler Row N

733–39 Lincoln Ave.

Charles. A. Wallingford, 1890

This sandstone row house, marooned in Colonial Revival country, offers a lively alternative to its restrained neighbors. It comes with all the requisite Victorian goodies—bays, balconies, terraces, towers, carved decorative panels, and a neat circular window thrown in for good measure.

*Horace E. Stevens–
Charles H. Bigelow Jr. House*

13 Horace E. Stevens–Charles H. Bigelow Jr. House ! N *L*

530 Grand Hill

Reed and Stem, 1895 / addition, ca. 1923

This powerful red brick house, built for an engineer who obviously believed in the Victorian gospel of weight and mass, is among the most impressive of its time in the Twin Cities. Although its pointed-arch windows evoke Gothic Revival, the house has almost none of the applied ornament or busy surface texturing typical of that style. Instead, it reads as a dense, sculpted object into which windows have been almost reluctantly chiseled. The front porch is also striking, as are the chimneys that rise like pylons to either side. The architect, Allen Stem, is not so well known as Cass Gilbert or Clarence Johnston, but he was in their league. Charles Bigelow, Jr., president of the Farwell, Ozmun and Kirk (FOK) Hardware Co., bought the house in 1923 and built a large rear addition that nicely matches the original design.

Cass and Julia Gilbert House

14 Cass and Julia Gilbert House N *L*

1 Heather Pl.

Gilbert and Taylor, 1890 / altered, ca. 1923

Gilbert and his wife, Julia, lived here from 1890 until they moved to New York City in 1900. With its gables, bays, and porch, the house falls into the picturesque mode that Gilbert—despite his renown as a classicist—typically handled with considerable finesse. The house today does

not look as it did when Gilbert designed it. In the 1920s an owner apparently infatuated with the then popular Tudor Revival replaced the original shingle cladding above the first story with stucco and half-timbering. The interior has also been significantly modified.

15 Goodkind Double House ! N *L*

5–7 Heather Pl.

Reed and Stem, 1910

A giant double house, rendered as an exercise in pure English romance and occupying a gorgeous site atop the Grand Ave. hill. Sprawling across its wooded grounds, the house unfolds in a nostalgic panorama of limestone, stucco, and half-timbering beneath a wood shake roof that curls in imitation of thatch. The house is in a Tudor variant sometimes called the Cotswold Cottage style, although the term *cottage* seems a tad insufficient in this case.

It was built for brothers Benjamin and William Goodkind, both of whom were connected with the Mannheimer Brothers Department Store in downtown St. Paul. Benjamin was president of the firm, while William served as secretary and treasurer. Benjamin lived in the larger of the two houses, at 7 Heather Pl. The only link between the houses is a bridgelike second-story passageway supported by heavy timbers and spanning a small central courtyard and fountain. The two sides of the property remain under separate ownership to this day. The grounds include a superb limestone retaining wall

Goodkind Double House

that extends hundreds of feet along Grand Ave., where there's also a winding stone staircase that leads up to the house.

16 Charles and Mary Ames House N *L*

501 Grand Hill

J. N. Tilton (Chicago), 1886

A Shingle Style house of many gables. Six are visible from the street, and others may lurk to the rear. Charles Ames was secretary of the West Publishing Co. when he and his wife, Mary, commissioned this house. F. Scott Fitzgerald, a friend of Ames's son, Theodore, described the home's backyard in one of his Basil Duke Lee stories.

17 Carl Schuneman House N *L*

489 Grand Hill

Stem and Haslund, 1925

One of the more monumental houses on Grand Hill, featuring rugged limestone walls and cut stone trim. The house, Tudor Revival in style, was built for a member of the family that owned Schuneman's Department Store in St. Paul. It's possible the house incorporates portions of an earlier mansion built in 1887.

18 Frederick Weyerhaeuser House N *L*

480 Grand Hill

William Channing Whitney, 1908

A Tudor Revival mansion designed for the lumber king near the end of his life by Minneapolis society architect William Channing Whitney. Like much of Whitney's work, the house is not especially exciting. Incidentally, the short street now called Grand Hill used to be a part of Grand Ave., which was crossed by Oakland Ave. here as it descended the long hill toward West Seventh St. The lower part of Oakland (along the hill) was renamed Grand in 1970, while this portion of Grand became Grand Hill. Such confused street genealogy is typical of St. Paul.

19 Robert Bement House N *L*

27 Summit Ct.

Gilbert and Taylor, 1888

Another of Gilbert's forays into eclecticism, built for a St. Paul businessman. The porch columns have Medieval-inspired capitals, the corner tower evokes the Shingle Style, while the design as a whole appears to be moving toward Colonial Revival.

20 George Squires House N *L*

19 Summit Ct.

Gilbert and Taylor, 1889

The type of symmetrical facades that Gilbert favored in the early 1890s first appeared on this house, built for a St. Paul attorney. It's one of at least nine houses Gilbert designed along Summit Ct., Heather Pl., and Grand Hill.

POI B Lawton Street Steps and house

Steps, between Grand Ave. and Grand Hill

1911 / restored, St. Paul Department of Public Works, 1992

House, 70 Lawton St.

2004

These 78 steps connect Grand Ave. to Grand Hill. Midway up the stairs is a house accessible only on foot. It replaced an earlier home owned by Conrad O. Searle, a St. Paul architect.

POI C Interstate 35E Parkway

Between Mississippi River and I-94

Minnesota Highway Department, 1956 and later

Construction of this interstate highway wiped out numerous homes and other buildings along the old Pleasant Ave. corridor. The freeway was supposed to have been opened in 1972, but fierce neighborhood opposition delayed completion until 1989. The long battle was resolved by a series of compromises that make this one of the country's most unusual stretches of interstate highway. It has only four lanes, the speed limit is 45 miles an hour, and it's designated a "parkway" from which large trucks are banned.

Jared Howe House

21 Jared Howe House

455 Grand Ave.

Louis Lockwood, 1907

Located next to the Lawton St. steps, this one of a kind house features a two-story front porch supported by stone and brick piers, a hipped roof over bracketed eaves, and a covered side entry with bottle-glass windows. Figuring out the house's style—which stirs Gothic, Classical, Arts and Crafts, and even Japanese-inspired elements into the mix—is no simple matter. Its closest architectural relatives appear to be colonial-era bungalows built by the British in India. Architect Louis Lockwood, born and trained in England, would have been familiar with the British bungalow style. Jared Howe, the first owner, was a lawyer and a bachelor, which may explain why the house's interior has something of the feel of a private gentlemen's club.

22 Apartments N

587 Grand Ave.

1925

Of the many vintage walk-up apartment buildings on Grand, this one has perhaps the most elaborate facade, a Renaissance Revival stage set that includes a pair of blind arches infilled with brick in a herringbone pattern to either side of the front door.

23 Henry Byllesby Row House N

21–27 South St. Albans St.

Clarence H. Johnston, 1892

A fine piece of Victorian street theater, named after the businessman who built it. The facades of each of the four units are treated differently but still combine to form a convincing whole. The row house is one of Clarence Johnston's first forays into the Tudor Revival variant known as Jacobethan, although there are Romanesque Revival elements as well.

Crocus Hill

Goodrich Ave. east of Dale St.

The block-long, blufftop street known as Crocus Hill has a peculiar house numbering system, even by St. Paul standards. Originally, the houses were numbered in order of construction, with 1 Crocus Hill being the oldest and so on. However, since many of the homes are second generation, the numbering system's link to chronology has now grown tenuous.

24 Clarence H. Johnston Jr. House N

11 Crocus Hill

1887 / remodeled, Clarence H. Johnston, Jr., 1912

Like his father, Clarence Johnston, Jr., was an architect, and this Arts and Craftsy house is one of his most successful creations.

Edmund Rice Jr. House

25 Edmund Rice Jr. House N

4 Crocus Hill

William Channing Whitney, 1886 / later remodelings

The street's oldest, largest, and most indisputably romantic house, situated at the end of Crocus Hill on a lot that commands a sweeping view of the river valley. Its original owner was Edmund Rice, Jr., a real estate agent who never lived here. The tower that rises above the layered roofline is a modern addition. Many changes were also made to the house in the 1920s.

26 Clarence H. and May Johnston House N

2 Crocus Hill

1884 / rebuilt, Clarence H. Johnston, 1909

The architect's own house and, like the man, rather unassuming. Johnston lived here until his death in 1936.

Diedrik Omeyer House

27 Diedrik Omeyer House N

808 Goodrich Ave.

Omeyer and Thori, 1889 / restored, Hengelfelt Restorations, 2004

Oh, those crazy Norwegians! The duo of Omeyer and Thori specialized in mad-dog Victorian houses, foaming with ornament. This is one of their prime extravaganzas, and it will clear your sinuses just by looking at it. The house was originally owned by architect Diedrik Omeyer, who with his partner in excess, Martin Thori, left fingerprints on gaudy Queen Anne houses all around St. Paul. For many years, this architectural wild thing was tamed by modern siding, but a restoration in 2004 brought it back to vibrant life. The restored front porch is especially fine.

28 Charles Bettingan House N

825 Goodrich Ave.

Louis Lockwood, 1900

A huge house that rambles all over its large lot but never settles on any particular style. The pivot point is a corner tower topped by a finial that seems to erupt out of a giant swirl of whipped cream. The first owner, Charles Bettingan, was an executive for a plumbing supply company.

29 House N

833 Goodrich Ave.

Augustus Gauger, 1891

A late Victorian house with tall, richly textured front gables divided into three layers. Christopher C. Andrews, who pioneered modern forestry practices in Minnesota (a state forest bears his name), once owned this home.

30 Charles and Elizabeth Meade House N

917 Goodrich Ave.

Mark Fitzpatrick, 1909

Instead of offering yet another take on Colonial Revival, architect Mark Fitzpatrick here found inspiration closer to home—in the work of Chicago architects Louis Sullivan and George Maher. The octagonal columns on the porch and the small niche above are in the manner of Sullivan, as are the squared-off, ornately carved capitals. But the house's broad proportions, widely spaced windows, and curious arched dormer show an even stronger affinity to homes designed by Maher in the early 1900s. Maher himself was no stranger to Minnesota, designing several important buildings in Winona as well as a mansion in the Lowry Hill neighborhood of Minneapolis.

31 St. Paul Academy and Summit School (Lower School)

1150 Goodrich Ave.

Clarence H. Johnston, 1924 / additions, 1951, 1958, 1963, and later

A Collegiate Gothic building, originally built for the Summit School for Girls, which in 1969 merged with the St. Paul Academy.

32 William Garland Houses N

846, 854–56 Fairmount Ave.

Omeyer and Thori, 1890

Here, St. Paul's principal providers of visual mayhem offer two more monuments to the art of the lathe and the jigsaw. William Garland, a trunk manufacturer, is listed as the original owner of both houses, in which other members of his family also lived at various times.

33 Frank B. Kellogg House ! N L

633 Fairmount Ave.

William H. Willcox, 1890 / addition, Allen H. Stem, 1923

In the 1920s, Frank Kellogg (for whom Kellogg Blvd. in St. Paul is named) negotiated the Kellogg-Briand Pact, an agreement in which over 60 nations renounced (but not for long) war. Kellogg, who served as secretary of state under President Calvin Coolidge, won the Nobel Prize Peace in 1930 for his efforts. Before moving onto the international stage, he was an attorney in St. Paul and Minnesota's first popularly elected U.S. senator.

His house, designated a National Historic Landmark in 1976, is as interesting for its architecture as for its history. The main part of the house, completed in 1890, was designed by William Willcox in a convincing amalgam of the Richardsonian Romanesque and Shingle styles. A brawny tower, built largely of pink quartzite from southwestern Minnesota, dominates the south side. To the east, overlooking the garden, the house is less forbidding, with a double gable rising above an inset arcade. In 1923, a large addition was constructed on the northeast side of the house, where the front entrance is now located.

34 Bushnell-West House N

91 Crocus Pl.

Charles E. Joy, 1888

A house with some wonderfully weird features, among them a stacked pair of dormers that appear poised to play a game of leapfrog across the roof. Why is it that no one ever seems to have had quite as much fun creating houses as the supposedly repressed Victorians?

35 David Aberle House ! N

54 Crocus Pl.

Edwin Lundie, 1927

Architect Edwin Lundie worked in the offices of Cass Gilbert and Emmanuel Masqueray before striking off on his own in about

Frank B. Kellogg House, 1910

Summit Hill

1920. Over the next 50 years he designed a series of exquisite houses in the Twin Cities and elsewhere in Minnesota, as well as a remarkable group of cabins and resort buildings along the

David Aberle House, 1929

north shore of Lake Superior. This house is one of Lundie's finest, done in the Cotswold Cottage variant of Tudor. It has beautifully laid-up walls of multicolored limestone, a slate roof, and a pinwheeling floor-plan designed to capture the site's views. As with all of Lundie's work, the details—note, for example the triangular fragments of slate shingles inserted at the corners of many of the eaves—are divine.

36 R. L. Wright House N

30 Crocus Pl.

Reed and Stem, 1899

A Renaissance Revival–style brick box that could easily pass for an apartment or club building. The house's use of multi-colored and -patterned brickwork is also noteworthy. The wrought-iron entrance porch is a modern addition.

37 Kenwood Parkway N

Near St. Albans St. and Osceola Ave.

This street, which forms a loop at the top of the bluffs, is one of the few in St. Paul with gateposts (don't worry: there are no guards, and the street is public). Among the fine homes here is the **Philip McQuillan House** (26 Kenwood Pkwy.), a Maheresque design from 1914.

38 Bush Memorial Children's Center N

180 South Grotto St.

1971

Low brick buildings with shed roofs give a quiet residential feel to this children's group home.

LOST 1 *From 1913 to 1966 this was the site of* **Visitation School and Convent,** *now located in Mendota Heights. Most of the brick walls here were originally part of the Visitation complex.*

39 Eugene Patterson House N

744 Osceola Ave.

Thomas Holyoke, 1912

With its wide eaves and low-pitched roof, this stone house has the relaxed feel of an Italian villa, although its sturdy forms and bold but simple detailing also show the influence of the Arts and Crafts movement. The small, off-center balcony over the front entrance is enchanting. The original owner was the vice president of a mortgage company.

Frank and Rosa Seifert House

40 Frank and Rosa Seifert House !

975 Osceola Ave.

Bentley and Hausler, 1914

One of St. Paul's largest and finest Prairie Style houses. Although not so dynamic as Frank Lloyd Wright's best Prairie designs, it's a strong and knowing work by a pair of gifted architects. Clad in tapestry brick and stucco, the house is a two-story cube with one-story projecting volumes that include porches on the south and west sides and a polygonal window bay in between. In contrast to the irregular first floor, the second story is symmetrical, with windows either centered or paired at the corners. Unfortunately, the eaves have been altered and don't extend out so far as they once did. Leaded glass and other ornamental details enrich the house inside and out. The home's first owner, Frank Seifert, is said to have operated a billiard parlor in downtown St. Paul. Bentley and Hausler went on to design one other Prairie house in St. Paul, at 1599 Portland Ave.

41 Bungalows

1042–80 Linwood Ave.

T. L. Blood and other builders, ca. 1908–11

Here between Lexington Pkwy. and Oxford St. is one of St. Paul's finest collections of small bungalows. What makes these homes so appealing is the quality of their detailing: many have half-timbering, some sport bargeboards, and leaded-glass windows are also common.

42 Malcolm McMillan House

1058 St. Clair Ave.

Ernest Hartford and Charles A. Hausler, 1915

This house is basically a Craftsman stucco box, but the side entry, the piers that project to either side of the front windows, and the applied bands of wood on the second story are all features you might expect to find on a high-style Prairie house.

43 House

970 Lombard Ave.

1948

A one-story modernist house behind an intimate courtyard.

44 Frederick Swift House

962 St. Clair Ave.

John Coxhead, 1888

Architect John Coxhead practiced in St. Paul for only five years, beginning in 1887, and many of his works are gone. But most of what survives, like this frothy

Frederick Swift House

Queen Anne concoction, is choice. An elaborate paint job highlights the house's amazing variety of textures, forms, and materials, although some decorative elements are presumably modern reconstructions.

45 Bingham House N

784 Linwood Ave.

James E. Niemeyer, 1927

The revival style du jour here is French Provincial. The white shutters add a quaint Storybook touch to the design.

46 Glenn Walding House N

709 Linwood Ave.

James E. Niemeyer, 1916

A severely plain house that must have seemed ultramodern when it was built. The Craftsman-Prairie mix here is stripped down to bare essentials: with some rejiggering of proportions and other adjustments, this house could pass as a precursor of the International Style to come. Walding was secretary of the St. Paul Mutual Hail and Cyclone Insurance Co., and perhaps he wanted a compact, unadorned house so as to present the smallest possible target to either form of disaster.

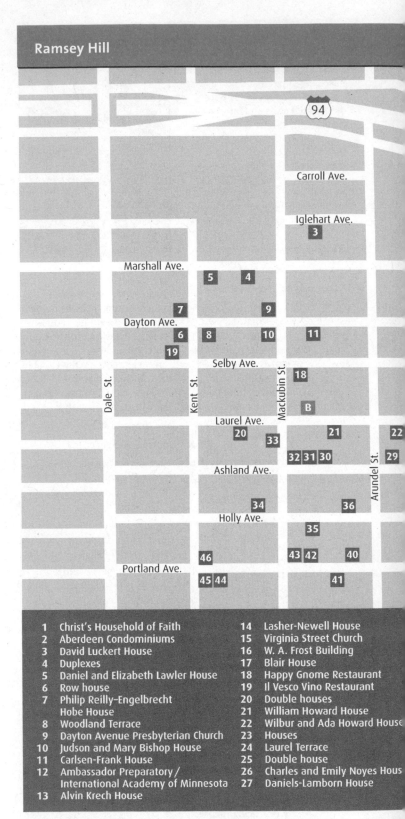

Ramsey Hill

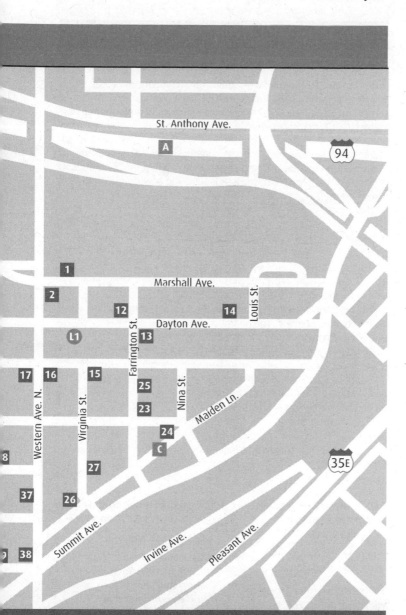

Ramsey Hill

Ramsey Hill

Located north of Summit Avenue and east of Dale Street, Ramsey Hill offers St. Paul's—and the Twin Cities'—greatest concentration of architect-designed, late nineteenth-century houses, many lying within one of the neighborhood's three historic districts. This gathering of Victorians is remarkable for its general level of preservation, its high architectural quality, and its extent. In few other places in the United States can you see, in one compact neighborhood, so many homes of this kind. On those extravagant summer days when the big houses drowse in their deep green yards, it is hard—at least for any midwesterner—to think of a more pleasant residential environment.

Although much of Ramsey Hill was built up in the 1880s and 1890s, houses appeared here as early as the 1850s, mainly along or near Summit and Dayton avenues. Development slowed after the financial panic of 1873, but by 1882 the boom was on. Close to downtown but protected by bluffs from commercial sprawl, the neighborhood was also well away from rail yards or industrialized areas. This combination of factors made it prime territory for upper middle-class settlement, especially along the streets south of Selby Avenue, which with its streetcar line became the neighborhood's main commercial thoroughfare. To the immediate north of Selby, along Dayton and Marshall, there are also many large homes as well as row houses and apartments.

More so than Summit Hill to the south, Ramsey Hill features a broad range of building types, including row houses, apartments, residential hotels, churches, schools, and institutional structures. Particularly noteworthy buildings include Laurel Terrace (1887), the finest row house in the Twin Cities; Blair House (1887), a large apartment hotel; and the Cass Gilbert–designed Dayton Avenue Presbyterian Church (1888).

POI A Interstate 94 Corridor and Rondo Avenue Neighborhood

I-94 between Rice St. and Lexington Pkwy.

This stretch of Interstate 94, which opened in 1967, was created by carving a block-wide gash between Rondo (now Concordia) and St. Anthony Aves., often described as the heart of St. Paul's historic black community. Yet it's worth noting that the old Rondo neighborhood was, in fact, quite mixed, with many whites—often from immigrant groups—among its residents. It was also architecturally diverse and included fine homes as well as others that could fairly be described as slums. By the time the interstate came through, however, blacks did indeed bear the brunt of the impact, accounting for 75 percent of the people displaced by its construction.

1 Christ's Household of Faith (St. Joseph's Academy) N L

355 Marshall Ave.

1863 / additions, 1871, 1877, and 1884 (Edward P. Bassford) / chapel and library wing, John W. Wheeler, ca. 1930

These stone and brick buildings were for over 100 years home to St. Joseph's Academy, a day and, at one time, boarding school for girls. Parts of the complex date to 1863, making it the state's oldest Catholic school building. It's also the largest surviving example of Italianate-style architecture in the Twin Cities.

The academy was founded in 1851 by the Sisters of St. Joseph of Carondelet, who 12 years later opened their first building here: a three-story stone structure at the southwest corner of the site. Additions followed to the north and east, also in the Italianate style. The most impressive

Christ's Household of Faith, 1936

section, constructed in 1877, is immediately to the east of the original building along Marshall. Four stories high, it features paired windows and a central two-story bay. The additions to the north date to the 1930s, by which time the academy functioned solely as a high school. The academy closed in 1972. The complex is now owned by Christ's Household of Faith, a religious community that uses the buildings for a school and as living quarters.

Historic Hill District N *L*

Created in 1976, this is St. Paul's oldest and largest locally designated historic district, taking in all or part of about 70 blocks. The district is roughly bounded by Interstates 35E and 94 and Dale St., although a section also extends west along Summit and Portland Aves. Much of this area falls within the boundaries of a nationally designated historic district of the same name that includes a sizable portion of the Summit Hill neighborhood as well. There is also a much smaller national district, Woodland Park, that overlaps the local district along Dayton and Marshall Aves.

2 Aberdeen Condominiums *L*

370 Marshall Ave.

Collaborative Design Group, 2005

A nostalgic condominium building that would have looked better with a well-defined cornice.

LOST 1 *The condominiums are named after the* **Aberdeen Hotel,** *an eight-story residential hotel that*

Aberdeen Hotel, 1937

once stood a block away at the southwest corner of Dayton Ave. and Virginia St. Designed by Willcox and Johnston, the Aberdeen opened in 1889 and initially attracted a well-heeled residential clientele. But the hotel's fortunes gradually declined, and it was a vacant hulk by the time of its demolition in 1944.

David Luckert House

3 David (George) Luckert House N *L*

480 Iglehart Ave.

David Luckert, 1858

One of the oldest buildings in the Historic Hill District, located along what used to be St. Anthony Rd., an early stagecoach route that linked St. Paul to Minneapolis. David Luckert, a German immigrant and skilled mason, constructed the house out of locally quarried limestone.

4 Duplexes N *L*

512–14 Marshall Ave. and 233–35, 237–39 North Mackubin St.

J. Walter Stevens?, 1908

These three duplexes, which are similar but have different parapet and porch designs, offer a well-detailed version of the Mission Revival style that enjoyed a brief fling in the Twin Cities around 1910.

5 Daniel and Elizabeth Lawler House N *L*

546 Marshall Ave.

John Coxhead, 1889

An imposing brick Queen Anne, fairly sedate by Coxhead's standards, with a hefty tower to one side and a two-story porch to the other. An oblong, shingle-clad attic dormer that curves out from the roofline is among the house's most distinctive features. The original owner, Daniel Lawler, was a Yale-trained lawyer who served as mayor of St. Paul from 1908 to 1910.

6 Row house N *L*

568–74 Dayton Ave.

Louis Lockwood, 1904

What a difference 16 years can make. Woodland Terrace just down the street is a model of Victorian exuberance. This row house, by contrast, is designed in the sedate and refined Georgian Revival style that became popular around 1900.

7 Philip Reilly–Engelbrecht Hobe House N *L*

565 Dayton Ave.

Abraham M. Radcliffe, 1881

A restored, richly ornamented wood-frame house built by lumber dealer Phillip Reilly, who undoubtedly got a good deal on all of the brackets, scallops, modillions, balustrades, and whatnot

used as adornments. The overall form of the house is Italianate, but much of the detailing—such as the incised carving and intricate bargeboards—is Eastlake. One of the house's later owners was Engelbrecht Hobe, a leader of St. Paul's Norwegian community.

8 Woodland Terrace N *L*

550–56 Dayton Ave. (also 198 Kent St.)

B. J. Buechner?, 1889 / renovated, ca. 1980s

A row house with patterned brickwork, sandstone staircases and trim, cast-iron ornament atop the gables, leaded-glass transoms, and just about everything else you'd expect of a Victorian dressed to kill. The arched entryways to the five townhomes are Romanesque Revival in character, but the building's busy roofline is of the Queen Anne persuasion.

Dayton Avenue Presbyterian Church

9 Dayton Avenue Presbyterian Church N *L*

505 Dayton Ave. (also 217 North Mackubin St.)

Gilbert and Taylor, 1888 / addition, Thomas Holyoke, 1911

Cass Gilbert's mother, Elizabeth, was a founder of this congregation and no doubt helped her son's firm secure the commission for this church. Clad in Lake Superior sandstone, the church is a strong design in the manner of H. H. Richardson, whose work influenced Gilbert and almost every other architect in the

United States. The rather squat corner tower is nicely integrated into the east side of the church, but the entry porch facing Dayton looks as though it was tacked on at the last minute. Within, there's a column-free auditorium with radial seating beneath a vaulted ceiling. An educational wing was added to the north of the church in 1911.

Judson and Mary Bishop House

10 Judson and Mary Bishop House N *L*

193 North Mackubin St. (at Dayton Ave.)

Abraham M. Radcliffe, 1882

No, Norman Bates doesn't live here, but if the psycho from *Psycho* was in the market for real estate in the Twin Cities, this French Second Empire pile might be the house of his dreams. It's a late example of the style. Although the house is essentially rectangular, an assortment of bays and angled projections forestall any foursquare monotony, while no fewer than 11 pedimented dormers jut out from the mansard roof. The house was built by Judson Wade Bishop, an engineer and Civil War general who later became manager of the St. Paul and Sioux City Railroad.

11 Carlsen-Frank House N *L*

482 Dayton Ave.

Peter Carlsen and Sylvia Frank, 1979

A witty infill house, teetering on the brink of pop architecture and therefore more interesting than the soberly nostalgic stuff now being built in the Hill District. Designed and owned by architects Peter Carlsen and Sylvia Frank, the house features a sweeping roofline and a win-

dowless corner cylinder that calls to mind the towers of nearby Victorians. Overall, the house shows the influence of Philadelphia architect Robert Venturi, a leading postmodern guru.

12 Ambassador Preparatory / International Academy of Minnesota (Frank and Anna Shepard House) *L*

325 Dayton Ave.

1882 / additions, ca. 1960s, 2006

A clunky 1960s addition hasn't helped the appearance of this substantial Queen Anne house, originally owned by Frank Shepard and his wife, Anna. Shepard was the son of David Shepard, who built much of the Great Northern Railway for James J. Hill. David Shepard resided in a large house (gone) across the street at 324 Dayton. Another large home built for a member of the family—Frank's son, David—is next door at 341 Dayton. It dates to 1901 and was designed by Louis Lockwood.

Alvin Krech House

13 Alvin Krech House N *L*

314 Dayton Ave.

Mould and McNicol, 1888 / restored, SALA Architects (Steve Buetow) and Robert Roscoe, 1996 and later

Another house with ties to the Shepard family, built for David Shepard's son-in-law, Alvin Krech. The architects, Charles Mould and Robert McNicol, designed several St. Paul mansions (most notably the John Merriam House that once stood near the State Capitol), but here they produced a real oddity. The house's rugged stone exterior and arched first-floor windows are typical of Romanesque Revival, but the cubic shape and almost flat roof are not. Most peculiar of all is the third floor, which features inset porches supported by dwarf columns with overscaled Byzantine capitals. The house was subdivided into a nest of apartments in the 1930s. It stayed that way until 1996, when a couple bought the house for ten dollars under a city revitalization program and then restored it as a single-family home.

Lasher-Newell House, 1936

14 Lasher-Newell House N L

251 Dayton Ave.

1864 / addition, J. Walter Stevens, 1886

With its tower and battlements, this stone house looks well equipped to repel invading hordes. Its central section, distinguished by prominent window hoods, dates to 1864 and is in the French Second Empire style. The tower, porte cochere, and western wing weren't built until 1886, after Stanford Newell acquired the house from its first owner. Architect J. Walter Stevens did a superb job of blending the new with the old while also distinguishing them in subtle ways. Thus, while the additions are built of the same limestone as the original house, the newer stone has a different finish. A lawyer and civic activist, Newell served as U.S. minister to the Netherlands and was a member of the St. Paul Park Board. Newell Park in St. Paul is named in his honor.

Selby Avenue (from Nina Street to Dale Street)

Platted in 1854, this historic avenue—long associated with the city's black community—is named after Jeremiah Selby, who owned an early farm on what is now the site of the St. Paul Cathedral. The avenue's character was largely determined by mass transit. A cable car line opened on Selby in 1888. It was electrified ten years later. Commercial and apartment development followed the streetcars, especially along the eastern end of the avenue.

Selby retained a comfortable mix of homes, apartments, and businesses into the 1950s. By the 1960s, however, the avenue began to decline, in part because of dislocation caused by the construction of Interstate 94 a few blocks to the north. A lack of new investment, a rising crime rate, and a racial disturbance in 1968 also contributed to the avenue's problems. In recent years, however, Selby has come back to life with new businesses and housing. Architecturally, the eastern end of Selby (between Summit Ave. and Dale St.) remains the most interesting.

Virginia Street Church

15 Virginia Street (Swedenborgian) Church N L

170 Virginia St.
(also 338 Selby Ave.)

Gilbert and Taylor, 1887 / addition, Clarence H. Johnston, 1922

One of Cass Gilbert's most charming works, as dainty as a child's playhouse and alive with small, sweet details. It has a base of river boulders, clapboard walls, shingled gables, and an octagonal bell tower featuring delicate lancet windows and what may be St. Paul's tiniest dormers. Within, there's a barrel-vaulted sanctuary with stenciled decoration. The parish hall added to the east end of the church in 1922 is faithful to the original design. The Swedenborgian congregation that built and still occupies this church was organized in 1873.

16 W. A. Frost (Dacotah) Building N L

366–74 Selby Ave.

Hennessey, Agnew and Cox (builders), 1889 / renovated, J. E. Erickson and Sons, 1975

A pleasing Victorian commercial-apartment building with walls of dark red brick rising above a base of pink Ohio sandstone. Originally known as the Dacotah Building, it takes its current name from a drugstore once located on the ground floor. The building was among the first in the Hill District to be renovated as the neighborhood began its turn-around in the 1970s.

Blair House, 1920

17 Blair House (Albion Hotel, Angus Hotel) N L

165 Western Ave. North (at Selby Ave.)

Hermann Kretz and William Thomas, 1887 and later / renovated, W. W. Orfield and Associates, ca. 1980s

Selby Avenue's largest Victorian—not the subtlest design you'll ever see but great fun nevertheless. With its rugged stone base, patterned brickwork, zooming turrets, ornate parapets and gables, pressed metal bays, and round corner tower (minus its original cap), the building is a catalog of Victorian styles. Constructed in stages, the building has a rational layout beneath all the architectural embroidery, its mass carved into four sections by deep, narrow light courts.

The building is named after the man who commissioned it, Frank Blair, secretary of the St. Paul Improvement Co., a real estate firm. Blair lost his naming rights just six years later, in 1893, when the building became the Albion Hotel. In 1911 it was purchased by Twin Cities transit tycoon Thomas Lowry, who renamed it the Angus Hotel. After years of decline as a residential hotel, the building closed in 1971 and faced possible demolition. In the 1980s, however, as the Hill District began to flourish, the building was renovated. It's now home to condominium units as well as commercial tenants.

18 Happy Gnome Restaurant (Engine House No. 5) L

498 Selby Ave.

Abraham M. Radcliffe, 1882 / addition, J. A. Clark, 1886

One of St. Paul's oldest surviving fire stations. It was built as Engine House No. 5 and expanded four years later to accommodate a ladder company as well. Last used as a fire station in 1930, the building went through a number of uses until it was converted to a restaurant in 1979.

19 Il Vesco Vino Restaurant (Trott-Birch House) N L

579 Selby Ave.

Hermann Kretz and Co., 1890

Now home to a restaurant, this Chateauesque double house is a rarity in the Twin Cities because of its height—a full three stories, with a fourth tucked beneath the steep roof. The rigorously symmetrical main facade culminates in a pair of gabled dormers to which floral ornaments are pinned like giant boutonnieres.

524–26 Laurel Ave.

20 Double houses N *L*

524–26, 534 Laurel Ave.

John Coxhead, 1888

A pair of idiosyncratic double houses. Atop each of the houses' distinctive oval towers is one of Coxhead's signature elements— an absurdly high, steep roof that resembles the mouthpiece of a cigarette holder blown up to enormous scale. You'll find a similar tower and roof on a Coxhead-designed house at 614 Dayton Ave.

Fitzgerald Condominiums, 1964

POI B Fitzgerald Condominiums (San Mateo Flats) ! N *L*

475–81 Laurel Ave.

Frederick A. Clarke, 1894 / addition (porches), Louis Lockwood, ca. 1905

A pair of standard late Victorian apartment buildings that carry one of the most famous addresses in St. Paul for the simple reason that F. Scott Fitzgerald was born in an apartment on the second floor of 481 Laurel on September 24, 1896. He lived here with his parents until 1898, when the family moved to Buffalo, NY, where they stayed for ten years before returning to St. Paul.

Now known as the Fitzgerald Condominiums, the buildings (originally sixplexes) were subdivided into 24 apartments and by 1970 were plagued by crime and drug problems. A few years later, 12 urban pioneers bought the buildings and renovated them, restoring the apartments to their original size. Among the first projects of its kind in the Hill District, it provided a model for many renovations to come. In 2004, 481 Laurel became the first building in the Twin Cities to be designated a national Literary Landmark by the Friends of Libraries U.S.A.

21 William Howard House N *L*

452 Laurel Ave.

ca. 1880

This Victorian dollhouse was probably built from a pattern book, and its modest size is part of what makes it so charming.

22 Wilbur and Ada Howard House N *L*

422 Laurel Ave.

1882 / enlarged, Denslow W. Millard, 1887

A visual encyclopedia of Victorian gingerbread. Sawn, turned, and carved woodwork sashays along the porch, around the windows, beneath the eaves, and even above the basement walls. Topping it all is a weird, towerlike roof projection with a large dormer.

307 Laurel Ave.

23 Houses N *L*

301, 307, 313 Laurel Ave.

1882–84 / restored, Robert Engstrom, ca. 1980

The Hill District's only identical triplets, known in the neighborhood as the "three sisters." Aside

Laurel Terrace

from their paint jobs, the one noticeable difference among them is that the house at 313 Laurel lacks a side porch, though it presumably had one originally.

24 Laurel Terrace (Riley Row) ! N L

286–94 Laurel Ave.

Willcox and Johnston, 1887

One of the finest Victorian row houses in the United States. With its bold lines, strong colors, and wealth of ornament, it is almost startling in its intensity. William Willcox and Clarence Johnston had been together for less than a year when they designed the row house, and it remains the greatest surviving monument of their brief (1886–89) but productive partnership.

Although it has no shortage of ornament, Laurel Terrace derives its power and presence from the simplicity of its basic forms. Unlike most Victorians, it has a strong horizontal emphasis, with each of its three stories defined by a different design element. On the ground floor, deep entrance arches dominate the composition. The second story features carefully grouped windows of similar size and shape. The third floor offers a line of gables to demarcate each of the original seven apartments. Tying the design together like a giant hinge is an inset corner tower topped by a steep conical roof outfitted with Gothic dormers. The impeccable detailing—in sandstone, granite, brick, slate, copper, wrought iron, and stained glass—includes a variety

of carved creatures, and there are even nymphs cavorting amid the column capitals.

Originally named after its first owner, William C. Riley, who was in the telegraph business and who lived across the street, Laurel Terrace can claim F. Scott Fitzgerald as its most famous former resident. As a boy, Fitzgerald lived in the row house between 1908 and 1909, first with his maternal grandmother and later with his parents.

25 Double house N L

156–58 North Farrington St.

Albert Zschocke, 1888

A wonderful design from the short-lived Albert Zschocke. This large double house is full of fanciful touches, including a front gable that swoops down into a pair of improbable curlicues, a long eyebrow window peering out from the roof, and a rounded corner tower with inset brick cylinders that are peculiar even by Victorian standards.

POI C Maiden Lane

West of Summit Ave. between Selby and Western Aves.

This picturesque little byway is essentially an alley for Summit Ave., and it's one of the few places in the Twin Cities where you feel as though you might have stumbled upon a tiny piece of Europe somehow transported across the pond. At one time, there were over 15 large carriage houses here.

Charles and Emily Noyes House, 1890

26 Charles and Emily Noyes House N *L*

89 Virginia St.

Gilbert and Taylor, 1887

Very probably St. Paul's first high-style Colonial Revival house. Cass Gilbert once worked for the New York firm of McKim, Mead and White, which introduced Colonial Revival on the East Coast. With its fussy detailing and elongated proportions, the house is by no means free of Victorian overtones. Even so, it must have been a novelty in its day. Charles Noyes founded a wholesale drug company known as Noyes Brothers and Cutler in Lowertown.

27 Daniels-Lamborn House N *L*

110 Virginia St.

1857 / remodeled and enlarged, Millard and Joy, 1891

The rear portion of this Colonial Revival house dates to 1857 and may well be the oldest property in the Historic Hill District. It was built at 267 Dayton Ave. for Joseph Daniels, an attorney. A later owner, Charles Lamborn, greatly enlarged the house in 1891, in part to accommodate a huge reception for his daughter's wedding. The house was moved here in 1907.

28 Michael Prendergast Double House N *L*

399–401 Ashland Ave.

Willcox and Johnston, 1887

A striking brick and stone double house that applies a classical appliqué to Romanesque Revival forms. The contrasting colors of the checkerboard frieze and arched entrances (which feature widely spaced quoins) make this one of the neighborhood's most vivid houses. Michael Prendergast was in the plumbing supply business and built the house as a rental property.

29 House N *L*

431 Ashland Ave.

Ole Ask (builder), 1890

This splendidly restored Queen Anne was moved here in 1977 from 825 Dayton Ave. Its builder, carpenter Ole Ask, may have taken the design from a pattern book.

30 Frederick Jackson House N *L*

467 Ashland Ave.

James Knox Taylor, 1882

A Shingle Style beauty by James Knox Taylor, who later partnered with Cass Gilbert. Taylor eventually became supervising architect of the U.S. Treasury.

Elizabeth Gilbert House

31 Elizabeth Gilbert House N *L*

471 Ashland Ave.

Cass Gilbert, 1884 / later remodelings

Cass Gilbert's first St. Paul house, built for his mother (although Gilbert himself lived here until his marriage in 1887). Gilbert began designing the Shingle Style house in 1882 when he was just 23 years old and working for the New York firm of McKim, Mead and White. In a letter to his friend and fellow architect Clarence Johnston, he wrote: "I am trying to study the whole thing with a loving regard for those that are to occupy it. It has become a little problem to do something which shall be artistic, not fashionable, sensible, genuine, and a place I shall not tire of myself." On the whole, he met those goals. Although the exterior has been modified (in a couple of instances by Gilbert himself), the interior remains largely intact.

32 Condominiums (St. John the Evangelist Episcopal Church) N *L*

495–99 Ashland Ave.

William H. Willcox (rear portion), 1883 / Thori, Alban and Fischer (front portion, St. Paul Universalist Church), 1907 / renovated, ca. 1980s

This stone structure was built as St. John the Evangelist Church and was later occupied by the St. Paul Universalist Church, Contender for the Faith Church, and other congregations. The rear portion, which has walls of gray rather than yellow limestone, is older than the church proper and was originally a school. Cass Gilbert and James Knox Taylor designed three additions to the first church here in the 1880s, but none of their work survives.

33 Firenze Apartments *L*

117 North Mackubin St.

James McLeod, 1900

A touch of Florence imported to St. Paul. The highlight is a rooftop loggia that rises from corbelled brick arches and features red and green terra-cotta panels adorned with shields and other motifs. The architect of this exotic concoction, James McLeod, was also the son-in-law of its builder, Dr. Rudolph Schiffman, who lived nearby on Summit Ave.

34 Holly Row N *L*

505–9 Holly Ave.

James Chisholm, 1888 / renovated, 1970s

A picturesque row house clad in sandstone. The tightly packed architectural crowd along the roofline includes four chimneys, two towers, a gable, and a dormer. Unsympathetic modern windows date to the 1970s when the building was renovated following a fire.

35 William George–Louisa McQuillan House N *L*

472 Holly Ave.

1895

A rather daunting stone house that's one of several built in St. Paul for Louisa McQuillan, F. Scott Fitzgerald's wealthy and apparently restless maternal grandmother. Like her house of the same period at 623 Summit Ave., this one has crenellations (atop the front bay window) and conveys an aura of no-nonsense solidity. Playwright August Wilson once lived here.

36 Everett Bailey House N *L*

459 Holly Ave.

James Knox Taylor, 1885 / Art: Chimney Sweep (wood sculpture), Scott Showell

A house in an admirable mix of styles, completed by James Knox Taylor just before he became Cass Gilbert's partner. The original owner, banker Everett Bailey, must have loved the place: he lived here until his death in 1953.

Commodore Hotel bar

37 Commodore Hotel N *L*

79 Western Ave. North

Alexander Rose, 1921 / bar, Werner Wittkamp, ca. 1940s

This gracious apartment hotel, now condominiums, is one of the largest buildings in the Hill District. Designed for a well-to-do clientele, the Commodore originally included a rooftop garden, a dining room, and other amenities. The Commodore was converted to condominiums after being damaged in a 1978 gas explosion. Inside are the partial remains of a boffo art deco barroom designed by Werner Wittkamp. The Russian-born Wittkamp, trained as a set designer, produced a number of suave buildings and interiors in the Twin Cities in the 1930s and 1940s.

38 James and Annie Skinner House N L

385 Portland Ave.

Clarence H. Johnston, 1902

This brick foursquare hints at a variety of styles—from Jacobethan to Colonial Revival to neoclassical—but relies on powerful massing to achieve its considerable effect. Details of note include the monumental columns and piers of the front porch, chimneys with distinctive flared tops, and a carriage house connected to the main house via an open passageway. James Skinner, the original owner, was in the fur business and also involved in banking.

Paul Doty House, 1973

39 Paul Doty House N L

427 Portland Ave.

Emmanuel Masqueray, 1915

One of only two houses in St. Paul known to have been designed by Emmanuel Masqueray, the French-born architect of the St. Paul Cathedral. With its exceptionally high roof and aura of continental suavity, the house certainly looks French, and it's not hard to imagine it standing somewhere on the outskirts of Paris. The highlight is a large front dormer that curves down into a parapet adorned with urns. Finished at about the same time as the Cathedral opened, this may well have been Masqueray's last residential work before his death in 1917. The original owner, Paul Doty, was vice president and general manager of the St. Paul Gas and Light Co.

40 Kirke-Murphy House N L

453 Portland Ave.

ca. 1889

A flamboyant brick-clad Queen Anne with patterned shingle work on the front gable and tower. William Kirke lived here for only a few years before moving to a house at 629 Summit Ave.

41 John White House N L

460 Portland Ave.

Cass Gilbert, 1885

Another of Gilbert's early houses that's very hard to peg to any particular style. The front porch, with its interplay of thin columns and thick piers, is quite striking.

42 Charles Bigelow III House N L

487 Portland Ave.

Thomas Holyoke, 1910

43 Fred R. Bigelow House N L

495 Portland Ave.

Thomas Holyoke, 1910

A pair of elegant Tudor Revival houses designed for Charles Bigelow and son Fred by Cass Gilbert protégé Thomas Holyoke. Charles Bigelow was president of the St. Paul Fire and Marine Insurance Co. (now St. Paul Travelers) from 1876 until 1911, when he was succeeded by his son, who ran the company until 1938.

44 Oscar Taylor Double House N L

544–46 Portland Ave.

Clarence H. Johnston, 1890

A dark, weighty double house, executed in rock-faced Lake Superior sandstone and very much in the spirit of H. H. Richardson. The tower, which has a recessed porch with a grillelike balustrade and dwarf columns beneath a witch's-hat roof, is one of the finest of its type in the Twin Cities.

Portland Terrace

45 Portland Terrace (Bookstaver Row House) N L

548–54 Portland Ave.

Gilbert and Taylor, 1888

Cass Gilbert's only surviving row house in St. Paul. The recessed arched entries on the building's eastern end and around the corner on Kent St. call to mind the work of H. H. Richardson, but overall the row house has the relaxed, comfortable feel of Colonial Revival. Among historic residents of the row house were Edward and Mollie Fitzgerald, who conceived their famous son while living here in late 1895.

St. John the Evangelist Episcopal Church, 1935

46 St. John the Evangelist Episcopal Church N L

Portland Ave. at Kent St.

Clarence H. Johnston, 1903 / remodeled, Clarence H. Johnston and Ralph Adams Cram, ca. 1919

guildhall, 60 Kent St.

Cass Gilbert, 1895

This church complex incorporates the work of both Cass Gilbert and Clarence Johnston. Gilbert's half-timbered guildhall along Kent St. was built first, in 1895, and served as a temporary worship space for the congregation, which moved that year from its old church on Ashland Ave. In 1902, Johnston designed the church proper. Built largely of local limestone, the church is dominated by a square tower with pinnacles at each corner—a type sometimes called a crown tower. Note the gargoyles, six to a side, that lurk near the top. Inside, the church includes a beautiful chancel that's the product of a 1919 remodeling by Johnston and Boston architect Ralph Cram (designer of nearby House of Hope Presbyterian Church).

Summit-University West

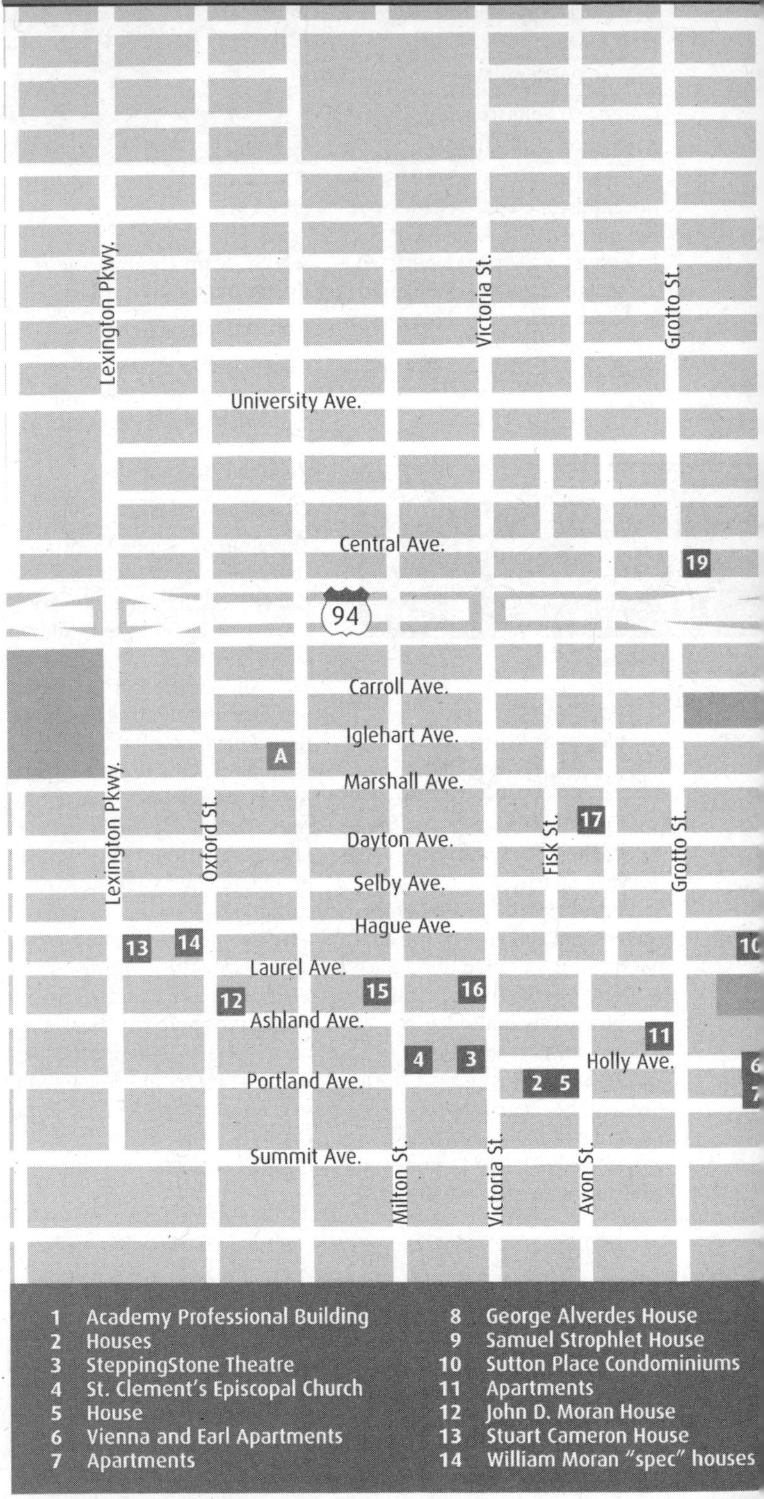

Lexington Pkwy.

Victoria St.

Grotto St.

University Ave.

Central Ave.

19

94

Carroll Ave.

Iglehart Ave.

A

Lexington Pkwy.

Oxford St.

Marshall Ave.

Fisk St.

17

Dayton Ave.

Grotto St.

Selby Ave.

Hague Ave.

13 **14**

Laurel Ave.

1C

12

15

16

Ashland Ave.

11

4 **3**

Holly Ave.

Portland Ave.

2 5

6

7

Summit Ave.

Milton St.

Victoria St.

Avon St.

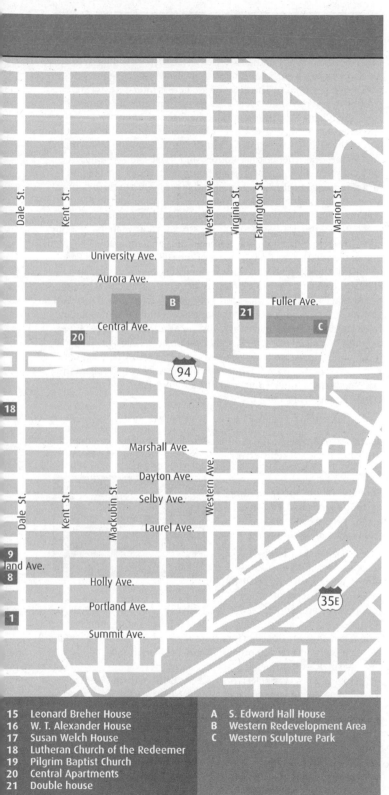

Summit-University

15 Leonard Breher House
16 W. T. Alexander House
17 Susan Welch House
18 Lutheran Church of the Redeemer
19 Pilgrim Baptist Church
20 Central Apartments
21 Double house

A S. Edward Hall House
B Western Redevelopment Area
C Western Sculpture Park

Summit-University West and North

To the north and west of the Historic Hill District, extending to Lexington Parkway, lies a portion of the Summit-University neighborhood with a split personality. The great divide here is Interstate 94, and crossing over it can almost seem like going from one city to another.

To the north of the interstate, in what became known as the Western Redevelopment Area, entire blocks were cleared and rebuilt beginning in the 1950s and continuing into the 1970s. Here you'll find many modern-era apartments, townhouses, and single-family homes as well as a scattering of older houses. Some of St. Paul's most historic African American churches are also in this area. Among the neighborhood's most intriguing places is Western Sculpture Park (1998), an unexpected homage to art and greenery located on Marion Street.

South of Interstate 94, the housing stock is mostly late nineteenth and early twentieth century, and some of it is of comparable quality to that of the Hill District (in fact, parts of the Hill and Woodland Park historic districts extend into this area along Dayton, Marshall, and Portland avenues). There are no overwhelming architectural monuments here, but you will find scores of houses designed by important St. Paul architects such as Clarence Johnston, Emmanuel Masqueray, Louis Lockwood, and Omeyer and Thori. At the western edge of the neighborhood, on Lexington Parkway, is one of the city's most spectacular bungalows: the Stuart Cameron House (1911). The neighborhood is also home to several noteworthy churches, among them the First Methodist Church (1910) and St. Clement's Episcopal Church (1895), both on Portland.

1 Academy Professional Building (St. Paul Academy)

25 North Dale St.

Thomas Holyoke, 1903 / addition, ca. 1960 / renovated, Ed Conley, 2006 / Art: F. Scott Fitzgerald (statue), Aaron Dysart, 2006

F. Scott Fitzgerald attended school in this building from 1908 to 1911, when it served as St. Paul Academy, then a private school for boys. The academy moved elsewhere in 1931, and the old school had a variety of occupants before it was converted to professional offices. A statue of Fitzgerald as a boy was placed on the building's front steps in 2006.

2 Houses N *L*

819, 823, 829 Portland Ave.

Omeyer and Thori, 1889

Three brick Queen Annes that anchor the middle of a block. The star of the trio is the middle house at 823 Portland. It's unusual by virtue of its two towers, the shorter and stouter of

which looks more like something from the Romanesque Revival

823 and 819 Portland Ave.

than the Queen Anne. The iron fence in front of the house is modern; it was made in Scotland and installed in 2005.

3 SteppingStone Theatre (First Methodist Episcopal Church) N *L*

873 Portland Ave.

Thori, Alban and Fischer, 1910

This updated version of a Roman temple, mounted on a high basement, is a rarity in the Twin Cities by virtue of both its style and its size. The colossal Ionic portico makes a big architectural statement and also forms a terminal vista at the end of Holly Ave. Beyond its impressive portico,

SteppingStone Theatre

the church is a simple design, with rows of regularly spaced windows along its side walls.

St. Clement's Episcopal Church

4 St. Clement's Episcopal Church N *L*

901 Portland Ave.

Cass Gilbert, 1895 / addition, Clarence H. Johnston, 1913

A lovely work by Cass Gilbert modeled on an English parish church. The Gothic elements are carried out simply, with buttressed walls of yellow limestone supporting a steeply gabled roof punctuated by delicate dormers. Rising from one side is a finely proportioned bell tower that culminates in a stone spire. The grounds include a lych-gate—an entry gate with benches to either side. The intimate worship space within features a hammer-beam ceiling, stencilwork, an oak rood screen, and Tiffany glass. Gilbert himself is said to have painted some of the altar decorations; he later complained when parts of the church were, in his words, "marred by other hands." The church was built with a $25,000 gift from Mrs. Theodore Eaton of New York. The dedication on October 6, 1895, attracted such eastern society elites as Mrs. J. P.

Morgan. A parish hall and a vestibule were added in 1913, but the historic church proper remains largely as built.

5 House

806 Holly Ave.

1890

A finely restored house caught somewhere between the Shingle and Colonial Revival styles, with a dollop of Queen Anne thrown in as well.

6 Vienna and Earl Apartments N *L*

682–88 Holly Ave.

Louis Lockwood, 1907

7 Apartments (boiler house)

47 North St. Albans St.

Louis Lockwood, 1907 / renovated, ca. 1982

These brick and concrete apartment buildings, luxurious in their day, are among the last works of the prolific St. Paul architect Louis Lockwood, who died in 1907 at age 43. They were constructed for Carl P. Waldon, a Swedish immigrant who started out as a bricklayer but later became a builder and developer. A boiler house to the rear was converted to apartments in the 1980s after being "Victorianized" with dormers, window hoods, and various ornamental features.

8 George Alverdes House

633 Holly Ave.

Hausler and Wright, 1919

A nice late Prairie Style house by Charles A. Hausler and one of the many partners he teamed up with over the years, Myrtus Wright. The house has a long one-story "prow" extending out from a two-story block that features a front bay with angled windows; a shorter one-story section is on the other side. As is typical of Prairie houses, the front door does not directly face the street. The first owner, George Alverdes, was the proprietor of a popular St. Paul restaurant that bore his name.

9 Samuel Strophlet House

633 Ashland Ave.

J. H. Strophlet (Pittsburgh), 1884

A sweet little cottage with unusual ornamental panels featuring inset circles. Built on Ninth St. in downtown St. Paul, it was moved here a short time later by its first owner, Samuel Strophlet.

10 Sutton Place Condominiums (Gilman Terrace)

697–703 Laurel Ave.

Hermann Kretz, 1892

A Victorian that's only half the building it used to be: its western portion, where there's a parking lot, was lopped off in the 1930s. Clad in red brick above a brownstone base, the building has two ornate wooden porches, balconies with iron railings, and checkerboard patterning beneath some windows. Architect Hermann Kretz was responsible for several large St. Paul apartment buildings of this period, including the Blair House nearby at Selby and Western Aves.

11 Apartments (Temple of Aaron and Jewish Educational Center)

744 Ashland Ave. and 741–59 Holly Ave.

Allen H. Stem (synagogue), 1916 / renovated after fire, 1952 / Liebenberg and Kaplan (educational center), 1930

These buildings, now apartments, once served as a synagogue and educational complex for the Temple of Aaron. The synagogue combines Byzantine and Romanesque elements in a way intended to set it apart from Christian churches. The educational center on Holly was one of the first Moderne-style buildings designed by Liebenberg and Kaplan, best known for their many theaters in the Twin Cities. Temple of Aaron relocated to a new synagogue in 1957, after

which Beth Israel Temple moved in for about 20 years.

12 John D. Moran House

1039 Ashland Ave.

Emmanuel Masqueray, 1909

This foursquare isn't as grand as the other Masqueray-designed house on Portland Ave., but it still stands out here. The handling of the brickwork, particularly on the second story, and the design of the front porch are unusual, and the house conveys a stately Beaux-Arts sensibility despite its modest size. The original owner, John D. Moran, ran a railroad construction company. The house fell vacant in the 1980s and was boarded up before being restored by new owners.

Stuart Cameron House

13 Stuart Cameron House

130 Lexington Pkwy. North

Alban and Hausler, 1911

A show-stopping Craftsman bungalow with just a hint of Swiss Chalet styling as well. The broad roof has a single half-timbered dormer and shelters a long porch with brick piers and tall wood-slat balustrades. Bargeboards, exposed rafters, acorn pendants, and leaded-glass windows are among the house's fine details. It was built for the superintendent of an ironworks company.

14 William Moran "spec" houses

1048, 1050 Hague Ave.

William H. Castner, 1890

Two marvelous Shingle Style houses built on speculation. The house at 1048 Hague is full of inventive details, including an eccentric array of windows and a polygonal tower that ties into a balcony nestled beneath a gable

1048 Hague Ave.

with flared eaves. The house at 1050 Hague is quite different, with a long roof that sweeps down over a corner porch, but it's just as enchanting as its neighbor.

15 Leonard Breher House

928 Laurel Ave.

William Linley Alban, 1909

A house that manages to wring something fresh and engaging out of the overworked Colonial Revival idiom. Small things make this design sing: the way the capitals of the paired Ionic porch columns curl up into brackets, the subtle flaring lines of the roof and gable, and, most of all, the swan's neck pediment that sits atop the small second-story window like a party hat.

16 W. T. Alexander House

876 Laurel Ave.

Omeyer and Thori, 1889

Another insanely festive house from St. Paul's Queen Anne wild men.

17 Susan Welch House

785 Dayton Ave.

Clarence H. Johnston, 1894

A monumental home that presides over its modest surroundings with regal aplomb. Colossal Ionic columns form a dignified temple front. Strong but simple detailing, including corner pilasters, reinforces the home's presence. The porte cochere on the west side of the house was originally balanced by a balustraded porch on the east side. Little is known about the house's original owner other than that she apparently did not wish to be upstaged by her neighbors.

POI A S. Edward Hall House N

996 Iglehart Ave.

1889

This small wood-frame house was the longtime home of a black barbershop owner and civic leader who played a key role in organizing the St. Paul Urban League.

18 Lutheran Church of the Redeemer

285 North Dale St.

Augustus Gauger, 1910 / addition, Slifer and Abrahamson, 1922 / addition, 1974

Clad in rock-faced limestone, this Gothic Revival church has a square tower of the "crown" variety that culminates in a kingly array of sprockets and finials. The congregation was founded in 1890 and built this church for $35,000, a tenth of what a 1974 addition cost. Nearby at 625 Marshall Ave. is a large stone house from 1903 that once served as the church parsonage.

19 Pilgrim Baptist Church N

732 Central Ave. West

William Linley Alban, 1928 / addition, 1949

Pilgrim Baptist is St. Paul's oldest black congregation, organized in 1866 by a group of former slaves led by Robert Hickman. This Gothic Revival church, dating to 1928, was built at a time when the city's 4,000 black residents were beginning to concentrate in the Rondo area. Another historic black church, **St. James African Methodist Episcopal,** is just down the street at 624 Central Ave.

20 Central Apartments

554 Central Ave. West

Brooks Cavin, 1964

A six-sided high-rise that juxtaposes inset and projecting balconies to create an interesting effect. The ogee arches at ground level are a peculiar touch.

POI B Western Redevelopment Area

Area roughly bounded by I-94, University Ave., Rice St., and Dale St.

City of St. Paul Housing and Redevelopment Authority, ca. 1950s and later

This area of redeveloped housing displays the design principles that guided urban planning in the 1960s and 1970s: a low-density mix of homes and apartments, lots of green space, cul-de-sacs rather than through streets, and midblock pedestrian pathways. In other words, the goal was to create an in-city suburb. It didn't turn out particularly well, but it's not awful either. What the area could use most now is mature trees to help soften its harsh edges.

21 Double house

360–62 Fuller Ave.

Omeyer and Thori, 1889

A giant Queen Anne double house that's now apartments. It once had an enormous floral carving beneath the roof peak, a broad classical pediment above the central attic window, and patterned shinglework in the front gables. These decorative features have vanished beneath modern siding.

POI C Western Sculpture Park

387 Marion St.

City of St. Paul (Jim Brewer), 1998

The idea here was to create a distinctive amenity in an area that consists largely of nondescript housing projects. Besides a rotating exhibit of 20 large sculptures, the park includes gardens, a play area, and a volleyball court. The City of St. Paul, the Fuller-Aurora Neighborhood Association, and Public Art St. Paul all played key roles in bringing about the park.

Western Sculpture Park

13

Frogtown, North End, & Como

Overview

This part of St. Paul, shaped by railroads, includes the old working-class neighborhoods of Frogtown and the North End as well as a more middle-class area around Como Lake. Along the southern border is University Avenue, a commercial artery that forms a linear neighborhood of its own. Never fancy places, Frogtown and the North End have many small, old houses on narrow lots. The most prominent monument here is St. Agnes Catholic Church (1912), its baroque tower visible for miles across the flat terrain.

No one knows for sure how Frogtown (officially Thomas-Dale) acquired its name. One theory holds that it's a slur upon the area's French settlers, sometimes called "Frogs." A more likely explanation is that the marshy ground here was once home to so many amphibians that *Frogtown* became the moniker of choice.

The neighborhood rapidly developed in the 1870s and 1880s as railroads and related industries became established. The St. Paul and Pacific Railroad built tracks here as early as 1862. In 1879 James J. Hill and other investors acquired the St. Paul and Pacific, reorganized it as the St. Paul, Minneapolis and Manitoba Railroad, and in 1882 built the Jackson Street Shops (now part of Empire Builder Industrial Park). After the railroad became the Great Northern in 1893, it constructed more shops (now gone) off Dale Street. These shops and their peripheral industries provided thousands of jobs, many of which were filled by European immigrants. Today, another wave of newcomers—mostly Southeast Asians—has changed the face of the neighborhood once again.

Like Frogtown, the North End grew with the railroads, especially after the Jackson Street Shops opened. Swedish, German, and Slavic immigrants were among those who poured into the area. Once a bastion of white ethnicity, the North End is now much more diverse, with Asians, blacks, Hispanics, and other minorities accounting for 45 percent of its population.

Rice Street has been the neighborhood's chief commercial thoroughfare since the 1880s, when horsecar service was inaugurated. By the 1890s, trolleys were running on both Rice and Jackson streets. Jackson never saw significant commercial development, however.

The North End's living population, about 25,000 people, pales in comparison to the 200,000 or so dead who rest within its boundaries. St. Paul's three largest cemeteries—Oakland, Calvary, and Elmhurst, all founded in the 1850s—form the corners of a triangle that encompasses much of the North End.

To the west of the North End is the Como neighborhood, which began attracting settlers in the 1840s. Among the early immigrants was Charles Perry, who hailed from the Alps near the Swiss-Italian border. It was Perry, looking back to his homeland, who gave Como Lake its name. The lake and the large park that grew around it form one key strand of the neighborhood's history. Railroading forms the other. The opening of the Northern Pacific's Como Shops (now Bandana Square) in 1885 brought in hundreds of new jobs and stimulated industrial, commercial, and residential development nearby.

One of the neighborhood's early residential enclaves was Warrendale, which today would be called an "upscale" community. Although never a great success, its legacy is visible in the row of Victorian homes on the southwest side of Como Lake. Today, Como remains a pleasant, mostly residential neighborhood. The oldest houses are concentrated around the lake, while farther north are tracts of Period Revival housing from the 1920s and bungalows from the 1950s.

Frogtown

From an architectural standpoint, Frogtown's distinguishing feature is its large number of small Victorian-era houses, some on lots only 25 or 30 feet wide, compared to the 40-foot width typical of St. Paul. The vast majority are simple wood-frame structures without any pretensions to high style. Many of the homes have been heavily remodeled, often with rear extensions. Historically correct (and usually expensive) restoration is not an option for most residents.

Even so, the neighborhood still has a good number of charming little houses, often tucked away on otherwise nondescript blocks. Brick "mechanic's cottages," as they were once called, are especially common here, but you'll also find a scattering of larger homes, a few historic apartments and row houses, along with one of the city's largest public housing projects—the Mount Airy Homes (1959).

The neighborhood's outstanding works of architecture, however, are churches. In addition to St. Agnes, Frogtown is home to at least two other noteworthy churches: St. Adalbert's (1911), built for Polish immigrants, and University Avenue Congregational Church (1908), designed by Clarence Johnston. Other important buildings here include the old Jackson Street Roundhouse (1907), now part of the Minnesota Transportation Museum, and the Wilder Foundation complex (ca. 1971 and later) on the site of the historic House of the Good Shepherd.

Much of Thomas-Dale's commercial life is concentrated along University Avenue, which because of its great length and importance to the city as a whole is the subject of its own section in this chapter.

1 Minnesota Transportation Museum, Jackson Street Roundhouse

Jackson St. and Pennsylvania Ave.

1907 and later / renovated, Julie Snow, 1993

This was the second roundhouse built at the Jackson Street Shops. The first, from 1882, was just to the west. Originally, this structure had 25 stalls for locomotives around a 70-foot-diameter turntable. The Great Northern Railway used the roundhouse until 1959, when locomotive servicing was moved elsewhere. The Minnesota Transportation Museum, which acquired the building in 1985, has restored the turntable and also maintains a gift shop here.

2 Empire Builder Industrial Park (St. Paul, Minneapolis and Manitoba Railroad Co. Shops Historic District) N *L*

23–27 Empire Dr. and 193 Pennsylvania Ave.

1882 / renovated, 1985 and later

In the late nineteenth century, railroads and their related industries employed one of every four wage earners in St. Paul. The three stone buildings

Jackson Street Roundhouse

Frogtown

1	Minnesota Transportation Museum, Jackson Street Roundhouse	15	House
2	Empire Builder Industrial Park	16	St. Paul Fellowship
3	Mount Airy Homes	17	Christ Lutheran Church on Capitol Hill
4	Amherst H. Wilder Foundation	18	State of Minnesota Building
5	St. Agnes Catholic Church	19	Farrington Place
6	Alley house	20	Old Home Foods
7	Row house	21	Rondo Outreach Library
8	Lucy's Bar	22	Lifetrack Resources Building
9	Frogtown Family Lofts	23	Commercial building
10	St. Adalbert's Catholic Church	24	Commercial building
11	House	25	Warehouse
12	Charles Buetow House	26	Bigelow Building
13	Small houses	27	Town House
14	Apartments	28	Midway Marketplace

Frogtown

Empire Builder Industrial Park

here—originally a machine shop, a pattern shop, and a storehouse, respectively—are remnants of that remarkable railroading era. Constructed of two-foot-thick limestone walls and heavy timber columns, they are also superb specimens of industrial architecture. They were once part of the Jackson Street Shops of the St. Paul, Minneapolis and Manitoba (later Great Northern) Railroad. Occupying 36 acres, the shops consisted of 25 structures for building and maintaining locomotives and freight and passenger cars. Skilled workers from silversmiths to cloth dyers to mechanics were employed at the shops.

When a merger produced the Burlington Northern Railroad in 1970, the shops became redundant and were thereafter used only for storage. In 1985 the St. Paul Port Authority acquired much of the site, demolished eight of the remaining buildings, and refurbished these three as part of the new Empire Builder Industrial Park.

3 Mount Airy Homes

Jackson and Mount Airy Sts.

Walter Butler Co. and others, 1959 / 1967 / renovated, ca. 1990s

This hilly area northeast of the capitol was once a neighborhood of ramshackle housing built along steep, narrow, crooked streets, with as much as 30 feet in elevation separating adjacent lots. Originally home to many Scandinavian immigrants, the neighborhood came to be known as the "Badlands" and was con-

sidered one of St. Paul's worst slums. In the 1950s, the city cleared everything away and began constructing the 298-unit housing project now called Mount Airy Homes. As built, the townhomes were grimly utilitarian structures that fairly shouted "public housing." In the 1990s, however, the St. Paul Public Housing Agency renovated the townhomes, improved the grounds, and built a community center (designed by McMonigal Architects). Mount Airy is now a far more inviting place.

Rice Street

(see under North End)

LOST 1 *The **Great Northern Railway Dale Street Shops** were once located near the northeast corner of Dale St. and Minnehaha Ave. The shops opened around 1902 and were used mainly for locomotive repair. The last of the shop buildings was razed in 1999.*

4 Amherst H. Wilder Foundation (including Wilder Square)

Area roughly bounded by Pierce Butler Rte., Lafond Ave., and Victoria and Chatsworth Sts.

*includes **Wilder Foundation Headquarters**, ca. 1971 / **Wilder Square Cooperative Housing,** 1975 and later / **Wilder Woods Gathering Pavilion (Alice Nicholson Pavilion),** Close Associates (Gar Hargens) and Hal Eckhart (artist), 2003*

In 1969 the Amherst Wilder Foundation bought the 17 acres

of hilly, wooded property here that forms the largest expanse of greenery in Frogtown. It renovated some of the buildings on the site and tore down others to create a headquarters campus. (Wilder announced plans in 2006 to relocate its headquarters elsewhere in St. Paul.) The foundation also developed a 163-unit cooperative housing community here in 1975 known as Wilder Square. The stucco-clad townhomes and apartments are nicely laid out to take advantage of the parklike grounds but offer little architectural interest. The grounds do harbor one architectural delight: a tiny pavilion features tree-trunk columns supporting a whimsically skewed version of a witch's-hat roof.

House of the Good Shepherd, 1890

LOST 2 *The Wilder Foundation property south of Minnehaha Ave. once belonged to the* **House of the Good Shepherd,** *founded in St. Paul in 1868. The institution, which moved into a new building here in 1883, was operated by the Contemplative Sisters of the Good Shepherd, who sought to reform unwed mothers, prostitutes, and girls thought to be "incorrigible." Judging by the size of the building—a huge Victorian Gothic affair with three towers and a central dome—there must have been a lot of fallen femininity in St. Paul. Other buildings were later added to the complex, which was razed after the Home of the Good Shepherd, as it is now called, moved in 1967 to suburban North Oaks.*

5 St. Agnes Catholic Church ! N L

548–50 Lafond Ave.

George Ries, 1897 / 1912 / renovated, MacDonald and Mack Architects and Conrad Schmidt Studios, 1985–88

The monument in Frogtown, and one of St. Paul's finest churches. Modeled on an Austrian monastery church, it has a

St. Agnes Catholic Church

soaring onion-domed bell tower that rises 205 feet above the neighborhood's flatlands. The tower, which like the rest of the church is clad in Indiana limestone, is unusual because of its location at the rear of the sanctuary. Also out of the ordinary is the church's tall basement, necessitated by Frogtown's notoriously high water table.

The front of the church is a marvelous baroque set piece. A monumental staircase leads to a terrace with three elaborately framed entrances and paired Ionic pilasters. Above the central entrance is an ornate window with niches to either side holding statues of St. Peter and St. Paul. Farther above is a pedimented gable where a larger statue of St. Agnes presides over the scene. Within, the long nave has vaulted ceilings and a 60-foot-high domed crossing. Completely redecorated in the 1980s, the baroque interior includes gilt column capitals, the extensive use of scagliola (a form of plastering that imitates marble), frescoes, and a marble altar with a baldachin (canopy). There are also brass chandeliers salvaged from the second Minnesota State Capitol after its demolition in 1939.

St. Agnes, at one time Minnesota's largest German parish, was founded in 1888. Work began on this church in 1897, when the basement was constructed. It was used for services while the parish raised money—about $200,000 in all—to build the full church. Work resumed in 1909, and the church was dedicated three years later at a four-hour-long service presided over by Archbishop John Ireland with the assistance of 32 priests.

6 Alley house

538 Blair Ave.

1901

This tiny alley house was once the kitchen wing of the larger house on the lot, moved here in 1901. The main house, Italianate in character, served in the 1880s as the rectory for St. Agnes Church and was also used as a school.

7 Row house

400–406 Van Buren Ave.

John Fischer, 1910

St. Paul's only concrete-block row house. The vaguely Colonial Revival design features three inset entries that add a jarring note of asymmetry to what is otherwise a very regular facade.

8 Lucy's Bar (Dietsch's Hall)

601 Western Ave. North

George Bergmann, 1890 / remodeled, ca. 1970s

There are actually two buildings here. The corner building, which has garishly painted brick arches atop its infilled second-story windows, was built by Joseph Steinkamp, who operated a saloon and other businesses. Later, the place became known as Dietsch's Hall and was used for neighborhood gatherings. The smaller adjoining building to the west on Thomas looks to be somewhat older than the saloon and was probably built as a shop with an apartment above.

9 Frogtown Family Lofts (Guiterman Brothers Men's Apparel, later Brandtjen and Kluge Printing Press Factory)

653 Galtier St.

Mark Fitzpatrick, 1910 / 1917 / renovated, 1992

A brick factory building where everything from men's clothes to printing presses was once made. In 1992 the building was converted into 36 large apartments for artists and their families.

St. Adalbert's Catholic Church

10 St. Adalbert's Catholic Church

265 Charles Ave.

Boyer Taylor and Tewes, 1911

A two-towered church, nothing elaborate, but still a sturdy and convincing display of faith. The brick mass of the church forms a dark contrast to the white towers that rise in three stages to tiny cupolas crowned by golden crosses. The simple front facade has three doors above which there were once three arched windows. St. Adalbert's was built for Polish immigrants who formed this parish in 1879. The old parish school on Edmund Ave. predates the church by ten years.

11 House

543 Sherburne Ave.

1885

An ornate house for Frogtown, with carved front porch brackets and heavy brick hoods over the upstairs windows. There's a fairly similar brick house just down the street at 571 Sherburne.

12 Charles Buetow House

567 Edmund Ave.

1885

Charles Buetow, a laborer, built this brick cottage for $650, and it's come down through the years wonderfully intact, even if the porch is sagging a bit.

Charles Ave. houses

13 Small houses

North side of Charles Ave. between Dale and Kent Sts.

1880s and later

A classic Frogtown block, packed with 17 houses, about as many as you'll find on any block in either St. Paul or Minneapolis. Some of the lots here appear to be no more than 25 feet wide.

14 Apartments

652–58 Sherburne Ave.

ca. 1906

This building's rough-faced blocks are laid up in a random ashlar pattern that imitates stone, and you have to look very closely to tell that the walls are in fact concrete. Across the street at 683 and 685 Sherburne are two other concrete-block apartment buildings.

15 House

727 Sherburne Ave.

1900 and later

A tiny house of uncertain provenance that looks to have been worked over by someone with a taste for unusual angles. Frogtown is particularly rich in this kind of vernacular mayhem.

POI A Former "shoe" house

743 Charles Ave.

1885

In 1996 the front of this house was covered with shoes by Detroit artist Tyree Guyton, working with neighborhood volunteers. The job of what might be called houseshoeing took 42 hours. Guyton called the project "Soul People," the idea being that the shoes represented the lost souls (and soles) of victims of urban violence. It was quite a sight. Later owners of the house, perhaps feeling the artist had gotten enough tread from his idea, removed the footwear.

St. Paul Fellowship, 1982

16 St. Paul Fellowship (University Avenue Congregational Church)

868 Sherburne Ave. (also 507 North Victoria St.)

Clarence H. Johnston, 1908

One of Frogtown's gems. Designed by Clarence Johnston, it's a sophisticated version of the so-called Carpenter Gothic style often used for small country churches. Key design elements here include a slightly tapered corner tower topped by a spire and a pair of steep gables with pointed-arch Gothic windows and lovely filigreed bargeboards that rise from brackets. The University Avenue Congregational Church was organized in 1895, and this was its third church building.

Frogtown

University Avenue
from Park Street to St. Paul City Limits

Thomas-Dale is one of seven St. Paul neighborhoods that University Avenue passes through between the East Side and the St. Paul city limits. For most of its route, University is St. Paul's busiest east-west artery (not counting Interstate 94). It's also one of the city's most interesting streets. With its rushing traffic, garish signs, and hodge-podge of buildings, University might be thought of as the city's id, an anti–Summit Avenue where beauty gives way to the gritty demands of commerce. Its eclectic array of architecture ranges from the State Capitol's sober magnificence to the garish delights of Porky's Drive-in. The commercial mix is equally diverse, in part because of an influx of Asian-owned businesses that began in the 1980s.

The avenue was named in the 1870s when St. Paul city leaders decided to establish it as a link to the University of Minnesota campus in Minneapolis. Originally, the plan had been to use what is now Minnehaha Avenue, a half mile to the north, for this purpose. Construction of the Minnesota Transfer Railroad yard blocked that route, however, and so a more southerly course was chosen. As early as 1873, civic dreamers envisioned the avenue as a wide boulevard à la the Champs-Élysées that would connect the two cities, but nothing ever came of the idea. In 1890 the first interurban streetcar line between St. Paul and Minneapolis opened along University, spurring development. Later, the avenue was widened to accommodate a growing volume of auto and truck traffic, and by the 1950s it had evolved into a classic American strip street.

University's most interesting buildings tend to be from the period between 1900 and 1930. Unfortunately, the avenue's greatest commercial monument, the huge Montgomery Ward Catalog Warehouse and Retail Store (1921) near Hamline Avenue, is gone, leveled in 1995 to make way for a drab big-box shopping center. As of 2007, plans were afoot to construct a light-rail line down University, a development that would surely add a new level of vitality to what is already one of the city's liveliest streets.

Christ Lutheran Church on Capitol Hill

17 Christ Lutheran Church on Capitol Hill (Norwegian Evangelical Lutheran Church)

105 University Ave. West

Buechner and Orth, 1913

Standing in the shadow of the State Capitol, this twin-towered building is a nice example of a small Renaissance Revival–style church. Built of yellow brick and white stone trim, the church's temple front features a pair of colossal Ionic columns rising from pedestals. The towers to either side culminate in open belfries in the form of miniature temples. The church is still home to the congregation that built it, although its name was changed to Christ Lutheran in about 1918.

18 State of Minnesota (Ford) Building

117 University Ave. West

John Graham (Seattle) with Kees and Colburn, 1914

This building began as a sub-assembly plant and service center for Ford Model T automobiles. At its peak, the plant turned out 500 cars annually, far fewer than a much larger plant Ford built in Minneapolis the same year. Assembly ended at both buildings by 1925, when Ford completed a new plant in the Highland Park neighborhood of St. Paul. Auto dealerships and other businesses occupied this building until 1952, when it was purchased by the State of Minnesota.

POI B Asian Main Street

University Ave. between Marion St. and Lexington Pkwy.

This two-mile-long stretch of University is sometimes called St. Paul's Asian Main Street. All told, it's home to about 100 Asian-owned businesses, reflecting the tremendous growth of the Asian community in St. Paul since the 1980s.

19 Farrington Place

312–16 University Ave. West

Albert Zschocke, 1889

One of the best Victorian-era buildings on University. Note the rounded bay windows on the west side of the building and the elegant little balcony between them.

Old Home Foods

20 Old Home Foods (Minnesota Milk Co.)

370 University Ave. West

1912 / addition and new facade, Charles A. Hausler, 1932

The art deco style was thought to be the height of modernism in its day and was often used to update the image of commercial and industrial buildings. Here, Charles Hausler took an earlier structure and gave it the full art deco treatment. He added a stepped-up entrance tower, encased the walls in a new stone skin, and threw in zigzag and chevron motifs along the cornice. There's also a fanciful bas-relief

sculpture near the top of the tower that depicts two children beside a very large milk bottle.

21 Rondo Outreach Library

461 North Dale St. at University Ave.

BKV Group, 2006

A new public library is incorporated into this 98-unit apartment building on a site once notorious as the home of a porn theater and bookstore. Combining a library with housing is a fine idea. Too bad, then, that the architecture is of the dull brick box variety with which St. Paul seems to have fallen in love in recent years. Something far more lively and colorful should have been built here.

LOST 3 *The Tudor Revival–style* **Faust Theater** *occupied this site until it was demolished in the 1990s following years of ignominious service as a venue for porn films.*

22 Lifetrack Resources Building (Owens Motor Sales Co.)

709 University Ave. West

1917 / additions, ca. 1921–23

With its row of seven elliptical arches and broad windows, this is one of the avenue's sharpest buildings. Constructed for the Owens Motor Co., an early Ford dealership, it was originally only one story high. A second floor was added and the building expanded to the east in the early 1920s. Like many commercial buildings of the period, it doesn't fit into any tidy stylistic category, although its brick- and tilework suggest an Arts and Crafts influence.

23 Commercial building (Victoria Theater)

825 University Ave. West

Franklin H. Ellerbe, 1915

Beaded and patterned brickwork distinguishes the facade of this small theater building, originally known as the Victoria.

The designer, Franklin Ellerbe, founded Ellerbe Architects (now Ellerbe Becket), which is today one of the largest architectural firms in the United States. The theater closed in the 1930s, and the building has served a variety of commercial uses since then.

908 University Ave. West, 1925

24 Commercial building (Brioschi-Minuti Studio and Showroom)

908 University Ave. West

Torelli Minuti, 1922

A small building constructed in 1922 for the Brioschi-Minuti Co., which specialized in ornamental plasterwork and architectural sculpture. The firm was founded in New York by two Italian immigrants, Carlo Brioschi and Adolpho Minuti. The duo moved to St. Paul in about 1909. They contributed ornamental work to the St. Paul Athletic Club, the State Capitol, the Minnesota Humanities Commission Building, and the Robert Street Bridge. This building, designed by Torelli Minuti (Adolpho's son), was intended to showcase the firm's work. It features ornamental panels and medallions, rooftop urns, and the company name carved above the front door. A successor firm, the Minuti-Ogle Co., is based in suburban Oakdale.

LOST 4 *Lexington Baseball Park* *once stood near the southwest corner of University Ave. and Lexington Pkwy. Built in about 1910, the park was home to the St. Paul Saints of the old American Association. It was torn down in 1960 after the Minnesota Twins arrived. As of 2007, this site was being redeveloped for a variety of uses,*

including a new headquarters building for the Amherst H. Wilder Foundation.

1222 University Ave. West, 1952

25 Warehouse (St. Paul Casket Co.)

1222 University Ave. West

Allen H. Stem, 1922

Now considerably the worse for wear, this large industrial building is a sophisticated design for its time. The central tower and corner piers have stepped buttresses that anticipate the art deco style, which didn't make its full-blown appearance in the Twin Cities until the late 1920s. Other details, such as the slight rounding of many of the building's edges, evoke the contemporaneous Gothic-tinged work of Boston architect Bertram Goodhue. The building was designed as a factory and showroom for a firm that began business in 1887 as the North St. Paul Casket Co. Eventually, the casket company itself perished, and the building is now used as a warehouse.

Bigelow Building, 1914

26 Bigelow Building (Brown and Bigelow Co.)

1286 University Ave. (450 North Syndicate St.)

Kees and Colburn, 1914 / portion razed, ca. 1980s

This nondescript, much-remodeled building once had two towers and a central entry flanked by colossal granite columns, set behind a well-tended lawn. It's all that remains of what was once the headquarters of the Brown and Bigelow Co. Founded in 1896 by Herbert H. Bigelow and Hiram Brown, the company (now located elsewhere in St. Paul) made specialty calendars, playing cards, and other promotional products. Norman Rockwell was among the artists who painted calendar art for the firm, although perhaps the most famous work ever commissioned by Brown and Bigelow was Cassius Coolidge's 1903 series of paintings of dogs playing poker.

Herbert Bigelow, the driving force behind the firm, was quite a character. He despised the federal income tax imposed in 1913. Convicted of tax evasion in the early 1920s, Bigelow served an eight-month stint in a federal prison (where he met a fellow inmate named Charles Ward, who later became Brown and Bigelow's president). Bigelow himself met a tragic end, drowning in 1933 while on a canoe trip near Ely, MN.

LOST 5 *Pioneer fur trader, steamboatman, and lover of fine horseflesh Norman Kittson built a racecourse, stable, and clubhouse here at the southwest corner of University and Hamline Aves. in 1881. Not given to false displays of modesty, he named his creation* **"Kittsondale."** *The stables were especially grand, containing 64 stalls in a cross-shaped brick building that sported a central tower. Kittson managed to enjoy the ponies for only a few years before dying in 1888. In about 1900 the stables were converted into a manufacturing plant; they were later used by a trucking company before being demolished in 1942.*

27 Town House (Kaiser Restaurant, Tip Top Tap)

1415 University Ave. West

1924 / remodeled, Werner Wittkamp, 1946

Now a gay bar, this building began as a laundry and later became a German restaurant.

When it was converted into a tavern called the Tip Top Tap in the 1940s, ace designer Werner Wittkamp was called in to liven things up. He didn't disappoint: over the entrance he installed a pair of curving canopies that look a bit like the result of a collision between the building and a small fleet of flying saucers. Within, much of Wittkamp's design also remains intact.

28 Midway Marketplace

University Ave. West between Hamline Ave. and Pascal St.

1995

When this big-box shopping center was being planned, there were promises that it would be more pedestrian friendly and "urbane" than the average suburban mall. Dream on. It's utterly generic except that the retail boxes are laid out in such a way that even navigating the place behind the wheel of a car isn't easy. Midway Marketplace is especially disappointing in view of this site's rich history and its location at one of the city's most important crossroads.

Montgomery Ward Catalog Warehouse and Retail Store, 1925

LOST 6 *Midway Marketplace occupies the site of the* **Montgomery Ward Catalog Warehouse and Retail Store,** *a 1.2 million-square-foot colossus that may have been the largest building in St. Paul's history. The "Northwest House," as Ward's called it, opened in April 1921. The complex consisted of a three-story administrative wing (soon remodeled into a retail store) along University and an eight-story warehouse to the rear where 25,000 catalog orders a day were being filled by the mid-1920s. Between the two sections was a 257-foot-high tower. Although the administrative-retail section included three entrances flanked* *by classical columns, the complex as a whole had a utilitarian look in keeping with its massive concrete-frame construction.*

As it turned out, the great house built by Montgomery Ward could withstand everything except the treacheries of time and fashion. Assailed by competition from specialty catalogs and other niche retailers, Ward's shut down its catalog operation in 1986. By 1995, the retail store on University was also closed and the complex was then demolished, despite neighborhood pleas to at least save the tower.

29 Midway Center

University Ave. West between Pascal St. and Snelling Ave.

ca. 1960 and later

A standard strip mall on a site that for years was home to the largest "trolley barn" in the Twin Cities.

LOST 7 *The Twin City Rapid Transit Co. maintained its sprawling* **Snelling Station and Shops** *here for almost half a century. More than 1,000 streetcars were built in the shops, mainly for use in St. Paul and Minneapolis, though some were sold to other cities. The northern section of the shop complex, where the mall now strands, was demolished in 1954, not long after the last streetcars were replaced by buses. Buildings on the southern part of the site were rebuilt for use as a bus garage, but these too were demolished in 2002 when the Metropolitan Transit Commission decided to relocate to a new facility.*

POI C Intersection of University and Snelling Avenues

This is believed to be the busiest intersection in Minnesota, with more than 64,000 vehicles passing through it on an average day.

30 Griggs-Midway Building (Griggs, Cooper and Co. Sanitary Foods Division)

1821 University Ave. West

Toltz, King and Day, 1912 / additions, 1919, 1925 / later renovations

Now used largely for offices and charter schools, this huge concrete-frame building was initially a canning factory said to be the largest of its kind in the world. The complex, which includes two ancillary structures, is an example of how even the most utilitarian architecture could be made "respectable" by draping it in a classical coat. The factory was built for Griggs, Cooper and Co., which later made candy and crackers here.

POI D Iris (Union) Park

University and Lynnhurst Aves.

ca. 1880 and later

Iris Park with its small artificial pond is a remnant of a much larger park once located here. Known as Union Park, it was developed in the early 1880s after the Chicago, Milwaukee and St. Paul Railroad completed its "Short Line" nearby and began providing commuter service. Entrepreneurs Herman Grote and John Hinkel bought 37 acres here and established the park, which included a pavilion for dancing, a bandstand, a merry-go-round, a small zoo, and an observation tower. Balloonists and high-wire acts also provided occasional entertainment. Housing gradually filled in the site, and Iris Park is now all that's left of the old amusement park.

Porky's Drive-in, 1976

31 Porky's Drive-in

1890 University Ave. West

Ray Truelson (builder), 1953

All hail the pink pig! With his black top hat tilted at a raffish angle, Porky is one of University's most beloved icons, and rightly so. He presides over just about the last restaurant of its kind in the Twin Cities. Porky's is a genuine 1950s drive-in, authentically garish down to the last detail. It was built by Ray Truelson in 1953 at a time when the American roadside still sported all manner of architectural wild things vying for motorists' attention. Truelson calculated that a building decked out in black and yellow checks (later softened to white and red) might do the trick. His first Porky's here proved so popular that three others were built in the Twin Cities.

As the roadside became enchained, however, mom-and-pop joints like Porky's vanished from the scene. Although all four Porky's eventually closed, this one avoided the wrecking ball, and in 1990 Truelson rescued the place from ruin. Today, it's still going strong.

Iris Park Place

32 Iris Park Place (Krank Manufacturing Co.) N *L*

1885 University Ave. West

Toltz, King and Day (Roy Childs Jones, chief designer), 1926

This building was constructed as a factory and showroom for the A. J. Krank Co., a firm that manufactured cosmetics, shampoos, and creams. To design his new factory, company founder Alfred J. Krank hired Toltz, King and Day, architects of the Hamm Building downtown. Like that building, Iris Park Place features superb terra-cotta ornament. Here, it appears around the entrances (where fantastic flower bowls perch atop brick piers), at the upper corners of the building, and in a series of panels above the first floor. The panels depict urns and vases from which flowers spill into colorful garlands. Presumably, this floral imagery

was intended to underscore the beautifying effect of the company's cosmetics.

The bloom didn't last long for Krank or for his company. A lover of fast cars, Krank had a fatal encounter with a trolley in September 1928 near Lake Minnetonka. In 1941 new owners moved a scaled-down version of the firm back to downtown St. Paul. This building was converted into offices in the 1980s.

33 Commercial building (Mutual Service Insurance Co.)

1919–23 University Ave. West

Ellerbe Associates, 1956 and later

An early example of architectural modernism in St. Paul. The building was originally three stories high and consisted of almost windowless stone-clad volumes linked to a glassy entrance pavilion and a stair tower sheathed in dark granite. It wasn't anything great, but it was a good work for its time. The later addition of two stories and new windows to the main volume didn't help the design, and the building now comes across as just another bland product of the fifties.

POI E Minnesota Transfer Railway bridge

University Ave. West between Prior and Cleveland Aves.

This bridge spans the tracks of the Minnesota Transfer Railway, established in 1882 to provide a central switching facility by which freight could be moved from one railroad to another. The railway played a key role in the industrial development of the Midway area. A general office building serving the railway was constructed in 1907 just east of this bridge, but it's now been replaced by a Menard's store. However, the railway's **roundhouse,** built between 1891 and 1907, still stands just to the south at 508 Cleveland Ave. North.

Frogtown

University-Raymond Commercial Historic District *L*

The newest historic preservation district in St. Paul, established in 2005. It encompasses more than 30 properties—mostly early twentieth-century commercial and industrial buildings near the intersection of University and Raymond Aves.

34 Midtown Commons (St. Paul Street Railway Co. Midway Carhouse) *L*

2324 University Ave. West

Charles Ferrin, 1891 and later / renovated, ca. 1990

A nicely renovated office building originally constructed as a streetcar barn following completion of the interurban line along University in 1890.

35 Twin City Janitor Supply (Red Wing Union Stoneware Co.) *L*

2345 University Ave. West

Kenneth Fullerton, 1930

An improbable piece of architectural theater. Behind this English cottage facade is a large warehouse and store built for a stoneware company.

Specialty Building

36 Specialty Building (Northwestern Furniture Exposition Building) *L*

2356 University Ave. West

Buechner and Orth, 1906 / 1917 / includes Cafe Biaggio (Ace Cafe), Ellerbe and Co., 1936

A chunky brick building that nonetheless manages to make a graceful turn around the corner at Raymond Ave. The entrance on University displays a classical pediment and pilasters but otherwise the building has little orna-

ment. It does, however, have the Cafe Biaggio (for many years the Ace Cafe), which resides behind a Streamline Moderne storefront installed in 1936.

Chittenden and Eastman Building

37 Chittenden and Eastman Building (M. Burg and Sons Co.) *L*

2402–14 University Ave. West

Walter R. Wilson, 1917

A commercial building that directly echoes the work of Chicago architect Louis Sullivan and his Prairie School followers, especially William Purcell and George Elmslie. As such, it was a progressive design for its time. The basic design scheme—broad bands of windows divided by piers with lavish foliate capitals, all set within a larger brick frame—is similar to Purcell and Elmslie's Merchants Bank of 1912 in Winona, MN. The ornament, which includes capitals with V-shaped motifs around the entrance, also shows the influence of Elmslie and Sullivan. For many years, the building was occupied by a national furniture wholesaler.

38 Court International Building (Willys-Overland Co., International Harvester Co.)

2550 University Ave. West

Mills Rhines Bellman and Nordhoff (Toledo), 1915 / renovated, Ankeny Kell Architects, ca. 1988

An impressive brick and concrete building, of no strong style but with hints of the Gothic in its tower. It originally served as a warehouse and assembly plant for the Willys-Overland Co. of Toledo, OH. International Harvester Co. acquired the building in the 1920s for use as a parts distribution center. In the 1980s, Ankeny Kell Architects of St. Paul converted the structure into offices, a renovation that included carving out two atriums to bring in natural light.

39 KSTP-TV Studios

3415 University Ave.

Liebenberg and Kaplan, 1949

The oldest portion of this cities-straddling building (yes, it's in both St. Paul and Minneapolis and has separate water and electrical lines, not to mention two zip codes) dates to 1949. The building is a good example of the late Moderne phase of art deco, which held on for a while after World War II before being eclipsed by other modernist styles.

Court International Building, 1935

North End

This neighborhood has two distinct residential zones, based—as almost everything in St. Paul seems to be—on age and elevation. The lower part, developed largely in the 1870s and 1880s, is much like Frogtown. Here the houses tend to be old, small, and much remodeled. North of Maryland Avenue, however, the neighborhood has a more modern character, with many houses from the 1920s and later, a lucky few of which command the heights along Wheelock Parkway.

The oldest portion of the North End is around Oakland Cemetery, where working-class houses from the 1880s, often built on narrow lots, predominate. Those east of the cemetery can be found along Agate Street and a dozen or so intersecting avenues that slope down toward Trout Brook valley. The blocks west of the cemetery, between Sylvan and Rice streets and farther out toward Western Avenue, are also packed with Victorian-era homes in varying states of repair.

The lavish restorations common in the Hill District are rare in this neighborhood. Instead, you're more likely to find aluminum, vinyl, or asbestos siding, chain-link fencing, historically incorrect windows, clashing additions, and other do-it-yourself handiwork unmediated by the superego of professional design. The results aren't always visually pleasing, but they're rarely dull. Despite all of the "modernizing" that's been inflicted on many of the houses, this part of the North End still conveys the sense of being a very old place (at least by Twin Cities standards).

Although the North End is not as architecturally rich as some other parts of St. Paul, it's home to at least one extraordinary building—St. Bernard's Catholic Church (1906), which is like nothing else in Minnesota. Other churches of note include St. Mary's Romanian Orthodox (1914) and Zion Lutheran (1888). The neighborhood boasts no mansions to speak of, but you will find a strange and tragic work of folk architecture—the Feyen House at 277 Burgess Street (1888). Another small gem is the Hugo House (1924), an intriguing Prairie Style design on Dale Street.

1 McDonough Townhomes

1544 Timberlake Rd. (Jackson St. and Wheelock Pkwy.)

Dimond Haarstick and Lundgren and others, 1951 / additions, 1959, 1965 / renovated, Adsit/Schrock DeVetter Architects and Close Landscape Architects, 2004–10

St. Paul's first public housing project and still its largest, with 580 units in over 100 townhouse-style buildings. The overall design, which features flat-roofed buildings arranged along winding streets with a separate sidewalk system, is typical of 1950s public housing. In 2002 the St. Paul Public Housing Agency began a project to renovate the homes inside and out, improve traffic circulation, and upgrade landscaping.

POI A Trout Brook Valley

This broad valley, through which the Mississippi River flowed thousands of years ago, forms the eastern boundary of the North End. It's been a transportation corridor since the early days of settlement. Railroads and later Interstate 35E used the long, easy grade here to climb out of the steep-bluffed Mississippi valley. Much of Trout Brook has been diverted underground, but north of Arlington Ave. there's a stretch of the creek that flows through wooded ravines and wetlands. Long-range plans call for opening up other portions of the brook as well.

Oakland Cemetery

2 Oakland Cemetery ! *L*

927 Jackson St.

1853 / Horace Cleveland and William M. R. French, 1874

Chapel, 75 East Sycamore St.

Thomas Holyoke, 1924

St. Paul's oldest formal cemetery, and a beautiful example of why graveyards are as much for the living as for the dead. Many early political, military, educational, and business leaders—including Alexander Ramsey, Henry Sibley, Norman Kittson, Harriet Bishop, and Charles E. Flandrau—are buried within Oakland's 100-acre expanse of lawn, woods, and gently curving roads. So, too, are Chinese immigrants, Civil War soldiers, firefighters, paupers, and orphans. Commemorating the dead are all manner of monuments in styles ranging from weepy Victorian Gothic to sleek art deco. Nowhere else in St. Paul will you find such a diverse architectural environment.

Oakland was founded as a nonsectarian cemetery in 1853 by a group of St. Paul's leading citizens, who purchased a 40-acre tract of rolling oak savannah just north of an informal graveyard known as Jackson Woods. Oakland's promoters proclaimed the site so remote that there was little chance "the hum of industry would ever disturb its rural quiet." By 1874, Oakland had grown to 80 acres and landscape architect Horace Cleveland was called in from Chicago to provide a new design. Cleveland responded by creating a garden cemetery common for the time. His design, with winding roads that follow the land's contours, remains largely intact today. The cemetery was so inviting that for many years it also functioned as a park.

Oakland's architectural ensemble is eclectic. The chapel, a stone Gothic Revival structure, isn't especially memorable, but there's much else of interest. The Victorian era, when sentiment ran thick as syrup, is particularly well represented by such graveyard classics as the gnarled tree trunk (with missing limbs signifying the dead) and the grieving angel. Obelisks, crosses, soaring eagles, and various kinds of heroic sculpture are also commonplace. There are even art deco tombs, the best of which, from 1933, marks the burial place of George McLeod.

3 Apartments (St. Paul Homeopathic Hospital)

784 Agate St.

1890

Behind the stucco here is a brick Romanesque Revival building that originally served as a hospital specializing in homeopathy, a type of medical treatment popular in the late nineteenth century and still practiced today. In the

North End

1   McDonough Townhomes
2   Oakland Cemetery
3   Apartments
4   Zion Lutheran Church / La Iglesia
    Luterana de Cristo el Redentor
5   Apartments
6   Lyton Park Place
7   Hiller Hoffman Sr. House
8   Frogtown Wireless
9   Minnesota Women's Building
10 Xcel Energy Building
11 Arvidson Block
12 Bluebird Apartments
13 Arlington Senior High School
14 Elmhurst Cemetery
15 Church of the Maternity of
    the Blessed Virgin
16 Leo S. Hugo House
17 St. Bernard's Catholic Church
18 St. Mary's Romanian
    Orthodox Church
19 Feyen House
20 Crossroads Elementary School
21 Front Hi-Rise
22 Calvary Cemetery

A   Trout Brook Valley
B   Wheelock Parkway
C   Viking Sign Supplies

L1 American Grass Twine Co.

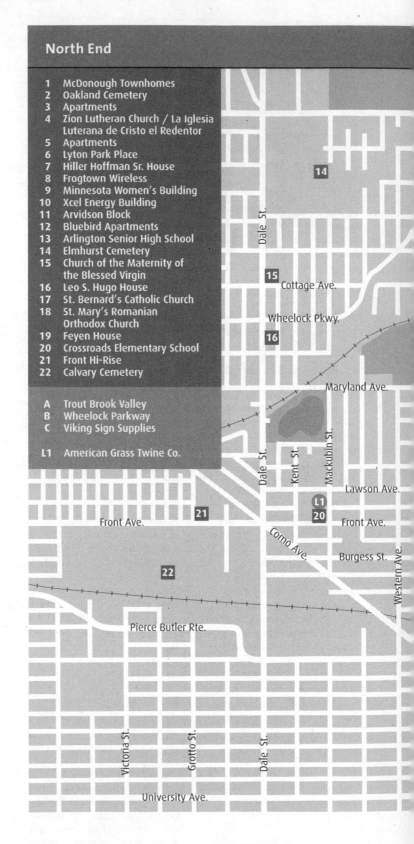

1890s Concordia College occupied the building briefly before moving to its present location in the Merriam Park–Lexington-Hamline neighborhood.

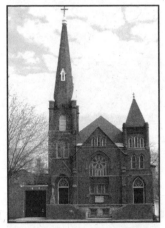

Zion Lutheran Church / La Iglesia Luterana de Cristo el Redentor

4 Zion (German Evangelical) Lutheran Church / La Iglesia Luterana de Cristo el Redentor

784 Jackson St.

Augustus Gauger, 1888 / addition, ca. 1964

A large brick Gothic Revival church at the southeast corner of Oakland Cemetery. The north tower's octagonal spire is one of the most graceful in the city, rising above four rocketlike turrets that seem poised to launch it toward the heavens. Zion Lutheran was organized in 1863 by German immigrants, and when it came time to design their new church, they hired one of their own—German-born architect Augustus Gauger.

5 Apartments (Ackerman Brothers Saloon and Grocery Store)

780 Jackson St.

Bergmann and Fischer, 1886

An old saloon and upstairs apartment whose first owners, brothers Rudolph and Edward Ackerman, made their living quenching the thirst of workers from the nearby Jackson Street

Shops. Although the building has been used strictly as apartments since 1914, it retains its original iron cornice stamped with the brothers' names.

6 Lyton Park Place

Lyton and Park Sts.

LHB Architects and Engineers, 1991

A well-designed group of 21 affordable houses. They replaced over 40 small, badly deteriorated properties that once occupied this site. Although the houses echo historic styles from Queen Anne to Craftsman, they don't come across as overly nostalgic.

7 Hiller Hoffman Sr. House

118 Manitoba Ave.

C. Christensen (builder), 1907

A big house for this neighborhood, Colonial Revival in style, with impressively hefty Ionic columns on the front porch. Hoffman owned a hardware store a block away on Rice St. and later built the Hoffman Block at 900 Rice.

Rice Street (north of University Avenue)

Legend holds that Rice St. was developed by James J. Hill in order to provide a direct route from his mansion on Summit Ave. to his farm in suburban North Oaks. A good story, but not true. Rice was actually graded as early as the 1870s, well before Hill became a financial titan and built his mansion. Once the street acquired horsecar and then streetcar service (the latter in 1891), its status as a commercial thoroughfare was assured. Named after pioneer St. Paul businessman and politician Henry M. Rice, the street is lined with small commercial buildings, mostly dating from around 1900, as well as some homes and apartments. In this respect, it's very similar to other streetcar "strip" streets that developed in St. Paul and Minneapolis in the late nineteenth century.

520 and 516–18 Rice St.

8 Frogtown Wireless

520 Rice St.

1889

This three-story Victorian has been junked up in various ways, but it still offers some fine architectural spectacle in the form of two dazzling arches beneath the cornice. The arches harbor terracotta shells enframed by elaborate layers of brick molding. The building next door at 516–18 Rice also dates to 1889.

9 Minnesota Women's Building

550 Rice St.

1884 / renovated, Sarah Susanka, ca. 1987 / renovated, Peter Kramer, ca. 2006

There are actually two buildings here. They were united beneath a common Italianate-style facade, probably not long after they were built. City records indicate both buildings date to 1884, but parts look older than that. The Minnesota Women's Consortium and two other groups renovated the buildings in the late 1980s for use as offices.

10 Xcel Energy (St. Paul Gas Light Co.) Building

825 Rice St.

Toltz, King and Day, 1925

A Classical Revival building in brick. Like most utility buildings of its time, it's very dignified and most attentive to its urban duties.

11 Arvidson Block

842 Rice St.

L. H. Larson (builder), 1889

A Victorian commercial building in which strips of vertical brick ornament and sandstone belt courses intersect to create a gridded facade. The ground floor, though modified, still sports its original cast-iron front. John Arvidson, the building's first owner, ran a grocery store and saloon here and lived upstairs. For many years, the building was home to the Caron-Fabre Furniture Co.

12 Bluebird Apartments (Hoffman Block)

900–904 Rice St.

1914

Built for Hiller Hoffman, Sr., this substantial brick block housed his hardware store as well as a movie theater known as the Bluebird, which operated until 1948. The building has been rudely modified at street level, and the original Chicago-style windows on the upper floors have been replaced. A health center, stores, and apartments now occupy the building.

13 Arlington Senior High School

1495 Rice St.

Winsor/Faricy Architects with Perkins and Will (Chicago), 1996

St. Paul's newest high school. With its tall narrow windows, the curving front facade has the look of a suburban office park building from the 1960s—not, perhaps, the best image for education. The school is divided into several "houses," which are visible on the outside as projecting rear wings. These break the building into manageable sections so that it doesn't seem overwhelmingly large, especially to younger students. At least, that's the idea.

POI B Wheelock Parkway

Lake Como to Lake Phalen

1909

The central portion of this parkway winds through the North End along the crest of steep hills between Dale and Rice Sts., where there are expansive views

North End

of the city. Along its route are many Period Revival houses from the 1920s and later as well as large ramblers from the 1950s. The parkway is named after Joseph Wheelock, who founded the *St. Paul Pioneer Press* and served as president of the St. Paul Park Board from 1893 until his death in 1906.

14 Elmhurst (German Lutheran) Cemetery

1510 North Dale St. (at Larpenteur Ave.)

1858 and later

Established in 1858 by two Lutheran churches in St. Paul, this cemetery was originally located just south of Lake Como and later relocated here. Now nondenominational, the cemetery took its present name in 1890. It doesn't have as much monumental funerary architecture as Oakland or Calvary cemeteries, but like all burial grounds it has stories to tell if you roam among the graves. The cemetery once had a pretty little Gothic chapel built in 1885, but it was torn down in 1998.

15 Church of the Maternity of the Blessed Virgin

1414 North Dale St.

Dreher Freerks Sperl Flynn, 1962

A reviewer for the 1980s Ramsey County Historic Sites Survey found this church so appalling that she wrote: "The architect was evidently trying to make a statement and ended up creating a monster." Ah, but it's a wonderfully interesting monster, hexagonal in plan, with blind arches in the limestone walls, ranks of tiny windows, and an entry arcade with spherical roofs. To the rear is a bell tower that culminates in a bronze cross mounted atop a pair of barrel vaults. There's no shortage of design here, even if not all of it seems to be going in the same direction.

Leo S. Hugo House

16 Leo S. Hugo House

1286 North Dale St.

Charles Saxby Elwood, 1924

With a few stylistic adjustments, this house might pass for something from the 1950s. But in fact it's a late Prairie Style house, based on a bungalow project called "Wee Haven" that architect Charles Saxby Elwood drew for a magazine in 1924. The house has many sophisticated touches, such as the overhanging eaves that interlock at different levels. Note, too, the abstract geometric ornament set into the stucco on either side of the front windows. Leo S. Hugo, a furnace installer, built the house for about $3,000, quite a bargain considering the quality of the design.

St. Bernard's Catholic Church, 1910

17 St. Bernard's Catholic Church ! N L

197 Geranium Ave. West

John Jager, 1906, 1914 / remodeled, ca. 1958 and later

An extraordinary church that can best be described as Art Nouveau–Prairie, delivered to St. Paul via Vienna, Chicago, and Minneapolis by John Jager, an architect born in Slovenia. Given this exotic blend of influences, it's no surprise that the church, built for a German Catholic parish organized in 1890, is like nothing else in the Twin Cities.

St. Bernard's Catholic Church interior, 1910

The twin-towered front, its windows divided by piers set beneath a broad shallow arch, has a proto-modern look suggesting the work of the Viennese architect Otto Wagner, under whom Jager studied. The towers are equally distinctive, starting out as squares and then pinching in to form octagonal belfries with round columns, a maneuver requiring some exceptional brickwork. Along the sides of the church, there's another novel touch: piers and overhanging eaves that feature wavy, Art Nouveau–style carved ornament. Within, the church is treated as a single large space united beneath a concrete, barrel-vaulted ceiling. The original interior, completed in 1914, was decorated with murals painted by artists from Germany; it was altered in 1958, which is also when a jarring steel canopy was installed over the front entrance.

The Vienna-trained Jager made his way in 1902 to Minneapolis, where his father and brother lived. The brother, a priest, was a close friend of St. Bernard's pastor, which is presumably how Jager landed the commission. One of the Twin Cities' essential buildings, St. Bernard's remains far and away the greatest work of Jager's career.

18 St. Mary's Romanian Orthodox Church

189 West Atwater St.

Buechner and Orth, 1914

A large Romanian immigrant community resided in the North End, where this little church opened in 1914. The state's first Romanian Orthodox church, it's said to be a replica of a church in San Nicholaul Mare, Romania. It has the usual onion-domed tower rising above stucco walls

St. Mary's Romanian Orthodox Church

trimmed with rock-faced concrete blocks. The clocks beneath the dome are fake, their hands all painted at four o'clock, possibly because that was the time of the first service held in the church.

Feyen House

19 Feyen House

277 Burgess St.

1888 / remodeled, Scot Feyen, ca. 1980s

An odd house with an odd story behind it. In the late 1980s, a young North End native named Scot Feyen transformed this modest wood-frame home, originally built by his great-grandfather, into a kind of mini-estate. He sheathed parts of the house in stone and boulders, built a long wall with iron gates along the front of the property, and meticulously landscaped the yard. He also bought other old homes and apartments nearby and began renovating them. By the late 1990s, however, his real estate empire began to unravel. His properties steadily deteriorated amid complaints he was renting to drug dealers and other undesirables. He eventually lost or was forced to sell most of the properties, including this house. In 2001, while awaiting trial on cocaine possession charges, he drowned in a pond in northern Wisconsin.

POI C Viking Sign Supplies (Chemical House No. 4, Engine Company No. 22)

293 Front Ave.

Havelock E. Hand, 1887

An old brick fire station of historical interest as the longtime home of an all-black fire company. St. Paul's first black fireman, William Godette, joined the department in 1885. Four other black men signed on over the next decade or so, and all served in a strictly segregated company based here until 1923. Two decades later, in 1943, the fire department was finally desegregated. This building ended its service as a fire station in 1958 and has had a variety of occupants since then.

20 Crossroads Elementary School

543 Front Ave.

Cuningham Group, 1999

The first new elementary school built in St. Paul since the 1970s, this rather hyper brick, glass, stucco, and metal building suggests education should be great fun. Nothing wrong with that, but the color palette inside is so aggressive that you have to wonder whether it's a distraction.

LOST 1 *Crossroads School occupies the site of a large manufacturing complex that was once home to the* **American Grass Twine Co.** *The company used wire grass, readily available in northern bogs and marshes, to make its product. Later, it reinvented itself by switch-*

ing to the manufacture of wicker furniture and rugs, also from wire grass. It then became known as the **Crex Carpet Co.** *At peak production, it employed nearly 500 workers, many of them women. After an initial success, Crex began to lose out to foreign competition and failed during the Great Depression. The last of the company's old brick industrial buildings was torn down in the 1990s.*

21 Front Hi-Rise

727 Front Ave.

Freerks Sperl and Flynn, 1969

The idea of building a senior citizens' high-rise overlooking St. Paul's largest cemetery may strike some as macabre, but here it is, 149 rooms with a view. The architecture—a well-designed example of the so-called Brutalist style of the 1960s—doesn't pull any punches either.

Calvary Cemetery

22 Calvary Cemetery

753 Front Ave.

1856 and later

This Catholic cemetery is St. Paul's largest, with 101,000 burials since its dedication in 1856 by Archbishop Joseph Cretin, who is himself among those who now rest here. The monuments at Calvary tend to be less grand than those at Oakland Cemetery, though you'll certainly find some impressive tombs here. Populist politician and potboiler novelist Ignatius Donnelly, Archbishop John Ireland, architect Emmanuel Masqueray, and brewers Theodore Hamm and Jacob Schmidt are among the cemetery's most illustrious occupants.

Como

Well before this neighborhood developed, Como Lake was an attraction, due largely to the efforts of a Pennsylvania transplant named Henry McKenty. Known by the sobriquet "Broad Acres," he forked out $6,000 in the 1850s to build the first road to the lake from downtown (following the general course of today's Como Avenue). Three resort hotels soon appeared, and McKenty also built his own home by the lake. Like other boomers, however, he was devastated by the financial panic of 1857 and eventually committed suicide (as did his wife and daughter).

Como Park dates to the 1870s, when the city council—acting on the advice of Chicago landscape architect Horace Cleveland—established a park board. In 1873 the board began buying land for the park. This step did not meet with universal acclaim. Prominent St. Paulites opposed the park, contending it would be of value only to real estate speculators hoping to sell lots nearby. Wisely, the board ignored these protests and went ahead, although development of the park didn't really begin until 1887, when the city finally provided money to prepare a design.

The residential neighborhoods around the park, including the Warrendale subdivision, developed largely because of improved public transportation in the 1880s. After completing the Como Shops, the Northern Pacific built a small rail station south of the lake in 1886 and provided commuter service to downtown until 1892, when a streetcar line opened on Como Avenue. Six years later, the Como-Harriet interurban line provided a connection to Minneapolis as well.

The neighborhood's outstanding work of architecture—and in many ways its symbol—is the Marjorie McNeely Conservatory (1915) at Como Park. Other important buildings include the Bandana Square complex (1885, renovated ca. 1985), the Charles Wallingford House (ca. 1886), Como Park Elementary School (1916), Mount Olive Lutheran Church (1926 and later), St. Andrew's Catholic Church (1927), and the Thomas Frankson House (1914).

1 Como Park !

Area approximately bounded by Como Lake and Hoyt, Hamline, and Como Aves.

1873 / park plan, Horace Cleveland, Frederick Nussbaumer, 1887 and later / Art: numerous statues, memorials, and other objects

One of the nation's great urban parks, a playground of the people that attracts more visitors than the Mall of America. Each year about 2.5 million people pour into the park, which spreads out across 450 acres west of Como Lake. With its zoo, conservatory, gardens, golf course, pavilions, picnic grounds, swimming pool, athletic fields, monuments, and historic buildings, the park has universal appeal, and it's a rare

Como Park

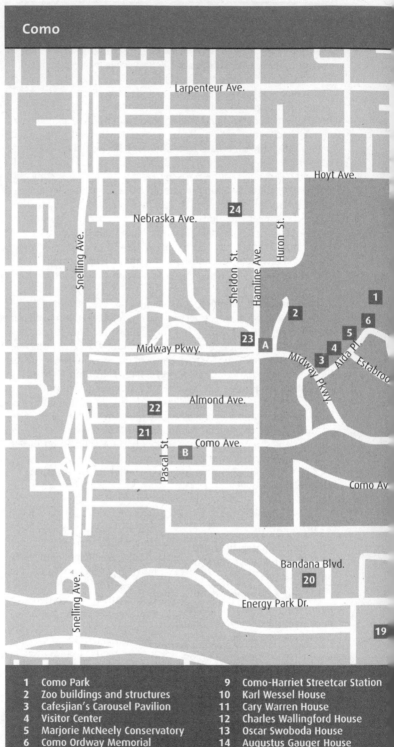

Como

Como

18 House
19 Energy Park
20 Bandana Square
21 Salvation Army Booth Brown House
    and Hope Transition Center
22 Mount Olive Evangelical
    Lutheran Church
23 Thomas Frankson House
24 George and Hannah Hazzard House

A Gateposts
B Yard art

L1 Aldrich Hotel

Twin Citian who hasn't been to Como at least once.

The city's park board acquired the first 300 or so acres for the park in 1873, but it wasn't until 1887 that Horace Cleveland began landscaping and laying out roads. Although some park drives still follow Cleveland's plan, much of Como's design is the work of Frederick Nussbaumer. Born in Germany and trained at leading European gardens, Nussbaumer met Cleveland in Paris in 1887. At Cleveland's urging, he immigrated to St. Paul and went to work as a park gardener. His talents were such that by 1892 he became the city's superintendent of parks. Under Nussbaumer, Como blossomed. His goal was to create a "recreation ground for all classes of people," and he succeeded admirably. In consultation with Cleveland, Nussbaumer laid out the park's winding roads along with its rolling meadows and groves of trees. He was also the force behind the conservatory, which he helped design.

Streetcars reached the park in 1892; six years later service was extended to Minneapolis via the Como-Harriet interurban line. With these new transit connections, the park's popularity soared. New attractions were added, including the zoo, established in 1897. By 1900, as many as 40,000 people visited the park daily on summer weekends. Although the park retains many of its historic features, it has inevitably changed over time. In the northern part of the park, for example, there was once a beautiful little pond known as Cozy Lake. The pond disappeared in 1928 when it was drained to make way for the park's 18-hole golf course.

Because of its age, size, and variety of attractions, Como has more architecture of note than any other park in the Twin Cities. It's also full of statuary, plaques, monuments, and man-made "natural" features such as a frog pond and the Hamm's Memorial Waterfall.

POI A Gateposts

Midway Pkwy. and Hamline Ave.

Clarence H. Johnston, ca. 1916

These brick and stone gateposts originally stood at the front entrance of the Oliver Crosby Estate ("Stonebridge") along Mississippi River Blvd. in St. Paul. The gateposts were moved here and rebuilt by the Works Progress Administration in 1937 after the estate was subdivided.

2 Zoo buildings and structures

Near Midway Pkwy. and Hamline Ave.

Seal (Monkey) Island, *St. Paul City Architect (Charles A. Bassford), 1932 / rebuilt, 1982 /* **Offices (Zoological Building),** *St. Paul City Architect (Charles A. Bassford), 1936 / renovated, HGA, 2003 /* **Bear grottoes,** *St. Paul City Architect (Charles A. Bassford), ca. 1930s /* **Barn for hoofed animals,** *St. Paul City Architect (Charles A. Bassford), ca. 1939*

Along with some restrooms, a small mill house, and a waterwheel, these are the oldest structures at the zoo, built under the auspices of the federal Works Progress Administration. The grottoes and barn display the rough stonework often used for WPA projects, as did the old Monkey Island before being rebuilt. The office building (originally the main zoo building) is a more formal Moderne-style work. The zoo embarked on a building program in the 1980s, completing four new exhibit structures. A recent addition—to the zoo and to the park as a whole—is a visitor center that opened in 2005.

3 Cafesjian's Carousel Pavilion

1245 Midway Pkwy.

Genesis Architects (Ken Piper), 2000

With its 68 hand-carved horses, the carousel within this festive structure is regarded as one of the finest in the United States. It was built in 1914 by the Philadelphia

Toboggan Co. and went round and round for 75 years at the Minnesota State Fair. Put up for sale in 1988, it was saved from being dismantled by a local group that raised over $1 million to buy and restore it. The carousel is named after Gerald Cafesjian, a retired St. Paul businessman who donated $600,000 toward the preservation effort.

4 Visitor Center

1225 Estabrook Dr.

HGA (Kara Hill), 2005

The park's newest building, which functions as a visitor center for the zoo and conservatory. It houses classrooms, an auditorium, a cafe and gift shop, and an exhibit called Tropical Encounters. The center incorporates "green" features, including a rainwater collection system and solar energy panels. Extending out from the rear of the conservatory, the building's most dramatic feature is a jagged, angular glass roof above the Tropical Encounters exhibit. Inside, the center works nicely, and overall it's a strong addition to Como Park's complement of buildings.

Marjorie McNeely Conservatory, 1964

5 Marjorie McNeely Conservatory ! N *L*

1325 Aida Pl.

Frederick Nussbaumer, Toltz Engineering Co., and King Construction Co. (New York), 1915 / renovated and restored, Winsor/ Faricy Architects, 1983 and later

One of the glories of St. Paul, and among only a dozen or so historic park conservatories of its size still standing in the United States. The 64-foot-high dome serves as the park's defining landmark. Always popular, the conservatory is especially appeal-

ing in deep winter, when its 31,000 square feet of greenery provide a welcome refuge of warmth, color, and blooming life.

Longtime St. Paul parks superintendent Frederick Nussbaumer was the motive force behind the conservatory. By the early 1900s, many of the nation's leading cities—including New York, Chicago, and San Francisco—had built such structures. Nussbaumer worked with St. Paul engineer Max Toltz to design the conservatory, which with its central dome and radiating wings follows the general model of its predecessors. The conservatory was renovated and restored over a ten-year period beginning in 1983. In 2002, it was renamed in honor of Marjorie McNeely, a founder of the St. Paul Garden Club, after her family donated $7 million to the Como Zoo and Conservatory Society.

6 Como Ordway Memorial Japanese Garden

1325 Aida Pl.

Masami Matsuda (Nagasaki, Japan), 1979 / renovated, 1991

A garden in the Sansui style with ponds, waterfalls, and a teahouse. Its design was a gift from Nagasaki, Japan, St. Paul's sister city.

7 Como Lakeside Pavilion

1360 Lexington Pkwy. North

Clarence H. Johnston, 1906 / renovated, City of St. Paul, 1993

One of the park's signature buildings, Classical Revival in style and featuring a large roofed porch that overlooks the lake.

Aldrich Hotel, 1870

LOST 1 *The **Aldrich Hotel,** built in about 1870, once occupied the site of the pavilion. It was one of three early resorts around Como Lake. All are long gone.*

8 Bridges N

Over former streetcar right-of-way at and near Lexington Pkwy.

William S. Hewett, 1904

These bridges are the second-oldest surviving reinforced concrete-arch spans in Minnesota. The larger of the two carries Lexington Pkwy. across the former streetcar right-of-way. The smaller bridge just to the east (now closed) was designed for pedestrian use. Reinforced concrete was a novel material in 1904, when engineers like Hewett were just beginning to use it.

9 Como-Harriet Streetcar Station

1224 Lexington Pkwy. North

1905 / remodeled, 1919 / renovated and restored, St. Paul Parks and Recreation Department and Hokanson/Lunning/Wende Associates, 2001

Built of boulder walls, this handsome little structure served as a station along the Como-Harriet streetcar line. Inside, there's a terrazzo floor with an inlaid map of the old Twin Cities streetcar system. The building is now used as a museum and rental pavilion.

Warrendale

Southwest side of Como Lake

ca. 1884 and later

In 1884, developer Cary Warren platted a 52-acre area south and west of Como Lake as a commuter suburb. Known as Warrendale, the development offered 218 lots and was served by the Northern Pacific Railroad, which built a depot near Chatsworth St. The commuter line was never a success; it stopped operating in 1892 when streetcars reached Como Park. Warrendale also proved short lived. Although a number of fine houses were built along the lake, the development never flourished. Only 30 lots had been purchased by the time Warren's company collapsed in the financial panic of 1893.

10 Karl Wessel House

1285 Como Blvd. West

Karl Wessel (builder), 1902

The backyard of this house (visible from Churchill St.) contains its most exceptional feature: a long trellis mounted on columns supported by concrete-block piers. The trellis, which shelters a formal walk, serves as a beautiful link between the house, its yard, and the street beyond. Its builder, Karl Wessel, was a German-born mechanical wizard who by the time he moved into this house had already achieved financial independence as an engineer specializing in textile machinery. Among other things, he invented the Crex carpet, made from marsh grass and manufactured until the 1930s in a nearby plant.

11 Cary Warren House

1265 Como Blvd. West

Augustus Gauger, 1888

Built for Warrendale's developer, this rather gawky Queen Anne lacks the grace of the Wallingford house just two doors down. Still, it appears to have hung on to most of its original features, although the tower cap is modern.

Charles Wallingford House

12 Charles Wallingford House

1259 Como Blvd. West

Charles A. Wallingford, ca. 1886

Warrendale's finest Victorian, done in the romantic manner of the Queen Anne houses of English architect Richard Norman Shaw. Defaced for many years by a stucco overlay, the house was restored beginning in the 1980s. Note the polygonal front tower with a chimney that sports a small stained-glass window. Flanking the chimney are picture windows with stained-glass transoms, one of which depicts a Viking longboat. Charles Wallingford, who designed this house and lived in it until 1903, trained as an architect in Indianapolis and moved to St. Paul in 1885.

13 Oscar Swoboda House

1231 Como Blvd. West

Charles Saxby Elwood, 1922

Like a number of Elwood's other designs, this home offers a simplified but distinctive take on the Prairie Style. Built for a St. Paul druggist, the house is one of many from the early twentieth century that filled Warrendale's vacant lots after the original development went belly up.

14 Augustus Gauger House

1183 Como Blvd. West

Augustus Gauger, 1886

German-born Augustus Gauger, one of nineteenth-century St. Paul's most prolific architects, was hired by the Warrendale Improvement Co. to design several houses in the new development. This Queen Anne was his own. The house has gone through a number of remodelings; the ornate front porch is a modern reconstruction.

St. Andrew's Catholic Church

15 St. Andrew's Catholic Church

1051 Como Ave.

Slifer and Abrahamson?, John W. Wheeler?, 1927

One of St. Paul's best Period Revival churches. The brick, stone, and tile church is Italian Romanesque in spirit, with many picturesque effects, including a scenic bell tower. Inside, it follows a Greek cross layout. The nave, transepts, and sanctuary are defined by large, banded arches of faintly Moderne character. Although prominent Catholic architect John W. Wheeler is known to have done work for St. Andrews, the church is usually attributed to Frederick Slifer and Frank Abrahamson, both of whom were once draftsmen for Emmanuel Masqueray, designer of the St. Paul Cathedral. It is thus no surprise that one of Masqueray's favorite motifs—the so-called "telephone dial" window—makes a prominent appearance on the front facade of St. Andrew's.

Como Park Elementary School, 1918

16 Como Park Elementary School

780 Wheelock Pkwy. West

St. Paul City Architect (Charles A. Hausler with Clarence Wigington), 1916 / additions, 1924 and later

Although it's been added onto—hideously in the case of a stuccoed wing tacked on in 1976—this school retains its imposing front entrance. Consisting of a monumental classical screen with paired Doric columns and projecting pavilions to either side, the entrance conveys a sense of great dignity and strength.

17 Casiville Bullard House N

1282 Folsom St.

Casiville Bullard, 1910

This brick foursquare was built by Casiville Bullard, one of the first known black masons to work in St. Paul. Born in Tennessee, Bullard was a highly skilled "corner mason"—responsible for laying the all-important first course of stone or brick—and worked on the State Capitol and many other projects in St. Paul and elsewhere in Minnesota.

18 House

1388 North Victoria St.

ca. 1860s and later

A historic farmhouse, greatly modified, and possibly the oldest building in the Como neighborhood. It was built as part of a farm that once occupied much of the land northeast of the lake. Just to the north of this house, along Arlington and Nebraska Aves., are two oversized, heavily wooded blocks with huge lots that may also be part of the old farm property.

19 Energy Park

Energy Park Dr.

1980 and later

A "brown fields" redevelopment in which a large tract of industrial, railroad, and public land, some of it contaminated by pollution, was transformed into an "urban village." The development includes offices, light industrial buildings, apartments, condominiums, and some retail space. At its heart are the four historic railroad shop buildings known as Bandana Square.

Bandana Square

20 Bandana Square (Northern Pacific Railroad Co. Como Shops Historic District) N *L*

Bandana Blvd.

Northern Pacific Railroad, 1885, 1901, 1911, and later / renovated, Winsor/Faricy Architects, 1985

In 1885 the Northern Pacific Railroad established a shop complex here devoted to the construction, repair, and refurbishing of pas-

senger cars. It was a huge operation: the railroad during its peak years maintained a fleet of over 1,100 coaches. The four shop buildings that survive as part of Bandana Square are built of yellow brick from Little Falls, MN, and were designed with monitor roofs to bring natural light deep into interior work spaces.

The largest of the four, called the Atrium Office Building, dates to 1885 and is at the rear of the site. Cruciform in shape, it was a woodworking and car erecting shop. To the south, in a building occupied by a hotel and a medical clinic, is the paint shop, built in 1885 and expanded in 1911. East of it is the new car shop, built in 1901, enlarged in 1911, and now an office and retail building. Nearby is the blacksmith shop (now offices), distinguished by its numerous chimneys. Other fragments of the shops complex also survive, including a water tower and a transfer table once used to shuttle cars from one shop to the next.

The shops shrank with the railroad's passenger business and closed in 1982, after which the surviving buildings were adapted to new uses by Winsor/Faricy Architects of St. Paul. The work was well done, although the retail portion of the complex never achieved much success.

POI B Yard art

1412 Como Ave.

Bob Kohnen, 1974 and later

A neighborhood landmark, this menagerie of wooden and cast concrete creatures includes eagles, deer, squirrels, bears, and what appears to be a pregnant (or maybe just a very rotund) troll.

21 Salvation Army Booth Brown House and Hope Transition Center (Salvation Army Rescue Home for Fallen Girls) N

1471 Como Ave.

Clarence H. Johnston, 1913 / 1923 / addition, ca. 1971

The original portion of this complex is an attractive Tudor Revival building with an off-center tower and half timbering. When it opened in 1913, it was known as the Rescue Home for Fallen Girls (that is, young woman who'd become pregnant out of wedlock). It later received a more morally neutral name and now functions as a residential treatment facility for adolescent girls.

22 Mount Olive Evangelical Lutheran Church

1460 Almond Ave.

1926 (basement) / Walter Huchthausen, 1942 (church) / addition, Bard and Vanderbilt, 1970

Built of rugged local limestone, this small church conveys a sense of monumental mass despite its modest size. Although the design falls within the realm of Gothic Revival, it's so stripped down that the church anticipates the simple modern A-frame style that became popular in the 1950s. The church as it was completed in 1942 is attributed to Walter Huchthausen, a professor of architecture at the University of Minnesota who died in combat during World War II.

23 Thomas Frankson House

1349 Midway Pkwy.

C. L. French, 1914

A large, mechanical-looking house that lacks the romantic spirit of the best Tudor Revival designs. Thomas Frankson, a lawyer turned real estate developer, platted many streets in this area (including Frankson Ave.). Something of a character, he once maintained a herd of buf-

falo in a pasture along a nearby street that he named, naturally, Bison Ave. Besides attending to his large ruminants, he also served as Minnesota's lieutenant governor from 1917 to 1921.

George and Hannah Hazzard House, ca. 1920

24 George and Hannah Hazzard House

1371 Nebraska Ave. West

ca. 1867

The only surviving house from the early days of development near Como Lake. At the time of its construction, it was a country manor, well beyond the more built-up areas of the city, although a few early resort hotels as well as Henry McKenty's mansion were not far away. Except for an unconvincing corner tower, the house is textbook Italianate, with bracketed eaves and tall narrow windows crowned by mock keystones. The front porch and rear wings are later additions.

The house was built for George and Hannah Hazzard. He was a railroad and steamboat agent who became a real estate speculator. She was a daughter of local pioneer Benjamin Hoyt, an early land claimant who in the 1840s lived in a log cabin in what is now downtown St. Paul. Nearby Hoyt Ave. is named after Hannah's brother, Lorenzo, who platted the street in 1872.

Como

1619

Overview

These neighborhoods occupy the southwestern part of St. Paul, extending from Lexington Parkway to the Mississippi River. Solidly middle class, they feature long straight streets lined with well-kept bungalows and Period Revival houses. Here, too, is St. Paul's college quarter, home to the University of St. Thomas, Concordia University, the College of St. Catherine, and Macalester College. Although largely built up by the 1920s, parts of these neighborhoods—especially in Highland—didn't completely fill in until the 1960s.

Highland was not only one of the last sections of the city to be developed but also among the first. The earliest arrivals were immigrants from the failed Selkirk Colony in Manitoba. They lived near Fort Snelling in the 1820s before a handful crossed the Mississippi and built houses near today's Elsie Lane along Mississippi River Boulevard. In 1840, however, they and other squatters were evicted by military authorities.

By 1854, all of present-day Highland was opened to settlement. Annexed by the city in 1887, Highland seemed destined for rapid growth once streetcar lines were extended down West Seventh Street and Randolph Avenue in 1891. But the depression of 1893 stalled development, although the opening of the College of St. Catherine in 1905 was a boost to the neighborhood. Highland's boom finally came in the 1920s, driven by the Ford Motor Co., which in 1925 completed its assembly plant along the Mississippi. Growth now seemed certain. The Great Depression retarded Highland's development once again, however, and housing construction didn't pick up until the mid-1930s.

Like Highland, Macalester-Groveland was once part of the so-called Reserve Township, and until the early 1900s it was mostly farmland. As St. Paul began its growth surge in the 1880s, the farms gradually gave way to development. The trustees of Macalester College were among the first agents of transformation. In 1881 they bought a 160-acre farm near Summit and Snelling avenues, set aside 40 acres for the college campus, then platted the remaining acreage into Macalester Park, an early commuter suburb that remains an oasis of green curves in the midst of the prevailing street grid.

The rest of Macalester-Groveland followed the usual pattern of growth along streetcar routes. The Grand Avenue line led the way, opening in 1890. One of the line's most active promoters was Archbishop John Ireland, who saw it as a vital link to the College of St. Thomas and a new campus he planned for the St. Paul Seminary. Much of Macalester-Groveland's housing dates to between 1910 and 1930, a period that saw the neighborhood expand block by block toward its western edge at the Mississippi.

As its triple name suggests, Merriam Park-Lexington-Hamline covers a wide range of urban territory. Within its boundaries are two late nineteenth-century commuter suburbs, two private colleges (including the state's largest, the University of St. Thomas), one of the nation's oldest private golf clubs, a commercial-industrial district centered around University Avenue, and a diverse housing stock that ranges from tiny bungalows to Victorian and Period Revival mansions to apartment towers.

Most of the neighborhood remained rural until 1880, when the Milwaukee Road's "Short Line" opened, providing commuter rail service to downtown Minneapolis and downtown St. Paul. Development quickly followed. Real estate tycoon John Merriam led expansion into the area, buying 140 acres around the site of the park that bears his name. Another, smaller residential development from the 1880s clustered around Union (now Iris) Park. At the south end of the neighborhood, Archbishop Ireland in 1885 established St. Thomas Aquinas Seminary, out of which the University of St. Thomas evolved.

Highland

Except for an expanding cluster of apartments and condominiums along the West Seventh Street–Shepard Road corridor, Highland consists largely of single-family houses. Many date from the 1920s and 1930s and come in all manner of Period Revival–style regalia. Among the few nineteenth century homes here is a farmhouse (ca. 1860s) built by William Davern, one of the neighborhood's earliest settlers.

Because much of Highland was laid out after the establishment of zoning codes (in 1922), housing is strictly segregated from other uses. As a result, Highland lacks the pleasing irregularities—a corner grocery store here, a church there—found in older sections of St. Paul. Parts of the neighborhood were also laid out with very long blocks (up to a quarter of a mile) that give it a distinctly suburban feel.

Highland's largest and most architecturally significant houses are concentrated on or near the river bluffs that form a great horseshoe along the neighborhood's eastern, southern, and western flanks. On the east, Edgcumbe Road and Montcalm Place have many Period Revival gems as well as the Moderne-style Robert Ahrens House (1938). The blufftops to the south along Upper and Lower St. Dennis roads feature many high-quality modern houses from the 1950s. To the west, on South Mississippi River and Mount Curve boulevards, you'll find an array of homes from the 1920s and later.

Highland's architectural highlights include Our Lady of Victory Chapel (1924) on the St. Catherine's campus, the Highland Park Water Tower (1928), two exceptional Moderne buildings from 1939—the Highland Theater and the Abe Engelson House—and the Temple of Aaron (1956) on Mississippi River Boulevard South.

1 Highland Towers Apartments

689 Snelling Ave. South and 1585 Highland Pkwy.

1959

Two classics from the late 1950s, complete with multicolored glazed brickwork and, along Snelling, what appear to be giant musical clefs mounted against a black background in a way that calls to mind velvet art.

2 Highland Park Junior and Senior High Schools

975, 1015 Snelling Ave. South

HGA, 1958 / 1967 / later additions

The firm of Hammel Green and Abrahamson was an early local outpost of functionalist modernism in the manner of Chicago architect Ludwig Mies van der Rohe. The junior high, completed in 1958, remains one of the Twin Cities' best, and first, examples of a Miesian modern school. Minimalist in style and featuring bands of windows set into brick

Highland Park Junior High School, 1957

walls with exposed steel columns, this kind of school became something like a standard model in the 1960s.

3 Old Mattocks (Webster) School

1015 Snelling Ave. South

1871

A rare surviving example of a one-room school built of stone. At the time of its construction at Snelling and Randolph Aves., it

Highland

Highland

was known as Webster School and was well out in the country. The name was changed to Mattocks—in honor of a local minister and school board member—after it became part of the St. Paul school system in 1887. It served as a school until 1929 and then did a 30-year tour of duty as an American Legion Post before being moved in 1964 to this site, where it's now used as a classroom for Highland Park Senior High School.

4 Highland Park

Snelling and Montreal Aves.

1925 and later

This spacious park, which was developed in the 1920s, includes nine- and 18-hole golf courses (the latter rebuilt in 2005 and renamed Highland National), picnic grounds, a swimming pool, and a Frisbee golf course.

5 Pavilion (golf clubhouse)

1403 Montreal Ave.

St. Paul City Architect (Frank X. Tewes), 1929

A handsomely detailed Period Revival building with a central arched entrance reached from an elevated terrace. Projecting wings to either side feature Palladian windows.

Highland Park Water Tower

6 Water Tower N

1570 Highland Pkwy.

St. Paul City Architect (Frank X. Tewes with Clarence Wigington), 1928

A local landmark built on the second highest point in St. Paul.

Constructed of brick and cut stone, this tapering octagonal tower is 134 feet high and holds 200,000 gallons of water in a steel tank. It features carved downspouts and shields beneath an arched observation deck open to the public on special occasions (the climb to the top is 151 steps). Designed by Clarence Wigington, the tower has been meticulously kept and is virtually unaltered since the day it was built.

LOST 1 *The low stone walls around the Lexington Park Apartments at the southwest corner of Lexington Pkwy. and Randolph Ave. are all that remain of the* **William Nettleton House,** *a country estate built in the 1870s. An Ohio native, Nettleton bought 130 acres here in 1871, constructed his house, and started a dairy farm. By 1880, however, he'd already begun to subdivide the property. He later moved with his family to Spokane, WA. It's not clear when the house was demolished, but it was gone by 1950, when the apartments were built. The so-called* **Highland Spring** *was also on this site; a company that bottled the 42-degree water was in business from 1900 to 1965.*

7 William Ingemann House

7 Montcalm Ct.

William Ingemann, 1928

William Ingemann was a St. Paul–born architect who worked for such notables as Cass Gilbert before establishing his own office in 1926. He was a top-notch designer of Period Revival homes in the 1920s and 1930s, including several located along Montcalm Pl. Ingemann and his wife, Dorothy Brink, also an architect and a highly skilled renderer, built this house in 1928. It's done in the manner of an English Arts and Crafts house, with plain stucco walls.

8 Robert Ahrens House

1565 Edgcumbe Rd.

Magnus Jemne, 1938

A severe but impressive house designed by St. Paul architect

Magnus Jemne, whose first foray into art deco was the Women's City Club in downtown St. Paul.

Robert Ahrens House

Here, he produced what may be the largest Moderne-style residence in the Twin Cities. The house has undulating, faceted walls of yellow brick, laid up in a pattern known as stack bond that conveys a sense of modernity. A two-story bay juts out from the south side of the house to capture sunlight from that direction. In keeping with its modernist esthetic, the house has no ornament, and it makes quite a statement in a neighborhood where conscientiously quaint Period Revival homes predominate.

9 Pierce Butler Jr. House

5 Edgcumbe Pl.

Lang Raugland and Lewis, 1923

With its plain walls and crisp forms, this "English" house shows that 1920s Period Revival architecture can look surprisingly modern. This house was built for Pierce Butler, Jr., a son of the U.S. Supreme Court justice of the same name and an attorney and civic leader in St. Paul.

10 Donald Haarstick House

1316 Bohland Pl.

Donald Haarstick, 1955

A brick and steel house built by and for a St. Paul architect whose firm was among the first in the city to embrace modernism after World War II. The cubelike house includes a side patio sheltered under a metal canopy and a sinuous, beautifully crafted brick wall in the front yard.

11 Donald and Elizabeth Lampland House

2004 Lower St. Dennis Rd.

Donald and Elizabeth Lampland, 1952

Although it looks quite conventional, this house was among the first in St. Paul to pursue the modernist dream of an open, flexible floor plan. Large trusses supported by the outside walls do most of the structural work, so that only one inside wall is load bearing. The other interior walls are partitions that can be moved about to create a variety of floor plans. Donald Lampland, an engineer and part owner of a lumber company, took architecture courses at the University of Minnesota with his wife, Elizabeth, after which the couple designed and built the house.

2168 Lower St. Dennis Rd.

12 House

2168 Lower St. Dennis Rd.

1956

A glassy house with a long sloping roof, set far back on its lot. Like most of the best houses of the 1950s, it conveys a sense of casual, comfortable modernism.

William and Catherine Davern House

13 William and Catherine Davern House N L

1173 Davern St.

ca. 1860s / remodeled and enlarged, Robert Elholm (builder), 1929

The oldest (south) part of this Greek Revival–Italianate house was built as a farm home for

William and Catherine Davern, who acquired the property in 1857. William Davern, an Irish immigrant, later cleared paths through his land: one eventually became Davern St. By 1880, Davern's land holdings totaled nearly 300 acres, although he'd sold most of his property for development by the time he died in 1913. In 1929 a new owner hired carpenter Robert Elholm to enlarge the farmhouse. Elholm added two bays to the north, and the work is so skillfully done that the house as a whole could easily pass for an original design from the 1860s.

14 House

1186 St. Paul Ave.

1948

This house has a small pent roof that parallels the projecting eaves above, creating two bold lines across the facade. It's quite a statement for such a modest home.

Mississippi River Boulevard

West Seventh St. to St. Paul city limits

1900 and later

The first portion of this scenic boulevard along the rim of the river gorge was built in 1900 near Shadow Falls Park at the end of Summit Ave. Other segments to the south were gradually added by the St. Paul Park Board amid constant battles with landowners. At one point, the board castigated the holdouts for their "purblind greed." Yet even the

purblind eventually saw the light, and in 1909 the boulevard was completed to West Seventh St. Unfortunately, plans to extend it to downtown St. Paul never panned out.

15 House (Hollyhocks Inn)

1590 Mississippi River Blvd. South

1906

One of the oldest homes on the boulevard, this much-remodeled mansion was once a notorious nightclub and gangster hangout. It was taken over in the 1930s by Jack Peifer, an underworld figure of considerable deviousness and charm. Under his proprietorship, the Hollyhocks—which in the 1930s was well out in the sticks—became St. Paul's hottest night spot. Peifer ran the club in high style until it was closed in 1934. Two years later, he committed suicide by swallowing a cyanide capsule after being convicted of kidnapping St. Paul brewer William Hamm, Jr.

16 Ford Twin Cities Assembly Plant and Power Plant

966 Mississippi River Blvd. South

Albert Kahn (Detroit), Stone and Webster (Boston, engineers), 1925 / remodelings and additions, ca. 1960s and later / includes **UAW-Ford-MnSCU Training Center**, *TKDA, 2001*

St. Paul real estate developer Lewis Britten was instrumental in luring Henry Ford to this site in

Ford Twin Cities Assembly Plant, 1940

the early 1920s with the promise of low-cost power from the new high dam. As designed by Detroit architect Albert Kahn, the plant was a 1,400-foot-long, one-story building punctured by a procession of large windows. Initially, the plant built Ford Model Ts and also made glass. In the 1960s, remodeling turned it into a mostly windowless box, but some of Kahn's original work can still be seen at the northern end. Below the plant is a powerhouse built by Ford in 1924. Its four turbines still produce all of the electricity used by the assembly plant.

In 2006, Ford announced it would close the plant, which assembles Ranger trucks and employs about 1,900 workers. The closing is set for 2008, and there will be extensive public debate over how best to redevelop the site, one of the finest in the Twin Cities.

17 Lock and Dam No. 1 (Ford Dam)

Mississippi River

Major Francis R. Shunk (engineer), 1917 / 1933 / 1983

Between St. Anthony Falls and downtown St. Paul, the Mississippi River drops more than 100 feet. In its natural state, this fast, rocky stretch of river prevented navigation north of St. Paul except in very high water. Not surprisingly, there was talk for years of building a dam in the gorge to extend navigation to Minneapolis and perhaps generate power as well.

The first dam was built three miles to the north in 1907. Known as the Meeker Island Dam, it opened the way for barges to reach Minneapolis, but it wasn't high enough to generate electric power efficiently. After much political maneuvering, Congress in 1910 approved a higher dam here. Completed in 1917, Lock and Dam No. 1 is a 30-foot-high, 574-foot-long concrete structure. A second lock was added in 1933; other improvements were made in the 1980s. A visitor center is on the Minneapolis side of the dam near Minnehaha Park.

18 Intercity (Ford) Bridge N

Ford Pkwy. over Mississippi River

Martin S. Grytbak with George M. Shepard and N. W. Elsberg, 1927 / widened, 1973 / renovated, 2004

The third of four elegant concrete-arch bridges built across the Mississippi River in Minneapolis and St. Paul between 1918 and 1929. This five-span bridge looks more airy and delicate than the others, in part because its vertical spandrels (columnlike elements connecting the main arches to the road deck) are paired, with the space between them left open.

19 740 River Drive Apartments

740 Mississippi River Blvd. South

Benjamin Gingold, 1961

At 21 stories the tallest in Highland, this was the first luxury high-rise apartment building in the Twin Cities, and its straightforward design has worn well.

Temple of Aaron

20 Temple of Aaron

616 Mississippi River Blvd. South

Percival Goodman (New York), 1956 and later / Art: "The Lifetime of a Jew" (stained glass), William Saltzman

Although not as well known as the contemporaneous Mount Zion Temple, this synagogue is an important Twin Cities building. It's the work of Percival Goodman, a New York architect and artist who sought to create a synagogue style suitable for Jewish worship in the modern age. Built of brick and wood, Temple of Aaron has a polygonal shape and swooping rooflines that echo the work of

Frank Lloyd Wright. The sanctuary has ten stained-glass windows and a beamed ceiling that displays Goodman's command of complex geometry. Temple of Aaron constructed this building after an earlier synagogue was damaged by fire in 1952.

21 Katherine Spink House

523 Cleveland Ave. South

Edwin Lundie, 1938

A Cape Cod cottage designed by the local master of Colonial Revival, Edwin Lundie.

22 Frederich and Catherine Knapheide House

2064 Randolph Ave.

1857 / remodeled, 1890, 1915, 1920s, and later

Portions of this extensively remodeled house date to 1857, making it the oldest in Highland. Frederich Knapheide, a German immigrant, and his wife, Catherine, built the house about a block to the west but moved it here in 1890 to make way for an extension of Randolph Ave. Virtually nothing remains of the house's original appearance.

23 College of St. Catherine

2004 Randolph Ave.

1904 and later

The College of St. Catherine was founded in 1904–5 by the Sisters of St. Joseph of Carondelet, led by Mother Seraphine Ireland, sister of Archbishop John Ireland. It is now the nation's largest Catholic women's college. St. Catherine's campus, which includes a cadre of original buildings as well as many modern additions, is the most handsome of any Twin Cities private college. The older buildings, mostly designed by John W. Wheeler (a cousin of the Irelands) are not dazzling, but they're of high quality. The biggest reason the campus is so inviting, however, is its quadrangle, which is quiet and pleasant and seems just the right size— no small accomplishment.

24 Whitby Hall and Jeanne D'Arc Auditorium

John W. Wheeler, 1914 / renovated, 2004

The auditorium, located just off Randolph Ave., is among the most impressive of Wheeler's early campus buildings. Its circular, domed hall seats 400 people.

25 Mendel Hall

Herbert A. Sullwold, 1927

Campus lore holds that this building was constructed in record time to thwart a plan by the City of St. Paul to extend Prior Ave. directly through the campus. It sounds like just the sort of coup the college's enterprising nuns might have pulled off.

26 Derham Hall N

John W. Wheeler, 1904

This brick administration building is the oldest on campus. With its pedimented Ionic portico, the building is dignified but not overbearing. It's named for Hugh Derham, a Rosemount man who contributed $20,000 toward its construction.

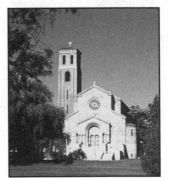

Our Lady of Victory Chapel

27 Our Lady of Victory Chapel ! N

Herbert A. Sullwold, 1924 / restored, Miller Dunwiddie Architects, 1998 / Art: tilework, Ernest Batchelder

A stunning church, full of novel and elegant touches. Although its form is derived from twelfth-century Romanesque architecture, the chapel is very much a child of the 1920s, when historic styles were reinterpreted to achieve

Our Lady of Victory Chapel interior

picturesque effects. Its richly decorated front porch is a fairly direct steal from the church of St. Trophime at Arles, France. The bell tower, however, is more Italian than French in character, while the church's distinctive cladding—randomly laid stone blocks outlined by red bricks— creates a kind of visual jazz that's more modern than Medieval.

Just as extraordinary is the chapel's barrel-vaulted interior, which has the dark, weighty, and mysterious feel of a very old stone church. Yet the walls, columns, and vaults are actually faced in tile made by California Arts and Crafts master Ernest Batchelder. The highlight is a perforated tile screen, almost Moorish in its intricacy, rising above the small choir loft.

28 The O'Shaughnessy

HGA, 1970

This large theater—a confrontational hunk of brick, concrete, and glass that closes off the east side of the quadrangle—remains the most important, and most controversial, of St. Catherine's modern-era buildings. Scaled in a way that emphasizes its brawn, it's a shot of architectural testosterone delivered to the heart of the campus, and it has a kind of bad-boy strut. The auditorium within can seat up to 1,800. The theater is named after Ignatius O'Shaughnessy, a St. Paul–born oilman who donated millions to St. Catherine's and to nearby St. Thomas University.

29 Carondelet Center (St. Joseph's Novitiate)

1890 Randolph Ave.

John W. Wheeler, 1912

Provincial House and Chapel

30 Provincial House and Chapel

1880 Randolph Ave.

John W. Wheeler, 1926

Although often perceived as part of the St. Catherine's campus, the buildings here are in fact separate, serving the Sisters of St. Joseph of Carondelet, St. Paul Province, who founded and operate the college. At the heart of the complex, these interconnected buildings make a cohesive architectural statement even though they were built at different times. Carondelet Center is the oldest. Its entry porch beneath a central gable follows the pattern Wheeler established with his earlier buildings at St. Catherine's. But when he designed the provincial house and chapel in the 1920s, Wheeler strove for a richer classical expression. The chapel's facade, inspired by French Renaissance architecture, is especially elegant, featuring a central pavilion with an arched entry and superbly detailed windows. The chapel conveys a sense of order, dignity, and calm— virtues you'd expect from a house of worship intended for nuns.

31 St. Paul Academy and Summit School (Middle and Upper School)

1712 Randolph Ave.

Thomas Holyoke, 1916 / addition, 1932–35 / addition, Benjamin Thompson and Associates, 1971 / addition (including new middle school, administration offices, and dining hall), Bentz/Thompson/ Rietow Architects with Graham Gund Architects (Boston), 2001

A small campus of brick buildings, the first of which was designed for St. Paul Academy in 1916 by Cass Gilbert disciple Thomas Holyoke in a pleasing Tudor Revival mode. Since then, several additions have sprouted up in varying styles. The addition completed in 2001 picks up the character of the original building without trying to slavishly imitate it.

John F. Linhard House

32 John F. Linhard House

1619 Scheffer Ave.

Kenneth Worthen, 1928

Architectural historians have coined terms such as *Hansel and Gretel* and *Storybook* to describe a certain kind of house from the 1920s that originated in Southern California, where motion picture set designers had long excelled at creating fantastic versions of historic architecture. This house, while not as insanely whimsical as its California progenitors, is an excellent local example of the Storybook style, offering irregular brick- and stonework and other pictorial effects. There's even a window stuck in the front chimney in blissful defiance of common sense.

33 A. S. Thome "Spec" House

1712 Highland Pkwy.

William Ingemann, 1929

The winning design in a 1926 competition sponsored by a group called the Better Homes Committee of St. Paul. Like other French-inspired houses of the time, it conveys a sense of delicate elegance.

Highland 2 Theatres

34 Highland 2 Theatres

760 Cleveland Ave. South

Myrtus Wright, 1939 / remodeled, 1978

One of St. Paul's last operating movie theaters and a fine if somewhat eccentric specimen of the Moderne style. The theater's provocatively asymmetrical facade pits a strong vertical element—in this case towers—against horizontals in the form of banded brickwork. The twin towers, a neighborhood landmark, consist of brick pylons of different heights with windows set between them and curving red and blue panels flaring out to one side. The ground floor incorporates a small shop with a rounded window next to the theater entrance.

35 Highland Village Apartments

845 Cleveland Ave. South

Walter Butler Co., 1940

Like the Fair Oaks Apartments in Minneapolis, these buildings are set amid beautifully maintained, campuslike grounds. The buildings, 12 in all, are also of high quality. Although the apartments and row houses aren't fancy, they convey a sense of timeless dignity by virtue of their solid construction and understated Colonial Revival detailing.

36 Lumen Christi Catholic Community (St. Leo the Great Catholic Church)

2055 Bohland Ave.

Bettenburg Townsend Stolter and Comb, 1965 / addition, 2005

One of St. Paul's more peculiar churches, a marble-clad octagon topped by a similarly shaped cupola. Inside, there's radial seating around the altar, a band of abstract stained glass high up on the walls, and, within the cupola, a mysterious blue dome.

37 "General Electric" House

1819 Bohland Ave.

Kenneth Fullerton, 1935 / later remodelings

This house was an award-winning design in a national "New American Home" competition sponsored by the General Electric Co. It's one of several steel-frame houses built during the 1930s by companies hoping to find new uses for steel as the housing market began to recover from the Depression. Originally, the house was a two-story, flat-roofed cube in the Moderne style, with a garage in front and a one-story wing to the rear. The house was later refaced with brick and given a shingled

mansard roof that completely obscures its original design.

38 House

1814 Hillcrest Ave.

Percy Dwight Bentley, 1928

A chaste, abstracted version of a Tudor-Norman Period Revival, with nary a hint of ornament. It's one of a pair of so-called "winter-built" houses erected by contractor Conrad Hamm to demonstrate techniques he'd developed for constructing homes even in the coldest of weather.

39 Abe and Mary Engelson House !

1775 Hillcrest Ave.

Harry Firminger (with Mary Engelson), 1939 / renovated, 2005

The Twin Cities' finest Moderne house. It was built for Abe Engelson, owner of a women's clothing store, and his wife, Mary, who played a big role in its design. The house's curving glass brick (rebuilt in 2005), rounded corners, and porthole window are all classic Moderne features. Its white stucco coat is a later addition, however; the walls were originally of white brick.

Mary Engelson reportedly worked out many of the house's details before turning over her plans to architect Harry Firminger. The Moderne seems to have been Firminger's favored style:

Abe and Mary Engelson House

he used it for another of his notable designs—the Farmers Union Grain Terminal Association headquarters (1947) in suburban Falcon Heights. Inside, the house's intricate floor plan brings together five levels like interlocking pieces of a puzzle box. This layered, complex plan isn't evident from the front of the house, which is something of a trickster in other ways as well. The stepped-up wall of glass brick, for example, looks to be following the line of a staircase, but in fact there are no stairs behind it.

POI A T. Eugene and Carol Thompson House

1720 Hillcrest Ave.

1928

This house's architecture is unremarkable. Its history is not. On the morning of March 6, 1963, Carol Thompson was beaten and stabbed to death here in what was to become the most highly publicized murder case in St. Paul's history. Her husband, attorney T. Eugene Thompson, was later accused of hiring two men to carry out the crime, and all three were eventually convicted of first-degree murder.

Macalester-Groveland

Despite the arrival of streetcars in the 1890s, most of this neighborhood wasn't developed until after 1900. An exception is the Macalester Park area, where you'll find a number of Victorian homes, including the David McCourt House (1887), designed by Cass Gilbert. Macalester-Groveland's oldest building, however, is a stone farmhouse (ca. 1867) on Mount Curve Boulevard built by German immigrant Frederick Spangenberg.

The bungalows, Craftsman foursquares, and Period Revival houses here generally date to between about 1910 and 1940 and were built largely as the tract housing of their era. They tend to be of average size, and most occupy standard 40-foot-wide lots. Yet their overall quality is such that they remain in great demand, as evidenced by their ever-escalating prices. Part of Macalester-Groveland's appeal is that it seems to have changed little over time, except that the trees (so long as they weren't elms) have grown larger and many houses have sprouted additions.

From an architectural perspective, the most fascinating portion of Macalester-Groveland is at its western edge, in the narrow strip between Cretin Avenue and Mississippi River Boulevard South. Here you'll find Woodlawn Avenue, a showcase for Period Revival houses, including the Emmett Butler House (1935), built almost entirely of steel, and the extremely peculiar Edward Bremer House (1925). A block from Woodlawn on Stonebridge Avenue is another surprise: a row of early modernist houses from the 1940s and 1950s nestled into a hillside. The houses occupy parts of the old Stonebridge estate, a magnificent property with a huge mansion built in 1916 for industrialist and inventor Oliver Crosby.

Some of Macalester-Groveland's other architectural highlights include Old Main (1884) at Macalester College, St. Mary's Chapel (1905) at the St. Paul Seminary, the charming California-style Randolph Heights School (1916) on Hamline Avenue, and the George and Mary Cahill House (1930), a one-of-a-kind stone structure on Sargent Avenue.

1 Macalester College

1600 Grand Ave.

1885 and later

Macalester was founded in 1874 as an outgrowth of two academies established by the Reverend Edward Neill, a pioneer Presbyterian clergyman. It's named after one of Neill's wealthy friends, Philadelphia businessman Charles Macalester, who donated a building for the college at its original location in Minneapolis. By 1885, however, the college had moved here and constructed its first building, Old Main. More buildings went up in the early 1900s, most of them clothed in a subdued version of Colonial Revival. Modernist buildings appeared in the 1960s, but since the 1980s the college has favored a more nostalgic brick look as exemplified by the DeWitt Wallace Library. The layout of the campus does little to unite its eclectic architecture. The biggest problem is that the campus is divided by busy Grand Ave., which was cut through in 1890 as part of a deal to extend streetcar service to the area.

2 Weyerhaeuser Memorial Chapel

Cerny and Associates (Duane Thorbeck), 1968

The finest modern building on campus, occupying a prominent site near Grand Ave. The building was controversial. Macalester students, known for their advanced views on just about everything, protested the loss of

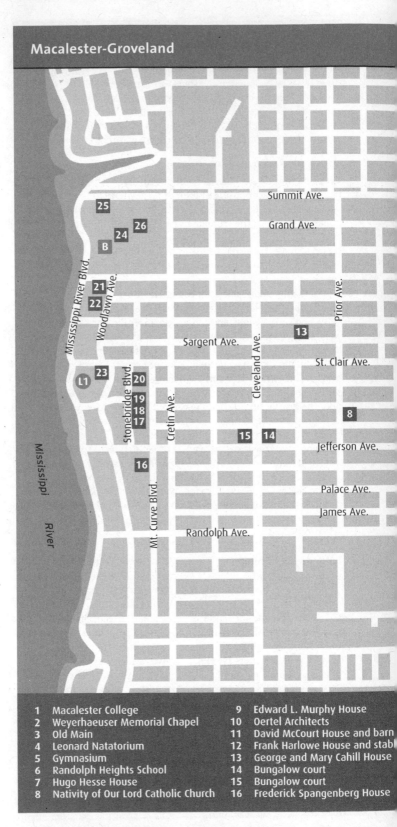

Macalester-Groveland

1   Macalester College
2   Weyerhaeuser Memorial Chapel
3   Old Main
4   Leonard Natatorium
5   Gymnasium
6   Randolph Heights School
7   Hugo Hesse House
8   Nativity of Our Lord Catholic Church
9   Edward L. Murphy House
10 Oertel Architects
11 David McCourt House and barn
12 Frank Harlowe House and stable
13 George and Mary Cahill House
14 Bungalow court
15 Bungalow court
16 Frederick Spangenberg House

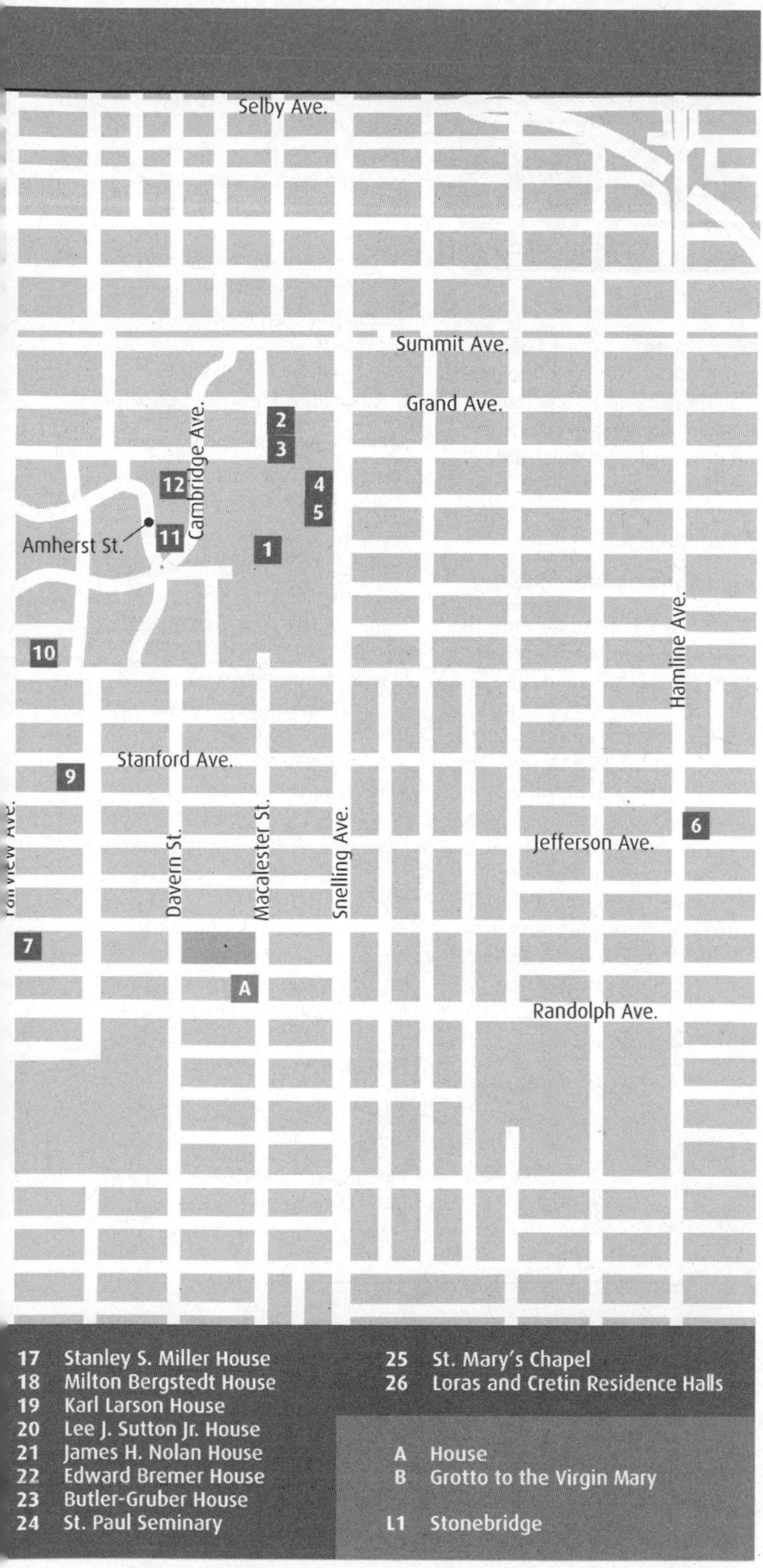
Selby Ave.
Summit Ave.
Grand Ave.
Cambridge Ave.
2
3
12
4
5
Amherst St.
11
1
10
Hamline Ave.
Stanford Ave.
9
6
Jefferson Ave.
Davern St.
Macalester St.
Snelling Ave.
7
A
Randolph Ave.

17 Stanley S. Miller House
18 Milton Bergstedt House
19 Karl Larson House
20 Lee J. Sutton Jr. House
21 James H. Nolan House
22 Edward Bremer House
23 Butler-Gruber House
24 St. Paul Seminary
25 St. Mary's Chapel
26 Loras and Cretin Residence Halls

A House
B Grotto to the Virgin Mary

L1 Stonebridge

trees to make way for the chapel. Set above a dry moat, the chapel has the aura of a classical temple,

Weyerhaeuser Memorial Chapel

albeit a temple stripped of all ornament, twisted into the shape of a hexagon, and sheathed in glass. Inside, treelike columns create a warm but muscular worship space.

3 Old Main N *L*

Willcox and Johnston, 1888

Still the heart of the campus, this old architectural warhorse suffered an amputation in the 1980s when its east wing (built in 1884) was demolished to make way for the DeWitt Wallace Library. The remaining section of the building dates to 1888, and it's a doughty Romanesque Revival pile featuring the usual arched entrance—in local limestone—and brick walls with terra-cotta and stone trim. The building now serves as Macalester's administrative offices.

4 Leonard Natatorium

Leonard Parker Associates, 1983

5 Gymnasium

William Ingemann, 1924 / renovated, ca. 1983

The Renaissance Revival–style gymnasium, by St. Paul's own William Ingemann, is the best of Macalester's early twentieth-century buildings. It's most impressive on the west side, where an inset arcade creates a strong, rhythmic effect. The adjoining natatorium (or swimming pool, in non-academic English) is pretty good, too, done in the postmodern mode of the mid-1980s.

6 Randolph Heights School

348 Hamline Ave. South

St. Paul City Architect (Charles A. Hausler), 1916

There's a Spanish flavor to this inviting school building, although it also evokes a classical sense of dignity with its columned central pavilion and flanking wings. A plaque above the front door depicts two children and carries this inscription: "Take Fast Hold of Instruction for She Is Thy Life." Alas, Hausler didn't follow this dictum when it came to his relations with the city council. He favored one-story elementary schools like this one, but they were costlier than multistory buildings, and his refusal to budge on the issue cost him his job as city architect in 1922.

POI A House

473 Macalester St.

1921

Cartoonist Charles Schulz, the ultimate source of the *Peanuts* craze that struck St. Paul in 2000,

Old Main, Macalester College, 1887

the year of his death, lived in this bungalow as a teenager. Though on the small side, it's typical of a housing type that's very common in Macalester-Groveland.

7 Hugo Hesse House

444 Fairview Ave. South

1925

A Storybook-style house with a mock thatched roof and fanciful stonework around doors and windows and even atop the chimney.

8 Nativity of Our Lord Catholic Church

1936 Stanford Ave.

O'Meara and Hills (St. Louis), 1938 / renovated, MacDonald and Mack Architects, ca. 2002

An imposing granite-clad church, built for a parish established in 1922 to serve what was then a rapidly growing part of St. Paul. The church's Gothic Revival architecture is familiar, but the multicolored stonework—seven kinds of granite—and forthright, powerful massing give it a monumental presence despite the lack of a tower.

9 Edward L. Murphy House

1774 Stanford Ave.

Percy Dwight Bentley, 1922

An early local example of the Spanish or, as it was often called, Mediterranean Revival style, built as an all-electric demonstration house. The projecting front portion with its overscaled window flanked by turned, balusterlike columns is especially striking.

10 Oertel Architects (Fridholm Office Building)

1795 St. Clair Ave.

Kenneth Worthen, 1928

This little beauty is so adorable that you want to give it a hug. Designed for a contractor as a double office building, it has a central gable, a hint of a tower, four arches (of different types and sizes), and a palette of materials that includes brick, stone, stucco, and half-timbering.

Oertel Architects

Macalester Park ("Tangletown")

Although this exceptionally pleasant neighborhood was platted in the 1880s, most of the houses that occupy its often odd-shaped lots were built in the early decades of the twentieth century. The houses themselves are, for the most part, less notable than the overall environment, which with its twisty streets and woodsy yards has the feel of an old East Coast suburb.

David McCourt House

11 David McCourt House and barn

161 Cambridge St.

Gilbert and Taylor, 1887 (barn, 1897) / renovated, David Heide, John Erler, Cliff Carey, and others, 2004

Recently restored, this house is the neighborhood's architectural centerpiece and the only one in Macalester-Groveland designed by Cass Gilbert. Although the house has a gambrel (double-sloped) roof typical of the Dutch Colonial, its corner tower, front dormer, and carefully detailed shingle cladding are all features of the Shingle Style. As always with Gilbert, there are distinctive touches, such as the shingled columns on the front porch and the unusual glass patterns in many of the windows. David McCourt, the original owner, was a dentist. The barn to the rear dates to 1897 and was also designed by Gilbert.

12 Frank Harlowe House and stable

123 Cambridge St.

H. Sackville Treherne, 1886

One of the oldest homes in Macalester Park. Behind it is a large stable. The house was built for a fruit merchant and designed by an architect who also served as the British counsel to St. Paul.

George and Mary Cahill House

13 George and Mary Cahill House ("The Castle") !

1999 Sargent Ave.

Mary Cahill (Charles Saxby Elwood drew plans for larger house), 1930 / renovated, Ron Buelow, ca. 2003

This house, which stands like a fortress atop a wooded hill, is among the Twin Cities' great architectural curiosities. Locally known as "the castle," it took on its odd appearance because of some very bad timing. The house was supposed to be a large Tudor Revival home for George Cahill, a St. Paul lawyer, and his wife, Mary. Architect Charles Saxby Elwood's design called for a tuck-under garage along Sargent, a stone-walled first floor, and half-timbered stucco above. But as construction began in 1929, the stock market crashed, and the Cahills had to scale back.

In a 1930 story, the *St. Paul Pioneer Press* attributed the house's design to Mrs. Cahill, who seems to have been a formidable character. "I've spent a lot

of time wheedling workmen, and getting my plans worked out on a cost plus basis," she told the newspaper, adding that because of the house's unconventional appearance, "sometimes I think I see the neighbors eyeing me queerly." No surprise there. The 1,700-square-foot house, renovated by an architect-owner in the early 2000s, is also unusual in that it was built with only one bedroom. The best view of the house is from a public staircase at Kenneth St. that runs along the west side of the property.

14 Bungalow court

336–38 Cleveland Ave. South

Jay Axelrod?, 1925

15 Bungalow court

333–35 Cleveland Ave. South

Elmer H. Justus, 1927

These bungalow courts face each other across Cleveland—the only such pair in the Twin Cities. The earlier one, at 336–38, is more interesting, with twin arches leading into a small but mysterious courtyard. Like so much else in the 1920s, the bungalow court proved to be a short-lived fad, at least in the Twin Cities, and none were built after about 1928.

Frederick Spangenberg House

16 Frederick Spangenberg House N *L*

375 Mount Curve Blvd.

1867

German immigrant Frederick Spangenberg bought 80 acres of land here in the 1860s and established a farm. Spangenberg built a log cabin as a temporary dwelling until he completed this stone farmhouse in 1867. The house, a simple provincial version of the Federal Style, is remarkably well preserved, in part because it stayed in the Spangenberg family for over a century. Aside from a Colonial Revival–style entrance added in the 1920s, the house looks much as it did when it was built, although other traces of Spangenberg's farm have long since vanished.

Stonebridge, 1932

LOST 1 *In the early 1900s, millionaire businessman, engineer, and inventor Oliver Crosby bought 40 acres along Mississippi River Blvd. and proceeded to build a magnificent estate. Known as **Stonebridge,** the estate's grounds extended from St. Clair to Jefferson Aves. and from the river boulevard to Mount Curve Blvd. Crosby, cofounder of the American Hoist and Derrick Co., hired Clarence H. Johnston to design a baronial Georgian-style mansion near what is now the southeast corner of Stanford Ct. and Woodlawn Ave. Completed in 1916, the house was impressive, but the estate itself was more so. The forested grounds included a huge greenhouse, two ponds, a tumbling brook, a grassy mall, and a sunken garden. The estate took its name from a stone bridge (which still stands on property at 280 Mississippi River Blvd. South) that crossed the creek.*

Crosby's tenure as lord of this realm proved brief. He died in 1922; his wife six years later. The heirs, faced with the cost of maintaining the property, immediately began subdividing it. In 1928 three streets—Woodlawn, Stanford, and Stonebridge—were built across portions of the estate; soon new houses began to appear. By 1944 what remained of the estate was tax forfeited while the great mansion

stood vacant. It was finally demolished in 1953.

Stonebridge Boulevard

Between about 1947 and 1957, 15 houses—modern in style, as evidenced by their mostly flat roofs—were built here on a hilly portion of the old Stonebridge estate. All but one were built along the east side of Stonebridge Blvd. Nowhere else in St. Paul will you find a comparable collection of architect-designed houses from the post–World War II era. The houses tend to be low-key and woodsy, and most have settled in comfortably amid the trees and thick foliage.

Stanley S. Miller House

17 Stanley S. Miller House

320 Stonebridge Blvd.

Norman C. Nagle, 1950

Clad in vertical redwood siding, this house steps merrily down the hillside, and it's a very inviting design. The house also features shed-roofed monitors that help bring light inside.

18 Milton Bergstedt House

300 Stonebridge Blvd.

Bergstedt and Hirsch, 1953

A boxy modernist house with an upthrust roof and a stone wall at the base. Milton Bergstedt was an architect whose firm also designed the house a few doors down at 324 Stonebridge (1957).

19 Karl Larson House

288 Stonebridge Blvd.

Karl Larson, 1947

Something of an odd duck among Stonebridge's modern flock. The house—which is built of red brick with blue and white trim—is vaguely Moderne in appearance and in certain ways resembles a small commercial building from the period. Karl Larson, the home's owner and designer, was a structural engineer.

20 Lee J. Sutton Jr. House

244 Stonebridge Blvd.

Norman C. Nagle, 1955

A two-story house, clad in vertical wood siding and featuring a cutout corner. Architect Norman Nagle was an assistant professor at the University of Minnesota and in 1952 became curator of architecture at the Walker Art Center in Minneapolis.

Woodlawn Avenue

This gently curving street a block back from Mississippi River Blvd. has a marvelous collection of Period Revival houses dating from the 1920s and 1930s, with a couple of real oddities thrown in for good measure. The area traversed by Woodlawn and neighboring streets is part of a subdivision called King's Maplewood that was platted just before World War I but wasn't extensively developed (except for the Stonebridge estate) until the 1920s.

21 James H. Nolan House

151 Woodlawn Ave.

Charles Saxby Elwood, 1923

One of the Twin Cities' last Prairie Style houses. As always with Elwood, the design is a bit peculiar. Prairie houses usually emphasize the horizontal line, but this one is more vertical, with a towerlike third floor room above the front entrance.

22 Edward Bremer House

181 Woodlawn Ave.

Kenneth Worthen, 1925

A weird house from St. Paul's outstanding designer of the 1920s. It features a peculiar mix of stucco and random stonework and a vaguely classical entrance that looks as though it was pasted on like so much wallpaper. But what really grabs your eye is the tower, which appears

Edward Bremer House

to have had its upper reaches sheared off in some calamity but which in fact was designed with a flat top, for reasons known only to Worthen, God bless him.

Butler-Gruber House

23 Butler-Gruber House

265 Woodlawn Ave.

Steel Construction Products Co., 1935

A unique house, built largely of steel by a St. Paul company that hoped to develop a profitable market for prefabricated metal homes. The house's welded steel frame is faced in porcelain enamel steel panels separated by strips of aluminum that mimic mortar. All doors and windows are also of steel. Despite its novel structure and Moderne elements, the house's design is actually somewhat conservative, with ornamental panels and other features that suggest the English Georgian style sometimes called Regency. The original owner, Emmett Butler, was in the iron ore business, which made living in a steel house highly appropriate. In 1946 a mechanical engineer named Francis Gruber purchased the property, and it's been in the family ever since.

24 St. Paul Seminary

2260 Summit Ave.

1894 and later

In 1885 Archbishop John Ireland founded a combined seminary and college at what is now the University of St. Thomas. But he'd long dreamed of establishing a fully independent seminary to train diocesan priests, and in 1894 he was finally able to do so here. The financial angel who made Ireland's dream a reality was James J. Hill, who donated $500,000 to construct and endow the seminary. Hill liked to stay close to his money, and it was inevitable that he would end up as a kind of general superintendent of the construction project, weighing in on almost every detail.

Cass Gilbert designed the seminary's first six buildings in a Renaissance Revival style that's as stiff as a Roman collar. The buildings, three of which survive, probably reflect the heavy hand of Hill, who had no use for architectural fuss and feathers. The campus, part of which is now occupied by the University of St. Thomas, also includes several modern-era buildings.

25 St. Mary's Chapel N *L*

2260 Summit Ave.

Clarence H. Johnston, 1905 / remodeled, Rafferty Rafferty Tollefson, 1988

This lovely chapel is modeled after a basilican church in Rome from AD 380. It's clad in rock-faced Kettle River sandstone with Indiana limestone trim. Beautifully detailed, the chapel has carved stonework, stained glass (including a rose window above the main entrance), marble floors, and a fine beamed ceiling. It was significantly altered in 1988 when the apse was removed

St. Mary's Chapel

and the interior reoriented as part of a plan that included constructing a new administration and residence complex for the seminary.

Cretin Residence Hall

26 Loras and Cretin Residence Halls

Cass Gilbert, 1894

Two of Gilbert's original campus buildings, now used as residence halls for the University of St. Thomas. The nearby Grace Hall, designed in 1912 by Emmanuel Masqueray, is quite similar.

POI B Grotto to the Virgin Mary

Finn's Glen

ca. 1910 / renovated and restored, 1993 / Art: bronze relief sculptures, Peter Lupori

Finn's Glen, a ravine named after an early settler, drops down into the Mississippi River gorge through the seminary's campus; at its upper end is a grotto with a statue, stone bridges, and winding walkways.

Merriam Park–Lexington-Hamline

1	Flannery Construction	
2	Central Baptist Church	
3	House	
4	George Carsley House	
5	Crosby Block	
6	House	
7	Edwin Moore House	
8	Triune Masonic Temple	
9	Olivet Congregational Church	
10	Ben and Rachel Awes House	
11	Charles Thompson Memorial Hall	
12	Merriam Park Branch Library	
13	Denis E. Lane House	
14	Albert Nason House	
15	St. Mark's Catholic Church	
16	Houses	
17	Richards Gordon Office Building	
18	George Pilmer House	
19	Concordia University	
20	Student Union	
21	Central High School	
22	Williams-Hesse House	
23	Henry Stempel House	
24	James M. Shiely House	
25	Albert Wunderlich House	
26	University of St. Thomas	
27	Ireland Hall	
28	Chapel of St. Thomas Aquinas	

29   O'Shaughnessy-Frey Library
     Center
30   John R. Roach Center for the
     Liberal Arts
31   Aquinas Hall
32   McNeely Hall
33   Edwin J. Binswanger House
34   Archibald C. Jefferson House
35   Kenneth Worthen House
36   "Eastcliff"
37   Edward and Ida Brewer House
38   Walter Coombs House
39   Nicholas R. Brewer House

A   Iris Park
B   Merriam Park
C   Shadow Falls
D   Town and Country Club
E   Meeker Island Dam

L1   Old Central High School
L2   Prince of Peace Lutheran
     Church for the Deaf

MerLexHam

Merriam Park–Lexington-Hamline

Among the first settlers here was Stephen Desnoyer, who claimed 320 acres along the Mississippi River north of present-day Marshall Avenue in 1843. Desnoyer, after whom a charming corner of the neighborhood is named, also operated an inn along the Red River oxcart trail, which followed roughly the same route though this part of St. Paul as Interstate 94 does today (a plaque along St. Anthony Avenue near Glendale Street commemorates the trail).

Both John Merriam and Archbishop John Ireland harbored great dreams for this neighborhood. Merriam hoped to see a new State Capitol here; Ireland envisioned a cathedral. As it turned out, these grand projects were built elsewhere, and the neighborhood instead developed in typical fashion once streetcar service arrived. A line opened along Selby, Marshall, and Prior avenues in 1891, but trolleys didn't reach the western end of the neighborhood until 1905.

The neighborhood's long period of development—some portions of Desnoyer Park date to the 1950s—accounts for its diversity of housing. Although there are impressive homes along Summit Avenue, near Merriam Park, and in Desnoyer Park, architectural honors go to a development from the 1920s known as Shadow Falls, after the park of that name along the river. Here you'll find a gorgeous collection of Period Revival houses. Two houses from 1926—Edwin Lundie's Binswanger House and a fantastic French-inspired concoction designed by Kenneth Worthen—are among Shadow Falls' many gems.

Other notable buildings in Merriam Park–Lexington-Hamline include Triune Masonic Temple (1911); the Denis E. Lane House (1910), a sophisticated bungalow; the Emmanuel Masqueray–designed Chapel of St. Thomas Aquinas (1918) at the University of St. Thomas; and an extraordinary folk folly, the George Pilmer House (1970s and later).

1 Flannery Construction

1375 St. Anthony Ave.

Roark Kramer Kosowski Design (Peter Kramer), 2005

An energy efficient building (note the solar panels on the roof) that also dares to have some fun. Finished in green, red, and blue stucco, the two-story building features an angular facade that overlooks Interstate 94 and displays the company's name in bold letters.

2 Central Baptist Church

420 North Roy St.

Alban and Hausler, 1913 / additions, 1947, 1974

An interesting stab at a Prairie Style church, with some vaguely classical features—such as the parapets over the entrances and along the roofline—mixed in for good measure.

424 Beacon Ave.

3 House

424 Beacon Ave.

William H. Castner, 1890

One of four Shingle Style houses in a row here (the others are at 428, 430, and 432 Beacon). They were all built around 1890 and are all encased, none too happily, in modern siding. This house's most distinctive feature, beneath the eaves on the south side, is a band of arched windows balanced atop a narrow, angular bay that drops all the way down to the foundation.

4 George Carsley House

451 Lynnhurst Ave. East

George H. Carsley, 1903

A Colonial Revival house in the Dutch manner, with a base of rough-faced stone and a steep gambrel roof above. George Carsley was a construction superintendent for architect Cass Gilbert.

POI A Iris (Union) Park

Area bounded by University, St. Anthony, Prior, and Fairview Aves.

1880 and later

The curving streets around Lake Iris were platted in 1884 as a residential development called Union Park, which filled in the site of an earlier amusement park. Today, this mini-neighborhood remains a pleasant oasis between two busy transportation corridors— University Ave. to the north and Interstate 94 to the south.

5 Crosby Block

1956 Feronia Ave.

Barber and Barber, 1888

In the 1880s, as "Short Line" commuter trains and later streetcars began to serve the Union (now Iris) Park and Merriam Park residential districts, a commercial hub developed around Prior and St. Anthony Aves. Several of the old buildings were razed to make way for Interstate 94 in the 1960s, but this one survived. It's a lovely Victorian, with carved ornaments beneath its broad arched windows (now partly filled in). As of 2007 the building was vacant.

6 House

1923 Iglehart Ave.

1890

A rare local example of a one-and-a-half-story Queen Anne house, animated by quaint details such as paired front windows sheltered by delicate pent roofs. Above and between the windows is a boxlike dormer that thrusts forward on brackets from a hipped roof. Farther up the roof is a gable with a semicircular window.

7 Edwin Moore House

1905 Iglehart Ave.

Augustus Gauger, 1885

A richly ornamented house, one of the earliest in the Merriam Park development. Its style, which has Italianate features such as window hoods, was somewhat conservative for the time, since Queen Anne was already in full flower elsewhere in St. Paul.

Triune Masonic Temple, 1979

8 Triune Masonic Temple N *L*

1898 Iglehart Ave.

Henry C. Struchen, 1911

One of the state's oldest and best-preserved Masonic temples, still in use today. The lodge was organized in 1891 and constructed this red brick building 20 years later. The building presents a dignified front, with four colossal Doric columns, a heavy cornice, and bracketed pediments above the doors and windows.

9 Olivet Congregational Church

1850 Iglehart Ave.

Clarence H. Johnston, 1907 / addition (school-office wing), Clarence H. Johnston, Jr., 1915

A charming church built around an open courtyard. The sanctuary occupies the brick portion of the building at the corner and connects to a school-office wing treated in a picturesque Tudor Revival style. The connecting element at the back of the courtyard has a small tower and gables

MerlexHam

decorated with bargeboards. Clarence Johnston wasn't an

Olivet Congregational Church

especially playful architect, but here he created a building that has a childlike feel, in the best sense of the word.

10 Ben and Rachel Awes House

1792 Iglehart Ave.

Ben Awes, 1999

An inventive infill house, long but only 20 feet wide, topped by a curving barnlike roof of silvery galvanized steel.

11 Charles Thompson Memorial Hall *L*

1824 Marshall Ave.

Olof Hanson (Seattle), 1916

In 1915, Charles Thompson, son of pioneer St. Paul banker Horace Thompson, died at age 51. Deaf since birth, Thompson had long been interested in establishing a club open to all deaf people. His wife, Margaret, also deaf, built this hall in his memory, hiring the nation's first deaf architect, Olof Hanson, to design it. The first clubhouse of its kind in the nation, it continues to serve the

deaf community today. The building, constructed largely of brick, is solid and unpretentious. Within are a variety of club-rooms, a caretaker's apartment, and a large hall.

Merriam Park Branch Library, 1930

12 Merriam Park Branch Library

1831 Marshall Ave.

MS&R Architects, 1993

This rather curious building fea-tures an oval entrance canopy and rotunda that symbolize the importance of reading by sug-gesting the shape of the eye. It also has incised ornamental stonework, a copper roof that folds down over the building like a snug hat, and ornamental bits and pieces from the 1930 Gothic Revival library that once stood here. The interior offers an Arts and Crafts ambiance with much cherry-stained woodwork.

13 Denis E. Lane House

2000 Marshall Ave.

Mark Fitzpatrick, 1910

A sophisticated bungalow built for a prominent real estate devel-oper who advertised himself as the "own your own home" man.

Denis E. Lane House

In this case, he built quite a home indeed, with the help of St. Paul architect Mark Fitzpatrick. The house's exceptional features include an inset second-story porch (originally open) and a complicated system of exposed columns, brackets, and beams that calls to mind the work of California's bungalow masters, the brothers Charles and Henry Greene.

POI B Merriam Park

Iglehart and Prior Aves.

ca. 1880s and later

Like the neighborhood, this pleasant park was named after John L. Merriam, who platted the area beginning in 1881. A commuter rail station was once located just north of the park.

14 Albert Nason House

2135 Iglehart Ave.

Clarence H. Johnston, 1908

A large and stodgy Tudor Revival house. Except for an offset front porch, the main facade is symmetrical—not really what you'd expect from a style based on the rambling eccentricities of English Tudor architecture. The house was built for Albert Nason, president of a real estate development company in St. Paul.

St. Mark's Catholic Church, 1920

15 St. Mark's Catholic Church

1991 Dayton Ave.

John T. Comes (Pittsburgh), 1919

This large parish was founded in 1889, the same year the first church was built here. However, the parish didn't develop in a big way until the Reverend J. A. Corrigan became pastor in 1911. He built a school in 1913, a rec-

tory in 1917, and this church in 1919. The Gothic Revival brick church—designed by John Comes, also architect of St. Luke's Catholic Church on Summit Ave.—is a neighborhood landmark. Its outstanding feature is a broad tower that rises to a gabled roof from which a thin spire erupts like a giant spike. Within, the church has plaster-vaulted ceilings but is otherwise quite simple, in keeping with its exterior.

16 Houses

1799, 1803 Dayton Ave.

1890

Before various remodelings—such as the addition of an enclosed porch at 1803—these Queen Annes were identical, both sporting fine bell-roofed towers. They are among the oldest houses on this stretch of Dayton.

17 Richards Gordon (Elementary School) Office Building

1619 Dayton Ave.

Ray Gauger, 1911 / renovated, ca. 1980s

A handsome school building converted to offices in the 1980s. Built of cream-colored brick, it features a pedimented entry pavilion that sports a rich array of botanical forms swirling around a bull's-eye window. The designer, Ray Gauger, was the son of Augustus Gauger, a prominent nineteenth-century architect in St. Paul. The building was named after the cofounder, in 1879, of the Gordon and Ferguson Co., a St. Paul firm that dealt in fur and leather goods.

18 George Pilmer House !

1467 Iglehart Ave.

1900 / remodeled, George Pilmer, ca. 1974–2005

A genuine folk folly created by a Scottish-born plasterer named George Pilmer. *Folly* in this case refers to an unorthodox structure built without architects or other design professionals. The first hint that this is no ordinary

MerlexHam

house appears at the sidewalk, where a wavelike wall rolls down from a small yard decorated by

George Pilmer House

a family of abstract sculptures. The centerpiece of Pilmerworld, however, is the house itself. Working alone, Pilmer transformed a prosaic bungalow into a stucco fantasy featuring swirls of color, a sculpted roofline, a parabolic-arched canopy over the front door, and porthole windows made from clear plastic salad bowls. The house reflects Pilmer's admiration for the work of Catalan architect Antoni Gaudi, famous for his sinuous, surreal buildings. Pilmer worked on the house for over 30 years before selling it in 2005.

19 Concordia University

275 North Syndicate St.

Art: Martin Luther *(bronze statue), 1921 (recasting of statue by Ernest Friedrich August Rietscher, 1861)*

The institution that evolved into Concordia University was founded in 1893 by the Lutheran Church–Missouri Synod as a high school. After a year in temporary quarters, the school moved to this site, where a state training school for boys had been located since the 1870s. Concordia became a four-year college in 1967 and added graduate programs in the 1980s. With the exception of its Student Union, Concordia offers a generally bland collection of buildings.

20 Student Union

1301 Marshall Ave.

Frederick Benz–Milo Thompson, 1972

A strong, if flawed, design. This angular, brick-clad, and virtually

windowless building relies on monitors at the corners to bring in light, but the scheme doesn't really work. The interior has an unpleasant, claustrophobic feel despite various spatial gymnas-

Concordia Student Union

tics, and you have to wonder whether function and comfort were compromised here in pursuit of an architectural ideal.

21 Central High School

275 Lexington Pkwy. North

Ellerbe Architects, 1979

The nadir of modern school architecture in St. Paul, a building so resolutely grim and uninviting that it suggests education can only be viewed as a form of incarceration.

Central High School, 1912

LOST 1 *The current school uses the structural frame (but nothing else) of the old **Central High School**— a splendid Collegiate Gothic building completed in 1912. It was the city's largest and finest high school building, and its destruction was a great loss.*

22 Williams-Hesse House

1384 Ashland Ave.

Guy Williams and Jackie Hesse, 2003

A modern take on the Craftsman foursquare, and a good example of an infill house that doesn't try to look "old" but still fits right in with the neighbors.

23 Henry Stempel House

1432 Portland Ave.

Jay Axelrod, 1923

A small house, vaguely Spanish in feel, with a monumental front veranda supported by chubby, tapering columns. The dormer above is a modern addition.

James M. Shiely House

24 James M. Shiely House

1460 Ashland Ave.

Charles Saxby Elwood, 1925

An intriguing blend of the popular English Cottage look of the 1920s with the rigorous geometries of Prairie Style. Architect Charles Elwood created this unlikely synthesis, and while it's possible to quarrel with some details—the second-story windows, for example, bunch up rather uncomfortably in places—there's no denying that the house is truly something different. Highlights include diamond-shaped triple windows at the peaks of the gables, a catslide roof over the front porch, and ornamental tilework used sparingly but effectively. The house was built for James M. Shiely, owner of a large trucking firm.

25 Albert Wunderlich House

1599 Portland Ave.

Bentley and Hausler, 1915

An object lesson in turning a Craftsman cube into a fashionable Prairie Style house: the trick lies in the details and how the pieces are put together. Here, Charles Hausler and Percy Dwight Bentley took the basic foursquare and transformed it into something exceptional. Its Prairie features include grouped corner windows, wide overhanging eaves, stucco walls above a high brick base defined by a continuous belt course, a side entrance, leaded glass with geometric patterns, and even a concrete planter à la Frank Lloyd Wright. The original owner, Albert Wunderlich, was a businessman who also served as an education commissioner for St. Paul.

Albert Wunderlich House

26 University of St. Thomas

Area bounded by Grand, Selby, Cretin, and Cleveland Aves., plus portions of St. Paul Seminary campus southwest of Cretin and Summit Aves.

ca. 1885 and later /
Art: Archbishop John Ireland (bronze statue), Michael Price, 1985 (in main quadrangle)

The University of St. Thomas began as a combination seminary and college founded in 1885 by Archbishop John Ireland. Today, it's the state's largest private college, enrolling over 10,000 students. Its campus here (there's also one in downtown Minneapolis) sprawls across more than 14 square blocks, including portions of the St. Paul Seminary complex.

The oldest buildings, on the northern half of campus, are angled away from the cardinal points of the compass. As the campus expanded to the south, however, it was realigned to match the street grid around it, and there's a well-defined quadrangle behind the buildings immediately north of Summit. Collegiate Gothic buildings faced in Minnesota limestone dominate the campus. Aquinas Hall, completed in 1931, established this style, which the university has generally followed ever since. The plus side of this approach is that the campus has a fairly uniform look. The minus side is that the university's devotion to Gothic drapery looks increasingly backward at a time when more modern architectural options are readily available.

Because of St. Thomas's growth, the campus seems to be perpetually expanding—long a sore point with neighbors. The university has already taken over much of the St. Paul Seminary and has also begun to construct new buildings along the south side of Summit.

27 Ireland Hall

Emmanuel Masqueray, 1912 / remodeled, Ellerbe Architects, 1945

A large, no-nonsense dormitory similar to the one Masqueray designed in the same year for the St. Paul Seminary, just across Summit Ave.

Chapel of St. Thomas Aquinas

28 Chapel of St. Thomas Aquinas !

121 Cleveland Ave. North

Emmanuel Masqueray (completed by Slifer, Abrahamson and Lundie), 1918 / remodeled, 1970s

Archbishop John Ireland dreamed of building a new cathedral here but had to settle for this chapel, which is very nice in its own right. Like the cathedral, it was designed by Emmanuel Masqueray, who died in 1917 just as construction began. Three of his former draftsmen completed the work. The chapel's site, angled off Cleveland Ave., doesn't give it a strong presence, which is unfortunate, since it's the best building on campus.

The Renaissance-inspired exterior features Masqueray's usual intricate brickwork but is otherwise quite restrained. Similar understatement characterizes the arched and pedimented front entrance, beneath one of the circular windows Masqueray so loved. The barrel-vaulted sanctuary within was initially quite plain. In the 1940s, stained-glass windows, wall paintings, and other decorative elements were installed in accordance with the master plan developed by the Reverend Walter LeBeau, longtime director of religion at St. Thomas.

O'Shaughnessy-Frey Library Center

29 O'Shaughnessy-Frey Library Center

Summit and Cleveland Aves.

Lang and Raugland, 1959 / addition, 1991

This Collegiate Gothic library may be the best of the campus's many buildings in that style. Named after St. Thomas benefactor Ignatius O'Shaughnessy, the library includes an extensive stained-glass and sculptural program. The glass mostly depicts God and the saints, but if you look closely you'll also find an image of Sherlock Holmes (a frequent visitor to Minnesota, according to one local author of dubious repute).

30 John R. Roach Center for the Liberal Arts (Albertus Magnus Science Hall)

2115 Summit Ave.

Ellerbe Architects, 1946 / addition (greenhouse), 1963 / renovated, 2000

31 Aquinas Hall

2115 Summit Ave.

Maginnis and Walsh (Boston), 1931 / remodeled, 1964

Aquinas Hall is the original Collegiate Gothic building on campus, done by the very able Boston firm that also designed the St. Paul Cathedral's sacristy in 1924. Aquinas is linked by a bridge to the somewhat later but stylistically similar John Roach Center. The arched passageway beneath the bridge serves as a major entry point into campus.

32 McNeely Hall

Summit and Cleveland Aves.

Opus Architects and Engineers, 2006

A new home for the university's business school delivered in the same old Collegiate Gothic package.

POI C Shadow Falls

Summit Ave. and Mississippi River Blvd.

At least half a dozen small, seasonal waterfalls, bearing romantic names like Fawn's Leap and Silver Cascade, once tumbled into the Mississippi River gorge between St. Paul and Minneapolis. Shadow Falls, lying deep within a long ravine, is probably the most pristine of the surviving waterfalls, and it gives its name to a small park as well as to the 1920s subdivision just to the north that contains some of the Twin Cities' most magnificent Period Revival homes.

Edwin J. Binswanger House

33 Edwin J. Binswanger House !

73 Otis Ln.

Edwin Lundie, 1926

Edwin Lundie designed houses that evoke a sense of the old way of building, elemental and beyond the whims of style. Whereas most Period Revival architects approached their work as a kind of theater, for Lundie it seems to have been more: a genuine effort to find meaning in the forms and techniques of the past. This house, in the Cotswold Cottage style Lundie often favored, is one of his best. Lundie was a craftsman at heart, and this house has above all else the feel of a thing beautifully made. The size and placement of every stone seems to have been carefully weighed so as to produce an intricate tapestry of textures and colors, and the result is Period Revival architecture at its most calm and intimate, shaped by a master's hand.

34 Archibald C. Jefferson House

71 Otis Ln.

Clarence H. Johnston, Jr., 1925

A willfully picturesque house that plays with all manner of styles, offering a bit of English Cottage here, some Tudor Revival there, and even a dab of classicism in the form of a double archway that connects to the garage. Like most Period Revival architecture, this house is history reimagined, a seductive but by no means archaeologically correct picture of the past, executed with great verve. The home's original owner operated a lumber business.

Kenneth Worthen House

35 Kenneth Worthen House !

54 Mississippi River Blvd. North

Kenneth Worthen, 1926

This house, best seen from its north side on Otis Ave., is among the high points of Period Revival architecture in the Twin Cities. The first county assessor to appraise the house found it so strange that he labeled it an "architectural freak." Maybe, but

the house's over-the-top quality—especially evident in its roof—accounts for much of its appeal. A fantastic exaggeration of a French-style mansard, the roof engulfs the house like a ten-gallon hat on a child. As with all of architect Kenneth Worthen's work, the house is beautifully put together, with gorgeous walls of gray and yellow limestone that play off against patterned brickwork around the windows. Fine details in copper, iron, and wood complete the composition. At about 2,800 square feet, the house isn't all that large, but, as they say in theater, it plays big.

"Eastcliff"

36 "Eastcliff" (Edward and Markell Brooks House) N

176 Mississippi River Blvd. North

Clarence H. Johnston, Jr., 1922 / addition, 1931

This 20-room mansion, a sprawling house in a modernized Colonial Revival style, has been used since 1960 as the official residence of the president of the University of Minnesota. It was probably designed by Clarence Johnston, Jr., who was handling most of the residential work for his father's firm by the 1920s. In 1987 the house became the focus of quite a furor over a costly remodeling project carried out by then university president Kenneth Keller, who resigned the next year. The house's original owner, Edward Brooks, was a lumberman. Family members donated the home to the university in 1958.

Marshall Avenue–Lake Street Bridge

(See under Powderhorn)

LOST 2 *A fine church designed by Ralph Rapson, Minnesota's most prominent architectural modernist, once stood at 205 Otis Ave. The **Prince of Peace Lutheran Church for the Deaf,** built in 1959, was a small but elegant brick temple beautifully sited on a wooded lot. It was torn down in 2006 to make way for a condominium project.*

POI D Town and Country Club

300 Mississippi River Blvd. North

Golf course, George McCree, 1893 and later

This hilly golf course along the Mississippi River north of Marshall Ave. is the oldest in Minnesota and reputed to be the second oldest in the United States still on its original site. The first clubhouse, long gone, was designed by Gilbert and Taylor in 1889.

POI E Meeker Island Dam (Lock and Dam No. 2) N

Mississippi River near Eustis St.

U.S. Army Corps of Engineers (Maj. Francis Shunk), 1907–12 (top five feet demolished)

Down in the Mississippi gorge, near where St. Paul and Minneapolis meet, lie the usually submerged remains of a lock and dam. Officially known as Lock and Dam No. 2, it was more commonly called the Meeker Island Dam. The 14-foot-high structure, completed in 1907, was the first dam anywhere on the river. Along with a second low dam then under construction, it was designed to raise the river level to permit navigation well into Minneapolis.

In 1910, however, Congress decided it would make more sense to build a single high dam in the gorge rather than two low ones that lacked the height needed to efficiently generate electricity. Two years later, the U.S. Army Corps of Engineers demolished the top five feet of the Meeker Island Dam. The second short dam was redesigned

as the higher Ford Dam and finally completed in 1917. The pool behind it submerged Meeker Dam and its island.

37 Edward and Ida Brewer House ("Not by a Dam Site")

383–87 Pelham Blvd.

ca. 1907 / Edward and Ida Brewer, 1918 and later

As part of the Meeker Island dam project, a Tudor Revival–style lockkeeper's house was built on the St. Paul side of the bluffs above the lock and dam. After the locks closed, the house stood vacant until 1918, when it was purchased by artist Edward Brewer and his wife, Ida. The Brewers moved the house here and incorporated it into an English Cottage–style home they were building on the site. The property also includes a studio built by Brewer, who, like his father, Nicholas, painted portraits but worked as a commercial artist as well.

38 Walter Coombs House

375 Pelham Blvd.

Robert Cerny, 1941

One of St. Paul's first modernist boxes. Though not terribly impressive, it is crisply designed, nicely sited, and apparently in excellent condition. Its designer, Minneapolis architect Robert Cerny, helped bring modernism to Minnesota in the 1940s and 1950s. His work was seldom exciting.

39 Nicholas R. Brewer House

510 Frontenac Pl.

William M. Linden Co., 1925

A Spanish-Moorish fantasy built for an artist who probably never lived in it. Painter Nicholas Brewer, known for his portraits, worked all around the United States but maintained his home base in St. Paul. In 1925 he commissioned this exotic-looking house on a hilly lot with views of the Mississippi. Its most distinctive feature is a pergola-like log

MerLexHam

Nicholas R. Brewer House

frame that extends across one corner of the roof. Oddly, it appears that Brewer never moved into the house; the first occupant of record is a man named Ernest Pierce, who didn't move in until 1937.

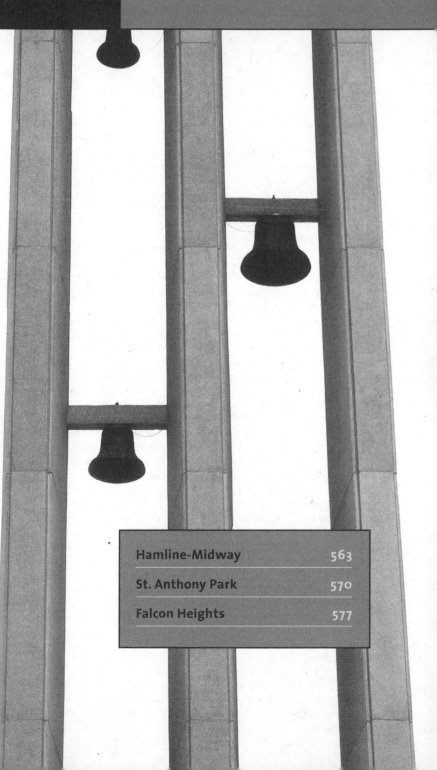

15

Hamline-Midway,
St. Anthony Park,
& Falcon Heights

Overview

Although Hamline-Midway, St. Anthony Park, and suburban Falcon Heights converge at the northwestern corner of St. Paul, they offer sharply contrasting architectural environments. Hamline-Midway is an unprepossessing working-class neighborhood, its flat grid of streets lined with modest houses, mostly from the early 1900s. It's also the site of Hamline University. St. Anthony Park, on the other hand, is all hills and curves. Victorian-era developers platted most of the neighborhood as an upper middle-class residential district, a character it's maintained to this day. Falcon Heights is distinctive by virtue of two huge institutional presences—the Minnesota State Fairgrounds and the University of Minnesota's St. Paul campus—that together consume over half the suburb's land.

Settlers began filtering into Hamline-Midway in the 1850s. By that time, Snelling Avenue, an old military route out of Fort Snelling, already bisected the area. Initially, only a scattering of farms occupied the prairie here, although real estate speculators, thick as locusts in those days, were already platting lots in expectation of a great boom just around the corner. As it turned out, the boom was a bit slow in coming.

The first significant development didn't begin until 1880, when Hamline University moved its campus to Snelling and Hewitt avenues. Old Main, which opened in 1884, was the first campus building. Houses soon appeared nearby, the oldest among them built as part of a commuter suburb once known as Hamline Village. Another big step occurred in the 1880s when the Minnesota Transfer Railway began operations at the western edge of the neighborhood. The railway, which served a large stockyard where the Amtrak Depot now stands, soon attracted industry and housing, especially near University Avenue. Much of Hamline-Midway wasn't developed until the early twentieth century, however. As usual, it was the arrival of streetcar service, beginning on University in 1890, that spurred growth by making the once distant area readily accessible to both downtown St. Paul and downtown Minneapolis as well as to other centers of employment.

The beginnings of St. Anthony Park go back to the 1870s, when most of the land was purchased by a group of real estate speculators led by William Marshall, a Civil War hero who served as governor of Minnesota from 1866 to 1870. Marshall dreamed of attracting the wealthy to his new suburb, which was conveniently located midway between downtown St. Paul and downtown Minneapolis and served by a rail line that connected them. In 1873 Marshall hired landscape architect Horace Cleveland to lay out St. Anthony Park with the requisite sinuous streets as well as estate-sized lots of five to ten acres.

As it turned out, Marshall's timing left something to be desired. The financial panic of 1873 plunged the nation into a recession, and Cleveland's design was never carried out. Another decade would pass before a reconstituted group of investors moved forward with development. This group formed the St. Anthony Park Co. in 1885 and platted the streets that remain largely unchanged today. The new layout followed Cleveland's picturesque ideals but subdivided the land into more or less standard-sized city lots. The company also hired architects and built dozens of houses—many of which survive—mainly south of Langford Park on either side of Raymond Avenue. Once streetcars arrived in the 1890s, commuter rail service was abandoned in St. Anthony Park, and the neighborhood began to follow the usual pattern of growth into the twentieth century.

Falcon Heights didn't become a municipality until 1949, but its history goes well back to the nineteenth century. The Gibbs Museum of Pioneer and Dakotah Life centers around one of the oldest houses (1854) in the Twin Cities, while the university's agricultural campus and the state fairgrounds were both established in the 1880s.

Hamline-Midway

With its flat terrain, gridded streets, and generally plain houses, Hamline-Midway doesn't offer a great many visual surprises. The great exception is St. Columba Church (1951), one of the most startling and original works of architecture in the Twin Cities. All but hidden away in the middle of an otherwise average block on Lafond Ave., the church is unknown even to many St. Paulites. Other notable neighborhood churches include Knox Presbyterian (1914), Hamline United Methodist (1928), and Jehovah Lutheran (1963).

Most of the neighborhood's everyday housing stock dates from 1900 to 1930. There are, however, some distinctive homes interspersed amid the usual bungalows, Craftsman foursquares, Tudors, and Colonials. Besides Victorians like the Oric O. Whited House (1887) on Englewood Avenue and the John Dewey House (1889) on Van Buren Avenue, you'll discover some intriguing houses from the first half of the twentieth century. These include a peculiar concrete-block house at 1462 Charles Avenue, a Moderne-style home at 1689 Edmund Avenue, and a one-story Spanish Revival hacienda at 1672 Blair Avenue.

Other important buildings in the neighborhood include the Giddens Alumni Learning Center (1972) at Hamline University and the Hamline-Midway Branch Library on Minnehaha Avenue (1930). And, of course, no visit to Hamline-Midway would be complete without a stop to gaze upon the Twin Cities' largest paint can, mounted in all its splendor atop a hardware store on Snelling.

Long a mostly white working-class neighborhood, Hamline-Midway—like St. Paul as a whole—saw significant growth in its minority population from 1990 to 2000. Among the neighborhood's distinctive ethnic characteristics is its concentration of Korean-owned businesses, including a grocery store and two restaurants.

Snelling Avenue

North of Interstate 94

By the time Snelling Ave. was named in 1856 in honor of Colonel Josiah Snelling (after whom the fort is named), its route was well established, first as an Indian path and later as a government road. Today, it's the busiest north-south artery in St. Paul. Snelling's architectural ensemble is diverse but, on the whole, not very impressive for a street of its size. Still, the avenue offers some small-scale architectural pleasures, though they can be hard to spot amid the rushing traffic.

1 Jehovah Lutheran Church

Snelling Ave. at Thomas Ave.
(1566 Thomas Ave.)

Harold Spitznagel Associates (Sioux Falls, SD), 1963

This church's patterned concrete walls, glassy recessed front en-

Jehovah Lutheran Church

trance, and simple cubic volume all mimic commercial buildings— especially department stores—of the era. It was designed at a time when many architects were under the spell of modernist masters like Ludwig Mies van der Rohe, who believed that just about anything, including a house of worship, could fit into a box. Still, this is an interesting and unusual church, quite different from any other in the Twin Cities, and its appearance is appropriate given its location on such a busy commercial street.

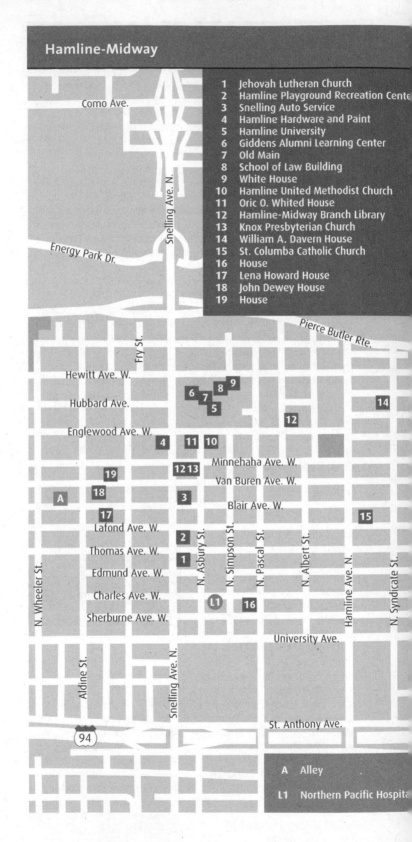

Hamline-Midway

1   Jehovah Lutheran Church
2   Hamline Playground Recreation Center
3   Snelling Auto Service
4   Hamline Hardware and Paint
5   Hamline University
6   Giddens Alumni Learning Center
7   Old Main
8   School of Law Building
9   White House
10 Hamline United Methodist Church
11 Oric O. Whited House
12 Hamline-Midway Branch Library
13 Knox Presbyterian Church
14 William A. Davern House
15 St. Columba Catholic Church
16 House
17 Lena Howard House
18 John Dewey House
19 House

A   Alley

L1 Northern Pacific Hospital

2 Hamline Playground Recreation Center *L*

Snelling Ave. at Lafond Ave. (1564 Lafond Ave.)

St. Paul City Architect (Charles A. Bassford with Clarence Wigington), 1940 / renovated, 1993

Among the best of the dozen or so playground structures designed by Clarence Wigington and built during the 1930s and 1940s with grants from the federal Works Progress Administration. Here Wigington employed a restrained variant of art deco sometimes called WPA Moderne.

3 Snelling Auto Service (Gratz Pure Oil Service Station)

670 Snelling Ave. North

P. Gepard, 1940

A sweet little survivor from an era when gas stations were downright tidy and "self service" would have been considered an oxymoron. The style here is English Cottage Revival.

4 Hamline Hardware and Paint

755 Snelling Ave. North

ca. 1950s

Mounted on the roof of this longtime neighborhood establishment is a roadside landmark in the form of a giant paint can, which used to revolve but in recent years has stopped. Fervent is the hope that one day it will twirl again.

5 Hamline University

Snelling and Hewitt Aves.

various architects, 1884 and later / Art: Bridgeman Memorial Court (relief sculptures), John Rood, 1954 / Leonidas Hamline (statue), Michael Price, 1995

Hamline is Minnesota's oldest university, founded in 1854 by Methodist bishop Leonidas Hamline, who's commemorated by a statue near the campus center. Originally located in Red Wing,

MN, the school experienced financial difficulties and closed for a time before relocating here in 1880. The lone architectural survivor from the campus's early days is Old Main, which opened in 1884. Numerous other buildings were added as the university grew—it enrolls about 4,000 students—and the campus now occupies about ten square blocks. Overall, the campus doesn't have a strong sense of design—the buildings seem to have fallen in place as needed—though there is a mall that extends north from Old Main to the new Klas Center athletic complex.

Giddens Alumni Learning Center

6 Giddens Alumni Learning Center

1556 Hewitt Ave.

*HGA, 1972 / includes entrance of former **library**, Clarence H. Johnston, 1907*

Perhaps the best modern building on campus, an energetic compilation of brick-clad volumes with monitors poking up through the roof. The old campus library was once on this site: its entrance was preserved within the learning center's lobby.

7 Old Main *L N*

1536 Hewitt Ave.

Warren H. Hayes, 1884

This towered brick pile is just what an old campus building should look like. It was constructed, quickly, when Hamline's first university hall burned down in 1883, just three years after opening. Architect Warren Hayes is best known locally for his Romanesque Revival churches, but here he did a fine turn in the Victorian Gothic style. The pointed arch windows, the bands of brownstone threading through

Old Main, Hamline University

the brick facades, and the steep-roofed tower with its dormers and spire are all signature features of the style, which strove for colorful and picturesque effects.

8 School of Law Building

1492 Hewitt Ave.

HGA, 1980

Fronted by a massive screen made up of angled concrete fins, this muscular piece of modernism suggests that whatever else the law may be, it's definitely not for sissies.

9 White (President's) House

830 Simpson St.

Clarence H. Johnston, 1903

Built by Hamline trustee Joseph Hackney and later donated to the university, this Classical Revival house was originally located a block or so away on Hewitt Ave. It was moved here in 1947 when a residence hall was built on its old site.

10 Hamline United Methodist Church

1514 Englewood Ave.

Slifer and Abrahamson, 1928 / Art: stone carving, Carlo Brioschi and Adolph Minuti, 1928 / stained glass, Andreas Ruud Larsen and Gaytee Studios, 1928 and later

A local landmark built after an earlier church burned down in

1925. Clad in Indiana limestone, the church follows familiar Gothic Revival models, although both

Hamline United Methodist Church

its nave and its transepts are shorter than usual. A splendid 160-foot-high copper spire atop the church sprouts gargoyles, crockets, and other Gothic paraphernalia. The church is also notable for the high quality of its sculpture, stained glass, and woodwork. Architect Frederick Slifer, who had trained under Emmanuel Masqueray and Cass Gilbert, was a member of the congregation.

11 Oric O. Whited House

1538 Englewood Ave.

1887

A brick and shingle Queen Anne with scroll brackets curling beneath the front gable. The original owner was a banker.

12 Hamline-Midway (Henry Hale Memorial) Branch Library

1558 Minnehaha Ave. West

St. Paul City Architect (Frank X. Tewes), 1930 / remodeled, 1985, 1990

A pleasing little Collegiate Gothic building, just fancy enough to let you know that going to the library should always be thought of as a special occasion.

13 Knox Presbyterian Church

1536 Minnehaha Ave. West

Alban and Hausler, 1914 / addition, 1957

This church is a hybrid, with Prairie Style features stirred into a Classical Revival mold. While the banded windows and geometric ornament are Prairielike, the overall composition—which includes end pavilions, a central parapet, and a cornice—has a restrained classical feel.

14 William A. Davern House

1288 Hubbard Ave.

1887

A Victorian delight, lifted out of the realm of the ordinary by four arches that enframe the open second-story porch. The arches, it must be said, hardly fit the overall design of the house, but, then again, architecture would be a dull thing indeed if the high-style decencies didn't get slapped around once in awhile by practitioners of the vernacular.

15 St. Columba Catholic Church !

1327 Lafond Ave.

Barry Byrne (Chicago), 1951

An extraordinary church from Barry Byrne, a designer whose formal schooling ended in the ninth grade but who during the course of his long career produced a body of work unique in American architecture. St. Columba is one of his last, and best, church designs. Along with Christ Lutheran Church (1949) in Minneapolis, it ranks as a high point of modern church architecture in the Twin Cities.

St. Columba parish built its first church here in 1915. As the congregation grew after World

St. Columba Catholic Church

War II, pastor Michael Casey hired Byrne to design a striking new church in the modern manner. Byrne did not disappoint. Angled into an unassuming mid-block site, St. Columba is notable for its unusual shape, its one-of-a-kind details, and the quality of the light that bathes its interior. Its pointed oval or "fish" shape is one that Byrne first used for a church in Kansas City, MO, in 1949. This shape, created by the overlapping of two circles, was an early Christian symbol. The distinctive bell tower wasn't Byrne's idea, however: Father Casey insisted on an "Irish" round tower for his church. The church's curving side walls, clad in smooth limestone, have tall, slitlike windows that

St. Columba Catholic Church interior

rise above low side aisles with horizontal bands of blue and yellow stained glass. There's also a small side chapel that juts off from the rear of the church.

The exterior detailing—from the slots cut into the tower to the granite crosses imbedded in the walls near the front entrance to the metal cladding on the main doors—is as idiosyncratic as the church's form. Like all of Byrne's best work, St. Columba evokes a highly personal vision, well removed from the ordinary avenues of architectural and religious expression.

The rather stark interior is notable for the quality of its light, which even on sunny days is mysterious and ethereal, inviting worship and contemplation. Within is also one of the few flaws in Byrne's design: an altar that seems undersized for such a large worship space.

1462 Charles Ave

16 House

1462 Charles Ave.

1911

Most concrete-block houses were built as foursquares, but this one has front and side gables as well as bands of cast ornament along the roofline, around the windows, and on the front porch.

LOST 1 *The block along Charles Ave. between Asbury and Simpson Sts. was once the site of the **Northern Pacific (later Samaritan) Hospital,** built in 1919. It was one of seven hospitals once maintained through a beneficial association established by the Northern Pacific to provide health care to employees at a nominal cost. The hospital*

was torn down in the late 1980s to make way for the townhomes that now occupy the site.

17 Lena Howard House

1672 Blair Ave.

1926

One of the city's most distinctive Spanish-Moorish Revival houses, small but with a lot going on. The front door lies behind a boldly arched central porch reached via a low-walled patio topped by a wooden pergola. Wall niches, plaques, and decorative ironwork complete the composition.

POI A Alley (old territorial road)

Block bounded by Blair and Van Buren Aves. and Wheeler and Aldine Sts.

ca. 1850s

The alley that cuts through this block on the diagonal is a rare remnant of an old territorial road that once linked St. Paul to St. Anthony (now Minneapolis).

18 John Dewey House

1684 Van Buren Ave.

1889

One of the loveliest pattern book Queen Anne houses in St. Paul. The porch—with its horseshoe arch, spooled spindlework, and scrolling brackets—is wonderful.

19 House

1663 Van Buren Ave.

1886

A tall Victorian with an unusual modern addition: a rooftop viewing platform set at a 45-degree angle to the street and reached by what looks to be a dizzying flight of stairs.

St. Anthony Park

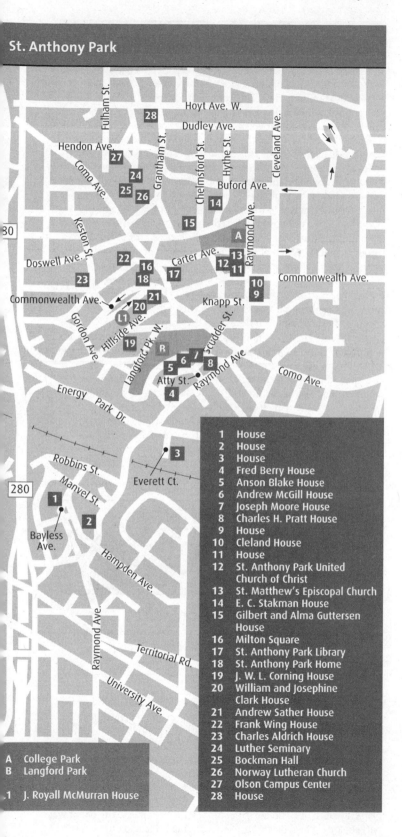

1	House
2	House
3	House
4	Fred Berry House
5	Anson Blake House
6	Andrew McGill House
7	Joseph Moore House
8	Charles H. Pratt House
9	House
10	Cleland House
11	House
12	St. Anthony Park United Church of Christ
13	St. Matthew's Episcopal Church
14	E. C. Stakman House
15	Gilbert and Alma Guttersen House
16	Milton Square
17	St. Anthony Park Library
18	St. Anthony Park Home
19	J. W. L. Corning House
20	William and Josephine Clark House
21	Andrew Sather House
22	Frank Wing House
23	Charles Aldrich House
24	Luther Seminary
25	Bockman Hall
26	Norway Lutheran Church
27	Olson Campus Center
28	House

A	College Park
B	Langford Park
.1	J. Royall McMurran House

St. Anthony Park

St. Anthony Park was the largest "genteel" residential enclave created in the Twin Cities during the Victorian era. Winding streets that rebuke the standard grid define the neighborhood's character. They sashay up and down hills, wander past small parks tucked into narrow valleys, and sweep past rows of frame houses occupying crooked, well-forested lots. Much of the neighborhood has the feel of an urban retreat, safe from the rude flux of the world, and it is indeed a pleasant place. This unruffled state of affairs was once maintained with the help of rules banning the sale of liquor within the neighborhood. Beer and wine have now infiltrated at select locations, but the communal peace does not appear to have been greatly disturbed as a result.

Although St. Anthony Park was designed primarily as a residential community, industry developed along the railroad tracks that cut through its heart. Much of the southern portion of the neighborhood, between the rail lines and University Avenue, remains devoted to commerce and industry. To the north, along Como Avenue, the neighborhood also attracted institutions, including Luther Seminary. The seminary's campus is home to the Old Muskego Church (1844), a rebuilt log structure moved here from Wisconsin.

Because it's largely residential, St. Anthony Park offers little in the way of monumental architecture. Most of its homes were built from about 1885 to 1930 and come dressed in all the usual styles. There are also a fair number of architect-designed modern homes. Among the neighborhood's outstanding houses are three large Queen Annes (1888–90) arrayed along the 2200 block of Scudder Street. The neighborhood's signature building may well be Milton Square (1909–12), a charming shop and restaurant complex on Como and Carter avenues. Nearby is the elegant St. Anthony Park Library (1917), one of three Beaux-Arts branch libraries in St. Paul built with money donated by Andrew Carnegie.

1 House

977 Bayless Ave.

Charles Buell, 1891

A member of the neighborhood's architectural charm squad. Its most captivating detail is a towerlike dormer that curves out to form a tiny balcony framing a window above the front porch.

2 House (Bethesda Norwegian Lutheran Church)

969 Raymond Ave.

1909 / remodeled, ca. 1970s

Before being converted to housing—work that was done in the tender spirit of a massacre—this concrete-block structure served as a church, initially for Norwegian Lutherans. Its wooden bargeboards, which decorate the gables like drooping icicles, are quite distinctive.

1048 Everett Ct.

3 House (Great Northern Passenger Depot)

1048 Everett Ct.

1888

Everett Ct. is a dead-end street lined on one side by houses built between about 1885 and 1890 by the St. Anthony Park Co. The street's prize, however, is at the very end: a house that began its life as a neighborhood depot for what would become the Great Northern Railway. The depot was originally located on the north side of the tracks, just west of Raymond Ave. It was moved here

Joseph Moore House

after commuter rail service to and from St. Anthony Park was discontinued in the 1890s.

4 Fred Berry House

1113 Raymond Ave.

1889

An architectural oddball, with a spike of a tower thrusting up from a beveled corner. Supported in part by a single column, the tower is reminiscent of a pirate resting on his peg leg.

5 Anson Blake House

2205 Scudder St.

William A. Hunt, ca. 1886–90

6 Andrew McGill House N *L*

2203 Scudder St.

William A. Hunt, 1888 / remodeled, ca. 1930s

7 Joseph Moore House

2201 Scudder St.

William A. Hunt, 1889

These towered Victorians form a fine architectural ensemble on their high, hilly lots; together they convey a picture of the genteel good life imagined by St. Anthony Park's founders. All three were designed by Minneapolis architect William A. Hunt, who soon moved on to Duluth. The trio's centerpiece is the Andrew McGill House, built not long after its

owner was elected governor of Minnesota in 1887. Joseph Moore was a business associate of McGill's and later his private secretary. Anson Blake was secretary of the St. Anthony Park Co. and the uncle of its president.

The McGill and Moore houses were once nearly identical. In the 1930s, however, the McGill House lost its porches and other decorative elements in a remodeling. The Moore House, by contrast, retains most of its original exterior features. The Blake House was always smaller than the other two and was encased in stucco for many years before being restored.

8 Charles H. Pratt House

1181 Raymond Ave.

P. S. Meacham, 1887

A small tower with a swirling ice cream cone top inexplicably erupts from the roof of this house, making it one of the neighborhood's curiosities.

9 House

1306 Raymond Ave.

2004

An infill house that doesn't try to be nostalgic. It's white, stuccoed, and modernistic; it has a barrel-vaulted metal roof; and it doesn't look at all bad next door to the Cleland House.

St. Anthony Park

10 Cleland House

2090 Commonwealth Ave.

C. W. Covington (builder), 1887

A nice example of the Shingle Style, with distinctive arched windows. The house across the street at 2095 Commonwealth was similar before being greatly altered after a fire.

11 House (Northern Pacific Passenger Depot)

2107 Commonwealth Ave.

1885

This old depot originally stood along the Northern Pacific tracks at the south end of Langford Park. It was moved around the turn of the last century and converted to use as a house. Commuter rail service was never successful in the Twin Cities, in part due to the lack of density in residential neighborhoods, and this station was closed once streetcars arrived in the 1890s.

12 St. Anthony Park United Church of Christ

2129 Commonwealth Ave.

Clarence H. Johnston, 1915 / restored, Setter Leach and Lindstrom, ca. 1997

13 St. Matthew's Episcopal Church

2136 Carter Ave.

Clarence H. Johnston, 1914 / addition, ca. 1990s

This is the only block in the Twin Cities where you'll find back-to-back churches by the same architect. Both are more or less Gothic Revival in style.

POI A College Park

Raymond and Carter Aves.

ca. 1907

As with most other parks in the neighborhood, this was once the site of a small pond. Preserved for park use in 1907, it's a charming spot—a little green glen ringed by trees.

14 E. C. Stakman House

1411 Hythe St.

Edwin Lundie, 1924

A shingle-clad house that shows how skillfully Lundie could manipulate Colonial Revival forms to achieve picturesque effects. He designed another Colonial house at 1452 Hythe.

Gilbert and Alma Guttersen House

15 Gilbert and Alma Guttersen House ("Burr Oaks")

2181 Doswell Ave.

Alban and Hausler, 1916

Although this large house falls into the general category of Craftsman, its symmetrical front facade, not to mention the canopy-*cum*–port cochere on the east side, gives it the monumental quality of a Beaux-Arts mansion.

Milton Square

16 Milton Square

2256–62½ Como Ave., 2226–42 Carter Ave.

Franklin H. Ellerbe, 1909 / Ellerbe and Round, 1912 / later additions

This complex of quaint, irregular buildings seems perfectly attuned to the neighborhood's spirit. It was built in two stages and originally included a pair of social halls (the Old Fireside Inn and Tamarack Lodge Hall, both gone) as well as shops and apartments. To accommodate these diverse uses, architect Franklin Ellerbe created an amiable gathering of shingled, stuccoed, and half-timbered buildings that wander around the corner of Como and Carter Aves. Over the years, there's been at least one addition to the complex, while the storefronts have received the inevitable remodelings. Even so, Milton Square remains the neighborhood's great charmer.

St. Anthony Park Library

17 St. Anthony Park Library N *L*

2245 Como Ave.

St. Paul City Architect (Charles A. Hausler), 1917 / addition, Philip Broussard, 2000

Like the Riverview Library on the West Side, this elegant building has an enormously dignified and gracious presence in the community. The library—essentially an oblong brick box with arched windows—evokes timeless images of classicism yet manages to be inviting at the same time. A children's reading room in the shape of a rotunda was added to the rear in 2000, and it works beautifully, complementing the original building but also making a statement of its own.

18 St. Anthony Park Home (Jean Martin Brown Receiving Home)

2237 Commonwealth Ave.

Ernest Kennedy, 1903 / additions, 1925, 1959, and later

Now a nursing home, this much-modified Tudor Revival building was originally constructed by the Children's Aid (later Children's Home) Society as a receiving home for children coming to Minnesota on the so-called orphan trains from New York City and elsewhere in the Northeast.

J. W. L. Corning House

19 J. W. L. Corning House

2266 Hillside Ave.

Clarence H. Johnston, 1917

A souped-up bungalow, with a more complex array of volumes than you normally find in homes of its type. It appears to have come down through the years beautifully intact.

20 William and Josephine Clark House

2251 Hillside Ave.

William and Josephine Clark, ca. 1901–4

One of the neighborhood's most impressive houses, its basement and first floor made of rubble stone. Because it rises from a hilly site, the stonework has the feel of a natural rock outcropping.

POI B Langford Park

Near Como Ave. and Knapp St.

ca. 1890

The largest of the half dozen or so ponds that once dotted St. Anthony Park was located here before it was filled in around 1890. The park is named after Nathaniel P. Langford, an early community investor who in the 1860s explored the area that would become Yellowstone National Park. He later served as the park's first superintendent.

LOST 1 *The home at 2268 Commonwealth Ave. occupies a portion of the site of the* **J. Royall McMurran House.** *The Shingle Style mansion rose from a rubble stone base (parts of which were incorporated*

*in the house now here) and presided
over a hilltop estate encompassing
the equivalent of 12 lots. Designed*

J. Royall McMurran House, 1888

*by Hodgson and Stem of St. Paul, it
was built in 1888 but burned to the
ground just 12 years later.*

21 Andrew Sather House

2252 Commonwealth Ave.

Andrew Sather (builder), 1923

Sather was a woodcarver, and
some of his handiwork is evident
on the wonderful bargeboards
that decorate the porch of this
house, which is otherwise a standard bungalow.

22 Frank Wing House

2267 Carter Ave.

1913

A house that combines Colonial Revival and Craftsman elements in an intriguing way.
Frank Wing was a cartoonist
who worked for several newspapers, including the *Tribune* in
Minneapolis and the *Pioneer
Press* in St. Paul. He also wrote
and illustrated books. Later in
his career, Wing befriended a
young St. Paul cartoonist named
Charles Schulz, who went on to
some success.

23 Charles Aldrich House

1323 Keston St.

Charles Aldrich, ca. 1890–95

A lovely house that eludes the
usual stylistic pigeonholes. Its
original owner, Charles Aldrich,
taught "mechanical training"
at the University of Minnesota
School of Agriculture but was
also a practicing architect. This
house is most notable for its elegant front porch.

24 Luther Seminary

2481 Como Ave.

1900 and later

The United Norwegian Lutheran
Church in America began building a seminary here in 1900, not
long after the Como-Harriet
interurban streetcar line opened.
Because of organizational changes,
the seminary has gone by a number of names over the years. Now
affiliated with the Evangelical
Lutheran Church in America,
the seminary took on its current
name in 1994. It enrolls about
800 full- and part-time students,
making it the nation's largest
Lutheran seminary. The campus
consists of two sections: an original portion south of Hendon Ave.
along Como and a newer section
to the north and west on the former site of Breck School. The
older part is the more attractive
of the two, its buildings clustered
along a wooded hillside.

Bockman Hall

25 Bockman Hall N

2375 Como Ave.

*Omeyer and Thori, 1901 /
addition, William Linley Alban,
1923 / later additions*

The seminary's oldest building, a
brick pile with colossal Corinthian
columns guarding the main
entrance. This temple front is
rather odd, however, in that a
portion of the top floor projects
out between the entablature and
the pediment above. The architects, Omeyer and Thori, are primarily known for their flamboyant Queen Anne–style houses,
but here they got the classical
religion.

Norway Lutheran Church

26 Norway Lutheran (Muskego) Church *L*

1844

Hidden away at the edge of the campus east of Bockman and Gullixson halls, this little log church was built by settlers at Muskego, WI (near Milwaukee), in 1844. It's believed to be the oldest Norwegian Lutheran church building in the United States. Purchased by the United Lutheran Church in 1904, it was dismantled, moved here, and reconstructed. The rough-hewn interior, formed by oak logs with black walnut columns, displays the craftsmanship of its builder.

27 Olson Campus Center

1490 Fulham St.

HGA, 1985

A series of low volumes set into the hillside and surrounded by an ingenious system of walkways that provide links to other parts of campus.

28 House

1543 Grantham St.

Edwin Lundie, ca. 1928

A Colonial Revival house, set sideways on its lot. As always with Lundie, the quality of the detailing is what elevates this house out of the realm of the ordinary.

Falcon Heights

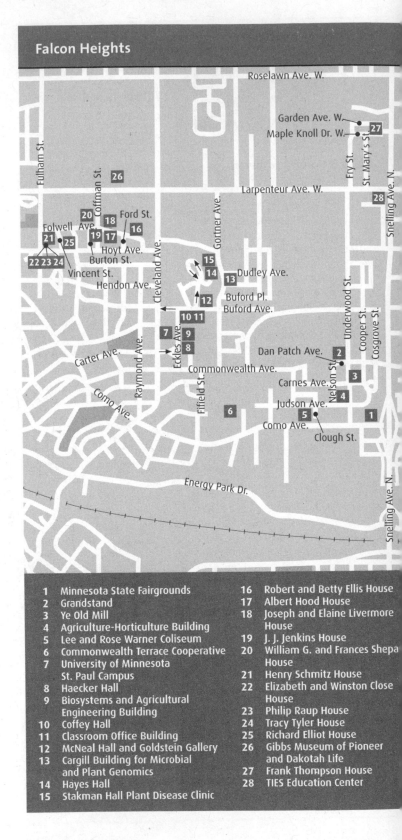

1   Minnesota State Fairgrounds
2   Grandstand
3   Ye Old Mill
4   Agriculture-Horticulture Building
5   Lee and Rose Warner Coliseum
6   Commonwealth Terrace Cooperative
7   University of Minnesota
    St. Paul Campus
8   Haecker Hall
9   Biosystems and Agricultural
    Engineering Building
10 Coffey Hall
11 Classroom Office Building
12 McNeal Hall and Goldstein Gallery
13 Cargill Building for Microbial
    and Plant Genomics
14 Hayes Hall
15 Stakman Hall Plant Disease Clinic

16 Robert and Betty Ellis House
17 Albert Hood House
18 Joseph and Elaine Livermore
    House
19 J. J. Jenkins House
20 William G. and Frances Shepa
    House
21 Henry Schmitz House
22 Elizabeth and Winston Close
    House
23 Philip Raup House
24 Tracy Tyler House
25 Richard Elliot House
26 Gibbs Museum of Pioneer
    and Dakotah Life
27 Frank Thompson House
28 TIES Education Center

Falcon Heights

This small suburban community, portions of which form a peninsula that juts into St. Paul along its northern border, is best known as home to the Minnesota State Fairgrounds and the University of Minnesota's St. Paul campus. However, Falcon Heights also includes a commercial district at the intersection of Larpenteur and Snelling avenues, as well as blocks of housing, some from as early as the 1920s but mostly dating to after World War II.

The state fairgrounds, home to several noteworthy Moderne-style buildings, is familiar territory to millions of Minnesotans. After years of wandering, the fair settled north of Como Avenue here in 1885. The site, originally 200 acres, had previously been occupied by the Ramsey County Poor Farm. Today, the fairgrounds encompasses more than 300 acres and extends all the way north to Larpenteur.

The university's St. Paul campus, directly north and west of the fairgrounds, was also founded in the 1880s, primarily as an agricultural school. It now spreads out across 540 acres and includes large test fields as well as a core of more than 100 buildings. Adjacent to the campus is University Grove, a unique neighborhood of houses designed by many of the Twin Cities' most prominent architects. Also close by the campus is Commonwealth Terrace (ca. 1950), one of the oldest and largest family housing cooperatives in North America.

Several individual properties of note can also be found in Falcon Heights. The Gibbs Museum of Pioneer and Dakotah Life, operated by the Ramsey County Historical Society, includes a farmhouse that dates to the 1850s. Not far from the farm is the Frank Thompson House (1915), one of the few Prairie Style homes located in the Twin Cities' suburbs. Falcon Heights can also boast of a significant Moderne-style office building, the old Farmers' Union Grain Terminal Association (1947) at Snelling and Larpenteur avenues.

1 Minnesota State Fairgrounds

North and west of Como and Snelling Aves.

1885 and later

Minnesota's first State Fair was held in 1859, but it wasn't until the 1880s that this site became its permanent home. More than 1.5 million people typically attend the annual event during its 12-day run that begins in August. Beloved for its stick-based, oil-drenched cuisine and seemingly timeless attractions, the fair is one of the nation's largest, and it's a rare Minnesotan who hasn't

Minnesota State Fairgrounds, 1975

passed through the gates at least once for a day of munching with the masses.

The fairground's first big building—on a site near today's intersection of Carnes Ave. and Underwood St.—was an exhibition hall crowned by a 120-foot-high wooden dome, which stood until a fire claimed it in 1944. Major bouts of construction occurred at the fairgrounds early in the twentieth century, during the 1930s (when the WPA did much of the work), in the years after World War II, and in the 1960s. However, buildings from every decade since 1900 occupy the grounds, which now sprawl across 340 acres.

No architectural masterpieces lurk among the fairground's collection of livestock barns, food stands, eating halls, and display buildings. Even so, the architectural free-for-all includes some impressive structures, especially Moderne monuments such as the Agriculture-Horticulture Building (1947) and the Lee and Rose Warner Coliseum (1952). The most interesting structure on the fairgrounds may be Ye Old Mill (ca. 1913–15), a historic tunnel of love.

2 Grandstand

Dan Patch Ave. and Nelson St.

Clarence H. Johnston, 1909 / 1919 / renovated, KKE Architects, 2002–4

One of the fairground's oldest buildings. It's been the scene of races, air shows, locomotive crashes, and even spectacles such as the *Fall of Troy* (staged in 1927 but without real Greeks). Nowadays, the entertainment is largely limited to concerts and fireworks.

3 Ye Old Mill

Carnes Ave. and Underwood St.

John H. Keenan (builder), ca. 1913–15

The oldest ride at the fair, this tunnel of love winds for a quarter of a mile in serpentine fashion, its wooden boats floating

in a 17-inch-deep channel. An engine turns a mill wheel that generates the current needed to

Inside Ye Old Mill, 1973

push the boats along. Still operated by the Keenan family, the ride is one of the fair's supreme nostalgic pleasures. Similar tunnels of love survive at only a few other venues, including the Iowa and Kansas state fairs.

Agriculture-Horticulture Building, 1947

4 Agriculture-Horticulture Building

Judson Ave. and Underwood St.

Kindy Wright, 1947

With its eight corridors radiating out from a central tower, this concrete building is one of the most recognizable on the fairgrounds. Kindy Wright, an architect and consultant for the fair from 1941 to 1975, designed several of its most prominent buildings. Moderne-style designs like this one and the nearby **4-H Building** (1940) seem to have been his specialty.

5 Lee and Rose Warner Coliseum

Judson Ave. and Clough St.

Kindy Wright?, 1952

Another of the fairgrounds' Moderne monuments, now used for shows year round. Built of reinforced concrete, it sports a series of buttress-like projecting ribs that support the vaulted roof. Relief panels depicting agricultural scenes provide the only ornamental note.

6 Commonwealth Terrace Cooperative

1250 Fifield St. at Como Ave.

ca. 1950s and later

This is among the oldest and largest family housing cooperatives in North America, providing 464 residential units for University of Minnesota students. The architecture—pure 1950s functionalism—won't thrill you, but at least it makes no pretenses about what it is.

7 University of Minnesota St. Paul Campus

Cleveland Ave. North and Buford Ave.

various architects, ca. 1880s and later

This campus, established in the 1880s as home to the university's agricultural programs, has a far more relaxed atmosphere than the main Minneapolis campus. Buffered by test fields to the north and east, the campus feels as though it's out in the country even though it's only miles away from the downtowns of both St. Paul and Minneapolis. No grand scheme similar to Cass Gilbert's mall on the university's East Bank campus is evident here, although various plans have shaped the siting of buildings over the years. A ridge paralleling Cleveland Ave. provides the most visible organizing feature. Some of the oldest buildings on campus crown this ridge, forming a central spine. Other buildings fan out to the south and east to complete the campus ensemble.

Architecturally, the campus offers the usual collegiate mishmash, although the mostly brick buildings along the spine make at least some effort to relate to one another. Among the better buildings on campus are those designed in the early twentieth century by Clarence H. Johnston, such as Coffey Hall (1906). In fact, as a group, they're a step above the dull brick boxes Johnston designed for the main university campus. The modern-era buildings here are generally less impressive, but there are a few of note, including Cargill Building for Microbial and Plant Genomics (2003), designed by Architectural Alliance.

8 Haecker Hall (Dairy Husbandry Building)

1364 Eckles Ave.

Clarence H. Johnston, 1923

9 Biosystems and Agricultural Engineering Building

1390 Eckles Ave.

Clarence H. Johnston, 1913

Coffey Hall

10 Coffey Hall

1420 Eckles Ave.

Clarence H. Johnston, 1906

These three brick buildings form a row along Eckles Ave. Though some details differ, they're essentially the same: all are three stories high and Renaissance Revival in style, have entry pavilions and decorative tilework, and feature hipped roofs with distinctive polygonal dormers.

11 Classroom Office Building

1994 Buford Ave.

Griswold and Rauma, 1972

Brick buildings with long bands of windows and shed-roofed atriums were much in favor in the 1970s, and here's a classic, if that's the right word, of the genre.

12 McNeal Hall (Home Economics Building) and Goldstein Gallery

1985 Buford Ave.

Clarence H. Johnston, 1915 / addition, Hodne-Stageberg Partners, 1975

Another of Johnston's Renaissance Revival buildings. The 1970s addition, with its banded windows and large cutouts, is well done.

Cargill Building for Microbial and Plant Genomics

13 Cargill Building for Microbial and Plant Genomics

1500 Gortner Ave.

Architectural Alliance, 2003

A slick example of eclectic modernism. The building offers a mix of cladding materials—stone, brick, glass, metal shingles, and corrugated metal—as well as a variety of forms, including a three-story cylinder that holds meeting rooms. As with many newer buildings, this one also incorporates numerous sustainable design features aimed at conserving energy use.

14 Hayes Hall (Agronomy Building)

1509 Gortner Ave.

Clarence H. Johnston, Jr., 1941

15 Stakman Hall Plant Disease Clinic

1519 Gortner Ave.

Clarence H. Johnston, Jr., 1941

Clarence H. Johnston, Jr., designed at least five campus buildings in the Moderne style. These two, on the eastern slope of the ridge that bisects campus, form mirror images of each other.

University Grove

Folwell and Hoyt Aves. between Fulham St. and Cleveland Ave. North

various architects, 1928 and later

This remarkable community of more than 100 architect-designed houses, situated on woodsy lots along gently curving streets, was founded as an enclave for University of Minnesota tenured faculty and administrators. It's best known for its many high-style modernist houses from the 1950s and 1960s. Architects Winston and Elizabeth Close (15 houses) and Ralph Rapson (eight houses) are especially well represented.

University Grove actually goes back to 1928, when a university official conceived of it as a way to attract and keep outstanding teachers and administrators. The neighborhood has several unusual features: residents own their homes but not their lots, which are leased from the university; there are shared commons that serve as children's play areas; every home has to be designed by an architect; and no home can be built costing more than a specified maximum amount (initially $10,000 but later much increased).

The first homes, in various Period Revival styles, were built around 1930 along Folwell and Hoyt Aves. between Fulham and Coffman Sts. More modern styles began to appear as early as the mid-1930s, but it wasn't until after World War II that modernism became the preferred style for new homes. In the 1960s, the community was extended four blocks east to Cleveland Ave. It was largely built out by 1970. Perhaps because they're similar in size and in their landscaping, the diverse houses here manage to coexist quite comfortably—a small miracle given that architectural modernism has never been renowned for its ensemble work.

16 Robert and Betty Ellis House

2111 Folwell Ave.

James Stageberg, 1968

A one-story house faced in vertical cypress boards with a drum-like tower rising from the center. The room within the tower was designed to accommodate the original owners' grand piano.

17 Albert Hood House

2160 Folwell Ave.

Ralph Rapson and Associates, 1964

By the mid-1960s, Rapson's houses were taking on the energetic look that became his trademark. This house moves in and out and up and down, its restless volumes organized around a front courtyard. It's said that Albert Hood was so fond of this house that he built an identical one a few years later when he moved to Iowa.

Joseph and Elaine Livermore House

18 Joseph and Elaine Livermore House

2179 Folwell Ave.

Ralph Rapson and Associates, 1969

Rapson at his most, well, Rapsonian. This small but busy house features deeply recessed windows, walls that project beyond the foundations, and a series of courtyards that separate its shed-roofed volumes. All in all, the most dynamic of Rapson's University Grove houses.

19 J. J. Jenkins House

2190 Folwell Ave.

Close Associates, 1957 / addition, Close Associates (Gar Hargens), ca. 2002

The original portion of this house is a good example of the functionalist designs that Winston

J. J. Jenkins House

and Elizabeth Close typically produced in the 1950s. The addition, which houses a library, is a cube clad in multicolored panels that look to have been arranged at random but in fact follow a proportioning system developed by the French architect Le Corbusier.

William G. and Frances Shepard House

20 William G. and Frances Shepard House

2197 Folwell Ave.

Ralph Rapson and Associates, 1957

Rapson's first house in University Grove. The flat roof and the courtyard between the house and garage are typical of his early work. Other houses designed by Rapson can be found at 1564 Burton St., 2118 and 2140 Folwell Ave., 2147 Hoyt Ave., and 1595 Vincent St.

Henry Schmitz House

21 Henry Schmitz House

2292 Folwell Ave.

Edwin Lundie, 1932

Lundie always had a poetic way with Colonial Revival houses, and that's certainly evident here. The front entrance to this shingle-clad house is particularly fine, with delicate pilasters and carefully scaled sidelights framing a wide door.

Elizabeth and Winston Close House

22 Elizabeth and Winston Close House

1588 Fulham St.

Close Associates, 1953

23 Philip Raup House

1572 Fulham St.

Close Associates, 1954

24 Tracy Tyler House

1564 Fulham St.

Close and Scheu, 1939

The squarish, two-story Tyler House is the first of Winston and Elizabeth Close's many homes in University Grove, while the flat-roofed Raup House next door is more typical of their mature work. The latter has a side entrance, wood and stucco cladding, a tuck-under garage, and a canopy that shields the west-facing windows from afternoon sun. The Closes' own house, an oblong two-story box sheathed in horizontal wood siding, makes ample use of natural light and summarizes their quiet, carefully crafted brand of modernism. Additional houses designed by the Closes, all dating from the 1950s and 1960s, can be found at 1578 and 1586 Burton St.; 2124, 2202, 2203, 2225, and 2286 Folwell Ave.; 2159 and 2285 Hoyt Ave.; and 1572 and 1580 Northrop St.

25 Richard Elliot House

1564 Vincent St.

Robertson and Jones, 1935

This two-story brick Moderne house was the first in University

Richard Elliot House

Grove to break away from the Period Revival styles of the 1930s. The iron canopy above the front door is an unusual feature.

26 Gibbs Museum of Pioneer and Dakotah Life N

2097 Larpenteur Ave. West

ca. 1854 and later

Operated by the Ramsey County Historical Society, this museum centers around a farmstead established here in 1849 by Heman and Jane Gibbs. The farmhouse itself began as a one-room structure made of logs and planks, built in 1854. Later, as the Gibbses expanded the house, they incorporated the original section into the walls of what is now a sitting room. The house, which is very plain in keeping with its rural origins, includes a large, L-shaped open porch. Other buildings in the museum complex are a reconstructed sod house, a replica of a Dakota bark lodge, two barns (one dating to 1910 and the other designed in the 1950s by Edwin Lundie), and a one-room schoolhouse built in 1878 in western Minnesota and moved here in 1966.

Frank Thompson House

27 Frank Thompson House

1607 Maple Knoll Dr. West

Bentley and Hausler?, 1915

A first-class brick and stucco Prairie Style house that includes a full complement of art-glass windows. The likely architects were Percy Bentley and Charles A. Hausler, who designed at least two other fine Prairie houses, both in St. Paul, in 1914–15. The house was built for Frank Thompson, who owned an electrical engineering company.

TIES Education Center

28 TIES Education Center (Farmers' Union Grain Terminal Association)

1667 Snelling Ave. North

Ray Gauger and Co. (with Harry Firminger), 1947 / additions, 1950s and later

This superb late art deco building was constructed in 1947 as headquarters of the Farmers' Union Grain Terminal Association (GTA), a large cooperative. It replaced a large country house known as "Crossroads," built for University of Minnesota botanist Fred W.

Snyder and designed by Emmanuel Masqueray, architect of the St. Paul Cathedral. Clad in Indiana limestone, the building mixes the Zigzag and Moderne phases of art deco, and it's one of the last great examples of these styles in the Twin Cities. It consists of a four-story central pavilion from which three-story wings extend along Snelling and Larpenteur Aves. Notable features include curving corner windows, decorative aluminum spandrels, and relief sculptures atop the entry pavilion. Within, there's a wood-paneled lobby with a symbolic design of ripening grain worked into the terrazzo floor. Although Ray Gauger and Co. is the architect of record, some sources attribute the design to Harry Firminger, an itinerant St. Paul architect known for his command of the art deco style.

The GTA, founded in 1938, merged with another cooperative to become Harvest States (now Harvest States Cenex) in the 1980s. TIES, a consortium established by 38 Minnesota school districts to provide technology and information services, now occupies the building.

Parker-Marshall House, 30 Irvine Pk., St. Paul, 1852

Greek Revival (1840s–1860s): Simple, square massing; gabled or hipped roof; trim band (representing classical entablature) beneath the eaves; front door with sidelights; columned portico (in more elaborate examples). Mostly houses. Once common, Greek Revival is now quite rare in the Twin Cities, although several dozen examples can still be found in the Irvine Park and West Seventh neighborhoods of St. Paul. Examples of the related **Federal Style**, a precursor of Greek Revival, are even rarer.

Sigma Phi Epsilon Fraternity, 400 Tenth Ave. Southeast, Minneapolis, 1856

Gothic Revival (1860–80): Irregular massing; steeply pitched roof; gables with decorated bargeboards; pointed-arch windows (not in all examples); porch with decorative pillars. Houses, churches. Few works in this style have survived intact in the Twin Cities. See also **Eastlake** and **Victorian Gothic**.

Burbank-Livingston-Griggs House, 432 Summit Ave., St. Paul, 1863

Italianate (1860s–early 1880s): Massing that ranges from squarish to quite irregular; hipped roof (sometimes with steep central gable); overhanging eaves with paired brackets; tall, narrow, and usually arched windows with heavy crowns (often called hoods); off-center tower (in larger examples). Houses, public and commercial buildings (where windows hoods are often the key identifying feature). Italianate buildings remain fairly common in older parts of St. Paul and Minneapolis. Also called **Italian Villa** style.

Alexander Ramsey House, 265 South Exchange St., St. Paul, 1872

French Second Empire (1860s–early 1880s): Closely related to Italianate but with one distinguishing feature: a prominent mansard roof. This style also tends to be a bit more ornate than Italianate. Houses, public and commercial buildings. The number of surviving examples in the Twin Cities is small.

Minnehaha Railroad Depot, 49th St. East and Minnehaha Ave., Minneapolis, ca. 1875

Eastlake (1870s–early 1880s): Like many Victorian styles, this one can be elusive to identify and not all architectural historians recognize it. Named after English architect Charles Eastlake, the style might best be characterized as a variant of Gothic Revival. Typical features include exposed structural members (such as corner braces), patterned wall surfaces often divided into horizontal fields, and delicate ornament in the form of knobs, cut-out or incised shapes, and other types of machined woodwork. This style, generally used for modest wooden houses and commercial buildings, is common in older working-class neighborhoods in the Twin Cities. Also known as **Eastlake Revival**.

Old Main, Hamline University, 1536 Hewitt Ave., St. Paul, 1884

Victorian Gothic (1875–85): Blocky massing; high, narrow windows, sometimes with pointed arches; agitated roofline with numerous gables, dormers, and chimneys; multicolored facades (often featuring red brick interlaced with white stone). This style was used for large commercial buildings, schools, churches, and mansions, while the earlier Gothic Revival was confined mostly to small, wooden structures. Quite a few Victorian Gothic buildings can still be found in the Twin Cities, although some of the most prominent examples, such as the Ryan Hotel in St. Paul, are gone.

Eugene and Christina Villaume House, 123 West Isabel St., St. Paul, 1895

Queen Anne (1880s–early 1890s): Picturesque massing with towers, turrets, bay windows, and other extrusions; steeply pitched roof, often with front-facing gable; patterned wall surfaces mixing a variety of materials; "gingerbread" ornament, usually in wood but sometimes in metal or terra-cotta; full-width front porch (in residential examples). Houses, commercial buildings, a few churches and public buildings. The Queen Anne style is what most people envision when they think of a typical Victorian house, and the style is extremely common in the Twin Cities. The related **Stick Style**, which features simplified massing and patterned facades defined by vertical and horizontal boards, is much rarer, as is an exotic variant known as **Moorish Revival**.

Minneapolis City Hall, 350 Fifth St. South, Minneapolis, 1889–1906

Richardsonian Romanesque (1885–1900): Massive stone or brick walls; round-arched windows and doorways; heavy round or square towers; floral ornament derived from Byzantine sources. Houses (usually mansions), apartments, churches, public and commercial buildings. Related to, but different from, an earlier style known simply as **Romanesque Revival**. Richardsonian Romanesque was the dominant style in the Twin Cities (and America) in the late 1880s and early 1890s. Scores of buildings in this style (most notably the Minneapolis City Hall) survive in the Twin Cities. The style was named after its creator, Boston architect H. H. Richardson. A late, somewhat lighter version of the style influenced by French examples is called **Chateauesque**.

Charles and Emily Noyes House, 89 Virginia St., St. Paul, 1887

Colonial Revival (1885–present): Generally rectilinear massing; gabled or gambrel (double-sloped) roof; central doorway with sidelights, classical detail, and often a portico; symmetrical windows, usually divided into small panes. Houses, apartments, commercial buildings. Inspired by early American architecture, this style remains popular even today, especially for houses, and is extremely common through-out the Twin Cities. Colonial Revival has innumerable variations, including **Georgian** and the elegant **Shingle Style**, which flourished briefly around 1890.

Grain Exchange Building, 400 Fourth St. South, Minneapolis, 1902

Chicago Commercial (1880s–1920s): As its name indicates, this style came out of Chicago during that city's rebuilding following the 1871 fire. This utilitarian style was used almost exclusively for skyscrapers, warehouses, and other commercial buildings. Typical features include steel- or iron-frame construction, minimal ornamentation, and exten-sive use of the Chicago window (a large picture window with double-hung windows to either side). Oddly, however, the style's most famous practitioner, Louis Sullivan, was also a great ornamentalist, and his distinctive work forms a subgenre known simply as **Sullivanesque**. Several outstanding examples of the Chicago Commercial Style, all in a Sullivanesque vein, survive in downtown Minneapolis.

St. Paul Central Library and James J. Hill Reference Library, 80–90 West Fourth St., St. Paul, 1917

Beaux-Arts Classicism (1890s–1920s): Foursquare, symmetrical massing; heavy stone or brick walls; classical columns and detailing, often with large cornices and ornamental panels; use of marble and other deluxe materials. Mansions, railroad stations, churches, public and commercial buildings. This was the dominant public style at the turn of the twentieth century. The style is sometimes called **Renaissance Revival** or **Classical Revival**. Many notable Beaux-Arts monuments (such as the State Capitol and the St. Paul Cathedral) remain.

Stuart Cameron House, 130 Lexington Pkwy. North, St. Paul, 1911

Arts and Crafts (late 1890s–present): Regular, squarish massing; low pitched gable or hipped roof (in two-story examples); wide eaves mounted on decorative brackets; open front porch with tapered columns; stained- or leaded-glass windows, often arranged in bands; wood or stucco finishing. Mostly houses. Also known as the **Craftsman**, **Bungalow**, or **Mission Style**, this was the most prevalent of all housing styles in the Twin Cities between 1910 and 1925 and was used for everything from inexpensive tract homes to Summit Avenue mansions. The style made a big comeback in the 1990s and remains popular today, especially for high-end, custom-designed homes.

John F. Linhard House, 1619 Scheffer Ave., St. Paul, 1928

Period Revival (1900–present): Picturesque massing; steep roof, often with ornamental chimneys; historical detailing drawn from French, English, Spanish, or Germanic sources. **Tudor Revival**, **Spanish Colonial Revival**, and **French Provincial** are all examples of this style, which has many variants, including the fanciful **Storybook** style. Houses, small commercial buildings. This style reached its peak in the 1920s and 1930s and was used for thousands of tract houses. Revival-style houses, generally inferior to earlier examples, are still being built today. A **Gothic Revival** variant, drawn from an earlier style of that name, was used primarily for churches well into the 1950s.

Purcell-Cutts House, 2328 Lake Pl., Minneapolis, 1913

Prairie (1905–20): Boxy, asymmetrical massing; low hipped roof with deep overhanging eaves; open floor plan; banded casement windows, often with stylized geometric patterns. Houses, a few churches and commercial buildings (mostly banks). This was one of the high-style versions of the Arts and Crafts movement, developed by Frank Lloyd Wright in Chicago and imported to the Twin Cities by William Purcell and George Elmslie. Some of the greatest examples of this style are located in Minnesota. Minneapolis alone has about a dozen houses designed by Purcell and Elmslie.

St. Paul City Hall and Ramsey County Courthouse, 15 Kellogg Blvd. West, St. Paul, 1932

Art deco (1925–early 1950s): Generally symmetrical massing, often with stepped-back, "wedding cake" profile; zigzag geometrical motifs; rich, colorful materials. Public buildings, skyscrapers, retail stores, theaters, a small number of houses. *Art deco* is a catchall term for two related styles—the early **Zigzag Moderne** (described above) and the later **Streamline Moderne**, which became popular in the 1930s and features rounded corners, smooth wall surfaces, and little or no applied ornament. Another art deco variant, used extensively for public buildings in the 1930s, is known as **PWA Moderne** (for Public Works Administration, a federal agency that undertook many building projects in the 1930s). Large numbers of art deco buildings remain in the Twin Cities. Frank Lloyd Wright devised his own version of the Moderne style that he called Usonian. One of his first Usonian homes, from 1934, is in Minneapolis.

IDS Center, 717 Nicollet Mall, Minneapolis, 1973

Modern (1930s–present): Massing that ranges from boxlike to highly sculptural; use of conspicuously "modern" materials like glass and steel; "curtain wall" construction; open floor plans; avoidance of traditional forms of ornament and detailing. Also known as the **International Style**. Office and commercial buildings, churches, schools, public buildings, houses. *Modern* is a catchall term that includes a bewildering variety of genres and subgenres, ranging from the loud, jazzy fast food joints of the 1950s (called **roadside architecture**) to the sleek, understated skyscrapers of the 1960s and 1970s. The rambler, ranch house, and split-level are vernacular versions of the style.

Gallier Plaza, 175 East Fifth St., St. Paul, 1986

Postmodern (1975–present): Hierarchical massing, often based on classical precedents; historically derived ornament, sometimes treated in an ironic or whimsical fashion; frequent use of rich, colorful materials; emphasis on context, which is a building's relationship to its surroundings. Skyscrapers, shopping malls, institutional and public buildings, houses. Much of what was built in the Twin Cities in the 1980s is postmodern in character. The style has pretty much run its course in high-style circles, but countless vernacular examples continue to be built.

Frederick R. Weisman Art Museum, 333 East River Pkwy., Minneapolis, 1993

Expressive Modernism (1990s–present): Nobody has quite figured out what to call the agitated, quirky, oddly angled buildings that began to dominate high-style architecture in the 1990s. One especially discordant branch of the style is sometimes called **Deconstructivism**. California architect Frank Gehry is the godfather of Expressive Modernism, which has many variants and which draws to some extent on early modern styles such as **Art Nouveau**, **Expressionism**, **Constuctivism**, and **Futurism**. So far, only a few full-blown examples of Expressive Modernism—among them Gehry's Weisman Museum at the University of Minnesota and the addition to the Walker Art Center in Minneapolis by the Swiss architectural firm of Herzog and de Meuron— have appeared in the Twin Cities.

Quick Fix in Wood: Rude Beginnings (1845–60)

The first buildings in the Twin Cities were simple structures reflecting the raw realities of pioneer life. Most were built of wood, although brick and local stone were also used, primarily for commercial structures. The Federal and Greek Revival styles predominated. However, the need to build quickly, and often cheaply, left little room for strong stylistic expression. Buildings of this period were not intended to last, and for the most part they haven't.

Minneapolis
Ard Godfrey House
John H. Stevens House
Aster Cafe
Our Lady of Lourdes Catholic Church
Martin-Morrison Block

St. Paul
Wright-Prendergast House
Parker-Marshall House
Simpson-Wood House
Anton Waldman House
Coney Island Restaurant buildings

Romancing the Stone: Picturesque Revivals (1860–80)

As the Twin Cities grew, buildings became larger and more ornate than they had been in pioneer days. New materials imported by rail (a link with Chicago was achieved in 1867) also expanded the range of expression. Three highly picturesque styles—Italianate, French Second Empire, and Gothic Revival (in both its regular and Eastlake form)—predominated during this era. Most architects of the time came from the master builder tradition and were not academically trained. Relatively few buildings from this period survive in the Twin Cities, but those that do are often major monuments.

Minneapolis
Sigma Phi Epsilon Fraternity
Grove Street Flats
Crown Roller Building
Washburn A Mill Complex

St. Paul
Burbank-Livingston-Griggs House
Alexander Ramsey House
Assumption Catholic Church
First Baptist Church
Straus Apartments

Exploding Cities: Architecture Comes of Age (1880–1900)

During the 1880s, St. Paul and Minneapolis were among the fastest growing cities in the world. The result was a tremendous building boom that attracted many outstanding architects. These talented and versatile designers, many of whom had been educated in Europe, turned out a huge array of high-quality buildings. Some of the Twin Cities' finest works of architecture—especially the fabulous mansions built by the *nouveau riche*—date from these decades. This flamboyant era saw a dizzying procession of styles, including the related Queen Anne, Stick, and Shingle. By the later 1880s Richardsonian Romanesque dominated the scene. It was soon supplanted by various Colonial and Renaissance Revival styles that gained popularity at the turn of the century.

Minneapolis	St. Paul
Chicago House	490 Summit
Hennepin Center for the Arts	Elizabeth Gilbert House
Minneapolis City Hall	Old Main, Hamline University
Frank Griswold House	Shipman-Greve House
Groveland Gallery	Pioneer Building
	St. Paul Building
	James J. Hill House

Beaux-Arts Meets Arts and Crafts (1900–20)

An era of consolidation, this period was dominated in the public domain by Beaux-Arts Classicism, a heavy and monumental style imported from France. Beaux-Arts was not the only style of the day, however. On the domestic front, where a variety of post–Victorian revival styles continued to be popular, this era introduced the Arts and Crafts style to the Twin Cities, most frequently in the form of the bungalow. The first two decades of the twentieth century also saw the rise and fall of the Midwest's only indigenous style of architecture— the so-called Prairie Style created by Frank Lloyd Wright and his followers in Chicago, most notably William Purcell and George Elmslie. The great Prairie houses of this period represent a summit of American domestic design.

Minneapolis	St. Paul
Schiek's Palace Royale	Landmark Center
Grain Exchange Building	Minnesota State Capitol
Basilica of St. Mary	Cathedral of St. Paul
Minneapolis Institute of Arts	St. Paul Central Library and
Purcell-Cutts House	James J. Hill Reference Library
	Ward and Bess Beebe House

A Little Zig, a Little Zag: Art Deco Delights (1920–50)

The Beaux-Arts movement lost steam after World War I and was quickly succeeded by the flashy, theatrical style that eventually came to be known as art deco. This style went through two phases—Zigzag Moderne and Streamline Moderne—with the latter especially popular in the Twin Cities. Art deco was chiefly used for theaters, office structures, and public buildings. Both St. Paul and Minneapolis can boast of major art deco monuments. Residential architecture at this time was still oriented toward various revival styles, although the Arts and Crafts style in its many guises remained popular well into the 1920s.

Minneapolis	St. Paul
Young Quinlan Building	Hamm Building
Rand Tower	Wold Architects
W Foshay Hotel	St. Paul City Hall and
Qwest Building	Ramsey County Courthouse
Malcolm and Nancy Willey House	Qwest Buildings
Minneapolis Armory	Highland 2 Theatres
	Abe and Mary Engelson House
	Clarence W. Wigington Pavilion

Wanting to Be Just Like Mies: The Modern Era (1950–75)

This period is associated in the public mind with glassy, flat-topped skyscrapers inspired by the work of the German-born Chicago architect Ludwig Mies van der Rohe. Modernists, who began to dominate the architectural scene in the Twin Cities in the early 1950s, generally took a highly rational approach to design, emphasizing strong, simple forms and structural expression while eschewing traditional applied ornament. However, modernism was never quite as homogeneous as its detractors contend. In fact, a wide range of buildings—some far more emotionally charged than the classic Miesian box—fall within the modernist fold.

Minneapolis
Christ Lutheran Church
ING 20 Washington
Walker Art Center
Marquette Plaza
IDS Center

St. Paul
St. Columba Church
Porky's Drive-in
Mount Zion Temple
Pioneer Press Building
Ecolab Center

Gaga over Gables: Postmodernism (1975–present)

After a quarter century, many architects got tired of modernism. By the mid-1970s, a group of *avant garde* designers began moving toward a more decorated, eclectic, and colorful style that was eventually labeled postmodernism. (Mies van der Rohe's famous dictum, "less is more," was restated by postmodern guru Robert Venturi as "less is a bore.") Unlike modernist architects, who tended to design their buildings as isolated objects in space, postmodernists emphasized "context" by striving to create buildings that would respond well to their surroundings. Postmodernists also liked to allude to, and even borrow from, traditional architectural styles. Although most high-style architects abandoned postmodernism by the early 1990s, the style remains popular in the Twin Cities for housing developments and continues to be favored by proponents of neotraditional town planning.

Minneapolis
WCCO-TV Building
Accenture Tower
Wells Fargo Center
Gaviidae Common
Federal Reserve Bank
Minneapolis Institute of Arts addition

St. Paul
Galtier Plaza
Minnesota Judicial Center
St. Paul Travelers Insurance Companies
Mears Park
Minnesota History Center

Modernism Returns: New Angles on Design (1990–present)

Even before the postmodern movement expired in high-design circles around 1990, a new style that might be called Expressive Modernism was beginning to gain popularity, with California architect Frank Gehry leading the way. Buildings in this style generally feature agitated, nonlinear forms with diagonal or skewed lines. They also make extensive use of rough-edged industrial materials. However, the style has many offshoots, and its varied practitioners appear to have no coherent philosophy beyond their desire to create novel forms.

Minneapolis
Leamington Municipal Ramp
    and Transit Hub
Frederick R. Weisman Art Museum
U.S. Courthouse and Federal Building
707 Second Avenue South
Walker Art Center addition
Minneapolis Public Library
Guthrie Theater

St. Paul
Minnesota Children's Museum
Xcel Energy Center
Science Museum of Minnesota

Annotated Bibliography

Abrahamson, Dean E., ed. *Under the Witch's Hat: A Prospect Park East River Road Neighborhood History.* Minneapolis: Prospect Park East River Road Improvement Association, 2003. A highly detailed history that provides information about many of the neighborhood's architecturally significant homes.

Adams, John S., and Barbara J. VanDrasek. *Minneapolis–St. Paul: People, Place and Public Life.* Minneapolis: University of Minnesota Press, 1993. Written by two geographers, this book provides a useful overview of the growth and development of the Twin Cities.

Anderes, Fred, and Ann Agranoff. *Ice Palaces.* New York: Abbeyville Press, 1983. Includes two chapters on St. Paul's many ice palaces.

Anderson, David, ed. *Downtown: A History of Downtown Minneapolis and Downtown St. Paul in the Words of the People Who Lived It.* Minneapolis: Nodin Press, 2000. Good stories about the days when the two downtowns were truly at the center of life in the Twin Cities.

Atwater, Isaac, ed. *History of the City of Minneapolis, Minnesota.* New York: Munsell and Co., 1893. A big subscription book of the kind popular in the nineteenth century. It offers intriguing sketches of the city's leading businessmen.

Banham, Reyner. *A Concrete Atlantis: U.S. Industrial Building and European Modern Architecture, 1900–1925.* Cambridge, MA: MIT Press, 1986. An excellent account of how American industrial architecture (including concrete grain elevators in the Twin Cities) influenced European design.

Belmont, Steve. *Cities in Full: Recognizing and Realizing the Great Potential of Urban America.* Chicago: Planners Press, 2002. A fascinating book that advocates much denser development of American cities. The author cites Minneapolis as a prime example of a city in need of more density.

Bennett, Edward H., with Andrew Wright Crawford. *Plan of Minneapolis.* Minneapolis: Minneapolis Civic Commission, 1917. A grand Beaux-Arts plan for Minneapolis that never came to be. The plan's huge, dreamlike renderings are splendid.

———, William E. Parson, and George Herrold. *Plan of St. Paul: The Capital City of Minnesota.* [St. Paul]: Commissioner of Public Works, 1922. Not nearly as grand as its Minneapolis counterpart, but it does offer some intriguing insights into how planners of the era hoped to change St. Paul for the better (mostly, they failed).

Berman, James, ed. *St. Anthony Falls Rediscovered.* Minneapolis: Minneapolis Riverfront Development Coordination Board, 1980. An early survey of buildings in the St. Anthony Falls Historic District.

Besse, Kirk. *Show Houses, Twin Cities Style.* Minneapolis: Victoria Publications, 1997. A history of St. Paul and Minneapolis movie theaters.

Blodgett, Geoffrey. *Cass Gilbert: The Early Years.* St. Paul: Minnesota Historical Society Press, 2001. Much information about the early St. Paul career of the man who designed the Minnesota State Capitol and many other monuments.

Borchert, John R., David Gebhard, David Lanegran, and Judith A. Martin. *Legacy of Minneapolis: Preservation amid Change.* Minneapolis: Voyageur Press, 1983. A rather disorganized book that nonetheless contains much interesting information about the city's architecture and history.

A Brief History of the Irvine Park District: The People and Architecture of an Extraordinary Neighborhood. St. Paul: Historic Irvine Park Association, 1986. A nicely illustrated pamphlet that covers all of the historic structures in one of St. Paul's oldest neighborhoods.

Bromley, Edward A. *Minneapolis Portrait of the Past.* 1890. Reprint, Minneapolis: Voyageur Press, 1973. Wonderful photographs showing the city's earliest days.

Brooks, H. Allen. *The Prairie School: Frank Lloyd Wright and His Midwest Contemporaries.* 1972. Reprint, New York: Norton, 1976. Still the best survey of the Prairie School, with much information about its chief Minnesota practitioners, William Purcell and George Elmslie.

Castle, Henry A. *History of St. Paul and Vicinity: A Chronicle of Progress.* 3 vols. Chicago and New York: Lewis Publishing Co., 1912. An encyclopedic work that amply displays the biases of its era. But it's an enjoyable read (in spots) and offers much information not readily available elsewhere.

Christen, Barbara S., and Steven Flanders. *Cass Gilbert, Life and Work: Architect of the Public Domain.* New York: Norton, 2001. Includes a chapter on Gilbert's career in St. Paul.

Conforti, Michael, ed. *Art and Life on the Upper Mississippi, 1890–1915: Minnesota 1900.* Newark: University of Delaware Press, 1994. Includes chapters on turn-of-the-century Minnesota architecture and a long essay on the work of Purcell and Elmslie.

Discover St. Paul: A Short History of Seven St. Paul Neighborhoods. St. Paul: Ramsey County Historical Society, 1979. Historical sketches illustrated with maps and photographs.

Down at the Lake: A Historical Portrait of Linden Hills and the Lake Harriet District. Minneapolis: Linden Hills History Study Group, 2001. A solid neighborhood history.

Earhart, Andrew G. *The Buildings of Saint Paul: The Mears Park Area.* St. Paul: The Author, 1992. Information on every building that faces the historic Lowertown park.

Eaton, Leonard K. *Gateway Cities and Other Essays.* Ames: Iowa State University Press, 1989. Includes a chapter on warehouses in St. Paul.

El-Hai, Jack. *Lost Minnesota.* Minneapolis: University of Minnesota Press, 2000. Includes entries on more than 50 vanished buildings in the Twin Cities.

Empson, Donald L. *Portrait of a Neighborhood.* St. Paul: Identified Treatment Area Committee, 1980. A walking tour of the Uppertown (sometimes called West Seventh Street) neighborhood, which contains many of St. Paul's oldest homes.

———. *The Street Where You Live: A Guide to the Place Names of St. Paul.* 1975. Reprint, Minneapolis: University of Minnesota Press, 2006. If you've ever wondered how St. Paul acquired so many unusual street names, you'll find the answers here.

Flanagan, Barbara. *Minneapolis.* New York: St. Martin's Press, 1973. The longtime newspaper columnist provides a breezy tour of her beloved Minneapolis.

Frame, Robert M. III. *James J. Hill's St. Paul: A Guide.* St. Paul: James J. Hill Reference Library, 1988. Identifies various St. Paul buildings associated with the fabled Empire Builder.

Gardner, John S., ed. *The Midwest in American Architecture*. Chicago: University of Illinois Press, 1991. Includes a long chapter on George Elmslie and his work in Minnesota and elsewhere.

Gebhard, David, and Tom Martinson. *A Guide to the Architecture of Minnesota*. Minneapolis: University of Minnesota Press, 1977. Now badly dated, this remains the only comprehensive guide of its kind. A new statewide architectural guide by other authors is in the works.

Harris, Moira. *Fire & Ice: The History of the St. Paul Winter Carnival*. St. Paul: Pogo Press, 2003. Much information on early ice palaces and other carnival structures.

Hart, Joseph (with photographs by Edwin L. Hirschoff). *Down and Out: The Life and Death of Minneapolis' Skid Row*. Minneapolis: University of Minnesota Press, 2002. A well-written account of the old Gateway District, illustrated with elegant photographs.

Hassler, Jon, and Doug Ohman. *Churches of Minnesota*. St. Paul: Minnesota Historical Society Press, 2006. Includes fine photographs of several important Twin Cities churches.

Hennessy, William B. *Past and Present of St. Paul, Minnesota*. Chicago: S. J. Clarke Publishing Co., 1906. Another big subscription book, offering lots of secondhand information with a few good photographs.

Hess, Jeffrey A., and Paul Clifford Larson. *St. Paul Architecture: A History*. Minneapolis: University of Minnesota Press, 2006. An excellent account of St. Paul's architectural history. The chapter on Period Revival architecture is especially informative.

Hession, Jane King, Rip Rapson, and Bruce N. Wright. *Ralph Rapson: Sixty Years of Modern Design*. Afton, MN: Afton Historical Society Press, 1999. A look at the life and work of Minnesota's best-known modern architect.

Hofsommer, Don L. *Minneapolis and the Age of Railways*. Minneapolis: University of Minnesota Press, 2005. A comprehensive look at how railroads helped shape the growth of Minneapolis in the nineteenth and twentieth centuries. Well written and illustrated, but probably a bit too detailed for the general reader.

Hudson, Horace B., ed. *A Half Century in Minneapolis*. Minneapolis: Hudson Publishing Co., 1908. Yet another compilation, with some interesting stuff lurking amid the standard salutes to wealth and progress.

Irish, Sharon. *Cass Gilbert, Architect: Modern Traditionalist*. New York: Monacelli Press, 1999. A biography of Minnesota's most famous architect.

Jacob, Bernard, and Carol Morphew. *Pocket Architecture: A Walking Guide to the Architecture of Downtown Minneapolis and Downtown St. Paul*. 1984. Rev. ed., Minneapolis: AIA Minnesota, 1987. Much of the information in this guidebook is now outdated.

Johnson, Frederick L., and David Thofern. *The Skyway Tour of Saint Paul History*. St. Paul: St. Paul Foundation and Minnesota Historical Society, 1991. A pamphlet describing historic sites and buildings that can be seen from the skyways.

Kane, Lucile M. *The Falls of St. Anthony: The Waterfall That Built Minneapolis*. 1966. Rev. ed., St. Paul: Minnesota Historical Society Press, 1987. The definitive account of how the milling industry developed around St. Anthony Falls and turned Minneapolis into the world's leading flour producer.

Kennedy, Roger G. *Historic Homes of Minnesota.* 1967. Rev. ed., St. Paul: Minnesota Historical Society Press, 2006. A number of prominent historic homes in the Twin Cities are included in this engaging book.

Kenney, Dave. *Twin Cities Album: A Visual History.* St. Paul: Minnesota Historical Society Press, 2005. A nice array of photographs and other images that provide an overview of the history of Minneapolis and St. Paul. There's also an informative text.

Kieley, Genny Zak. *Heart and Hard Work: Memories of "Nordeast" Minneapolis.* Minneapolis: Nodin Press, 1997. A largely anecdotal look at one of Minneapolis's oldest ethnic neighborhoods, now home to many artists.

————. *Pride and Tradition: More Memories of Northeast Minneapolis.* Minneapolis: Nodin Press, 2000. More about Northeast Minneapolis.

————. *Roots and Ties: A Scrapbook of Northeast Memories.* Minneapolis: Nodin Press, 2003. Still more about Northeast's good old days.

Koeper, H. F. *Historic St. Paul Buildings.* St. Paul: City Planning Board, 1964. This booklet, published as the preservation movement was just getting under way, identified nearly 100 St. Paul buildings thought to be historically and architecturally significant. Alas, not all of them survived the 1960s.

Kudalis, Eric, ed. *100 Places Plus 1: An Unofficial Architectural Survey of Favorite Minnesota Sites.* Minneapolis: AIA Minnesota, 1996. Various essayists describe their favorite buildings and places in Minnesota.

Kunz, Virginia. *St. Paul: Saga of an American City.* Woodland Hills, CA: Windsor Publications, 1977. A glossy "corporate history" that tends to plow familiar ground.

————. *The Mississippi and St. Paul: A Short History of the City's 150-Year Love Affair with Its River.* St. Paul: Ramsey County Historical Society, 1987. A look at how the Mississippi River shaped St. Paul's development and vice versa.

Lanegran, David, and Ernest Sandeen. *The Lake District of Minneapolis: A History of the Calhoun-Isles Community.* St. Paul: Living Historical Museum, 1979. A history of what continues to be one of Minneapolis's most fashionable neighborhoods.

————, with Judith Frost Flinn. *St. Anthony Park: Portrait of a Community.* St. Paul: District 12 Community Council and St. Anthony Park Association, 1987. A well-researched history that offers a good deal of information about the neighborhood's historic homes and buildings.

Larson, Paul Clifford. *Minnesota Architect: The Life and Work of Clarence H. Johnston.* Afton, MN: Afton Historical Society Press, 1996. A detailed study of Johnston, who designed numerous important buildings in St. Paul and at the University of Minnesota. Includes a complete catalog of his work.

————, with Susan Brown, eds. *The Spirit of H. H. Richardson on the Midland Prairies: Regional Transformations of an Architectural Style.* Minneapolis and Ames: University of Minnesota Art Museum and Iowa State University Press, 1988. A series of essays examining the influence, in the Twin Cities and elsewhere, of the great Boston architect Henry Hobson Richardson.

Lathrop, Alan. *Churches of Minnesota: An Illustrated Guide.* Minneapolis: University of Minnesota Press, 2003. Includes information about a number of significant churches in the Twin Cities.

Legler, Dixie, and Christian Korab. *At Home on the Prairie: The Houses of Purcell and Elmslie.* San Francisco, CA: Chronicle Books, 2006. Wonderful color photographs, by Korab, of Purcell and Elmslie's houses, including those in the Twin Cities.

Lindley, John M. *Celebrate St. Paul: 150 Years of History.* Encino, CA: Cherbo Publishing Group, 2003. The latest history of St. Paul, profusely illustrated.

Maccabee, Paul. *John Dillinger Slept Here.* St. Paul: Minnesota Historical Society Press, 1995. Everything you ever wanted to know about St. Paul's gangster era in the 1920s and 1930s. Includes excellent maps.

McClure, Harlan E. *A Guide to the Architecture of the Twin Cities: Minneapolis and St. Paul, 1820–1955.* New York: Reinhold Publishing Co., 1955. Outdated, but interesting for its take on the first generation of "modern" architecture here.

Martin, Judith, and Antony Goddard. *Past Choices / Present Landscapes: The Impact of Urban Renewal on the Twin Cities.* Minneapolis: Center for Urban and Regional Affairs, 1989. A straightforward account of how urban renewal dramatically altered St. Paul and Minneapolis.

————, and David Lanegran. *Where We Live: The Residential Districts of Minneapolis and Saint Paul.* Minneapolis: University of Minnesota Press, 1983. Lots of good information on neighborhoods in the Twin Cities.

Millett, Larry. *The Curve of the Arch: The Story of Louis Sullivan's Owatonna Bank.* St. Paul: Minnesota Historical Society Press, 1985. Includes a biographical sketch of George Elmslie, the great Prairie School architect who designed many houses in Minneapolis.

————. *Lost Twin Cities.* St. Paul: Minnesota Historical Society Press, 1992. A look at the Twin Cities' many vanished buildings.

————. *Strange Days, Dangerous Nights: Photos from the Speed Graphic Era.* St. Paul: Borealis Books, 2004. Newspaper photographs from St. Paul in the 1940s and 1950s that contain much lurid gore but also show what the city looked like before the age of urban renewal.

———— (with photographs by Jerry Mathiason). *Twin Cities Then and Now.* St. Paul: Minnesota Historical Society Press, 1996. Historic photographs of more than 70 street scenes paired with new pictures taken from the same locations.

Mulfinger, Dale. *The Architecture of Edwin Lundie.* St. Paul: Minnesota Historical Society Press, 1995. An overview of the work of Lundie, a master architect known for his romantic stone and wood houses.

Murphy, Patricia, and Susan Granger. *Historic Sites Survey of Saint Paul and Ramsey County, 1980–1983: Final Report.* St. Paul: St. Paul Heritage Preservation Commission and Ramsey County Historical Society, 1983. A survey of significant architecture in St. Paul and Ramsey County. The report contains errors and omissions, but it's an invaluable reference document.

Newson, Thomas N. *Pen Sketches of St. Paul, Minnesota, and Biographical Sketches of Old Settlers, from the Earliest Settlement of the City, up to and including the Year 1857.* St. Paul: The Author, 1886. The title says it all. A big, quirky book that is usually interesting and in places downright amusing.

Nord, Mary Ann, comp. *The National Register of Historic Places in Minnesota.* St. Paul: Minnesota Historical Society Press, 2003. Lists every Minnesota building on the register.

Olson, Russell L. *The Electric Railways of Minnesota*. Hopkins: Minnesota Transportation Museum, 1977. Written by a trolley buff, this study describes in exhaustive detail the Twin Cities' late, great streetcar system.

Orfield, Myron. *Metropolitics: A Regional Agenda for Community and Stability*. Washington, DC: Brookings Institution Press, 1997. A book about how to stem urban decline in St. Paul, Minneapolis, and elsewhere. Many interesting maps.

Pennefeather, Shannon M., ed. *Mill City: A Visual History of the Minneapolis Mill District*. St. Paul: Minnesota Historical Society Press, 2003. A handsomely illustrated book published to coincide with the opening of the new Mill City Museum.

Peterson, Penny A. *Hiding in Plain Sight: Minneapolis' First Neighborhood*. Minneapolis: Marcy-Holmes Neighborhood Association, n.d. Good information about the Fifth Street Southeast Historic District in Minneapolis.

Peterson, Richard, and Paul Clifford Larson. *Terra Cotta in the Twin Cities*. St. Paul: Northern Clay Center, 1993. A guide to buildings adorned with terra-cotta, which was widely used as an architectural material between 1880 and 1930.

Powderhorn Park: Nature, People and Community. [Minneapolis]: The Horn Newspaper, Powderhorn Park Neighborhood Association, and Powderhorn Park Activities Council, 1990. An informal look at one of Minneapolis's most diverse neighborhoods.

Prairie School Architecture in Minnesota, Iowa, Wisconsin. St. Paul: Minnesota Museum of Art, 1982. Six essays on Prairie School architecture, lavishly illustrated with photographs and drawings.

Pyle, J. G., ed. *Picturesque St. Paul*. St. Paul: Northwestern Photo Co., 1888. Great photographs of old-time St. Paul, assembled by the man who wrote the first biography of James J. Hill.

Richards, Hanje. *Minneapolis–St. Paul Then and Now*. San Diego, CA: Thunder Bay Press, 2001. Lots of photographs, but not much in the way of explanatory text.

Richter, Bonnie, ed. *Saint Paul Omnibus: Images of the Changing City*. St. Paul: Old Town Restorations, Inc., 1979. A nice booklet that explores the city's architectural history.

Rosheim, David. *The Other Minneapolis, or the Rise and Fall of the Gateway, the Old Minneapolis Skid Row*. Maquoketa, IA: Andromeda Press, 1978. A fascinating look at a down-at-the-heels but historically significant part of Minneapolis destroyed by urban renewal in the 1960s.

Sandeen, Ernest. *St. Paul's Historic Summit Avenue*. 1978. Reprint, Minneapolis: University of Minnesota Press, 2004. Although Sandeen's architectural judgments are a bit eccentric, this book is a delight to read and remains the best guide to St. Paul's most famous thoroughfare. Includes a catalog of houses on the avenue.

Schmid, Calvin F. *Social Saga of Two Cities: An Ecological and Statistical Study of Social Trends in Minneapolis and St. Paul*. Minneapolis: Council of Social Agencies, Bureau of Social Research, 1937. Conceived as a Depression-era project, this is one of the most informative books ever written about the Twin Cities. Especially valuable are the superb maps and charts.

Schulyer, Montgomery. *American Architecture and Other Writings.* William H. Jordy and Ralph Coe, eds. Cambridge, MA: Harvard University Press, Belknap Press, 1961. Schuyler was an outstanding turn-of-the-century architecture critic. Includes a fascinating 1891 essay on buildings in St. Paul and Minneapolis.

Shutter, Marion D., ed. *History of Minneapolis, Gateway to the Northwest.* 3 vols. Chicago and Minneapolis: S. J. Clarke Publishing Co., 1923. This plump compendium, best taken in small doses, provides useful information about the city's early movers and shakers.

Slade, George Richard. *Banking in the Great Northern Territory: An Illustrated History.* Afton, MN: Afton Historical Society Press, 2005. A regional history that includes photographs and descriptions of many old bank buildings in the Twin Cities.

Stevens, John H. *Personal Recollections of Minnesota and Its People, and Early History of Minneapolis.* Minneapolis: Privately published, 1890. Stevens, who was among the first residents of Minneapolis, laid out the downtown street grid still in use today.

Stipanovich, Joseph. *City of Lakes: An Illustrated History of Minneapolis.* Woodland Hills, CA: Windsor Publications, 1982. The most recent full-dress history of the city and on the whole well done. Includes many photographs.

Taylor, David Vassar, and Paul Clifford Larson. *Cap Wigington: An Architectural Legacy in Ice and Stone.* St. Paul: Minnesota Historical Society Press, 2001. A good account of the life and work of St. Paul's first black architect.

Torbert, Donald R. "Minneapolis Architecture and Architects, 1848–1908: A Study of Style Trends in Architecture in a Midwestern City Together with a Catalogue of Representative Buildings." PhD diss., University of Minnesota, 1951. A good source of information about early Minneapolis architects.

———. *Significant Architecture in the History of Minneapolis.* Minneapolis: City Planning Commission, 1969. Torbert did pioneering research in local architectural history, but an extreme modernist bias often clouded his judgment.

Trent, Vera. *Tracing the Steps of Historic St. Paul.* St. Paul: St. Paul Foundation, 1991. A downtown walking tour with emphasis on the city's early history.

Trimble, Steve. *In the Shadow of the City: A History of the Loring Park Neighborhood.* Minneapolis: Minneapolis Community College Foundation, 1989. A nicely written history of perhaps the most urbane neighborhood in Minneapolis.

Vandam, Elizabeth. *The Doors of Tangletown.* Snoqualmie, WA: Sponte Valere Books, 2002. A book about the Washburn Park neighborhood along Minnehaha Creek in south Minneapolis.

Vincent, Jeanne Anne. "St. Paul Architecture, 1848–1906." Master's thesis, University of Minnesota, 1944. An early study of St. Paul's historic architecture. Includes many photographs.

Warner, George E., and Charles M. Foote, comps. *History of Ramsey County and the City of St. Paul, including the Explorers and Pioneers of Minnesota, by Edward D. Neill, and Outlines of the History of Minnesota, by J. Fletcher Williams.* Minneapolis: North Star Publishing Co., 1881. A useful compendium, even if the title seems nearly as long as the book.

Westbrook, Nicolas, ed. *A Guide to the Industrial Archaeology of the Twin Cities*. St. Paul and Minneapolis: Society for Industrial Archaeology, 1983. Fascinated by bridges, dams, factories, railroad yards, and the like? If so, you'll enjoy this guide.

Westbrook, Virginia. *Historic Lowertown: A Walking Tour*. St. Paul: St. Paul Heritage Preservation Commission, 1988. If you're interested in taking a stroll around the historic Lowertown warehouse district, this pamphlet will come in handy.

Williams, J. Fletcher. *A History of the City of Saint Paul to 1875*. 1887. Reprint, St. Paul: Minnesota Historical Society, 1983. A good "snack" book, filled with colorful stories of early St. Paul.

Wingerd, Mary Lethert. *Claiming the City: Politics, Faith, and the Power of Place in St. Paul*. Ithaca, NY: Cornell University Press, 2001. One of the best books ever written about St. Paul. It offers a convincing explanation for why St. Paul is in many ways so different from Minneapolis.

Writers' Program, Works Progress Administration. *Minneapolis: The Story of a City*. 1940. New York: AMS Press, 1948. A typical product of the Federal Writers' Program sponsored by the Works Progress Administration.

———. *The Bohemian Flats*. 1941. Reprint, St. Paul: Minnesota Historical Society Press, 1986. A lively account of the neighborhood that once occupied the Mississippi River flats just south of St. Anthony Falls.

Young, Biloine Whiting, and David Lanegran. *Grand Avenue: The Renaissance of an Urban Street*. St. Cloud, MN: North Star Press, 1996. A rather informal book that explains how the once seedy avenue came back to life as St. Paul's most upscale shopping venue.

Zahn, Thomas R., and Associates. *Historic Dayton's Bluff Driving Tour*. St. Paul: Historic Dayton's Bluff Association, 1992. A pamphlet devoted to St. Paul's most recently created historic district, located on the East Side.

Index

Every building and site described in the Guide is listed as a primary entry in the index, both by previous and current names. Some street names beginning with "North," "South," "East," or "West" are inverted and alphabetized under the keyword part of the street name (e.g., "North St. Albans St." is alphabetized as "St. Albans St. North"). Building and street names beginning with numbers are alphabetized as if spelled out. The names of people, firms, organizations, and government offices involved in creating the works listed in the Guide appear in **semibold type**. Unless otherwise indicated, they are architects, associated artists, or builders. Names of geographic areas or communities within the greater Twin Cities appear in *boldface italic*. A page reference in **boldface** indicates a photograph of the building, area, or other work.

The following abbreviations appear in the index:

Admin.	Administration	Condos.	Condominiums	Mpls.	Minneapolis
Amer.	American	Corp.	Corporation	Natl.	National
Assn.	Association	Ct.	Court	NE	Northeast
Assocs.	Associates	Dept.	Department	Pkwy.	Parkway
Apts.	Apartments	Dr.	Drive	Rd.	Road
Bldg.	Building	H.S.	High School	RR	Railroad/Railway
Blvd.	Boulevard	Hosp.	Hospital	SE	Southeast
Bros.	Brothers	Ins.	Insurance	St.	Street
Cem.	Cemetery	Intl.	International	Univ.	University
Co.	Company	MN	Minnesota		

Picture Credits

Rick Bronson: 54, 82 left, 83 left

Diane D. Brown: 32, 39 left, 40 left, 46 left, 49 left, 60, 81, 99 left, 101 top, 121 left and bottom right, 130, 147 left, 149, 158, 161 left, 163 right, 170, 184 left, 188 left and right, 193 left, 194 right, 196 right, 224 top, 225 bottom right, 229 top, 231, 232 top and bottom, 233 right, 256 left and right, 258 right, 260, 277, 280 right, 281 left and right, 285, 286 bottom, 293 left, 297 left and right, 302, 420 right, 431 right, 460 left, 464, 474 right, 476 right, 478 right, 495 left, 498, 521 left, 531 bottom right, 550, 556, 567 top, 571, 572 bottom, 579, 581 middle right, 583, 587 top, 593 bottom

Vincent J. DiGiorno: 398

David Enblom: 224 right, 225 top right, 230 left, 233 left, 234 left and right, 235, 236 left, 238, 239, 243 bottom left and right, 325 top, 329, 345 top, 348 bottom, 353, 360, 378, 388 top right, 444 left, 448 left, 449, 507, 520, 522, 542 left, 543 bottom, 544 left, 545 right

Farrell photographic: 59 right, 148 right, 150 bottom

Bob Firth: 74 bottom

Brian M. Gardner: vi, vii, 15, 25, 229 bottom, 309, 315, 316, 317 left, 318 left and bottom, 319, 321, 322 left, 324, 325 bottom, 330 left and right, 331 top, 333 top and right, 345 right, 347, 349, 350, 351 top and bottom, 370 left and right, 371 left, 372, 373 right, 382 left and right, 383, 388 bottom right, 390 right, 396 bottom, 397 left, 399, 404, 405, 406, 419 top, 431 left, 484, 488, 494, 497 left, 503, 511, 512 top, 513 top and bottom right, 514, 515, 531 left and top right, 533, 535 right, 547 bottom, 552 left and bottom, 554 left and top right, 557 left, 558 right, 563, 565, 568, 570, 590 top, 593 top

Chris Gregerson: 26, 33, 36 bottom left and right, 40 right, 337

Jessica Hackner: 192, 193 right, 194 bottom left

George Heinrich: 49 right, 101 bottom

Joe Hoover: 336 right, 359 left, 368 bottom right, 369 top and bottom, 371 right, 373 left, 420 left, 425 top and bottom right, 427, 429 left, 450 right, 463 right, 472, 530, 536 right, 547 top, 566 right, 573 left, 574 right, 575

Tom Johnson: 168 left and right, 169 left and right, 171 right and bottom

Bill Jolitz: 23, 38 left, 42, 52, 53, 56, 61 top, 65, 72, 77, 91, 98 top, 111, 122, 123, 128, 131, 132 left, 134, 139 right, 153, 175 top and bottom right, 179, 189, 200, 201 left and bottom right, 203, 207, 208 top, 210, 211 left, 213 left and right, 217, 225 left, 236 right, 237, 240, 241 left and bottom right, 244 right, 247, 252 right, 255, 257 left and right, 264 top and right, 268 bottom left, 269 left and right, 270, 278 bottom right, 286 top, 287, 292, 295 left, 296 left and top and bottom right, 299, 300 right, 301 right, 303 left, 363, 407 left, 408, 409 right, 410 bottom, 411 left, 413, 414 top, 419 bottom, 422, 459, 485 top and bottom, 486, 489, 491, 496, 499, 525, 536 left, 561, 566 top, 572 top, 573 right, 581 left and top and bottom right, 582 left and bottom right, 587 bottom, 588 top, 589 bottom, 590 bottom, 591 top

Phyllis A. Kedl: 97, 98 bottom, 100 top, 103 left and right, 108 left and right, 446, 461 left and bottom, 467, 471 bottom right, 473 left, 477, 481 left

Edward J. Kodet, Jr., FAIA: 214, 301 left

Paul Clifford Larson: 346, 375, 376, 387, 412 top, 421, 426, 432 right, 434, 451 right, 460 right, 463 left, 466 right, 473 right, 476 top left, 487, 504 left and right, 510, 537, 543 top, 544 right, 546 top and bottom, 555 left and bottom, 557 right, 558 left, 560, 567 bottom, 585 top

Colleen McGuire: 48, 55, 140, 143

Courtesy Mall of America: 178

Frank Mazzocco: 27 top left, 34 top, 71, 73, 82 right, 83 left, 274 top left, 275 left, 276, 282, 283

Minneapolis Institute of Arts, Bequest of Anson Cutts: 275 bottom right

Jim Mornes, AIA, courtesy Architectural Alliance: 580

David Oakes: 357

Doug Ohman: 106, 339 right, 340, 386, 441, 534, 535 left, 592 top

Pioneer Press archives: 397 right, 578 top

Gene Schwope: 155, 160 top, 163 top

Pat Schwope: 159, 162, 164

Steven Sikora: 142 top and bottom

University of Minnesota Archives: 129

All others, MHS collections

Maps by Map Hero—Matt Kania

AIA Guide to the Twin Cities was designed by Cathy Spengler Design, Minneapolis.
Typesetting by Cathy Spengler; Allan Johnson, Phoenix Type, Milan, Minnesota;
and Will Powers, Minnesota Historical Society Press.
Printed by Transcontinental Printing, Louiseville, Quebec .